www.wadsworth.com

wadsworth.com is the World Wide Web site for Wadsworth Publishing Company and is your direct source to dozens of online resources.

At *wadsworth.com* you can find out about supplements, demonstration software, and student resources. You can also send e-mail to many of our authors and preview new publications and exciting new technologies.

wadsworth.com
Changing the way the world learns®

*This book is dedicated
to those who have provided me with the encouragement,
example, and inspiration to reach far beyond what I thought possible
To my family,
my students,
my teachers,
and my colleagues*

Research Strategies
for Education

Douglas C. Wiseman

Professor Emeritus

Plymouth State College

Wadsworth Publishing Company

I(T)P® An International Thomson Publishing Company

Belmont, CA • Albany, NY • Boston • Cincinnati • Johannesburg • London • Madrid
Melbourne • Mexico City • New York • Pacific Grove, CA • Scottsdale, AZ • Singapore
Tokyo • Toronto

Education Editor: Dianne Lindsay
Editorial Assistant: Valerie Morrison
Marketing Manager: Becky Tollerson
Project Editor: Tanya Nigh
Print Buyer: Barbara Britton
Permissions Editor: Bob Kauser
Production: Sara Dovre Wudali, Gustafson Graphics
Art and Design Coordinator: Jay Purcell
Copy Editor: Linda Ireland, Gustafson Graphics
Illustrator: Berk Haan, Gustafson Graphics
Compositor: Gustafson Graphics
Printer: R R Donnelley & Sons

Printed in the United States of America
1 2 3 4 5 6 7 8 9 10

For more information, contact Wadsworth Publishing Company, 10 Davis Drive, Belmont, CA 94002, or electronically
at http://www.wadsworth.com

International Thomson Publishing Europe
Berkshire House
168-173 High Holborn
London, WC1V 7AA, United Kingdom

International Thomson Editores
Seneca, 53
Colonia Polanco
11560 México D.F. México

Nelson ITP, Australia
102 Dodds Street
South Melbourne
Victoria 3205 Australia

International Thomson Publishing Asia
60 Albert Street
#15-01 Albert Complex
Singapore 189969

Nelson Canada
1120 Birchmount Road
Scarborough, Ontario
Canada M1K 5G4

International Thomson Publishing Japan
Hirakawa-cho Kyowa Building, 3F
2-2-1 Hirakawa-cho, Chiyoda-ku
Tokyo 102 Japan

International Thomson Publishing Southern Africa
Building 18, Constantia Square
138 Sixteenth Road, P.O. Box 2459
Halfway House, 1685 South Africa

Library of Congress Cataloging-in-Publication Data
Wiseman, Douglas C.
    Research strategies for education / Douglas C. Wiseman.
        p.   cm.
    Includes bibliographical references and indexes.
    ISBN 0-7668-0013-X (alk. paper)
    1. Education—Research—Handbooks, manuals, etc.   2 Education—
Experimental methods—Handbooks, manuals, etc.   I. Title.
LB1028.W526   1999
370'.72—dc21
                                                    98-48148
                                                    CIP

 This book is printed on acid-free recycled paper.

Reviewers

Richard Antonak, Ph.D.
University of North Carolina
Charlotte, NC

John Bruno, Ph.D.
State College
Buffalo, NY

P.J. Karr-Kidwell, Ph.D.
Texas Women's University
Denton, TX

Dennis Kear
Wichita State University
Wichita, KS

Claudia Flowers
University of North Carolina
Charlotte, NC

Contents

Preface

What is research? How does one conduct effective literature reviews? Who is responsible for engaging in research activities? What distinguishes qualitative from quantitative research? How does one plan and execute a viable research design? What determines the significance and generalizability of research findings? While there are many principles that are shared by those who conduct research, there are also many opinions about how to best generate understanding on the part of those who are in the process of learning research skills. One needs but to examine the various textbooks on the market to appreciate the varying perspectives authors bring to this subject.

Research Strategies for Education has evolved from over thirty years of teaching and research. Experiences useful to authoring this book have arisen from observations, conferencing, course evaluations, reviewing publishers' manuscripts, and supervising more than nine hundred graduate research projects. Although this book has been prepared primarily for graduate students enrolled in their first educational research course, it is also designed for practicing teachers, administrators, guidance counselors, and other clinicians who recognize the need to use research as a basis for decision making about policies, processes, products, and programs.

The intent of this book is to present students and practitioners with the tools necessary to interpret the literature and carry out applied research projects—projects designed to answer questions appropriate to their areas of study or responsibility. Most research texts are designed around theoretical models. It is the mission of this author to present objectives; key terms; and enabling strategies using action models, including qualitative and quantitative research, sample projects where the reader will pursue a design from inception to analysis and interpretation, developmental activities, and recommended readings that include examples of published research utilizing the procedures described. Integrated within the chapters on descriptive and experimental research are examples of statistical treatments that can be applied to the data generated through those processes.

The text is divided into four parts. Part I, Nature and Purpose of Research, contains five chapters: Selection and Definition of a Problem, Ethical and Legal Considerations in Research, Preparation of a Research Plan, Sampling Procedures, and Selecting Instruments of Assessment.

Part II, Descriptive Research Methods, includes three chapters: Survey Procedures, Correlation Procedures, and Other Descriptive Procedures (Qualitative, Case Study, Historical, Causal-Comparative, Philosophical, and Test and Measurement).

Part III, Experimental Research Methods, has three chapters: Single-Group Designs, Two-Group Designs, and Other Experimental Procedures (Single-Subject, Multiple-Baseline, Alternating-Treatment, Cohort, Multiple-Group, and Factorial).

Part IV, Postanalytical Considerations, also has three chapters: Using the Computer for Data Analysis, Preparing the Research Report, and Evaluation of a Research Report.

At the beginning of each chapter are lists of objectives and key terms. Disbursed throughout the chapters are checkpoint questions and study notes. Developmental activities and recommended readings are presented at the conclusion of each chapter. These are provided in response to the complaint that I have heard (and had) about other texts that neglect to address the necessary linkages between theory and practice.

Appendix materials include a table of random numbers, table of appropriate sample sizes, chi square table, and tables that reveal critical values for *r*, *t*, and *F*. The appended section concludes with a standard score conversion table. These tables are followed by a glossary of key terms and an index.

Accompanying the text is an instructor's guide, which includes recall- and recognition-type items selected to measure the attainment of the objectives and other topics of significance within the chapters. Each item has been validated through jury review, and internal consistency and stability coefficients greater than .90 have been obtained for the entire battery.

If the premise is correct that school practitioners should be expected to understand and conduct research, it should follow that they must be taught the strategies for doing so in a meaningful and systematic way. Because of the range of experiences they bring to the topic, it is imperative that tools and techniques be integrated in ways that are nonthreatening. Toward that end, this text has been written.

Acknowledgments

Among those who helped make possible the creation of this text, I must first thank President Donald Wharton, Plymouth State College; Dr. A. Robin Bowers, Dean; and Dr. Virginia Barry, Chair of the Department of Education, who granted me a one-semester leave to begin its development. I am also indebted to

—my teachers who brought meaning to the importance of learning;

—my students and colleagues who have taught me a great deal about the art and science of teaching;

—my wife, Donna; my mother; and other members of my immediate and extended family whose encouragement and support were so vital to a project of this magnitude;

—the many reviewers who provided thoughtful advice during the evolutionary stages of the project; and

—Jay Whitney, Erin O'Connor Traylor, Dianne Lindsay, Valerie Morrison, Linda Ireland, Sara Dovre Wudali, Karen Leet, Mara Berman, and the other professionals at Delmar and Wadsworth Publishers, whose guidance and support helped to make this task a labor of love.

To all of them I offer my heartfelt gratitude.

NATURE AND PURPOSE OF RESEARCH

CHAPTER 1

Selection and Definition of a Problem

OBJECTIVES

After reading this chapter, you should be able to:

- Define research and discuss its primary and secondary purposes.
- Classify research according to purpose.
- Classify research according to method.
- Distinguish between descriptive and experimental research.
- Identify and discuss various descriptive procedures.
- Distinguish between comparative, noncomparative, and interrupted time series designs.
- Distinguish between fields of interest, problem areas, and differentiating factors.
- Describe the differences between research and statistical (null) hypotheses.
- Write a problem statement and hypothesis for both a descriptive and an experimental study.
- Identify and discuss the eight sources of related literature.
- Define key terms, and answer the checkpoint questions.

KEY TERMS

Abstracts

Applied Research

Basic Research

Book Guides

Case Study

Causal-Comparative Research

Comparative Group

Correlation Research

Descriptive Studies

Dictionaries

Differentiating Factors

Directories

Educational Resources Information
    Center (ERIC)

Encyclopedias

Ethnographic Research

Experimental Studies

Field of Interest

Handbooks

Historical Research

Newspaper Index

Noncomparative Group

Null Hypothesis

Periodical Index

Philosophical Research

Problem Area

Problem Statement

Qualitative Research

Quantitative Research

Research Hypothesis

Survey

Test and Measurement Research

Textbook Sources

Variables

INTRODUCTION

George Burns once said, "It's what we learn after we know it all that really counts." At first glance, this remark is likely to invoke a hardy chuckle, particularly given our knowledge of Mr. Burns's propensity for wit. But there is more to it than that. Further examination will likely reveal that this comment can easily be referenced to advancing one's knowledge regarding school practice and reform. Suddenly, a more sobering thought is before us.

But how does one acquire information in a way that can make a difference? It is through the art and the science of thoughtful research. Its practice empowers decision makers to be more informed about the choices before them. Yet, there are some K–12 school teachers and administrators who express the notion that research should be the practice of those in colleges and universities. This is a very shortsighted view in that it is unlikely that anyone would be more informed of the nature of the conditions in the school than those who are employed there. Further, it is the view of some school practitioners that research is a process that is limited to experimental designs—designs that require the administration of treatments and the employment of sophisticated statistical procedures. While there is a place for experimentation, this is but one form of research. Surveys, case studies, historical investigations, and correlation procedures are examples of other methods that can be used to acquire necessary information about topics of interest.

Although tradition, personal experience, intuition, and the opinions of others should not be discounted in one's search for truth, each is likely to be inadequate as the only basis for arriving at decisions (Fullan & Stiegelbauer, 1991; Phillips, 1980). In this chapter, you will be introduced to the process of scientific and disciplined inquiry—specifically, the language and the logic of research used in reading and conducting studies.

CLASSIFICATION OF RESEARCH BY PURPOSE

The *primary* purpose of research is to produce findings that are valid to the group(s) under study (internal validity). *Secondly,* its purpose is to produce inferences from those findings that can be applied to other populations (external validity). Both of these purposes are a product of the preciseness with which the investigator carried out the study. Incorporated within the overall purpose of having findings that are valid and generalizable, research can be classified into one of five categories: applied, basic, qualitative, quantitative, and research and development (R & D).

Applied research is done with the specific purpose of solving an existing problem, usually one arising in the workplace. It is a category of research often equated with action research in which an investigation is carried out to examine (and improve) a process, product, or program in a particular setting. The major difference between applied research and action research is that, in the latter, there is no intention to generalize the results.

Basic research, often referred to as theoretical or pure research, serves to add to the pool of knowledge that exists on general or specific topics. In short, it aims to increase one's knowledge of basic principles, advance methodology and scientific inquiry, and identify theories for testing in the workplace.

Qualitative research is a category of research that emphasizes the meaning of events as expressed by those who experience them. Often referred to as **ethnographic** (or naturalistic) **research,** it requires carefully taken field notes (which are often accompanied by photographs/videos) of observations made in naturalistic settings. Following prescribed criteria (Altheide & Johnson, 1994), these notes (and pictures) are analyzed with a view toward verbalizing findings and revealing trends.

While qualitative studies purport to employ expressive language in describing observations, the purpose of **quantitative research** is to gather numerical data on observed behavior with a view to subjecting the findings to statistical analysis.

Research and development has as its purpose the design of new products (for example, computer programs, media materials, teacher training aids) to address specific needs. Once created, the materials are field-tested, evaluated, and revised until specified criteria of quality and effectiveness are satisfied.

CLASSIFICATION OF RESEARCH BY METHOD

This textbook does not endorse one method of research at the expense of another. Each method has its place; each method has its value. If an administrator is interested in knowing the attitudes of teachers toward morale within the school, the *survey* is likely to be the design of choice. On the other hand, if a high school guidance counselor is interested in knowing whether there is a statistical relationship between student achievement in social studies and achievement on a Scholastic Aptitude Test, a *correlation study* would be appropriate. An elementary school classroom teacher who wants to know whether massed practice is as effective as spaced practice in generating achievement in spelling would likely choose to do an *experiment*. Selecting the method, then, is dependent on the topic to be investigated.

Briefly defined, *research is a carefully prescribed process of collecting and analyzing data*. This process is systematic, purposeful, and predicated on the careful application of the scientific method. It is always possible to generate data that are subject to question because of assorted, unplanned-for problems arising with the subjects or the setting during the course of the investigation; however, the careful planning of the design and control of the **variables** will increase the likelihood that the findings will be objective, reliable, and valid.

Given that one goal of all scientific endeavors is to arrive at solutions that are verifiable, it is necessary to follow carefully designed and monitored steps—steps that employ the scientific method. These steps are offered in the following list.

1. Select and define the problem. The researcher must articulate a specific goal for the investigation. Normally, this takes the form of a clear and measurable hypothesis.

2. Create the research plan. The plan (design) for the study will dictate the specifics of the procedures to be followed. These procedures include the selection of subjects, instrument(s) of assessment, and processes for sampling, gathering, and analyzing data.

3. Collect the data and prepare them for analysis.

4. Analyze the data. Data analysis involves the use of one or more statistical procedures (if the study is quantitative) or a trend analysis procedure (if the study is qualitative).

5. Express findings, conclusions, and recommendations.

While there are additional steps to take, depending upon the specific requirements of the research method being used, the five steps listed here are common to *all* designs. Again, the design one selects is dictated by the problem to be solved. (Processes for creating these designs will be presented in Chapters 6–11.) Knowing and understanding the various designs, and the implementation procedures unique to each, is important to both the conductor and the consumer of research. The conductor needs to know the elements of each design in order to select the process that will allow for an effective examination of the problem to be investigated. The consumer must have knowledge of the various designs in order to judge effectively the validity of the research and the implications of the findings to his employment setting.

The various research methods (designs) fall under either of two umbrella categories: descriptive or experimental. **Descriptive** studies examine the past or current status of individuals, institutions, or processes. There is no attempt to manipulate, influence, or control the variables in any way. Utilizing carefully designed survey or recording forms, the researcher relies on information obtained from prime and secondary sources. On the other hand, **experimental studies** do more that describe what was or what is. They examine cause-and-effect relationships. For example, if a classroom teacher is interested in knowing whether frequency of computer usage in her seventh-grade Introduction to Literature class influences achievement, she is asking about the causal nature of the relationship between computer usage and class achievement. To answer this question, the teacher would administer the treatment (independent) variable—computer usage—and measure its effect upon the dependent (outcome) variable—class achievement. There are various factors, other than computer usage, that could influence student achievement, including frequency with which students study, teaching competence, parental influence, and validity of the instruments of assessment to arrive at final grades. Techniques for controlling such extraneous influences become part of the research design.

In short, if you are manipulating variables, the study is experimental; if not, the study is descriptive. The following text introduces the various research methods (designs) that fall into these two categories.

Descriptive Studies

Case study research has, as its purpose, the investigation of one, unique individual, group, or institution. It requires detailed observations and recordings over a period of time. The priorities of this method are to enhance understanding of what, when, where, how, and why.

Causal-comparative research, also referred to as ex post facto research, attempts to determine reasons for the present status of things. Alternative causes are examined after they have occurred. Rather than manipulating treatments, as is the case with experimental designs, the research focuses on what has occurred differently for comparative groups of subjects. For example, if it were observed that some students did well on the statistics portion of a pretest in a research design class and that others did not, one might be interested in determining the cause. Assume that an examination of their undergraduate transcripts reveals that those who did well shared one common thread: each of them had completed successfully an undergraduate course in statistics. On the other hand, it is observed that those who did not do well in the statistics portion of the pretest shared a common thread as well: none of them had completed an undergraduate statistics course. One could assume, therefore, that the cause of doing well is completing successfully an undergraduate course in statistics. Simply stated, completing an undergraduate statistics course appears to be the cause of doing well in the statistics portion of the pretest. This would be an example of a causal-comparative study. There is no manipulation of the variables.

Correlation research investigates the relationship between two or more variables. It requires that one collects data on at least two variables for an identical group of subjects and, using a specific statistical procedure (discussed in Chapter 7), computes a coefficient between the measures. The purpose of correlation research is twofold: (1) to identify the extent of the statistical relationship between the variables, and (2) to use the coefficient representing this relationship to make predictions from one variable to another. A variable is a concept (for example, attribute or behavior) that can assume different values depending upon how it is used in the study. Examples of variables include achievement, family income, intelligence, and motivation.

Historical research attempts to establish facts and arrive at conclusions concerning persons, places, and events of the past. One goal of the study of history is to gain a better understanding of present circumstances.

Philosophical research examines the principles of laws that underlie knowledge and reality, and the processes that govern thought and behavior. The philosophical method involves critical thinking beyond the realm of fact-finding science. It requires that the researcher reflect upon the conclusions of science in order to develop more comprehensive position statements.

Survey research is the systematic collection, analysis, interpretation, and report of pertinent facts and findings about the current status of persons, processes, products, or programs. Through the use of interviews and written questionnaires, information is gathered with a view toward identifying relative strengths and weaknesses of topics under study.

Test and measurement research utilizes processes appropriate to the creation and revision of instruments of assessment (for example, achievement tests, attitude scales, personality inventories). Procedures include developing objectives, tables of specifications, and questions; jury validation; pilot testing; and item analysis.

In Part II of this book, the reader will find a thorough discussion of the selection criteria and procedures appropriate to each of these methods.

Experimental Studies

Noncomparative group research, often referred to as a "nondesign" because there is no control group, attempts to examine the effects of a treatment upon a dependent variable. Noncomparative group studies may be done with or without pretests.

Comparative group research investigates the effects of a treatment upon a dependent variable, but in contrast to a noncomparative design, there is a control group—that is, a group that does not receive the treatment (for example, new method). Comparative group studies may be done with or without pretests.

Interrupted time series research, utilizing data trends, requires several repeated measurements on the same subjects prior and pursuant to the administration of the treatment. Assessing the effect of a treatment upon the dependent variable, this research may be done with or without a control group.

Although there are alternatives to the experimental methods introduced here, these, used alone or in combination, constitute the procedures most often desired by those doing studies requiring the administration of treatments. Table 1–1 provides a summary of their important features. Part III of the text will reveal the techniques critical to the selection and employment of experimental methodology. Discussion is presented on each of these designs as entities and, where applicable, how they may be used in combination. For example, a noncomparative pretest-posttest design could be extended into a repeated treatment design:

O X O X O X O X O

In such a design, treatments are repeated after all but the final observation/ measurement.

✓CHECKPOINT

Please respond to each item below by identifying the descriptive or experimental method that you believe is likely to be the design of choice.

A category of research in which:

1. one is interested in determining the derivation of corporal punishment as a method of discipline at School Administrative Unit #48.
2. one is interested in seeking the extent of statistical relationship between achievement in social studies and mathematics for sixth-grade students at Mt. Kearsarge Elementary School.
3. an individual is tracked over a six-week marking period in order to discover behavioral trends.
4. two groups had similar averages at the onset of the study. The one that received the treatment did *not* improve significantly over the group from which the treatment was withheld.
5. one wants to measure the existing attitudes of teachers toward student morale at Nashua High School.

Answers

How do you think that you did? Were you in the "comfort zone" with regard to offering responses? Here are the answers you should have given.

1. Historical
2. Correlation
3. Case study
4. Pretest-posttest control-group
5. Survey

If you have any doubts about the appropriateness of these answers, examine the descriptions of each research method again. Having this base knowledge is important because the following text will introduce the procedures for arriving at a **problem statement** for the research you may have an interest in doing.

INVESTIGATING ONE'S FIELD OF INTEREST

Problems suitable for investigation exist everywhere. They can be found in the classroom, the teachers' room, or the living room. Wherever your interest is aroused, a problem is in the making. Where does your interest lie? Is it in teaching within such areas of speciality as art, English, foreign languages, health, mathematics, music, natural science,

Table 1–1: **Summary of Features of Selected Experimental Designs***

Design	Diagram	Number of Groups
Noncomparative posttest only	X O	One
Pretest-posttest	O X O	One
Comparative posttest only control-group	X O O	Two or more
Pretest-posttest control-group	O X O O O	Two or more
Interrupted time series repeated measures	O O O X O O O	One
Repeated measures control-group	O O O X O O O O O O O O O	Two or more

*O = tests/observations; X = treatment

physical education, social science, or special education? Is it administration—perhaps guidance and counseling, or school nursing? Each of these areas represent a **field of interest.** The first task, then, is identify your field of interest.

Having established your field of interest, you need to identify a **problem area.** As a classroom teacher, you might be interested in discovering the best method to generate student knowledge and understanding of causes of the Civil War. As a special education supervisor within a school district, you may want to know the attitude of the teachers toward inclusionary education. A high school principal may need to determine whether formal training for teachers is necessary in order for them to use successfully the new computer software for submitting student grade reports.

If you are a first-year graduate student enrolled in a research design course, you may be uncertain about what problem to select. You might find this to be one of the most difficult tasks. While there is no lack of problems in education to be solved, it is partly a matter of not being familiar enough with the literature. In this case, what you need to do is look at references such as the following for guidance:

American Educational Research Association. (1931–present). *Review of educational research*. Washington, DC: Author, and Mitzel, H. (Ed.) (1992).

Encyclopedia of educational research. New York: Macmillan (1992).

You might also discuss general interests with faculty and other students, or review textbooks and journals within your major field of interest. Each of these sources will help you to generate ideas.

In short, whatever your field of interest, the problem should be so clearly stated that anyone reading the problem statement would know exactly what you have in mind. Lack of clarity is certain to cause problems for you later. It is very easy to lose focus when the problem is stated in vague terms. For example, suppose you are interested in doing a study in the spring semester of the current academic year to determine the attitude of teachers in the school district about inclusionary education. Do you mean all teachers, whether or not they have students with exceptionalities in their classrooms, or are you concerned only about the attitudes of those teachers who have children with coded disabilities? Is it important to know whether teachers have prior experience in working with students with exceptionalities, or whether they have been trained to work with these children? Be clear; be precise. To do so means that you need to consider identifying **differentiating factors** (also called delimitations). In this example, one might want to clarify the problem by specifying:

1. the name of the school administrative unit and grade levels.
2. whether the target of the study would be full- or part-time teachers.
3. whether the teachers to be included are trained or untrained.
4. whether the teachers need to be experienced or inexperienced.
5. whether the students in the classroom(s) have coded exceptionalities.

As a result of these considerations, the problem statement could read: This study will examine the attitudes of all K–8 classroom teachers within School Administrative Unit (SAU) #48 toward inclusionary education for children with exceptionalities.

 NOTE: The use of the term *all* (K–8 classroom teachers) implies that (1) level of training or experience, (2) full- or part-time status, or (3) whether they have students in their classes who are coded by exceptionality, are not differentiating factors in this study.

Arising out of the problem statement would be the hypothesis for the study. Hypotheses are classified as either research or statistical (null). A **research hypothesis** is used with descriptive studies. In the example on inclusionary education, one would use such a hypothesis, since the study is descriptive. This research hypothesis would read:

> Assuming a valid data-gathering process, it is hypothesized that a survey conducted of SAU #48, K–8 teachers during the spring term of the current academic year, will reveal their attitudes toward inclusionary education.

A tenth-grade social science teacher is becoming disenchanted with the method he has been using to teach about causes of the Civil War. Quite by chance, he comes across an article in a professional journal that proposes the use of new computer software, designed specifically for studying causes of the Civil War, which has recently come on the market (and would be available on loan for one year). Given the fact that the teacher is responsible for two sections of the same course, he decides to try the software with one of them in order to test its effectiveness. To conduct such a study, he should use a statistical **(null) hypothesis,** namely:

> It is hypothesized that the computer software (Variable A) will be as effective as current practice (Variable B) in enhancing knowledge and understanding of the Civil War.

If the findings are not held to be significant (using statistical procedures to be described in Part III), the researcher would accept the null hypothesis; that is, there is no real difference in the two methods. It appears, therefore, that any statistical difference in the numerical values generated by the posttest can be attributed to chance alone. On the other hand, if the findings are significant, the teacher would reject the null hypothesis in favor of one of the alternatives. Either (Variable A), the use of computer software, is superior to (Variable B), the current practice, or vice versa. Being significant means that something other than chance has affected the findings in favor of the method generating the greater numerical values.

Note #1: If the null hypothesis is accepted, the inference can be made that the use of the software is as effective as current practice in generating knowledge and understanding of causes of the Civil War. Thus, the teacher may choose to continue the use of the software in order to avoid his own disenchantment with current practice. Assuming that it is practical for the school district to purchase the software (after the loan period has expired), the increased motivation of the teacher alone may be argument enough for its use being continued.

Note #2: There is a difference between statistical significance and practical significance. In this example, the teacher may find that the use of the computer software is statistically more effective than current practice in enhancing knowledge and understanding of the Civil War, but the school district may not be able to afford to purchase the software (upon termination of the loan period). Thus, the findings are significant, but not practical.

Note #3: In experimental studies, it is recommended that one use the null rather than the directional hypothesis for two basic reasons: (1) it implies neutrality on the part of the researcher, and (2) many of the statistical tables are based upon a test for no preference. The directional hypothesis takes the position, at the onset of the study, that one method is superior to another. While the researcher may have a hunch, it is best not to commit. (Assume for a minute that you are trying to gain support for your study from the parents of the children who are enrolled in your social science classes. It is unlikely that many parents would be supportive of your subjecting their children to what you are declaring as an inferior teaching method.)

✔CHECKPOINT

Write a null hypothesis for the following scenario:

> Recent studies carried out in Europe show that the use of amphetamines in treating hyperactivity may be a dangerous practice, and in the United States, practitioners report that behavior modification is successful in treating a variety of behavioral disorders, including hyperactivity.

Answer

Your null hypothesis statement should look something like this: It is hypothesized that behavior modification techniques will be as effective as amphetamines in reducing hyperactivity.

✔CHECKPOINT

How could the specificity of the null hypothesis expressed in the previous Checkpoint be enhanced?

Answer

Use differentiating factors described earlier, for example, age, gender, grade level; term, semester, marking period; name of K–8, secondary school for hyperactive children; location. Now, to increase your own understanding, attempt to arrange your own scenario.

Acknowledging that this part represents but an introduction, more will be said about these processes in Parts II and III, where you will examine sample topics and be guided through specific procedures for creating complete research designs for these topics (from the statement of the problem to data analysis, findings, conclusions, and recommendations).

Review of Related Literature

Once a problem has been identified, it is natural for the investigator to want to get the research underway as soon as possible. It is important to keep in mind, however, that a prerequisite to successful research is the investment of time in surveying what is already known about the subject. This review of the literature involves the identification, location, and analysis of documents that contain information pertaining to that problem. In alphabetical, not priority, order, this includes the use of abstracts, book guides to the literature, dictionaries, directories, encyclopedias, handbooks, newspaper and periodical indexes, and textbook sources. The following text provides examples of some of these sources and additional information that may be helpful in determining the appropriateness of the source.

Abstracts. These publications provide the reader with salient, nonevaluatory descriptions of published or unpublished documents. Normally, **abstracts** include a statement of the problem, a brief description of the population sample, research methods, and a summary of important findings. Examining an abstract can be very helpful in determining whether the complete document is appropriate to your needs and worth procurement. Among the various sources of abstracts are:

Black, D. (Ed.). (1965). *Guide to lists of master's theses*. Chicago: American Library Association. This source includes two main lists of master's theses: by institution and by special fields. The entries within the special fields lists are accompanied by annotations.

Dissertation abstracts international. (1938–Present). Ann Arbor, MI: University Microfilms. Published monthly, this source contains abstracts of doctoral dissertations submitted by over three hundred cooperating colleges and universities. Many libraries provide online database searching of DAI through such vendors as Bibliographic Retrieval Services Information Technologies; CompuServe Information Service, Inc.; and Dialog Information Services, Inc.

The **Educational Resources Information Center (ERIC)** has two major publications:

Current index to journals in education (CIJE). (1969–Present). This publication provides information on articles from nearly eight hundred education journals.

Resources in education (RIE). (1966–Present). This source identifies and provides abstracts for unpublished documents, including course syllabi, curriculum guides, and papers presented at conferences.

Dunbar and Beary (1994) and Zinfon (1996) are among those who offer instructions for accessing ERIC documents. The Educational Resources Information Center maintains clearinghouses that collect, abstract, and distribute information within their respective areas of responsibility. These areas are assessment and evaluation, disabilities and gifted education, information and technology, teaching and teacher education, and urban education.

Psychological Abstracts (1927–Present) is published by the American Psychological Association. Although readers will observe that the focus is on psychology rather than education, most find a great deal of overlap between these two fields. The summaries of articles deemed to be most useful to educational researchers are those found within two of the twelve known areas of psychology, namely, developmental psychology and educational psychology.

The process for accessing both educational and psychological documents is very much the same. Your library will likely have both sets of the materials in traditional print, but you will find an increasing number of libraries with the capabilities for making CD-ROM searches. (A CD is a compact disc that "plays" visual information instead of music; ROM refers to "read-only memory," implying that you can read, interact with, and print but not change the contents of the disc.) A major distributor of a CD-ROM version of the data is SilverPlatter. The SilverPlatter system contains thousands of references to research articles and reports in education (ERIC) and psychology (PsycLit). Zinfon (1996) suggests the following basic instructions for doing a CD-ROM search for ERIC and PsycLit materials.

To search records:

1. Look up your subject term(s) in the brown Thesaurus of ERIC Descriptors or the green Thesaurus of Psychological Index Terms. Use only these terms first. They are called "descriptors." Enter your term as a subject descriptor (as opposed to a randomly occurring keyword) by hyphenating it as follows:

   intelligence-tests

   pretesting-

2. Type your subject terms whenever the bottom of the screen says FIND. If you do not see the FIND prompt, press the F2 key. Press ENTER after you type each term.

3. To narrow or specify your subject further, combine descriptors with the Boolean operators AND, OR, or NOT.

 NOTE: The term *Boolean* is from the name George Boole, an English mathematician and logician. He showed the relationship between mathematics and logic in *Mathematical Analysis of Logic* (1847) and *Investigation of the Laws of Thought* (1854).

For example:

Shaded Area(s) Indicates Retrieval

(CMT / NCMT Venn diagram, both shaded)	Certified Music Teachers (CMT) OR Noncertified Music Teachers (NCMT)	Articles that include either
(CMT / NCMT Venn diagram, none shaded)	Certified Music Teachers (CMT) AND Noncertified Music Teachers (NCMT)	Articles that include both
(CMT / NCMT Venn diagram, CMT shaded)	Certified Music Teachers (CMT) NOT Noncertified Music Teachers (NCMT)	Articles that include certified music teachers, but not noncertified music teachers

4. To combine terms that you have already entered, type the set numbers [that is, the number sign (#) and the set numbers] of those terms; for example, #1 AND #2.

5. Likewise, to combine a term already entered with a new one, type the set number of the first term, followed by AND, then the new term; for example, #2 AND test-validity.

To display records:

1. To view records found, press F4.

2. The DOWN ARROW key moves the cursor down one line. Press the PGDN key to move to the next screen of the record, or press the plus (+) key to move to the top of the next record. To move back to the top of the previous record, press the minus (–) key.

3. As you scroll through the records, press ENTER to MARK each record you wish to print out later. Make sure the blinking cursor is on some part of the record you want to mark.

To print records:

1. Press the F6 key, or the letter P.

2. The PRINT OPTIONS window will appear showing the default print settings. The system is set to print the basic citation, the abstract, and the descriptors for each item, as shown by CITN,AB,DE in the FIELDS TO PRINT line.

3. If you have previously MARKED each record you wish to print, the RECORDS TO PRINT line will already indicate MARKED. To print these records, simply press ENTER.

4. If you did not MARK your records, or if you wish to make other changes in print options, press C.

5. Another window will appear with directions for making changes. If you did not mark your records, use the TAB key to move to the RECORDS TO PRINT space, then type in the numbers you wish to print; for example: 1-12, or 3, 8, 14, 15, 19-23, etc.

6. After making all changes in the PRINT OPTIONS window, press ENTER. The window will reformat with the changes you made. Press ENTER again to accept changes and begin printing.

7. To search other topics, or make new combinations of terms, press F2. If you have finished searching, press F7.

Book guides to the literature. These publications will direct the researcher to sources of information. Among the most popular of **book guides** are:

Durnin, R. G. (1982). *American education: A guide to information sources*. Detroit, MI: Gale Research.

Freed, M. N. (Ed.). (1989). *The educator's desk reference: A sourcebook of educational information and research*. New York: Macmillan.

Kennedy, J. R. (1979). *Library research guide to education: Illustrated search strategy and sources*. Ann Arbor, MI: Pierian Press.

O'Brien, N. P., & Fabiano, E. (1991). *Core list of books and journals in education*. Phoenix, AZ: Oryx Press.

Woodbury, M. (1982). *A guide to sources of educational information* (2nd ed.). Arlington, VA: Information Resources Press.

Dictionaries. These sources are used to define educational terms and concepts. Observe, however, that you should refrain from using standard **dictionaries** of the type normally found in one's home. The definitions in them are too generic. You will want definitions that apply to education. As an illustration, look up the word *stress* in a standard dictionary, then look it up in a dictionary of education. There is greater stress on the metal of airplanes with increasing "G" forces; there is teacher stress; or stress can be a point of emphasis. A list of recommended dictionaries follows:

Good, C. V. (Ed.). (1973). *Dictionary of education* (3rd ed.). New York: McGraw-Hill.

Hawes, G. R., & Hawes, L. S. (1982). *The concise dictionary of education*. New York: Van Nostrand Reinhold.

Shafritz, J. M., Koeppe, R. P., & Soper, E. W. (1988). *The facts on file dictionary of education*. New York: Facts on File.

Directories. These publications are used as sources for names, addresses, and telephone numbers. Among the directories recommended for researchers are:

Burek, D. M., et al. (1994). *Encyclopedia of associations* (28th ed.). Detroit, MI: Gale Research.

Moody, D. (1993). *Patterson's American education*. Mount Prospect, IL: Educational Directories. This directory covers 30,000 secondary schools; 3,000 private and Catholic secondary schools, and over 7,000 postsecondary schools. It is organized by geographical location.

Moody, D., et al. (Eds.). (1993). *Patterson's elementary education*. Mount Prospect, IL: Educational Directories. This directory covers 60,000 elementary schools and 11,300 private and Catholic elementary schools. It is organized by geographical location.

Encyclopedias. Some **encyclopedias** to consider for your search include:

Husen, T., & Postlethwaite. T. N. (Eds.). (1994). *The international encyclopedia of education* (2nd ed.). New York: Pergamon Press.

Knowles, A. S. (1977). *The international encyclopedia of higher education*. New York: Pergamon Press.

Kurian, G. T. (Ed.). (1988). *World education encyclopedia*. New York: Facts on File.

Mitzel, H. (Ed.). (1992). *Encyclopedia of educational research* (6th edition). New York: The Free Press.

Reynolds, C. R., & Fletcher-Janzen, E. (Eds.). (1990). *Concise encyclopedia of special education*. New York: Wiley.

Sills, D. L. (Ed.). (1968). *International encyclopedia of social sciences*. New York: Macmillan.

Thomas, R. M. (Ed.). (1990). *The encyclopedia of human development and education: Theory, research, and studies*. New York: Pergamon Press.

Handbooks. These publications attempt to provide a one-volume overview of generally accepted facts and procedures. Especially valuable for bibliographic leads are the following **handbooks:**

Cameron, J., et al. (Eds.). (1983). *International handbook of education systems*. Volume 1: Europe and Canada; Volume II: Africa and the Middle East; Volume III: Australia and Latin America. New York: Wiley.

Harrison, C. (1988). *Public schools USA: A comparative guide to school districts* (2nd ed.). Princeton, NJ: Peterson's Guides.

Kapel, D. E., Gifford, C. S., & Kapel, M. B. (1991). *American educators' encyclopedia*. New York: Greenwood.

Pearson, J. B., & Fuller, E. (1969). *Education in the states: Historical development and outlook*. A project of the Council of Chief State School Officers. Washington, DC: National Education Association.

Postlethwaite, T. N. (Ed.). (1988). *The encyclopedia of comparative education and national systems of education*. New York: Pergamon Press.

Requirements for certification of teachers, counselors, librarians, administrators for elementary and secondary schools (58th ed.). (1993–1994). Chicago: The University of Chicago Press.

Wittrock, M. C. (Ed.). (1985). *Handbook of research on teaching* (3rd ed.). A project of the American Educational Research Association. New York: Macmillan.

Newspaper and periodical indexes. These indexes identify sources in which pertinent articles can be found. In addition to the *Current Index to Journals in Education* (CIJE), published by the Educational Resources Information Center (referenced earlier under Abstracts), the most popular and useful of the **newspaper index** and **periodical index** documents are:

Christian science monitor index. (1945–Present). Ann Arbor, MI: UMI, A Bell & Howell Company. This index provides abstracts and comprehensive indexing of all articles of research significance. With eight-month, along with quarterly and annual, cumulations, the coverage includes book reviews, business and financial news, commentaries, editorials, feature articles, and news items.

Education index. (1929–Present). New York: Wilson. This index lists bibliographical information on references appearing in education periodicals, as well as in bulletins, yearbooks, and other educational reports.

Newsbank. (1981–Present). New Canaan, CT: NewsBank, Inc. This is a reference service providing access to articles from newspapers of over four hundred and fifty United States cities. Full-text articles of research value are selected from the newspapers and reproduced on microfiche each month. A printed index to the microfiche is published monthly, and cumulated quarterly and annually. The broad categories into which articles are organized include, among others, Arts and Literature, Business and Economic Development, Consumer Affairs, Education, Employment, Environment, Government, Health, Housing and Land Development, International Affairs and Defense, Law and Legal Systems, People, Political Development, Science and Technology, Social Relations, Transportation, and Welfare and Social Problems.

New York times index. (1851–Present). New York: Wilson. With semimonthly, quarterly, and annual cumulations, this source contains abstracts of the significant news, editorial matter, and special features published in the daily and Sunday newspapers. The entries are classified under appropriate subject, geography, organization, and personal name headings. While the *New York Times Index* and the *Readers' Guide to Periodical Literature* (referenced below) do not index articles in professional journals, these sources can still be useful in enabling the researcher to assess public and editorial sentiment on issues of concern.

Readers' guide to periodical literature. (1900–Present). New York: Wilson. With semimonthly and annual cumulations, this source indexes articles in nontechnical references, such as *Newsweek, Reader's Digest,* and *U.S. News and World Report.*

Social science citation index (SSCI). (1974–Present). Philadelphia, PA: Institute for Scientific Information. This index identifies reports having to do with education and behavioral science. One of the values of this particular index is that if, for example, D. Anderson published research in 1980 on teacher attitudes toward

inclusionary education, the SSCI would provide a listing of subsequent research reports that made reference to Anderson's work.

Textbook sources. These are sources that identify the names of the authors, titles, publishers, and copyright dates of books published in assorted fields of interest and problem areas. Highlighting any roster of **textbook sources** is:

Books in Print. (Current). New Providence, NJ: Bowker.

This is considered to be the best source for identifying older and recent publications that are currently in print.

SUMMARY

Advancing one's knowledge in order to effect optimum school practice and reform is a product of carefully designed research. While tradition and experience are aids to understanding truth, they cannot replace thoughtful applications of the scientific method.

There are various dimensions to research. It can be classified according to purpose—that is, whether it is applied, basic, qualitative, quantitative, or research and development. Research can also be classified according to whether it is descriptive or experimental.

Following an introduction in this chapter to various descriptive and experimental methodologies, the process of selecting and refining a problem statement was presented. This led to a discussion of research and statistical hypotheses—in particular, their construction and when each is used. The chapter concluded with a section on sources of information that were offered in order to aid the reader in accessing documents and completed studies on topics of concern.

Rather strict conventions are used in educational research in order to help ensure that findings are valid. Therefore, it is important that the contents of Chapter 1 are known and understood before embarking further. You had the opportunity to respond to "checkpoint" questions in order to help you test your acquired knowledge as you progressed through the chapter, and now you are provided with a series of summary laboratory assignments. You will be at an advantage if you take the time to respond to each of these items before beginning Chapter 2, which covers the ethics of research.

RECOMMENDED LABORATORY ASSIGNMENTS

1. Respond to each of the objectives cited at the beginning of the chapter.

2. Meet with fellow graduate students and colleagues in order to share ideas about possible research topics.

3. Arrange to interview department chairpersons, school principals, business managers, and school superintendents in order to learn of their perceptions regarding priority research topics for the district.

4. Meet with school and nonschool employees who have carried out applied research projects in order to discuss their interests and experiences.

5. Review the recommended readings.

6. Prepare a problem statement and hypothesis for a topic requiring descriptive research. Give consideration to differentiating factors in your statements. Be able to identify and defend the use of the case study, causal-comparative, correlation, historical, philosophical, survey, or test and measurement research process that would be necessary to use in order to gather the data for your topic.

7. Prepare a problem statement and hypothesis for a topic requiring experimental research. Give consideration to differentiating factors in your statements. Be able to indicate whether you would use a comparative or noncomparative group design, and whether you would employ a pretest. Defend your response to colleagues and supervisors.

8. Do a literature review for the topic you chose in response to question 6 or 7, or for both topics. Which of the sources did you find most useful for your research interest(s), and why?

RECOMMENDED READINGS

Bereiter, C. (1994). Implications of postmodernism for science, or, science as progressive discourse. *Educational Psychologist, 29,* 3–12.

Brandt, R. (1992). On research on teaching: A conversation with Lee Schulman. *Educational Leadership, 49*(7), 14–19.

Buttram, J. L. (1990). Focus groups: A starting point for needs assessment. *Evaluation Practice, 11*(3), 207–212.

Cohen, D. K., & Ball, D. L. (1990). Relations between policy and practice: A commentary. *Educational Evaluation and Policy Analysis, 12*(3), 249–256.

Connelly, F. M., & Clandinin, D. J. (1990). Stories of experience and narrative inquiry. *Educational Researcher, 19*(5), 2–14.

Denzin, N. K., & Lincoln, Y. S. (1994). Introduction: Entering the field of qualitative research. In N. K. Denzin & Y. S. Lincoln (Eds.), *Handbook of qualitative research* (pp. 230–252). Thousand Oaks, CA: Sage.

Eisner, E. (1991). *The enlightened eye: Qualitative inquiry and the enhancement of educational practices.* New York: Macmillan.

Erickson, F. (1986). Qualitative methods in research on teaching. In M. C. Wittrock (Ed.), *Handbook of research on teaching* (3rd ed.). New York: Macmillan.

Houston, J. E. (Ed.). (1990). *Thesaurus of ERIC descriptors* (12th ed.). Phoenix, AZ: Oryx Press.

Jaeger, R. M. (1988). *Complementary methods for research in education.* Washington, DC: American Educational Research Association.

Lytle, S., & Cochran-Smith, M. (1992). Teacher research as a way of knowing. *Harvard Education Review, 62,* 447–474.

Sawin, E. (1992). Reaction: Experimental research in the context of other methods. *School of Education Review, 4,* 18–21.

Walberg, H. J. (1986). Synthesis of research on teaching. In M. Wittrock (Ed.). *Handbook of research on teaching.* (3rd ed., pp. 214–229). New York: Macmillan.

Wang, M. C., Haertel, G. D., & Walberg, H. J. (1993). Toward a knowledge base for school learning. *Review of Educational Research, 63,* 249–294.

Winkler, K. (1992). Researchers leave labs, flock to schools for a new look at how students learn. *Chronicle of Higher Education, 39*(8), 6–7.

REFERENCES

Altheide, D. L., & Johnson, J. M. (1994). Criteria for assessing interpretive validity in qualitative research. In N. K. Denzin & Y. S. Lincoln (Eds.), *Handbook of qualitative research* (pp. 485–499). Thousand Oaks, CA: Sage.

Dunbar, M., & Beary, M. (1994). *Basic instructions for using ERIC on CD—Easy menu searching*. Unpublished document, Library Services, Florida International University, Miami, FL.

Fullan, M. G., & Stiegelbauer, S. (1991). *The new meaning of educational change* (2nd ed.). New York: Teachers College Press.

Phillips, D. C. (1980). What do the researcher and the practitioner have to offer each other? *Educational Researcher, 9*(11), 19.

Zinfon, L. (1996). *Basic guide to searching ERIC and PSYCLIT*. Unpublished document, Office of Bibliographic Instruction, Plymouth State College, Plymouth, NH.

CHAPTER **2**

Ethical and Legal Considerations in Research

OBJECTIVES

After reading this chapter, you should be able to:

- Discuss the importance of ethical standards in human subject research.
- Distinguish between the Buckley Amendment and the National Research Act of 1974.
- Discuss the implications of the preambles to the ethical standards of the American Educational Research Association.
- Identify five standards of the Ethics Code as prescribed by the American Psychological Association.
- Identify and discuss six strategies that are recommended for protecting human subjects.
- Identify and discuss the essential ingredients of an informed consent letter.
- Identify the questions that are common to informed consent research proposal forms.
- Distinguish between the terms *beneficence* and *credibility*.
- Discuss conditions under which a researcher may find it necessary to suspend her study.

KEY TERMS

Accuracy

Accurate Disclosure

Active Deception

American Educational Research Associaiton (AERA)

American Psychological Association (APA)

Beneficence

Benefit-to-Risk Ratio

Buckley Amendment

Code of Conduct

Confidentiality

Conflict of Interest

Credibility

Double-Blind

Ethical Safeguards

Exculpatory

Full disclosure

Honesty

Human Subjects Research Committee (HSRC)

Informed Consent

Integrity

Legal Safeguards

National Research Act

Passive Deception

Principles

Privacy

Protection

Research Assistant

Risks

Single-Blind

Standards

INTRODUCTION

In Chapter 1, you were introduced to guidelines for selecting and defining a research problem. Although experience will bring increased levels of comfort to the process, you should feel some degree of confidence in your ability to delimit your options. As you were thinking about possible areas of inquiry, did you give any thought to whether ethical issues were at stake? Perhaps you were even wondering if there were legal implications to carrying out a study that came to mind. There are studies that could likely subject the participants to physical, mental, or emotional risks, therefore making them unethical to attempt. Some studies may even be contrary to current law. The purpose of this chapter is to address some of the ethical and legal issues that are necessary to consider in any proposed investigation.

GUIDING PRINCIPLES

Research should enhance the human condition. This holds true as much for the process of gathering information as it does for the findings generated by the investigation. In any research design, plans must be made to ensure that **ethical** and **legal safe-guards** are in place. Yet, it is not uncommon to find examples in the literature wherein research participants have been subjected to risk. Why is it that there appear to be no clear-cut answers to the question of whether a study is ethical? Examine each of the following questions and see if you can make a determination.

1. Can a researcher legitimately deceive those who are participating in the research by not laying out in detail the entire purpose of the study?

2. Can a researcher require that subjects introduce substances into their bodies in order to determine the effect of these substances upon cardiovascular endurance?

3. Can individuals who are prone to epileptic convulsion be allowed to participate in a study in which flashes of light in a dark room are produced at predetermined intervals in order to test their effect on the onset of seizures?

4. Can a select group of students within a tenth-grade social studies class be denied access to computers in order to reaffirm a theory that test scores will decline if computers are not used?

5. Can test results be posted on a classroom door in order to observe levels of anxiety expressed by students with high, average, and low scores?

6. Can actors be introduced into a prison in order to assess the extent to which their staged brawling produces measurable (or unmeasurable) chaos among the inmates there?

How did you make out? Did you feel as though you needed more information? Probably so, but what information would you want? It should be clear that the solution to each question may depend upon a number of things. In the vast majority of cases, researchers do resolve such matters and make intelligent decisions about the propriety of carrying out certain investigations.

Among the associations that have responded to public and professional concern about some of the practices that have been revealed in published, as well as unpublished, papers is the **American Educational Research Association (AERA).** In 1992, the AERA published forty-five **standards** as a guide to educational researchers, editors-reviewers, and institutional review boards. The preambles to each of the six topics within which the standards can be found are as follows.

1. Responsibilities to the Field

> Preamble. To maintain the **integrity** of research, educational researchers should warrant their research conclusions adequately in a way consistent with the standards of their own theoretical and methodological perspectives. They should keep themselves well informed in both their own and competing paradigms where those are relevant to their research, and they should continually evaluate the criteria of adequacy by which research is judged.

2. Research Populations, Educational Institutions, and the Public

> Preamble. Educational researchers conduct research within a broad array of settings and institutions, including schools, colleges, universities, hospitals, and prisons. It is of paramount importance that

educational researchers respect the rights, **privacy,** dignity, and sensitivities of their research populations and also the integrity of the institutions within which the research occurs. Educational researchers should be especially careful in working with children and other vulnerable populations. These standards are intended to reinforce and strengthen already existing standards enforced by institutional review boards and other professional associations.

3. Intellectual Ownership

   Preamble. Intellectual ownership is predominantly a function of creative contribution. Intellectual ownership is not predominantly a function of effort expended.

4. Editing, Reviewing, and Appraising Research

   Preamble. Editors and reviewers have a responsibility to recognize a wide variety of theoretical and methodological perspectives and, at the same time, to ensure that manuscripts meet the highest standards as defined in the various perspectives.

5. Sponsors, Policy Makers, and Other Users of Research

   Preamble. Researchers, research institutions, and sponsors of research jointly share responsibility for the ethical integrity of research, and should ensure that this integrity is not violated. While it is recognized that these parties may sometimes have conflicting legitimate aims, all those with responsibility for research should protect against compromising the standards of research, the community of researchers, the subjects of research, and the users of research. They should support the widest possible dissemination and publication of research results. AERA should promote, as nearly as it can, conditions conducive to the preservation of research integrity.

6. Students and Student Researchers

   Preamble. Educational researchers have responsibility to ensure the competence of those inducted into the field and to provide appropriate help and professional advice to novice researchers.

A second organization, the **American Psychological Association (APA),** has published an Ethics Code, or **code of conduct,** for those engaged in supervising or producing research. Of the eight standards described in *Ethical Principles of Psychologists and Code of Conduct* (1992), the following five are particularly relevant to the conduct of research itself:

1. Ethical standards (Standard 1)
2. Evaluation, assessment, or intervention (Standard 2)
3. Privacy and confidentiality (Standard 5)
4. Teaching, training, supervision, research, and publishing (Standard 6)
5. Resolution of ethical issues (Standard 8)

When, as designers of research, you begin to create your own individual or group plans, close adherence to ethical **principles** cannot be overstated. I strongly recommend that you, or the institution in which you are employed, obtain copies of *Ethical Standards of the American Educational Research Association,* and the Ethics Code that is published by the American Psychological Association. Study them carefully. They will serve as valuable sources to you and your colleagues.

STRATEGIES FOR THE PROTECTION OF HUMAN SUBJECTS

To this point in the chapter, attention has focused upon principles underlying ethical practices. With these guidelines in mind, the discussion now turns to six ethical issues through which, if attended to by those supervising, producing, and using research, the preservation of research integrity will receive high marks.

Accuracy

The investigator has the responsibility to describe all pertinent processes used to gather and analyze the data, and to present the findings that were generated (whether or not they conform to one's expressed or unexpressed desires). **Accuracy** includes more than proofing the language of the problem statement and hypothesis, corroborating the dates of sources used in related literature, verifying tabular entries, and checking mathematical calculations. The researcher must also consider the potential for misinterpretation of the findings and conclusions and make every effort to communicate the procedures and results so that misunderstanding is minimized. If the researcher clarifies such things as the following, the reader of the research report is less likely to draw invalid inferences through *ignorance* or by *accident*.

1. Date and time of the investigation. Was the study carried out in the fall semester with the posttest administered just before Christmas break? Was the study conducted with a 9:00–10:00 A.M. class, or did it take place immediately after lunch? These conditions could generate different results, not because of the treatment, perhaps, but because of energy levels and interest of the subjects.

2. Character and size of the population or sample used in the study. *Character* includes such things as age, ability level, gender, grade level, economic status, experience, earned degrees, and number of siblings. Whether or not these differentiating factors are pertinent to your study, it is critical that the character of your specific study group be made clear.

3. Instrumentation used to gather data. Were the tests or surveys used in the study standardized, or did they have to be created by the investigator? If the instruments were standardized, who was the publisher? What evidence is there that the findings of validity for the standardized testing instruments are relevant to the group in *this* investigation? If the instruments had to be developed by the researcher, how was validity established?

4. Analytical procedures. What statistical procedure did you use to analyze the data? Did you use a descriptive statistic (for example, mean, median, or mode)

in order to simply describe the central tendency of the scores? Or did you employ an inferential statistic (for example, t test, or analysis of variance) in order to relate the findings to the larger population from which your sample study group was selected?

Confidentiality

In 1974, an important piece of human rights legislation was passed by Congress. The Family Educational Rights and Privacy Act (known as the **Buckley Amendment**) put into law the principle of **confidentiality.** Among its provisions is that the personal records of individuals cannot be revealed unless written permission is acquired from them or, if under age, from their parents or legal guardians. Illustrative of what have been found to be more prevalent among the violations of this amendment include:

1. Posting achievement scores by name or complete social security number
2. Displaying the work of individuals as examples of good or poor practice
3. Requesting individuals who completed a test to score the papers of others
4. Distributing scored papers to a group in a way that enables them to view the recorded achievement of others
5. Describing the performance of one individual to a third person who does not need or have the right to know such information
6. Examining the written records of an individual without being granted the authority to do so

A request for consent must indicate the purpose of the disclosure, the information that may be disclosed, and to whom it would be made available. Confidentiality can be guaranteed by making certain that the data cannot be linked to an individual subject by name. Among the ways by which one's privacy can be secured are the following:

1. Having subjects furnish information anonymously
2. Having a researcher-initiated identifier that is destroyed when response is received. (An identifier is useful if it becomes necessary to send a follow-up to a written survey that was not returned by the due date.)
3. Having subjects use their own code numbers or aliases. (Code numbers or aliases are necessary if you want to be able to match individual pretest to posttest performance.)
4. Having subjects enter their individual responses on a computer
5. Using a third party to link data to names, who then gives results to the researcher (without names attached)
6. Reporting group, not individual, data

For complete information on the provisions of the Buckley Amendment, contact the Family Educational Rights and Privacy Office, 200 Independence Avenue, SW, Washington, DC 20201.

Deception

To a certain extent, all research on human subjects involves some deception. For obvious reasons, it is important that participants in a study do not know exactly what the researcher expects them to do in particular situations; otherwise, there is likely to be acquiescence, which would then compromise the validity of the investigation. Since it is important that participants not know what the researcher expects, the practice of "not telling all" is *passive* **deception** and should be of no ethical concern. The researcher is not lying; rather, she simply is not mentioning something that the subject should not know about at the onset of the study. (If you are concerned about the matter, you can tell the participants that the expected results are being kept secret until the completion of the study in order not to affect their behavior.)

On the other hand, if the researcher intentionally creates a false impression in the minds of participants by lying to them or by using accomplices, this is known as *active* **deception.** For some studies, one could argue that active deception is necessary. For example, if a researcher wants to observe how students react to overt cheating in the classroom, it may be necessary to use a confederate (accomplice) who is assigned responsibility for cheating at predetermined times. (Finding natural occurrences in the classroom would not be wanted or desired.) The question is: How is a researcher to determine whether the deception used in a particular study is ethically justifiable? Is it likely, in this example, that cheating (by the accomplice) would encourage cheating by others? Would we want that? In short, is there an advantageous **benefit-to-risk ratio**? The following discussion may help to clarify this matter.

1. Deception should not be used unnecessarily. Even if getting the information without the use of deception would be more costly in time or money, the practice of deception should be avoided.

2. The research should be important to the public at large. It is not justifiable to engage in active deception simply to satisfy the interest of a few scholars. There should be significant social benefit as a result of the research, such as that done by Milgram (1963) in which volunteers were ordered by an authority figure to administer shock treatments to a research confederate in order to test for the existence of "blind obedience." (The "volunteers" were unaware that the effects of the "shock treatment" upon the confederate were fabricated.) The study was done due to expressed concern about the "blind obedience" of much of the German population during World War II to genocidal orders of the Nazi regime. How likely is it that people will perform life-threatening or, at the very least, painful tasks if encouraged to do so by their leaders? Do individuals show any remorse after they have carried out their "assignments"? In Milgram's study, desensitization was provided in order to convince volunteers of the deception that occurred and the reason for it, and in order to remove undesirable effects.

To a great extent, the ethical concerns about this study have centered around the potential for emotional harm to the participants. No one denies that the risk was there, or that the participants, though permitted to terminate their involvement at any time, experienced painful emotional reactions. On the other hand, the defenders of the study claim that the research produced benefits unattainable in other ways and, further, that long-term follow-up programs have revealed no negative after-effects in the participants. In short, it seems that the argument of "just following orders" used in the War Crimes Trials could be accurate—*not good,* but accurate. Surely if a rational society desires to prevent similar situations from arising in the future, these situations must first be understood. The question is: Was the temporary discomfort of a few volunteers worth the risk? You be the judge.

Disclosure

Those who are being sought as research participants should be informed accurately about the general nature of the research, as well as unusual procedures to which they may be subjected. *Accurate* **disclosure,** however, is not synonymous with *full* **disclosure.** As indicated in the discussion of deception, full disclosure would provide subjects with information that could invalidate the findings of the study. In research that involves entire classes of students, it is generally unnecessary to obtain permission from parents or legal guardians. Normally, it is sufficient to obtain permission from the school principal. In any event, get the permission in writing. For most studies, an informed consent letter would include:

Not OK

1. Reference to the fact that subjects have a free choice about whether they wish to participate in the study. Subjects should not feel coerced as a consequence of their being in a class taught by someone who is doing the research.

2. Language that readers of the letter can understand. The words used should not be so scientific that one would require technical training in order to understand them. General vocabulary should also be at the level of the reader. It is not very helpful to anyone if readers do not understand what you are telling or asking of them.

3. No language that is **exculpatory**—that is, language that is designed to free the researcher from liability should negligence be determined.

4. A reasonable explanation of the research—accurate, but not necessarily full.

5. Procedures to be used to maintain confidentiality.

6. Procedures to follow in case of injury. (This is particularly necessary in studies that are designed to measure such qualities as cardiovascular endurance.)

7. A contact person. Such a person should be identified for potential participants in the event they have questions about the study.

An example of a letter and postcard used to enlist cooperation on the part of directors for a study dealing with program evaluation can be found in Figures 2–1 and 2–2.

Honesty

If research is to enhance the human condition, it is absolutely essential that facts and findings be reported truthfully. Although it may seem unnecessary to address the issue of **honesty,** it is with alarming frequency that one can read of data being manipulated in order to yield findings that researchers or sponsors of grants are

Figure 2–1: **Sample Informed Consent Letter**

Date

Dear _____:

As a graduate student at Indiana University, I am presently developing the frame-work for a doctoral dissertation entitled *A Critical Evaluation of Undergraduate Professional Preparation in Physical Education for Men and Women in Selected Colleges and Universities of New England.* The scorecard that will be used in the evaluation is the result of multiple studies conducted by its authors, Doctors Karl W. Bookwalter and Robert J. Dollgener. This scorecard has been validated by authoritative and pertinent references. It includes areas, subareas, and items, each appropriately weighted, thus affording specific evaluation information for each institution.

The purpose of this letter is to ask your cooperation in making this study. This cooperation would consist of (1) a personal interview (approximately two hours in length, (2) permission to observe some of your facilities and equipment, and (3) completion of the enclosed postal card. You will be contacted by telephone in order to establish a date for the visitation.

Be assured that any findings regarding your institution will remain anonymous at all times with the exception that you personally will be provided with results per-taining to your institution upon the completion of the study. This information will include (1) relative strengths and weaknesses, and (2) national position accord-ing to areas, subareas, and total scores.

Should you have any questions, please do not hesitate to call, e-mail, or write. Pertinent addresses and numbers are located on the attached card. Thanking you in advance for your thoughtful consideration of this matter, I remain

Sincerely yours,

Douglas C. Wiseman
Attachment
Enclosure

looking to find. Such "fixing" of data is inexcusable. It can (1) set back scientific progress in that it makes all research suspect, (2) generate improper practices because of information thought to be correct, and (3) establish inappropriate base-lines for new research.

As Charles (1995) points out: "That bona fide researchers would risk loss of repu-tations and careers by tampering with data shows how high the stakes are in certain

Figure 2–2: **Self-addressed Postal Card**

❏ I am willing to grant you time for an interview   Date: _____
     and will make our facilities available.   (Month)   (Day)

I have arranged for you to interview:
Dr/Mr/Mrs/Ms _____   Position: _____
School Address: _____
                 (Building)   (Room Number)

Telephone: Business: _____
                    (Area Code)   (Number)   (Extension)

         Home: _____
                    (Area Code)   (Number)

Please arrange to have this interview during the:
First - Second - Third - Fourth Week of: _____
           (Circle One)   (Month)

kinds of research, especially those involving career advancement and large sums of money." (p. 10) Any temptation, regardless of its attractiveness, must be set aside without hesitation.

The practice of honesty in research, however, is not limited to issues of data and the reporting of findings. It also relates to *plagiarism*. Taking someone else's ideas and claiming them as one's own is stealing one of the most precious holdings of a scientist. Quite simply, if you get an idea from another individual, identify the source. Not only are you then giving credit to the person who deserves it, you are also providing additional reference material to the reader of your report. If the findings of a study are to generate ideas of quality, giving appropriate credit where credit is due will help to make that happen. Remember, one's integrity as a scholar is at stake with every entry of the pen or computer keyboard. You have the controls, and no one can take them away from you.

Protection

Under the **protection** of law and professional ethics, subjects and consumers have the right to assume that researchers will be accurate and honest; that they will keep individual records confidential; and that they will not deceive or disclose inaccurate information. But rather than rely upon one's good will alone, you need to know that subjects are also protected by the **National Research Act** of 1974. Enacted the same year as the Buckley Amendment, the intent of this law is to protect human subjects against emotional, mental, or physical harm by requiring that proposed research be approved by an authorized group within the institution in which the research is proposed to take place (Weinberger & Michael, 1976). The law is very specific about the fact that individuals should not feel compelled to participate in research, and if subjects are not of age, informed consent must be granted by parents or legal guardians (Michael & Weinberger, 1977).

Most colleges and universities have a **Human Subjects Research Committee (HSRC).** If not, an existing committee must be assigned the responsibility to review research proposals as they arise. Normally, the prospective researcher would submit a written proposal to the committee chair who, in turn, schedules a review meeting with the committee. If deemed necessary, the prospective researcher is invited to attend. Pursuant to a thorough examination of the proposal, one of the following decisions is made:

1. The committee finds that the researcher appears to have taken the necessary steps to protect the rights, safety, and welfare of the research subjects.

2. The committee finds that research procedures described in the application do *not* meet the minimum standards for the protection of the rights, safety, and welfare of human subjects. (The researcher has the right to clarify, revise, or resubmit the project application for further committee consideration and approval.)

3. The committee would like the researcher to appear before it to clarify or provide further information about [topic is specified].

At Plymouth State College of the University System of New Hampshire, a document is made available to all faculty, staff, and administrators who are contemplating research or who, as instructors, are considering a class assignment in which their students do the research themselves. In Figures 2–3, 2–4, and 2–5, copies of pertinent documents in this regard are offered for your examination.

For your information, an example of an **informed consent** form that can be used with subjects directly is shown in Figure 2–6. Examples of other forms may be found in the academic offices of colleges and universities. You should not hesitate to contact officials there in order to request a review of samples.

OTHER CONSIDERATIONS IN RESEARCH ACTIVITIES

In addition to the six strategies described in the preceding text for protecting human subjects, there are other considerations to which a thoughtful researcher needs to give attention. Some are obvious; others are less so. At the risk of boring some readers with what they might claim are commonsense matters, the following discussion identifies several such items to ensure that we share common insights and, therefore, are able to initiate research activities from the same frame of reference.

Beneficence

The motive of one's research should never be to cast doubts on the credibility of the work of others. Although contrary findings may arise, **beneficence** requires that research be neither designed nor reported in a manner that would incline the reader to cast blame, coerce, criticize, disparage, find fault, or stifle. Research should serve and enlighten, but not at the personal or professional expense of others. Be mindful of and control whatever **conflict of interest** issues exist for you.

Figure 2–3: **Informed Consent Research Proposal Form**

Federal regulations and college policy require that proposals which involve human subjects in research must be reviewed by the Human Subjects Research Committee. Please respond to the following questions and return this form, when complete, to the Research Office.

Name of Principal Investigator: _____

Department: _____

1. Brief description of the project.

2. Indicate how informed consent is to be obtained. Provide a copy of the informed consent documents you will use in your research. (Examples of typical informed consent documents accompany these instructions.)

3. How will confidentiality of subject data be assured as they are collected and, if they are to be retained, over the length of time that they are to be retained?

4. List all foreseeable risks which may be encountered by the subjects and the justification for the project in terms of benefits to be realized which might outweigh the risks, and steps taken to reduce any potential risks.

Credibility

It is contrary to worthy use of time to conduct research that, when completed, lacks **credibility.** In order to avoid this undesirable perception, the research problem must:

1. Have conceptual soundness, and be capable of being investigated. Is the research design likely to provide an answer to the question being addressed? In short, are the data-gathering and analyzing strategies appropriate for the topic being investigated?
2. Comply with ethical principles *and* satisfy the requirements of the Buckley Amendment and the National Research Act of 1974.

Figure 2–4: **Committee Response to Research Proposal**

The Committee for Human Subjects Research has reviewed your proposal state-ments for the research:

Title: _____

_____

Researcher: _____

Date Submitted: _____   Date Returned: _____

☐   The committee finds that the research appears to have taken the necessary steps to protect the subjects.
☐   The committee finds that the procedures described do *not* meet mini-mum standards. You have the right to clarify, revise, or resubmit the project application.
☐   The committee would like to have you appear before it to clarify (or provide additional information) concerning:

_____

_____

_____

_____

The committee reserves the right at any time to review procedures used with human subjects as the research progresses. If deemed appropriate, the commit-tee may require a final project report.

3. Lead one to conclusions that are clear—conclusions that are based upon find-ings that could be replicated if the study were carried out again under identical conditions.

Suspending Research

It may be necessary for the investigator to suspend the research before it is com-plete. Earlier in the chapter, it was noted that subjects have the right to withdraw from a study at any time for any reason. The researcher also may have a reason to *stop* the study. Suppose, for example, that one is testing a null hypothesis that a tra-ditional method of instruction is as effective in generating achievement as is a new instructional method that has been recently introduced in a professional journal. Although the study has been designed to last through the first three marking periods of the academic year, it is determined, on the occasion of a final examination for the first marking period, that one group is performing significantly better than the other. At the end of the second marking period, the difference is even greater. Would you want to continue to expose one of the groups to what appears to be an inferior

Figure 2–5: **Form for Student Projects**

This research has been reviewed and approved by my instructor/advisor(s), who is/are:

Name: _____ Title: _____

Department: _____

Name: _____ Title: _____

Department: _____

Name: _____ Title: _____

Department: _____

Figure 2–6: **Sample Informed Consent Form**

I have examined the information describing the study in which you would like me to participate and herein express my consent to do so, with the following provisions:

1. I can withdraw from the study at any time for any reason;

2. That individual results will be kept confidential, and that any final report will include group data only; and

3. If I desire, a copy of the final report will be sent to me as soon as it is available.

Signature: _____ Date: _____

Mailing address: _____

_____

_____

method, thus causing the potential for significant delays in their achievement for the year? It seems that these preliminary findings argue for suspending the study under the original design. Given the significance of findings at the conclusion of the first marking period, you might want to redesign the study by flip-flopping the treatment for the second marking period so that the group demonstrating lower achievement now receives the more effective method. This action would also provide you with the opportunity to test the credibility of the original findings with a different group.

TRAINING RESEARCH ASSISTANTS

Whenever a study is going to be undertaken that requires any form of assistance from other individuals, it is necessary that formal training be provided for them. Any colleague, teacher, administrator, graduate student, or other person who is going to be working with you during the course of the investigation should be considered a **research assistant,** and should be made knowledgeable about pertinent dates, times, places; the nature of the study (including legal and ethical implications); and the specific role they will have in it.

For example, if a study involves conducting a series of interviews at various classroom or school sites, part of the training should include having your assistant(s) go through simulated interviews in order to ensure that the questions are being asked in accordance with the research design and are being introduced in a clear and professional manner. It is important to note during the training that if questions are raised by those being interviewed, there are consistent, preplanned responses available. Conduct during the interview process must be consistent from site to site; otherwise, the validity of the investigation can be compromised. If there are different interpretations of the questions being asked, the data that are gathered become meaningless in any group-to-group comparative analyses.

If, on the other hand, an experiment is going to be conducted to examine, for example, the effect of an ergogenic aid upon one's cardiovascular endurance, the research assistant should not, by oral or body language, give clues to the subject(s) about whether the aid or a placebo is being administered. Again, the study can be compromised. In a **single-blind** method, the subject should not know whether she is receiving one ingredient or the other. To refine the process even further, a **double-blind** method is often used in which neither the subject nor the individual administering the dosages knows what is being given. In this instance, the research assistant is not made aware of the nature of the substance in order to control for the threat of researcher expectancy affecting the internal validity of the study.

In both of these illustrations, training will help your research assistants to become thoroughly familiar with the procedures, and prepared to use them during the course of the entire investigation. Monitoring their practices will help the researcher to ensure that all processes are in keeping with the research design.

SUMMARY

Thoughtful researchers will adopt a plan that will include giving attention to the ethical and legal implications of their research. In this chapter, attention was assigned to guiding principles, including references to responsibilities to the field; research populations, educational institutions, and the public; intellectual ownership; editing, reviewing, and appraising research; sponsors, policy makers, and other users of research; and students and student researchers. Strategies for the protection of human subjects were then offered, particularly as they pertain to accuracy, confidentiality, deception, disclosure, and honesty. Sample forms relating to informed consent were presented and discussed, as were sources of information. The chapter concluded with a discussion of beneficence, credibility, conditions under which a study may need to be suspended, and the importance of training research assistants. The information presented here should aid all who are interested in ensuring that the ethical and legal standards of research activities are satisfied.

RECOMMENDED LABORATORY ASSIGNMENTS

1. Thoughtfully examine copies of *Ethical Standards of the American Educational Research Association,* and the Ethics Code published by the American Psychological Association.

2. For a problem statement prepared in response to suggestions in Chapter 1, prepare an informed consent letter that would be distributed to the subjects of your study.

3. Meet with college or university officials in order to determine the typical composition of the Human Subjects Research Committee. Request that you be allowed to sit in on some of their deliberations.

4. Assuming that you would like to conduct a study within an institution, prepare responses for an informed consent research proposal form. Ask if a review committee within the institution will examine your document in order to determine whether all pertinent legal and ethical safeguards have been met.

5. Arrange to meet with school and nonschool employees to discuss their insights into the ethical and legal implications of their research activities, and the controls they put in place in order to control for such matters.

6. Review three to five pieces of published research. Make a list of ethical and legal questions that you believe could have arisen during the course of those studies. If explanations are not provided within the written reports, contact the authors or publishers directly.

7. Write to two to three different publishers of research in order to procure descriptions of their procedures for evaluating manuscripts before them. Upon receipt of these documents, examine the references that are made to legal safeguards and professional ethics.

8. Review the recommended readings.

RECOMMENDED READINGS

Adair, J. G., Dushenko, T. W., & Lindsay, R. C. (1985). Ethical regulations and their impact on research practice. *American Psychologist, 40,* 59–72.

American Psychological Association, Committee for the Protection of Human Participants in Research. (1982). *Ethical principles in the conduct of research with human participants* (2nd ed.). Washington, DC: Author.

Baumrind, D. (1985). Research using intentional deception. *American Psychologist, 40,* 165–174.

Boruch, R. F., & Cecil, J. S. (1979). *Assuring the confidentiality of social research data.* Philadelphia: University of Pennsylvania Press.

Bower, B. (1990). Subliminal deceptions. *Science News, 138,* 124.

Cassell, J. (1982). Harm, benefits, wrongs, and rights in fieldwork. In J. Seiber (Ed.), *The ethics of social research* (pp. 7–32). New York: Springer-Verlag.

Cassell, J., & Wax, M. (Eds.). (1980). Ethical problems in fieldwork. *Special issue of Social Problems, 27.*

Ceci, S. J., & Peters, D. (1984). Letters of reference: A naturalistic study of the effects of confidentiality. *American Psychologist, 39,* 29–31.

Committee on Scientific and Professional Ethics and Conduct. (1977). Ethical standards of psychologists. *APA Monitor, 8,* 22–23.

Deyhle, D. L., Hess, G. A., Jr., & LeCompte, M. D. (1992). Approaching ethical issues for qualitative researchers in education. In M. D. LeCompte, W. L. Millroy, & J. Preissle (Eds.), *The handbook of qualitative research in education* (pp. 597–641). San Diego, CA: Academic Press.

Federal policy for the protection of human subjects; notices and rules, Part II. (1991). *Federal Register, 56,* 28001–28032.

Grisso, T., Baldwin, E., Blanck, P. D., Rotheram-Borus, M. J., Schooler, N. R., & Thompson, T. (1991). Standards in research: APA's mechanism for monitoring the challenge. *American Psychologist, 46,* 758–766.

Holmes, D. S. (1976). Debriefing after psychological experiments: I. Effectiveness of post-deception dehoaxing. *American Psychologist, 31,* 868–875.

Hudgins, H. C., & Vacca, R. S. (1991). *Law and education* (3rd ed.). Charlottesville, VA: Michie.

Kimmel, A. J. (1980). *Ethics and values in applied social research.* Newbury Park, CA: Sage.

Koocher, G. P., & Keith-Spiegel, P. C. (1990). *Children, ethics, & the law.* Lincoln, NE: University of Nebraska Press.

Laosa, L. M. (1991). The cultural context of construct validity and the ethics of generalizability. *Early Childhood Research Quarterly, 6,* 313–321.

Levin, J. R., & Marshall, H. H. (1993). Publishing in the Journal of Educational Psychology: Reflections at midstream. *Journal of Educational Psychology, 85,* 3–6.

Lincoln, Y. S., & Guba, E. G. (1989). Ethics: The failure of positivist science. *Review of Higher Education, 12,* 221–240.

Milgram, S. (1975). *Obedience to authority: An experimental view.* New York: Harper & Row.

Mitchell, R. G. (1993). *Secrecy and fieldwork.* Newbury Park, CA: Sage.

Shulman, J. (1990). Now you see them, now you don't: Anonymity versus visibility in case studies of teachers. *Educational Researcher, 19*(6), 11–15.

Sieber, J. E. (1992). *Planning ethically responsible research.* Newbury Park, CA: Sage.

Smith, L. M. (1990). Ethics in qualitative field research: An individual perspective. In E. W. Eisner & A. Peshkin (Eds.), *Qualitative inquiry in education: The continuing debate* (pp. 258–276). New York: Teachers College Press.

Taylor, S. J. (1987). Observing abuse: Professional ethics and personal morality in field research. *Qualitative Sociology, 10*(3), 288–300.

Wax, M. L. (1991). The ethics of research in American Indian communities. *American Indian Quarterly, 15,* 431–456.

REFERENCES

American Educational Research Association. (1992). Ethical standards of the American Educational Research Association. *Educational Researcher, 21,* 23–26.

American Psychological Association. (1992). Ethical principles of psychologists and code of conduct. *American Psychologist, 47*(12), special insert.

Charles, C. M. (1995). *Introduction to educational research* (2nd ed.). White Plains, NY: Longman.

Michael, J. A., & Weinberger, J. A. (1977). Federal restrictions on educational research: Protection for research participants. *Educational Researcher, 6*(1), 3–7.

Milgram, S. (1963). Behavioral study of obedience. *Journal of Abnormal Psychology, 67,* 371–378.

Plymouth State College, Human Subjects Research Committee. (1996). *Informed consent research proposal form.* Unpublished document, Author, Plymouth, NH.

Weinberger, J. A., & Michael, J. A. (1976). Federal restrictions on educational research. *Educational Researcher, 5*(11), 3–8.

CHAPTER **3**

Preparation of a Research Plan

OBJECTIVES

After reading this chapter, you should be able to:

- Discuss the major components of a research plan.
- Identify and discuss the pertinence of the four subproblems found in a research design template, and the five guiding questions common to each of them.
- Describe factors implicit to preparing time schedules and operating budgets.
- Distinguish between direct and indirect costs.
- Identify and discuss factors that govern the selection of one's research design, and the important terms for which one needs to offer definitions.
- Identify and discuss factors that go into writing needs for studies, literature reviews, and hypotheses.
- Describe factors that go into testing basic assumptions.
- Distinguish between the following terms: internal and external validity; history and maturation; expectancy, selection, and statistical regression; mortality and instability; and instrumentation and pretesting.
- Discuss the relationships of sampling, person, place, and time to the external validity of a study.

- Describe procedures for addressing threats to internal and external validity.
- Create a template for the problem statement prepared in response to the recommendations of Chapters 1 and 2.
- Define key terms, and answer the checkpoint questions.

KEY TERMS

Basic Assumptions	*Literature Review*
Design Alternatives	*Maturation*
Direct Costs	*Need for the Study*
Expectancy	*Objectivity*
Experimental Mortality	*Pretesting*
External Validity	*Reliability*
Gantt Chart	*Sampling*
History	*Selection*
Hypothesis	*Statistical Regression*
Indirect Costs	*Template*
Instability	*Tentative Budget*
Instrumentation	*Threats to the Study*
Internal Validity	*Validity*
Inter-Rater Reliability	

INTRODUCTION

At this juncture, you should be in a position to understand the factors that contribute to the preparation of a problem statement. You should also be aware of your responsibilities for ensuring that ethical and legal standards are satisfied. These issues, along with a thorough review of related literature, are at the foundation of any investigation. This chapter takes you to the next level; that is, it prepares you to design plans in a way that guarantees that the steps taken during the course of the study are appropriate and capable of producing valid data.

A research plan is a detailed description of a proposed study designed to investigate a specific problem. The plan must be completed before a study is begun. Although research plans are known by various names, they generally are comprised of common elements. The approach in this chapter is to present these elements in two phases. Phase 1 addresses the processes for preparing a time schedule, tentative budget, statement of the problem, need (justification) for the study, review of related literature, hypothesis, basic assumptions, possible threats to the study, design alternatives, and definitions of terms. Phase 2 describes the specific steps that must be taken in order to implement the study successfully. You will find that these strategies have been arranged according to the four subproblems appropriate to *any* investigation: (1) permission for study and selection of subjects; (2) selection of instrument of assessment; (3) administration of study and collection of data; and (4) analysis of data, and presentation of conclusions and recommendations.

To make this effort meaningful, reference throughout Phase 1 and Phase 2 is made to *inclusionary education* as a sample problem area within the sample field of *special education*. At pertinent times, a discussion of procedures for alternative research designs is presented. As you proceed through the material, give thought to how this information could translate to a study that would be of particular interest to you. For the scenario of this chapter:

- The *problem* to be investigated is the attitudes of all K–8 classroom teachers within School Administrative Unit (SAU) #48 toward inclusionary education (mainstreaming) for children with exceptionalities.

- The *research hypothesis* is that, assuming a valid data-gathering process, a survey conducted of SAU #48, K–8 teachers during the spring term of the current academic year will reveal their attitudes toward inclusionary education.

PHASE 1

Time Schedule

In order to complete your study within the time parameters available, a thoughtfully prepared time management schedule is extremely important. When one looks at the entire battery of tasks that must be completed in order to arrive at a final report, it is very easy to become overwhelmed. Too often, this becomes the deterrent for beginning researchers. On the other hand, if you limit your attention to one or two events at a time, the entire process becomes workable, as well as enjoyable. It is truly exciting to see the various stages of the study unfold.

Basically, a time schedule is a matrix that identifies the major phases of the proposed study in relation to corresponding estimated completion dates. One approach for recording these relationships is known as the **Gantt chart** method (Carlisle, 1979). In the example in Figure 3–1, the activities to be completed are listed in sequence down the left side of the page, and the months (dates) are noted across the top. Since the scenario of the chapter provides that the actual survey of the teachers will take place in the spring term, all preliminary work must be completed by January. The researcher must also be mindful of the times during the year when school personnel will not be available at their places of employment because of school vacations, workshops, in-service training days, and so on, and when teachers will be very busy and not able to devote the attention necessary to complete the survey form(s), such as times immediately before or after vacation periods, when schoolwide standardized tests are being administered, and so on.

Figure 3–1: **Modified Gantt Chart for Proposed Study on Inclusionary Education**

	Dates									
Activities	**Sep**	**Oct**	**Nov**	**Dec**	**Jan**	**Feb**	**Mar**	**Apr**	**May**	**Jun**
Permission to conduct study	X									
Selection of subjects		X								
Selection of instrument		X	X	X						
Administration of study					X	X				
Analysis of data							X			
Report preparation								X	X	
Report distribution										X

It can be seen from the chart that it is unnecessary to complete one task before beginning another. For example, one might begin looking for a suitable instrument to measure attitudes before written permission from all pertinent sources has been received.

Regardless of the nature of the study—whether it is a survey to measure the attitudes of teachers toward inclusionary education, or a pretest-posttest control-group design to compare the math achievement of seventh-grade students who are neurologically impaired with those who are not (see Chapter 10, Two-Group Designs)—it is important to include, in the early phase of the research plan, a system that will allow one to isolate major tasks while meditating on the big picture.

Tentative Budget

When planning for the various components of the study, it is necessary to consider both the **direct** and **indirect costs** and to develop a **tenative budget.** For example, if the researcher wants to administer the survey by way of face-to-face interviews, the researcher may need to be released from some portion of his own teaching schedule in order to match his availability with that of his subjects. This might require that a substitute be hired to cover his classes. Can he afford to pay for a substitute, or had he better plan to administer the study through on-campus mail? Although the researcher may perceive the latter procedure to be less desirable, it may be all that he can afford (both in time and money). Further, it is important for him to remember that a study administered through the mail is far better than not doing the study at all.

If, on the other hand, the researcher can rely upon an administrator within the school to assist him in conducting the face-to-face interviews, his direct costs will be substantially lower. However, an administrator may inadvertently cause reactions to some of the questions on inclusionary education (for example, the ones generating findings that could cost money) to vary from what they might have been under other survey conditions. Because of this potential threat to the validity of the study, it might be wise to seek a grant. If one is received, alternative interview arrangements can become more feasible. If the school board or the state department of education consider the study to be of significance, the researcher may be able to get the necessary funding. As you can see, there are a number of variables to take into account when planning one's budget.

The *direct* costs are expenses that come out of the researcher's own pocket. *Indirect* costs are those that are borne by others. To illustrate, if the researcher were granted permission to use the school Xerox machine to duplicate the number of survey instruments needed for the study, the cost would be absorbed by the school's duplicating budget and, thus, would be an *indirect* cost to him.

Let us assume that, upon examining alternative funding sources, it has been determined that although no money is available from the state or district to support the researcher's release time, he can (1) use the duplicating facilities of the school within which the study will take place to copy the number of survey forms needed, (2) have the services of the secretary to the district coordinator of special education to distribute and collect the survey forms, and (3) use a computer for data analysis and word processing. In addition, the superintendent of schools has agreed to make her offices available for duplicating and distributing the final report to all members of the school board, school and district administrators (including the coordinator of special education), and all K–8 elementary/middle school teachers who participated in the study. So with these factors in mind, a tentative budget can be prepared. For an example of such a budget, see Figure 3–2.

Statement of the Problem

As indicated in Chapter 1, one's problem statement should be clear and precise:

> This investigator is interested in assessing the attitudes of all K–8 classroom teachers within School Administrative Unit (SAU) #48 toward inclusionary education (mainstreaming) for children with exceptionalities.

Figure 3–2: **Tentative Budget for Proposed Study on Inclusionary Education**

BUDGET	Amount
Direct costs	
Mileage	$ 10.00
Indirect costs	
Duplication of survey materials	$ 40.00
(40 copies × 5 pages × $0.20)	
Computer time	$ 50.00
Duplication of survey report	$100.00
(50 copies × 10 pages × $0.20)	
Overhead (secretary/staff office time)	$100.00
Grand Total:	$300.00

2

Note in this illustration that (1) the name of the school administrative unit is specified; (2) school grade levels are indicated; (3) "all K–8 classroom teachers" implies that individuals within the specified grades will be sought as subjects regardless of whether they are trained in special education, have experience working with children who have exceptionalities, or have students in their classrooms with coded exceptionalities; and (4) the study deals with teacher attitudes, not knowledge.

It is important to realize that budget can influence the *scope* of a study. For example, suppose there were ten different schools within the district that accommodated children, grades K–8. It might be that, because of the limited number of "support" dollars available, the researcher would find it impossible to assess the attitudes of *all* the teachers employed in these schools, in which case the study could be designed for a random sample of them (see Chapter 4, Sampling Procedures). Under this set of circumstances, the problem statement would have to be modified to represent what the researcher has found it financially possible to do. Again, however, a study conducted with a random sample of K–8 teachers within SAU #48 is better than no study at all.

Need (Justification) for the Study

What **need for the study** exists? Why do this study? Is inclusionary education as important a topic to the general public as it is to the researcher? Does this issue hold as much significance locally as it is does on the national level? In particular, how critical is this topic to School Administrative Unit #48 and the K–8 teachers employed there? What are the attitudes of the teachers toward federal and state legislation governing the education of children with exceptionalities? Do the teachers feel that the laws are being translated to practice within their school(s)? Is the financial support sufficient to accommodate the needs of the class and resource rooms? Finally, to the extent that inclusionary practices are in place, are they enabling students with *all* levels of ability to benefit from the processes and programs?

An important step to making such determinations would be to design a study that provides for the examination of teacher attitudes toward these specific issues. From the information acquired, (1) in-service workshops can be planned, (2) a need might be established to reconsider the designation of dollar values currently assigned to specific budget lines, and (3) the importance of applied research on related topics could be determined.

Beginning the process, however, requires that a critical examination of related literature be undertaken. From that review, one can learn of the programs and practices in other school systems and, with valuable knowledge in hand, prepare the need (justification) for the study. The following statement is illustrative of justification for this investigation:

> Over twenty years ago, PL 94-142, the Education for All Handicapped Children Act, mandated that children with disabilities be educated in the least restrictive environment. This statement in the law should have continued [the least restrictive environment] in which the child's needs can be met (Baker, Wang, & Walberg, 1995; Costello, 1991; Cratty, 1989; Fuchs, Fuchs, & Bishop, 1992; Sherrill,

1993; Wiseman, 1994). In an article by Sherman (1996), it was pointed out that including children in the mainstream of education is a civil rights issue. It is more than ensuring that institutions arrange inclusionary circumstances because of moral correctness.

Whereas Public Law 94-142 (1975) mandates that all states provide a free and appropriate education for all handicapped children between the ages of three and twenty-one, and whereas SAU #48, in meeting the requirements of the law, is interested in ensuring the quality of the curriculum and instruction for all students enrolled there, this writer finds need to survey the K–8 classroom teachers in order to assess their attitudes toward inclusionary education (mainstreaming). It is from the information generated by this study that: sources and direction of attitudes can be determined, meaningful in-service training can be planned, budget dollars can be redistributed as needed, and applied research on the effectiveness of the in-service training programs can be implemented.

For legitimate reasons, it may be necessary to provide additional information about inclusionary education and its relevance to the school administrative unit. Very often, one will find that the need for more data is dependent upon the audience for whom the statement of justification for the study is being prepared. If little is known about the issues of concern, you may find it necessary to provide additional background on the nature and evolution of the problem, particularly at the local level. Few can argue with the premise that programs should be child-centered, and that every child coming through the system has the right to enjoy its benefits. If one can demonstrate that needed, critical insights can be acquired through the study (at very little cost), it is likely that endorsement of the proposal will follow.

Review of Related Literature

Albert Einstein once said, "It is impossible to solve a problem with the same mind that created it." It is in this regard that **literature reviews** take their rightful place. Stated another way, the more one learns about the topic, and the findings of prior investigations, the better prepared one will be to address the problem at hand. Not only should one be interested in knowing the results of prior studies, but it is also important to know:

1. The design(s) used to gather data

2. The character (for example, demographics) of the study group

3. The site of the study

4. The statistical procedures used to analyze the data

5. The recommendations for further study that arose out of the findings

In addition, reviews of related literature uncover other references within their respective bibliographical listings. If one can find even one study that has been reported on a related topic, the reference list of that report will yield additional sources of information.

Graduate students, in the early stages of their research design course, have said, "I can't find any studies related to my problem statement; maybe I should change my topic." Quite frequently these students need to widen their search by using other descriptors. If this approach does not produce related information, it may be that the lack of studies in a related topical area argues for the students doing one. It is also important for beginning researchers to know that although little information may be found on studies related to curriculum development in a given discipline, for example, art, gains can be made if one uncovers curriculum studies in other disciplines, such as mathematics. Many of the procedures used to create and evaluate math curricula parallel those that need to be employed when studying the field of art. An examination of curriculum studies in mathematics, social science, English, health, and so on may well produce findings that would be appropriate to include in the related literature section of your paper.

Another issue that requires noting is that of examining and reporting findings that appear to conflict with one another. Do *not* limit your reports of studies to those that coincide with what you hope to reveal in your own investigation. Much like the neutral position one takes when expressing the null hypothesis (no difference) in experimental study designs, it is important to remain objective when reporting on the findings of other studies. Present all observed sides of the case. When you arrive at the findings section of your own report, it can be indicated that your findings support or contradict what was found in related literature. In either instance, additional information is made available to readers and those contemplating new studies on the subject.

To conduct your search of related literature, examine the sources described in Chapter 1—that is, abstracts, book guides to the literature, dictionaries, directories, encyclopedias, handbooks, newspaper and periodical indexes, and textbook sources. Be sure to include accessible online databases. Depending upon the topic, you may want to reveal the findings of different times in history. In the study on inclusionary education, it may be important to note that the problem is not new, and that studies on the matter have been conducted at different times since the passage of Public Law 94-142 in 1975, with varying results. This can underscore the fact that the issues are not yet resolved. Teachers may feel unqualified to work with children having exceptionalities and, thus, have a negative attitude about the propriety of the requirement. Perhaps they feel that their classes are already overloaded and that, without teacher aides, they cannot serve the needs of the average children, let alone those with coded exceptionalities. There are many variables that can contribute to the attitudes one may have about inclusionary education. All substantive findings should be included in any report of the researcher's literature search.

Another consideration for literature reviews is that there is no magic number of studies that should be included. Much depends upon your own professional and personal standards, as well as the expectations of those for whom you are writing your report. In addition, some topics have been studied extensively; others have not. Consequently, the number of studies that are available will vary. In the author's graduate research design course, students are required to prepare a design for a topic within their specific field of study, with a general requirement that they review between ten and fifteen references. Additional considerations bearing on this requirement are (1) the amount of time that is available to students during the semester in which the course is scheduled, and (2) the availability of references. The important thing is that the students find representative samples of what is available. The same can be said for manuscripts of journal articles and unpublished conference papers that the author has reviewed. On the other hand, in advising those involved with graduate theses and dissertations, the author's expectations have been much greater. In this case, particularly with doctoral dissertations, the review of related literature on the subject must be exhaustive.

In the final analysis, you should consider the following in your literature review:

1. Use a computer as much as possible, not only for doing your searches, but for filing your information as well. Database software can sort data a number of ways, including alphabetically, and by least-to-most recent. In addition, general management and editing of the material can be greatly simplified (see Chapter 12, Using the Computer for Data Analysis).

2. Examine reports of the subject from different periods of history. This is particularly useful in studies where evolutionary trends are important to identify.

3. Conduct systematic reviews of the reports you select for examination. Be mindful of the fact that incomplete notes will require locating the source(s) again. Although what you record may appear sufficient at the time, unless you attend to the information in brief notes without extensive delay, specifics will be forgotten, for example, the exact wording of statements you want to quote, names of pertinent sources, dates, and so on.

4. Be as accurate as possible, particularly regarding (a) the findings, (b) who gets credit for statements found within the document, (c) spellings of proper names, (d) dates and times of events, (e) names of all contributing authors of the report, and (f) names and addresses of the publisher(s).

5. Integrate the findings of the related literature so that relationships between the studies that you have examined are clear. Not only does this make for interesting reading, it reveals the extent of agreement that appears to exist. Although isolated abstracts of studies have a place, that place is not within the related literature section of a report (see Chapter 13, Preparing the Research Report, specifically as it relates to preparing abstracts). For example, it might be stated that:

> In the 1980s, it was advocated that students with mild to severe and profound disabilities be accommodated in the regular classroom with the rest of the student body (Biklen, 1988; Strully & Strully, 1985; Thousand, Fox, Reid, Godek, Williams, & Fox, 1986; Villa & Thousand, 1988; Will, 1985). By the 1990s, this concept had grown to one in which teaching methods and curricula normally found within the traditional classroom began to change in order to meet the heterogeneous needs of the students enrolled there (Neary, Halvorsen, Kronberg, & Kelly, 1992; Stainback & Stainback, 1992; Thousand, Villa, & Nevin, 1994). Although heterogeneous schools are often considered a contrast to providing a continuum of educational placements based upon what is deemed to be the least restrictive environment (Kirk, Gallagher, & Anastasiow, 1997; Sherrill,

1993; Wiseman, 1994), until recently, most of the debate about the value of inclusion has surfaced without information on the effects of the various service delivery models on the students themselves (Baker, Wang, & Walberg, 1995; Lipsky & Gartner, 1995; Villa & Thousand, 1995), and without input from school personnel charged with the implementation of these models (Coates, 1989; Hasazi, Johnston, Ligget, & Schattman, 1994; McLaughlin, 1991; Semmel, Abernathy, Butera, & Lesar, 1991).

6. Consider the works of individuals whose names appear regularly in the research literature. Without reference to prominent researchers in the field, those reading your report are likely to assume that your search was incomplete, and in fact, it probably was.

7. Show the relationship between the literature and the topic you are investigating. It is very important that the relevance be clear to the reader. Quite frequently, a gap appears to exist between the topic of research that one is doing and the report on studies others have produced. Further, when you get to the findings of your study, relate them to what the literature review has revealed. Do your findings agree or disagree with those of previous studies? Connections should be made clear for the readers.

Hypothesis

You learned in the first chapter that an experimental study requires a statistical (null) **hypothesis.** However, the survey on inclusionary education is *descriptive,* not experimental; therefore, a research hypothesis would be used. An illustration of such a hypothesis for the scenario of this chapter is as follows:

> Assuming a valid data-gathering process, it is hypothesized that a survey conducted of SAU #48, K–8 teachers during the spring term of the current academic year will reveal their attitudes toward inclusionary education.

Basic Assumptions

It is very important that, to the extent possible, all **basic assumptions** be satisfied *before* one's study actually begins. Otherwise, one may find rather late that the investigation cannot be completed per its original design and, as a consequence, appropriate adjustments cannot be made. For example, I would not be able to conduct a survey of the K–8 teachers within SAU #48 if I did not have permission to do so. In other words, one basic assumption that has to be satisfied is that I will have *permission* to conduct the study. According to school policy, I might have to get this permission from the department head, school principal, and/or superintendent of schools, as well as from the teachers themselves. Another basic assumption that would have to be addressed is whether I have *time* within my work and personal schedule to prepare, administer, and analyze the surveys. Can I meet the *direct costs* of the study as suggested in my estimated budget? In addition to these items, there are other assumptions that should be considered before beginning the study, for example:

- that it will have been determined that the survey instrument is valid for *this* study;
- that the administration will find it possible to satisfy its commitment to absorb selected predetermined costs of the study within its operating budget;
- that it has been determined that the K–8 teachers will find it possible within their schedules to respond to the questions in a timely fashion;
- that everything possible will be done to conduct the study in a manner appropriate to its design, and to ensure that the methods for administering the survey of K–8 teachers will elicit attitudes that are valid; and
- that the final report will provide information that is useful to the planning of in-service workshops, and future applied research.

If one were doing research that required the use of equipment, an assumption would have to be made that the equipment has been calibrated properly and will be available for use when needed. For obvious reasons, one would want to *test* for equipment availability and calibration to ensure that such is the case.

It is important to think about these issues *before* you begin the study and, where possible, to get resolution. One should make a serious effort to reduce the number of situations that could arise during the course of a study that have not been considered in advance. If you have prepared a problem statement for a study within your own field of interest (per suggestions of Chapter 1), it would now be helpful for you to consider the basic assumptions that should be taken into account before pursuing the study further. Is it likely that all of them can be satisfied, or do you think that you will find yourself "flying by the seat of your pants"? In a *tight* research design, **threats to the study** are eliminated or, at the very least, minimized.

Possible Threats to the Study

In many ways, attention to satisfying the basic assumptions for a study will alleviate many of the threats to its internal and external validity. (You will recall from Chapter 1 that **internal validity** refers to the ability of an investigation to produce findings that are valid to the group under study, while **external validity** refers to the extent to which the findings of that study can be generalized to other populations.) Such threats, while of major concern in experimental studies because of the investigator's desire to attribute significant findings to receiving (or not receiving) a treatment, do warrant attention by those conducting descriptive studies as well.

Threats to Internal Validity. The following is a list of possible threats to the *internal* validity of a study.

1. History. **History** represents an event in one's environment that arises during the course of a study. An example of such a threat would be if the school board decided, the week before the survey on inclusionary education was to be distributed to the teachers, that, for every child with a coded disability in the class, the teacher would receive some stipulated sum of money in order to offset the amount of time required to attend after-school planning meetings. For rather obvious reasons, such an event could influence teacher attitudes toward "the value of inclusionary education."

For another example of history as a threat, suppose one were conducting a study on the effect of incorporating computer software in a class on the causes of the Civil War. If some parents decided to purchase personal computers for their children, the results of the study might change—not because of the use of computers in class, but because of the interest generated by computers within the home.

An important issue to keep in mind is that the longer a study is, the greater the chance that history will be a problem. After all, the greater the length of time it takes to investigate an issue, the greater is the opportunity for something to happen.

Keep in mind that one can attempt to control for threats of history by determining, in advance, the likelihood that certain compromising events will occur, such as parents buying new computers for their homes, public television networks broadcasting after-school specials on related topics, and so on. For example, if it is determined that, three weeks into the study, *all* children will have new computers in their homes, parental intervention could become a feature of the study. If an afternoon special was going to relate to the topic of your investigation, you might consider contacting the network for permission to tape the broadcast, and make it available for everyone to see (thus, it would become a part of the study design). If, instead, you announced to your students that you did not want them to watch the special, what do you think would happen? Not only would some be inclined to watch, there would be a serious ethical question about research that encouraged students not to watch public broadcasting programs that related to school topics (for fear that they would learn more than they were supposed to).

2. Selection. **Selection** is a threat when subjects are selected in a way that does not provide for representation of the population in question. If one could study the entire population, there would not be any selection bias. On the other hand, if a sampling procedure is used that does not provide all members of a population with an equal opportunity to be selected, a selection bias exists. For example, if the surveys were distributed to only those K–8 teachers who have been trained in special education, no insights would be gained from those who were not so trained, and thus, the validity of the findings would be compromised. Granted, the research would assess the attitudes of those who were trained; but it would not assess the attitudes of *all* teachers, as stipulated in the problem statement.

The threat of selection also exists if one does an experimental study with two groups and (a) the treatment is not randomly assigned to one of them, or (b) a pretest is not given to each group participating in the study. Without knowing the relative status of the subjects before the study begins, one might attribute any difference in the achievement of the two groups to a treatment when, in fact, the group that received the treatment was more knowledgeable about the topic to begin with. As you would expect, this threat (while not necessarily actualized) would be present if previously formed groups (such as classes in school) were selected for use in a study. (See Chapter 4, Sampling Procedures, for a discussion of strategies for dealing with *convenience samples.*)

3. Maturation. **Maturation** occurs most readily when a study extends over a long period of time. Similar to the effects of history, research is more likely to be influenced by maturation if the study proceeds over extended periods. Subjects of the study are more likely to develop in ways that are not under the control of the investigator. Using the example of the study on inclusionary education, imagine that a local college is offering an evening division graduate course on "Learning Environments for Exceptional Children." Some of the K–8 teachers decide to register for the class. If the survey was distributed to the teachers in January for a return date deadline in June, it is likely that the knowledge gained over the full-semester course would affect their attitudes. Certainly, knowledge is expected to influence attitudes, but in this instance, the findings of the study would be clouded because not only would some teachers be taking the course and others not taking it, but also, of those taking the course, some might complete the survey in January while others might wait until the beginning of June (because they are attending the class and would like to be able to use some of the information acquired when answering the questions). The "window of opportunity" for completing the survey is too big. The responses to the questions should be based on the attitudes that exist at a specific time common to all participants in the study.

One could do an experimental study in order to assess the effects of attending a graduate class upon teacher attitudes. A pretest could be administered to two groups of teachers in order to measure the status of their attitudes at the beginning of the study. One group of teachers would be considered a control group, and the other group of teachers would attend the class (the experimental group). Following the completion of the class, an equivalent posttest would be administered to both groups of teachers, and a pre- and posttest, within and between group comparison of the teachers who attended the class and those who did not would be made. In this study, the researcher could measure the attitudes as they existed prior to any (graduate class) treatment, and then compare the attitudes of the two groups after one of them had attended the class. Here, the intent of the study is different, so the research design is different. Although there are other concerns, including the determination of which group would take the class, the possibility of such a study is clear.

4. Instrumentation. **Instrumentation** is a threat when an instrument of assessment lacks the necessary validity, reliability, and objectivity (also known as **interrater reliability**) to acquire information pertinent to the study. **Validity,** the most important characteristic of any test, refers to the degree to which that test measures what it purports (claims) to measure. If the instrument to measure attitudes toward inclusionary education had been jury-validated for use with preprofessionals—that is, individuals who have been certified to teach but are yet unemployed—it would be invalid for this study. If a standardized test on mathematics had been validated for students who are entering their seventh year of school, it would not be valid for use with students who are entering their eighth year of school. Validity is audience-specific, time-specific, and place-specific. Yes, *place*-specific. If a 600-yard run/walk test had been validated for use by ninth-grade girls on a one-fourth mile outdoor asphalt track, the times generated by those girls would not be appropriate for use as norms for ones taking the test on the hardwood floor of a 50- by 84-foot indoor high school gymnasium.

Reliability refers to the consistency of a measurement. If an instrument is assessing one's attitudes on Wednesday morning, it should generate the same scores if administered on Thursday morning (if the test is consistent, and truly measuring attitudes). Such factors as allowing subjects in a study anywhere between one week and a semester to respond to questions on attitudes toward inclusionary education would likely contaminate the responses because of intervening variables (such as attending the class "Learning Environments for Exceptional Children" described earlier in the section on "maturation").

It is also important to realize that an instrument can be reliable without being valid. For example, if a researcher assembled teachers in the library under the guise of administering an attitude questionnaire but, when they arrived, administered a thirty-second push-up test instead, validity for that study would not be present. However, if the researcher administered that same push-up test a week later, it would be likely that he would get consistent scores. Therefore, the test is reliable, but not valid (unless the study was designed to measure extensor arm strength through the use of a thirty-second push-up test).

Objectivity refers to the degree to which two or more observers arrive at the same scores for a subject. Although this is not an issue with *standardized tests* (a term used interchangeably with the expression *instrument of assessment*) scored by a computer, it can be a problem in studies that are designed to record the observation of subject behavior. If an instrument of observation is generating data that are objective, one's scores should not be dependent upon the bias of an observer. In other words, if an instrument is objective, two trained observers using it at the same time should get similar scores when rating the behavior of a subject. If, for example, an instrument used to assess teacher attitudes toward inclusionary education employed a 1–5 Likert-type rating scale (see Chapter 5, Selecting Instruments of Assessment), it is likely that any two trained research assistants examining the responses would arrive at the same scores. Objectivity would be present. (For example, if a subject circled number 3 on the 1–5 rating scale, one could be certain that any two research assistants would arrive at a score of 3 for that question; room for error in the interpretation of the response is not a possibility.) A lack of objectivity could exist, however, if that instrument contained open-ended (completion, discussion, essay, or enumeration-type) questions. Unless very specific scoring criteria were prepared for use by the research assistants, there could be a lack of agreement in what the score to a question should be; thus, objectivity would be affected. This is not to say that essay-type questions in survey research are to be discouraged. To the contrary, open-ended questions provide for responses that are not attainable in any other way.

In Chapter 5, a thorough discussion of procedures for acquiring quality testing instruments is presented. Unless the instrument of assessment in any study satisfies minimum standards of validity, reliability, and objectivity, data generated by that instrument are likely to be meaningless.

5. Statistical Regression. **Statistical regression** can threaten the internal validity of a study if one or more of the groups in the research score particularly high or low in a pretest. To illustrate, assume that forty individuals are randomly assigned to two equal groups of twenty. It has than been determined by random selection that one of the groups will receive the treatment. When a standardized pretest is given, it is found that one of these groups scores within the 90th percentile; the other scores within the 50th percentile. Given these findings, one would expect that differences in rate of growth during the study would exist between the two groups. After all, the potential for greater growth would exist in the group that had originally scored within the 50th percentile.

In the case of the study on inclusionary education, if none of the teachers selected for the investigation had ever received training in special education, one might expect that attitudes toward inclusionary practices would be poorer than they would be for a group where ongoing training is common practice within the school administrative unit.

6. Experimental Mortality. **Experimental mortality** refers to changes that take place in the composition of the group during the course of a study. These changes can arise within a school for any number of reasons. The most common reasons include: (a) students moving away from the school district, (b) students having to leave school for a term because of illness, (c) students being pulled out of the regular classroom in order to participate in accelerated or enrichment programs for the gifted, (d) students frequently missing classes because of participating in off-campus athletic events, and (e) students being added to the class rolls because their parents recently moved into the school district. For obvious reasons, the greater the length of a study, the greater the likelihood that experimental mortality will occur and, thus, influence the internal validity of the study. Since this threat is more pertinent to studies that extend over a period of time, it would not be expected to pose a problem for the survey research illustrated in this chapter.

Pretesting can also be a threat to internal validity. At the same time, however, it can be used in an attempt to control for experimental mortality. For example, students could be paired on the basis of pretest scores and placed in two different groups. If a student in one of the groups could no longer attend class, you would know his counterpart in the other group. Although you could not arbitrarily choose to exclude him from participating in class, it would be possible to exclude that person's score when analyzing the results of the posttest. As you can see, there is no total control for experimental mortality, short of not allowing the counterpart to continue in class, which, for obvious reasons, is not an option.

✓ CHECKPOINT

What two threats, other than *experimental mortality,* are more likely to affect internal validity because of the duration of the study?

Answers

Your answers should have been:

1. History
2. Maturation

If you had problems arriving at the two answers in the preceding Checkpoint, re-examine numbers 1 through 5 under the head "Possible Threats to the Study" in the preceding text.

7. Pretesting. This can become a threat when responses of a group on an assessment instrument (usually a posttest) are affected because of their having taken a pretest. This is particularly a threat if the time between the testing dates is of short duration. In such cases, subjects may improve their performance on the posttest with or without exposure to instructions or experimental treatment in the interim period. They simply remember the questions, or, learning from the nature of the pretest that they are going to be the subject of a study on inclusionary education, they may be motivated to do unassigned reading on the subject. Further, the pretest may prompt increased debates in the teachers' room. Although these practices are not part of the instructions or treatment, they could influence attitudes about inclusionary education.

8. Instability. **Instability** refers to chance factors that arise during the course of the investigation. These factors include such things as:

1. An employee being advised, on the morning of the day that he is planning to complete a questionnaire on attitudes, that he has been nominated by the school principal to be State Teacher of the Year

2. The on-campus mail system breaking down and questionnaires being sent to incorrect offices, causing delays in their receipt by study participants

3. A fire alarm going off while students are taking a pre- or posttest

4. A piece of equipment breaking down during the experimental phase of the study

5. The principal having to hire a substitute for a teacher who becomes ill during the critical phase of a study in which he is the instructor

These are factors for which it is very hard, if not impossible, to plan. They would not be called threats of instability if they were naturally occurring events. However, thoughtful regard for such circumstances, in *advance* of their occurring, will enable one to more intelligently prepare responses for such contingencies should they surface during the course of the investigation.

9. Expectancy. **Expectancy** is a threat that can impact results when the researcher has a bias about the outcome of the study. Body language, tone of voice, and general enthusiasm toward the activities of one of the groups in the study can all have a bearing on the performance of the subjects therein. Although the investigator may have a hunch about what the findings will reveal, it is critical to the validity of the outcome that research objectivity be maintained. One way to ensure that your presence will not have a bearing on the performance of subjects is to train research assistants to serve in your place. In the case of the proposed study on inclusionary education, it would be appropriate to arrange to have an individual other than the researcher serve as the contact person for deliveries and returns of the questionnaires, particularly since the teachers may know that the researcher is a proponent of totally integrated classes. The researcher's presence may or may not influence their responses, but he should not take the risk. (You will recall that arrangements have been made for the secretary to the district coordinator of special education to deliver and collect the survey instruments.)

10. Interaction of Two or More of the Other Threats. For example, the maturing of a subject during the course of a study may cause him to read more, watch more news on television, or tune in to after-school specials broadcast through public television networks. If an extended study taking place in a classroom relates to a topic that becomes of increased interest to one making out-of-class decisions, maturation and history are interacting. Certainly, it would be ideal if topics of debate in a classroom prompted students to seek to learn more about them after school or on weekends. The problem is that students mature differently, and the activities available to them beyond school vary just as much. Unless the research design includes equivalent out-of-class assignments for all, the interactive threats of maturation and history are going to influence the results of the study to some degree. How much? It may never be known. Learning will take place, but how much of it can be attributed to the classroom treatment would be difficult, if not impossible, to calculate.

In the case of the study on inclusionary education, the interaction of instrumentation, regression, and expectancy would occur if the researcher used an invalidated instrument to measure the attitudes of K–8 teachers who had little or no training in special education, with the hope of later showing how their participation in inservice workshops would improve their attitudes on the merits of integration. If teachers had no training in special education, it would be probable that their understanding of the values of integration would improve if subjected to a workshop designed for that purpose.

In addition to the methods already described for controlling for threats to internal validity (for example, giving thoughtful regard to the length of the study; avoiding bias as it relates to sample selection and expectancy; ensuring that the instrument of assessment is valid, reliable, and objective for the study; and screening for competencies at the onset of the study when pretesting is not considered a threat to acquiring valid scores on a posttest), random sampling will control for all of the threats to internal validity except: (1) experimental mortality, (2) instability, and (3) expectancy. It is assumed that if individuals are randomly selected from a finite population, their characteristics (and those of the study protocol) will parallel the circumstances intrinsic to the study of the larger group. At the same time, randomization will *not* control for the fact that someone may drop out of the study (experimental mortality), for chance factors that may arise without warning during the course of the study (instability), or for the possibility that the researcher has an uncontrolled bias (expectancy).

Threats to External Validity. On the matter of external validity, researchers and consumers are often interested in generalizing findings of a study to other groups. The extent to which this is a legitimate practice depends upon the relationship of the circumstances of that study to the circumstances of the group(s) for which inferences are going to be attempted. The following is a list of possible threats to making such generalizations and, therefore, can serve as a benchmark for assessing the *external* validity of a study.

1. Sampling. **Sampling** is the process of selecting subjects to participate in a study. Unless an entire finite population of subjects is going to be used in a study, it is critical that, at the very least, every member of that population has an equal opportunity to be selected for the study group. Otherwise, it would be inappropriate to expect that the findings related to that group (sample) could be inferred to the population in any meaningful way. If it were determined in the study on inclusionary education, for example, that (a) face-to-face interviews were the only way to get the information needed, (b) it was too costly in time and money for the researcher to meet personally with *all* the K–8 classroom teachers, and (c) the researcher did not want to rely upon research assistants to conduct the interviews, it would be necessary to get a random sample of the teachers. Unless the researcher ensured that each and every member of the K–8 teaching population had an equal opportunity to be selected to be part of the sample, it would be inappropriate to generalize the findings to the entire group.

2. *Person(s)*. This threat relates to the fact that if inferences from a sample group are going to be drawn to other groups, the selection characteristics of the individuals comprising the sample and those of the population group(s) should be comparable. Simply put, the findings on the attitudes of K–8 teachers can be generalized to other groups *if* pertinent characteristics of the individuals comprising all pertinent groups are similar. For example, if the researcher examined the attitudes of experienced, certified K–8 classroom teachers who were "untrained" in special education, the findings of that group could be inferred to other "untrained" teachers who met all the other standard certification and experiential requirements.

3. *Place(s)*. To illustrate an example of this threat, the findings of studies conducted in open classrooms can only be generalized to individuals who are located within other open classrooms, and who meet all other pertinent requirements. If an investigation were done to study the effect that running on a treadmill (at a predetermined length of time, speed, and inclination) had upon the cardiovascular endurance of linebackers on a first-year college student varsity football team, the findings would not be generalizable to linebackers in another first-year college football program (or the same linebackers for that matter) who were being tested outdoors on a cinder track. Since the place would be different, the conditions would be different. Although the results might be the same, that cannot be assumed.

When planning for the survey on inclusionary education, the researcher should be mindful of the fact that the filling out of a questionnaire in the school lunchroom between bites of a sandwich provides different conditions than does the filling out of the questionnaire in the relaxed environment of a family room at home. Attitudes on virtually any subject may vary depending upon the conditions of the place where issues are considered. It would be wise for the researcher, in this case, to arrange for the subjects to respond to the questions in a common, relaxed environment. To the extent possible, the influence of extraneous variables should be minimized.

4. *Time(s)*. Being able to generalize findings can also be threatened by such things as (a) time of the day, (b) day of the month, (c) whether the study is conducted immediately before, during, or after particularly stressful (or relaxing) events, and (d) duration of the study. A study to assess the effect of a behavior modification system on hyperactive students may generate different results, depending upon whether the observations take place before or after lunch. Likewise, the results of a measure of teacher attitudes toward inclusionary education may not be generalizable to similarly trained and experienced teachers located elsewhere without referencing the time that the questionnaires were administered.

Consideration of sampling, person(s), place(s), and time(s) has a bearing on whether the findings of any study can be generalized to other populations. Therefore, to control for these threats to external validity, the researcher should make reference to these items in any oral or written research report so that the consumer of the research can make intelligent decisions about the appropriateness of the findings in his particular set of circumstances. (See Chapter 13, Preparing the Research Report.)

Design Alternatives

There are many factors that govern the research design that will be selected for use in an investigation, such as: familiarity with options available, competencies of the researcher, availability of time and resources, and the degree of support from subjects and their program directors. The most important factor in choosing among the different **design alternatives,** however, is the *purpose of the study*.

If the researcher wanted to assess the current attitudes of teachers toward inclusionary education without regard for (1) comparing them to other groups, or (2) judging the effect of some treatment upon them, the design of choice would be a *survey*.

However, if the researcher wanted to determine the effect of an in-service workshop upon teacher attitudes, he might consider using a randomized posttest only control-group procedure. With this technique, the population of K–8 teachers would be randomly assigned to one of two groups; one of the groups would be randomly selected to participate in a workshop, and the other would proceed with its activities as usual. Then, at the conclusion of the workshop period, an equivalent posttest would be administered to both groups in order to test the null hypothesis. If it was found that (a) groups were comparable in their attitudes at the beginning of the study, (b) pertinent threats to internal validity had been controlled, and (c) on the posttest, the group attending the workshop demonstrated significantly more favorable attitudes toward inclusionary education than did their counterparts, the difference would be attributed to attendance at the workshop. This design would be *experimental*.

On the other hand, if the researcher wanted to examine evidence of the past in order to determine whether the attitudes of K–8 classroom teachers of preceding eras toward inclusion were observed and recorded, he would employ an *historical* design. An examination of attitudinal changes of one subject over an extended period of time would require the use of a *case study*.

Question: If you were interested in assessing the degree and direction of attitude changes over an extended period of time for *one* of the K–8 classroom teachers, which design would you be tempted to use?

Although various factors may have a bearing on exercising one's choice, design preference is determined, for the most part, by the *purpose* of the investigation. Does that point seem clear to you? Pursuant to your study of Parts II and III of this text, you will be in a position to make various determinations about the appropriateness of designs for studies you may desire to pursue.

Definitions of Terms

Early in the study, it is helpful to define important terms, and terms for which there may be more than one definition. Not only does defining terms help the researcher stay focused, it later helps the readers of the research report know exactly what is meant when the terms are used. For example, most people reading this text would assume that a *test* is a measure of achievement or intelligence. In writing this text, however, the author has defined a *test* as an *instrument of assessment*. If that point were not made clear, some readers could be confused by the use of this term. Therefore, tests (instruments of assessment) can be designed to measure any of the following: achievement, aptitudes, attitudes (or perceptions), intelligence, or interests. (See Chapter 5, Selecting Instruments of Assessment.)

For purposes of the study described in the scenario of this chapter, *inclusion* means the same as *mainstreaming*—that is, the integration of children with exceptionalities into the curricular, cocurricular, and extracurricular activities that are normally scheduled for all children. Although some may quarrel with the specifics of this definition, the use of these specifics is the researcher's choice to make. Since the study is the researcher's, he has the right to define terms as he wishes. While consideration should be given to standard practices and "general use in the profession," you have the same right in your study.

✓CHECKPOINT

The following ten questions are designed to sample your familiarity with threats to the internal and external validity of a study. While responding to these items, refrain from looking back at the reading. At the end of the list of questions, answers are provided. At that time, reread the material if your responses do not agree with the answers given.

1. When a testing instrument demonstrates that it measures what it claims to measure, it is known to have _____ .

2. When two or more evaluators agree about the relative merit of one's response, it can be said that the test question has _____ .

3. When an instrument of assessment measures some variable in a consistent way, it is known to have _____ .

4. A threat to the *internal* validity of a study in which external factors, such as watching an afternoon television special, may influence the results is known as _____ .

5. A threat to the *internal* validity of a study that may arise when subjects are forced to withdraw from the study is known as _____ .

6. A threat to the *internal* validity of a study when subjects in one of the groups score unusually high in a pretest is known as _____ .

7. When a sampling procedure is used that does *not* provide all members of a population with equal opportunities to be chosen, the threat is called

_____ .

8. Unplanned events that arise during the course of an investigation contribute to a threat known as _____ .

9. A threat to the *external* validity of a study when one attempts to draw inferences to settings that are unrelated to those under study is known as

_____ .

10. The threat of _____ to the *external* validity of a study exists when one considers drawing inferences from findings that emerge in the fall semester, to the spring semester of an academic year.

Answers

The correct answers to the above questions are:

1. Validity

2. Objectivity (or inter-rater reliability)

3. Reliability

4. History

5. Experimental mortality

6. Statistical regression

7. Selection

8. Instability

9. Place

10. Time

If you earned a score between 8 and 10, you did an *excellent* job and should feel comfortable with your ability to identify the threats presented in the chapter—unless you missed the two questions dealing with *external* validity, in which case you should review that particular information again. If you had 5 to 7 responses correct, you should be pleased in knowing that you were able to recall at least one-half of the names assigned to the threats described in the questions. At the same time, you may want to spend some time reading the material again, particularly as it relates to the items you answered incorrectly. If you scored less than 5, you had the majority of the questions wrong. In this case, you need to study all of the threats again. Understanding the impact of these threats is considered a prerequisite to outlining strategies for carrying out a proposed study—strategies that are presented in the next section of this chapter.

Although knowing the labels assigned to the various threats is not nearly as important as knowing their influence if they are not controlled, one measure of your insights on the matter is your ability to identify their descriptions. In the report of one's completed study, reference is generally made to the identity of those threats that were controlled or uncontrolled.

PHASE 2

A **template** that portrays a valid sequence of procedures for conducting a study can be likened to a good road map. You might know where you want to go, but unless you have carefully designed plans for getting there, problems can surface that will jeopardize the outcome. Preparation of the template requires that the right questions get asked. For each of the subproblems identified within the introduction section of this chapter, responses to the following questions need to be prepared: (1) *What* do I need to know? (2) *Where* will I find it? (3) *How* will I find it? (4) What needs to be done to *organize and analyze* the information? (5) What *conclusions* should one expect (under optimum conditions)?

As you read through the entries from left to right in Figure 3–3, a sample design template for a study on inclusionary education, give thought to the procedures that would have to be considered for other studies, such as one for which you may have already prepared a problem statement.

The template is nothing more than a blueprint for carrying out a study. During the conduct of the investigation, problems may arise that require procedural adjustments. For the most part, this should not cause undue concern. By having a thoughtful plan of action, one is better prepared to meet arising contingencies, since each step necessary to conducting the investigation has been selected *after* consideration has been given to alternative designs.

SUMMARY

The purpose of this chapter was to provide you with the insights and skills to prepare thoughtful research plans. As the various sections unfolded, it should have become apparent that responding to each of the elements that has been presented is requisite to successfully addressing one's research problem. From the birth of an idea to the concluding statement in the design template, the steps that are taken progress through a fairly predictable sequence. While it is possible to commence work on the budget before the Gantt chart is complete, both should be in place before proceeding to the actual identification of the individual subjects for the research. At the same time, the beginning researcher should understand that a review of related literature is an ongoing process. One should be seeking constantly to learn more about the work of others.

As you were reading the chapter, hopefully you began to refine your ideas about the requirements of your own research problem. Did you think about what it would take to match the components of Phases 1 and 2 in this chapter with what *you* would need to address in order to carry out your study?

It is recommended that time schedules, budgets, problem statements, justifications, literature reviews, hypotheses, and basic assumptions be managed in harmony with initiatives to control for threats to internal and external validity. Coupled with adherence to the standards of ethical and legal practices described in Chapter 2, the beginning researcher should be well on the way to understanding what it takes to conduct studies of quality.

 ## RECOMMENDED LABORATORY ASSIGNMENTS

1. Review the recommended readings.

2. For the literature review you conducted in response to the recommendation of Chapter 1, integrate the findings of ten to fifteen studies. If there were opposing results, include them in your section summary.

3. At the conclusion of Chapter 1, it was recommended that you prepare problem statements and hypotheses for both a descriptive and an experimental study.

Figure 3–3: **Design Template for Study on Inclusionary Education**

Subproblems	What	Where	How	Organize/Analyze	Conclusions
Permission/Selection of subjects	1. Whether administrative authorities will allow study to proceed	From school district superintendent and building principal	By describing orally and in writing the purpose of study	Receive *written* permission to proceed with study	Permission has been granted
	2. Whether teachers will be willing to participate in study	From teachers themselves	By describing study in writing	Receive *written* agreement to participate in study	Agreement is received
	3. Timelines for conducting study	Within the design of study	By following a Gantt chart	Ensure that timelines are reasonable to follow	Timelines are established
Selection of instrument	1. Whether 5–7 professionals in general and special education would be willing to serve on a jury to validate an attitude questionnaire	From colleagues at the institution where I am employed	By meeting with selected individuals to describe the study, and seeking their agreement to participate	Make a list of names and mailing addresses of willing participants	A roster of jury members is identified
	2. Whether I have a valid instrument for the study. (It has been determined that a valid, standardized test to measure teacher attitudes toward inclusionary education does *not* exist. Hence, I must create my own.)	From the review made by members of the jury	By preparing and distributing research objectives, table of specifications, and items to jury members	Obtain returns from jurors and make adjustments to questionnaire as recommended	Instrument is valid

Figure 3–3: **Design Template for Study on Inclusionary Education (continued)**

Subproblems	What	Where	How	Organize/Analyze	Conclusions
	3. Whether second SAU would be willing to assist me in determining reliability and objectivity of instrument	At SAU that has characteristics similar to those of SAU selected for participation in study	By contacting pertinent authorities to discuss purpose	Obtain *written* agreement	Agreement is granted
	4. Whether instrument is reliable and objective	From personnel within the second SAU	By administering the instrument on two occasions, the first of which is assessed by second evaluator and myself	*Objectivity* will be determined by seeking 90% agreement between two evaluators on the first testing occasion; *reliability* will be determined by seeking 80% agreement of my evaluation of first and second administrations of the instrument	Instrument is reliable and objective
Administration of study/Collection of data	1. Whether study has been carried out in a manner appropriate to its design, including control for threats to internal validity: (a) history, (b) selection, (c) maturation, (d) instrumentation, (e) regression, (f) mortality, (g) pretesting, (h) instability, and (i) expectancy	At locations where study is designed and administered	By monitoring procedures for gaining permission; procuring sample; selecting instrument; distributing and collecting questionnaire. (External validity is not a pertinent issue unless consideration is given to generalizing the findings to other groups.)	*History, maturation, mortality, pretesting:* nonthreats; *selection, regression:* controlled by using K–8 teacher population; *instrumentation:* controlled by jury validation and pilot testing; *expectancy:* controlled by using secretary to distribute and collect questionnaires; *instability:* monitored and noted	Study has been carried out, per design

Figure 3-3: **Design Template for Study on Inclusionary Education (continued)**

Subproblems	What	Where	How	Organize/Analyze	Conclusions
	2. That data have been collected from at least 70% of the respondents and are ready for analysis	From the questionnaires returned to me	By examining the questionnaires to ensure their suitability for analysis	Responses to Likert-type items will be entered into a computer, responses to discussion questions will be prepared for qualitative analysis	Data are ready for analysis
Analysis of data/ Conclusions/ Recommendations	1. The attitudes of K–8 teachers toward inclusionary education	From the data generated by the study	By applying appropriate quantitative and qualitative analytical procedures	Quantitative data will be analyzed by calculating modes, percentages of attainment, and chi square; qualitative data will be analyzed through trend analysis	Data have been analyzed on attitudes toward inclusionary education; attitudes are known
	2. The conclusions that can be drawn from analysis of the quantitative and qualitative data available to me	From the findings of the analyses	By examining all findings appropriate to the purpose of the study	Modes, percentages of attainment, chi square values, and trends will be synthesized	Conclusions have been prepared
	3. The recommendations, appropriate to the findings and conclusions, have been generated	From the conclusions	By carefully studying the statements made in the conclusions	Prepare list of recommendations	Recommendations have been prepared on topics for workshops and future study

Considering the ethical and legal implications of your specific interests, for one of those studies, prepare:

   a. a time schedule.

   b. a tentative budget.

   c. a statement of justification.

   d. a list of basic assumptions.

   e. a list of possible threats to its internal validity, and how you would control for them.

   f. an identification of factors that would need to be considered to maintain its external validity.

   g. evidence that contrasting designs were examined, and the basis upon which a final determination was made.

   h. definitions of important terms.

   i. a template that includes responses to all pertinent subproblems, as well as to the questions related to: what, where, how, organization and analysis, and conclusions.

NOTE: *Refinement* of your sampling and instrumentation procedures can be delayed until Chapters 4 and 5 have been read. Further, it is understood that you may not yet be in a position to identify the preferred analytical options necessary for data analysis—that is, organization and analysis section of the fourth subproblem, analysis of data/conclusions/recommendations. This information is presented in Parts II and III of the text. For the time being, that section of the template can be left unattended.

4. Arrange to meet with fellow graduate students, colleagues, as well as school and nonschool employees who have carried out applied research, in order to review and discuss your plans to date.

RECOMMENDED READINGS

Berg, K., & Latin, R. (1994). *Essentials of modern research methods in health, physical education, and recreation.* Upper Saddle River, NJ: Prentice-Hall.

Bordens, K. S., & Abbott, B. A. (1995). *Research design and methods: A process approach* (3rd ed.). Mountain View, CA: Mayfield.

Brink, P. J., & Wood, M. J. (1994). *Basic steps in planning nursing research: From question to proposal* (4th ed.). Boston: Jones & Bartlett.

Chronbach, L. J. (1982). *Designing evaluations of educational and social programs.* San Francisco: Jossey-Bass.

Creswell, J. W. (1994). *Research designs: Qualitative and quantitative approaches.* Thousand Oaks, CA: Sage.

DeBakey, L. (1976). The persuasive proposal. *Journal of Technical Writing and Communication, 6,* 8–9.

Drew, C. J., Hardman, M. L., & Hart, A. W. (1995). *Designing and conducting research: Inquiry in education and social science* (2nd ed.). Needham Heights, MA: Allyn & Bacon.

Firestone, W. A. (1987). Meaning in method: The rhetoric of quantitative and qualitative research. *Educational Researcher, 16*(17), 16–21.

Fowler, F. J. (1984). *Survey research methods*. Beverly Hills, CA: Sage.

Goodwin, C. J. (1995). *Research in psychology: Methods and design*. New York: Wiley.

Gordon, R. (1981). *Interviewing: Strategies, techniques, and tactics*. Homewood, IL: Dorsey.

Hedrick, T. E., Bickman, L., & Rog, D. J. (1993). *Applied research design: A practical guide*. Newbury Park, CA: Sage.

Jaeger, R. M. (Ed.). (1988). *Complementary methods for research in education*. Washington, DC: American Educational Research Association.

Krathwohl, D. R. (1991). *How to prepare a research proposal* (3rd ed.). Syracuse, NY: Syracuse University Press.

Locke, L. F., Spirduso, W. W., & Silverman, S. J. (1993). *Proposals that work* (3rd ed.). Newbury Park, CA: Sage.

Majchrzak, A. (1984). *Methods for policy research*. Newbury Park, CA: Sage.

Marshall, C., & Rossman, G. R. (1989). *Designing qualitative research*. Newbury Park, CA: Sage.

McHugh, M. C., Koeske, R. D., & Frieze, I. H. (1986). Issues to consider in conducting nonsexist psychological research: A guide for researchers. *American Psychologist, 41,* 879–890.

Oja, S. N., & Smulyan, L. (1989). *Collaborative action research: A developmental approach*. London: The Falmer Press.

Schatzman, L., & Strauss, A. L. (1973). *Field research: Strategies for a natural sociology*. Englewood Cliffs, NJ: Prentice-Hall.

Schumacher, S., & Esham, K. (1986). *Evaluation of a collaborative planning and development of school-based preservice and inservice education, Phase IV*. (ERIC Document Reproduction Service No. ED 278 659). Richmond: Virginia Commonwealth University, School of Education.

Sieber, J. E. (1992). *Planning ethically responsible research*. Newbury Park, CA: Sage.

Taylor, S. J., & Bogdan, R. C. (1984). *Qualitative research methods: The search for meanings* (2nd ed.). New York: Wiley.

Westmeyer, P. M. (1994). *A guide for use in planning, conducting, and reporting research projects* (2nd ed.). Springfield, IL: Thomas.

REFERENCES

Baker, E., Wang, M., & Walberg, H. (1995). The effects of inclusion on learning. *Educational Leadership, 52*(4), 33–35.

Biklen, D. (Producer). (1988). *Regular lives* [Video]. Washington, DC: State of the Art.

Carlisle, H. M. (1979). *Management essentials: Concepts and applications*. Chicago: Science Research Associates.

Coates, R. D. (1989). The Regular Education Initiative and opinions of regular classroom teachers. *Journal of Learning Disabilities, 22,* 532–536.

Costello, C. (1991). *A comparison of student cognitive and social achievement for handicapped and regular education students who are educated in integrated versus a substantially sep-arate classroom.* Unpublished doctoral dissertation, University of Massachusetts, Boston.

Cratty, B. J. (1989). *Adapted physical education in the mainstream* (2nd ed.). Denver, CO: Love.

Fuchs, L., Fuchs, D., & Bishop, N. (1992). Instructional adaptation for students at risk. *Journal of Educational Research, 86*(21), 70–84.

Hasazi, S., Johnston, P., Liggett, A., & Schattman, R. (1994). A qualitative policy study of the least restrictive environment provision of the individuals with disabilities education act. *Exceptional Children, 60,* 491–507.

Kirk, S. A., Gallagher, J., & Anastasiow, N. (1997). *Educating exceptional children* (8th ed.). Boston: Houghton Mifflin.

Lipsky, D., & Gartner, A. (1995). The evaluation of inclusive education programs. *National Center on Educational Restructuring and Inclusion Bulletin, 2*(2), 1–7.

McLaughlin, M. V. (1991). The Rand change agent study: Ten years later. In A. R. Oden (Ed.), *Education policy implementation* (pp. 143–145). Albany, NY: State University of New York Press.

Neary, T., Halvorsen, A., Kronberg, R., & Kelly, D. (1992, December). *Curricular adaptations for inclusive classrooms.* California Research Institute for the Integration of Students with Severe Disabilities, San Francisco, CA.

Semmell, M., Abernathy, T., Butera, G., & Lesar, S. (1991). Teacher perceptions of the regular education initiative. *Exceptional Children, 57,* 9–22.

Sherman, A. (1996). Mainstreaming: Where did we fail? *Palaestra, 12*(2), 25–27.

Sherrill, C. (1993). *Adapted physical activity, recreation, and sport: Crossdisciplinary and life-span* (4th ed.). Dubuque, IA: Brown & Benchmark.

Stainback, S., & Stainback, W. (1992). *Curriculum considerations for inclusive classrooms.* Baltimore: Brookes.

Strully, J., & Strully, C. (1985). Teach your children. *Canadian Journal on Mental Retardation, 35*(4), 3–11.

Thousand, J., Fox, T., Reid, R., Godek, J., Williams, W., & Fox, W. (1986). *The homecoming model: Educating students who present intensive educational challenges within regular edu-cation environments* (Monograph No. 7-1). (ERIC Document Reproduction Service No. ED 284 406). Burlington, VT: University of Vermont, Center for Developmental Disabilities.

Thousand, J., Villa, R., & Nevin, A. (1994). *Creativity and collaborative learning: A practical guide to empowering students and teachers.* Baltimore: Brookes.

Villa, R., & Thousand, J. (1988). Enhancing success in heterogeneous classrooms and schools: The powers of partnership. *Teacher Education and Special Education, 11,* 144–154.

Villa, R., & Thousand, J. (1995). The rationales for inclusive schooling. In R. Villa & J. Thousand (Eds.), *Creating an inclusive school* (pp. 28–44). Alexandria, VA: Association for Supervision and Curriculum Development.

Will, M. (1985, December). *Educating children with learning problems: A shared responsibili-ty.* Paper presented at the meeting of Wingspread Conference on The Education of Special Needs Students: Research Findings and Implications for Practice, Racine, WI.

Wiseman, D. C. (1994). *Physical education for exceptional students: Theory to practice.* Albany, NY: Delmar.

CHAPTER 4

Sampling Procedures

OBJECTIVES

After reading this chapter, you should be able to:

- Describe the differences between finite and infinite populations.
- Distinguish between random and nonrandom sampling procedures.
- Discuss the limitations of nonprobability sampling techniques.
- Describe the lottery and table of random numbers methods for procuring valid population samples.
- Demonstrate the procurement of a sample from the table of random numbers.
- Determine minimum sample sizes for given population values.
- Identify, distinguish, and discuss the steps for selecting simple, stratified, cluster, stratified cluster, and systematic random samples.
- Identify and discuss the Hawthorne, John Henry, and placebo effects as they relate to research samples and findings.
- Distinguish between convenience, purposive, and quota samples (including advantages and disadvantages of each).
- Define key terms, and answer the checkpoint questions.

KEY TERMS

Block Sampling	*Nonprobability Sampling*
Cluster Random Sample	*Placebo Effect*
Convenience Sample	*Probability Sampling*
Finite Population	*Purposive Sample*
Haphazard Sampling	*Quota Sample*
Hawthorne Effect	*Raffle Method*
Infinite Population	*Random Sampling*
Intact Group	*Simple Random Sample*
John Henry Effect	*Stratified Cluster*
Judgmental Sampling	*Stratified Random Sample*
Lottery Method	*Systematic Random Sample*
Minimum Sample Size	*Table of Random Numbers*

INTRODUCTION

In the preceding chapters, you have been introduced to strategies for translating problem statements into workable research plans. While you may recall that reference has been made to subject selection, you will also remember that the specific procedures for doing so have been deferred to this point in time. While the procedures themselves are not complex, they nonetheless require close attention without the encumbrances of other issues; thus, they are presented in a separate chapter. Once the knowledge presented in this chapter is acquired, the information can be integrated, as pertinent, with other processes described to date.

If one desires to draw conclusions about a population of subjects, one may choose to observe that group in its entirety. This is the ideal procedure because, under these circumstances, the researcher does not have to rely upon indicators of a sample group as a basis from which to draw inferences. The researcher would know how the entire population would perform because each and every member of that group was subjected to the research. As you might expect, however, it is not always possible to test (observe) *everyone*. Individual members of that population may not be identifiable or, if identifiable, may not be available. To complicate matters, the researcher may have insufficient resources to include all subjects in her study, even if they were known and available. As a consequence, it is important to know about the sampling alternatives that exist. By knowing and exercising the appropriate options, the investigator will be in a position to make *direct* observations of valid population samples and, through the use of inferential statistics, be able to estimate the extent to which the findings would be replicated if the entire population had been studied. This chapter will discuss various **probability sampling** and **nonprobability sampling** techniques, but first it is important to distinguish between finite and infinite populations.

FINITE VERSUS INFINITE POPULATIONS

A **finite population** is one in which all of its members can literally be counted. Examples include:

- All eighth-grade students currently enrolled at Carpenter Middle School. The names of these children can be identified by examining grade registration records retained by the eighth-grade teacher(s) and the school principal.

- All full-time teachers currently employed within School Administrative Unit #48. The names of these teachers can be identified through the records maintained within the office(s) of the school principal(s) and/or superintendent of schools.

- All children within School Administrative Unit #48 who have coded learning disabilities. This information would be on file with the district coordinator of special education, school principal(s), and/or superintendent of schools.

- All graduate students currently enrolled in the course "Research Design." This information is retained by the instructor of the course and the college registrar.

Do these examples make the point clear? In order for one to use **random sampling** techniques, a finite population must exist. Since each and every member of the population must have an opportunity to be selected in order to have a random sample, one must first know the identity of these individuals. Remember, a random sample can only be obtained from a finite population.

An **infinite population** is one in which its members cannot be counted. Although, in theory, the group may exist, its individual members cannot be identified. As a consequence, it is impossible to make a random selection from that population. Examples of infinite populations include:

- All students who will enroll in the eighth grade at Carpenter Middle School within the next five years. Although efforts could be made to make predictions by looking at the rolls of students who are currently registered in the third through seventh grades within the school system, one cannot be absolutely sure about the students' specific names because of the numbers of children who will be entering and leaving the school district during the five-year period. There is no question that predictions of future class sizes are made in order to facilitate decisions on faculty lines and supply purchases. However, these numbers are derived from general trends and experience, not from random sampling.

- The teachers who will be employed full-time by School Administrative Unit #48 for each of the next five years. Again, a guess can be made about who they might be, but there is no way to be sure. It might be possible to identify the names of the teachers who are planning to retire during that period, but there is no way to know at this time who their replacements might be. New faculty lines may even emerge. Further, some teachers may resign to teach in another school system. How could one possibly know at this time who those teachers will be and who would be hired to take their places?

- The names of those students who will be coded with learning disabilities within each of the next five years. One could examine current records and, from the findings, make reasonable predictions. Again, however, it would be impossible to select a random sample from that group because, at this point in time, the population of students with coded learning disabilities for each of the next five years does not exist.

- The names of graduate students who will be enrolled in the course "Research Design" through each of the next five years. A survey could be taken of current college undergraduate students in the region in order to inquire about their interest in pursuing a graduate degree within a specific institution. At best, however, this would provide but an estimate. It still would not be possible to identify the names of enrolled students until they in fact register. It would be possible to identify a population of undergraduate students who express an interest in graduate studies, but that does not address the issue in question. Not having that information makes it impossible to obtain a random sample.

Is the distinction between finite and infinite populations clear to you? This would be a good time for you to create your own examples of each of these. Remember, the specific membership of a finite population is identifiable, whereas the specific identity of members comprising an infinite population is not. While individuals from an infinite population may be chosen to constitute a sample study group, it would not be a random (probability) sample.

TYPES OF RANDOM (PROBABILITY) SAMPLES

Random sampling is a process that provides for each and every member of the population to have an equal and independent opportunity to be chosen. It requires that the result of one selection is independent of the result of any other selection.

Depending upon a number of factors, one can opt to employ any of the following sampling methods: (1) simple, (2) stratified, (3) cluster, (4) stratified cluster, and (5) systematic.

Simple Random Sample

The **simple random sample** is one that has been created by ensuring that each member of the population was in a position to be chosen during the entire phase of the selection process. There are three basic procedures that can be used to generate a random sample: (1) the lottery method, (2) the table of random numbers method, and (3) the computer method.

Lottery Method. With the **lottery method,** often referred to as the **raffle box method,** each member of the population is assigned a number. These numbers are then placed upon tabs of paper which, in turn, are dropped into a container, and thoroughly mixed. A tab of paper is drawn, the number of the population member is recorded, and then that tab is tossed back and mixed with other pieces of paper in the container. Replacing the tab of paper is an important feature of the raffle method in that it ensures that every number (individual) has an equal and independent opportunity to be selected until the desired sample size is reached. For example, if there were 100 members of a finite population, 100 corresponding tabs of paper would be tossed into a raffle box. If one did not replace each tab after each draw, the probability of being selected would change: it would change from one out of 100, to one out of 99, to one out of 98, to one out of 97, and so on. This would violate the principles of equal and independent sampling opportunities. If, by chance, a number is selected a second time, it is disregarded, because that number has already been recorded, and that tab of paper is tossed back into the container and the process is continued.

As indicated earlier, each name must have the same probability of being selected throughout the selection process. This is at the foundation of valid sampling theory. The raffle box method, while simple, is a very good way to select random samples. However, if the population size is considered by the researcher to be inordinately large, she may not want to labor through the process of labeling, selecting, identifying, and replacing tabs of paper. Instead, she may want to use a table of random numbers.

Table of Random Numbers Method. With the **table of random numbers** method, numbers are again assigned to each member of the population. This time, however, the system of numbering is a bit different—not complex, but different. To illustrate, assume that there are 200 identifiable members in a finite population. This time, instead of simply assigning numbers 1–200, one would use 000–199 in order to have them coincide with the range of integers provided for within the rows and columns of random number tables. It is unnecessary for one to alphabetize names before assigning numbers to them; in fact, the names do not need to be arranged in any particular order. It is not considered wrong to do so, but it is unnecessary to the random numbers sampling process. The one value that an alphabetized list does have is that it helps to ensure that everyone's name in the population has been included on the roster. See Table 4–1, Abbreviated Table of Random Numbers. (For a more extensive table, see Appendix A.)

Notice, in Table 4–1, that there are rows and columns. The rows are read across the table (horizontally); the columns are read down (vertically). Entrance into the table may be accomplished in any number of ways. Any of these ways can be correct, providing that pure chance dictates the process. For example, one might begin by blindly pointing a finger to a spot on the table, and proceed to read down using the number of columns that corresponds to the number of digits assigned to the last person in the population. A second way is to use any two consecutive digits of the serial number on a dollar bill. Suppose the bill has the serial number B 30881842 I. Using the last two digits, the numbers 4 and 2, the number 4 might tell one to begin in the fourth row; the number 2 might tell one to begin in the second column. If the researcher so desired, the number 4 could represent the column, and the number 2 could represent the row. There is no requirement about which is the row and which is the column.

Table 4–1: **Abbreviated Table of Random Numbers**

Rows			Columns		
1	10480	15011	01536	02011	81647
2	22368	46573	25595	85393	30995
3	24130	48360	22527	97265	76393
4	42167	93093	06243	61680	07856
5	37570	39975	81837	16656	06121
6	77021	06907	11008	42751	27756
7	99562	56420	69994	98872	31016
8	96301	91977	05463	07972	18876
9	89579	14342	63661	10281	17453
10	85475	36857	43342	53988	53060
11	28918	69578	88231	33276	70997
12	63553	40961	48235	03427	49626
13	09429	93969	52636	92737	88974
14	10365	61129	87529	85689	48237
15	07119	97336	74048	08178	77233

While there are hundreds of computer-generated random number tables (of various sizes), in Table 4–1, there are fifteen rows and twenty-five columns (five columns in each of five blocks). Therefore, for row 4 and column 2, one would begin one's sample search with the number 2. (Direct your attention to the intersection of row 4 and column 2 on the table.) Here are two other examples. If one were to begin in row 4, column 3, the search would start with the number 1. On the other hand, if one were to begin with row 4, column 4, one would start the search with the number 6.

✓CHECKPOINT

Beginning with row 9, column 16, in Table 4–1, with what number would you begin your search?

Answer

You would begin your search with the number 1. If you had any problems coming up with this answer, reread the paragraph preceding this Checkpoint or talk to your colleagues. While knowing this particular answer is not critical to mastering the principles of sampling theory, understanding how it was found may help to establish an important foundation for the illustration in the text that follows.

Earlier it was stated that if the population was comprised of 200 people, one would number them 000–199. (Zeros are always assigned to the first person on the population roster.) Following the same logic, if you had a population of 100, its members would be assigned numbers of 00–99. (Notice that two digits are used in the numbering process here because the last individual in the 100-person population would be assigned a 99.)

To apply these principles, assume that a researcher would like to conduct interviews of *all* 287 K–12 public and private school teachers within a given geographical region of central New Hampshire. Because the researcher does not have the resources that would allow her to arrange face-to-face meetings with each of them, the next best procedure would be the selection of a random sample. First, each of the teachers in the population would be assigned a number between 000 and 286 (see Table 4–2, Finite Population, N = 287). Using the answer to the preceding Checkpoint question—beginning in Table 4–1 with row 9, column 16 (truncated to three integers)—Table 4–2 indicates that the *first* person who would be selected to be in the sample would be Rick Hutchins, since he was assigned the number 102. Reading down in Table 4–1, the next three digits after 102 are 539. Since there are only 287 in the population, the number 539 does not apply, so it can be disregarded. Reading down to the next number, 332, it turns out that this number has not been

Table 4–2: **Finite Population, N = 287**

000 Mary Bourgeault	118 Jason Holder	159 Kathie Moulton
001 Peter Cofran	119 Gary Goodnough	--- etc.
002 Virginia Barry	120 Catherine Baumann	--- etc.
003 Patricia Lindberg	121 Wendy Palmquist	172 Bob Tuveson
004 Kenneth Heuser	122 Stephen Weissmann	173 Debbie Tobine
005 Kate Coupe	123 David Switzer	174 Mary Campbell
006 Michael Fischler	124 David Zehr	175 Richard Hage
007 Bryon Middlekauff	--- etc.	176 Gail Carr
008 Eldwin Wixson	134 Gary Richey	177 Donald Wharton
--- etc.	135 Chris Clarke	--- etc.
034 Philip Wei	136 Stephen Bamford	--- etc.
--- etc.	137 Martha Riess	267 Khuan Chong
081 Stacy Yap	138 Mark Wiseman	268 John Clark
082 Donna Anderson	139 Robert Swift	269 Barbara Blaha
--- etc.	140 Dennise Bartelo	270 Cindy Smoot
--- etc.	--- etc.	278 Shawn Griffin
100 Kathy Lambert	151 Nancy Aldrich	279 John Carr
101 Sally Boland	152 Virginia Garlitz	280 Lori Stoffel
102 Rick Hutchins	153 Joy Butler	281 Jeanne Dubino
103 Patricia Cantor	154 Lynn Davis	--- etc.
104 Gerard Buteau	155 Robin Bowers	--- etc.
105 Ann Marie Jones	156 Katharine Fralick	--- etc.
--- etc.	--- etc.	286 Tim Keefe

assigned to any member of the population either, so it is also disregarded. The next number down is 034, which belongs to Philip Wei in Table 4–2, so he becomes the second person in the sample. The third is Stacy Yap. (Can you see how this name was determined? It was first necessary to disregard the numbers 927 and 856.)

This process is continued until the necessary sample size has been selected. After you have made your entry into the table at the appropriate row/column intersection, use whatever columns to the immediate right are necessary to correspond with the number of digits assigned to the members of the population. In other words, if you get to the bottom of the page and still do not have the necessary sample size, begin at the top of the page with the next consecutive set of columns, read down, and continue in that fashion until the sample is of necessary size. (Using this system, the fourth person in the sample discussed in the previous paragraph would be Jason Holder.) If you do not have the desired sample size upon reaching the end of the page, go to the beginning of the page and continue.

The process for selecting random samples is not as complicated as it may seem. The following is a summary of the essential steps.

Step 1. Identify the population.

Step 2. List all members belonging to that population.

Step 3. Assign each member on the list a consecutive number beginning with zero—that is, for a population of 100, 00–99; a population of 150, 000–149, a population of 500, 000–499, and so on.

Step 4. Determine the necessary sample size (to be discussed later in the chapter).

Step 5. Select an entrance point on a table of random numbers. (Close your eyes and point, or randomly select two digits on a dollar bill, credit card, social security number, telephone directory, or vehicle registration tag.) Once the base intersection point is determined, choose the appropriate number of integers, and begin to make your selections.

Step 6. Read down the columns; if the number corresponds to a number assigned to any of the members of the population, that person becomes a member of the random sample. If a number you come to in the table is a repeat, disregard it and read on. (This may happen because you are using a table of random numbers. If one were to eliminate numbers that were repeated, the table could no longer be considered *random*.) Likewise, if the number you come across in the table is greater than the highest number assigned to any of the members in the population, disregard it as well. If you get to the bottom of the column before reaching the necessary sample size, go to the top of the next corresponding set of columns to the right or, if necessary, to the beginning of the page.

Step 7. Continue with step 6 until the desired sample size is reached.

Once the selection of the sample has been achieved, further random selections can be made, such as for experimental designs in which it may need to be determined (a) which half of the sample will be assigned to group one of two groups, and then (b) which of the two groups will receive the treatment. It is important for the reader to realize that there is nothing magic about whether you read up, down, or across columns, or whether you go to the next corresponding set of columns at the top of the page, or whether you choose to overlap them in some way. What is provided here is a set of guidelines. The important thing is that choices are randomized, and then made consistent within any given sample search.

The Computer Method. In recent years, the computer has become increasingly popular as a tool for selecting random samples. Once the researcher identifies a finite group of subjects, the computer can be programmed to make the selections. With due consideration to the principles of random selection, programs can be written or purchased that will generate desired sample sizes. (See Chapter 12, Using the Computer for Data Analysis, for a discussion of the multiple capabilities of computers in research activities.)

On several occasions, reference has been made to generating *desired* sample sizes. What is a desirable sample size? As you would surmise, too small a sample is unlikely to reflect the characteristics of the population it has been chosen to represent. Although a temptation may exist to reduce one's workload by keeping things simple, the information gained from an inappropriately small sample size is likely to be invalid to the larger group. If a random sample is to represent the population from which it was selected, it must be large enough to satisfy a probability that a trait distribution of the population would be found there. The question is: How large does the random sample have to be so that the likelihood of this relationship would exist? Unless the entire population is used in the study, it is unlikely that one will ever know. However, there are ways to increase the probability of such an occurrence.

While Bartz (1976) and Best and Kahn (1993) suggest that sample *size* is less important than the *care* taken during its selection, Charles (1995) points out that a sample of less than thirty is unlikely to reflect characteristics similar to what would be found in its population. The validity of any number, however, rests in part with whether the population is homogeneous or heterogeneous. On this matter, Leedy (1997) suggests that the more homogeneous the population is with regard to the trait to be measured, the smaller its random sample can be and still represent pertinent total-group idiosyncrasies. At the same time, the type of study one is planning to do will dictate, to some degree, the size of the sample necessary. For example, Roscoe (1975) has stated that some experimental studies with tight controls may be valid with as few as fifteen subjects per group. For some descriptive-type studies, Gay (1996) suggests using sample sizes of ten to twenty percent. She goes on to say that causal-comparative and correlational research should have a minimum of thirty subjects.

Although there are various theories on the matter, one general guideline is *the larger the sample, the better*. This statement is not very helpful, however, to one who is faced with making specific decisions. To this end, Krejcie and Morgan (1970) have generated data leading to the display in Table 4–3. While adjustments may have to be made depending upon such things as: (1) the specific nature of the descriptive or experimental study being designed, (2) the homo- or heterogeneity of the population being sampled, and (3) the fact that some individuals who have been selected will withdraw their previously expressed interest to participate, the values provided in the table represent general *minimum* standards as to how large the random sample needs to be in order to be ninety-five percent certain that the results of the study could not be jeopardized because of sample size alone.

A careful examination of Table 4–3 will reveal a number of important considerations. Among these are the following:

1. The smaller the population size, the greater the percentage of people that need to be selected in order for ninety-five percent confidence to be established. For

Table 4–3: **Abbreviated Table of Sample Sizes (S) Required for Selected Population Sizes (N)**

N	S	N	S	N	S
10	10	210	136	1000	278
15	14	220	140	1100	285
20	19	230	144	1200	291
25	24	240	148	1300	297
30	28	250	152	1400	302
35	32	260	155	1500	306
40	36	270	159	1600	310
45	40	280	162	1700	313
50	44	290	165	1800	317
55	48	300	169	1900	320
60	52	320	175	2000	322
65	56	340	181	2200	327
70	59	360	186	2400	331
75	63	380	191	2600	335
80	66	400	196	2800	338
85	70	420	201	3000	341
90	73	440	205	3500	346
95	76	460	210	4000	351
100	80	480	214	4500	354
110	86	500	217	5000	357
120	92	550	226	6000	361
130	97	600	234	7000	364
140	103	650	242	8000	367
150	108	700	248	9000	368
160	113	750	254	10000	370
170	118	800	260	15000	375
180	123	850	265	20000	377
190	127	900	269	30000	379
200	132	950	274	50000	381

example, if you have a population (N) of 10, your sample (S) size should also be 10 (100%). On the other hand, if N equals 500, your S need be but 217, or 43.4%. An N of 1,000 would require an S of 278, or 27.8%.

2. When a population (N) of less than 50 exists, one should consider using all of the subjects instead of sampling them. If, for legitimate reasons, it is deemed necessary to select a sample (S), one might consider sampling subjects "out of" instead of "into" the study. For example, if $N = 30$, the first two subjects selected at random would be excluded. This leaves the required $S = 28$, and accordingly, each member of the population (N) had an equal and independent opportunity to be selected.

3. Since all population (N) values between 10 and 50,000 have not been listed, it becomes necessary to make an adjustment. While mathematical interpolation is possible, it is simply recommended that when your N value falls between the expressed N values on table, use the recommended sample (S) for the higher N. For example, if your $N = 287$, use $S = 165$. Using the larger S will ensure that minimum (95%) standard is satisfied.

For the mathematicians and computer programmers among you, it needs to be said that there are other procedures for determining sample sizes that go beyond the scope of this text (Cohen, 1988). While Table 4–3, and the related discussion, may appear to oversimplify the process, knowing this material will enable you to satisfy most research sampling needs. Where unique considerations of the determination of appropriate sample sizes are pertinent to specific descriptive or experimental research models, amplification will be provided in Parts II and III.

Stratified Random Sample

The **stratified random sample** is one in which identifiable subgroups are included in the same proportion as they can be found in the population from which the sample was selected. You may have noted that, of the first four persons selected from Table 4–2 to represent the 287 teachers, three were men. If, by chance, that same ratio of men to women continued to be chosen throughout the selection process, the number of men in the final sample may not be in proportion to what exists in the population. Suppose, for example, that out of the 287 teachers, 160 are men. This represents 55.75% of the total, which is the proportion one should approximate in the sample. It is obvious that a chance drawing of three men for every one woman (75%) throughout the selection process (215 or 216 men to 71 or 72 women) would not be appropriate if proportional representation is to occur. While some studies may not require *gender* specificity, others may. A thorough review of what is reported in the literature, along with the personal experience of you and others, will help to make this determination.

For purposes of illustration, assume that the survey is going to address the extent to which the perception of sexual bias exists within the schools where these teachers are employed. Since a review of the literature has revealed that classroom inequities continue to exist in some school systems (Streitmatter, 1994), it would be inappropriate to rely on simple random sampling techniques alone to generate representative proportions of men and women. Given that the researcher wants to be able to generalize the findings to the entire population of teachers from which the sample is to be selected, this would be the time to use a *stratified* random sample. The process would be as follows.

Step 1. Prepare a roster of 127 women and a roster of 160 men.

Step 2. Assign the women numbers 000–126; assign the men numbers 000–159.

Step 3. Examine Table 4–3, sample sizes required for selected population sizes, to determine the sample size needed for the population of 287. Because $N = 287$ is not listed on the table, move to the next highest N value, 290. The table shows that the sample (S) needed is 165.

Step 4. Compute the percentage the sample (S) is of the population (N): 165/290 = 56.9, or 57%.

Step 5. Multiply the number of women (127) by 57%. This equals 72.39 (73 women). Multiply the number of men (160) by 57%. This equals 91.2 (92 men). Seventy-three women and 92 men yield a total of 165, which is the total number of men and women needed to satisfy the requirements of S.

Step 6. Randomly select 73 women from the roster of women, and randomly select 92 men from the roster of men.

Step 7. A stratified random sample of K–12 teachers has now been chosen; the researcher is in a position to proceed with the study.

Because of the nature of a study, it may be deemed necessary to stratify the population even further. In the study just described, the researcher might also want to ensure that teachers with six or more years of teaching experience within the system are distinguished from those with five years or less for purposes of proportional representation (see Figure 4–1).

In consideration of the display in Figure 4–1, the procedures for proportioning the population of teachers beyond the level of gender to years of experience would be as follows.

Step 1. Prepare a roster of women with six or more years of experience within the system (for example, N = 100). Number them 00–99.

1. Compute the percentage of this number (100) out of the total population (287). The answer is 34.84%.
2. Multiply 34.84% by the desired sample (S) size, 165. The answer is 57.49 (57).
3. Randomly select 57 persons from the roster of women who have six or more years of experience within the system.

Step 2. Prepare a roster of women with five or less years of experience within the system (for example, N = 27). Number them 00–26.

1. Compute the percentage of this number (27) out of the total population (287). The answer is 9.41%.
2. Multiply 9.41% by the desired sample (S) size, 165. The answer is 15.53 (16).
3. Randomly select 16 persons from the roster of women who have five or less years of experience within the system.

Step 3. Prepare a roster of men with six or more years of experience within the system (for example, N = 100).

1. Compute the percentage of this number (100) out of the total population (287). The answer is 34.84%.
2. Multiply 34.84% by the desired sample (S) size, 165. The answer is 57.49 (57).
3. Randomly select 57 persons from the roster of men who have six or more years of experience within the system.

Figure 4–1: **Graphic Display of Considerations for Gender and Years of Experience**

Population ($N = 287$)———

    Women ($N = 127$)———

          6+ Years ($N = 100$)

          5– Years ($N = 27$)

    Men ($N = 160$)———

          6+ Years ($N = 100$)

          5– Years ($N = 60$)

Step 4. Prepare a roster of men with five or less years of experience within the system (for example, $N = 60$).

1. Compute the percentage of this number (60) out of the total population (287). The answer is 20.91%.

2. Multiply 20.91% by the desired sample (S) size, 165. The answer is 34.50 (35).

3. Randomly select 35 persons from the roster of men who have five or less years of experience within the system.

NOTE: By adding the answers of the number 2s in steps 1–4 together, one will arrive at the desired sample (S) size for the population (N); that is, 57 + 16 + 57 + 35 = 165 (see Table 4–3).

To this point, simple random and stratified random sampling have been presented as ways to identify teachers for participation in the study. While both of these procedures are notable, either would likely require a great deal of traveling. (Since random selections are being made, it is unlikely that the professional addresses of the teachers taking part in the study would be in any one, or even two, of the schools within the participating school districts. Further, it would be unreasonable to expect those being interviewed to come to the researcher's place of employment.) If the researcher (1) was concerned that some of the teachers who were not selected (within any given school) might be upset because of the appearance of the researcher not being interested in their views, (2) wanted to reduce the amount of travel on anyone's part, or (3) thought it was important to have the information as quickly as possible, she could consider using cluster (or block) random sampling.

Cluster Random Sample

The **cluster random sample** is one that is comprised of randomly selected groups rather than individuals. First, the researcher identifies a population of clusters, and then she makes random selections from those blocks (or groups) of subjects. Examples of such clusters include: all tenth-grade classes in Los Angeles County, all private elementary schools in Chicago, and all public 9–12 secondary schools in Boston. Once random selections of clusters are made, every member of each of those

clusters is included in the study. Instead of randomly selecting individuals from a roster of 287 K–12 classroom teachers, for example, the researcher would randomly
select schools and include *all* the teachers employed at the schools which were
selected. The following are some examples of studies where cluster random sampling
would be the method of choice.

- A researcher is interested in examining the effectiveness of computer software
  on the enhancement of knowledge and understanding of the Civil War. It would
  be unlikely for her to receive teacher or administrative approval for a study that
  required some portion of students from each of several classes to be removed
  in order to integrate computer software into their instruction. It is more probable that permission would be granted if one requested the use of **intact group**
  (cluster) classrooms.

- A researcher is interested in conducting face-to-face interviews of K–12 teachers in Maryland in order to assess their attitudes toward state-mandated reforms.
  Rather than randomly choosing the names of teachers from a master roster, it
  would expedite matters, at much less cost, to use randomly selected cluster
  groups. The researcher could then travel to the schools that were selected and
  interview all the teachers employed there.

Both of these research interests are suitable to the use of cluster sampling procedures, but what of the study on the 287 K–12 teachers in central New Hampshire?
Would it be more efficient to design that study around cluster sampling? If one is
interested in using less time and fewer resources to conduct the study, the answer is
yes. If cluster random sampling were used, the steps would be as follows.

Step 1. Identify the population (*N*) of teachers in central New Hampshire. *N* = 287.

Step 2. Determine the desired sample (*S*) size for *N*. *S* = 165.

Step 3. Identify the clusters of schools in which the teachers are employed (for
example, *four* grade K–8 elementary schools, *two* grade K–6 elementary schools, *two*
grade 7–8 middle schools, and *two* grade 9–12 high schools—for a total of *ten*
schools). Prepare a roster of these schools.

Step 4. Assign each of the 10 schools (clusters) a number of 0–9.

Step 5. Compute the average number of teachers per cluster. While the schools
would vary from one another in terms of the number of teachers they employ, the
average would be 28.7 (287/10).

Step 6. Determine the number of clusters one needs to randomly select by dividing the desired sample (*S*) size (165) by the average number of teachers (28.7). The
answer is 5.75 (or 6) clusters.

Step 7. Using the lottery or table of random numbers method, select *six* clusters.
(Six schools, with an average of 28.7 teachers per school, exceeds the desired minimum sample size of 165 for this study.)

Step 8. The six clusters (blocks) have been chosen, and the researcher is in a position to proceed with the study. Arrangements can now be made to schedule interview sessions with the teachers in each of the six schools.

While this method does *not* provide the chance for each of the 287 teachers to be
selected independently, the opportunity for random selection does exist for the
schools in which they are employed. There is, however, a major shortcoming of cluster sampling, or **block sampling,** of which you should be aware. With some studies,

what is going to be described in the following scenario would not be an issue. In the matter of interviewing teachers on their perceptions of sexism within the schools, however, a problem may exist. You see, it is possible that the six clusters selected for inclusion in the study could be comprised of elementary schools alone. Remember, although the researcher wants random selections to occur, chance alone may yield six schools, none of which include grade 9–12 high schools. This would mean that the researcher would not learn of perceived practices at the high school level. As a consequence, the researcher may want to consider an alternative sampling procedure in order to ensure that each of the four categories of schools would be included. The alternative procedure is a combination of the cluster and stratification methods.

Stratified Cluster Random Sample

The **stratified cluster** random sample method works as follows.

Step 1. Identify the population (N) of teachers in central New Hampshire. $N = 287$.

Step 2. Determine the desired sample (S) size for N. $S = 165$.

Step 3. Identify the categories of school clusters in which teachers are employed, and the number of schools within each category:

- *Four* grade K–8 schools
- *Two* grade K–6 schools
- *Two* grade 7–8 schools
- *Two* grade 9–12 schools

Step 4. Assign each of the schools within each cluster a number:

- K–8 schools: 0–3
- K–6 schools: 0–1
- 7–8 schools: 0–1
- 9–12 schools: 0–1

Step 5. Compute the average number of teachers per school. The answer is 28.7 (287/10).

Step 6. Determine the number of schools one needs to randomly select by dividing the desired sample (S) size (165) by the average number of teachers (28.7). The answer is 5.75 (or 6) clusters. Given that the number 6 represents 60% of the total number of schools in the population, the researcher would then take 60% of the number of schools in each cluster category:

- 60% of four grade K–8 schools = 2.4
- 60% of two grade K–6 schools = 1.2
- 60% of two grade 7–8 schools = 1.2
- 60% of two grade 9–12 schools = 1.2

Step 7. Since step 6 indicated that six schools should be included in the sample, a determination is made that the following number of schools will be selected from each category in order to reach the minimum desired sample (S) size:

- Three grade K–8 schools: 3×28.7 teachers/school = 86.1
- One grade K–6 school: 1×28.7 teachers/school = 28.7
- One grade 7–8 school: 1×28.7 teachers/school = 28.7
- One grade 9–12 school: 1×28.7 teachers/school = 28.7

Total sample of teachers: 172.2

Step 8. Since 172.2 exceeds the minimum standards for sample size determined in step 2, random selections of the specified number of schools from each of the cluster categories will provide the representative roster of teachers. The researcher is now in a position to proceed with the study.

Systematic Random Sample

Using the terms *systematic* and *random* in the title of a sampling process offers a paradox that requires explanation. In using a **systematic random sample,** a group is formed by taking every *nth* person on a list. The distinction between systematic and other sampling procedures discussed so far (that is, simple and stratified) is that all members of the finite population do not have an independent opportunity to be selected *throughout the sampling process*. Once the first person on the list is identified, the rest of the individuals who will comprise the sample has been predetermined. However, by randomizing the list and using a number that has been randomly selected (from a list of 1–10, for example), one can procure a systematic random sample. According to Vockell and Asher (1995), "the resulting sample is essentially the same as a random sample, unless there is a systematic bias in the way the names appear on the list" (pp. 177–178). Given the following scenarios, however, one can imagine the kinds of selection bias that could arise:

- Using a telephone directory. In addition to having an alphabetized listing that, in itself, would be a problem, not everyone in a community would be eligible to be selected because only those whose names are associated with having telephones would be on the roster published by NYNEX.

- Taking every 1st, 3rd, 5th, 7th, 9th, and so on, student in a class in which girls and boys have been assigned alternate seating throughout the room. In this case, the sample would be comprised of boys or girls only.

- Getting an alphabetized list of district teachers by academic departments. If the selection interval was randomly determined to be eight and there were fewer than eight teachers in some departments, it would be possible for the selections to exclude representation from these departments.

A major problem of systematic sampling is that there is the possibility for certain subgroups within the population to be automatically excluded from the sample. Fortunately, this threat can be identified by asking the provider of the list how the roster has been presented. It will save time if adjustments can be made before the list gets in your hands. But, in any event, the list *must* be randomly rearranged.

The following steps, which refer to the finite population of 187 teachers who have been identified for a study on gender discrimination, are illustrative of the procedures to take in order to minimize the effects of selection bias.

Step 1. Randomly order the population (*N*) of teachers. *N* = 287.

Step 2. Determine the necessary sample (*S*) size. *S* = 165.

Step 3. Determine the *n interval* by dividing the size of the population (*N*) by the desired sample (*S*) size: *n interval* = 1.78. This information alerts the researcher that it will be necessary to use the entire population in order to get the desired sample. If the 1.78 was rounded to 2, and one proceeded to select every second subject from the population roster, the **minimum sample size** would not be reached.

NOTE: It can be observed in Table 4–3, sample sizes required for selected population sizes, that a finite population (*N*) of 400 would need to be present before it would be possible to select every *second* subject to complete the sample.

Choosing Between Types of Random (Probability) Samples

It is important to think carefully about the character of the population before a determination is made concerning the type of sampling method to employ. Elements of the population critical to any study can be established, in large part, by talking with experienced researchers, carefully reading related literature, and examining one's own professional experiences. If it is established that (1) critical features in the population exist, (2) it is important to have these features represented in the study, and (3) simple random sampling cannot be counted on alone to ensure their presence in the sample, alternative methods appropriate to that end are available.

CHECKPOINT

As a review, respond to each of the following questions on sampling procedures:

1. You have discussed your topic with experienced researchers, carefully examined related literature, and meditated on your own professional experiences. With findings in hand, it is determined that the finite population for your study is homogeneous on all pertinent demographics, for both the teachers and the institutions in which they are employed. Assuming that you would have neither time nor resources to include all members of the population in the study, which of the five sampling processes would be the method of choice?

2. Using Table 4–1, the abbreviated table of random numbers, and reading *down* starting in row 12, columns 1 and 2, which of the following persons, from a finite population of 15, would be selected to be the *first* member of your sample?

00 - Carole	05 - Sherry	10 - Andy
01 - Thomas	06 - Lois	11 - Bonnie
02 - Ralph	07 - Myrna	12 - Anna
03 - Justin	08 - Thomas	13 - David
04 - Sally	09 - Jeanne	14 - Trystan

3. Considering the size of the population cited in question 2, how would you arrive at the composition of the sample?

Answers

1. Since the teachers and the institutions in which they are employed have been deemed homogeneous, and since time and resources are issues, the *cluster* sampling procedure would appear to be the preferred method. While other factors may govern the decision, the researcher should consider expediting the study by making it easier to collect whatever data are being sought. This can be done by arranging research activities in a fewer rather than a greater number of places.

2. The first person selected to be a member of the sample would be *Jeanne*. The first number at the row/column intersection point is 63. Since the finite population (*N*) is not that large, you must read down to the next number, which is 09. That number has been assigned to Jeanne.

3. According to Table 4–3, sample sizes required for selected population sizes, a finite population of 15 requires a sample size of 14. Given that each member of the population had an equal and independent opportunity to be chosen, it would expedite the process to exclude Jeanne on the basis of her random selection and, thus, consider the remaining 14 as the sample group. This procedure is more efficient than laboring through the process of randomly selecting 14 out of 15 subjects. Can you imagine doing this while using the lottery method? As you might expect, one would be better off to use a table of random numbers. If you did choose your sample by proceeding through the table, *Andy* would be the second person selected to be in the sample (using the information provided in question 2), and *Myrna* would be the third.

As indicated earlier in the chapter, finite populations of subjects do not always exist. As a consequence, it can become necessary to employ nonrandom (nonprobability) methods. These methods are discussed in the following section.

TYPES OF NONPROBABILITY SAMPLES

There are three primary nonprobability sampling techniques that are available for use. Although they may be found under different titles, their roles are clear: none of them depend upon the existence of a finite population. Yes, there are limitations. At the same time, however, these methods provide ways of getting information that may not be accessed through other means. These three sampling methods are known most commonly as: (1) convenience, (2) purposive, and (3) quota.

Convenience Sample

This technique is one that consists of working with individuals or groups that happen to be available for the study. At one level, a **convenience sample** may be nothing more than asking questions of people as they are exiting a building—be it a school, shopping mall, or supermarket. The success of this procedure is dependent upon the number and characteristics of those who choose to respond to the questions. Since the size of S is likely to be small, the results are often misleading. **Haphazard sampling** is another name that Reaves (1992) assigns to this procedure. Frequently, this label is *apropos,* and in such instances, the researcher must use extreme caution when attempting to draw inferences from the results. The following scenario is another example.

An editor of a local newspaper is interested in knowing the attitudes of high school students in the town toward recent local election results. A reporter gets administrative permission to survey the classes, but the only time that she can get to the school is during her lunch hour. It has been decided by her boss that, given time limitations, she should plan to visit an intact tenth-grade class homeroom at 12:15 P.M., fifteen minutes before the students are scheduled to leave for the cafeteria. It is expected that a summary of the findings can then be prepared in time for the morning edition of the paper. Do you believe that this convenience sample would provide valid information about the election? Probably not, and for two basic reasons: (1) it is unlikely that the attitudes of *one* intact tenth-grade class could be generalized to the rest of the student body at any given time, and (2) it would be inappropriate for one to assume that administering a survey during a fifteen-minute time period just before lunch would likely generate thoughtful responses. Just the fact that a time was scheduled to meet with students in the last fifteen minutes of their homeroom period may be cause to diminish the value of the study in the eyes of those being surveyed. This would hold true for virtually any subject.

The use of volunteers also constitutes a convenience sample. Although some research must depend upon volunteers, the inferences from the findings of those studies are generally limited to other groups of volunteers. Even if one gets a random sample from a finite population of volunteers, the best that one can do is draw inferences to that specific population. The reason for this is that volunteers are often plagued with what is called the **"Hawthorne" effect,** named for the problem that was demonstrated some years ago at the Hawthorne Plant of the Western Electric Company in Chicago (Roethlisberger & Dickson, 1939). While not limited to studies being conducted with volunteers, this effect can arise when subjects (a) tend to respond in certain ways because of the special attention they are getting, (b) are aware of their participation in the research, and (c) know of the hypothesis for the study. After all, those who volunteer generally have a special interest in the subject. As a consequence, the findings of that group may be different than what would be found in the general population.

Aside from the obvious pitfalls found in these illustrations, convenience sampling can be taken to another level. Let me explain. Earlier in the section on random sampling, it was indicated that an intact classroom would qualify as a cluster. The limiting factor in being able to determine the identity of one such class through random procedures, however, is that a population of such classes (beyond the one that is currently being taught) may not exist. Thus, if the researcher is to do the study, she must use the one that is available (convenient). Further, if it can be determined that students currently enrolling in that class have similar characteristics to those who have enrolled in the class in the past, it might be reasonable to assume that students who would be registering for that class in the future would be alike in most respects as well (particularly if prerequisites for admission into that class are not altered). Though an imperfect system, one might consider its use in the following scenario.

Assume that one is interested in examining a new method for presenting course content to a group of students and, from the findings, making a determination about the appropriateness of using that method with subsequent classes. If a class were available, it might be possible to randomly assign an experimental treatment to one-half of its membership and compare findings at the end of a predetermined period of time. The teacher/researcher could even plan to flip-flop the treatment for the second half of the term so that (a) no student is deprived the opportunity to experience the effects of the treatment, and (b) opportunities become available for the teacher/researcher to examine the replicability of the findings.

Consider the example referenced earlier in the book in which a tenth-grade social science teacher is interested in examining the effectiveness of computer software on the enhancement of knowledge and understanding of causes of the Civil War. In this instance, it was indicated that the teacher was responsible for two sections of the same course. Following that assumption, the treatment (computers) could be randomly assigned to one of them (for example, through the toss of a coin). In most cases, having a control group (the one that does *not* receive the treatment) provides for a stronger research design. It is always possible, however, that individuals who know that they are going to be compared against "the treatment" may try harder (Saretsky, 1972). This is called the **"John Henry" effect** (named after a folk hero who, upon learning that he and his colleagues on the railroad were going to be replaced by a steam drill, set out to "beat the machine").

Without getting into the specifics of the design at this time, the teacher/researcher would plan to examine testable hypotheses and, from the findings at the conclusion of the study, draw inferences about its value (compared to the traditional method that was applied to the control group). There is no question that meaningful information could be acquired as a result of using the two classes that were available (convenient).

NOTE: To counterbalance the Hawthorne and John Henry effects, some researchers use a *placebo* selected to generate the impression among *all* subjects that they are being treated similarly. In medical research, for example, one might find a group receiving calcium lactate to counterbalance the psychological effects of an alternate group receiving amphetamine sulfate. (Both of these substances have similar appearances.) In educational research, the **placebo effect** is being practiced when subjects are unaware that they or others have been singled out for experimental treatments. Without knowing the specifics of the design, all subjects assume they are being treated alike.

Another example of a convenient sample would be an entire first-year college class. If a researcher was interested in examining the effectiveness of incorporating the use of portfolios in required composition classes, it could be arranged for the teachers of those classes in the fall semester to provide for their use by all incoming first-year students. This group would constitute a cohort. Data from the *prior* fall semester, when first-year students did *not* use portfolios in their composition classes, could be examined. At the end of the study period, data would be available that would enable one to determine whether portfolios appeared to have a bearing on student writing. Unless marked changes were made in admission standards or the applicant pool, one could assume that students enrolling in college from one year to the next are very much alike in their basic writing skills. Given that assumption to be reality for the periods under study, one would be in a position to make enlightened recommendations about the appropriateness of the requirement in subsequent composition classes. Again, the incoming first-year college class is not a random sample, but useful information could be acquired (particularly considering the size of N). While randomization is not present in convenience sampling, there are some reasons to support the useful place of convenience sampling in the cause of meaningful research.

Purposive Sample

This technique uses a sample population that is comprised of individuals whom the researcher *believes* would be representative of those found in a given population. Also referred to as **judgmental sampling** (Ary, Jacobs, & Razavieh, 1990; Charles, 1995; Gay, 1996), the **purposive sample** method engages a process which, according to Patton (1990) and Schumacher and McMillan (1993), is designed to generate a group that is "information rich." If the process is successful, the selected sample will be sufficiently knowledgeable about the phenomena being studied and, therefore, should represent the character of the population in a meaningful way.

Applying this principle, one might want to do an ethnographic study in which an investigation is designed to research the characteristics of educators who have received national distinguished teaching awards. Given that the researcher determines it impossible to procure a random sample of that group (even if its members could be identified with resources available), a decision is made to pick ten such recipients, believing that they possess the characteristics and knowledge that make for successful teachers. In practice, however, not all researchers would agree about what makes for a "good teacher" and, as Kalton (1983) states, would cause a sample to be "subject to a risk of bias of unknown magnitude" (p. 91). The only way that a researcher can be certain that she will identify individuals who will represent the characteristics of a population is to first identify the characteristics possessed by the members of that population. If an effort were made to identify the actual population of award-winning teachers, the researcher would then be able to use simple, stratified, cluster, or systematic random sampling. Certainly, one of these, alone or in combination, would be the procedure of choice. Again, however, the researcher may find that she does not have the time or the resources to carry out such a process; thus, purposive sampling becomes her preferred choice for this study.

Quota Sample

This technique is one in which individuals or groups are chosen to be in direct proportion to their frequency in the population. Although similar to convenience sampling in many respects, the **quota sample** method differs from convenience sampling because selections are made in a way that provides for the characteristics of the resulting sample to be a miniature approximation of what would be found in the population. For example, if the researcher knows that seventy percent of the certified public school teachers in Massachusetts are employed in urban areas, then seventy percent of the sample should be comprised of teachers who are employed within urban schools. In quota sampling, the representative group is not created by random selection; instead, it is created by convenience. The general procedures for quota sampling include the following.

Step 1. Identify the characteristics of the population that are germane to the study; for example, gender, years of experience, and highest degree earned.

Step 2. Using information from such sources as the state department of education, determine the size of each relevant segment of the population.

Step 3. Calculate the proportion of each of these segments. For example, if thirty percent of the population of women teaching in urban settings have ten or more years of teaching experience and a master's degree, thirty percent of the women selected for whatever size sample is chosen to represent urban K–12 schools would need to have those same characteristics.

Step 4. Identify those who have the characteristics found in step 3 in order to fill the quotas.

The quality of quota sampling rests with those who are selected to fill the various slots. Since each subject does not have equal and independent opportunity to be selected, sincere efforts must be made to ensure that all pertinent characteristics are in place in direct proportion to their presence in the population. Otherwise, the findings generated from the study can be very misleading. In spite of the shortcomings, quota sampling has its place because of the opportunity it provides for completing studies that otherwise might not be possible. While convenience does tend to dictate who will be selected to participate in quota-directed studies, experience with the process can help one avoid some of the problems common to nonprobability sampling.

SUMMARY

Sampling is a process of selecting a specific number of individuals from a population, preferably in such a way that those individuals will represent the larger group from which they were chosen. The greater the sample differs from the population, however, the greater the potential for invalid generalizations. With finite populations, it is possible to procure *random* samples. Depending upon the nature of the study, characteristics of the population, and time and resources available, decisions are made about the appropriate random sampling procedure to employ: simple, stratified, cluster, stratified cluster, or systematic.

When individual members of a population cannot be singled out for random selection, the researcher has to rely on nonprobability techniques, including: convenience, purposive, and quota. Although there are weaknesses implicit to nonrandomized sampling techniques, they do provide opportunities for researchers to do studies that otherwise would not be possible. Whether random or nonrandom sampling procedures are used, care must be taken to ensure that the group comprising the sample is thoughtfully acquired.

RECOMMENDED LABORATORY ASSIGNMENTS

1. Review the recommended readings.

2. Meet with fellow graduate students and colleagues in order to discuss the advantages and disadvantages of probability and nonprobability sampling.

3. For an existing (or fictitious) finite population, list what you believe to be characteristics pertinent to the study topic for which you have already created a template. Once the members of that population have been *identified,* select:

   a. a simple random sample (using a table of random numbers).

   b. a stratified random sample (which will guarantee proportional representation of all pertinent characteristics of the population).

   c. a cluster random sample.

   d. a stratified cluster random sample.

   e. a systematic random sample.

4. Upon examining the composition of each of the five sample groups, make a determination about which you believe would be the most appropriate for your proposed study. Defend your position with fellow students and colleagues.

5. Determine whether any Hawthorne, John Henry, or placebo effects will have a bearing upon your study. If so, outline your plans to address the problems.

6. Review the relationship each of the sampling procedures presented in this chapter has to controlling the threats to internal and external validity (presented in Chapter 3).

7. For the template prepared in response to recommendations of Chapter 3, examine your entries as they relate to *selection of subjects.* As deemed necessary, refine your sampling procedures.

8. Arrange to meet with fellow graduate students, colleagues, as well as school and nonschool employees who have carried out applied research, in order to review and discuss your plans.

RECOMMENDED READINGS

Badia, P., & Runyon, R. P. (1982). *Fundamentals of behavioral research.* Highstown, NJ: McGraw-Hill.

Bourke, P. D. (1984). Estimation of proportions using symmetric randomized response designs. *Psychological Bulletin, 96,* 166–172.

Cochran, W. C. (1985). *Sampling techniques* (2nd ed.). New York: Wiley.

Edwards, A. L. (1974). *Statistical methods* (4th ed.). Fort Worth, TX: Rinehart & Winston.

Henry, G. T. (1990). *Practical sampling.* Newbury Park, CA: Sage.

Jaeger, R. M. (1984). *Sampling in education and the social sciences.* New York: Longman.

Kish, L. (1965). *Survey sampling.* New York: Wiley.

Lowry, D. T. (1979). Population validity of communication research: Sampling the samples. *Journalism Quarterly, 56,* 62–68, 76.

Permut, J. E., Michel, A. J., & Joseph, M. (1976). The researcher's sample: A review of the choice of respondents in marketing research. *Journal of Marketing Research, 13,* 278–283.

Rosenthal, R., & Rosnow, R. L. (1975). *The volunteer subject.* New York: Wiley.

Strauss, A., & Corbin, J. (1990). *Basics of qualitative research: Grounded theory procedures and techniques.* Newbury Park, CA: Sage.

Stuart, A. (1984). *The ideas of sampling* (3rd ed.). New York: Macmillan.

Sudman, S. (1976). *Applied sampling.* New York: Academic Press.

Welch, W. W., Walberg, H. J., & Ahlgren, A. (1969). The selection of a national random sample of teachers for experimental curriculum evaluation. *School Science and Mathematics, 69,* 210–216.

Yin, R. K. (1989). *Case study research: Design and methods.* Newbury Park, CA: Sage.

REFERENCES

Ary, D., Jacobs, L. C., & Razavieh, A. (1990). *Introduction to research in education* (4th ed.). Philadelphia: Holt, Rinehart & Winston.

Bartz, A. (1976). *Basic statistical concepts in education and the behavioral sciences.* Minneapolis, MN: Burgess.

Best, J., & Kahn, J. (1993). *Research in education* (7th ed.). Needham Heights, MA: Allyn & Bacon.

Charles, C. M. (1995). *Introduction to educational research* (2nd ed.). White Plains, NY: Longman.

Cohen, J. (1988). *Statistical power analysis for the behavioral sciences* (2nd ed.). Hillsdale, NJ: Lawrence Erlbaum.

Gay, L. R. (1996). *Educational research: Competencies for analysis and application* (5th ed.). Englewood Cliffs, NJ: Prentice-Hall.

Kalton, G. (1983). *Introduction to survey sampling.* Newbury Park, CA: Sage.

Krejcie, R. V., & Morgan, D. W. (1970). Determining sample size for research activities. *Educational and Psychological Measurement, 30,* 607–610.

Leedy, P. D. (1997). *Practical research: Planning and design* (6th ed.). Columbus, OH: Merrill.

Patton, M. Q. (1990). *Qualitative evaluation and research methods* (2nd ed.). Newbury Park, CA: Sage.

Reaves, C. C. (1992). *Quantitative research for the behavioral sciences.* New York: Wiley.

Roethlisberger, F. S., & Dickson, W. J. (1939). *Management and the worker.* Cambridge, MA: Harvard University Press.

Roscoe, J. T. (1975). *Fundamental research statistics for the behavioral sciences* (2nd ed.). New York: Holt, Rinehart & Winston.

Saretsky, G. (1972). The OEO P.C. experiment and the John Henry effect. *Phi Delta Kappan, 53,* 579–581.

Schumacher, S., & McMillan, J. H. (1993). *Research in education: A conceptual introduction* (3rd ed.). New York: HarperCollins.

Streitmatter, J. (1994). *Toward gender equity in the classroom: Everyday teachers' beliefs and practices.* Albany, NY: State University of New York Press.

Vockell, E. L., & Asher, J. W. (1995). *Educational research* (2nd ed.). Columbus, OH: Merrill.

CHAPTER 5

Selecting Instruments of Assessment

OBJECTIVES

After reading this chapter, you should be able to:

- Distinguish between concurrent-, construct-, content-, and predictive-related validity.
- Describe how stability and equivalence can be determined when estimating the reliability of a test.
- Identify and discuss four procedures by which the evidence of internal consistency for a test can be established.
- Discuss why the Spearman-Brown prophecy formula should be used with split-half estimates of reliability.
- Demonstrate the use of Cronbach alpha procedure and the Kuder-Richardson 20 and 21 formulas for establishing estimates of the internal consistency of a test.
- Describe the roles of standard error of measurement and error bands when establishing the accuracy of a test score.
- Identify primary sources of standardized tests and be able to use these sources effectively when judging the quality of assessment instruments.

- Write a behavioral objective that includes a statement of condition, performance, and criterion for success.
- Describe procedures for creating and validating practitioner-made testing instruments.
- Determine item difficulty, discrimination, and, when using multiple-choice questions, whether alternatives are functioning.
- Distinguish between the four scales of measurement, and give examples of data that would be indicative of each.
- Define key terms, and answer the checkpoint questions.

KEY TERMS

Behavioral Objectives	Jury
Coefficient Alpha	Kuder-Richardson 20
Concurrent-Related Evidence	Kuder-Richardson 21
Construct-Related Evidence	Measurement Error
Content-Related Evidence	Mental Measurements Yearbook (MMY)
Correlation Coefficient	
Cronbach's Alpha	Nominal Scale
Cronbach's Coefficient Alpha	Ordinal Scale
Data	Pilot Study
Dissertation Abstracts International (DAI)	Predictive-Related Evidence
	Product-Moment r
Educational Testing Service (ETS)	Prophecy Formula
Education Index (EI)	Psychological Abstracts (PsycLit)
Empirical Research	Rank-Order Correlation
Equivalence-Related Reliability	Ratio Scale
Error Band	Split-Half Reliability
Internal Behavior	Stability-Related Reliability
Internal Consistency	Table of Specifications
Interval Scale	Test Critiques
Item Analysis	Tests
Item Difficulty	Tests in Print (TIP)
Item Discrimination	Triangulation

INTRODUCTION

The **data** that are gathered during the course of one's research are only as good as the instruments used to generate them. To conduct research without valid instrumentation can be likened to an exercise in futility. Therefore, it is critical that thoughtful attention be given to this very important phase of one's research design; otherwise, the findings arising from the process are likely to be meaningless.

In relating the principles of assessment to the practices of research, this chapter will address both the *selection* of standardized, and the *creation* of practitioner-made, measuring devices. On the one hand, standardized tests that are very appropriate for use in one's research may be found in the literature. In fact, there may be hundreds of published tests that, on the surface, may appear to be acceptable. Close scrutiny of these instruments, however, may reveal that many of them are inappropriate given the expressed purpose of the study and the characteristics of your population or sample. With the hundreds of aptitude, attitude, intelligence, interest, and knowledge tests being advertised in assorted bulletins, catalogs, and journals, it is not easy to make wise choices.

It seems to bait the obvious to say that intelligent decisions in regard to choice of instrumentation can only be made when the researcher maintains his focus upon *who* and *what* needs to be measured. Although a given standardized test may be valid for a very important educational function, it may not be valid for who and what needs to be measured in your study. In fact, upon thoroughly reviewing the literature, it may be determined that instruments valid for your study have not been created. For example, if you are interested in assessing the attitudes of K–6 teachers in regard to the feasibility of integrating art, literature, and music within the school curriculum, it is unlikely that a standardized attitude scale on that subject has been published. In this circumstance, it would become necessary for you to develop your own.

In addition to identifying prime sources within which standardized measuring devices are indexed and profiled, and discussing criteria for the selection of these devices, this chapter presents procedures for writing, validating, and field-testing assessment instruments of your own. Both standardized and practitioner-made tests hold a rightful place in research activities. The important thing is ensuring, to the extent possible, that the instrument is *valid* to the study. To that end, this chapter has been written.

CHARACTERISTICS OF VALID INSTRUMENTS

Instrumentation

In Chapter 3, you learned that the internal validity of a study is influenced by a number of factors, one of which is *instrumentation*. If measuring devices used to collect data lack the ability to consistently measure what they purport to measure, it is unlikely that the findings will be very useful to the researcher or the consumer. In short, the results will lack *validity*.

Research is **empirical**—that is, it is based on what can be perceived by the senses and rejects that which cannot be verified. Once the researcher has decided upon what is to be measured, the task is to employ a test that will zero in on the information needed, rather than on extraneous variables of little consequence to the study design. What, then, characterizes tests that will lead to verifiable findings?

According to the American Educational Research Association (AERA), American Psychological Association (APA), and National Council on Measurement in Education (NCME) (1985), there are four categories of evidence that demonstrate the validity of test results: (1) **concurrent-related evidence,** (2) **construct-related evidence,** (3) **content-related evidence,** and (4) **predictive-related evidence.** As Gall, Borg, and Gall (1996) point out, validity is a unitary concept. Therefore, these categories should not be thought of as types of validity, but rather as the ways by which one can gather evidence. For concurrent-, construct-, content-, and predictive-related validity, the appropriateness of the measuring device must be established in *advance* of its use in the actual research. As noted in Chapter 3, the selection of one's measuring instrument is a major component of a research design template.

Concurrent Validity. Concurrent validity refers to the degree to which performance on one test relates to performance on a previously validated test. If a group of individuals takes both instruments at approximately the same time, concurrent validity is present if the members of the group perform equally well (or poorly) on both instruments. If the data generated by the two instruments are *interval*[*] in nature, the numerical coefficient (r) representing the relationship would be generated through the use of a technique known as Pearson product-moment correlation (described in Chapter 7, Correlation Procedures).

The higher the numerical value, the greater the relationship.[**] For example, a researcher may have found a standardized test that appears to be valid for his study. However, it is reported in the test manual that two and one-half hours are required to administer the test. Given the fact that the researcher has received permission to use an intact class for study, and the class is scheduled to meet for fifty minutes, it would require that he attempt to make arrangements for students to miss their next two classes in the day in order to meet time requirements. It should be expected that this request would not receive hearty endorsements from the teachers of the next two

---

[*]A thorough discussion of the nature of nominal, ordinal, interval, and ratio data is presented at the end of this chapter.

[**]**Correlation coefficients** range from 0.0 to ±1.0. Since detailed descriptions of the meanings of coefficients (and how they are calculated) are presented in Chapter 7, Correlation Procedures, it is sufficient to say at this point that, in general, a *low* correlation is considered to be 0.0 to 0.29; a *medium* correlation is 0.30 to 0.69; and a *high* correlation is 0.70 to 1.00. In this regard, when judging the coefficients (within the high range) for validity, reliability, and objectivity, one would hope to find a 0.70, 0.80, and 0.90, respectively. Although validity is the most important characteristic of any test, a high coefficient is more difficult to come by. The consistency of a measurement and the extent to which scorers agree on the merit of responses are considered to be easier to find, and thus, one can expect to find higher standards for reaching estimates of satisfaction.

classes. Further, a serious question arises about whether it is even appropriate to ask that students be excused from other studies.

If the researcher created a test that could be administered in a fifty-minute period, he might find during a preresearch pilot study of the two tests (conducted after school hours) that a correlation of the two reveals a high statistical relationship. If this were the case, the practitioner-made test could then be used during the actual research. After all, if the recently created researcher's test correlated highly with a previously validated test, that would mean that there is concurrent-related evidence that the new test is also valid.

Construct Validity. Construct validity refers to the degree to which an instrument of assessment measures a trait that is not *directly* observable. Examples of constructs include: anxiety, creativity, giftedness, honesty, integrity, leadership, and social intelligence. While external behavior is relatively easy to observe, **internal behavior** (a construct) cannot be seen directly. One can only observe its effect. Therefore, when deciding upon a test of a given construct, it must be determined at onset that the test purports to measure behavior generally deemed to be identifiable with the internal behavior one wants to examine.

To gather evidence of construct validity, it is first necessary to begin with descriptions of how those possessing varying degrees of the construct of concern are likely to behave. For example, suppose that a test publisher advertises that a given instrument of assessment will measure giftedness among tenth-grade students. How does the consumer know whether that test will actually measure this construct? Practitioners who work with gifted students claim that those who are creative have the ability to: (a) give a *variety* of answers to a given question (fluency), and (b) give appropriate, yet *unique,* responses (originality) (Callaghan, 1978, Kirk, Gallagher, & Anastasiow, 1997; Torrance, 1981). If it has been determined that the instrument of observation will enable its user to record the performances of students in regard to these matters, the findings should differentiate between students who demonstrate giftedness and those who do not, in which case it can be said that the measuring device has construct validity.

Since more than one piece of evidence is important to establishing construct validity, the findings of independent studies, including those on the instrument that provide evidence of concurrent validity (as well as content and predictive validity to be presented in the sections that follow), will help to strengthen the argument that the instrument measures what is purported.[†] Construct-related validity does not yield a correlation coefficient. Instead, its determination arises out of informed judgments—judgments that are based upon the ability of the instrument to differentiate the construct being studied from other constructs.

Content Validity. Often equated with *face* validity, content validity refers to the extent to which experts believe that the instrument of assessment addresses the

---

[†]When one employs more than one data-gathering procedure in order to judge the validity of an outcome, the process is known as **triangulation.**

research objectives or, in the instance of the school curriculum, whether students have mastered a representative sample of course or unit objectives. The question is: Does the test appear valid? As Vockell and Asher (1995) point out, "Content [related] validity is assured by logically analyzing the domain of subject matter or behavior that would be appropriate for inclusion on a data collection process and examining the items to make sure that a representative sample of the possible domain is included" (p. 109). In the case of the classroom achievement test, the person making this judgment is the teacher. After all, who would be in a better position to judge the appropriateness of the questions to the course objectives than the teacher of the course? In this case, the teacher is the expert—in effect, a jury of one. In the practice of research, however, it would be important to have more than one individual look at the questions against the objectives. This helps to reduce the effect of researcher bias. If each member of the jury, working independently, believes that the items address the objectives, it can be said that the instrument has content-related validity. As is the case with construct validity, one does not calculate a correlation coefficient; rather, the findings are based upon the combined judgments of independent experts that the questions appear to address a representative sample of the research objectives.

A step-by-step process for establishing the content-related validity of practitioner-made tests is described later in the chapter.

Predictive Validity. Predictive validity is the degree to which estimated performance becomes a reality. The expression *predictive validity* implies that there is a difference in time between the gathering of measurement data on a predictor, and the criterion against which those original data are to be validated. One's research interests may be to develop an instrument of assessment that will enable the user to make intelligent predictions about subsequent performance. A common illustration of an instrument used to predict subsequent performance is the scholastic aptitude test (SAT). The extent of such a relationship can be determined by administering one form of the test to high school seniors who are going on to college. On the basis of individual performances, a correlation coefficient is calculated between the original SAT scores and the college cumulative grade point averages (CGPA). The question is: Did those students who scored above the average of their group in the SAT also score relatively high in their CGPA? Conversely, did those students who scored below the average of their group in the SAT also score relatively low in their CGPA? The findings will allow one to determine the extent to which that form of the SAT accurately predicted the college performance of those students who took the test.

Another example of an attempt to establish predictive-related validity would be for a researcher to create an analytically scored writing test that would be given to students as they are about to exit junior high school. The purpose of the test would be to determine the ability of that instrument (variable A) to predict student ranking upon graduation from high school (variable B). The cumulative scores generated through the process of analytical scoring will be correlated against high school ranks. Since the data in variable B are ranked (ordinal), the statistical process for establishing the extent of this relationship would be Spearman rank order (*rho*) correlation. This procedure will be described in Chapter 7, Correlation Procedures.

Reliability

A major component of the validity of any measuring device is *reliability*. In other words, if reliability is found to be lacking during the process of assessment, validity is compromised. While a reliable test may have little to do with the purpose of a test, in order for a test to measure what it purports to, it must be able to do so consistently (see Chapter 3, Preparation of a Research Plan). There are three categories of evidence that point to the existence of reliability for a test: (1) stability, (2) equivalence, and (3) internal consistency.

Stability. **Stability-related reliability** refers to the degree to which scores generated by a test administered on one occasion can be replicated when that same test is administered at a later date. In advance of using any particular test in one's research, it is important to know how consistently that test would measure whatever it is designed to measure. One would not want the data that are generated to be a product of time or the testing atmosphere. When alternate (equivalent) forms of a measuring device are not available, test-retest (stability) procedures will provide an opportunity to examine evidence as to the reliability of the instrument. The basic steps for examining the stability of a test are as follows.

Step 1. Administer the test to a selected group of individuals.

Step 2. Following some time interval (for example, one to two weeks), administer the identical test to the same group of individuals.

NOTE: It is important that the interval between the testing sessions not be too short or too long. To some extent, it is a judgment call based upon *your* experience and that of *others*. If the interval is too short or too long (for example, when examining the stability of an achievement test), subjects may respond based upon their memory of previous answers or, on the other hand, may have sufficient time to learn more about what is being tested. Be mindful of the fact that the stability of achievement test data can only be determined if the conditions of the subjects and the testing atmosphere are close to identical on the two testing occasions. Otherwise, the data that are generated cannot be expected to be consistent, regardless of the quality of the measuring device.

Step 3. Compute a correlation of the two sets of scores (see Chapter 7, Correlation Procedures).

Step 4. Interpret the results.

Equivalence. **Equivalence-related reliability** refers to the extent to which *two* forms of a measuring device are able to demonstrate evidence that they generate similar, if not identical, results. If two groups of subjects are participating in a study, the researcher may not want to run the risk of administering the same test to both of them (because of the possibility of questions or answers being revealed by members of one of the groups after they have taken the test). As a consequence, it may be desirable for the investigator to have *alternate* forms of the instrument. Both forms of the device would be prepared in advance of the actual study and subjected to the following procedures.

Step 1. Administer one form of the test to a selected group of individuals.

Step 2. Shortly thereafter (if not at the same session), administer the alternate form of the test to the same group of individuals.

Step 3. Compute a correlation of the two sets of scores (see Chapter 7, Correlation Procedures).

Step 4. Interpret the results.

Internal Consistency. This refers to the extent to which the questions comprising a single version of a test appear to be measuring for the same thing. Since it is not always possible to construct equivalent versions of a measuring device, nor always convenient for the researcher (or a group of individuals) to arrange for more than one testing session, the components of a single test can be used to estimate **internal consistency.** Using individual items or parts of the test, mathematical formulae are applied that generate a coefficient. The most common techniques used to estimate reliability through internal consistency measurements are: (1) **split-half,** (2) **Cronbach's alpha,** (3) **Kuder-Richardson 20,** and (4) **Kuder-Richardson 21.**

1. Split-half estimates of reliability can be determined by the following steps:

1. Administer the test to a selected group of individuals.

2. Divide the test into two halves. This can be accomplished by either (a) scoring the odd-numbered items separately from the even-number items, or (b) scoring the first half of the test separately from the second half of the test. The latter procedure is not recommended when:

   • items throughout the test get progressively more difficult (power test), or
   • when there is a change in the form of the question asked throughout the test. For example, students may have a more difficult time with multiple-choice than with essay questions. Therefore, if the multiple-choice questions are at the beginning of the test, one would expect scores generated from those questions to be lower.

   An additional factor to consider is that if the test is inordinately long, fatigue may set in for the subjects as time progresses. As you can see, odd-even scoring will avoid these particular problems.

3. Compute two scores for each subject, one for each half of the test.

4. Compute a correlation for the two sets of scores (see Chapter 7, Correlation Procedures).

5. To the results of step 4, apply the Spearman-Brown **prophecy formula.** Since longer tests tend to be more reliable than shorter ones, this correction will adjust the findings for procedures that require the correlation of two halves of a test.

NOTE: The reason that longer tests tend to be more reliable is that the increased number of questions will test a larger sample of the material. The more that is asked, the greater the chance that some answers will be known; the greater the opportunity, therefore, to discriminate between the more and less informed. To take the point to an extreme, if there was only *one* question in an examination, it would be likely for a subject to get a perfect score when the only information known by that individual was the answer to that single question. On the other hand, an individual who spent a great deal of time studying the subject may have learned all but what was asked in that one item. Can you see how the validity of the instrument would be influenced by a lack of reliability?

The Spearman-Brown formula for estimating the reliability of a test when one half is correlated with the other half is as follows:

$$r \text{ (total test)} = \frac{2r \text{ (split half)}}{1 + r \text{ (split half)}}$$

Assuming that the correlation coefficient representing the relationship of the two halves of a forty-question test is .60 (which, in effect, constitutes the correlation between two twenty-question tests), the estimated reliability of the entire (forty-question) test would be .75. This can be observed by the following illustration:

$$r \text{ (total test)} = \frac{2(.60)}{1 + .60} = \frac{1.20}{1.60} = .75$$

The findings indicate that the split-half estimate of .60 has been corrected to .75. You will learn in Chapter 7 that one would hope for a minimum of .80 when estimating reliability. As a result, the value of .75 does not satisfy the minimum recommended standard. Further, it has been observed by Gay (1996) that the correction formula "tends to give a higher estimate of reliability than would be obtained using other procedures" (p. 149). Thus, the actual reliability of the measuring device being contemplated for use by the researcher is likely to be lower than what the .75 even indicates.

2. *Cronbach's alpha,* also referred to as **coefficient alpha** and **Cronbach's coefficient alpha** (Cronbach, 1951), enables one to estimate internal consistency when the scoring of items on a test is *not* limited to 1 point (for correct) or 0 points (for incorrect) responses. (When items are scored 1 or 0, Cronbach alpha and KR20, which is presented later in this section, would yield identical values.) If the sophistication of one's answer to any of the questions within the test provides for the respondent to earn variable points (for example, 1, 2, 3, 4, or 5), the Cronbach alpha procedure would be appropriate. Unlike the split-half procedure, this technique: is *not* dependent upon having each half of a test scored separately; does *not* require the calculation of a correlation coefficient; does *not* require the use of the Spearman-Brown prophecy formula; and generates a coefficient that is conservative. The formula for arriving at an estimate of a test's reliability through the process of Cronbach's alpha is as follows:

$$Alpha = \frac{n}{n-1} \left(\frac{SD^2 - \Sigma SD_i^2}{SD^2} \right)$$

where n = number of items (questions) on the test. N = the number of respondents (Σf).

SD^2 = variance of scores on the test [square of the SD (standard deviation)]. (See Chapter 7 for pertinent definitions and alternative methods for computing the standard deviation.)

SD_i^2 = sum of the variances on each item, that is:

$$\Sigma SD_i^2 = \frac{\Sigma fX^2 - \dfrac{(\Sigma fX)^2}{N}}{N}$$

The following is an example of one item on a survey dealing with sexism:

I believe that the practice of sexism exists within my school district:	Number of Points (X)
(A) Strongly agree	5
(B) Agree	4
(C) Undecided	3
(D) Disagree	2
(E) Strongly disagree	1

In Table 5–1, you will find sample data for computing *item* variance. Included are the responses of 165 teachers responding to the previous item. Using the data in Table 5–1, the following steps would apply to computing item variance:

1. Square the ΣfX, and divide by N (or Σf).

2. Subtract the answer (found in step 1) from ΣfX^2.

3. Divide the answer (found in step 2) by N (or Σf).

4. The finding of item variance is .789.

The same procedure used to obtain this value would be followed for each of the other items on the test (and, for consistency, truncation would be maintained at three places). The variances for each of the items would then be summed and entered into Cronbach's alpha formula:

$$SD_i^2 = \frac{2065 - \dfrac{(565)^2}{165}}{165} = \frac{2065 - \dfrac{319225}{165}}{165}$$

$$= \frac{2065 - 1934.696}{165} = \frac{130.304}{165} = .789$$

3. Kuder-Richardson 20 provides an estimate of the reliability of a test based upon the number of questions, item difficulty, and variance of the scores (standard deviation squared). Although Kuder and Richardson (1937) developed a number of formulas for estimating the reliability of a test, formula 20 (named after the numbering

Table 5–1: **Sample Data for Item on Sexism**

X	f	X²	fX²	fX
5	20	25	500	100
4	50	16	800	200
3	80	9	720	240
2	10	4	40	20
1	5	1	5	5
	--------	--------	--------	--------
	$\Sigma f = 165$		$\Sigma fX^2 = 2065$	$\Sigma fX = 565$

in their original article) is given preference by most practitioners. As is the case with calculations that are made through other procedures, reliability coefficients range between 0.0 and 1.0. The formula for arriving at an estimate of reliability through the process of KR20 is as follows:

$$KR20 = \frac{n}{n-1} \left(\frac{SD^2 - \Sigma PQ}{SD^2} \right)$$

where n = number of items (questions) on the test.
SD^2 = variance of scores on the test [square of the SD (standard deviation)]. (See Chapter 7 for pertinent definitions and alternative methods for computing the standard deviation.)
P = proportion of those who responded correctly.
Q = proportion of those who responded incorrectly $(1 - P)$.

In Table 5–2, you will find sample data for a five-item test administered to ten subjects. (The small number of items and subjects is for illustrating the procedure only.) Assuming the *variance* of the scores to be 2.25, the following steps would apply to computing KR20 (using the information from Table 5–2):

1. Divide n by $n - 1$ (the number of items on the test).

2. Subtract the ΣPQ from the variance.

3. Divide the answer obtained in step 2 by the variance.

4. Multiply the answer obtained in step 3 by the answer obtained in step 1.

5. Interpret the results.

$$KR20 = \frac{5}{4} \left(\frac{2.25 - .870}{2.25} \right) = 1.25 \left(\frac{1.380}{2.25} \right) = 1.25 \,(.613) = .766$$

4. Kuder-Richardson 21 provides another estimate of internal consistency. Unlike KR20, however, one does not need to compute the *difficulty* of each item. In this procedure, the information needed is: the number of items on the test, the arithmetic average (mean), and the variance of the scores (standard deviation squared). The values

Table 5–2: **Sample Data for Computing KR20**

Item	Number of Students Responding Correctly	Proportion Responding Correctly (P)	Proportion Responding Incorrectly (Q)	PQ
1	8	.80	.20	.1600
2	2	.20	.80	.1600
3	7	.70	.30	.2100
4	5	.50	.50	.2500
5	9	.90	.10	.0900

			ΣPQ =	.8700

of KR20 and KR21 would be identical only if the items throughout the test were of equal difficulty (equal *P* values). When the difficulty level varies, KR21 underestimates the internal consistency coefficient. The formula for KR21 is as follows:

$$KR21 = \frac{n}{n-1}\left(1 - \frac{M - \frac{(M)^2}{n}}{SD^2}\right)$$

where n = number of items on the test.

M = mean (arithmetic average) of the scores on the test.

SD^2 = variance of scores on the test [square of the SD (standard deviation)].

Given a *mean* of 40 and a *variance* of 25 on a fifty-item test, the following is an illustration of the application of the KR21 formula:

$$KR21 = \frac{50}{49}\left(1 - \frac{40 - \frac{(40)^2}{50}}{25}\right)$$

$$= 1.020\left(1 - \frac{40 - \frac{1600}{50}}{25}\right) = 1.020\left(1 - \frac{40 - 32}{25}\right)$$

$$= 1.020\left(1 - \frac{8}{25}\right) = 1.020\left(1 - .32\right) = 1.020\,(.68) = .693$$

Although discussion of reliability to this point has focused on an entire test, it is also possible to estimate the reliability of scores on the test. The expression used to indicate this estimate is *standard error of measurement*. The essence of the procedure is to generate an **error band** for the scores. For example, if a given subject earned a score of 60, is it likely that if he took the test again, the score would also be 60. A small error band would indicate a high reliability level for any score on the test. If the test was perfectly reliable—that is, a +1.00—there would be no error band. In the example, the estimated score would be the same—that is, a 60. On the other hand, if the test had poor reliability, the **measurement error** would be large. To determine the standard error of measurement (*SE*), all one needs to do is apply the following formula using the standard deviation (*SD*) and the internal consistency estimate of reliability (*r*) for the test.

$$SE = SD\sqrt{1 - r}$$

If the *standard deviation* for the test was 4 and the KR20 value was .75, the *SE* = 2.0.

$$SE = 4\sqrt{1 - .75} = 4\sqrt{.25} = 4\,(.50) = 2.0$$

The error band is formed by adding 2.0 to, and subtracting 2.0 from, each score. In other words, if a subject earned a test score of 60, the error band for that score would be 58–62. This means that if that subject took the test again, one would estimate that his score would fall between 58 and 62.

 NOTE: Upon examination of the formula, it can be seen that if the test had perfect reliability (+1.0), there would be *no* measurement error and, thus, *no* error band. On the other hand, if there was no estimate of reliability for the test, the estimate of the range for a subject's score on a subsequent administration of that test would be as high as the first score, plus and minus the standard deviation. [You will learn in Chapter 7 that the *standard deviation* of a test is a product of group heterogeneity. The greater the variability (or variance) in performance of the members of a group, the larger will be the standard deviation.] If, in the illustration, the test lacked reliability (0.0), the standard error of measurement would be 4.0. The error band for a score of 60 would be 56–64. That means that the best estimate of that subject's score on a subsequent administration of the test would be anywhere between 56 and 64. It can be seen that if the test lacks reliability, the measurement error is as large as the standard deviation.

Another major component of the quality of a measuring device is *objectivity* (also referred to as *inter-rater reliability*). As indicated in Chapter 3, the objectivity of a test is a product of the degree to which two or more observers arrive at a similar score for a subject. The greater the opportunity for scorers to disagree on the merits of a response, the lower the objectivity of the test is likely to be. In computer-scored standardized tests, the objectivity is perfect (+1.0) because there is no chance, short of input errors or computer breakdown, for objective scoring to be compromised. When there are open-ended items (for example, essay questions), however, two or more scorers may have different views on the point value that should be assigned to the answer. A method to estimate the objectivity of a testing instrument is to have two individuals score the tests, and arrange the data so that they can be correlated (see Table 5–3).

Using Pearson product-moment correlation procedures (to be described in Chapter 7), a coefficient (range of 0.0 – ±1.0) would be generated. The higher the coefficient,

Table 5–3: **Test Scores Assigned by Two Evaluators**

Subjects	Scorer A Variable X	Scorer B Variable Y
J. Smith	82	84
K. Walen	81	81
P. Hartman	90	88
D. Tobine	92	91
M. Campbell	88	89
L. Olcott	87	85
T. Randall	91	92
D. Smarsik	84	85
R. DeCotis	89	90
H. Hyde	80	82

the greater the estimate of test objectivity. Higher objectivity contributes to validity because if a test is truly measuring what it purports to measure, it should not matter who among the trained scorers is assigned the task of examining the responses. Once estimates of validity, reliability, and objectivity for a measuring instrument are known, the researcher is in a position to make intelligent decisions about the appropriateness of that instrument for use in his research.

✓CHECKPOINT

The following questions are designed to sample your familiarity with validity, reliability, and objectivity. While responding to these items, refrain from looking back at the reading. At the end of the list of questions, answers are provided. At that time, you should reread the material if your responses do not agree with the answers given.

1. When knowledgeable individuals express the view that a measuring device appears to relate directly to the research objectives, it can be said that the device demonstrates _____-related evidence for validity.

2. What form of evidence for validity exists when the results of one test correlate highly with the results of a previously validated test when both instruments are administered to the same subjects at approximately the same time?

3. When a researcher desires to assess traits that cannot be observed directly, what form of evidence for test validity needs to be sought?

4. What evidence for reliability is the researcher seeking when he administers the same test on two occasions to an identical group of subjects?

5. When a researcher administers the KR20 formula to a set of test data, he is attempting to establish _____-related evidence for reliability.

6. Which internal consistency technique for estimating reliability is being utilized when the researcher employs the Spearman-Brown prophecy formula?

7. The difference between KR20 and KR21 for estimating the internal consistency of a measuring instrument is that, in the latter formula, the _____ of each item does *not* have to be calculated.

8. If a test has a standard deviation of 6 and a KR20 value of +.75, the standard error of measurement would be _____.

9. If the measurement error (*ME*) for a test was 5, what would be the error band for a score of 70?

10. When a researcher and his colleague each evaluate the responses given by subjects to questions on a test, what specific quality of the device is being estimated?

Answers

The correct answers to the questions are:

1. Content
2. Concurrent
3. Construct
4. Stability
5. Internal consistency
6. Split half
7. Difficulty
8. $3 \ [6 \sqrt{1 - .75} = 6 \sqrt{.25} = 6 \ (.5) = 3]$
9. 65–75 (70 plus and minus 5)
10. Objectivity

The use of valid, reliable, and objective tests is critical to the success of any research endeavor. As indicated at the onset of this chapter, the data that emerge from one's research are only as good as the instruments used to generate them. The section that follows provides information on making informed selections from the tests that have already been prepared by others. Through a thoughtful examination of the information that is provided about a particular test, you may discover that it is especially appropriate for use in your research.

STANDARDIZED INSTRUMENTS OF ASSESSMENT

One of the first things that a researcher should do upon establishing a problem statement is to examine the literature in order to determine whether a standardized instrument exists that would be valid for the purpose of the study. The value of a standardized testing instrument is that procedures for administering and scoring the device have already been developed in order to ensure consistency in all testing situations.

There are a number of sources to which one can refer in order to determine the existence of such an instrument. Included among the most useful of sources are the following:

***Tests in Print* (TIP)** and ***Mental Measurements Yearbooks* (MMY),**[‡] published by the Buros Institute of Mental Measurement, located at the University of Nebraska—Lincoln. While the TIP volumes do not contain reviews or evaluative material on tests, they do provide descriptive and bibliographic information. Further, they can be used as an index to the MMY. Begin by consulting the Index of Titles in TIP for the name of the test. Look under the entry number indicated for the test description, and record all references to the MMY series that you can find. In particular, look for the phrase *for a review* or the term *References*. Sample references from TIP would look like this:

- 7:243   You will find the reference to the test in the *Seventh Mental Measurements Yearbook* under entry 243.
- T2:987   You will find the reference to the test in *Tests in Print II* under entry 987.
- PA 74:1478 You will find information about an article concerning the test in *Psychological Abstracts,* volume 74, citation 1478.

Look at each of the *Mental Measurement Yearbooks* to which a reference is made and examine the evaluative reviews found there. Also, consider examining journal articles to which the reader is referred.

Keyser-Sweetland Test Series, published by PRO-ED in Austin, Texas. This series includes *Tests: A Comprehensive Reference for Assessments in Psychology, Education, and Business* (hereafter referred to as **Tests**) and **Test Critiques,** which provide a classified listing of literally thousands of tests in the areas of business, education, and psychology. Each test entry includes a statement of the purpose of the test, a description of the test, relevant cost and availability information, and the primary owner/publisher of the test. The purpose statement provides a physical description of the forms, format, manner of administration, and other special features of the test. While volumes of *Tests* do not contain any test evaluations, this information can be found in *Test Critiques*. The steps to take in order to retrieve the test information referenced within these sources are the following:

- Look in the Test Title Index of the *Tests* volumes for pertinent bibliographic information.
- Locate volume 8 of the *Test Critiques* series. (This volume contains a cumulative index to the entire set.) Locate the name of your test in the Index of Test Titles (located in the back of the volume). The reference number will refer you to the appropriate volume and page number of this set (for example, VI:225) that contains an essay on the test.

[‡] Although the term *yearbook* implies an annual publication, such is not the case. For example, the eleventh MMY was published in 1992, and the twelfth in 1995.

- At the end of the essay, note any list of references to journal articles and sections of books that contain information on the test.

It is important to keep in mind that the evaluatory reviews provided in the *Mental Measurements Yearbooks* and *Test Critiques* have been written by independent test authorities. By design, these individuals are not to have had any prior personal or professional relationship with the authors or the publishers of the tests.

While these sources are considered primary when researchers want to sort through the various published tests available (Fitzpatrick, 1996; Gay, 1996; Sax, 1989; Thorndike, 1997), there are also various periodical indexing and abstracting sources that may reveal tests suitable for use. These include the following:

***Dissertation Abstracts International* (DAI),** published by University Microfilms in Ann Arbor, Michigan. This source provides abstracts of theses that have been completed—theses in which the author may have had to validate his own measuring instrument. Given the specifics of a doctoral candidate's study, a test that would be appropriate to the student's problem area may not have existed at the time of his search; consequently, the student may have needed to develop his own. It may be that, with permission, the instrument he created could be used or modified for use in your study.

***Education Index* (EI).** This source provides citations to journal articles. First, search under the heading "Tests and Scales," then look for the individual test name.

Educational Resources Information Center (ERIC). This source provides a machine-readable data file searchable on CD-ROM. Included are citations and abstracts to journal articles and documents in the CIJE and RIE indexes in one database. (For specific access procedures, see the "Review of Related Literature" section under the heading "Investigating One's Field of Interest" in Chapter 1.)

Educational Testing Service (ETS) collection. This source provides information on tests published by ETS. Information is available in print from Educational Testing Service in Princeton, New Jersey, and is on microfiche located within college and university libraries. Probably the most useful of these collections is *Tests in Microfiche*. Beginning in 1975, ETS began distributing an index of unpublished tests; copies of these tests have been placed on microfiche. According to Thorndike (1997), by the end of 1995, the collection included more than one thousand instruments, and that number has been increasing at a rate of approximately twenty-five tests per year. In order to supplement its *Tests in Microfiche* service, ETS has recently incorporated the services of the internet in order to identify the measuring instruments in its test collection.

***Psychological Abstracts* (PsycLit).** This source provides a machine-readable data file searchable on CD-ROM. By using the name of the individual test in the "DE" field, one can find citations and abstracts to psychological journal articles. (For specific access procedures, see the "Review of Related Literature" section under the heading "Investigating One's Field of Interest" in Chapter 1.)

It can be expected that published, standardized tests have been administered to a sample group of *typical* subjects and evaluated by their designers in regard to: (a) clarity of directions, and (b) the validity of the test items with regard to the attributes they are designed to measure. In some instances, these instruments are suitable for qualitative as well as quantitative research. There may also be more than one form of the test, which is useful to know when one is considering pre- and posttesting or the use of multiple-group designs). The publisher usually provides: (a) a manual that describes the procedures that were followed to establish validity, (b) the reliability coefficients for all the forms of the test that exist, and (c) the procedures that were followed for norming the test scores. The manual is also expected to contain general and specific directions for test administration, as well as norms against which one's scores can be compared.

With unpublished standardized tests, however, it is rare to find a manual or, if one exists, to find that it attends to all of the elements attended to in published works. At the same time, this may not matter to a researcher if the items in the test appear to address the objectives of the study. The researcher may want to critically examine this assumption by: (a) utilizing a group of experts **(jury)** to gather content-related evidence for the test by having them judge its merits against the research objectives, or (b) correlating the test against another for which validity has already been established in order to gather concurrent-related evidence that it measures what is purported.

Since there are many published and unpublished measuring instruments to be found in test sources of the type described in the preceding text, the researcher should exercise caution when considering the options available. There are many factors that should be taken into account when attempting to make test selection judgments. Wiseman (1994, p. 474) suggests an example of a form that can be used to compare alternatives available (see Table 5–4).

Finding a suitable standardized test that can be used, whether it is published or not, may be less costly and is almost always less time-consuming for the researcher than going through the process of creating his own. Depending upon the complexity of the behavior one chooses to examine, it is likely to be more difficult to develop a measuring device from scratch than to use (or modify) one that already exists. At the same time, however, the specifics of one's research may require a test that is more precise. For example, since publishers are interested in marketing their tests in as many institutions as possible, the test may cover too broad a spectrum of content. In addition, when items begin to get answered successfully by an increasing number of subjects, these items are often deleted from the test. The reason publishers take this action is so the norm average (for example, 500 in the ETS scale) can remain fairly consistent from year to year. If the norm average gets too high, assuming that the maximum score for a test remains constant, it will become increasingly difficult to discriminate between individuals at the upper end of the scale. Unfortunately, the excluded questions may have been particularly valid for the specific purposes of one's research. In short, if an instrument containing the items a researcher needs is not available, it will be necessary for the researcher to create one.

PRACTITIONER-MADE INSTRUMENTS OF ASSESSMENT

Measuring instruments that have been prepared by the researcher makes it possible to have items that are tailored specifically to the purpose of the investigation.

Table 5–4: **Standardized Test Evaluation Form**

Title of Test: _____

Purpose of Test: _____

Author(s): _____

Publisher (and Address): _____
_____

Date of Publication: _____ Date of Last Revision: _____

Target Group(s): _____ Number of Forms: _____ Norms: <u>Yes</u> or <u>No</u>

Type(s) of Validity: _____ Evidence of Validity, . . . according to:

   Mental Measurements Yearbook: _____
_____
_____

   Test Critiques: _____
_____
_____

   Other (Reference: _____): _____
_____

Type(s) of Reliability: _____ Evidence of Reliability, . . . according to:

   Mental Measurements Yearbook: _____
_____
_____

   Test Critiques: _____
_____
_____

   Other (Reference: _____): _____
_____

Standard Error of Measurement: _____ Ease/Cost of Administering Test: _____
_____
_____

Durability of Materials: _____
_____

Would You Recommend the Use of This Instrument (Why or Why Not)? _____
_____
_____
_____
_____

Although creating a measurement instrument is a time-consuming process, the product one acquires can be well worth the effort. To carry out this mission requires that one follow a carefully prescribed sequence of events. Identification and discussion of these procedures are presented as follows.

Clarifying Objectives

The objectives of the research must be clarified and expressed in measurable terms. Instead of using such broad terms as *understand* and *appreciate* in your objectives, consider using such action verbs as *classify, create, define, demonstrate, describe, diagram, discuss, distinguish, identify, list, match, prioritize, rate,* and *write*. These terms can more easily be matched to the wording of a test item. For example, question 1 might read:

> Identify four ways by which one can establish evidence for the validity of a test.

It is also valuable to the assessment process if the objectives are written in *behavioral* terms, that is, if they include reference to a: (a) *statement of condition,* (b) *statement of behavior/performance,* and (c) *criterion for success.* For example, a **behavioral objective** might be:

> As a result of successfully completing the course "Research Design," it is with 100% accuracy that each student will be able to identify four ways to establish evidence for the validity of a testing instrument.

The *statement of condition* is: As a result of successfully completing the course "Research Design." The *statement of behavior/performance* is: each student will be able to identify four ways to establish evidence for the validity of a testing instrument. The *criterion for success* is: 100% accuracy.

It can be seen that the question concerning test validity relates directly to the objective. When test questions are written against the objectives of the research, it is much easier to judge their appropriateness to the instrument.

For the study on inclusionary education introduced in Chapter 1, an example of a behavioral objective would be:

> As a result of completing the survey on inclusionary education, each respondent will have had the opportunity to identify the composition of the evaluation and placement team, and the roles each member can play in the development and administration of individualized programs within the school district.

The *statement of condition* is: As a result of completing the survey on inclusionary education. The *statement of behavior/performance* is: identify the composition of the evaluation and placement team, and the roles each member can play in the development and administration of individualized programs within the school district. The *criterion for success* is: each respondent will have had the opportunity.

A corresponding question would be:

> Place a letter in column 1 that corresponds to the identity of the person whom you believe has <u>current</u> responsibility for chairing the Evaluation and Placement Team during the course of a hearing within the district. Place a letter in column 2 that corresponds to the identity of the person whom you believe <u>should have</u> responsibility for chairing that team meeting when a hearing is taking place.

Columns

1   2

_   _   A. Child's parent/guardian

         B. School principal

         C. Special education coordinator

         D. Teacher making the referral

In the first example (re: course in "Research Design"), it can be observed that one question could be written to address the entire objective. This category of objective is called *restrictive*. In the second example (re: study on inclusionary education), more than one question could be written to address the objective. This category of objective is called *inclusive*. Both forms of objectives have their place in research. It is just a matter of how specific the researcher believes he needs to be, given the nature of the study.

Preparing a Table of Specifications

Preparation of a **table of specifications** helps to ensure that all pertinent objectives are addressed in the instrument, and given weight according to their relative importance. The table of specifications is a road map for constructing the instrument of assessment. It helps to ensure that the test writer does not place more or less emphasis on areas than had been intended. It also helps the jury to judge whether the research objectives are being addressed. (See Table 5–5 for an example of an abbreviated table of specifications for a study on inclusionary education.)

In Table 5–5, the *row* across the top lists the objective by number. The *column* on the left represents the categories of questions that are being considered for inclusion in the instrument. The values in the body of the table represent the number of questions that correspond to the specific objectives. By examining the totals, it can be seen that (a) there are twice the number of alternative-response (multiple-choice) questions than either of the other two types of questions, (b) there are a total of twenty questions in the instrument, and (c) objective 4 is receiving greater emphasis in the instrument than are the other objectives. If these are the emphases that the researcher desires, then he should feel free to proceed.

Table 5–5: **Abbreviated Table of Specifications for Study on Inclusionary Education**

Questions	1	2	3	4	Total
			Objectives		
Alternative response	5	2	1	2	10
Enumeration	0	0	0	5	5
Discussion	0	3	2	0	5
Total:	5	5	3	7	20

Constructing the Questions

The questions should be constructed in a way that corresponds to the entries on the table of specifications. As the researcher is proceeding, he may discover a better way to address a specific objective than using the type of question on which he had originally planned. There is nothing wrong with altering one's original plans, providing the new question will do a better job. (Remember, a road map for writing questions is nothing more than a guide—a blueprint for action.) Further, keep in mind that there are items, other than the ones offered as examples in Table 5–5, that might be useful to a particular study. These include: checklists, completion (fill-in-the-blanks), Likert-type rating scales, matching, and true-false, to name a few.

Assuming the objective (re: evaluation and placement teams) for the study on inclusionary education was the first of five, the related alternative-response question (offered as an illustration) would be the first of the questions that would be prepared in that category.

Finally, give careful thought to the number of items that are going to be included in the measuring instrument. How much time will it take to answer twenty questions? An instrument that is too long is likely to discourage respondents who do not have a great deal of time in their schedules. If it is assumed that it takes an average of one and one-half to two minutes to respond to each of the twenty questions presented in the sample table of specifications, thirty to forty minutes would have to be set aside to respond to the survey.

In planning the amount of time that should be allocated to complete the survey, it is important to realize that some items will take longer to answer than others. A single discussion item, for example, will ordinarily take longer to complete than will an alternative-response-type question. How many pages will the instrument require? Informed estimates can be acquired through the use of a jury and pilot test.

Establishing a Jury of Experts for Review

A jury of "experts" should review the instrument against the objectives and table of specifications in order to establish an estimate of content validity. While the objectives and table of specifications are being written, somewhere between five and seven individuals should be contacted to serve as jury members for the test. These persons should be identified on the basis of their expertise in the field of study. For example, in the study on inclusionary education, one would want to include individuals who are able representatives of such groups as administrators, classroom teachers, parents, special education coordinators, those who have prepared tests, and those who have studied related problems. Upon reviewing the research problem and considering the requirements of validation, each of these people will be in a position to determine whether he has the time and the energy to participate.

Once a roster of jury members has been established, each member is sent a copy of directions and deadlines, along with a draft of: (a) the cover letter, (b) objectives, (c) the table of specifications, and (d) questions comprising the test. Each of the jury members works independently and forwards his findings back to the researcher. The returns are collated and reviewed, and items are revised per recommendations of the jury members. Editorial changes can be addressed "in-house." However, if it is deemed that substantive changes need to be made, the jury would be contacted again to examine the second draft. As a result of these efforts, the evidence of content validity will become increasingly apparent.

Obtaining Evidence of Reliability

The next step in the process is to obtain evidence that will attest to the reliability of the instrument. This requires that a pilot test be conducted. Normally, the size of a pilot group approximates ten percent of the size of the group for whom the test is being designed. The characteristics of the pilot group should be similar to those of the population, but the group should not be a sample (random or otherwise) that has been selected from the population. It should be an independent group that has agreed to participate in the **pilot study**. Included in the findings that can be generated from this process are the following.

Estimates of Reliability (using split half, Cronbach alpha, Kuder-Richardson 20, or Kuder-Richardson 21). If the instrument is administered more than once, it will be possible to compute an estimate of stability (test-retest). If alternate forms of the test have been prepared, one can estimate reliability through the process of analyzing equivalence (alternate forms).

Estimates of Objectivity (inter-rater reliability). This can be established by having a second individual independently examine responses on the test. As indicated earlier in the chapter, an estimate of the objectivity of the test can then be prepared by correlating both sets of scores.

Quality of Individual Questions. This can be assessed through a process known as **item analysis**. There are three ways to do this:

1. Looking at each of the choices within the alternative-response (multiple-choice) questions to see whether *alternatives are functioning*. In an achievement test, this is particularly important because if one or two choices in a four-item multiple-choice question can be eliminated because they make little sense to the respondents, what is really remaining is a two-choice question where there is a fifty-fifty chance of answering correctly. If the researcher desires to discriminate between those who know the answer from those who do not, all of the alternatives should be attractive to the uninformed. While not a pure science, one guideline is that if fewer than ten percent of the respondents choose any one of the alternatives, the researcher should consider rewriting that alternative.

   In a survey of aptitudes, attitudes, and interests, however, the goal of the instrument is different. The only reason to examine alternatives on an instrument designed to measure these particular qualities is to be sure that a sufficient number of choices are available to satisfy the preferences the respondent may want to express.

2. Looking at the difficulty (*diff*) of each item (see discussion under the Kuder-Richardson 20 procedure for estimating internal consistency of a test). You may remember that examining **item difficulty** can be accomplished by

dividing the number of subjects who answered the item correctly by the number of subjects who made the attempt. The range of possibilities is between 0.0 and 1.00.

Example 1: 10 subjects correctly answered question 1.
30 subjects made an attempt to answer question 1.
diff = 10/30 = .33.

Example 2: 15 subjects correctly answered question 1.
30 subjects made an attempt to answer question 1.
diff = 15/30 = .50.

Example 3: 30 subjects correctly answered question 1.
30 subjects made an attempt to answer question 1.
diff = 30/30 = 1.00.

While it may appear to be a contradiction in terms, it can be seen that the higher the difficulty coefficient, the easier the item. In a test in which the researcher hopes to discriminate between subjects, questions should be rewritten when data from a pilot study reveal an item that was too difficult (0.0–.20) or too easy (.80–1.0). On the other hand, if the researcher is attempting to use a question to assess mastery of a particular topic, he will not be interested in attempting to discriminate between those taking the test. Under these circumstances, a desirable item would generate a difficulty coefficient of 1.0.

3. Looking at whether the item is discriminating (*disc*) between those individuals who scored highest and lowest in the total test. If the item is valid to the test, the subjects with higher scores (for example, the upper one-third of those taking the test) should have answered it correctly. Conversely, those who have the lowest scores (for example, the lower one-third of those taking the test) should have answered it incorrectly. The middle group is not used in the analysis because its members did not distinguish themselves in any particular direction.

There are various ways by which one can estimate the discriminating power of an item; each of them provides the researcher with a process that is consistent to itself. With that in mind, the following procedure is suggested:

1. After total scores have been assigned to each test, divide the group into upper and lower thirds. For example, if thirty subjects attempted the test, the upper and lower thirds would each consist of ten people.

2. Look at question 1 and count the number of people in the upper one-third who answered it correctly. Then, for that same question, count the number of people in the lower one-third who answered it correctly.

3. Enter the answers from step 2 into the following equation:

$$disc = \frac{Upper\ one\text{-}third}{Upper\ one\text{-}third\ and\ lower\ one\text{-}third}$$

4. Repeat the process until coefficients are estimated for each item on the test.

NOTE: The range of possibilities is between 0.0 and 1.00. *Positive* **item discrimination** exists when the coefficient is *greater* than .50. *No* item discrimination exists when the coefficient *equals* .50. *Negative* discrimination exists when the coefficient is *below* .50. Therefore, the higher the value of the coefficient, the greater the estimate of the discriminating power of a given item. If the estimate of discrimination for an item is .50 or below, the researcher should consider rewriting the item.

Example 1:   All of the ten students in the upper one-third answer the item correctly. None of the students in the lower one-third answer the item correctly.

$$disc = \frac{10}{10 + 0} = \frac{10}{10} = 1.00$$

Example 2:   Five of the ten students in the upper one-third answer the item correctly. Five of the ten students in the lower one-third answer the item correctly.

$$disc = \frac{5}{5 + 5} = \frac{5}{10} = 0.50$$

Example 3:   None of the ten students in the upper one-third answer the item correctly.
One of the students in the lower one-third answers the item correctly.

$$disc = \frac{0}{0 + 1} = \frac{0}{1} = 0.00$$

Example 4:   None of the ten students in the upper one-third answer the item correctly.
Ten of the students in the lower one-third answer the item correctly.

$$disc = \frac{0}{0 + 10} = \frac{0}{10} = 0.00$$

While the application of these procedures may appear to be tedious, it is important that the researcher can feel confident in the measuring instrument he elects to use. If an analysis of data generated by the pilot study causes substantive changes to be made in the questions, the researcher may want the jury to re-examine the most recent draft.

In short, the more thorough the analyses, the greater the credibility that can be attached to the data collection process. Once the findings of the jury and the pilot study have been instituted, the final edition of the measuring device can be made ready for subsequent distribution (per guidelines of the Gantt chart and research template). An overview of the process for validating the instrument would be presented in the *procedures* section of the final research report (see Chapter 13, Preparing the Research Report).

PROPERTIES OF DATA

Depending upon the nature of the instrument selected for use, the data generated may vary in their properties. According to Hopkins and Glass (1978), these properties cause values to be: (1) distinct from one another (for example, name/identification code, gender, or degrees held); (2) relative to one another (for example, ranking of high school graduates, or top ten women tennis players in the world); (3) related to each other in identifiable units (for example, scores on a 100-item, 100-point achievement test); or (4) proportional to one another (for example, distance covered on a running long jump, or time required to assemble a fifteen-piece puzzle). Psychometricians refer to these properties as *measurement scales*. Since assessment in education ordinarily requires that researchers assign values to such things as aptitudes, attitudes, knowledge, and skills, it is important that they understand those things that differentiate one form of scale from another. Being able to attach meaning to these scales makes it possible to make informed choices about the appropriateness of selected analytical treatments. There are four measurement scales: (1) nominal, (2) ordinal, (3) interval, and (4) ratio.

Nominal Scales

A **nominal scale** provides for the classification of data. Considered the most primitive form of measurement, it does not allow for quality ratings to be attached to those things that have been categorized. Instead, persons or objects with common characteristics are placed together into groups of equal value. One group is no better or worse than another. At the same time, these groups (or categories) can be true or artificial. A *true category* is one in which the groups are formed naturally (for example, gender, married or unmarried, public or private school). If a person in the study were enrolled in a public school, he would go in one category; if not, he would go in the other. An *artificial category,* on the other hand, is formed by the researcher according to his own specifications (for example, tall or short, heavy or light, bright or dull, fast or slow). If the operational definition of *tall* is 5'10" or greater, anyone who is at or above that height would be placed in the *tall* category. Everyone else would be in the *short* category. It is also possible to have more than two categories, for example: *tall,* 5'10" or greater; *medium,* 5'6" to 5'9"; *short,* 5'5" and below. Researchers label these categories by name, letter, or number, but this is for the sake of convenience only.

Since categories are not quality-driven, statistical analysis is limited. Although computing the mean ($\Sigma X/N$) is considered to be a very basic procedure, one cannot calculate this value with *nominal* data. Computing the arithmetic average of being married or unmarried, for example, is not a possibility. One can, however, compute such things as the mode (the most frequently observed category), percent of attainment (number of married individuals/total number of individuals, times 100), and the chi square test (a comparison of expected to observed proportions). More will be said about these and other statistical alternatives for use with nominal data in Part II.

Ordinal Scales

An **ordinal scale** provides for ranking the values in any given category from high to low. Although *how much* greater one value is from another cannot be determined, one can order the values in a way that identifies them as being greater than, equal to, or less than other values. When ranking high school graduates, for example, the valedictorian would be ranked #1, the salutatorian would be ranked #2, and others throughout the class would be ranked from #3 to total *N*. The interval between each of these ranks, however, is not necessarily equal. For example, the difference between ranks #1 and #2 may be very different than the difference between ranks #15 and #16. Since intervals between ranks have the potential to be of various sizes, one is again limited to selected statistical analyses. One can compute the median (50th percentile), any other percentile, and **rank-order correlation** (with a second distribution of scores for the same individuals). *Ordinal* data possess all the characteristics of nominal data and more; therefore, one can compute the mode, percentage of attainment, and the chi square test as well. More will be said about these and other statistical procedures that are appropriate to use with ordinal data in Part II.

Interval Scales

An **interval scale** contains all the characteristics of nominal and ordinal scales but, in addition, includes equal appearing intervals. The interval between each number is constant. At the same time, however, there is no *absolute* zero or *absolute* 100 (or 200, and so on). In interval scales, minimum and maximum scores are arbitrarily determined. Because an individual gets a score of 100 on a test does not mean that the instrument measured all that he knows about the subject. Likewise, if a person gets a zero on a test, it does not mean that he does not know anything about the subject. This is one of the main reasons why it is important to exercise care when deciding upon a measuring instrument for use in one's research. Each question should be a valid, reliable, and objective measure of the quality being assessed.

Given that there are equal intervals between each of the values in interval scales, it is possible to employ more sophisticated analytical procedures, including the mean, standard deviation, and product-moment correlation (referenced earlier in the chapter), and the *t* test and analysis of variance (ANOVA) (to be introduced in Part III). The statistical procedures appropriate for nominal and ordinal scales are appropriate for use with interval scales as well. The reverse is not true, however. A statistic that is introduced for use with interval data cannot be used with ordinal or nominal data because it requires the existence of equal intervals. More information on analytical procedures appropriate for use with interval data will be provided in Parts II and III.

Ratio Scales

A **ratio scale** represents the most refined level of measurement. In addition to possessing the characteristics of the aforementioned scales, because there is a true zero point, values can be expressed as ratios. For example, when timing children's disposition to remain still during "quiet time," one might find that: (a) John is able to remain quiet and Mike is not (nominal scale), (b) John was quieter than Mike (ordinal scale), (c) John was quiet for ten minutes and Mike was quiet for two minutes (interval scale), or (d) John remained quiet five times longer than Mike did (ratio scale).

The statistics appropriate for use with nominal, ordinal, and interval scales can also be used with ratio scales (see Table 5–6). Since ratio scales require an absolute zero, few topics with such data properties are the subject of research in education (other than those requiring the assessment of time or distance).

SUMMARY

The selection of appropriate instruments of assessment is at the foundation of good research practice. Without valid, reliable, and objective measuring instruments, the researcher cannot hope to procure information that will satisfy the purposes of his study. This chapter has addressed factors critical to the informed selection and development of such devices, including: (1) processes for establishing evidence of test validity, reliability, and objectivity; (2) sources of standardized tests and criteria for judging their appropriateness; (3) specific techniques for creating and validating practitioner-made test items and instruments; and (4) the various data properties generated by these instruments.

Whether the instrument the researcher elects to use is standardized or self-made, of utmost importance is its ability to generate data that are valid to the operational definition of what is to be measured. If the investigator uses only data collection processes that relate directly to the research problem, he should feel comfort in knowing that the findings will do so as well.

 ## RECOMMENDED LABORATORY ASSIGNMENTS

1. Review the recommended readings.
2. Arrange to meet with fellow graduate students and colleagues in order to discuss the advantages and disadvantages of standardized testing instruments.

Table 5–6: **Sampling of Statistics for Use with Measurement Scales**

| | Measurement Scales | | | |
Statistic	Nominal	Ordinal	Interval	Ratio
Mode	‑‑‑‑‑‑	‑‑‑‑‑‑	‑‑‑‑‑‑	‑‑‑‑‑‑
Percent of attainment	‑‑‑‑‑‑	‑‑‑‑‑‑	‑‑‑‑‑‑	‑‑‑‑‑‑
Chi square test	‑‑‑‑‑‑	‑‑‑‑‑‑	‑‑‑‑‑‑	‑‑‑‑‑‑
Median		‑‑‑‑‑‑	‑‑‑‑‑‑	‑‑‑‑‑‑
Percentiles		‑‑‑‑‑‑	‑‑‑‑‑‑	‑‑‑‑‑‑
Rank-order correlation		‑‑‑‑‑‑	‑‑‑‑‑‑	‑‑‑‑‑‑
Mean			‑‑‑‑‑‑	‑‑‑‑‑‑
Standard deviation			‑‑‑‑‑‑	‑‑‑‑‑‑
Product-moment correlation			‑‑‑‑‑‑	‑‑‑‑‑‑
t test			‑‑‑‑‑‑	‑‑‑‑‑‑
Analysis of variance			‑‑‑‑‑‑	‑‑‑‑‑‑

3. Using the evaluatory criteria from Table 5–4, examine the references *Mental Measurements Yearbook* and *Test Critiques* to see what information they have on standardized tests from each of the following five categories:

   a. Achievement tests

   b. Aptitude tests

   c. Attitude tests/scales

   d. Intelligence tests

   e. Interest, personality, or adjustment tests

   Discuss the findings with fellow students and colleagues. For each of the five categories, identify what you believe to be the instrument of choice. Be able to defend the reasons for your selections.

4. Construct an instrument of assessment for a topic of your choice. During the process, include each of the following:

   a. List of research objectives

   b. Table of specifications

   c. Ten to twenty test items

   d. Jury review (for estimate of content validity), and item revision (as necessary)

   e. Pilot study

   f. Test analysis (for estimate of internal consistency), and item analysis (for estimates of item difficulty, discrimination, and, in the case of multiple-choice questions, whether alternatives are functioning)

   Review strategies and findings with fellow students and colleagues, including any problems encountered during the procurement of jury and pilot study groups. Discuss procedures for improving the jury and pilot group selection process.

5. Carefully examine the entries in your research template as they relate to *selection of instrument* (prepared in response to Recommended Laboratory Assignment 3(i) in Chapter 3). Given the information in this chapter, consider whether you have made the best possible choice for a measuring device that would be valid to your proposed study. As deemed appropriate, refine your responses.

6. Arrange to meet with fellow graduate students, colleagues, as well as school and nonschool employees who have carried out applied research, in order to review and discuss your plans to date.

7. Prepare a chart similar to that in Table 5–6 in readiness for including additional statistical procedures as they are introduced in Parts II and III. A completed chart will (a) reveal a summary of analytical procedures appropriate to the four measurement scales, and (b) offer assistance to those who have yet to make a decision on the statistical process to identify in their research plans.

RECOMMENDED READINGS

Berk, R. A. (Ed.). (1986). *Performance assessment: Methods and applications*. Baltimore: The Johns Hopkins University Press.

Bloom, B. S., et al. (1956). *Taxomony of educational objectives. Handbook I: Cognitive domain.* New York: Longman.

Borich, G. D., & Madden, S. K. (1977). *Evaluating classroom instruction: A sourcebook of instruments.* Reading, MA: Addison-Wesley.

Brainard, E. A. (1996). *A hands-on guide to school program evaluation.* Bloomington, IN: Phi Delta Kappa.

Brennan, R. L. (1984). Estimating the dependability of the scores. In R. A. Berk (Ed.). *A guide to criterion-referenced test construction* (pp. 292–334). Baltimore: The Johns Hopkins University Press.

Bruininks, R. H., Woodcock, R. W., Weatherman, R. F., & Hill, B. K. (1985). *Scales of independent behavior.* Chicago: Riverside.

Campbell, J. P., Dunnette, M. D., Arvey, R. D., & Hellervik, L. V. (1973). The development and evaluation of behaviorally based rating scales. *Journal of Applied Psychology, 57,* 15–22.

Center for the Study of Evaluation/Center for Research on Evaluation, Standards, and Student Testing (CRESST). (n.d.). *Alternative assessments in practice.* Los Angeles: CRESST.

Conoley, J. C., & Impara, J. (Eds.). (1995). *The twelfth mental measurements yearbook.* University of Nebraska–Lincoln, NE: Buros Institute of Mental Measurements.

Crocker, L., & Algina, J. (1986). *Introduction to classical and modern test theory.* New York: Holt, Rinehart & Winston.

Feldt, L. S., & Brennen, R. L. (1989). Reliability. In R. L. Linn (Ed.). *Educational measurement* (3rd ed.). New York: American Council on Education.

Feldt, L. S., Forsyth, R. A., Ansley, T. N., & Alnot, S. D. (1993). *Iowa tests of educational development, Forms K and L.* Chicago: Riverside.

Fetterman, D. M. (1989). *Qualitative approaches to evaluation in education: The silent scientific revolution.* Westport, CT: Praeger.

Goldman, B. A., & Mitchell, D. F. (1990). *Directory of unpublished experimental mental measures: Vol. 5.* Dubuque, IA: Brown.

Hammill, D. D., Brown, L., & Bryant, B. R. (1992). *A consumer's guide to tests in print* (2nd ed.). Austin, TX: PRO-ED.

Harcourt Brace. (1996). *Stanford achievement test series* (9th ed.). Orlando, FL: Author.

Hersen, M., & Bellack, A. S. (Eds.). (1988). *Dictionary of behavioral assessment techniques.* New York: Pergamon.

Hogan, T. P., & Mishler, C. (1980, Fall). Relationships between essay tests and objective tests of language skills for elementary school students. *Journal of Educational Psychology, 17*(3), 219–227.

House, E. R. (1980). *Evaluating with validity.* Beverly Hills, CA: Sage.

Keiser, R. E., & Prather, E. N. (1990). What is the TAT? A review of ten years of research. *Journal of Personality Assessment, 52,* 309–320.

Keyser, D. J., & Sweetland, R. C. (Eds.). (1984–1994). *Test critiques (Vols. I–X).* Austin, TX: PRO-ED.

Keyser, D. J., & Sweetland, R. C. (Eds.). (1990). *Tests: A comprehensive reference for assessments in psychology, education, and business* (3rd ed.). Austin, TX: PRO-ED.

Likert, R. (1932). A technique for the measurement of attitudes. *Archives of Psychology, 140.*

Lustberg, R. S., Molta, R., & Naccari, N. (1990). A model using the WISC-R to predict success in programs for gifted students. *Psychology in the Schools, 27,* 126–131.

Mehrens, W. A., & Lehmann, I. J. (1987). *Using standardized tests in education* (4th ed.). New York: Longman.

Messick, S. (1993). *Foundations of validity: Meaning and consequences in psychological assessment.* Princeton, NJ: Educational Testing Service.

Messick, S. (1995). Validity of psychological assessment: Validation of inferences from persons' responses and performances as scientific inquiry into score meaning. *American Psychologist, 50*(9), 741–749.

Moreland, K. L., Eyde, L. D., Robertson, G. J., Primoff, E. S., & Most, R. B. (1995). Assessment of test user qualifications: A research-based measurement procedure. *American Psychologist, 50*(1), 14–23.

Osgood, C. E., Suci, G. J., & Tannenbaum, P. H. (1957). *The measurement of meaning.* Urbana, IL: University of Illinois Press.

Parker, K. (1983). A meta-analysis of the reliability and validity of the Rorschach. *Journal of Personality Assessment, 47,* 227–231.

Robinson, J. P., Shaver, P. R., Wrightsman, L. S., et al. (Eds.). (1990). *Measures of personality and social psychological attitudes.* San Diego, CA: Harcourt Brace Jovanovich.

Salvia, J., & Ysseldyke, J. E. (1995). *Assessment* (6th ed.). Boston: Houghton Mifflin.

Schumacher, S., Esham, K., & Bauer, D. (1988). *Professional knowledge objectives for preservice teachers as selected by school and university educators: Implications for program development and evaluation.* Paper presented at the American Association of Colleges of Teacher Education Annual Meeting, New Orleans, LA.

Shepard, L. A. (1993). Evaluating test validity. In L. Darling-Hammond (Ed.), *Review of research in education. Vol. 19* (pp. 405–450). Washington, DC: American Educational Research Association.

Stock, W. A., Okun, M. A., Haring, M. J., Miller, W., Kenney, C., & Ceurvorst, R. W. (1982). Rigor in data synthesis: A case study of reliability in meta-analysis. *Educational Researcher, 11*(6), 10–14.

Thurstone, L. L., & Chave, E. J. (1929). *The measurement of attitude.* Chicago: The University of Chicago Press.

Worthen, B. R., Borg, W. R., & White, K. R. (1993). *Measurement and evaluation in the schools.* New York: Longman.

Zern, D. (1967). Effects of variations in question phrasing on true-false answers by grade-school children. *Psychological Reports, 20,* 527–533.

REFERENCES

American Educational Research Association, American Psychological Association, and National Council on Measurement in Education. (1985). *Standards for educational and psychological testing.* Washington, DC: American Psychological Association.

Callaghan, C. (1978). *Developing creativity in the gifted and talented.* Reston, VA: Council for Exceptional Children.

Cronbach, L. J. (1951). Coefficient alpha and the internal structure of tests. *Psychometrika, 16,* 297–334.

Fitzpatrick, R. E. (1996). *Tools for test selection and evaluation.* Unpublished document, Office of Bibliographic Instruction, Plymouth State College, Plymouth, NH.

Gall, M. D., Borg, W. R., & Gall, J. P. (1996). *Educational research* (6th ed.). White Plains, NY: Longman.

Gay, L. R. (1996). *Educational research: Competencies for analysis and application* (5th ed.). Englewood Cliffs, NJ: Prentice-Hall.

Hopkins, K. D., & Glass, G. V. (1978). *Basic statistics for the behavioral sciences.* Englewood Cliffs, NJ: Prentice-Hall.

Kirk, S. A., Gallagher, J. J., & Anastasiow, N. J. (1997). *Educating exceptional children* (8th ed.). Boston: Houghton Mifflin.

Kuder, G. F., & Richardson, M. W. (1937, September). The theory of the estimation of test reliability. *Psychometrika, 2,* 151–160.

Sax, G. (1989). *Principles of educational and psychological measurement and evaluation* (3rd ed.). Belmont, CA: Wadsworth.

Thorndike, R. M. (1997). *Measurement and evaluation in psychology and education* (6th ed.). Columbus, OH: Merrill.

Torrance, E. (1981). Cross cultural studies of creative development in seven selected societies. In J. Gowan, Khateno, & E. Torrance (Eds.), *Creativity: Its educational implications* (2nd ed.). Dubuque, IA: Kendall/Hunt.

Vockell, E. L., & Asher, J. W. (1995). *Educational research* (2nd ed.). Columbus, OH: Merrill.

Wiseman, D. C. (1994). *Physical education for exceptional students: Theory to practice.* Albany, NY: Delmar.

PART **II**

DESCRIPTIVE RESEARCH METHODS

CHAPTER **6**

Survey Procedures

OBJECTIVES

After reading this chapter, you should be able to:

- Define survey research.
- Identify and discuss the step-by-step procedures for creating an effective design for survey research.
- Distinguish between interviews, questionnaires, and observations.
- Describe time sampling, interval recording, and continuous recording as procedures for gathering observational data.
- Describe considerations essential to preparing fixed-choice and open-ended questions, including: standard-, corrective-, and interpretive true-false; multiple-choice; matching; master list; completion; enumeration; essay; rating scales; and checklists.
- Discuss the relevance of jury validation and pilot studies to survey research. As a frame of reference, be able to describe the processes described in this scenario: *The investigation of undergraduate professional preparation in those colleges and universities of New England offering programs leading to certification in learning disabilities.*

- Identify and describe various survey instruments that can be used to assess knowledge, attitudes, and perceptions.
- Identify and discuss potential threats to the *internal* and *external* validity of a survey.
- Distinguish between *qualitative* and *quantitative* processes for analyzing data and, with regard to the latter, be able to compute the mean, median, mode, percentage of attainment, percentiles, standard deviation, and chi square.
- Create a research design template for survey research on a topic of your choice.
- Define key terms, and answer the checkpoint questions.

KEY TERMS

Checklists

Chi Square Test

Completion-Type Questions

Continuous Recording

Corrective True-False

Cross-Sectional Studies

Enumeration Questions

Essay Questions

Exploratory Questions

Face-to-Face Interviews

Fixed-Choice Questions

Interpretive True-False

Interval Data

Interval Recording

Longitudinal Studies

Master List Questions

Matching Questions

Mean

Median

Mode

Multiple-Choice Questions

Nominal Data

Observations

Open-Ended Questions

Ordinal Data

Percentiles

Percent of Agreement

Percent of Attainment

Prime Sources

Qualitative Data Analysis

Quantitative Data Analysis

Questionnaires

Rating Scales

Standard Deviation

Standard True-False

Structured Questions

Survey Research

Threats to External Validity

Threats to Internal Validity

Time Sampling

Weighted Rating Scale

INTRODUCTION

In Part I, Nature and Purpose of Research, you were introduced to considerations essential to establishing a foundation for research activities. Pertinent information was provided for selecting and defining a problem, and ethical and legal issues in problem selection; how to prepare a research plan; sampling procedures; and selecting, preparing, and validating instruments of assessment. With the information from those chapters as background, it is time to move ahead with strategies for carrying out a study.

As indicated in Chapter 1, there are two general research methods under which all designs fall: *descriptive* and *experimental*. In Part II, discussion will focus on descriptive research. This chapter, in particular, will address one of these procedures known as the *survey*, which, as you learned in Part I, is the method of choice in situations in which one wants to elicit facts about the *current status* of persons, processes, products, or programs. Typically employing *applied* rather than *basic* research theories, information is gathered through the use of interviews, questionnaires, and observations, with a view toward relating the acquired information to solving problems of local concern. It is from this information that thoughtful decisions can be made— decisions that can influence the principles and practices of education.

The initial section of this chapter focuses upon the purpose of survey procedures. This section is followed by discussion of strategies for developing and administering a survey, a description of survey devices, and selected qualitative and quantitative analytical procedures. Given that the survey is among the most common of all research methods (Ary, Jacobs, & Razavieh, 1990; Gay, 1996), it is here where Part II begins.

PURPOSE OF SURVEY PROCEDURES

On the surface, **survey research** may appear to be quite mundane. After all, how difficult can it be to prepare a few questions for distribution to a group of volunteers? When the facts are known, however, it becomes readily apparent that carefully designed survey procedures require a great deal of planning and effort. This holds true whether the instrument contains a single question (such as "Should the United States join an organization of nations for the control of atomic power?") or multiple questions (such as those to be found in the Kuder General Interest Survey—Form E, 1991). Although it is obvious that more time is necessary to validate a multiple-question instrument than an instrument containing a single question, the point is that care must be taken to ensure that the questions, regardless of their number, are the best ones possible to address one's research interest, and that: (1) the people who are asked to respond to the questions are the **prime sources** of the information being sought, (2) the questions on the survey are being asked in a way that is nonthreatening, (3) data are analyzed and reported upon accurately, and (4) anonymity is preserved, when guaranteed as a condition of subject participation.

A survey is a carefully prescribed procedure to gather information from a group of individuals in order to determine their status (for example, attitudes, interests, demographics, and so on) with regard to one or more variables. It is important to realize, however, that the information gained represents a target group's situation at a particular point in time. Their status may change, depending upon the circumstances that intervene between one assessment occasion and another. While the facts of a particular date in history remain constant, events of the present are ever-changing. What is available through survey research procedures, therefore, is a snapshot of present circumstances. These "pictures" can be obtained through **cross-sectional studies,** in which specific issues are examined at a particular point in time, or through **longitudinal studies,** wherein these issues are examined at different times. For example, if a researcher wanted to determine the attitudes of teachers within a school district toward state-mandated assessment, she could conduct a cross-sectional survey by arranging to administer a questionnaire to the teachers in each of the schools within an administrative unit in October of the current academic year. If, on the other hand, the researcher was interested in determining whether attitudes toward state-mandated assessment remain constant or change in a three-year period, the researcher would conduct a longitudinal survey by gathering information in October of this year, and again in October, three years from now.

There are three basic methods that can be employed to gather information in survey research: (1) interview, (2) questionnaire, and (3) observation. Each method may be used separately or in combination. Their selection depends upon the nature of the information desired, the instruments available for use to acquire the information, and the resources available. If the study group is considered to be relatively small and the factors being considered in the study are many and complex, an *interview* would probably be the preferred method. On the other hand, if the study group is large and the factors to be examined are limited in scope, the **questionnaire** would likely be the technique of choice (Crowl, 1996).

One concern with questionnaires is not receiving responses within the time limits that have been imposed in the cover letter. For obvious reasons, it may be necessary to conduct a follow-up. Therefore, a few days after the time limit specified in the letter has expired, it is recommended that you contact the nonrespondents by sending a follow-up letter, along with another copy of the questionnaire and another self-addressed envelope (Heberlein & Baumgartner, 1981). Since it appears that the first letter did not do the job, it is useful to construct another. For example, if a professional appeal was used in the initial letter, it might be worthwhile to consider a personal appeal in the follow-up letter. While the use of postal cards (instead of letters) have been used as reminders, Worthen and Brezezinski (1973) found, in their study on techniques for increasing return rates, that they were less effective, even though they contained the same message.

Although an interview is nothing more than an oral questionnaire, one most often thinks of a questionnaire as one that is distributed through the mail. An interview employs a **face-to-face** or telephone conversation designed to elicit responses to prepared **open-ended** or **fixed-choice** questions.

NOTE: Open-ended questions are those for which a respondent *supplies* an answer (for example, completion or essay questions) rather than *selecting* one from among fixed choices (for example, Likert-scale, multiple-choice, or matching questions). Although open-ended questions are more difficult to score because of the range of response possibilities, they have their place in survey research, depending upon the nature of the information sought.

In addition to the fact that the interview provides an opportunity for the researcher to offer clarification to questions that appear ambiguous, another advantage of the interview over the written questionnaire method rests with its ability to provide data on a variety of topics. To this end, interviews can be:

1. **structured,** in which responses are sought for very specific questions.

2. **exploratory** (unstructured), in which questions arise out of responses given by those who are being interviewed. The investigator probes with a general question, records the response, and, on the basis of that answer, makes a decision about what to ask next. The disadvantage of the exploratory method is that, since a variety of follow-up questions may be asked of different individuals, it may be inappropriate to compare their responses.

3. a combination of the structured and exploratory methods, wherein the interview would include questions of both types.

Observation is a process by which desired information is obtained by observing, and possibly video recording (for subsequent analysis), the occurrence or nonoccurrence of defined behaviors. The method of choice for many investigators who desire to evaluate student behavior in the classroom, observation may employ **time sampling, interval recording,** or **continuous recording** techniques.

When utilizing time sampling, the researcher literally "samples" student conduct at specific points in time during the course of a class period. The researcher may deem it useful to predetermine the times to observe the child, and prepare a chart on which student behaviors can be recorded (see Figure 6–1). There is no specific number of occasions when the observer should record behavior; however, to the extent that the teaching of the class lesson is not compromised, the more observations the better. With expected classroom behaviors listed across the top of the recording form, and specific minutes that have been determined at random written on the left of the form, the observer places a check mark within the column that best represents the behavior of the child at the moment in question. At the end of the class period, the researcher examines whatever trends may be revealed. Time sampling is used most often when the teacher/researcher is alone in the classroom and she does not have the luxury of observing a given student over a block of time.

With interval recording, the researcher examines the students throughout a time interval, such as the first five minutes of class, the five minutes immediately following the assignment of in-class paperwork, the last five minutes of class, or any time interval in between. Of course, the most reliable observation system would be for the researcher to observe (or cause to be observed) the behavior of a student over an interval of the entire class period (continuous recording). As you would expect, however, this process would require the presence of a second (unobtrusive) observer or, perhaps (with permission), a video camera.

Instead of preparing a chart to observe one student, the teacher/researcher might want to arrange a chart for observing all students, in which case all possible minutes of a class period would be placed across the top of the chart, and a roster of the

Figure 6–1: **Chart for Recording Samples of Student Classroom Behavior**

| | | Student Behaviors | | | |
Minute(s)	On Task	Day Dreaming	Whispering	Vacates Seat	Disrupts Class
3	--------	--------	--------	--------	--------
7	-------	--------	--------	--------	--------
15	--------	--------	--------	--------	--------
17	--------	--------	--------	--------	--------
25	--------	-------	-------	--------	--------
40	-------	--------	-------	--------	--------
42	-------	--------	-------	--------	--------
51	--------	--------	-------	--------	--------

students in the class would be listed down the left side of the chart. Then the researcher could do one of two things: (1) select a specific behavior to observe on a particular day, and place a check next to the student under the column representing the time the behavior occurred; or (2) use a symbol to represent a behavior, such as: (O), on task; (D), day dreaming; (W) whispering; (V) vacates seat; and (RC), disrupts class. With the latter approach, the appropriate symbol would be recorded for the child under the appropriate minute as the behavior arose. (One alternative to using a symbol for on-task behavior is to leave a blank when on-task behavior is occurring; this reduces the amount of recording one has to do.)

Observations in the field (often referred to as ethnographic studies) provide valuable opportunities for qualitative-type analyses (Vockell & Asher, 1995). In place of or in addition to recording data on a form, one might elect to take field notes where words and numerical values, or both, are later analyzed through qualitative *and* quantitative techniques.

Keep in mind that the time of the day may have a bearing on the extent of disruptive behavior one may find, as will pre- and postvacation periods (Crowl, 1996). As with any study, it is important that these factors be taken into account before generalizations are made from the findings. If the assessment of a behavior is based on clearly defined definitions of what is to be observed (and when), the researcher can expect to find valid, reliable, and objective results.

Interviews, mailed questionnaires, and observations are used in virtually all professional fields, including the arts, economics, education, political science, and sociology. Once a problem has been identified, related literature reviewed, and the research hypotheses stated (see Chapters 1 and 2), the researcher must give thoughtful consideration to subject selection (Chapter 4), instrumentation (Chapter 5), and preparation of the design template (Chapter 3).

For any researcher utilizing interviews or mailed questionnaires as the method of survey, it is vital that the individuals being asked the questions be the prime sources of the information desired. Corrigan (1997) refers to this as *participatory* research. If one wants to know why selected students are frequently tardy, the ones who are tardy are the ones who should be asked. Perceptions may be offered by administrators, classroom teachers, parents, social scientists, and others, but the facts are probably best known by those who are tardy. The same principle would hold true if you wanted to know any of the following:

- The standards that officials within the Educational Testing Service (ETS) follow when deleting items from selected forms of scholastic aptitude tests
- The criteria that school board members apply when they make their decisions on what items to cut from the budget
- The key qualifications superintendents of schools look for in applicants for teaching positions
- The routes followed by bus drivers as they make their way through the early morning hours to pick up children for school
- The reason parents volunteer to assist schools in their teacher-aide programs

Again, there are many individuals, in addition to the prime sources, that a researcher could seek out in order to learn of their insights on these matters—and that might be important if the researcher wanted to know what their perceptions were, or wanted to study the relationship of their perceptions to reality. If a researcher wants to acquire the *facts,* however, the best sources of information are the persons who are experiencing them. Two classic examples of using invalid information sources would be the following:

- A television network conducting a survey of television viewers to ascertain whether they felt that the findings of the jury in the O. J. Simpson civil trial were correct. How could they possibly have an informed opinion? The civil trial was not televised. Unless they were present in the courtroom and attentive throughout the proceedings, these individuals could not be expected to be knowledgeable in regard to all the testimony in the case.
- Sending a questionnaire to superintendents of schools within selected school administrative units in order to have them indicate the percentage of time teachers spend preparing for their classes. While the superintendents would have a general idea, they would not be the prime sources of the information. For obvious reasons, the best sources of that data would be the teachers themselves. The information from superintendents would be useful only if the researcher were interested in assessing school policies or the perceptions of superintendents on the matter, or in relating those policies or perceptions to information procured from other sources (for example, school board members, principals, parents, students, or the teachers themselves).

NOTE: One concern of an investigator in the latter scenario might be that the teachers might overstate the time they spend preparing for classes, unless anonymity is assured. After all, it would be unlikely that respondents would be interested in identifying themselves as teachers who were spending minimum amounts of time in that activity. If, however, the sample of teachers responding to the survey were large enough (the larger the better), the mean, median, and mode amount of time spent would be the statistics of choice. By reporting *group* averages, confidentiality would be preserved, and the findings could be considered to be a fairly accurate benchmark of the information desired.

In brief, survey research is used to examine present status. Using the best tools possible with the most informed subjects possible will likely generate the information that is sought. The next section addresses specific strategies for developing and administering a survey, and includes descriptions of various types of questions, as well as sample questionnaires that can be used to gather survey data.

STRATEGIES FOR DEVELOPING AND ADMINISTERING A SURVEY

In keeping with the procedures described in Chapter 3, Preparation of a Research Plan, the steps for designing survey research can be clearly delineated. It is with these procedures in mind that the following strategies are presented. Imagine, for example, that:

1. a faculty member is interested in creating a research plan for a survey in one of the following areas of inquiry:
   a. her teaching competence as revealed by students;
   b. grading practices;
   c. student teaching competence as revealed by a cooperating teacher within a school;
   d. appropriateness of a film or video to classroom instruction before it is selected for use; or
   e. contributions of student peers to group project work;

2. an administrator is interested in creating a research plan for a survey in one of the following areas of inquiry:
   a. her administrative competence as revealed by the instructional staff,
   b. annual professional and service activities of her faculty;
   c. organizational climate within the elementary school;
   d. student perceptions of the health curriculum; or
   e. faculty perceptions of the foreign language curriculum;

3. a guidance counselor is interested in creating a research plan for a survey in one of the following areas of inquiry:
   a. substance abuse among students;
   b. faculty satisfaction with the general education program;
   c. applied economics rural expansion project within the state;
   d. business/school partnerships within the state; or
   e. handwashing practices after using bathroom facilities; and

4. a member/officer of a professional organization is interesting in creating a research plan for a survey in one of the following areas of inquiry:

 a. institutional compliance with accreditation standards;

 b. effectiveness of presentations at a regional conference;

 c. restructuring of a professional association;

 d. evaluation of the individual holding the position of executive secretary in the association; or

 e. evaluation of undergraduate professional preparation programs leading to certification in learning disabilities.

While it may seem apparent that the demands of some of these topics would be greater than those of others, the general strategies for carrying out the study would hold true for any of these topics. The only variation would rest with the breadth of attention one would find necessary to assign to each of the processes.

Per the recommendations of Chapter 3, Preparation of a Research Plan, the research design would be arranged in two phases. Phase 1 would begin with the preparation of a tentative time schedule (Figure 3–1) and budget (Figure 3–2) for conducting the investigation. Although preliminary determinations are always subject to change as tasks unfold, having basic guidelines in place at the onset of design development helps to provide focus. At the very least, it causes the investigator to think about matters of concern in advance of their becoming issues during the course of an investigation. By addressing time and budget issues early in the process, plans for how the survey is to be administered can be thoughtfully considered.

NOTE: The author is reminded of his experience when doing his doctoral dissertation (Wiseman, 1970). His plans included traveling to seventeen New England colleges and universities in order to evaluate their professional preparation programs in teacher education. During the year in which he was hoping to do this study, he was teaching full-time and coaching three intercollegiate athletic teams: soccer (fall), wrestling (winter), and tennis (spring). Realizing that if he was to conduct face-to-face interviews at each of the sites (which was his procedure of choice), it would be necessary for him to arrive on the respective campuses sometime during the week. Otherwise, it would be unlikely that the prime sources that he needed to see would be available on site. Fortunately, the dean allowed him to collapse his five-day teaching/coaching schedule into four days, which allowed him to travel to his destinations on Thursday evening, thus making it possible to schedule interviews beginning at 8:00 A.M. on Friday. On the weekends that he had intercollegiate contests, he remained with the teams.

It can be seen that if he had not sought and received permission early in the planning stages to be away from campus on Fridays (except on the weekends when he had games/meets scheduled), he would have had to prepare plans for what he deemed to be a less preferred method for carrying out the study, that is, distributing the survey questions through means other than face-to-face interviews (for example, telephone interviews or mailed questionnaires).

Pursuant to creating tentative time and budget lines, the remaining elements of Phase 1 of the survey research plan are ready to be clarified.

Statement of the Problem

As indicated in Chapter 1, Selection and Definition of a Problem, it is extremely important that the problem statement be written clearly so that any individual reading it would know exactly what the practitioner/researcher intends to do. Clear problem statements, such as the following, also help the researcher to stay focused:

> The purpose of this investigation is to evaluate the status of undergraduate professional preparation in those colleges and universities of New England offering programs leading to certification in learning disabilities.

NOTE: During the process of preparing the problem statement, it is important to revisit budget issues. For example, if one wanted to conduct on-site interviews and learned through an examination of reference documents (for example, *The College Blue Book*) that there were *thirty* different colleges and universities in New England that offered undergraduate professional preparation programs leading to certification in learning disabilities, one might have to modify one's original interests. Because of financial and time restraints, it might be necessary to conduct the survey through the mail or by way of telephone—or, instead of traveling to all pertinent colleges and universities, to limit travel to a random (or stratified random) sample of them.

Statement of the Need (Justification) for the Study

Why is it important that this topic be investigated? Can the findings of the survey be applied to the practitioner/researcher's own professional work assignment, or is the information considered necessary to advance the pool of knowledge about education in general? To the extent that the expression of need can be documented by the facts and figures of pertinent and timely sources, this will add to the credibility of one's justification for the study. (See Chapter 1 for examples of sources.)

Review of Related Literature

This is an extremely important ingredient of one's research plan. It is here that you are able to report upon those studies that have already been completed that relate to your own survey topic. Not only can you *summarize* the reported works of others, but you and the readers of your research plan can acquire information about such things as the following:

1. History and recency of related studies
2. Identity of those who have published in similar fields of inquiry
3. Approaches used to gather data (interviews, questionnaires, or observations)
4. Extent to which there are similar and opposing findings

5. Qualitative and quantitative processes used to treat information

6. Study group demographics

7. Identity of institutions and other places where related studies have been undertaken

Statement of the Hypothesis

The next logical step in the sequence of one's plan is to state the hypothesis. The hypothesis one states should arise logically out of the problem statement and one's knowledge of previous research. As a result of its confirmation or rejection, doors are opened to future research on the topic. Simply stated, a concise, well-written hypothesis will:

1. help the investigator to maintain direction throughout the research process;

2. make it easier for the readers of one's research to understand the essence of the study; and

3. bring focus to the findings and conclusions once the data have been analyzed.

✓CHECKPOINT

Would one employ a *statistical* (null) hypothesis or a *research* hypothesis with survey research?

Answer

Your answer should have been to use a *research* hypothesis, since the hypothesis is for survey research, which is a *descriptive* study. The statistical (null) hypothesis is used with experimental studies in which one introduces a treatment in order to assess its influence upon a dependent variable. In survey research, one is not introducing any treatment; instead, one is investigating things as they are. There is no attempt nor desire to manipulate a variable.

In the example of evaluating undergraduate programs leading to certification in learning disabilities (referenced earlier under "Statement of the Problem"), the research hypothesis would read:

> Assuming a valid data-gathering process, it is hypothesized that a survey to evaluate the status of undergraduate professional preparation in those colleges and universities of New England offering programs in learning disabilities during the Spring Semester, 1998, will reveal the extent to which state certification standards are being addressed.

Basic Assumptions

At this point in the research, all suppositions that can be anticipated are identified. This encourages the investigator to test the realities of carrying out the study as desired. All assumptions that have a bearing on the survey should be set forth openly and without reservation (Bogdan & Biklen, 1982; Leedy, 1997; Lunneborg, 1994). As indicated in Chapter 3, it is important that all basic assumptions be reviewed *before* the study actually begins, since failure to do so can cause major problems during the implementation stage. In survey research, the following illustrations are typical of the assumptions that should be satisfied.

Time. The researcher must have the ability to conduct the study in the time allotted. If she is employed full-time outside of the home, it may be necessary to get release time to conduct the study. For example, traveling to the sources of the information for on-site interviews may be necessary. If conducting telephone interviews, it is often best to do so during working hours so that interviewees can be contacted at their worksites where they have access to the information you may be seeking, rather than at home where the information they need to answer certain questions may not be available.

Resources. The researcher must have the resources to carry out the study according to the design. If traveling to the individual worksites for face-to-face interviews is the procedure of choice, not only will the investigator need the time, she will also need resources for such things as gas mileage, overnight accommodations, and meals. The investigator should calculate the distances to the various visitation sites and estimate housing and meal costs early in her planning. If it is determined that the costs will be prohibitive, alternative data-gathering procedures can be considered.

 NOTE: During the data-gathering phase of the author's doctoral dissertation, he traveled 8,058 miles to seventeen different colleges and universities throughout New England in order to conduct on-site interviews. On some occasions, it was necessary to travel to an institution two or three times. Fortunately, he was able to arrange some housing at less expensive, on-campus residence sites. While it was necessary to eat "out" some of the time, he consumed many sandwiches that he had brought along and, on some occasions, was invited into the school dining hall for breakfasts, lunches, and dinners.

One of the program directors invited the author into his home for overnight and meal accommodations. The author has corresponded with him many times on a variety of professional issues since that weekend. As you might suspect, traveling to the worksites of those you are interviewing makes it possible to meet many wonderful people. This is one of the many concomitant outcomes of conducting on-site survey research. Even though the expenses of the on-site interviews were greater than what they would have been had he used the telephone or mail, the author will never regret the choice that was made. Further, in surveys where evidence is required, one may find that being on site is the only feasible way to get supportive documentation for responses that are offered.

Permission. The researcher must obtain permission to carry out the study. In addition to getting permission to visit and interview the prime sources of information, it may also be necessary to obtain permission from one's own work supervisors, particularly when hours of the workday or days of the workweek need to be used to administer the study.

Enough cannot be said about identifying the prime sources of information for one's study. In the case of evaluating college and university undergraduate professional preparation programs leading to certification in learning disabilities, one might determine, through the examination of pertinent and special education standards, that the following areas should be subjected to analysis:

1. General institutional and departmental practices—general institutional policies; professional affiliations and accreditation; and admissions policies and practices

2. Staff standards—number; qualifications in their major field; experience; and teaching and service

3. Curriculum policies and practices—general education; foundation sciences; general professional education; and special professional theory

4. Library, technology, and media services—library (general features, library services, reference sources); technology (general features; instruction and materials; equipment, facilities, and access); and media services (general features; instruction and materials; equipment, facilities, and access)

5. Supplies and equipment—location and availability; supplies (kind and number); and equipment (kind and number)

6. Facilities—general features; administrative; instructional; and service

The logical question at this point would be: "Who are the prime sources of information for each of these six areas of concern?" One way to find that out would be to contact program directors within each of the institutions and ask for the job titles, names, and addresses of these individuals. Once that information is known, each source can be contacted in order to arrange an appointment for an interview. See Figure 6–2 for an identity of prime sources of information for the six areas identified here.

Validity, Reliability, and Objectivity. The researcher must employ a valid, reliable, and objective assessment instrument. In Chapter 5, Selecting Instruments of Assessment, procedures were described for validating practitioner-made measuring devices. Although it is possible, it is not likely that standardized instruments will be found that have been validated for very specific survey interests. Therefore, it is often necessary for the researcher to prepare her own questions.

Types of Questions for Survey Research

There are many types of questions that one might use for survey research. In some instances, the teacher/researcher is interested in surveying the present level of *knowledge* a group of students has about a specific content area and, as a consequence, will select types of questions that are geared to that end. The following sections provide examples of such items, considerations for their preparation, directions for students, and sample questions.

Figure 6-2:   **Sample Roster of Prime Sources for Survey Research**

Areas	Prime Sources
1. General institutional and department practices	President Academic Dean Dean of Student Affairs Director of Admissions Director of Academic Support Director of Financial Aid Department Chair Faculty Campuswide student leaders Students enrolled in classes
2. Staff standards	Academic Dean Chair, Affirmative Action Department Chair Campuswide student leaders Students enrolled in classes
3. Curriculum policies and practices	Academic Dean Chair, Curriculum Committee Department Chair Campuswide student leaders Students enrolled in classes
4. Library, technology, and media services	Director of the Library Director of Media Services Director of Computer Services Department Chair Campuswide student leaders Students enrolled in classes
5. Supplies and equipment	Academic Dean Director of Purchasing Department Chair Students enrolled in classes
6. Facilities	Academic Dean Facilities Director Department Chair Students enrolled in classes

Standard True-False. With **standard true-false** items, it is recommended that the researcher follow the guidelines presented here.

  1. Avoid specific determiners such as "always" and "never." The use of such adverbs can give clues to the correct answers. Further, very few things are *always* so or *never* so. As a consequence, when these terms are used in a question and the respondent does not *know* the answer, her best guess would be to mark the answer as *false* (and, unless thoughtful consideration is given to the use of these terms in the question, she will probably be right). Remember, it is unlikely that the evaluator will ever know whether a respondent got the correct answer by guessing—therefore making it impossible to determine whether the concept is known and understood.

2. *Be careful that questions requiring true and false responses are not arranged in patterns that are predictable.* For example, one instructor actually created tests in which the first question was always true, the second question was always false—no matter how many examinations he administered during the course of a marking period.

3. *Avoid writing questions that are quoted directly from a textbook.* This form of question requires little more than memorization of text material.

4. *Remember that more knowledgeable individuals tend to "read things" into standard true-false test questions.* Consequently, such individuals may score lower than those who are less informed about the subject.

5. *Keep in mind that, traditionally, longer sentences tend to be true; shorter sentences tend to be false.* A significant variance in question length should be avoided when writing the items; otherwise, test-wise respondents will begin to make their true or false choices on the basis of the length of the questions—particularly if some are inordinately longer or shorter than the others.

6. *Avoid "trick" words.* They tend to trip the individuals who actually know the material.

7. *Direct the respondents to use a plus (+) symbol for a true statement and a zero (0) symbol for a false statement* (if not employing computerized response sheets). This leads to less confusion than when one's choices are written as *t* and *f*. (Depending upon one's penmanship, it can be difficult to distinguish between the two.)

8. *Have a minimum of twenty questions.* Although there is a fifty-fifty chance of guessing an answer correctly on a standard true-false question (given the fact that there are but two alternatives from which to select a correct response), it is unlikely that the uninformed respondent will continue to guess correctly as the number of items increases.

9. *Allow approximately fifteen to twenty seconds per item.* The estimated time that it takes for one to respond to and review each question, regardless of its type, is important to take into account during test construction. Giving this matter due consideration helps the evaluator to judge the number of items that can be administered to an average respondent within the time available (or desired). One way to arrive at this estimate is to time the respondents during the pilot test.

> Directions: Read each statement carefully. If the statement is true, place a plus (+) sign into the space provided to the left of the numbered item. If the statement is false, place a zero (0) in the corresponding space.
>
> Example: ___ 1. The degree to which a testing instrument is consistent in measuring whatever it is designed to measure is known as objectivity.

Corrective True-False. With **corrective true-false** items, it is recommended that the researcher follow these guidelines.

1. Consider the principles appropriate to writing any true-false questions (particularly recommendations 1 through 7 in the preceding section).

2. Acknowledge that this type of true-false item is likely to reduce successful guessing (particularly if the question is false). In this type of item, if the respondent is unable to correct the underlined words, she will not get credit for the item.

3. Do not over-underline words within the statement. Underlining too many words allows the respondent to change the intent of the question. As a consequence, the researcher is not measuring what she wants to measure.

4. Be mindful of the fact that items that are false require that respondents offer a correction to the underlined words. As a consequence, more time will be needed to respond to these items. Assessing the time during a pilot test is the most reliable way to make such an estimate, but as a general rule, allow up to thirty seconds for questions that are false (require correction).

> Directions: Read each statement carefully. If the statement is true, place a plus (+) sign into the space provided to the left of the numbered item. If the statement is false, place a (0) in the corresponding space, and change the <u>underlined</u> word or words in order to make the statement correct.
>
> Example: ___ 1. The degree to which a testing instrument measures what it purports to measure is known as <u>reliability</u>.

Interpretive True-False. With **interpretive true-false** items, it is recommended that the researcher follow the guidelines presented in the following text.

1. Consider the principles appropriate to writing any true-false questions (particularly recommendations 1 through 7 in the preceding section on standard true-false items).

2. Be mindful of the fact that, in addition to reducing the likelihood of successful guessing, these items provide an opportunity for the respondent who may have misunderstood or "read into" an item to offer a successful defense for the response she gave (even if it does not agree with what the investigator had in mind by the question). In the interpretive true-false question, the respondent is required to defend her answer whether it is thought to be true *or* false. In this form of question, no words are underlined, except to show emphasis, such as when one is using negatives. We all know that students and others may know the information but end up getting a certain number of questions incorrect because of a lack of question clarity. If the teacher/researcher is truly interested in learning what the student knows, the interpretive true-false item may be the preferred alternative of the true-false variety.

3. Plan for the respondent to use approximately one minute to answer each of the interpretive true-false questions. It can be expected that one will require more time to defend an answer in this form of question than what would be required to correct an underlined word or words (as with *false* corrective true-false questions), particularly if the requirement includes having the respondent use complete sentences when offering a defense.

4. Provide adequate space beneath the item to allow respondents to offer their defenses.

5. Consider using this form of true-false question when giving a posttest or final examination (because little, if any, opportunity is available at the end of a term to go over the examination with the respondents). Should misunderstandings of some of the questions exist, the respondents' defenses for their responses should address the majority of the problems.

> Directions: Read each statement carefully. If the statement is true, place a plus (+) sign into the space provided to the left of the numbered item. If the statement is false, place a zero (0) in the corresponding space. In each instance, you are to defend your response in the space provided beneath the item.

> Example: ___ 1. Estimates of objectivity are best determined by correlating the results of two forms of the same test.

Multiple-Choice. With **multiple-choice** items, also referred to as multiple-alternative, alternative-response, or fixed-choice questions, it is recommended that the researcher use the following guidelines.

1. *Avoid using specific determiners such as "a" or "an" in the stem of the question.* They can give clues to the correct answer (because of grammatical considerations).

> **NOTE:** The stem of the item is the question itself (which is followed by the choices from which the respondent selects her answer).

2. *Request that respondents give the "best" answer as opposed to the "correct" answer.* Quite often, and by design, there is more than one correct answer in a group of alternatives.

3. *Use four to five alternatives, and try to make the "distractors" as plausible as possible.* It is important that respondents do not eliminate alternatives because these choices lack plausibility. Under such circumstances, the respondent may get the item correct because the alternatives made little to no sense. As a consequence, the person scoring the test will not know whether the respondent *knew* the information. During the pilot study, plausibility can be determined by examining the alternatives of each question to see if they were selected by anyone. If a respondent is able to eliminate two of the four choices provided in a question, she will have a fifty-fifty chance of getting the item correct—much like a standard true-false item. If this happens during the pilot study, the item should be revised.

4. *Include all alternatives on the same page.* They should be placed in chronological or alphabetical order.

5. *Avoid opinion items when measuring knowledge/achievement* (for example, "Which of the following individuals is the *best* composer?" According to whom or what criteria?).

6. *Underline negatives appearing in the stem of the item in order to make the intent of the question clear* (for example, "Which of the following is <u>not</u> a measure of central tendency?").

7. *Exercise caution to ensure that patterns of correct answers are not predictable* (for example, where the letter "B" or some other option is the correct answer most

of the time). In instances where alphabetical or chronological ordering is not pertinent, alternatives should be randomly assigned to A, B, C, or D (or A, B, C, D, or E if you are preparing questions with five alternatives).

8. *Plan to allow thirty to forty-five seconds per item.*

> Directions: Read each statement carefully. Select the <u>best</u> answer and place its letter into the space provided to the left of the numbered item.

> Example: ___ 1. The content validity of a practitioner-made test can be determined most effectively by:
> A. administering the test on two occasions.
> B. correlating the first half with the second half of the test.
> C. developing an alternative form of that test and computing the relationship between the two.
> D. having a jury review the test items against the research objectives and table of specifications.

Matching. With **matching** items, it is recommended that the researcher consider the following guidelines.

1. *Make each set of matching questions as homogeneous as possible.* While there may be more than one set of matching questions within an instrument of assessment, each set should be geared toward the measurement of a single concept, such as names of people, dates of events, or places.

2. *Place the phrases in the left column, and the shorter response alternatives in the right column.* This reduces the amount of reading time required to respond to a question. With less reading time allocated to a question, more questions can be asked within the time available. In general, the more questions that are asked, the greater the opportunity for acquiring evidence for the reliability of the instrument.

3. *Put no more than five to ten questions in each set.*

4. *Prepare more alternatives than there are questions.* For example, with five questions, there should be seven to eight alternatives; with ten questions, there should be approximately fifteen alternatives. This reduces the likelihood that respondents can correctly guess the answers to some of the questions through the process of elimination.

5. *Place all of the questions and alternatives on the same page.* Time is wasted if respondents have to flip from one page to another in order to read through the list of questions and alternatives.

6. *Arrange the options in the second column in alphabetical or numerical order.* This procedure is important so that the respondent does not have to waste valuable time searching for a response.

7. *Plan to allow three to four minutes for five questions and seven alternatives; seven to eight minutes for ten questions and fifteen alternatives.* This is assuming that answers are used only once. Under this condition, once an answer is recorded in the appropriate space, the respondent no longer needs to consider that particular alternative. As a consequence, the reading time becomes less as the length of the option list decreases.

Directions: Read each statement carefully. From the list at the right, select the <u>best</u> answer and place its letter into the space provided to the left of the numbered item. Answers may be used only once (with the possible exception of "none of the above").

Example:

___ 1. The most frequently found score in a distribution.	A. Chi square
___ 2. A measure of the variability of a group of test scores.	B. Mean
___ 3. A measure of central tendency that accounts for the weight of each score.	C. Measurement error
___ 4. A value that represents the degree of accuracy of a test score.	D. Median
___ 5. A value that tests significance between expected and observed responses.	E. Mode
	F. Standard deviation
	G. None of the above

Master List. With **master list** items, it is recommended that the researcher follow the guidelines provided here.

1. *Avoid using specific determiners.* Clues should not be given unnecessarily to those who are taking the test.

2. *Prepare the questions in a way that will require multiple responses to some of the items.*

3. *Employ well-thought-out scoring procedures.* Since there may be more than one answer to a question, the evaluator should subtract a point from what the question is worth for each incorrect entry up to the total number of points that are possible for that question. For example, if three answers (worth one point each) are appropriate for one of the questions, and a respondent offers four answers (one of which is wrong), she would earn a total of two points (three correct answers, minus one incorrect answer, equals a score of two). There should be a penalty for those who simply produce rosters of responses, hoping that the correct answers will be among them.

4. *Arrange to have all the questions and alternatives on the same page.*

5. *Arrange the list of options in alphabetical (or numerical) order.* As is the case with multiple-choice and matching-type questions, the respondent should not have to waste an unnecessary amount of time looking for the correct answer (assuming that she knows it).

6. *Consider its use when it is desirable to screen for a great deal of information (in a relatively short period of time) with a single set of questions.*

7. *Plan for approximately forty-five seconds for each item* (when the number of fixed alternatives approximates ten).

Directions: Read each statement carefully. From the list at the top, select the <u>best</u> answer (or answers) and place their letters into the spaces provided to the left of the numbered items. Answers may be used more than once, and while there may be more than one answer to a question, there is a penalty for guessing.

Example: A. Master list   F. Multiple-choice item
          B. Matching item   G. Reliability
          C. Mean   G. Standard deviation
          D. Median   H. True-false item
          E. Mode   I. None of the above

___ 1. Where the use of specific determiners leads to inappropriate clues.

___ 2. A test item that requires the use of homogeneous alternatives.

___ 3. Should have at least twenty items to reduce the impact of successful guessing.

___ 4. The most frequently earned score in a distribution.

___ 5. Measure(s) of central tendency.

___ 6. The degree to which a test is consistent in its ability to measure.

___ 7. Provides opportunities for use of multiple answers to a single question.

___ 8. Provides an indicator of the variability of test scores.

___ 9. Necessary to compute when calculating measurement error.

___10. Instance(s) where invalid distracters contribute to higher test scores.

Enumeration. With **enumeration** items, it is recommended that the researcher consider the following guidelines.

1. Provide an example of an answer in the stem of the question. This provides an opportunity for the individual taking the test to restrict her thinking to specific areas of inquiry.

2. Be mindful of the fact that respondents are less likely to guess the answer correctly because they cannot rely upon fixed alternatives from which to select a response. They must supply (recall) their own responses.

3. Plan for fifteen to thirty seconds for each entry that is to be made (depending upon the degree of thought that must go into the response).

Directions: Read each statement carefully, and place your responses into the spaces provided beneath each item.

Example: 1. One measure of central tendency is the *mean*. Identify <u>two</u> others.

          A. _____

          B. _____

 NOTE: Higher levels of thinking could be assessed in this question by asking the respondents to *identify* and *discuss* two other measures of central tendency.

Completion. With **completion-type** items, it is recommended that the researcher use the guidelines presented in the following text.

1. Provide space for the response to the left of the numbered item. This helps to facilitate scoring because the answer sheet can then remain aligned with the *left* column during the correction process.

2. Be willing to accept more than one correct answer and, if that is done, to write the acceptable answer on the answer sheet. This will help to maintain objectivity when scoring subsequent papers by ensuring that any other person who gave that answer will receive credit for it. (To help maintain consistency when evaluating answers, it may be necessary to go back over previously corrected papers to be certain that the "new" answer was not overlooked.)

3. Do not take off full credit for spelling errors (unless the test is specifically a test on spelling). One instructor asked the following question: "A shunting forward of the 5th lumbar vertebrae is known as _____." The response that he was looking for was "spondylolisthesis." If a student misspelled it, she did not receive any credit for the item. If a student gave the answer "spinabifida," the item was also marked totally wrong. It seems that the respondent who knew that the answer was spondylolisthesis (who spelled it wrong) knew more than the individual who gave the answer as spinabifida. Accordingly, partial credit probably should have been given. All educators should be concerned about spelling, but should it be deemed more important than the content they are structuring the test to measure?

4. Plan for the respondents to have somewhere between ten and twenty seconds to respond to each question.

> Directions: Complete each statement by placing your response into the space provided to the left of the numbered item.
>
> Example: _____ 1. The sum of the scores divided by their number is known as the_____.

Discussion (Essay). For **essay** items, it is recommended that the researcher follow these guidelines.

1. Recognize the fact that a respondent who is unfamiliar with the information being requested may guess, bluff, or ramble. As a consequence, an individual who has a gift for writing may end up receiving more credit for a response than should be the case. This issue can be addressed by awarding credit for each of the points made by the respondent (up to the total value of the question). By having a roster of possible correct responses on the answer sheet, objectivity in scoring can be enhanced. Remember from the discussion in Chapter 5, Selecting Instruments of Assessment, the objectivity of a question can always be "tested" by having more than one trained evaluator read the answer. Other ways to help ensure objectivity in scoring is to: assign identification numbers that the respondents will use to identify themselves on the test paper, have respondents place their names on the back of the test papers, and score one question for all respondents before attempting to evaluate their responses to other questions.

2. Be mindful of the fact that, while the essay form of question is relatively easy to construct, it is among the most difficult of questions to correct (in terms of time and objectivity).

3. Remember that respondents who write slowly or have difficulty organizing their thoughts and answers are severely penalized in timed essay tests. For those who fall in this category, it would be appropriate to consider untimed tests.

4. Consider the time allocated. This means the amount of time allocated for each essay question on the basis of the number and relative importance of the question, and the amount of time the respondent has to complete the entire instrument of assessment.

> Directions: Read each question carefully, and thoughtfully consider your ideas before putting them on paper.

> Example: Write a one-page essay that reveals the essential differences between qualitative and quantitative research methods. Your response will be evaluated in terms of its organization, comprehensiveness, and relevance.

Checklists and Rating Scales in Survey Research

Since surveys are often carried out with the specific purpose of measuring attitudes, there are a number of considerations in regard to the choice of questions to be used. While the types of questions discussed in the preceding text may be written to address attitudes, the **checklist** and **rating scale** are among the procedures most frequently used to elicit attitudinal information. Each may be used alone or in combination with the other.

Although it is not always limited to two choices, the checklist, for the most part, is a two-category, fixed-choice item (yes or no; agree or disagree). The problem is that very few things can be answered with one of two choices. One exception is demographic information, for example:

> Gender: Male_____   Female ____
> Married: Yes_____   No ____

With issues such as curriculum, however, either/or responses can be cloudy. For example, suppose the following item was asked:

> Are objective as well as subjective measures used to determine the progress of students in attaining program objectives?
>
>   Yes_____   No ____

In rating an identical curriculum, one person may say *yes* to the question because she believes it is done in the *majority* of the classes, while another person may say *no* because, although it is done in the majority of the classes, it is not done in *all* of them. Therefore, if a five-point rating scale were used, the reliability of the responses would be likely to increase. For example, the same question could be asked as follows:

> Are objective as well as subjective measures used to determine the progress of students in attaining program objectives?
>
>   1   2   3   4   5
>
> where 5 = 100% of the classes.
>   4 = 75% of the classes.
>   3 = 50% of the classes.
>   2 = 25% of the classes.
>   1 = 0% of the classes.

By requesting that the respondent circle her preferred choice, the intensity of her feelings on the matter can be determined. The rating scale allows for gradations between 0% and 100%.[*]

Since research projects may want to examine the matter of desirability, importance, or feasibility with respect to whether something "new" should be considered (for example, for the institution, program, and so on), it can be helpful to the respondents if word descriptors are attached to the rating values. In short, descriptors are provided as a "key" in the directions in order to add meaning to the numbers (much like the earlier example in which 5 = 100% of the classes, 4 = 75% of the classes, and so on). For examples of descriptors, see Figure 6–3 for ranking on *desirability,* Figure 6–4 for ranking on *importance* (compared to other needs in the program), and Figure 6–5 for ranking on *feasibility*.

Figure 6–3: **Sample Descriptors for Issues on Desirability**

Rank	Criteria	Descriptor
5	Highly desirable	Educational benefits far outweigh educational costs
4	Desirable	Educational benefits are greater than educational costs
3	Neutral	Educational benefits equal educational costs
2	Undesirable	Educational costs are greater than educational benefits
1	Most undesirable	Educational costs far outweigh educational benefits

Figure 6–4: **Sample Descriptors for Issues on Importance**

Rank	Criteria	Descriptor
5	Very important	Has a direct effect on the program
4	Important	Will have a significant impact on the program, but not until other matters are addressed
3	Moderately important	May have some impact on the program
2	Unimportant	Is likely to have little impact on the program
1	No importance	Will have no measurable effect on the program

---

[*]Among the more common standardized rating scales are those proposed by Guttman (1944), Likert (1932), and Thurstone & Chave (1929).

Figure 6–5: **Sample Descriptors for Issues on Feasibility**

Rank	Criteria	Descriptor
5	Very feasible	Very feasible considering resources needed and available; capable of being utilized and dealt with successfully
4	Moderately feasible	Feasible when other priorities are addressed, but somewhat dependent upon additional resources being made available
3	Feasible	Can be accomplished but would require substantial support beyond what is available (given present level of resources)
2	Feasible, but with prejudice	Is doubtful that the matter could be accomplished, regardless of receipt of additional resources that would be required
1	Not feasible	Even if additional resources were available, it would not be feasible to spend time on the issue

Earlier in the chapter, survey topics that might be of interest to faculty, administrators, guidance counselors, and members/officers of professional organizations were presented as suggested problem areas. The reader will now find examples of instruments suitable for use by these various categories of professionals. Figures 6–6 through 6–9 provide illustrations of instruments that can be used in studies designed to measure teaching effectiveness. Specifically, they can be used by those interested in surveying the perceptions students have about the competence of their teachers.

Figure 6–10 is an example of a **weighted rating scale.** In this instance, the document is designed to evaluate student teachers. Acknowledging that some qualities are more important than others, the assigned rating is multiplied by the weighting in order to generate an item score. For example, if, under the general category "Personal Qualifications," *general appearance* was assigned a rating of 3, that 3 would be multiplied by 1 (the weight of that item), yielding a total of 3. On the other hand, if a rating of 3 was assigned to *voice,* the 3 would be multiplied by 2, which would yield a total of 6. In this illustration, "voice" is considered to be more important than "general appearance" during classroom teaching.

Quite often, classroom teachers group students within their classes for project work. Equally as often, instructors find themselves unsure about the relative contributions of each of the members of the group to the group process. Figure 6–11 is an illustration of an instrument that can be used as part of a study to gather perceptions from each of the group members with regard to this matter. The names of all members of a group are placed on the lines, and each student is asked to rate everyone within the group (including him- or herself in order to retain anonymity). The average of the ratings for each individual can then be incorporated into the calculation of a student's final grade. The importance of that average rests with the confidence you have in the reliability of the entries made by each of the students.

Figure 6–6: **Sample Open-ended Questionnaire**

STUDENT EVALUATION OF INSTRUCTOR AND COURSE

INSTRUCTOR: _____ COURSE:_____

SEMESTER/YEAR:_____   .

1. In the space below, indicate your opinion about the **course** itself.

2. In the space below, indicate your opinion about the **instructor** of the course.

3. To what degree do you feel this course contributes in understanding, and skills useful in improving your competence as a future teacher in a public school facility or a person in your chosen area of work?

4. In retrospect, which sessions and activities contributed **most** to the value of this course?

5. In retrospect, which sessions or activities contributed **least** to the value of this course?

6. Please write specific suggestions for improving the course—student participation and involvement, instruction, etc.   .

Faculty members and administrators are often called upon to assess films and videos in order to determine their appropriateness for classroom use. When considering various teaching materials, it is usually helpful to have a form upon which impressions can be documented for future use. Figure 6–12 is an example of such a form.

Figure 6–13 is an example of an instrument used to gather information about how course grades are assigned. This device may be administered by a teacher in order to survey the practices of other teachers, by an administrator to determine grading practices of her teachers within a school, or by someone interested in surveying practices within a number of institutions in order to provide a basis for summarizing prevalent practices. Although the illustration relates to classes in physical education, the form could be adapted for use within any academic discipline.

Figure 6–14 is a sample of an instrument of survey that can be used to gather information about the various activities in which faculty members have been engaged during the course of an academic year. While it provides useful summary data for administrators, it is also useful for faculty in that it encourages them to think about their annual accomplishments.

Figure 6–7: **Sample Three-part, Fixed-choice, and Open-ended Questionnaire**

STUDENT EVALUATION FORM

Directions: Bear in mind that these are your opinions. If you have no basis for such, or if the question does not apply to your case, leave the response blank. Your responses are to be made on the accompanying computer sheet. Use a soft lead pencil and do <u>not</u> sign your name.

Part A: Your response to each of questions 1–5 should be: 1 = poor; 2 = below average; 3 = average; 4 = above average; 5 = excellent.

1. The instructor's provision for the development of appropriate skills in the subject area is:

2. The instructor's ability to explain course material is:

3. The instructor's interest in the subject is:

4. The instructor's knowledge of course material is:

5. The instructor's organization of course material has been:

Part B: Your response to each of questions 6–26 should be: 1 = never; 2 = infrequently; 3 = frequently (meant to be an "average" rating); 4 = nearly always; 5 = always. If the question does not apply to your case, leave the response blank.

6. Does the instructor allow students to express their own views without fear of reprisal?

7. Does the instructor show responsibility in meeting class?

8. Does the instructor demonstrate enthusiasm for subject?

9. Does the instructor make himself available to students outside class?

10. Has the instructor been fair in his dealings with you?

11. Does the instructor exhibit a friendly and approachable attitude?

12. Does the instructor create interest and stimulate thinking in students?

13. Does the instructor present material in terms that are understandable to students?

14. Does the instructor make reasonable assignments that are helpful in promoting the understanding of subject matter?

15. Does the instructor give meaningful answers to questions?

16. Are classes an aid to your mastery of the subject matter?

17. Are course objectives clearly stated?

18. Does the instructor stick to the subject matter rather than use the class as a forum for the instructor's personal opinions about topics bearing little or no relationship to the subject?

19. Does the instructor stimulate an interest in learning?

20. Does the instructor use the class time effectively?

Figure 6–7: **Sample Three-part, Fixed-choice, and Open-ended Questionnaire (continued)**

21. Does the instructor seem concerned about your intellectual development?

22. Does the instructor assign grades fairly?

23. Does the instructor communicate a knowledge of the subject matter?

24. Does the instructor clarify course objectives?

25. Does the instructor construct tests that consistently measure course materials presented?

26. Does the instructor communicate the relevance or significance of subject?

Part C: The following numbers (27–35) may be used for questions provided by your professor and/or the department.

27.

28.

29.

30.

31.

32.

33.

34.

35.

The document in Figure 6–15 is an example of a checklist that is designed to reveal problem areas within a curriculum. While the illustration pertains to health, it is easily adaptable for use in other academic disciplines. It is on the basis of findings from this checklist that topics are revealed for further investigation.

The purpose of the display in Figure 6–16 is to determine the opinions of recent high school graduates about the health program in the school district. Certainly, there are fewer categories of individuals who would be more able to judge the effectiveness of the program than that of the participants in it. Combining this information with that gathered from other sources should provide curriculum evaluators with sound bases for decision making. As with other illustrations in this chapter, this form can be modified to address other fields of study.

The instrument in Figure 6–17 is designed to measure attitudes about the values of integrating technology across the curriculum. Given the permeation of computers throughout our society, one might assume that the schools have a major responsibility to keep administrators, faculty, and students abreast of evolving methods and materials so that they will be equipped to stay ahead of the evolution. It is the purpose of the device displayed in Figure 6–17 to gather information from educators about their attitudes on the relationship of technology to learning in the schools.

Figure 6–8: **Sample Seven-part, Fixed-choice Questionnaire with an Opportunity for Comments**

DESCRIPTION OF FACULTY MEMBER

Instructor: _____ Department: _____

Course Number and Title: _____ Semester/Year: _____

The following statements reflect some of the ways teachers can be described, both in and out of the classroom. Some of these statements may not apply to the teacher under consideration, due to such factors as the nature of the course being taught or lack of basis for comparison.

For the instructor named above, please circle the number that you feel is most descriptive of him or her, using NA if you feel that a particular statement is not applicable. **Do not sign your name.** Remember, the purpose of this evaluation is to help members of the faculty in improving their teaching methods, so be honest.

A. <u>Definition of Course</u>: In structuring the course, the instructor

	Low High	Doesn't Apply or Don't Know
1. establishes objectives at outset of course	1 2 3 4 5	NA
2. states objectives for each class session	1 2 3 4 5	NA
3. identifies what he/she considers important	1 2 3 4 5	NA
4. gives tests that reflect course objectives	1 2 3 4 5	NA

Comments:_____

B. <u>Subject Mastery</u>: In dealing with students, the instructor

5. is fair and impartial	1 2 3 4 5	NA
6. stresses important points in lectures or discussions	1 2 3 4 5	NA
7. stimulates substantial effort toward learning	1 2 3 4 5	NA
8. presents facts and concepts from related fields	1 2 3 4 5	NA
9. has mastery of course content	1 2 3 4 5	NA

Comments:_____

C. <u>Efficiency and Effectiveness of Presentation</u>: In presenting material, the instructor

10. uses class time constructively and efficiently	1 2 3 4 5	NA
11. explains clearly	1 2 3 4 5	NA
12. is well prepared	1 2 3 4 5	NA
13. stimulates students to take another course with him/her	1 2 3 4 5	NA
14. emphasizes understanding rather than memorization	1 2 3 4 5	NA

Figure 6–8: **Sample Seven-part, Fixed-choice Questionnaire with an Opportunity for Comments (continued)**

15. is careful and precise in answering questions   1 2 3 4 5   NA

16. keeps seminar sessions focused on the topic   1 2 3 4 5   NA

17. utilizes/recommends textbooks that facilitate learning of content   1 2 3 4 5   NA

Comments: _____

D. Open-mindedness: In conducting classes, the instructor

18. considers points of view other than his/her own   1 2 3 4 5   NA

19. enables students to disagree and ask questions   1 2 3 4 5   NA

20. effectively encourages students to participate   1 2 3 4 5   NA

Comments: _____

E. Sensitivity to Students: In relating to students, the instructor

21. stimulates them to discuss related topics outside of class   1 2 3 4 5   NA

22. is not confused by unexpected questions   1 2 3 4 5   NA

23. has interest in and concern for the quality of his/her teaching   1 2 3 4 5   NA

24. has a genuine interest in students   1 2 3 4 5   NA

25. is accessible to students out of class   1 2 3 4 5   NA

26. takes into account students' individual needs   1 2 3 4 5   NA

Comments: _____

F. Personal Characteristics: In providing a classroom setting, the instructor

27. maintains an atmosphere of good feeling in the class   1 2 3 4 5   NA

28. is enthusiastic about his/her subject; seems to enjoy teaching   1 2 3 4 5   NA

29. seems to have self-confidence   1 2 3 4 5   NA

30. varies the speed and tone of his/her voice   1 2 3 4 5   NA

Comments: _____

G. Student Background: (For each question, #31–35, circle one response)

31. Was this course required in your degree program?   (a) Yes   (b) No

32. What is your gender?   (a) Male   (b) Female

33. What is your overall GPA?   (a) 1.9 or less   (b) 2.0–2.2   (c) 2.3–2.7
                        (d) 2.8–3.3   (e) 3.4–4.0

Figure 6–8: **Sample Seven-part, Fixed-choice Questionnaire with an Opportunity for Comments (continued)**

```
    34. What is your class level?    (a) Freshman          (b) Sophomore
                                     (c) Junior            (d) Senior
                                     (e) Certification only  (f) Graduate student
    35. Your class attendance:       (a) Good      (b) Fair     (c) Poor

    Comments: _____
    _____
    _____
    _____
    _____
    _____
    _____
    _____
    _____
```

Establishing Credibility

Regardless of the types of questions and instruments selected for use in a survey, it adds to the credibility of the entire data-gathering process if one has thoughtfully incorporated the use of a jury and pilot group during the process of their creation. To do so requires the translation of the steps for validation described in Chapter 5, Selecting Instruments of Assessment. In brief, the process requires that the researcher perform the following tasks.

1. *Clarify the objectives of the research.*
2. *Prepare a table of specifications.* The table should include: (a) the types of questions you want to include in the instrument, and (b) the objectives that need to be addressed. For an example, see Table 5–5 and Table 6–1. It can be observed from Table 6–1 that each category (objective) has been weighted according to its relative importance to the professional preparation of students majoring in the field of learning disabilities. In other words, there will be more questions or more points assigned in the area of "curriculum policies and practices" than any of the other areas. The researcher apparently believes that the most important component of professional preparation relates to the courses taught, both requirements and electives. Although other practitioner-researchers may disagree, the second most important component of one's preparation is deemed to rest with the qualifications and teaching competence of the faculty (staff standards). Considered third in importance is the library, technology, and media services, followed by general institutional and departmental practices. Equally ranked as lowest in relative importance are supplies and equipment, and facilities. This is not to say that these two areas are unimportant, but rather that they are the least important of the areas to be surveyed in this study.

Figure 6-9: **Sample Five-section, Fixed-choice, and Open-ended Questionnaire**

STUDENT INSTRUCTIONAL REPORT

This questionnaire gives you an opportunity to express anonymously your views of this course and the way it has been taught. Indicate the response closest to your view by <u>circling the appropriate letter or letters</u>.

Section I Items 1–20. Circle one response letter or letters for each question.

NA (0) = <u>Not Applicable or Don't Know</u>. The statement does not apply to this course or instructor, or you simply are not able to give a knowledgeable response.

SA (1) = <u>Strongly Agree</u>. You strongly agree with the statement as it applies to this course or instructor.

A (2) = <u>Agree</u>. You agree more than you disagree with the statement as it applies to this course or instructor.

D (3) = <u>Disagree</u>. You disagree more than you agree with the statement as it applies to this course or instructor.

SD (4) = <u>Strongly Disagree</u>. You strongly disagree with the statement as it applies to this course or instructor.

1. The instructor's objectives for the course have been made clear.   NA SA A D SD

2. There was considerable agreement between the announced objectives of the course and what was actually taught.   NA SA A D SD

3. The instructor used class time well.   NA SA A D SD

4. The instructor was readily available for consultation with students.   NA SA A D SD

5. The instructor seemed to know when students didn't understand the material.   NA SA A D SD

6. Lectures were too repetitive of what was in the textbook(s).   NA SA A D SD

7. The instructor encouraged students to think for themselves.   NA SA A D SD

8. The instructor seemed genuinely concerned with students' progress and was actively helpful.   NA SA A D SD

9. The instructor made helpful comments on papers or exams.   NA SA A D SD

10. The instructor raised challenging questions or problems for discussion.   NA SA A D SD

11. In this class I felt free to ask questions or express my opinions.   NA SA A D SD

12. The instructor was well prepared for each class.   NA SA A D SD

13. The instructor told students <u>how</u> they would be evaluated in the course.   NA SA A D SD

14. The instructor summarized or emphasized major points in lectures or discussions.   NA SA A D SD

Figure 6–9: **Sample Five-section, Fixed-choice, and Open-ended Questionnaire (continued)**

15. My interest in the subject area has been stimulated by this course.   NA SA A D SD

16. The scope of the course has been too limited; not enough materials have been covered.   NA SA A D SD

17. Examinations reflected the important aspects of the course.   NA SA A D SD

18. I have been putting a good deal of effort into this course.   NA SA A D SD

19. The instructor was open to other viewpoints.   NA SA A D SD

20. In my opinion, the instructor has accomplished (is accomplishing) his objectives.   NA SA A D SD

Section II Items 21–31. Circle <u>one</u> response number for each question.

21. For my preparation and ability, the level of difficulty of this course was:
    1 Very elementary
    2 Somewhat elementary
    3 About right
    4 Somewhat difficult
    5 Very difficult

22. The workload for this course in relation to other courses of equal credit was:
    1 Much lighter
    2 Lighter
    3 About the same
    4 Heavier
    5 Much heavier

23. For me, the pace at which the instructor covered the material during the term was:
    1 Very slow
    2 Somewhat slow
    3 Just about right
    4 Somewhat fast
    5 Very fast

24. To what extent did the instructor use examples or illustrations to help clarify the material?
    1 Frequently
    2 Occasionally
    3 Seldom
    4 Never

25. Was class size satisfactory for the method of conducting the class?
    1 Yes, most of the time
    2 No, class was too large
    3 No, class was too small
    4 It didn't make any difference one way or the other

Figure 6–9: **Sample Five-section, Fixed-choice, and Open-ended Questionnaire (continued)**

26. Which one of the following <u>best</u> describes this course for you?
    1 Major requirement or elective within major field
    2 Minor requirement or required elective outside major field
    3 College requirement but not part of my major or minor field
    4 Elective not required in any way
    5 Other

27. Which <u>one</u> of the following was your most important reason for selecting this course?
    1 Friend(s) recommended it
    2 Faculty advisor's recommendation
    3 Teacher's excellent reputation
    4 Thought I could make a good grade
    5 Could use pass/no credit option
    6 It was required
    7 Subject was of interest
    8 Other

28. What grade do you expect to receive in this course?
    1 A
    2 B
    3 C
    4 D
    5 Fail
    6 Pass
    7 No credit
    8 Other

29. What is your approximate cumulative grade-point average?
    1 3.50–4.00
    2 3.00–3.49
    3 2.50–2.99
    4 2.00–2.49
    5 1.50–1.99
    6 1.00–1.49
    7 Less than 1.00
    8 None yet—freshman or transfer

30. What is your class level?
    1 Freshman
    2 Sophomore
    3 Junior
    4 Senior
    5 Graduate
    6 Other

31. Gender:
    1 Female
    2 Male

Figure 6–9: **Sample Five-section, Fixed-choice, and Open-ended Questionnaire (continued)**

Section III Items 32–39. Circle one response letter for each question.

NA (0) = Not applicable, don't know, or there were none
 E (1) = Excellent
 G (2) = Good
 S (3) = Satisfactory
 F (4) = Fair
 P (5) = Poor

32. Overall, I would rate the textbook(s)   NA E G S F P
33. Overall, I would rate the supplementary readings   NA E G S F P
34. Overall, I would rate the quality of the exams   NA E G S F P
35. I would rate the general quality of the lectures   NA E G S F P
36. I would rate the overall value of class discussions   NA E G S F P
37. Overall, I would rate the laboratories   NA E G S F P
38. I would rate the overall value of this course to me as   NA E G S F P

39. Compared to other instructors you have had (secondary school and college), how effective has the instructor been in this course? (Circle <u>one</u> response number.)

   1. One of the most effective (among the top 10%)
   2. More effective than most (among the top 30%)
   3. About average
   4. Not as effective as most (in the lowest 30%)
   5. One of the least effective (in the lowest 10%)

Section IV Items 40–49. If the instructor provided supplementary questions and response options, use this section for responding. Circle only <u>one</u> response number for each question.

40. NA (0) 1 2 3 4 5 6 7 8 9
41. NA (0) 1 2 3 4 5 6 7 8 9
42. NA (0) 1 2 3 4 5 6 7 8 9
43. NA (0) 1 2 3 4 5 6 7 8 9
44. NA (0) 1 2 3 4 5 6 7 8 9
45. NA (0) 1 2 3 4 5 6 7 8 9
46. NA (0) 1 2 3 4 5 6 7 8 9
47. NA (0) 1 2 3 4 5 6 7 8 9
48. NA (0) 1 2 3 4 5 6 7 8 9
49. NA (0) 1 2 3 4 5 6 7 8 9

Section V Students' Comment Section
If you would like to make additional comments about the course or instruction, use a separate sheet of paper. You might elaborate on the particular aspects you liked most as well as those you liked least. Also, how can the course or the way it was taught be improved? PLEASE GIVE THESE COMMENTS TO THE INSTRUCTOR

Figure 6-10: **Sample Four-part, Weighted Rating Scale for Assessing Student Teachers**

Supervised Student Teaching
Evaluation Report

Student Teacher_____

School _____City or Town_____

Subject _____Cooperating Teacher _____

Directions: Circle the number which <u>best</u> describes the student you are rating. Multiply this number by the weight value to obtain total value for the item. Add the total value column to obtain a grand total.

			Weight Value	Total Value
A. Personal Qualifications	1. General Appearance	1 2 3 4 5	1	
	2. Voice	1 2 3 4 5	2	
	3. Poise, Refinement, Social Grace	1 2 3 4 5	2	
	4. Initiative, Resourcefulness, Creativity	1 2 3 4 5	3	
	5. Sense of Humor	1 2 3 4 5	1	
B. Professional Qualifications	1. General Scholarship	1 2 3 4 5	2	
	2. Knowledge of Subject Matter	1 2 3 4 5	3	
	3. Understanding of Methods	1 2 3 4 5	3	
	4. Acceptance and Use of Criticism	1 2 3 4 5	2	
	5. Professional Interest	1 2 3 4 5	2	
C. Teaching Techniques	1. Daily and Long-Range Planning	1 2 3 4 5	3	
	2. Use of Plans	1 2 3 4 5	2	
	3. Preparation and Use of Materials	1 2 3 4 5	1	
	4. Provision for Individual Needs	1 2 3 4 5	2	
	5. Skill in Questioning, Discussion	1 2 3 4 5	3	
	6. Ability to Maintain Order in the Classroom	1 2 3 4 5	3	
D. Classroom Management	1. Provision for Physical Comfort	1 2 3 4 5	1	
	2. Care of Classroom	1 2 3 4 5	1	
	3. Effectiveness of Relationship with Others	1 2 3 4 5	2	

Numerical Total_____
No. of Absences_____
No. Tardy _____

Courtesy of Plymouth State College, Plymouth, NH.

Figure 6–11: **Sample Peer Rating Scale**

Peer Evaluation

    The purpose of this instrument is to provide you with the opportunity to offer your assessment of the relative contributions each member has made to the efforts of your group. Realizing that an <u>individual</u> may have varying priorities that govern the amount of time and effort s/he is willing to devote to the group process, the outcomes do represent an aggregate of the contributions of all. In order to recognize the extent of individual contributions to the process, you are requested to circle the number which *best* describes your perceptions of the efforts of your colleagues. Please use the following key when considering a response (<u>and include yourself in the rating</u>):

    Compared to others in the group, this individual,

    5 - exerted group leadership; assumed responsibility for tasks without being urged to do so; was totally dependable; completed work without delay; volunteered her or his time to complete specific tasks; attended <u>all</u> scheduled group meetings.

    4 - exerted some leadership skills; was willing to do things without undue pressure; could depend upon him or her to complete work in a reasonable amount of time; attended <u>all</u> group meetings pertinent to topics associated with his/her areas of responsibility.

    3 - performed in a way that would characterize someone who was interested in the project, but would do little more than what was requested of her or him: there was no <u>unreasonable</u> delay in completing assigned tasks; attended <u>most</u> group meetings if topic to be discussed related to her/his areas of responsibility.

    2 - <u>seemed</u> uninterested in the work of the group; upon prodding, would agree to do task, but there <u>was a delay</u> in its completion that caused group to find it difficult to complete its work in a timely fashion; did <u>not</u> attend many of the group meetings.

    1 - expressed disinterest in work of the group; did <u>not</u> volunteer nor assume any task requiring individual effort; failed to attend <u>most</u> of the group meetings; generally would characterize individual as being undependable.

Rating Scale

	Lo				Hi
_____	1	2	3	4	5
_____	1	2	3	4	5
_____	1	2	3	4	5
_____	1	2	3	4	5
_____	1	2	3	4	5
_____	1	2	3	4	5
_____	1	2	3	4	5
_____	1	2	3	4	5
_____	1	2	3	4	5
_____	1	2	3	4	5
_____	1	2	3	4	5
_____	1	2	3	4	5
_____	1	2	3	4	5
_____	1	2	3	4	5

Figure 6–12: **Sample Film/Video Rating Form**

<u>Film Analysis</u>

Reviewer: _____

Film Title: _____ Copyright: _____

Publisher: _____ <u>Color B/W</u>
(Circle One)

Sound: <u>Narration Dialogue Combination</u>
(Circle One Only) Length: _____ Min

Cost: Rental: _____ Purchase: _____ Grade Level: _____

	Excellent					Poor
	5	4	3	2	1	0
Content Appropriateness						
Method of Presentation						
Contemporary Format						
Comprehensiveness						
Usefulness						

General Comments:
Strong Points - _____
Weak Points - _____
Other - _____

Strongly recommend: _____ For Rental: _____ For Purchase: _____
Recommend: _____ For Rental: _____ For Purchase: _____

Table 6–1: **Abbreviated Table of Specifications for Study on Professional Preparation in the Field of Learning Disabilities**

Questions	Demographics	Objectives						Total
		(1)	(2)	(3)	(4)	(5)	(6)	
Alternative response	5	15	25	30	20	5	5	105

Key: Objective Area (1): General institutional and departmental practices
Objective Area (2): Staff standards
Objective Area (3): Curriculum policies and practices
Objective Area (4): Library, technology, and media services
Objective Area (5): Supplies and equipment
Objective Area (6): Facilities

Figure 6–13: **Sample Instrument for Surveying Grading Practices**

Survey of Grading Practices

Please fill out this survey regarding grading practices employed in physical education classes. To respond, place a check mark in the space adjacent to each question/statement.

PERSONAL COLLEGE EXPERIENCE: The following questions ask you to reflect on experiences you may have encountered as a physical education student.

I had the following courses in measurement (check all that apply):

____ Measurement outside the PE department as an undergraduate
____ Measurement within the PE department as an undergraduate
____ Measurement outside the PE department as a graduate student
____ Measurement within the PE department as a graduate student
____ No measurement but a statistics class
____ No measurement or statistics classes

What standards for determining grades on **individual tests, assignments, etc.** did you most encounter as an **undergraduate** physical education student? (Check only one)

____ Criterion-referenced (grade based on preset standards)
____ Normal curve (grade based on performance relative to class)
____ Natural break (rank all scores and base grades on breaks within the distribution)
____ Percentile ranks
____ Other

What practices for assigning **course grades** in theory classes did you most encounter as an **undergraduate** physical education major? (Check only one)

____ Totaling of points earned on tests, assignments, etc.
____ All coursework (tests, assignments, etc.) was equally weighted and grades were averaged.
____ Exams were weighted most and other coursework was given lesser weights. A weighted average was then determined.
____ Grading practices were never clearly defined.
____ Other; please explain _____

As an **undergraduate** physical education student, what was the relative frequency with which the following attributes were used in theory classes to determine your overall course grade?

	Frequently	Occasionally	Never
Attendance	____	____	____
Attitude	____	____	____
Effort	____	____	____
Homework	____	____	____
Improvement	____	____	____

Figure 6–13: **Sample Instrument for Surveying Grading Practices (continued)**

Written exams	____	____	____
Participation	____	____	____
Potential	____	____	____
Quizzes	____	____	____
Research paper	____	____	____
Extra credit	____	____	____
Other_____	____	____	____

STANDARDS YOU EMPLOY TO DETERMINE GRADES FOR COURSEWORK

What type of exam do you primarily give in your theory classes? (Check one)

____ Essay
____ Short answer
____ Multiple-choice
____ True/false
____ Combination of above; please explain _____
_____
____ Other

What grading standard do you employ in assigning grades for specific course-work in your theory classes?

____ Criterion-referenced (grade based on preset standard)
____ Normal curve (grade based on performance relative to class(es) in that course)
____ Natural break (rank scores and base grades on breaks in the distribution)
____ Percentile ranks
____ Other; please explain _____
_____

When determining grades based on a normal curve, I

____ Add or subtract a set number of points from every student's score as needed.
____ Transform scores to an ideal curve using a preset mean and standard deviation.
____ Not applicable; I do not grade on a curve.
____ Other; please explain _____
_____

When determining grades based on criterion-referenced standards, I

____ Assign grades based on percentage correct (e.g., 90–100% = A, etc.).
____ Assign grades based on percentile ranks.
____ Assign grades based on norms I have collected from my classes over time.
____ Not applicable; I do not use criterion-referenced standards.
____ Other; please explain _____
_____

Figure 6–13: **Sample Instrument for Surveying Grading Practices (continued)**

Which factors do you evaluate on essay exams and/or papers? (Check all that apply)
____ Content
____ Grammar
____ Spelling
____ Style
____ Critical thinking
____ Creativity
____ Not applicable; I do not give essay exams or assign papers.
____ Other; please explain _____
_____

I evaluate a multiple-choice test after it has been given by: (Check all that apply)
____ Conducting an item analysis
____ Estimating reliability
____ Other; please explain _____
_____

The grades students receive in a theory class should reflect their performance in relation to other students in that class.
____ Strongly disagree
____ Disagree
____ Neutral
____ Agree
____ Strongly agree

ASSIGNING OVERALL COURSE GRADES
To what extent do you perceive that subjective factors influence the final course grades you assign in theory classes?
____ None
____ Minimal
____ Somewhat
____ Significantly

Prior to weighting coursework to determine final course grades, I: (Check one)
____ Convert observed scores to *T* scores.
____ Convert observed scores to *z* scores.
____ Convert observed scores to percentage correct.
____ Convert observed scores to grade point equivalents.
____ Divide observed scores by group's standard deviation.
____ Do not alter observed scores.
____ Not applicable; I do not weight observed or transformed scores.

Students not **meeting the minimum standards** of a theory course should receive an overall course grade of **F** regardless of effort.
____ Strongly disagree
____ Disagree

Figure 6–13: **Sample Instrument for Surveying Grading Practices (continued)**

_____ Neutral

_____ Agree

_____ Strongly agree

Do you curve final course grades?

_____ Yes

_____ No

Do you use a computer to help you determine final course grades?

_____ Yes

_____ No

When you determine a student's overall course grade, what percentage of their final grade is each of following? (Please estimate a percentage)

_____ Attendance	_____ Lab work
_____ Attitude	_____ Midterm exams
_____ Effort	_____ Participation
_____ Extra credit	_____ Potential
_____ Final exam	_____ Quizzes
_____ Homework	_____ Research paper(s)
_____ Improvement	_____ Other

What is the typical distribution of overall course grades in your theory classes? (Please estimate a percentage)

_____ As

_____ Bs

_____ Cs

_____ Ds

_____ Fs

Personal Information

Gender: _____ Male _____ Female

_____ Age

_____ Highest degree earned? What specialization? _____

_____ Total years' teaching experience

_____ Yes _____ No Are your majors (teaching area) required to take a measurement class?

_____ Yes _____ No Are you currently teaching a measurement class?

_____ Yes _____ No Have you taught measurement in the past?

How often have you published articles that focus on a measurement issue?

_____ Never

_____ Occasionally

_____ Frequently

Thank you for taking the time to complete this survey. Please return it as soon as possible and preferably by: _____. Your contribution is much appreciated. Misplaced the addressed stamped envelope? Mail survey to:

_____

_____

_____

Figure 6–14: **Sample Annual Activity Report**

Annual Faculty Report

NAME: _____ ACADEMIC YEAR: _____

DEPARTMENT: _____ DUE IN CHAIR'S OFFICE_____

PLEASE ATTACH A COMPLETE CURRICULUM VITAE IN ATTACHED FORMAT IF YOU HAVE NOT SENT ONE TO THE DEAN'S OFFICE WITHIN THE LAST 3 YEARS

SKILL AND EFFECTIVENESS IN TEACHING/LIBRARIANSHIP/ADVISING

1. List all the courses you have taught during this current academic year. Star (*) any that you taught for the first time. Underline those courses for which written student evaluations were/will be conducted.

2. Briefly describe special activities, improvements or innovations in teaching carried out this academic year, e.g., development of General Education courses, participation in Writing Across the Curriculum (WAC), introducing computing into a course, revising a class to include women or minorities, fostering active learning, engaging in classroom research, and so on.

3. List the number of advisees you currently have:
   Undergraduate_____   Graduate_____

4. Specify special activities, improvements of innovations in advising carried out this year.

5. Include any other pertinent information related to your teaching/librarianship/advising.

SCHOLARSHIP/PROFESSIONAL ACTIVITY

1. Briefly describe any research/experimentation for course development or improvement.

2. Briefly describe any ways you involved students in scholarly/professional activity.

3. Briefly describe efforts in research/publication.
   a. List up to three areas of current professional interest of research.

Figure 6-14: **Sample Annual Activity Report (continued)**

b. Cite any refereed publications, juried art shows or musical performances, or other analogous professional accomplishments.

c. Cite any papers or speeches delivered and/or non-refereed publications.

4. Specify conferences, workshops, seminars in which you played an active role as a scholar/professional. Give particulars where appropriate.

5. List any consulting based on professional accomplishment and reputation.

6. List membership in professional/scholarly organizations.

7. Indicate any other pertinent information about your scholarship/professional activity.

SERVICE (Directly/Indirectly Related to the Institution)

1. List department committees on which you serve, or other departmental service. Indicate office held where appropriate.

2. List institution-wide committees on which you serve. Indicate office held where appropriate.

3. List outreach activities.

4. List offices or activities with professional/scholarly organizations.

5. List community services you perform, with or without remuneration, which relate to your area(s) of professional expertise.

6. List consulting services you perform, with or without remuneration, which relate to your area(s) of professional expertise.

7. List any other pertinent information with regard to service.

Courtesy of Plymouth State College, Plymouth, NH.

Figure 6–15: **Sample Checklist for Assessing the Curriculum**

SUGGESTED OUTLINE OF A CURRICULUM EVALUATION CHECKLIST

The following evaluation checklist for health education programs suggests methods of assessing curriculum development in this area.

Item	Yes	No
1. Does the health education curriculum meet the agreed upon objectives?	_____	_____
2. Does the health education curriculum provide for the keeping of records in order to portray student progress?	_____	_____
3. Is evaluation used to help each student in the health education program find out where he/she is in relation to the program objectives?	_____	_____
4. Are objective as well as subjective measures used to determine the progress of students in attaining program objectives?	_____	_____
5. Are the students protected by periodical medical examinations in order to assess present health status?	_____	_____
6. Does the health education curriculum provide for the administration of physical fitness tests to evaluate the degree of fitness of each student?	_____	_____
7. Does the health education curriculum provide for cognitive testing of students to see how much knowledge has been obtained?	_____	_____
8. Does the health education curriculum provide for the testing of social adjustment of each student?	_____	_____
9. Are the attitudes and interests of the students evaluated?	_____	_____
10. Does the health education curriculum provide for mobility of students based on needs and interests?	_____	_____
11. Does the health education curriculum provide for teacher evaluation (by students/faculty/administration)?	_____	_____
12. Does the health education program provide for the recognition of curriculum problems and then try to bring about change?	_____	_____
13. Is there a standing curriculum committee?	_____	_____
14. Are school/community health committees/councils in place?	_____	_____
15. Is there a provision for ongoing evaluation of programs in reference to satisfying objectives according to an established schedule?	_____	_____

Figure 6–16: **Sample Instrument for Surveying Recent High School Graduates**

High School Health Survey

The teachers would like to know what you think are the strengths and weaknesses of the health program so that we can best serve our students in the future. Please answer the following questions to the best of your ability. Your input is greatly appreciated. Thank you.

Age: ___
Gender: Male ___ Female___
In which grade did you enter the School District? (circle one):

7　8　9　10　11　12

In what town do you presently live? _____
What health-related courses have you taken at _____ High School? (Check all that apply.)
____ Health
____ Biology
____ Behavioral Science
____ Other (Please specify):_____

Part I: Please answer the following questions for each of the ten Health Content Areas. (Circle your responses)

A. How much instruction did you receive in school?
 1.) none
 2.) minimal
 3.) sufficient information <u>without</u> enough discussion and debate
 4.) sufficient information <u>with</u> enough discussion and debate

B. How often have you used the education you received to make personal decisions?
 1.) never used
 2.) sometimes used
 3.) often used
 4.) used to make major decisions or life changes

C. To the best of your recollection, when (in what grades) did you receive instruction? List more than one, if appropriate.
 1.) before grade 7
 2.) grades 7–8
 3.) grades 9–10
 4.) grades 11–12

D. When (in what grades) do you think instruction should be given? If you think the topic should be repeated, check more than one.
 A) before grade 7　 B) grades 7–8　 C) grades 9–10　 D) grades 11–12

　　　　　　　　　　　　　　　　　A　 B　 C　 D

1. <u>Personal Health</u>: body systems, aging, physical　 ____ ____ ____ ____
 fitness, lifestyles

Figure 6–16: **Sample Instrument for Surveying Recent High School Graduates (continued)**

2. <u>Emotional Health</u>: self-concept, stress management, depression, other mental illness ⸺ ⸺ ⸺ ⸺

3. <u>Diseases</u>: AIDS, other sexually transmitted diseases, infectious diseases, heart disease, etc. ⸺ ⸺ ⸺ ⸺

4. <u>Nutrition</u>: food choices, nutrients, diets, eating disorders, food labeling, weight control ⸺ ⸺ ⸺ ⸺

5. <u>Substance Use & Abuse</u>: illegal drugs, alcohol, tobacco, prescription & over-the-counter drugs ⸺ ⸺ ⸺ ⸺

6. <u>Safety</u>: accident prevention, first aid, CPR ⸺ ⸺ ⸺ ⸺

7. <u>Community Health</u>: local health resources and services ⸺ ⸺ ⸺ ⸺

8. <u>Consumer Health</u>: consumer protection, quackery, propaganda ⸺ ⸺ ⸺ ⸺

9. <u>Environmental Health</u>: pollution, world health ⸺ ⸺ ⸺ ⸺

10. <u>Family Life</u>: life cycles, sexuality, reproduction, marriage, parenting ⸺ ⸺ ⸺ ⸺

<u>Part II</u>: Drugs and sexuality are two health topics that are covered in detail and appear to be of high interest to students. Therefore, it is important to look at these topics more closely. Please answer the following questions for each drug and sexuality topic.

A. How much instruction did you receive in school?
   1.) none
   2.) minimal
   3.) sufficient information without enough discussion/debate
   4.) sufficient information with enough discussion/debate

B. How often have you used the education you received to make personal decisions?
   1.) never used
   2.) sometimes used
   3.) often used
   4.) used for major decisions or life changes

C. To the best of your recollection, when (in what grades) did you receive instruction? Circle more than one, if appropriate.
   1.) before grade 7
   2.) grades 7–8
   3.) grades 9–10
   4.) grades 11–12

D. When (in what grades) do you think instruction should be given? If you think this topic should be repeated, check more than one.
   A) before grade 7   B) grades 7–8   C) grades 9–10   D) grades 11–12

Figure 6–16: **Sample Instrument for Surveying Recent High School Graduates (continued)**

	A	B	C	D
1. self-esteem and peer pressure	—	—	—	—
2. risk factors for drug addiction	—	—	—	—
3. decision making	—	—	—	—
4. effects of drugs and alcohol	—	—	—	—
5. caffeine, over-the-counter & prescription drugs	—	—	—	—
6. gateway drugs: alcohol, tobacco & marijuana	—	—	—	—
7. hard drugs: cocaine, narcotics, hallucinogens, amphetamines & barbiturates	—	—	—	—
8. drugs and driving	—	—	—	—
9. drugs and sex	—	—	—	—
10. reproductive biology	—	—	—	—
11. AIDS and other sexually transmitted diseases	—	—	—	—
12. love, marriage, divorce	—	—	—	—
13. birth	—	—	—	—
14. birth control	—	—	—	—

<u>Part III</u>: Please answer questions 1 and 2 based on the health topics listed below.

1. <u>Personal Health</u>: body systems, aging, physical fitness, lifestyles
2. <u>Emotional Health</u>: self-concept, stress management, depression, other mental illness
3. <u>Diseases</u>: AIDS, other sexually transmitted diseases, infectious diseases, heart disease, etc.
4. <u>Nutrition</u>: food choices, nutrients, diets, eating disorders, food labeling, weight control
5. <u>Substance Use and Abuse</u>: illegal drugs, alcohol, tobacco, prescription and over-the-counter drugs
6. <u>Safety</u>: accident prevention, first aid, CPR
7. <u>Community Health</u>: local health resources and services
8. <u>Consumer Health</u>: consumer protection, quackery, propaganda
9. <u>Environmental Health</u>: pollution, world health
10. <u>Family Life</u>: life cycles, sexuality, reproduction, marriage, parenting

1. In your opinion, in what <u>five</u> (5) health areas should students be the *most* informed. List them in priority order, the most important first.

    1. _____
    2. _____
    3. _____

Figure 6–16: **Sample Instrument for Surveying Recent High School Graduates (continued)**

4. _____

5. _____

2. In your opinion, are there any health topics you feel should not be dealt with by the school?

   Yes ____   No ____   If so, please list them.

   _____   _____   _____

   Why? _____

   _____

3. What health-related events, discussions, assemblies, speakers, or classroom activities do you remember as being particularly informative or useful to you during your years in the _____ School District?

   _____

   _____

   _____

4. On the whole, how would you rate the Health Education you received in each school within the district? (Circle one for each school, or non-applicable, NA)

   Elementary: Excellent   Good   Average   Fair   Poor   NA
   Jr. High: Excellent   Good   Average   Fair   Poor   NA
   Sr. High: Excellent   Good   Average   Fair   Poor   NA

5. From what other sources have you obtained health information? (Check all that apply to you.)

   ____ family   ____ peers
   ____ religious group   ____ school counselors
   ____ media (TV, radio)   ____ physicians
   ____ personal reading   ____ school nurse
   ____ guidance support groups   ____ community counselor
   ____ other: _____

6. Are there other health programs or services that you feel should be available for students at _____ High School? Please list them.

   _____

   _____

   _____

   _____

7. Use the space below for any additional comments, suggestions, and/or constructive criticism that you feel will help us better serve the students in the _____ School District.

   _____

   _____

   _____

   _____

   _____

Figure 6–17: **Instrument to Assess the Attitudes of Educators Toward Technology-use and Learning**

Educational Technology Survey Instructions

The questionnaire contains 90 inquiries on technology-use in education and is divided into *four categories of interests:* I. Principles, II. Opinions, III. Methods, and IV. Practices. These will be related to the *categories of sources* determined by your answer to question 1a below.

1a. My position is: 1   2   3   4   5
   (1) Teacher
   (2) Administrator
   (3) Staff Member
   (4) Specialist
   (5) Other (specify) _____

SCORING CRITERIA FOR RANKING ON AGREEMENT

This table contains some parameters to assist you in picking a response to each inquiry on a rank scale of 1 to 5. Throughout, one **(1)** is always **firmly disagree,** and five **(5) solidly agree.**

Score	Rank	Criteria
1	Firmly disagree	No priority in Educational Technology. No measurable effect on learning. Cannot be implemented. Unprecedented allocation of resources is needed. Politically unacceptable.
2	Disagree	Low priority. Has little impact. Some indication this cannot be implemented. Large-scale increase in available resources needed. Major political roadblocks.
3	Somewhat agree	Third order priority. May have impact. Contradictory evidence this can be implemented. Increase in available resources would be needed. Political roadblocks.
4	Agree	Second order priority. Significant impact. Some indication this can be implemented. Available resources would have to be supplemented. Some political roadblocks.
5	Solidly agree	First order priority. Has measurable effect on learning. Can be implemented. Definitely within available resources. No major political roadblocks.

****

I. Rate these **PRINCIPLES** from: (1) Firmly disagree to (5) Solidly agree
   1. Technology offers great opportunities to reform and
      improve education.   1 2 3 4 5

Figure 6–17: **Instrument to Assess the Attitudes of Educators Toward Technology-use and Learning (continued)**

2. Technology is an integral part of today's global society.	1 2 3 4 5
3. Technology does not replace the good teacher but instead enhances their abilities and capabilities.	1 2 3 4 5
4. New technologies will enable teachers to teach more effectively and enhance student learning in remarkable ways.	1 2 3 4 5
5. Computers, like books, are another evolution of instructional technology.	1 2 3 4 5
6. Technology's major purpose is to improve learning and <u>not</u> create a new content area.	1 2 3 4 5
7. Technology can be integrated across all curriculum areas.	1 2 3 4 5
8. Technology-use in the curriculum reflects the changing needs of students and the new expectations of society.	1 2 3 4 5
9. Technology awareness/proficiency should be considered when hiring new faculty, staff, or administrators.	1 2 3 4 5
10. Technology will improve the productivity of students and educators.	1 2 3 4 5
11. Using technology, schools will provide for the current and future needs of our students.	1 2 3 4 5
12. Schools can use technology to reach for more powerful learning goals and school reform.	1 2 3 4 5
13. Technology will not transform schools, rather schools must learn to harness technology to allow them to keep pace with change.	1 2 3 4 5
14. Technology will impact upon the mission of preparing students to be productive citizens in an information-based society.	1 2 3 4 5
15. Technology is an ever-growing resource in a media-saturated world and access to information is becoming more swift making schools avid consumers.	1 2 3 4 5
16. Technology will be used to enhance the productivity of educators.	1 2 3 4 5

****

II. <u>Rate these **OPINIONS** from: (1) Firmly disagree to (5) Solidly agree</u>

17. Technology-use decisions in curriculum development are driven mainly by fiscal considerations.	1 2 3 4 5
18. Curriculum reform and technology integration are influenced most by community and business leaders.	1 2 3 4 5
19. Top-down leadership by school administrators should concentrate on educating the community about technology-use.	1 2 3 4 5
20. ITV and distance learning are cost effective ways to use technology in schools.	1 2 3 4 5
21. Educational technology is becoming synonymous with networked multimedia personal computers.	1 2 3 4 5

Figure 6–17: **Instrument to Assess the Attitudes of Educators Toward Technology-use and Learning (continued)**

22. A shotgun approach of using whatever technologies are available and cheapest, works as well as planning for areas of opportunities. 1 2 3 4 5
23. Technology planning is primarily about buying equipment and reorganizing the curriculum. 1 2 3 4 5
24. Technology-use planning goals should be supportive of curriculum reform outcomes. 1 2 3 4 5
25. Accountability for carrying out various components of a school or district's technology plans should be stated clearly and adhered to. 1 2 3 4 5
26. Technology planning is an evolutionary process requiring an on-going review and modification as curriculum needs change. 1 2 3 4 5
27. Community support for integrating new technology into the curriculum depends upon keeping them well informed about planning. 1 2 3 4 5
28. Commitment to technology integration requires a sense of shared ownership by all teachers. 1 2 3 4 5
29. A sense of ownership of, and commitment to, technology-use in schools must be shared by parents, students, and the community. 1 2 3 4 5
30. Technology is the newest tool for wholesale restructuring of the classroom. 1 2 3 4 5
31. Consensus among teachers and curriculum developers is needed before technology-use programs are adjusted or terminated. 1 2 3 4 5
32. Other programs that compete with technology cause continuous modification and changes in the timelines for implementation. 1 2 3 4 5
33. Alternative funding sources—bonds or grants—should be considered in order to stabilize implementation. 1 2 3 4 5
34. Favorable community support for technology is a major factor for successful implementation of the technology plan. 1 2 3 4 5
35. Teacher support for technology implementation has significant impact on budgeting for computers in classrooms. 1 2 3 4 5
36. The School Board support for technology expenditures weighs heavily upon implementation. 1 2 3 4 5
37. Teachers, administrators, parents, and businesses share similar views about the current requirements for technology-use in education. 1 2 3 4 5
38. Similar views about the roles and missions of schools and educational change and innovation are shared by teachers. 1 2 3 4 5

****

III. Rate these **METHODS** from: (1) Firmly disagree to (5) Solidly agree
39. Initially, deployment of computer resources in either a lab or classrooms should be planned in order to meet specific instructional and learning goals. 1 2 3 4 5

Figure 6–17: **Instrument to Assess the Attitudes of Educators Toward Technology-use and Learning (continued)**

40. A technology lab run by a media specialist or instructional aide is an effective way to teach keyboarding and computer literacy.   1 2 3 4 5

41. Putting technology-use into subject-oriented courses that are taught by regular classroom teachers provides meaningful learning.   1 2 3 4 5

42. Specialized areas within the curriculum where technology is sought by teachers and staff should be put into an evolving technology plan.   1 2 3 4 5

43. A full- or part-time director/coordinator with expertise in technology-use is required at each school.   1 2 3 4 5

44. Using a single vendor who understands the school's needs for equipment and services would provide better support.   1 2 3 4 5

45. Potential costs for upgrading equipment, installation, maintenance, and training should be considered in the school/district's technology plan.   1 2 3 4 5

46. Technology should be acquired incrementally and integrated gradually into the curriculum.   1 2 3 4 5

47. Establish a pilot program/site for the first-year implementation phase using only teachers who are eager to use technology.   1 2 3 4 5

48. A deliberate training schedule while at school allows teachers an opportunity to explore technology.   1 2 3 4 5

49. A "buddy teacher" system encourages faculty and staff to share ideas, frustrations, and successful technology-use practices.   1 2 3 4 5

50. Staff development requires customized training activities matching the needs, learning styles, schedules, and experience levels of teachers and staff.   1 2 3 4 5

****

IV. Rate these **PRACTICES** from: (1) Firmly disagree to (5) Solidly agree

51. New technologies will enable teachers to teach more effectively.   1 2 3 4 5

52. New technologies will enhance student learning opportunities.   1 2 3 4 5

53. Technology will allow students and educators the ability to find, manipulate, and manage information.   1 2 3 4 5

54. Reading skills are the most fundamental requirement and precursor for using technology-based learning tools.   1 2 3 4 5

55. Incorporating technology as an integral part of the curriculum should span various learning styles and abilities.   1 2 3 4 5

56. Technology-use in the classroom increases students' aspirations to achieve new levels of excellence.   1 2 3 4 5

57. Students need technology tools and electronic/ telecommunications resources to help them learn and achieve in the future.   1 2 3 4 5

Figure 6–17: **Instrument to Assess the Attitudes of Educators Toward Technology-use and Learning (continued)**

58. Technology encourages a more horizontal classroom organizational structure making the teacher a facilitator and able to learn from students. 1 2 3 4 5

59. The relationship between classroom organization and computer use is mutually influential. 1 2 3 4 5

60. Computers extend, rather than replace, instruction by good teachers. 1 2 3 4 5

61. Computer-facilitated environments extend the power of students to analyze and understand information. 1 2 3 4 5

62. Computers can help students understand how information is collected, stored, and synthesized to solve problems. 1 2 3 4 5

63. Classroom use of shared computer resources establishes skills for cooperative work—a vital skill for participation in our society. 1 2 3 4 5

64. Teachers establish functional learning environments by relating the computer activities to other educational tasks the students perform. 1 2 3 4 5

65. Technology makes it possible to create learning situations where students can engage in activities they find interesting for their own reasons. 1 2 3 4 5

66. Entertaining learning activities can still accomplish the goals of teachers and give students control over their educational destiny. 1 2 3 4 5

67. Linking computer use with other classroom work allows teachers to present lessons in a mutually supporting context. 1 2 3 4 5

68. When students have guided access to quality problem-solving technology resources, they become more active learners. 1 2 3 4 5

69. Computers in the hands of good teachers can be an extremely effective tool for reshaping the educational process. 1 2 3 4 5

70. Technology will provide teachers with expanded resources to meet the varying abilities of the students enrolled in their classes. 1 2 3 4 5

71. The teaching/learning process will be enhanced for all students and teachers with a wide variety of technology-use in schools. 1 2 3 4 5

72. Integration of technology will facilitate learning by shifting emphasis away from assimilation of facts to the construction of relevant knowledge. 1 2 3 4 5

73. Integration of technology will facilitate the implementation of an interdisciplinary curriculum and adaptation to changing objectives easily. 1 2 3 4 5

74. Integration of technology throughout the curriculum will personalize learning to accommodate different styles and intelligence quotients. 1 2 3 4 5

75. Technology-use addresses cognitive, affective, and psychomotor learning, as well as enhancing creativity, critical thinking, and problem solving. 1 2 3 4 5

Figure 6–17: **Instrument to Assess the Attitudes of Educators Toward Technology-use and Learning (continued)**

76. Instructional use of technology will make learning fun by producing a desired shift from teacher as dispenser of knowledge to a facilitator of learning.   1 2 3 4 5

77. Technical competence of teachers, administrators, and support staff is an imperative for successful integration of technology in the curriculum.   1 2 3 4 5

78. Students need to be able to express themselves using a variety of interactive media and learn when each medium is most appropriate.   1 2 3 4 5

79. A school-wide information system will improve communication, decision-making, organizational efficiency, in addition to learning.   1 2 3 4 5

80. Technology initiatives should be focused and aligned with curricular goals and development, as well as instructional management.   1 2 3 4 5

81. Computer-based instruction (CBI) used for drill and practice does not engage learners because of insufficient interactiveness.   1 2 3 4 5

82. Computer-based technologies derived from research in cognitive science with integrated multimedia, promote engaged learning.   1 2 3 4 5

83. Someday, computers using artificial intelligence may help learners think through very complex and authentic problems.   1 2 3 4 5

84. Integrated learning systems (ILS) with interdisciplinary multimedia encyclopedias are traditional instructional approaches targeted to basic skills.   1 2 3 4 5

85. Regardless of the type of distance learning technology used, students learn equally as well as those who receive "face-to-face" instruction.   1 2 3 4 5

86. The Internet is becoming a major vehicle for distance education because it promotes engaged learning using interactive networked technologies.   1 2 3 4 5

87. Technology provides access to knowledge and learning resources to K–12 schools that were previously available at only colleges and universities.   1 2 3 4 5

88. Technology allows students and teachers to be powerful communicators, enabling them to produce original knowledge and share it with the world.   1 2 3 4 5

89. Technology is transforming society; therefore, schools do not have a choice as to whether they will incorporate it, only how well they will do it.   1 2 3 4 5

90. Internet access encourages students to do research and construct real-world knowledge during project-based collaborative learning.   1 2 3 4 5

Courtesy of J. DeMinico, Glen, NH.

In general, the following criteria should be considered when assigning weights (point values) to areas and questions within a measuring instrument:

- Cruciality or indispensability
- Direct relationship to the program and its purpose
- Difficult to obtain or retain
- Number of areas and items in the instrument

The demographics category will provide the researcher with background information about those who are responding to the questions. This section would include such things as: gender, position title, years of experience in the position, highest degree held, and major field of study. It should also be noted that the total number of points assigned to the six categories (objectives) is 100. It is not required that a value of 100 be established as a maximum for any instrument, but this number does lend itself to quick calculations (for example, percentiles) should they be desired.

3. Construct the alternative-response questions that will best address the categories (objectives) of the study. While open-ended questions are desirable for getting certain kinds of information, for purposes of the illustration on the assessment of programs on learning disabilities, it has been determined by the investigator that questions offering fixed responses will be the item of choice. If the jury feels differently, this point should surface during the validation process. Among the areas for questioning the investigator might consider for each of the six areas related to the study are:

Area 1: General Institutional and Departmental Practices

- A well-formulated statement of institutional aims, objectives, and philosophy is published and readily available.
- Departments or schools and students are represented in institutional policy making.
- Definite policies on salary, promotion, leaves of absence, sabbatical leaves, and tenure exist and are available.
- A minimum number of credit hours is required for graduation with an undergraduate degree.
- A minimum of one year (thirty semester, or equivalent, hours) is required in residence before one can qualify for the baccalaureate.
- The institution is an accredited member of a recognized association of higher educational institutions, including state, regional, and NCATE.
- For admission, the student must present character references, a record of graduation from an accredited high school, and pass a standardized entrance examination.
- A statement of objectives for the department is published and available.
- A departmental committee gives continuous or, at the least, annual consideration to curriculum needs.

Area 2: Staff Standards

- A full-time staff member is assigned as the head of the department.
- Adequate number of full-time staff members is assigned to the instruction of the recommended curriculum for the professional preparation program in learning disabilities.

- Staff members are adequate to maintain proper class size (not over thirty-five in a class; special technique classes in proportion).
- Adequate clerical staff are provided to properly expedite correspondence, reports, word processing, budget accounting, and the like.
- Adequate maintenance and sanitation personnel are provided at all times.
- The majority of the professional staff holds a doctoral (or other terminal) degree.
- All teaching faculty hold at least the master's degree, with a major in the field of their instructional duties.
- Faculty members are provided with monetary incentives to participate in post-graduate study and professional travel.
- Most of the instructional staff have taught in their field at the secondary or elementary level.
- Methods teachers have taught at least two years in the public schools in the area of their methods courses.
- There is a diversity of institutions in which the faculty members have earned their degrees.
- A planned program of in-service training for the staff exists.
- Administrative, academic advising, research, and committee duties are considered in determining teaching load.
- Staff members are affiliated with their appropriate state and national special professional organizations (for example, Council for Exceptional Children).
- Full-time staff members are given the equitable salaries, ranks, and tenures in keeping with other departments (or schools).

Area 3: Curriculum Policies and Practices

- For graduation, a minimum of sixty semester (or equivalent) hours must be acquired in general education courses.
- For graduation, a minimum of nine semester (or equivalent) hours must be acquired in written and oral communication (three of which must be satisfied through a major course requirement).
- For graduation, a minimum of nine semester (or equivalent) hours must be acquired in the social sciences.
- For graduation, a minimum of nine semester (or equivalent) hours must be acquired in the humanities.
- For graduation, a minimum of six semester (or equivalent) hours must be acquired in the natural or physical sciences; three semester (or equivalent) hours must be acquired in mathematics (above the level of introductory college algebra).
- For graduation with a major in learning disabilities, a minimum of forty semester (or equivalent) hours is outlined with proper indication of progression and balance.
- For graduation with a major in learning disabilities, a minimum of twelve semester (or equivalent) hours must be acquired in the foundation sciences (six of the credits may be double-counted to satisfy general education requirements).
- For graduation with a major in learning disabilities, a minimum of six semester (or equivalent) hours must be acquired in anatomy and physiology.

- For graduation with a major in learning disabilities, the program of studies will demonstrate that it requires LD (learning disability) certification-level competency in the following areas:
  — Diagnostic testing
  — Developing individual education plans (IEPs)
  — Receptive, associational, and expressive processes
  — Developing, evaluating, and modifying curriculum
  — Basic individual and group counseling skills (appropriate for use with students, parents, and other teachers)
- For graduation with a major in learning disabilities, a minimum of eighteen semester (or equivalent) hours must be acquired in educational theory and psychology courses.
- For graduation with a major in learning disabilities, a minimum of eight semester (or equivalent) hours must be acquired in supervised, full-time field work or student teaching in a combination of regular and special education classrooms, and extending over at least an eight-week period.

Area 4: Library, Technology, and Media Services

- The general library is centrally located.
- A department library is readily available and properly serviced.
- Computer clusters are adequate in number and properly serviced.
- The school and department budgets for the library, technology, and media services are adequate and fully utilized.
- The faculty aids in the selection of library materials and technology for classroom use.
- Space for library study is adequate and properly lighted, heated, and ventilated.
- Instruction is provided on the use of the library and computer clusters.
- Textbooks in general professional and special education, as well as in learning disabilities, are adequate in number, kind, and recency.
- Reference materials are adequate in number, kind, and recency.
- Current issues of journals and periodicals are available in-house or through interlibrary loan.
- Standardized test materials are properly secured, and updated on an annual basis.
- Instruction is offered in the use of technology, including: laser and disc players, camcorders, computers and peripherals, telecommunication hard- and software, and multimedia.
- Classrooms are equipped for using projection materials, including transparencies, opaque documents, computer-assisted instruction, as well as audio and video recordings.

Area 5: Supplies and Equipment

- A central purchasing agent serves all programs, but the number and quality of equipment and supplies are determined by the department concerned.
- Regular inspections and inventories of supplies and equipment are made, with particular consideration given to condition, quantity, and safety.
- Maintenance personnel are assigned to care for, issue, and repair equipment and supplies.

- Anthropometrical calipers, tapes, weight scales, and stadiometers are available in sufficient numbers and condition for class and research use.

Area 6: Facilities

- All facilities meet the safety and sanitation measures and are well lighted, ventilated, and heated.
- An adapted-remedial physical education room is conveniently located with respect to service facilities.
- There is one administrator or committee that coordinates the use and development of facilities for all.

4. *Once the questions have been prepared, arrange for a jury of experts to review them against the objectives and table of specifications in order to obtain evidence of instrument validity.* In the example of the study on the education of those majoring in the field of learning disabilities, it would be important for the jury to be comprised of individuals who are deemed "experts" in the categories represented by the instrument. For example, one of the members should have demonstrated through writing or presenting at conferences that she is well versed in general institutional and departmental practices. Finding one who also has had formal accreditation team training and experience would be ideal. A minimum of one person should be included who has been formally trained and certified in the field of learning disabilities. Likewise, other members should be selected on the basis of their expertise in one or more of the areas being surveyed.

5. *Gather evidence that will demonstrate the reliability of the instrument.* In the instance of the example of the investigation on professional preparation programs in learning disabilities, two evaluators, employing the identical jury-validated instrument, would be called upon to conduct independent studies at an institution that satisfies all pertinent selection criteria. The data generated would be analyzed in one of two ways.

1. If the data generated are **ordinal** or **interval** in nature, the reliability would be estimated through the use of procedures that would lead to a correlation coefficient. (With ordinal data, one would use rank-order correlation; with interval data, one would use either rank-order or, preferably, product-moment correlation.)

2. If the data generated are **nominal** in nature, the reliability would be estimated through a calculation of the number of answers that are in agreement on the two independent evaluation forms. Then, by dividing the number of answers that are in agreement by the total number of answers possible, and multiplying by 100, a **percentage of agreement** would be determined.

Using one of these methods, the researcher would want to have a minimum of .80 through a correlation, or 80% through percentage of agreement.

If a researcher were surveying the *knowledge* a group of individuals had about a particular subject, evidence of reliability would best be obtained through a test-retest, alternate-form, or split-half technique (see Chapter 5, Selecting Instruments of Assessment).

In addition to the four basic assumptions addressed earlier—namely, the researcher has the ability to conduct the study in the time allotted; the researcher has the resources to carry out the study per the design; the researcher has obtained permission to carry out the study; and the researcher will employ a valid, reliable, and objective assessment instrument—there are four others that should be taken into account:

1. The data must be analyzed, interpreted, and reported accurately. The researcher may want to use qualitative methods, a combination of qualitative and quantitative methods, or quantitative methods alone. In any case, thoughtful analysis followed by accurate reporting is quintessential. (A description of pertinent *qualitative* and *quantitative* analytical methods is presented later in this chapter. For now, it is important to accept the fact that all reasonable steps must be taken to ensure that the data are analyzed accurately.)

2. The findings of the study must be of importance, not only to the researcher, but also to the advancement of knowledge that may lead to further investigations on the subject.

3. The items in the testing instrument must distinguish between successful and unsuccessful practices.

4. The requirements for becoming certified to work with children who have learning disabilities are standards worthy of attainment.

✓ CHECKPOINT

In examining the illustrations of various recall- and recognition-type items, you may have observed that some of them focused upon topics that were presented in previous chapters. As a review, then, see if you can answer the following five items.

1. Standard true-false:

The degree to which a testing instrument is consistent in measuring whatever it is designed to measure is known as objectivity.

2. Corrective true-false:

The degree to which a testing instrument measures what it purports to measure is known as reliability.

3. Interpretive true-false:

Estimates of objectivity are *best* determined by correlating the results of alternate forms of the same test.

4. Multiple-choice:

The content validity of a practitioner-made test can be determined most effectively by:

A. administering the same test to the same group of individuals on two separate occasions.

B. correlating the first half with the second half of the test.

C. developing an alternative form of that test and computing the statistical relationship between the two.

D. having a jury review the test items against the research objectives and table of specifications.

5. Completion: The sum of the scores divided by their number is known as the _____.

Answers

The answers to each of the above items are as follows:

1. Standard true-false: The answer is *false*. When a test is consistent in its ability to measure, that instrument is known to have *reliability*. (See question 3 for information on objectivity.)

2. Corrective true-false: The answer is *false*. Change the underlined word to *validity*.

3. Interpretive true-false: Since estimates of objectivity cannot be determined through correlating the results of alternate forms of the same test, the only correct answer to this question is *false*. In this regard, two of the ways that a response to this item could be defended are:

- estimates of objectivity are best determined by correlating the scores assigned by two evaluators when grading the same test.

- estimates of reliability (equivalence) are best determined by correlating the results of alternate forms of the same test.

4. Multiple-choice: The answer is D. Administering the same test to the same group of individuals on two separate occasions (A) is reliability (*stability*). Correlating the first half with the second half of the test (B) is known as reliability (*internal consistency*), which would then be corrected with the Spearman-Brown prophecy formula. Developing an alternative form of that test and computing the statistical relationship between the two (C) would also be a process for estimating reliability (*equivalence*).

5. Completion: The answer is *mean*. Add up all the scores and divide that sum by the total number of scores.

How did you do? If you had difficulty with any of these questions, go back and read that information again. For those of you who had each of the answers correct, *congratulations*. You did very well to remember those concepts from the prior chapters.

The components of the first five of the eight steps necessary to complete Phase 1 for designing survey research have been described in the preceding pages (statement of the problem, statement of the need for the study, review of related literature, statement of the hypothesis, and basic assumptions). Let us now examine the remaining steps in the process: possible threats to the study, design alternatives, and definitions of terms.

Possible Threats to the Study

While threats to a study are often thought to be a feature of experimental studies alone, there is no question that they still need to be anticipated in survey research. The threats described in Chapter 3, Preparation of a Research Plan, are identified in Figure 6–18. Accordingly, the reader is advised about whether the threat is considered to be of concern with regard to the scenario on professional preparation programs in the field of learning disabilities. It can be seen from Figure 6–18 that seven of the fourteen threats are deemed to be potentially problematic—that is, they are factors that could compromise the validity of the findings or interpretations (unless appropriate offsetting strategies are employed).

As you may remember from Chapter 3, Preparation of a Research Plan, four of these seven threats (instrumentation, instability, expectancy, and interaction) relate to the internal validity of the study. The remaining three (persons, place, times) are potential threats to its external validity. These seven things are deemed to be threats because they are not automatically controlled by the design of the study as are the other elements listed in Figure 6–18, namely, history, selection, maturation, statistical regression, mortality, pretesting, and sampling. The following text discusses all fourteen elements.

Figure 6–18: **Concerns for Threats to Validity in a Cross-sectional Survey**

Threats	Considered a Threat	Not Considered a Threat
Internal Validity		
History		X
Selection		X
Maturation		X
Instrumentation	X	
Statistical regression		X
Mortality		X
Pretesting		X
Instability	X	
Expectancy	X	
Interaction	X	
External Validity		
Sampling		X
Person(s)	X	
Place	X	
Time(s)	X	

Instrumentation. Unless the instrument contains the necessary validity, reliability, and objectivity, the data generated from that device could be virtually meaningless. To attempt to control for this threat, the instrument is going to be reviewed by a jury and field-tested for inter-rater reliability.

Instability. Factors such as having the instrument delivered to incorrect offices can cause delays in the ability of the prime sources to respond in a timely fashion. To control for this threat, all instrumentation will be carried out through the process of face-to-face interviews. The researcher will deliver the interview materials herself. Should a prime source be ill or, because of a schedule conflict, find herself unable to participate in an interview, interviews with that prime source will be rescheduled (rather than meet with a designated associate). While other "chance" factors could occur (such as those described in Chapter 3, Preparation of a Research Plan), every effort will be made to deal with them in an appropriate way. By anticipating what these possibilities might be, the researcher will be better prepared to address them should they arise.

Expectancy. It is always possible that, unless the interview questions are presented in a nonthreatening way (and without apparent expectations of what the responses should be), this threat would arise. Hence, sincere efforts will be made to conduct the interviews in a way that would decry any appearance of bias.

Interaction. If the threats of any combination of instrumentation, instability, and expectancy are present, interactions could occur. For example, if the researcher has not determined estimates of instrument validity and reliability in advance of the actual study, through the process of jury analysis and pilot test, respectively, she (and those being interviewed) may lack confidence in the ability of the instrument to gather information that is appropriate for the study. As a consequence, there may be an expectancy (or bias) regarding how those being interviewed will respond to some of the questions being raised. Since controls are in place for *two* of the three possible **threats to internal validity** pertinent to this study, namely, instrumentation and expectancy, the threat of interaction is basically nonexistent (regardless of issues of instability that may arise).

Person(s). Because of the importance of respecting anonymity, the reader of the report will not have access to the names of the institutions or of the prime sources. Consequently, she might be inclined to assume that the findings of this study could be inferred to any population group. To combat the potential of this **threat to external validity,** sufficient information will be provided to alert the reader that the data have been generated by participating New England institutions offering professional preparation programs in the field of learning disabilities, and that because of confidentiality, all information is being reported as group data.

Place. Because the reader of the report will not have access to the names of the institutions, she might assume that the findings could be inferred to institutions in general—wherever they may be. While the identity of individual schools will *not* be revealed, the report will make clear that the conditions of the interviews were constant for each of the schools offering the professional preparation program under study. It will also be made clear in the report that the findings for this program should not be inferred to professional preparation programs in other fields of study.

Time(s). Because the reader of the report may be inclined to generalize the findings to surveys conducted at any time, the report will specify the time of the year when the data were collected. It should be apparent that the conditions of an institution could change during a given span of time because of any number of things, including: number and composition of the faculty, new facilities being built, or additional acquisitions in the way of computer hard- and software. This investigation, however, represents a snapshot of events as they existed at a particular point in time. In the report, it will be important to indicate what that time was.

History. This is controlled because the survey is being administered to each school at a particular point in time. There is no opportunity for events in the environment to arise during the course of the study—before and after the study, perhaps, but not on the "snapshot" occasion of the interviews.

Selection. This is controlled because the entire population of institutions in New England offering professional preparation programs in learning disabilities will be asked to participate in the study. Assuming agreement on the part of the program directors, *all* of the institutions will be scheduled for participation. If written agreement to participate is not obtained from a director of a particular program, no attempt will be made to draw inferences about that institution.

Maturation. This is controlled because, like history, it is a condition that becomes a potential problem when a study is protracted over time. Since the survey in question is to evaluate programs at a particular point in time, there is little to no opportunity for those participating in the study to "mature," while the snapshot is being taken, to the extent that findings would be jeopardized.

Statistical Regression. This is controlled because there is no pretest. As you may remember from Chapter 3, this condition exists when individuals in a study perform particularly high or low on a pretreatment examination. In the case of the survey scenario being considered in this chapter, the researcher is not interested in determining the degree of program quality at a particular point of time in advance of the interview sessions. In short, an assessment is going to be made of existing conditions without reference to the past.

Mortality. This is controlled because the study will not proceed unless prime sources provide all the information pertinent to their areas of responsibility. If those individuals become ill or, because of other reasons, are unable to complete the interview, the meetings will be rescheduled. Since the study is not designed to be extended over time, mortality is not expected to be an issue.

Pretesting. This is controlled because, as indicated earlier, pretests are not part of the design for this investigation.

Sampling. This is controlled because it is planned that all institutions in New England offering professional preparation programs in learning disabilities will be included in the investigation. If, by chance, permission is not granted for interviews at any one of these institutions, no attempt will be made to draw inferences about their respective programs. Findings and generalizations will only be made for those institutions that choose to participate.

Design Alternatives

Given the interest of the investigator in examining the current status of professional preparation programs in learning disabilities, it was determined that the survey would be the research design of choice. For the purpose of *this* particular investigation, it was deemed that neither the case study, causal-comparative, correlation, experimental, historical, philosophical, nor test and measurement designs would be appropriate. Secondly, since the survey is designed to investigate six rather broad program areas, the investigator will plan to conduct face-to-face interviews.

Definitions of Terms

During the early planning stages of a study, it is important that the investigator give thought to those terms that may need clarification. Not only may the terms be unique to one's study, they may be words for which there is more than one definition. For example, the word *stress* would mean one thing to practicing behaviorists, but would mean something quite different to a music teacher, to one dealing with phonetics, or to an engineer. Consequently, it is not uncommon for individuals, because of their professional backgrounds, to bring their own definitions to some of the words that they read.

In the study on professional preparation programs in the field of learning disabilities, there are at least twenty-two such words that require definitions:

Administrators	Institutions (private)
Certification	Institutions (public)
Computer-assisted instruction	Learning disabilities
Content validity	Lecturer
Enrollment type	Policies
Face-to-face interview	Practices
Foundation sciences	Prime sources
Full-time faculty	Professional preparation
General education	Staff
General professional education	Supportive documents
Institution type	Technology

Once definitions have been assigned to these words, Phase 1 of the research plan will be brought to a close, and it will be time to prepare the template (Phase 2). As you may remember from Chapter 3, the template is the place where one determines how the investigation will proceed—that is, the point at which specific strategies for acquiring critical information necessary to carrying out the study are identified.

A SURVEY PRACTICUM

In order to present the sequencing necessary to prepare a "road map" for a study, the discussion will focus on the investigation that has been designated as a reference point throughout this chapter—that is, the study on professional preparation programs in the field of learning disabilities. A sequence of pertinent questions for each of the four subproblems common to any investigation will be posed (see Chapter 3, Preparation of a Research Plan). The intent is that you will be able to relate these questions to any survey topic in which you may have an interest. For obvious reasons, some items will apply; others will not. In all cases, however, their relevance to survey research (using a face-to-face interview model) will be readily apparent.

For each of the questions regarding the four subproblems, the investigator would prepare responses to each of the following:

- Where the answers will be found
- How the answers will be found
- Procedures for organizing and analyzing the information for further use
- Conclusions that would follow from the procedures and allow the researcher to proceed to the next subproblem

Subproblem 1: Permission/Selection of Subjects

1. What institutions in New England offer a professional preparation program in learning disabilities?
2. What are the names and professional mailing addresses of the program directors?
3. Who among the program directors will grant permission for face-to-face interviews?
4. Will supportive documents be made available for examination upon request?
5. What are the names and professional mailing addresses of the prime sources for the six areas identified in the study?
6. Who among the prime sources will grant permission for face-to-face interviews?
7. What are the timelines for conducting the study?

Subproblem 2: Selection of the Instrument

1. What are the specific research objectives for the survey?
2. What is the configuration of the table of specifications?
3. What five to seven professionals would be willing to serve on a jury to validate the instrument of assessment to be used in the face-to-face interviews?
4. What are the administrative directions and the timetable for completing the search for estimates of content validity?
5. Can the instrument of assessment claim that it has estimates of content validity?
6. What institution that meets all pertinent selection criteria would be willing to serve as a subject of a pilot study to determine the inter-rater reliability of the instrument of assessment?
7. Who would be willing to serve as a second evaluator of the instrument of assessment?
8. What is the timetable for completing the pilot study?
9. Can the instrument of assessment claim that it has obtained estimates of inter-rater reliability?
10. Will the instrument of assessment and recording forms be available and in necessary quantities?

Subproblem 3: Administration of Study/Collection of Data

1. Will the study be carried out in a manner appropriate to its design, including control for threats to *internal* validity:

   a. Instrumentation
   b. Instability
   c. Expectancy
   d. Interaction

2. Will face-to-face interviews and supportive documents produce the information needed to complete the study successfully?
3. Will all pertinent data be collected and recorded on forms prepared for that purpose?
4. Will the data be arranged in an order appropriate for analysis?

Subproblem 4: Analysis of Data/Conclusions/Recommendations

1. To what extent did each of the institutions meet the standards reflected in the questions of the instrument of assessment in the areas of:

   a. General institutional and departmental practices
   b. Staff standards
   c. Curriculum policies and practices
   d. Library, technology, and media services
   e. Supplies and equipment
   f. Facilities

2. What are the relative strengths and weaknesses of each of the institutions with regard to the six areas represented in the instrument of assessment?
3. How did institutions compare to each other with regard to:

   a. State
   b. Public or private
   c. Institution type: college or university
   d. Enrollment type: 0–999; 1,000–4,999; 5,000–9,999; 10,000–19,999; 20,000 and up

4. What conclusions can be drawn from the analysis of the quantitative and qualitative data available?
5. Will the recommendations, appropriate to the findings and conclusions, be stated correctly in keeping with control for threats to *external* validity:

   a. Person(s)
   b. Place
   c. Time(s)

ANALYZING DATA

Until this point, discussion has targeted the *purpose* of survey procedures, *strategies* for developing and administering a survey (Phase 1 of a research design), and a survey *practicum* (Phase 2 of a research design). The next step is to present examples of the various **qualitative** and **quantitative** procedures one can employ to analyze the data generated by the instrument used in a survey. As you may have already surmised from your reading, there are various ways that perceptions or facts gathered through a survey can be analyzed. Depending upon the nature of the data one has available, information can be analyzed either by qualitative or quantitative methods.

Qualitative Analytical Methods

In qualitative procedures, the emphasis is on *words* rather than *numbers*. For example, there may be occasions during face-to-face interviews, that requests were made to see supporting documents. It is the *narrative* in these documents that, while not quantitative in nature, can still provide useful information to the investigator and the reader of the research report. By examining trends in the various documents and collating the findings, the researcher is able to enhance the report that otherwise would be based upon numbers alone. Through a critical analysis of the documents, the findings can produce an anecdotal account of various topics, including how the numbers were generated and what they mean. Ultimately, this can provide the reader with an enhanced perspective of the report of the programs under study that otherwise would have been limited by a singular quantitative description.

To illustrate how supportive documents can be used, imagine that the investigator, while asking questions related to the NCATE accreditation status of the institution, determined that it was important to look at the institution's most recent self-study report. In examining the document, the reader was referred to several exhibits. While examining one of these exhibits, it was revealed that the institution had recently been cited for its exemplary general education program. To support the finding, information was provided about the features of the program that made it particularly strong. In preparing the findings of her research, the researcher, instead of limiting her comments to affirming that a minimum of sixty semester (or equivalent) hours are required in general education courses in order to graduate from the institution, could use a narrative to speak of the quality of the requirement. Doing so would add a "dynamic" to the report that otherwise might not exist.

One concern that the reader may have is that the use of qualitative analysis can fly in the face of objectivity. True, it can! Remember, however, that the data that are analyzed objectively are not compromised by a qualitative assessment of narrative information. In fact, the two methods can complement each other. There should be little concern that objectivity of the study would be in question when: (1) numerical values are recorded during the course of a study, (2) appropriate statistical measures are employed to analyze those values, (3) the findings of the analysis of those values are thoughtfully displayed, and (4) the conclusions can be supported by the findings. Adding qualitative information to the report merely adds testimony to the context within which those numbers were found. It can bring "character" to what might otherwise be a rather bland report. (See Chapter 8, Other Descriptive Procedures, for a thorough discussion on gathering and organizing qualitative research information for subsequent analysis.)

Quantitative Analytical Methods

There are a variety of statistical analyses that are appropriate for survey-generated data. At the same time, however, you may remember from Chapter 5 that these analyses are governed by the *kinds* of data arising out of the instrument. If, for example, responses to a survey can be either "yes," "no," or "undecided" (nominal data), among the statistics that could be applied to these data would be the **mode** (*Mo*), the most frequent response in the distribution; **percent of attainment** (*POA*), the number of those who responded to any given question, divided by the total number of respondents, times 100; or a **chi square** (*Chi²*), which is an analysis of the data in a way that will determine if statistical significance can be found between *expected* and *obtained* results (also referred to as *goodness of fit*).

Using the study on professional preparation programs in the field of learning disabilities as an illustration, these analyses would be appropriate for at least one of the questions that would likely be prepared to assess Area 1, General Institutional and Departmental Practices. Under the area dealing with accreditation, the question might read:

> Check one:
> The institution is an accredited member of a recognized association of higher education:
>
> _____ The state
> _____ The state and region
> _____ The state, region, and NCATE

In addition to reporting the status of a given institution regarding its accreditation, it would be possible to merge the responses from all of the participating institutions. Assume that there are twelve institutions in New England offering a professional preparation program in the field of learning disabilities, and that the breakdown of responses to the question was as follows:

- *Two* institutions reported:　the state
- *Two* institutions reported:　the state and region
- *Eight* institutions reported:　the state, region, and NCATE

The findings would show that:

- The mode (*Mo*) is:　　　　state, region, and NCATE.

More institutions fell into that category than into any other single category. A distribution may be monomodal (one mode, as is the case in this example), bimodal (two modes), trimodal (three modes), or multimodal (four or more modes). There are also instances where no category (or score) is indicated more than any other. This would be a nonmodal distribution. The findings would also show that:

- The percent of attainment (*POA*) for the state accreditation is:　　16.6%.
- The percent of attainment (*POA*) for the state and region is:　　16.6%.
- The percent of attainment (*POA*) for the state, region, and NCATE is: 66.6%.

 NOTE: A percent of attainment (*POA*) is found by dividing the frequency of responses in a category (*f*) by the total number of institutions (*N*), and multiplying by 100.

$$POA = \frac{f}{N} \ (100)$$

Finally, the findings would reveal that:

- The chi square (*Chi²* or X^2) value is: 6.000.

In order to determine whether this finding is significant, one would refer to Appendix C, Chi Square Table, degrees of freedom (*df*) = 2. It can be observed that a value of X^2 = 6.000 is significant at the .05 level of confidence (*loc*). It *equals* or *exceeds* the entry at the intersection of .05 *loc* and 2 *df*. (To be determined significant, the value of 5.991 noted in the table must be equaled or surpassed.)

> **NOTE:** When making a decision about how far one should carry out the calculations, look at the reference table (in this case, chi square). Since the table displays numbers into the thousands, one should carry out one's work to the third place as well, and truncate. Do not carry to four places and round back to three. It would be inappropriate to report significance on the basis of a rounded-off value.

Since the number in the table is 5.991, a value of 6.000 would be significant at the .05 *loc*. There appears to be a lack of "fit" between observed and expected frequencies. At the same time, however, a 6.000 is *not* significant at the .02 *loc* because a value of 7.378 at that level would be required. In brief, the interpretation of the findings would be:

> Within the limitations of the fixed choices provided by this question, the researcher has found significance at the .05 *loc*. It appears that something *other than chance* has influenced the differences between observed and expected values (in favor of institutions with state, regional, and NCATE accreditation).

The formula for computing chi square is:

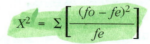

$$X^2 = \Sigma \left[\frac{(fo - fe)^2}{fe} \right]$$

For a demonstration of its use, you are referred to Table 6–2.

> **NOTE:** There are two rows in this chi square model. Rows (*r*) are read across. They are the rows labeled: observed frequencies (*fo*) and expected frequencies (*fe*). Columns (*c*) are read down, and there are three of them: state; state and region; state, region, and NCATE.

While each test of significance has its own procedure for determining degrees of freedom, the chi square method is: $(r - 1) (c - 1)$. The best way to explain why the number 1 is subtracted from the number of rows and the number of columns is to provide an illustration. Suppose

Table 6–2: **Calculations of a Chi Square Value for the Question on Accreditation**

	State	State and Region	State, Region, and NCATE
Observed frequencies (*fo*)	2	2	8
*Expected frequencies (*fe*)	4	4	4
**(*fo* − *fe*)	2	2	4
(*fo* − *fe*)^2	4	4	16
$\dfrac{(fo - fe)^2}{fe}$	1	1	4

$$\Sigma \left[\frac{(fo - fe)^2}{fe} \right] = 6 \qquad\qquad df = 2\ (r - 1)\ (c - 1)$$

*Expected frequencies are expressed in a way that assumes that there would be no difference in the number of institutions falling into the various categories; that is, 4, 4, and 4 (for a total of 12).
**For (*fo* − *fe*), an absolute rather than relative difference is calculated. In other words, there will be *no* minus signs.

for example, you are charged with the responsibility of arriving at three numbers which, if summed, would equal the number 25. You might decide that the first number is 6 and the second number is 10. Once those two numbers have been selected, you have lost one degree of freedom because of one restriction—that is, that the third number must be 9. In other words, 3 minus 1.

As you can observe, the mode represents a very basic level of analysis. It identifies the most frequent variable in the distribution. By presenting percents of attainment, however, the researcher is moving a bit higher into the analysis hierarchy by showing, by way of a proportion, how that variable relates to the whole. Yes, the mode was state, region, and NCATE, but by expressing the fact that the mode represents 66.6% (of the respondents), additional information is being provided for the reader.

 NOTE: Considering the accreditation question for the twelve institutions in the study, suppose that *five* were state, region, and NCATE; *four* were state and region; and *three* were state. The mode would still have been state, region, and NCATE (because it was the most frequently found variable in the distribution), but it would have represented only 41.66%, less than one-half the size of the group. If the researcher only reported the *mode,* the reader would have no idea of the percent that value represented.

Now, by adding a chi square to the analysis, one is able to report whether that finding is statistically significant. In the earlier example, a value of $X^2 = 6.000$ was found to be significant at the .05 level of confidence. To use a metaphor, by moving up the "food chain," more and more "nourishment" can be provided for the reader.

✓ CHECKPOINT

Presented with the following information:

1. Compute a chi square value.

	Group 1	Group 2	Group 3	Group 4	Group 5
fo	23	15	17	20	25

2. Interpret the finding (using the chi square table of significance in Appendix C).

Answers

The answers to the above questions are:

1. The chi square value is 3.400. First, it would have been necessary to assign *fe* values of 20 to each of the columns, since it is important to assume that there would not be any difference in what one would expect to find for the five groups. The 20 is found by summing the values in the *fe* row, and dividing that number by 5; thus, 100/5 equals 20. Given this information, the computation would be set up as follows:

	Group 1	Group 2	Group 3	Group 4	Group 5
fo	23	15	17	20	25
fe	20	20	20	20	20
$(fo - fe)$	3	5	3	0	5
$(fo - fe)^2$	9	25	9	0	25
$\frac{(fo - fe)^2}{fe}$	.45	1.25	.45	0	1.25

$$\Sigma \left[\frac{(fo - fe)^2}{fe} \right] = 3.400 \quad df = 4 \; (2 - 1) \; (5 - 1)$$

2. Applying the data to the chi square table (Appendix C), the finding is *not* held to be significant. (In the table, the X^2 value for $df = 4$; .05 *loc* is 9.488, which is greater than the obtained value of 3.400.) There appears to be a "fit" between observed and expected frequencies. Consequently, any observed difference between the obtained and expected values can be attributed to *chance alone*.

If you had any difficulty arriving at these answers, review the steps described earlier in the chapter. You might also consider setting up another set of *fo* values for analysis. Relate the steps used in the calculations from this chapter to your own data. With regard to the interpretations of the findings, if the calculated value *equals* or *exceeds* the number in the table (beginning with the .05 *loc,* for the given *df*), significance has been found and the findings are due to something *other than chance.* On the other hand, if your value does *not* reach the value in the table (for the selected *loc* and *df*), the findings can be attributed to *chance alone.*

So far the discussion has focused on examples of statistical procedures that are appropriate to *nominal* data. Now the discussion will turn to examples of other statistical analyses that could be applied to survey-generated *ordinal* data. Suppose each institution that agreed to participate in the study on professional preparation programs in the field of learning disabilities was ranked from top to bottom on the basis of total score (see Table 6–3).

 NOTE: The **median** (*Mdn*) is the 50th **percentile.** If the researcher wanted to calculate the median of the scores for this survey, she would take 50% of *N* (the total number of scores in the distribution).

$$Mdn = .50 \ (N)$$

In this case, .50 (*N*) = 6. She would count up from the bottom until the 6th score is reached. The number found is the 50th percentile. In Table 6–3, 50% of the institutions earned a score of 77 or less; therefore, the score 77 is the 50th percentile (also known as the median).

In some textbooks on statistics, you would be told that the median is 77.5 for the data in Table 6–3—that is, the midpoint between the 6th and 7th score. However, this author agrees with those who subscribe to the principle that the 50th percentile (median) should be a score that was literally earned—that is, the point *at* and *below which* 50% of the scores can be found.

With regard to Table 6–3, then, 50% of the institutions earned a value of 77 (the median) and below. By the same token, the percentile rank of the score 77 is 50%. Equivalency has been demonstrated.

Earlier in the chapter, reference was made to estimating inter-rater reliability through the process of correlation. By having two different evaluators administer the survey at a pilot study institution, one would end up with a pair of scores for each institution. These data could then be analyzed through the process of: percent of agreement, described earlier in the chapter, *or* correlation. As you may remember, if the correlation coefficient reaches a minimum of .80, an estimate of reliability would have been established, and the study is ready to proceed (assuming qualities of content validity have already been assured). The process for calculating the correlation coefficient, however, will be deferred until Chapter 7, Correlation Procedures.

Many of the instruments used in a survey will generate interval data. One example would be where the teacher/researcher is interested in surveying the *knowledge* of a group of students regarding some field of study. Since plans for the instrument

Table 6–3: **Total Scores, Ranks, Percents of Attainment, and Percentile Ranks for Twelve Institutions Participating in the Study on Professional Preparation of Students**

Institution # (a)	Score (b)	Ranks (c)	Percents of Attainment (d)	Percentile Ranks (e)
3	95	1	95%	100.00%
10	87	2.5	87%	91.66%
6	87	2.5	87%	91.66%
11	84	4	84%	75.00%
1	80	5	80%	66.66%
12	78	6	78%	58.33%
7	77	7	77%	50.00%
2	74	8	74%	41.66%
5	73	9	73%	33.33%
8	70	10	70%	25.00%
4	68	11	68%	16.66%
9	65	12	65%	8.33%

Key: (a) Institution is identified by number in any general report in order to maintain the confidentiality of each institution.

(b) This column represents the total score earned by each institution out of one hundred possible points.

(c) This column represents the ranking of each institution on the basis of total scores. In the instance of tie scores, the would-be ranks are averaged and that number is assigned to each institution. If there were *no* ties, the institution with the best score would get a rank of 1; the second best, a rank of 2; the third best, a rank of 3; the fourth best, a rank of 4, and so on.

(d) This column displays the percents of attainment (*POA*) for each institution. This number is computed by dividing the earned score (*ES*) by the possible score (*PS*). To convert the answer to a percent, this number is then multiplied by 100.

$$POA = \frac{ES}{PS} (100)$$

Percents of attainment are criterion-referenced values in that they are not dependent upon the scores of other institutions. As a consequence, the criterion becomes the total points an institution can earn on the instrument of assessment. In this instance, the total number of points is one hundred.

(e) This column represents the percentile rank (*PR*) of each institution. The value is determined by counting the cumulative frequency (*fc*) of institutions earning a particular target score and below, and dividing that value by (*N*), which is the total number of institutions in the study. To convert the answer to a percentile rank, this number is then multiplied by 100.

$$PR = \frac{fc}{N} (100)$$

For example, two institutions earned a score of 68 and below. Divide the number 2 by 12, the total number of institutions in the study, and multiply by 100. The answer is 16.66%. Unlike the calculations for percents of attainment, this value *is* dependent upon how other institutions placed in the survey. Thus, percentile ranks represent norm-referenced values.

of survey for professional preparation programs did not provide for questions that would generate interval data, another illustration will be used.

Imagine that ten students are enrolled in an honors class. A pretest is given in order to establish some preliminary baselines for instruction. As a result of this diagnostic measure, scores are generated and placed into a frequency distribution for analysis (see Table 6–4). There are *three* measures of *central tendency* that could be found for the data in this distribution, namely, the **mean** (M, $\bar{M}$, or $\bar{X}$), the median (*Mdn*), and the mode (*Mo*). The median was discussed under ordinal data, and the mode was presented under nominal data. Remember, any statistic introduced at the nominal level may be used with ordinal, interval, and ratio data. Likewise, any statistic introduced at the ordinal level may be used with interval and ratio data. (See Table 5–6 in Chapter 5.) Since this discussion focuses on interval data with an example of pretest scores, this is the time to introduce the calculation of the *mean*.

The *mean* (common symbols are M, $\bar{M}$, and $\bar{X}$) is considered to be the most reliable measure of central tendency because it takes into account the individual weighting of each and every score. Using a raw score formula, one can find the mean by summing the scores (X) and dividing by their number (N):

$$M = \frac{\Sigma X}{N} = \frac{421}{10} = 42.1$$

If the statistical analysis will include more than finding the mean, and most likely it will, use a frequency distribution of the type described. Otherwise, unordered scores can merely be added and averaged without regard to placing them in a column in descending order.

NOTE: In some studies, the lowest score would be the best score, for example, when one is timing events. If such is the case, it is recommended that the lowest score be placed at the top of the distribution. This is to facilitate the calculation of the median and other percentiles, referenced under ordinal data.

The **standard deviation** (common symbols are *SD* and σ) is a measure of the variability of the distribution of test scores. A mathematician might observe by examining the raw score formula, below, that the answer represents the square root of the average of the deviations from the mean of the distribution.

$$SD = \sqrt{\frac{\Sigma X^2}{N} - M^2}$$

For Table 6–4, the calculations for the standard deviation would be as follows:

Step 1. Square each score (for example, the square of the score 50 is 2500; the square of the score 48 is 2304, and so on).

Step 2. Sum the squared scores and divide by N.

Step 3. Square the mean (arithmetic average).

Step 4. Subtract the squared mean value from the average of the squared scores.

Table 6–4: **Scores Earned by Ten Students on an Honors Class Pretest**

Students	Scores (X)	X^2
A	50	2500
B	48	2304
C	46	2116
D	44	1936
E	43	1849
F	41	1681
G	39	1521
H	38	1444
I	37	1369
J	35	1225

Step 5. Compute the square root. This will generate the standard deviation, which is an indication of the dispersion or spread of the scores.

In a homogeneously grouped distribution, the standard deviation will be smaller than in a heterogeneous group of scores. (If you do not recall how to compute the square root, consult a table of square roots, which can be found in the appendices of many statistics and educational measurement textbooks.)

For the scores in Table 6–4, the standard deviation is found as follows:

$$SD = \sqrt{\frac{\Sigma X^2}{N} - M^2}$$

$$= \sqrt{\frac{17945}{10} - 1772.41}$$

$$= \sqrt{17945 - 1772.41}$$

$$= \sqrt{22.09}$$

$$SD = 4.70$$

Of the various analyses described to date, the mean and the standard deviation are among the most important because their answers are used as a foundation for many other formulas. For example, means and standard deviations are used in:

1. Product-moment correlation (see Chapter 7, Correlation Procedures)

2. t test (see Part III, Experimental Research Methods)

3. Analysis of variance (see Part III, Experimental Research Methods)

It is also necessary to compute the mean and standard deviation for use in various standard scores (that is, *T* score, *z* score), as well some of the inferential statistics not described in this book.

How does one *draw the line* regarding what statistics to present in a research design text such as this? There is a threefold answer to this question. The statistical procedures that are presented in this text are those that: (1) are most commonly used by beginning researchers and, as a consequence, provide enabling strategies for statistically analyzing most of the data that would be generated by them; (2) are very often used as a basis for analyzing data that are subsequently reported in journal articles (in other words, the techniques presented in this book will enable the reader to understand the procedures and interpretations presented there); and (3) will help to set the stage for understanding the more advanced procedures that are described in graduate-level statistics textbooks.

✓CHECKPOINT

Compute the answers for the items listed below for the following set of numbers: 75, 80, 73, 66, 79, 77, 76, 72, 74, and 78.

_____ **1.** The mean of the distribution

_____ **2.** The median of the distribution

_____ **3.** The mode of the distribution

_____ **4.** The standard deviation of the distribution

_____ **5.** The 40th percentile

Answers

Your answers should have been:

1. The mean of the distribution is 75.

2. The median of the distribution is 75.

3. The mode of the distribution is *nonmodal.*

4. The standard deviation is 3.87.

5. The 40 percentile is 74.

NOTE: Remember that when computing the median and a percentile, the distribution of scores should first be ordered—in this case, from high to low.

SUMMARY

In this chapter, you were introduced to those research strategies essential to designing successful surveys. Various topics that were presented include: the definition and the purpose of research; the selection of prime sources; the process of conducting interviews, questionnaires, and observations; the use of structural and exploratory (nonstructured) questions; techniques for jury validation and pilot studies; controlling for threats to internal and external validity; and, while utilizing a scenario for investigating professional preparation programs in learning disabilities, the step-by-step procedures for preparing the actual research design.

Given the fact that a study is only as good as the instrument used to collect information, a description of various categories of questions was presented, namely: standard-, corrective-, and interpretive true-false; multiple-choice; matching; master list; as well as completion, enumeration, and essay questions. The respective roles of interval scales and checklists requiring two or more responses were then offered as examples of data-gathering processes. The discussion of these various question types culminated with a presentation of sample questionnaires that incorporated many of the question formats described earlier. The chapter concluded with a discussion of various qualitative and quantitative analytical procedures.

Survey research provides a method for gathering information about present practices attainable in no other way. Therefore, acquiring a working familiarity with the essential processes for designing a successful project will make it possible for practitioners to carry out applied research activities in their schools. Although the product of survey research can be an end unto itself, more importantly, it can become a means to an end to the extent that the findings set the stage for further studies, and the enhancement of the process and the product of educational reform.

RECOMMENDED LABORATORY ASSIGNMENTS

1. Review the recommended readings.

2. Arrange to meet with fellow graduate students and colleagues in order to discuss the strategies for designing survey research.

3. If you have not prepared a survey research template for a problem statement, it is suggested that you do so at this time (either alone, or in collaboration with no more than two other people). All the elements of Phase 1 and Phase 2 should be addressed, including:

   a. Time schedule

   b. Tentative budget

   c. Statement of need (justification) for the study

   d. Integration of eight to ten related literature articles

   e. Statement of hypothesis

   f. List of basic assumptions

   g. List of possible threats to its *internal* validity, and how you would control for them

   h. Identification of factors that would need to be considered to maintain its *external* validity

   i. Evidence that contrasting designs were examined, and the basis upon which a final determination was made

   j. Definitions of important terms

    k. Template that includes responses to all pertinent subproblems, as well as to the questions related to: what, where, how, organization and analysis, and conclusions. (You should also be in a position to recommend qualitative and/or quantitative analytical procedures.)

4. Working with fellow classmates or colleagues, acquire rosters of scores that can be used to calculate measures of central tendency, standard deviation, percents of attainment, percentile ranks, and chi square. Working independently, compute answers, and then compare results. Should there be discrepancies in the findings, assist each other in determining the sources of the difficulty.

5. For a set of research objectives, prepare a table of specifications, and a sample set of two of each form of question described in the chapter—except the master list, for which you should prepare one fixed-alternative set consisting of eight to ten questions. Ask five to seven fellow students or colleagues to examine the questions against the objectives and table of specifications. Make adjustments to the questions, as recommended.

6. Conduct a sample pilot study in which ten individuals (possessing demographics similar to those of the individuals for whom the final instrument of assessment is designed) will respond to the questions in a way to provide you with data for analysis. Incorporate the principles of item analysis that were introduced in Chapter 5, Selecting Instruments of Assessment. Where applicable, request that a second evaluator administer the instrument as well in order to test for inter-rater reliability.

7. Arrange to meet with fellow graduate students, colleagues, as well as school and nonschool employees who have carried out survey research, in order to review and discuss your plans.

RECOMMENDED READINGS

Abney, F. G., & Hutcheson, J. D., Jr. (1981). Race, representation, and trust: Changes in attitudes after the election of a black mayor. *Public Opinion Quarterly, 45,* 91–101.

Alreck, P. L., & Settle, R. B. (1995). *The survey research handbook* (2nd ed.). Burr Ridge, IL: Irwin.

Anderson, L. W. (1981). *Assessing affective characteristics in the schools.* Boston: Allyn & Bacon.

Anderson, L. W. (1988). Attitudes and their measurement. In J. P. Keeves (Ed.), *Educational research, methodology, and measurement: An international handbook.* Oxford: Pergamon Press.

Angelo, T. A., & Cross, K. P. (1993). *Classroom assessment techniques: A handbook for college teachers.* San Francisco: Jossey-Bass.

Bakeman, R., & Gottman, J. M. (1986). *Observing interaction: An introduction to sequential analysis.* New York: Cambridge University Press.

Bennett, R. E., & Ward, W. C. (1993). *Construction versus choice in cognitive measurement.* Hillsdale, NJ: Lawrence Erlbaum.

Berdie, D. R., Anderson, J. F., & Niebuhr, M. A. (1986). *Questionnaires: Design and use* (2nd ed.). Metuchen, NJ: Scarecrow Press.

Bourque, L. B., & Clark, V. A. (1992). *Data processing the survey example.* Newbury Park, CA: Sage.

Bradburn, N. M., Rips, L. J., & Shevell, S. K. (1987). Answering autobiographical questions: The impact of memory and inference on surveys. *Science, 236,* 157–161.

Converse, J. M., & Presser, S. (1986). *Survey questions: Handcrafting the standardized questionnaire.* Newbury Park, CA: Sage.

Converse, J. M., & Schuman, H. (1974). *Conversations at random: Survey research as interviewers see it.* New York: Wiley.

Council of American Survey Research Organizations. (1982). *Report of the CASRO completion rates task force.* Unpublished report.

Devaus, D. A. (1986). *Surveys in social research.* Boston: Allen & Unwin.

Diez, M. E. (1997, Winter). Assessment as a lever in education reform. *National Forum, 77*(1), 27–30.

Edgar, E., Levine, P., & Maddox, M. (1988). *Statewide follow-up studies of secondary special education students in transition.* Unpublished manuscript, University of Washington, Seattle, WA.

Evertson, C. M., & Green, J. L. (1986). Observation as inquiry and method. In M. C. Wittrock (Ed.), *Handbook of research on teaching* (3rd ed.). New York: Macmillan.

Fink, A. (1995). *The survey handbook.* Thousand Oaks, CA: Sage.

Fowler, F. J. (1988). *Survey research methods* (2nd ed.). Newbury Park, CA: Sage.

Frey, J. H., & Oishi, S. M. (1995). *How to conduct interviews by telephone and in person.* Thousand Oaks, CA: Sage.

Gordon, R. (1992). *Basic interviewing skills.* Itasca, IL: Peacock.

Goswami, D., & Stillman, P. R. (Eds.). (1987). *Reclaiming the classroom: Teacher research as an agency for change.* Upper Montclair, NJ: Boynton, Cook.

Hanson, A. J. (1997, January). Writing cases for teaching: Observations of a practitioner. *Kappan, 78*(5), 398–403.

Harris, M. B. (1995). *Basic statistics for behavioral science research.* Needham Heights, MA: Allyn & Bacon.

Henerson, M. E., Morris, L. L., & Fitz-Gibbon, C. T. (1987). *How to measure attitudes.* Newbury Park, CA: Sage.

Hogelin, G. (1988). The behavioral risk factor surveys in the United States 1981–1983. In R. Anderson, J. K. Davis, I. Kickbush, D. V. McQueen, & J. Turner (Eds.), *Health behavior research and health promotion* (pp. 111–124). Oxford: Oxford University Press.

Jaeger, R. M. (1988). Survey methods in education. In R. M. Jaeger (Ed.). *Complementary methods for research in education* (pp. 303–336). Washington, DC: American Educational Research Association.

Langdon, C. A. (1996, November). The third Phi Delta Kappa poll of teachers' attitudes toward the public schools. *Kappan, 78*(3), 244–250.

Lavrakas, P. J. (1987). *Telephone survey methods: Sampling, selection, and supervision.* Newbury Park, CA: Sage.

Levine, P., & Edgar, E. (1994). Respondent agreement in follow-up studies of graduates of special and regular education programs. *Exceptional Children, 60,* 334–343.

Loftus, E. (1979). *Eyewitness testimony.* Cambridge, MA: Harvard University Press.

Magnusson, D., Bergman, L. R., Rudinger, G., & Torestad, B. (Eds.). (1991). *Problems and methods in longitudinal research: Stability and change.* New York: Cambridge University Press.

Rea, L. M., & Parker, R. A. (1992). *Designing and conducting survey research.* San Francisco: Jossey-Bass.

Reid, J. B., & DeMaster, B. (1972). The efficacy of the spot-check procedure in maintaining the reliability of data collected by observers in quasi-natural settings: Two pilot studies. *Oregon Research Bulletin, 12*(8).

Salant, P., & Dillman, D. A. (1994). *How to conduct your own survey.* New York: Wiley.

Schatz, M. A., & Best, J. B. (1987). Students' reasons for changing answers on objective tests. *Teaching of Psychology, 14,* 241–242.

Schwarz, P. N., & Sudman, S. (1996). *Answering questions: Methodology for determining cognitive and communicative processes in survey research.* San Francisco: Jossey-Bass.

Sedman, S., & Bradburn, M. M. (1982). *Asking questions: A practical guide to questionnaire design.* San Francisco: Jossey-Bass.

Sexton, D., Lobman, M., Constans, T., Snyder, P., & Ernest, J. (1997, Spring). Early interventionists' perspectives of multicultural practices with African-American families. *Exceptional Children, 63*(3), 313–328.

Sirkin, R. M. (1995). *Statistics for the social sciences.* Thousand Oaks, CA: Sage.

Thach, L. (1995). Using electronic mail to conduct survey research. *Educational Technology, 35*(2), 27–31.

Uitenbroek, D. G. (1996, December). Sports, exercise, and other causes of injuries: Results of a population survey. *Research Quarterly for Exercise and Sport, 67*(4), 380–385.

Wehmeyer, M., & Schwartz, M. (1997, Winter). Self-determination and positive adult outcomes: A follow-up study of youth with mental retardation or learning disabilities. *Exceptional Children, 63*(2), 245–255.

Witte, R. S. (1989). *Statistics* (3rd ed.). New York: Holt, Rinehart & Winston.

REFERENCES

Ary, D., Jacobs, L. C., & Razavieh, A. (1990). *Introduction to research in education* (4th ed.). Philadelphia: Holt, Rinehart & Winston.

Bogdan, R. C., & Biklen, S. K. (1982). *Qualitative research for education: An introduction to theory and methods.* Boston: Allyn & Bacon.

Corrigan, D. (1997, February). *The role of educational leaders in creating collaborative education, health, and human service systems.* Paper presented at the opening ceremony in celebration of the new Certificate of Advanced Graduate Studies, Plymouth State College, Plymouth, NH.

Crowl, T. K. (1996). *Fundamentals of educational research* (2nd ed.). Chicago: Brown & Benchmark.

Gay, L. R. (1996). *Educational research: Competencies for analysis and application* (5th ed.). Englewood Cliffs, NJ: Prentice-Hall.

Guttman, L. (1950). The basis for scaleogram analysis. In S. Stouffer et al. (Eds.), *Measurement and prediction.* Princeton, NJ: Princeton University Press.

Heberlein, T. A., & Baumgartner, R. (1981). Is a questionnaire necessary in a second mailing? *Public Opinion Quarterly, 45,* 102–108.

Leedy, P. D. (1997). *Practical research: Planning and design* (6th ed.). Columbus, OH: Merrill.

Likert, R. (1932). A technique for the measurement of attitudes. *Archives of Psychology, 52*(140).

Lunneborg, C. E. (1994). *Modeling experimental and observational data.* Belmont, CA: Wadsworth.

Thurston, L. L., & Chave, E. J. (1929). *The measurement of attitudes.* Chicago: University of Chicago Press.

Vockell, E. L., & Asher, J. W. (1995). *Educational research* (2nd ed.). Columbus, OH: Merrill.

Wiseman, D. C. (1970). *A critical evaluation of undergraduate professional preparation in physical education for men and women in selected colleges and universities of New England.* Unpublished doctoral dissertation, Indiana University, Bloomington, IN.

Worthen, B. R., & Brezezinski, E. J. (1973, February). *An experimental study of techniques for increasing return rate in mail surveys.* Paper presented at the annual meeting of the American Educational Research Association, New Orleans, LA.

CHAPTER 7

Correlation Procedures

OBJECTIVES

After reading this chapter, you should be able to:

- Describe the purposes of correlation research.
- Distinguish between a positive and a negative relationship.
- Diagram and interpret a scattergram.
- Distinguish between *no* and *total* regression from an X to a Y distribution of scores.
- Define, compute, and interpret the use of Spearman rank-order correlation (*rho*).
- Define, compute, and interpret the use of Pearson product-moment correlation (*r*).
- Compute measurement error (*ME*) and coefficient of determination (*CD*).
- Demonstrate the application of the Spearman-Brown prophecy formula to a split-half reliability coefficient.
- Define, compute, and interpret the use of a biserial correlation (*rbis*).
- Define, compute, and interpret the use of a tetrachoric correlation (*rtet*).

- Define, compute, and interpret the use of a phi coefficient (ϕ).
- Define, compute, and interpret the use of a coefficient of contingency (C).
- Define, compute, and interpret the use of a partial correlation ($r12.3 \ldots x$).
- Describe the use of a multiple correlation (R).
- Create a research design template for a correlation study on a topic of your choice.
- Define key terms, and answer the checkpoint questions.

KEY TERMS

Abscissa	*Positive Relationship*
Biserial Correlation	*Prediction Studies*
Coefficient of Contingency	*Product-Moment Correlation*
Correlation Studies	*Scatter Diagram*
Critical Values for r	*Spearman-Brown Prophecy Formula*
Dichotomized Variables	*Tetrachoric Correlation*
Linear Relationships	*Total Regression*
Multiple Correlation	*X Axis*
Negative Relationship	*Y Axis*
Ordinate	*Zero-Order Correlation*
Partial Correlation	*Zero Relationship*
Phi Coefficient	*z Score*

INTRODUCTION

In Chapter 6, Survey Procedures, techniques were described for enabling the practitioner-researcher to acquire information on whether and to what extent a variable (or variables) are distributed within a sample or population. In short, information was offered on: (1) data-gathering methods such as interviews, questionnaires, and observations; (2) preparing questions for instruments of assessment; (3) sample questionnaires; and (4) qualitative and quantitative analytical procedures. From the information gathered, it was shown how findings can be revealed, including: trends, rankings, percents of attainment, averages, and levels of significance.

Although surveys hold a distinctive place in applied research methods, they do <u>not</u> provide for assessing the extent to which two or more variables are related among a single group of subjects. It is for this reason that Chapter 7 has been written. The process of correlation provides another tool for carrying out descriptive research when the investigator is interested in examining relationships between variables, including the gathering of evidence on the: (1) concurrent and predictive validity of testing instruments; (2) equivalence, inter-rater, split-half, and stability reliability of tests; (3) statistical association between variables, such as *knowledge and attitudes about health* or *annual salary and composite scores on the National Teacher Examination;* and (4) predictability of scores from one test to another.

While data gathered at the nominal and ordinal levels are useful in school settings (and provide bases for numerous statistical treatments), interval and ratio data allow for the application of more sophisticated techniques of analysis. As a consequence, one can learn more about the variables under study. So, in addition to describing procedures for computing rank-order (*rho*) correlation (useful as a statistical process when one has ordinal data), Chapter 6 will present information on procedures known collectively as correlation-regression analysis, including: Pearson product-moment (r), biserial (r_{bis}), tetrachoric (r_{tet}), phi (ϕ), coefficient of contingency (C), partial correlation ($r_{12.3\ldots x}$), and multiple correlation (R).

Pursuant to a further examination of the purposes underlying the conduction of **correlation studies,** the reader will find strategies for their design, followed by a correlation practicum, and procedures for analyzing and interpreting data arising from the correlation process.

PURPOSE OF CORRELATION PROCEDURES

Frequently, a practitioner-researcher is interested in examining more than one variable in order to determine whether there is some degree of association between them. For example, when applying the scenario from Chapter 6 regarding professional preparation programs in the field of learning disabilities, the researcher might be interested in learning whether institutions that scored *above the average* of their group in Area 1, General Institutional and Departmental Practices, also scored *above the average* of the group in Area 3, Curriculum Policies and Practices.

A second example would be to look at the relationship between the ratings of student teachers (Figure 6–10) and their final numerical average upon completing a required upper-division course in classroom management. Still other examples would be to examine the relationship between:

- The performances of a group of sixth-grade students in language arts and social science mid-term examinations
- Self-confidence and the length of time coded, special education students have spent in mainstreamed classroom environments
- Ranks of graduating high school seniors and the annual salary for their first full year of employment
- Two identical aptitude tests administered one year apart
- High school and college grade-point averages

Finally, as indicated in Chapter 5, Selecting Instruments of Assessment, correlation procedures are also used to estimate certain varieties of test validity (concurrent, predictive) and test reliability (equivalence, inter-rater, split-half, stability).

Correlation research involves the examination of two or more sets of data for a single group of subjects. When employing a simple two-variable, correlation procedure, the arrangement of the data sets is often referred to as a bivariate distribution (Harris, 1995; Howell, 1982; Kachigan, 1986; Kiess, 1989; Leedy, 1997). It is called *bivariate* because there are scores for two variables for each subject in the study. Efforts are then made to determine if, and to what extent, a relationship exists between them. If, for example, a **positive relationship** is found between the achievement of a group of sixth graders on language arts (*LA*) and social science (*SS*) mid-term examinations, it means that those who scored above the average of their group in language arts also tended to score above the average of their group in social science. It also means that those who scored below average in the one variable also tended to score below average in the other. Depending upon the intensity of the relationship, the coefficient would be found somewhere between a 0.00 and a +/– 1.00. For a graphic display of a *positive* relationship, see Figure 7–1.

Plotting is done with reference to two lines (coordinate axes): the horizontal or **abscissa (X axis)** and the vertical or **ordinate (Y axis).** Figure 7–1 shows that John earned a score of 78 in language arts (Variable *X*) and a score of 67 in social science (Variable *Y*). When he and each of the other subjects have their scores plotted on the **scatter diagram** (also referred to as a *scattergram* or *scatter plot),* evidence of a **linear relationship** begins to emerge. (Each dot on the diagram represents a pair of scores.) From an examination of the data, one can see a positive association between language arts and social science scores. In simple language, those who scored above the average of their group in one variable also scored above the average of their group in the other variable.

In studies in which the investigator is interested in examining the relationship between variables, it is usual to label one as the *independent* variable and plot it on the horizontal (X axis). Accordingly, the second variable would be labeled the *dependent* variable and plotted on the vertical (Y axis). Since the lowest of the earned scores are placed near the intersect of the X and Y axes, and increase in magnitude

Figure 7–1: **A Graphic Representation of a Positive Relationship**

Subjects	Variables X (LA)	Y (SS)
John	78	67
Carole	77	66
Joan	79	68
Tim	75	64
Cynthia	76	65

to the most distant point of the horizontal and vertical lines, a scattergram in which plots representing pairs of scores are scattered from lower left to upper right, such as the one in Figure 7–1, would provide a display of a positive relationship. By examining the pattern of score points in the figure, a visual and conceptual picture of the direction of the relationship between the two variables is obtained. In short, the scatter diagram provides a pictorial representation of a relationship which, when subjected to appropriate statistical procedures (to be described later in the chapter), will generate a correlation coefficient.

In this illustration, it seems clear that the correlation is *perfectly linear,* that is, the student who scored highest in variable *X* (Joan) also scored highest in variable *Y;* the student who scored second highest in variable *X* (John) also scored second highest in variable *Y,* and so on, down to the student who scored lowest in variable *X* (Tim), who also scored lowest in variable *Y.* As a consequence of this finding, one can show a direct line (without regression) from variable *X* to variable *Y,* as in Figure 7–2.

 NOTE: With a perfect correlation between two variables, the prediction line from a score on one variable (*X*) would *not* regress toward the mean on the second variable (*Y*). However, with less than a perfect correlation between the two variables, the regression line would move toward the mean. (This holds true whether the correlation is positive *or* negative.) If there was *no* relationship between the variables, there would be a

Figure 7–2: **Illustration of a +1.00 Relationship (No Regression to Mean)**

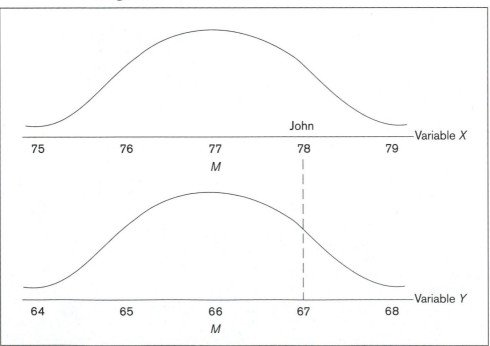

total **regression** to the actual (or predicted) mean on the second variable. In other words, if there was no correlation between the two variables (X and Y), one's best estimate of how a subject would do on the Y variable is that he would earn an average score. The closer a relationship is to 0.0, the less able one is to use the correlation coefficient as a basis for making a prediction. (More will be said about this matter later in the chapter.)

However, the fact that there may be a positive relationship between these two variables does not mean that one is the *cause* of the other. A decision to make such an assumption is based on the premise that improved achievement in language arts will *cause* score increases in social science. If that were the case, efforts could be applied to increase student achievement in language arts with the belief that grades would also increase in social science. Although knowing how to read is important to success in *all* subjects, students must read the assigned material for the course or, *regardless of how well they read,* their scores in social science cannot be expected to be very high.

Any thoughts that an individual may have about attributing cause-and-effect relationships to the results of a simple correlation procedure must be held suspect. In the preceding example, it may be that students who do well in social science do so because they are excited about the computer-assisted instruction that may have just been introduced there and, as a consequence, do better with their word processing skills, which, in turn, enhances achievement in the language arts class. There may also be variables beyond these two classes that are impacting upon student achievement. Can you think of any such examples? Some possibilities include:

1. Parents/guardians purchasing home computers
2. Absenteeism because of illness, student senate meetings, clubs, athletics, and so on
3. After-school television specials on topics being studied in some of the classes
4. Improved study habits
5. Social maturation
6. Grandparents instituting an award system for higher grades on report cards

NOTE: It has been reported that, of those individuals born in 1850 who later dined on pickles, there has been a 100% mortality rate. One might conclude that there is a relationship between pickle consumption and death. Although there may be a relationship between the two variables (death and pickle consumption), the probable cause of their deaths would likely be related to old age. After all, if the subjects were still living, they would be close to one hundred and fifty years old.

Correlation research provides the researcher with an opportunity to estimate just how much the variables are related. Expressed as a coefficient, if the two variables are highly related, the value would approach either a +1.00 or a −1.00. (One is as significant as the other; the plus (+) or minus (−) signs merely show the direction of the relationship.) As indicated earlier, if individuals who score above the average of their group in one variable also score above the average of their group in a second variable, the correlation coefficient would be somewhere between +0.01 and +1.00. On the other hand, if individuals who scored above the average of their group in one variable scored below the average of their group in the second variable, the correlation coefficient would be somewhere between –0.01 and –1.00. For a graphic display of a ***negative*** **relationship,** see Figure 7–3.

In this scenario, John earned a score of 78 in language arts (variable *X*), and a score of 65 in social science (variable *Y*). When John and each of the subjects have their scores plotted on the scatter diagram, a negative relationship begins to surface. As individuals scored above the average of their group in language arts, they scored below the average of their group in social science. A computation of a correlation coefficient, using a product-moment method, would reveal a –1.00. In this instance, we have a perfect *negative* linear relationship between the two variables. Again, one can show a direct line from variable *X* to variable *Y*. Unlike Figure 7–2, however, Figure 7–4 shows the potential for a prediction to a score below the arithmetic average of the group.

The more intense the relationship, the higher the coefficient will be (up to and including +/– 1.00). If there was *no* apparent statistical relationship between the variables, the coefficient would tend to approach 0.00. In other words, individuals who score a particular value on one variable (*X*) are likely to score anywhere along the distribution of scores on the second variable (*Y*). In short, there is no trend in the pattern of the score plots (see Figure 7–5).

To show a complete regression to the mean, which would occur in a circumstance in which there was no relationship between variable *X* and variable *Y*, the reader is referred to Figure 7–6.

As you can see, the stronger the relationship, the closer the numerical value will be to a +/–1.00, and the more accurate are the predictions one might make about that relationship. Further, when high relationships are found between variables, there is a stronger rationale for considering experimental studies in order to study causes and effects (see Part III, Experimental Research Methods).

Figure 7–3: **A Graphic Representation of a Negative Relationship**

	Variables	
Subjects	*X* (LA)	*Y* (SS)
John	78	65
Carole	77	66
Joan	79	64
Tim	75	68
Cynthia	76	67

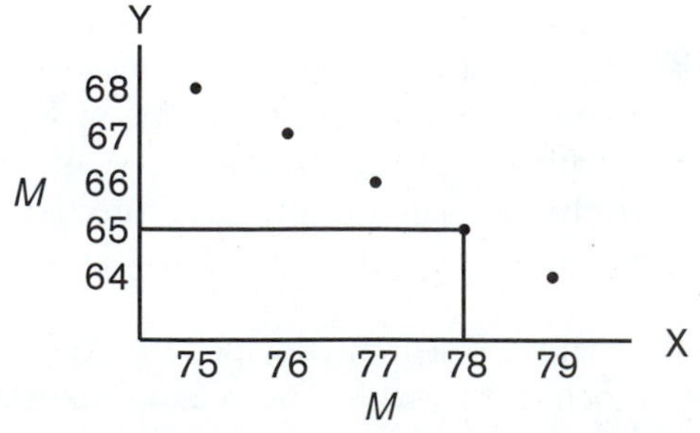

Figure 7–4: **Illustration of a –1.00 Relationship (No Regression to Mean)**

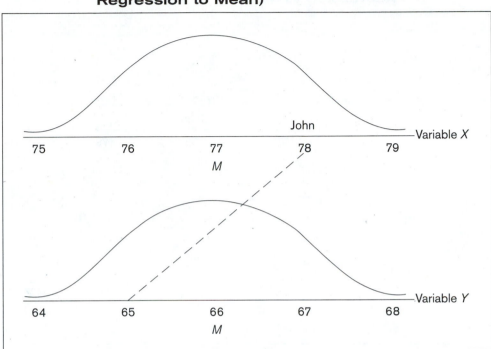

Figure 7–5: **A Graphic Representation of a Relationship Approaching 0.00**

Subjects	Variables	
	X (LA)	Y (SS)
John	78	68
Carole	77	64
Joan	79	66
Tim	75	65
Cynthia	76	67

In short, correlation studies are done in order to:

1. Determine relationships between variables

2. Use the relationships for the purpose of making predictions

3. Establish a basis for experimental investigations

Figure 7–6: **Illustration of a 0.00 Relationship (No Regression to Mean)**

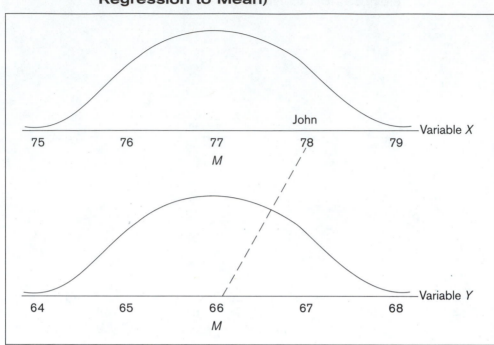

✓CHECKPOINT

The following pair of scores were earned by ten (10) students on mathematics (variable *X*) and biology (variable *Y*) examinations.

Students	Mathematics Variable *X*	Biology Variable *Y*
Alan	93	91
Cindy	96	86
John	92	88
Steven	90	80
Emily	84	82
Catherine	88	83
Tony	60	74
Becky	52	74
Trystan	83	77
Bart	92	85

The following assignments are designed to enable you to test yourself in regard to your understanding of the *construction* and *interpretation* of a scatter diagram. Good luck! Answers and discussion will follow.

1. Plot a scatter diagram representing the intersect points of variables X and Y. Place only the earned scores on the graph.

2. Compute the mean for variable X, and draw a vertical line from that value.

3. Compute the mean for variable Y, and draw a horizontal line from that value.

4. Place the Roman Numeral I in the upper right-hand quadrant, and insert a *plus* (+) sign.

5. Place the Roman Numeral II in the upper left-hand quadrant, and insert a *minus* (−) sign.

6. Place the Roman Numeral III in the lower left-hand quadrant, and insert a *plus* (+) sign.

7. Place the Roman Numeral IV in the lower right-hand quadrant, and insert a *minus* (−) sign.

8. Through the process of observation, determine whether a relationship appears to exist between the X and Y variables. If so, is the relationship *positive* or *negative?*

Answers

The findings would be plotted on a scatter diagram as follows:

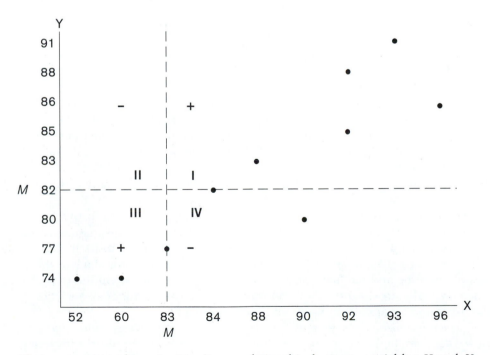

There appears to be a *positive* linear relationship between variables X and Y. By counting the tally marks in each of the four quadrants, it can be seen that there are more intersect points in quadrants I and III than in quadrants II and

IV. (If there were more tally marks in quadrants II and IV than in quadrants I and III, the relationship would be negative. If there were near equal number of tally marks in each of the four quadrants, the relationship would approach **zero,** or no correlation.) Although a coefficient can be computed directly through a scattergram, the process is considered cumbersome and inefficient. As a consequence, it is recommended that one employ the formula systems described later in this chapter.

As an alternative to studies that would require two-variable product-moment correlation procedures, practitioner-researchers may decide upon topics that require more sophisticated statistical strategies. For example, they may be interested in examining the following.

1. The relationship between two variables when one of the variables can be dichotomized, that is, divided into two parts. This procedure is known as **biserial correlation** (r_{bis}). For example, a superintendent of schools may want to know whether there is a relationship between attitudes toward inclusionary education and workshop training (that is, those who have attended training and those who have not). Simply stated, does an increase in training correlate with more favorable attitudes toward inclusionary education? Since r_{bis} is not limited to a range of 0.0 to +/–1.0, the findings do not lend themselves to comparisons with values arising out of other correlation procedures. Nonetheless, the resulting coefficient does provide evidence of a positive or negative association between the dichotomized and criterion variables.

2. The relationship between two variables when both of them can be dichotomized, that is, a **tetrachoric correlation** (r_{tet}). Tetrachoric procedures are particularly useful when one wishes to determine the relationship between two traits when scores are not readily attainable but, rather, are capable of being separated into two categories. For example, a guidance counselor might be interested in following a group of high school students who have gone on to college in order to determine whether there is a relationship between successfully completing a high school course in linguistics with a grade of C or higher, and earning a grade of B or higher in a required, first-year college composition course. The subjects could be arbitrarily dichotomized on both variables: (a) successfully completing a linguistics course with a grade of C or higher, *yes* or *no,* and (b) earning a B or higher in a required, first-year college composition class, *yes* or *no.* The use of r_{tet} assumes that the two variables are capable of generating scores that could be placed into a frequency distribution. In this example, scores (A through F) could be acquired for those enrolling in the high school linguistic and the first-year college composition courses. On the other hand, when data fall into *natural* rather than *arbitrary* categories, a different analytical procedure would be appropriate—the phi coefficient (ϕ).

3. The relationship between variables when they fall into distinct (rather than artificial) categories. In this situation, one should consider computing **phi coefficient (ϕ).** The Director of Student Affairs at a local college is interested in knowing whether there is a relationship between owning a word processor and passing the required course "Introduction to the Academic Community." For students participating in the study, the data are generated as: owning the word processor, *yes* or *no;* and passing the course, *yes* or *no.*

4. *The relationship between two variables when each can be classified into two or more categories.* This research interest could employ a correlation statistic known as the **coefficient of contingency** (*C*). For example, a classroom teacher may be interested in knowing whether there is a relationship between final course grades (A, B, C, D, or F) earned by students, and their letter grades for a prerequisite course taken a semester earlier. While the computation process is similar to that of a chi square test (discussed in Chapter 6, Survey Procedures) in that it depends upon a comparison of *expected* and *observed* frequencies, the findings do not remain constant for the same data when they are spread over a greater number of categories. For example, when *K* equals the number of categories, the *maximum* coefficient of contingency (*C*) is found by the formula:

$$\sqrt{\frac{(K-1)}{K}}$$

Maximum values according to table sizes resulting from number of categories would be as follows:

- 2 × 2 table: .707
- 3 × 3 table: .816
- 4 × 4 table: .866
- 5 × 5 table: .894
- 6 × 6 table: .912
- 7 × 7 table: .925
- 8 × 8 table: .935
- 9 × 9 table: .942
- 10 × 10 table: .948

NOTE: A 2 × 2 table has 2 rows and 2 columns; a 3 × 3 table has 3 rows and 3 columns; a 4 × 4 table has 4 rows and 4 columns; and so on.

Because of the limits imposed by maximum values, coupled with the fact that many individuals have difficulty interpreting a *C* value (Garrett, 1958), a chi square test procedure is often preferred by the researcher.

5. *The relationship between two variables while other variables are held constant.* This research interest would require the use of a **partial correlation** procedure (r*12.3* . . . *x*). The number of symbols to the right of the first decimal point indicates the number of variables that are being held constant. This and multiple-correlation processes represent an extension of liner, two-variable correlation designs. For purposes of illustration, suppose that a Director of Health and Physical Education for a school district is interested in knowing whether there is a relationship between final grades in social science (variable *X*) and health knowledge (variable *Y*), with age

(variable *Z*) held constant. Since a correlation between any two traits is likely to be positive when studying students across an age span (for example, twelve to eighteen), holding age constant will help to control for the influence that age may bring to the relationship. It is important to realize that any correlation between two variables may be misleading due to their dependence upon a third (or more) variable. For example, when studies are done with heterogeneous age groups, the correlation is likely to be positive and quite high. As students grow older, it is expected that they will acquire more general knowledge.

When one variable is held constant, it is called a *first-order* partial correlation; when two variables are held constant, it is called a *second-order* partial correlation; and so on. A simple product-moment correlation is called a **zero-order** **correlation** because there are *no* variables held constant. One advantage of a partial correlation is that it enables the practitioner-researcher to factor out the effects of unwanted variables. A second, and perhaps more striking, advantage is that its use makes it possible for one to set up a multiple-correlation (and regression) equation. From the findings generated by this approach, one is able to make more refined predictions. Procedures for computing multiple-correlation and regression analysis can be found in advanced statistics books; they are beyond the scope of coverage in this text.

6. The relationship between one variable and a combination of other variables. When a researcher is interested in this type of study, he should consider using a **multiple-correlation** process [R*1*(*23* . . . *x*)]. Multiple *R* enables the investigator to assess the relationship between one variable (*criterion*) and a group of others. The variable not included within the parentheses is the criterion to be estimated or predicted; the variables found within the parentheses are the independent variables. Unlike the bivariate Pearson's product-moment *r*, the coefficient here is *always* a positive number. A multiple-correlation process would be applicable to the following: A college advisor is interested in determining the accuracy of predicting one's graduating grade-point average (variable 1) from verbal aptitude scores upon admission into the college (variable 2) *and* one's first-year cumulative grade-point average (variable 3).

Each of the six procedures discussed in the preceding text has a specific purpose, and its selection is determined by the nature of one's study. Understanding the contributions each process can bring to one's correlation analysis is helpful in a number of ways, including:

1. Conducting one's own correlation study
2. Setting the stage for subsequent computer analysis of research data
3. Interpreting the findings generated by others
4. Evaluating the appropriateness of the analyses used by others in their own work (as reported in conference proceedings, unpublished papers, and articles)

With the exception of multiple *R,* these statistical methods for analyzing the data generated through the correlation processes will be presented later in the chapter. A requisite to that section in the chapter, however, is understanding the protocol for developing and administering a correlation study. Once the initial plans for designing the investigation are in place, and a sample practicum is reviewed in order to reinforce design strategies, the researcher will be in a position to make a decision about the appropriate statistical measure to use for his own study.

STRATEGIES FOR CONDUCTING RELATIONSHIP (CORRELATION) STUDIES

Following the techniques described in Chapter 3, Preparation of a Research Plan, the steps for designing correlation research can be clearly delineated. It is in keeping with these procedures that the following strategies are presented.

In addition to the areas of inquiry suggested earlier in the chapter, consider the following to be illustrative of other topics one might be interested in examining for which the use of correlation procedures could be employed.

1. A faculty member is interested in creating a research plan for a correlation study in one of the following areas of inquiry:

    a. Student grades on first *and* second examinations of the marking period

    b. Strength *and* age, height, and weight (combined)

    c. Stability of a social science test administered to seventh graders

    d. Association of English *and* Spanish examination scores for eleventh-grade girls whose IQs are 115 or higher

    e. Years of service *and* merit ratings of school teachers

2. An administrator is interested in creating a research plan for a correlation study in one of the following areas of inquiry:

    a. Final grades of students in social *and* natural sciences

    b. Department budget requests for the current *and* the preceding year, *without* regard to faculty/staff salaries

    c. National Teacher Examination scores *and* student achievement in mathematics classes taught by teachers with *five* or more years of experience within the district

    d. Student achievement in team-taught *and* single-instructor biology classes

    e. Student grades *and* in-season varsity athletic participation

3. A guidance counselor is interested in creating a research plan for a correlation study in one of the following areas of inquiry:

    a. Number of free hot lunches dispensed to students in the school cafeteria *and* school attendance

    b. Age at which students are admitted into first grade *and* subsequent performance on a holistically scored writing sample

    c. Frequency of cigarette smoking *and* tardiness among ninth-grade students

    d. Scores earned on the Scholastic Aptitude Test *and* attendance at SAT training sessions

    e. Association between earning a B or higher in an introductory French class *and* enrolling in elective upper-division foreign language courses

4. A member/officer of a professional organization is interested in creating a research plan for a correlation study in one of the following areas of inquiry:

    a. Age of members *and* qualities preferred in candidates for the association presidency

    b. Association between rankings of men's ice hockey teams in the last two years

    c. Association between alcoholism *and* health knowledge of fathers and sons residing in central New Hampshire

    d. Marital adjustment scores *and* education level of husbands

    e. Association fees *and* sustained membership

These topics do not lend themselves to identical correlation procedures. For reasons that probably seem quite clear, some of them would lead to more intensive analysis than would others. At the same time, however, the general strategies for designing a research template would remain constant.

    Per the guidelines of Chapter 3, Preparation of a Research Plan, the design would be arranged in two phases. Phase 1 includes a tentative time schedule (Figure 3–1) and a budget (Figure 3–2). Although specific entries in each of these may require revision as the research unfolds, it is still necessary to establish a frame of reference from which the researcher will create his plans.

    Without repeating all the documentation of Phase 1 as it relates to designing a *survey* (see Chapter 6), pertinent steps and entries for conducting a *correlation study* will be provided by employing a scenario for the question: Is there an association between participation in training sessions *and* teacher attitudes toward inclusionary education?

Statement of the Problem

    An example of a statement of the problem would be:

> The purpose of this investigation is to examine the relationship between teacher attitudes toward inclusionary education and attendance at a workshop training session offered by School Administrative Unit #48.

Statement of the Need (Justification) for the Study

Why is it important that this study be done? Would knowing the association of the variables in question be of any consequence to the practitioner/researcher or others? Can the findings be useful in arriving at topics for future in-service training sessions? To the degree that "need" can be established by the facts reported in related studies, the previous experience of you and others within the school or district, or both, the credibility for conducting this particular investigation would be advanced.

Review of the Literature

As indicated in several preceding chapters, this is an extremely important element of one's research plan. A review of the literature makes it possible for the practitioner-researcher to discover what has been reported by others. Not only will the reader learn of the findings, a review of the analysis portion of the unpublished paper or article will offer clues to the various ways data have been treated. One can acquire useful ideas in this regard. (See Chapter 1, Selection and Definition of a Problem, Chapter 3, Preparation of a Research Plan, and Chapter 6, Survey Procedures, for other information pertinent to conducting literature reviews.)

Statement of the Hypothesis

Since a correlation study is considered descriptive, one would use a *research* hypothesis.

 NOTE: A correlation study falls within the rubric of descriptive research because one is not introducing a treatment in order to test its effect upon a dependent variable; rather, one is conducting the study in order to assess the association of the variables *as they are,* without making efforts to manipulate them.

Considering the scenario on studying the association between attitudes toward inclusionary education and attendance at training sessions, the hypothesis can be stated:

> Assuming a valid data-gathering process, it is hypothesized that a correlation study on teacher attitudes toward inclusionary education and attendance at a training session, offered by School Administrative Unit #48 during the Spring Semester, 1998, will cause their association to be revealed.

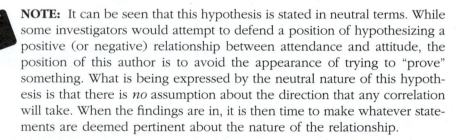 **NOTE:** It can be seen that this hypothesis is stated in neutral terms. While some investigators would attempt to defend a position of hypothesizing a positive (or negative) relationship between attendance and attitude, the position of this author is to avoid the appearance of trying to "prove" something. What is being expressed by the neutral nature of this hypothesis is that there is *no* assumption about the direction that any correlation will take. When the findings are in, it is then time to make whatever statements are deemed pertinent about the nature of the relationship.

Basic Assumptions

This is the section of Phase 1 where the researcher addresses the suppositions that set forth whether the study can proceed. Among the assumptions to take into consideration for the scenario under discussion are the following:

1. The researcher has the ability to conduct the study in the time allotted.
2. The researcher has the resources to carry out the study, per design.
3. The researcher will obtain permission to conduct the study.
4. The researcher will employ valid, reliable, and objective instruments to gather the data.
5. The teachers who are attending the workshop will complete the attitude test.

6. The teachers who are *not* attending the workshop will complete the attitude test.

7. The data generated by the study will be analyzed using appropriate statistical procedures.

8. The study will generate information that is useful to the planning of in-service training workshops for teachers in the future.

Possible Threats to the Study

Since it is planned for those who *are* and *are not* attending the workshop to complete the test on attitudes toward inclusionary education on the same day (at a time to be designated immediately following the training workshop), the same threats to internal and external validity that were considered for survey research (see Chapter 6) would be applicable to this study. As previously stated, sincere attention to their control would be emphasized. These threats are:

1. *Internal validity*

- *Instrumentation.* Efforts will be made to control for instrumentation by conducting jury and field-testing procedures.
- *Instability.* Efforts will be made to control for instability by anticipating all possible "chance" contingencies and preparing plans for dealing with them.
- *Expectancy.* Efforts will be made to control for expectancy by administering the assessment instrument to all teachers without appearance of bias. Teachers will be scheduled to appear for the test at the same time. The proctors of the test will not know who has and who has not attended the training workshop.
- *Interaction.* Efforts will be made to control for interaction by providing for controls for the other threats. As indicated in Chapter 6, if controls are in place for instrumentation and expectancy, the threat of interaction is nonexistent (regardless of issues of instability that may surface). For the threat of interaction to be present, there must be two or more threats operating within the study.

2. *External validity*

- *Person(s).* Efforts will be made to control for the threat of person(s) by describing in the report all pertinent *group* characteristics of those who participated in the investigation.
- *Place.* Efforts will be made to control for the threat of place by making it clear in the report that, whatever the findings, they relate only to the training and other pertinent circumstances within School Administrative Unit #48.
- *Time(s).* Efforts will be made to control for the threat of time(s) by making it clear in the report that the findings represent the association between attitudes and training only at a particular point of time in history.

Design Alternatives

Given the interest of the researcher in examining the *relationship* between attendance at a training workshop and attitudes toward inclusionary education, it has been determined that *correlation* research would be the procedure of choice. Neither the case study, experimental, historical, philosophical, survey, nor test and measurement designs would be appropriate for the purposes of this study. Further, when consideration is given to the fact that one of the variables, training, can be dichotomized into attendance and nonattendance, it becomes clear that the specific correlation procedure should be biserial *r*. In other words, a relationship between two variables is being studied (attitudes and training), and one of the variables (training) can be subclassified into two categories.

Definitions of Terms

It is very important that essential terms be defined early in the design process. As with any research, a formal definition of terms enables the researcher, the subjects, and readers of the report to remain focused on what is meant by the terms that are being used. With regard to the correlation study on training and attitudes toward inclusionary education, it has been determined that there are at least ten terms that should be defined:

Association	Inclusionary education
Attendance	Relationship
Attitude test	School Administrative Unit #48
Biserial *r*	Teachers
Correlation research	Training session

A CORRELATION PRACTICUM

In accordance with the principles of design development (see Chapter 3, Preparation of a Research Plan), this section presents a sequence of pertinent questions for each of the four subproblems common to any investigation, namely: permission/selection of subjects; selection of the instrument; administration of the study/collection of data; and analysis of data/conclusions/recommendations. While some of the questions identified for attention would not apply to all correlation investigations, their general relevance is clear, and they should guide any researcher who is interested in designing studies dealing with relationships.

For each of the questions regarding the four subproblems, the investigator would prepare responses to each of the following:

- Where the answers will be found
- How the answers will be found
- Procedures for organizing and analyzing the information for further use
- Conclusions that would follow from the procedures and allow the researcher to proceed to the next subproblem

Subproblem 1: Permission/Selection of Subjects

1. Do I have permission to conduct the study?
2. What is the date and time that the training workshop is being scheduled?
3. What is the format of the workshop?
4. What teachers will be eligible to attend?

5. What teachers are planning to attend and would be available to take the test on attitudes toward inclusionary education?

6. What arrangements will be made for teachers who did *not* attend the workshop to take the test on attitudes toward inclusionary education?

7. What are the timelines for conducting the study?

Subproblem 2: Selection of the Instrument

1. What are the specific research objectives for the correlation study?

2. What is the configuration of the table of specifications for the attitude test?

3. Is there a validated and field-tested instrument that exists to measure attitudes toward inclusionary education?

4. What five to seven professionals would be willing to serve on a jury to validate the whole instrument, its parts, or new questions created by the investigator?

5. What are the administrative directions and the timetable for completing the search for estimates of content validity?

6. Can the instrument of assessment claim that it has estimates of content validity?

7. Which individuals, who meet all pertinent selection criteria, would be willing to serve as subjects for a pilot study to determine estimates of the instrument's internal consistency (reliability)?

8. What statistical treatment would be appropriate for determining estimates of reliability?

9. What is the timetable for completing the pilot study?

10. Can the instrument of assessment claim that it has obtained estimates of internal consistency (reliability)?

11. Will the instrument of assessment be available and in necessary quantities?

Subproblem 3: Administration of Study/Collection of Data

1. Will the study be carried out in a manner appropriate to its design, including control for threats to *internal* validity:

  a. Instrumentation
  b. Instability
  c. Expectancy
  d. Interaction

2. Will the arrangements made for administering the attitude test make it possible to procure the information needed to complete the study successfully?

3. Will tests be distributed and collected per design of the study:

  a. to those who attended the training workshop?
  b. to those who did *not* attend the training workshop?

4. Will the tests be scored objectively?

5. Will the data be arranged in an order appropriate for analysis?

Subproblem 4: Analysis of Data/Conclusions/Recommendations

1. What are the attitude scores of the teachers:

  a. for those who attended the training workshop?
  b. for those who did *not* attend the training workshop?

2. What is the appropriate correlation procedure for addressing the relationship between the variables in the study? (See the section on design alternatives under the heading "Strategies for Conducting Relationship (Correlation) Studies" in the preceding text of this chapter.)

3. What is the *rbis* for the variables?

4. What observations can be made from the findings of the correlation analysis?

5. Will the recommendations, appropriate to the findings and conclusions, be stated correctly in keeping with control for threats to *external* validity:

  a. Person(s)

  b. Place

  c. Time(s)

ANALYZING DATA

Until this point, the discussion in this chapter has focused on the purposes of correlation procedures, strategies for their design, and the presentation of a correlation practicum, at which time procedural questions related to carrying out a specific study on the relationship between training and attitudes were identified. The foundation is now in place for the creation of a template for any relationship study you may have in mind to do (see Chapter 3, Preparation of a Research Plan). At the same time, however, more needs to be said about the employment of specific statistical procedures—procedures that are dependent upon the nature of the variables being examined. Beginning with a statistical analysis appropriate to a *biserial* correlation (*rbis*), examples are then presented for other correlation methods introduced within this chapter.

Biserial Correlation (*rbis*)

Given the nature of the study on the relationship between workshop training and attitudes on inclusionary education, a decision has been made to analyze the data through the process of biserial *r*. By carefully following the steps of the illustration of the correlation process for analyzing a set of representative data, you will understand how to apply the techniques to information generated by a study you might devise that requires similar statistical analyses.

Table 7–1 illustrates the computation of *rbis*. Column (A) shows a list of scores for those teachers who attended the training workshop (*fp*), and column (B) shows a list of scores for those teachers who did *not* attend the workshop (*fq*). Using the values in these columns, the computation of biserial *r* is described in the following steps.

Step 1: Compute the mean (*Mp*) of the scores earned by the trained group.

$$Mp = \frac{\Sigma X}{N} = \frac{2142}{27} = 79.333$$

Step 2: Compute the mean (*Mq*) of the scores earned by the untrained group.

$$Mq = \frac{\Sigma X}{N} = \frac{1662}{23} = 72.260$$

Table 7–1: **Display of Raw Data for Trained and Untrained Teachers**

Teachers	Columns (A) *fp*	(B) *fq*	Teachers	Columns (A) *fp*	(B) *fq*
A.B.	91		O.L.		75
B.D.	89		B.J.		74
D.E.		89	D.K.		74
C.E.	88		L.D.		74
E.G.	88		T.N.	74	
A.E.	87		J.A.		72
G.T.	87		N.C.		70
M.M.	87		P.B.		70
D.E.		86	U.L.	70	
E.B.		86	V.G.	70	
H.O.	86		R.E.		69
I.Q.	86		W.P.	69	
J.C.	85		T.D.		68
K.P.	84		V.G.		68
L.B.	83		I.Y.	68	
M.J.	82		B.Z.	67	
N.E.	81		Y.F.		67
O.F.	81		K.I.		66
P.D.	80		M.H.		66
F.O.		78	B.A.	66	
Q.H.	78		O.J.		66
G.I.		77	Q.T.		65
R.K.	76		S.L.		65
S.M.	75		B.B.	64	
B.H.		75	U.K.		62

Step 3: Compute the standard deviation (σt) of all the scores.

$$\sigma t = \sqrt{\frac{\Sigma X^2}{N} - M^2}$$

$$= \sqrt{\frac{292940}{50} - 5788.166}$$

$$= \sqrt{5858.8 - 5788.166}$$

$$= \sqrt{70.634}$$

$$= 8.404$$

NOTE: If you do not remember how one determines the values of ΣX or ΣX^2, review Chapter 5, Selecting Instruments of Assessment.

Step 4: Determine the proportion (p) of those teachers who were trained.

$$p = \frac{Np}{Nt} = \frac{27}{50} = .54$$

Step 5: Determine the proportion (q) of those teachers who were untrained.

$$q = \frac{Nq}{Nt} = \frac{23}{50} = .46$$

Step 6: Determine the height of the ordinate (u) of the normal curve at the point that separates those who were trained from those who were untrained (that is, 4.0% below the mean) (see Figure 7–7). Assuming those who are trained (p) represent 54% of the teachers, and given the fact that 50% represents the midpoint of any normally distributed set of scores (that is, 54% – 50% = 4%), one would now examine Table 7–2 in order to find the point representing the height of the normal curve ordinate (u) dividing the two parts, p and q—that is, 4%. It can be seen from the table that the ordinate (u) value for 4% (.04) is equal to .397.

Figure 7–7: **Distribution of Percent of Trained and Untrained Teachers with Relation to a Normal Distribution**

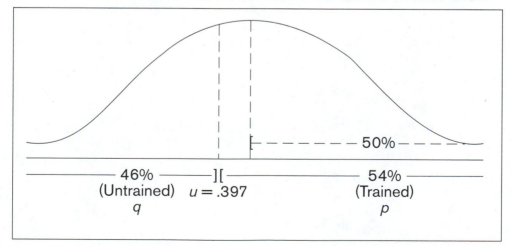

Table 7–2: **Ordinates (u) for Given Distances Measured from the Mean of a Normal Distribution**

Area from the Mean	Ordinates (u)	Area from the Mean	Ordinates (u)
.00	.399	.26	.311
.01	.399	.27	.304
.02	.398	.28	.296
.03	.398	.29	.288
.04	.397	.30	.280
.05	.396	.31	.271
.06	.394	.32	.262
.07	.393	.33	.253
.08	.391	.34	.243
.09	.389	.35	.233
.10	.386	.36	.223
.11	.384	.37	.212
.12	.381	.38	.200
.13	.378	.39	.188
.14	.374	.40	.176
.15	.370	.41	.162
.16	.366	.42	.149
.17	.362	.43	.134
.18	.358	.44	.119
.19	.353	.45	.103
.20	.348	.46	.086
.21	.342	.47	.068
.22	.337	.48	.048
.23	.331	.49	.027
.24	.324	.50	.000
.25	.318		

Step 7: Having computed Mp, Mq, σt, p, and q, one can now find the biserial r coefficient by substituting in the formula, as follows:

$$rbis = \frac{Mp - Mq}{\sigma} \times \frac{pq}{u}$$

$$= \frac{79.333 - 72.260}{8.404} \times \frac{(.54)(.46)}{.397}$$

$$= \frac{7.073}{8.404} \times \frac{.248}{.397}$$

$$= .841 \times .624$$

$$= .524$$

Step 8: Interpret the result:

> Within the limitations of this investigation, it appears that a positive relationship exists between attending a training workshop and higher earned scores on a test to measure attitudes toward inclusionary education.

An *alternate* formula for computing biserial *r* can be used when one has computed the mean of the total group of scores. In some respects, one may find the process to be less cumbersome and more efficient. Given a mean for the total group of scores to be *Mt* = 76.080, *rbis* would be calculated with this alternative technique as follows:

$$rbis = \frac{Mp - Mt}{\sigma} \times \frac{p}{u}$$

$$= \frac{79.333 - 76.080}{8.404} \times \frac{.54}{.397}$$

$$= \frac{3.253}{8.404} \times 1.360$$

$$= .387 \times 1.360$$

$$= .526$$

It can be seen that this finding confirms the previous finding within a value of .002.

Since *rbis* is not limited to a range of 0.00 to +/−1.00, it is considered to be inappropriate to make comparisons with coefficients arising through other correlation procedures. However, when:

1. *N* is large,

2. the proportions (*p* and *q*) are not too much in variance with one another, and

3. it can be assumed that the trait that has been dichotomized would be continuous were additional information available (for example, *degrees* of training received by those attending workshops),

then a biserial *r* is a good estimate of product-moment *r*.

 NOTE: The *rbis* coefficient does *not* have a standard error of estimate, so the only prediction (estimate) the researcher might want to make about a teacher's performance would be that he would score at the mean value of the category for which the prediction is being made (for example, trained or untrained). In other words, if a teacher wanted to anticipate what his score would be if he were trained, the researcher's best estimate of that answer would be 79.333. Conversely, if the researcher wanted to predict what the attitude score would be for an untrained teacher, the predicted value would be 72.260.

The chapter will now present alternative analytical procedures that are appropriate for use with other correlation studies in which relationships are being examined. To make the illustrations meaningful, examples are drawn from the various correlation topics introduced earlier in this chapter. Before moving on to these processes, review the correlation modalities that have been discussed to date.

✓ CHECKPOINT

See if you can assign names to each of the following correlation methodologies. Each of them was discussed earlier in the chapter. Correct answers will be provided upon conclusion of the exercise.

1. A correlation procedure that can be used with ordinal, interval, *and* ratio data. It is based upon the principle that, while each pair of scores are capable of being ordered, there is no requirement that there be an equal value distance between them.

2. A linear, *zero-order* correlation procedure that examines the degree of relationship between *two* variables.

3. A procedure that examines the relationship between *two* variables when *each* of them can be *dichotomized*.

4. A procedure that provides for the examination of the relationship between variables when they fall into *distinct* (rather than *artificial*) categories.

5. A process that allows for an examination of the relationship between *two* variables when *each* of them can be subdivided into *two or more* categories.

6. A process for examining the relationship between *two* variables when *other* variables are held *constant*.

7. A study of the relationship between *one* variable and a *combination* of others.

Answers

The correct answers for the above items are as follows:

1. Rank order (*rho*)
2. Product-moment (*r*)
3. Tetrachoric *r* (*rtet*)
4. Phi coefficient (φ)
5. Coefficient of contingency (*C*)
6. Partial *r* (r*12.3* . . . *x*)
7. Multiple *r* (*R*)

If you had problems with the identification of any of these items, it is recommended that you return to pertinent sections of the chapter for a more extensive review of these various correlation procedures.

With a knowledge of the various correlation models, now you are ready to examine some of the more common statistical procedures that can be applied to their analysis.

Spearman Rank Order (*rho*)

Spearman[*] rank order (*rho*) is used when one wants to examine the relationship of a pair of data without regard for the gaps between adjacent scores in each of the distributions. For example, a practitioner-researcher may want to rank individuals or groups in order of aesthetic quality, general athletic ability, social adjustment, or some other factor that does not lend itself to direct measurement. Pieces of art may be judged and ranked against a criterion, as can athleticism and adjustment, but it would be very difficult, if not impossible, to assign numerical scores to them (for example, 70, 71, or 72; 84, 85, or 86; 95, 96, or 97; and so on) as one can do when evaluating the performance of an individual on some achievement test. As a consequence, the correlation process becomes one of examining the association of ranks without regard to the interval of distance between the values within each of the distributions. Rank-order correlation analyses reveal the relationship *between* the ranks of the two distributions, not the relationship *within* the ranks of a distribution.

To demonstrate the use of *rho,* assume that the researcher is interested in examining the relationship between the ranks of twenty-five state high school men's ice hockey teams at the conclusion of the 1996–1997 (variable *X)* and 1997–1998 (variable *Y)* seasons. Table 7–3 provides the hypothetical data upon which the *rho* analysis will be made.

NOTE: (1) Although it is not necessary to arrange the schools in order for variable *X,* that has been done for the data in Table 7–3.

(2) The ranks are assigned in accordance with how institutions compare to others. For example, Salem would have been ranked 25th even if it had not won any games.

(3) For a review of procedures for dealing with situations in which there are identical scores (for example, won-lost-tie records), refer to the discussion pertaining to Table 6–3 in Chapter 6.

Utilizing the formula:

$$rho = 1 - \frac{6(\Sigma D^2)}{N(N^2 - 1)}$$

---

[*]Charles Spearman is credited with the development of the rank-order correlation technique.

Table 7–3: **Data for Computing Rank-Order Correlation Analysis**

Institutions	Variable *X*				Variable *Y*				D	D²
	Won	Lost	Tied	Rank	Won	Lost	Tied	Rank		
Berlin	22	0	0	1	20	2	0	1	0	0
Nashua	21	0	1	2	19	1	2	2	0	0
Plymouth	21	1	0	3	18	2	2	3	0	0
Concord	20	0	2	4	17	4	1	4	0	0
Meredith	20	1	1	5	16	5	1	5	0	0
Manchester	20	2	0	6	14	8	0	8	2	4
Ashland	19	0	3	7	13	9	0	9	2	4
Haverhill	19	1	2	8	10	12	0	12	4	16
Derry	19	2	1	9	9	13	0	13	4	16
Penacook	19	3	0	10	8	13	1	14	4	16
Hudson	17	3	2	11	15	6	1	6	5	25
Laconia	17	4	1	12	12	10	0	10	2	4
Bristol	17	5	0	13	6	16	0	16	3	9
Littleton	14	7	1	14	15	7	0	7	7	49
Amherst	14	8	0	15	5	15	2	17	2	4
Bow	12	9	1	16	11	11	0	11	5	25
Conway	12	10	0	17	7	14	1	15	2	4
Campton	10	11	1	18	5	16	1	18	0	0
Exeter	10	12	0	19	5	17	0	19	0	0
Gilford	9	12	1	20	4	17	1	20	0	0
Enfield	8	13	1	21	4	18	0	21	0	0
Kingston	8	14	0	22	3	16	3	22	0	0
Lisbon	7	13	2	23	3	17	2	23	0	0
Milford	7	15	0	24	3	18	1	24	0	0
Salem	6	14	2	25	3	19	0	25	0	0

where D^2 represents the squared differences between the ranks, and N represents the number of institutions that have been assigned ranks, the computations would proceed as follows:

$$rho = 1 - \frac{6(176)}{25(624)}$$

$$= 1 - \frac{1056}{15600}$$

$$= 1 - .067$$

$$= +.933$$

Findings: There appears to be a high positive relationship between the ranks of variable X and variable Y. Men's ice hockey teams that ranked well at the conclusion of the 1996–1997 season also tended to rank well at the conclusion of the 1997–1998 season. Likewise, those who ranked low at the conclusion of the 1996–1997 season also tended to rank low at the conclusion of the 1997–1998 season.

REMINDERS: (1) Rank-order correlation studies provide for a coefficient that falls between 0.00 and +/–1.00. Irrespective of the sign, the findings are shown as:

High correlation: 0.70–1.00
Medium correlation: 0.30–0.69
Low correlation: 0.00–0.29

(2) A *negative* correlation is as significant as a *positive* correlation. The sign merely shows the *direction* of the relationship.

(3) The *rho* statistic can be used with ordinal, interval, *and* ratio data.

Pearson Product-Moment Correlation (*r*)

Pearson[**] product-moment correlation (r) is used when the practitioner-researcher is interested in examining the relationship of two variables, the data of which have been described as interval or ratio. This procedure is particularly useful when assessing such things as:

1. Concurrent or predictive validity

2. Alternate form (equivalence), inter-rater, internal consistency (split-half), and test-retest (stability) reliability

3. Relationships between performances on a test measuring one variable (for example, history) and a test measuring another variable (for example, biology)

4. The error of measurement for a test or test score

5. Predictability of a student's score from one test to another

6. The coefficient of determination (common variance) for the related pairs of scores

Remember, however, that relationship studies of the type described require that the instruments of assessments yielding a pair of scores must have been administered to the same group of individuals. One cannot study the statistical relationship of achievement scores generated by two different groups of individuals with traditional correlation procedures. Interests in that regard would be left to other statistical measures.

For purposes of illustration, assume that a teacher is interested in determining the reliability of a test that has been given but once to a group of students. One approach

---

[**]Karl Pearson (1857–1936) is credited with the development of the **product-moment correlation** technique.

he might take is to employ Cronbach alpha or Kuder-Richardson (KR20 or 21) techniques described in Chapter 5, Selecting Instruments of Assessment. Another technique would be to use the Pearson product-moment correlation method described here.

A one-hundred-point social science examination has been administered to a group of tenth-grade students. The instructor records the scores for the first one-half of the test (variable X), and then records them for the second one-half of the test (variable Y). From the two columns of data, he proceeds to calculate the coefficient (see Table 7–4).

 NOTE: Given the fact that the processes for calculating the mean and standard deviation have been presented previously, these values will be provided for you. Should you desire a reminder, review Chapter 5, Selecting Instruments of Assessment.

Using the formula:

$$r = \frac{\dfrac{\Sigma XY}{N} - [Mx \times My]}{\sigma x \times \sigma y}$$

where ΣXY is found by summing the scores in the XY column, N represents the total number of individuals in the study, Mx is the arithmetic average of the X distribution, My is the arithmetic average of the Y distribution, σx is the standard deviation of the X distribution, and σy is the standard deviation of the Y distribution, the computation would proceed as follows:

$$r = \frac{\dfrac{17161}{10} - [42.1 \times 40.0]}{4.70 \times 7.62}$$

$$= \frac{1716.1 - 1684}{35.814}$$

$$= \frac{32.1}{35.814}$$

$$= +\ .896$$

The correlation coefficient representing the relationship of variable X and variable Y represents the finding for two halves of a test only. You may recall from Chapter 5, when a correlation coefficient is calculated on the basis of one-half of a test against another, one must use the **Spearman-Brown prophecy formula** in order to estimate the reliability of the entire test.

 NOTE: Since greater numbers of test questions lead to higher reliability, one-half of a test correlated against the other one-half of that same test

Table 7–4: **Data for Computing Internal Consistency Reliability**

Students	Variable X	Variable Y	XY
A.D.	50	48	2400
D.A.	48	48	2304
C.E.	46	47	2162
P.Z.	44	42	1848
L.K.	43	43	1849
M.D.	41	43	1763
O.P.	39	35	1365
D.W.	38	36	1368
N.Q.	37	36	1332
T.H.	35	22	770
	$M = 42.1$	$M = 40.0$	$\Sigma XY = 17161$
	$\sigma = 4.70$	$\sigma = 7.62$	

would generate a very conservative reliability coefficient; hence, the need to use the prophecy formula.

Using the formula,

$$r_p = \frac{2r}{1 + r}$$

where r_p represents the prophesied reliability for a complete test, and r represents the correlation coefficient of variables X and Y (the two halves of the test), the computation would proceed as follows:

$$r_p = \frac{2(.896)}{1 + .896}$$

$$= \frac{1.792}{1.896}$$

$$= + .945$$

Findings: There is evidence of a high degree of internal consistency (reliability) for this test.

NOTE: A coefficient should be at least .80 in order for estimates of reliability to be satisfied.

From the finding of estimates of reliability, one can then employ other measures, such as the following.

Significance. Is the rp = .945 significant? For this determination, refer to Appendix D, **Critical Values for r.** For *df* (*N* − 2) = 8, significance is:

loc	Significant (Yes or No)
.05	Yes
.01	Yes
.001	Yes

$p < .001$

NOTE: For *df* = 8 (Appendix D), one needs to equal or exceed:

.6319 at the .05 *loc*
.7646 at the .01 *loc*
.8721 at the .001 *loc*

Findings: It appears that significance (*p*) is evident at a point less than the .001 level of confidence. In other words, the researcher would be wrong *less* than one time in one thousand in saying that there was a finding of significance. There appears to be little question that the social science examination has internal consistency.

Measurement Error. What is the measurement error (*ME*) for a value of .945? In other words, what is the estimate of accuracy for any given test score within the two halves of the examination? Is it likely that, if students took the same test again under similar conditions, they would earn the same score?

Using the formula:

$$ME = \sigma \sqrt{1 - r}$$

where σ represents a standard deviation, and r = rp (the reliability of the test), the computations for the measurement error for each one-half of the test would proceed as follows:

Using the standard deviation for the *first* one-half of the test:

$$ME = 4.70\sqrt{1 - .945}$$

$$= 4.70\sqrt{.055}$$

$$= 4.70 \times .234$$

$$= 1.099$$

Using the standard deviation for the *second* one-half of the test:

$$ME = 7.62\sqrt{1 - .945}$$

$$= 7.62\sqrt{.055}$$

$$= 7.62 \times .234$$

$$= 1.780$$

Findings: For the *first* one-half of the test, the measurement error is 1.099. This means that the accuracy of each score in the first one-half of the test is equal to X +/– 1.099. If a student earned a score of 41, his actual score could be anywhere between 39.901 and 42.099. For the *second* one-half of the test, the measurement error is 1.780. This means that the accuracy of each score in the second one-half of the test is equal to X +/– 1.780. If a student earned a score of 43, his actual score could be anywhere between 41.220 and 44.780.

It can be seen that the error of measurement is less in the first one-half of the test. This implies that the earned score is more likely to be an accurate indication of what the students know than is the case with the second one-half of the test. Further, note that the smaller the variability of the test scores (standard deviation) within a distribution, the greater the accuracy in predicting what a true score will be. In other words, there is a smaller margin of error because the *error band* is smaller. If there was a *perfect* positive correlation, there would not be any measurement error (regardless of the size of the standard deviation). This can be shown by:

$$ME = 10\sqrt{1 - 1.00}$$

$$= 10\sqrt{0}$$

$$= 10 \times 0$$

$$= 0$$

On the other hand, if there was *no* reliability for a given test, the measurement error would be as large as the standard deviation. This can be shown by:

$$ME = 10\sqrt{1 - 0.00}$$

$$= 10\sqrt{1.00}$$

$$= 10 \times 1.00$$

$$= 10$$

Prediction. How well can one predict from one test to another? If a researcher knows the relationship of two variables (as revealed on a pilot test), he can use the results of one test (variable X) to estimate how well one is likely to do on a second test (variable Y). This represents one form of a **prediction study,** in which one makes a prediction to a second test and, when that second test has been taken, determines how accurate the prediction turned out to be. The procedures for arriving at a predicted value include the following:

1. Compute the **z score** for the raw score *from which* you want to make the prediction. Using the formula:

$$z \text{ score} = \frac{x - m}{\sigma}$$

where *x* represents the raw score, *m* represents the mean of the distribution, and σ represents the standard deviation of the distribution, the *z* score is computed as:

$$z \text{ score} = \frac{41 - 42.1}{4.70} = \frac{-1.1}{4.70} = -.234$$

2. To determine the *predicted z score (Zp)*, multiply the correlation coefficient by the student's *z* score on the first test (*r* = *rp* = .945):

$$Zp = .945 \times -.234 = -.221$$

This finding indicates that the best estimate data predicts that the student who earned a −.234 *z* score on the first test would earn a −.221 *z* score on the second test. Because there is *less* than a perfect relationship between the two tests, the student's score would regress toward the mean—that is, the mean of a *z* score distribution = 0.00.

 NOTE: Since *z* scores include both positive and negative numbers, they may not be easily understood by a reader of your report. Consider for a moment a situation in which you indicate that a predicted test score for a student would be −.221. Few people, other than those who work with such numbers, would know what that means. As a consequence, it is often useful to convert a *z* score to another standard value—a value for which many individuals have a frame of reference. For converting *z* scores to other standard scores, refer to Appendix G, Standard Score Conversion Table.

Coefficient of Determination. What is the coefficient of determination (common variance)? Although the finding of a statistical correlation does not, in its own right, provide for the researcher to state cause-and-effect relationships between the two variables (*X* and *Y*), it is possible to estimate the percentage of the variance for variable *Y* that is *associated* with the variance of variable *X*. In the instance of a reliability coefficient of .945, the coefficient of determination (*CD*) is found by squaring that value:

$$CD = .945(.945) = .893 = 89.3\%$$

Findings: The coefficient of determination (*CD*) estimates that slightly more than eighty-nine percent of the variability of variable *Y* is accounted for by the variability of variable *X*. Approximately eleven percent of what is operating in variable *X* can be attributed to factors *external* to the parameters of this study.

Tetrachoric Correlation (rtet)

Tetrachoric correlation (*rtet*) is used when one is interested in determining an estimate of the relationship between two variables when both of them can be dichotomized. Its use can be illustrated with the example offered earlier of a guidance counselor seeking to determine whether there is a relationship between successfully completing a high school course in linguistics with a grade of C or higher *and* earning a grade of B or higher in a required first-year college composition course (see Table 7–5).

For a simple approximation of *rtet,* divide the product of [(A)(D)] by the product of [(B)(C)] and refer the finding to Table 7–6. Substitute the values from Table 7–5 as follows:

$$\frac{AD}{BC} = \frac{400}{100} = 4.0$$

By applying the 4.0 to Table 7–6 (Davidoff & Goheen, 1953), the estimated *rtet* value becomes .50.

Findings: There is a positive relationship between successfully completing a high school linguistics class with a grade of C or higher *and* completing a first-year, college composition class with a grade of B or higher.

While the utilization of the full equation for computing tetrachoric correlation is complex, the process described is considered an appropriate alternative for most circumstances. One final note: If the product of *BC* is *larger* than the product of *AD,* determine the ratio of *BC/AD,* and add a minus (–) sign.

Phi Coefficient (ϕ)

Phi coefficient (ϕ) is used when data are capable of being subdivided into *discrete* categories, and do *not* represent normal distributions. When the variables in these categories are considered independent, ϕ, as an alternative to r*bis* (in which data can be considered continuous), is considered to be a more appropriate statistic. Since the findings are considered equivalent to those of a product-moment correlation procedure, the coefficient can be checked for significance against the same table

Table 7–5: **Data for Computing Tetrachroric Correlation**

| | | Variable X High School Grade of C or Higher | | |
		No	Yes	Totals
	Yes	10 (B)	20 (A)	30 A & B
Variable Y				
College Grade of B or Higher	No	20 (D)	10 (C)	30 C & D
	Totals:	30 B & D	30 A & C	60

Table 7–6: **Estimated Values of Tetrachoric *r* (rtet)**
Corresponding to the Ratio *AD/BC*

AD/BC	rtet	AD/BC	rtet	AD/BC	rtet
0–1.00	.00	2.42–2.48	.34	7.76–8.11	.68
1.01–1.03	.01	2.49–2.55	.35	8.12–8.49	.69
1.04–1.06	.02	2.56–2.63	.36	8.50–8.90	.70
1.07–1.08	.03	2.64–2.71	.37	8.91–9.35	.71
1.09–1.11	.04	2.72–2.79	.38	9.36–9.82	.72
1.12–1.14	.05	2.80–2.87	.39	9.83–10.33	.73
1.15–1.17	.06	2.88–2.96	.40	10.34–10.90	.74
1.18–1.20	.07	2.97–3.05	.41	10.91–11.51	.75
1.21–1.23	.08	3.06–3.14	.42	11.52–12.16	.76
1.24–1.27	.09	3.15–3.24	.43	12.17–12.89	.77
1.28–1.30	.10	3.25–3.34	.44	12.90–13.70	.78
1.31–1.33	.11	3.35–3.45	.45	13.71–14.58	.79
1.34–1.37	.12	3.46–3.56	.46	14.59–15.57	.80
1.38–1.40	.13	3.57–3.68	.47	15.58–16.65	.81
1.41–1.44	.14	3.69–3.80	.48	16.66–17.88	.82
1.45–1.48	.15	3.81–3.92	.49	17.89–19.28	.83
1.49–1.52	.16	3.93–4.06	.50	19.29–20.85	.84
1.53–1.56	.17	4.07–4.20	.51	20.86–22.68	.85
1.57–1.60	.18	4.21–4.34	.52	22.68–24.76	.86
1.61–1.64	.19	4.35–4.49	.53	24.77–27.22	.87
1.65–1.69	.20	4.50–4.66	.54	27.23–30.09	.88
1.70–1.73	.21	4.67–4.82	.55	30.10–33.60	.89
1.74–1.78	.22	4.83–4.99	.56	33.61–37.79	.90
1.79–1.83	.23	5.00–5.18	.57	37.80–43.06	.91
1.84–1.88	.24	5.19–5.38	.58	43.07–49.83	.92
1.89–1.93	.25	5.39–5.59	.59	49.84–58.79	.93
1.94–1.98	.26	5.60–5.80	.60	58.80–70.95	.94
1.99–2.04	.27	5.81–6.03	.61	70.96–89.01	.95
2.05–2.10	.28	6.04–6.28	.62	89.02–117.54	.96
2.11–2.15	.29	6.29–6.54	.63	117.55–169.67	.97
2.16–2.22	.30	6.55–6.81	.64	169.68–293.12	.98
2.23–2.28	.31	6.82–7.10	.65	293.13–923.97	.99
2.29–2.34	.32	7.11–7.42	.66	923.98–	1.00
2.35–2.41	.33	7.43–7.75	.67		

(Appendix D, Critical Values for *r*), or converted to a chi square value and referred to Appendix C, Chi Square Table.

The computation of ϕ can be illustrated with the example referenced earlier in the chapter in which a Director of Student Affairs is interested in knowing whether there is a relationship between owning a word processor (variable *X*) and passing the required course "Introduction to the Academic Community" (variable *Y*). Table 7–7

Table 7–7: **Data for Computing the Phi Coefficient**

		Variable X		
		Yes	No	Totals
Variable Y	Yes	30 (B)	70 (A)	100
	No	70 (D)	30 (C)	100
	Totals	100	100	200

provides the data for which the analysis will be made. By substituting the values in the table, the phi coefficient is computed as follows:

$$\phi = \frac{AD - BC}{\sqrt{(A + B)(C + D)(B + D)(A + C)}}$$

$$= \frac{(70)(70) - (30)(30)}{\sqrt{(70 + 30)(30 + 70)(30 + 70)(70 + 30)}}$$

$$= \frac{4900 - 900}{\sqrt{(100)(100)(100)(100)}}$$

$$= \frac{4000}{\sqrt{100,000,000}}$$

$$= \frac{4000}{10,000}$$

$$= .40$$

Findings: There is a positive relationship between owning a word processor and passing the course "Introduction to the Academic Community." With $df = 198$ ($N - 2$), a ϕ of .40 is held to be significant at $p < .01$.

To test for significance at an equivalent chi square (X^2) value, the process is:

$$X^2 = N\phi^2$$

$$= 200 \, (.40)^2$$

$$= 200 \, (.16)$$

$$= .32$$

which, for 1 df (R − 1)(C − 1), shows the finding to be significant at $p < .01$.

Coefficient of Contingency (C)

Coefficient of contingency (C) is used when the two variables under study can be classified into two *or more* categories. Consider the example of a classroom teacher wanting to determine whether there is a relationship between final course grades (A, B, C, D, or F) earned by students in a French II class (variable X) and their letter grades for a prerequisite course in French I taken a semester earlier (variable Y). In Table 7–8, each cell contains the *actual grades earned* by the ninety students, and their *expected grades* (displayed within brackets). The data are based upon the hypothesis that the *expected* grades (those in brackets) will approximate the *earned* grades.

   The analytical process begins by determining the proportion of students who earned a grade of A on variable Y (out of the possible number of grades distributed). For example, 10 students out of 90 earned a grade of A in the prerequisite course (variable Y). By multiplying this ratio by the total number of students who earned an A on variable X, one has the number of individuals who earned an A in the French II course who could be expected to have earned a grade of A (by chance alone) in the prerequisite French I course. Given that 10/90 (10) = 1.11 is the number of students who earned a grade in variable X (who can be expected to have earned a grade in variable Y on the basis of chance alone), the expected value is then compared against the *two* students who actually earned a grade of A in *both* classes. Similarly, expected values are determined for the rest of the cells in the table. When each of the expected values is calculated, the observed cell entry is squared and divided by its expected value. The total of these quotients yields S, and from S and the total number of students (N), the coefficient of contingency (C) is determined. The formula for this determination is as follows:

$$C = \sqrt{\frac{S - N}{S}}$$

Table 7–8: **Data for Computing Coefficient of Contingency**

		Variable X					
		A	B	C	D	F	Totals
	A	2 [1]	3 [4]	4 [5]	1 [0]	0 [0]	10
	B	4 [3]	3 [4]	8 [8]	3 [4]	2 [1]	20
Variable Y	C	3 [5]	8 [6]	12 [11]	4 [5]	3 [3]	30
	D	1 [1]	5 [4]	6 [6]	7 [5]	1 [4]	20
	F	0 [0]	1 [2]	0 [0]	5 [6]	4 [2]	10
	Totals	10	20	30	20	10	90

Now the coefficient for the data related to students who have completed French I and II classes can be computed. The calculation of *expected values* is as follows:

10/90 (10) = 1.11	30/90 (10) = 3.33	10/90 (10) = 1.11
10/90 (20) = 2.22	30/90 (20) = 6.66	10/90 (20) = 2.22
10/90 (30) = 3.33	30/90 (30) = 9.99	10/90 (30) = 3.33
10/90 (20) = 2.22	30/90 (20) = 6.66	10/90 (20) = 2.22
10/90 (10) = 1.11	30/90 (10) = 3.33	10/90 (10) = 1.11
20/90 (10) = 2.22	20/90 (10) = 2.22	
20/90 (20) = 4.44	20/90 (20) = 4.44	
20/90 (30) = 6.66	20/90 (30) = 6.66	
20/90 (20) = 4.44	20/90 (20) = 4.44	
20/90 (10) = 2.22	20/90 (10) = 2.22	

Then the value of S is computed as follows:

$\frac{(2)^2}{1.11} = 3.60$	$\frac{(1)^2}{2.22} = 0.45$	$\frac{(7)^2}{4.44} = 11.03$
$\frac{(4)^2}{2.22} = 7.20$	$\frac{(4)^2}{3.33} = 4.80$	$\frac{(5)^2}{2.22} = 11.26$
$\frac{(3)^2}{3.33} = 2.70$	$\frac{(8)^2}{6.66} = 9.60$	$\frac{(0)^2}{1.11} = 0.00$
$\frac{(1)^2}{2.22} = 0.45$	$\frac{(12)^2}{9.99} = 14.41$	$\frac{(2)^2}{2.22} = 1.80$
$\frac{(0)^2}{1.11} = 0.00$	$\frac{(6)^2}{6.66} = 5.40$	$\frac{(3)^2}{3.33} = 2.70$
$\frac{(3)^2}{2.22} = 4.05$	$\frac{(0)^2}{3.33} = 0.00$	$\frac{(1)^2}{2.22} = 0.45$
$\frac{(3)^2}{4.44} = 2.02$	$\frac{(1)^2}{2.22} = 0.45$	$\frac{(4)^2}{1.11} = 14.41$
$\frac{(8)^2}{6.66} = 9.60$	$\frac{(3)^2}{4.44} = 2.02$	$S = 116.43$
$\frac{(5)^2}{4.44} = 5.63$	$\frac{(4)^2}{6.66} = 2.40$	

Finally, the *coefficiency of contingency (C)* is calculated:

$$C = \sqrt{\frac{S - N}{S}}$$

$$= \sqrt{\frac{116.43 - 90}{116.43}}$$

$$= \sqrt{\frac{26.43}{116.43}}$$

$$= \sqrt{.22}$$

$$= .46$$

Findings: By examining the cells diagonally from the upper left to the lower right (A-A; B-B; C-C; D-D; F-F), it can be seen that, in all but one instance (B-B), the observed frequencies exceeded the expected frequencies. Of the remaining twenty cells, fifteen displayed cases in which the expected frequencies equaled or exceeded the observed frequencies. Hence, the observed (actual) entries are less than the number to be expected by chance alone. The size of the coefficient rests with the degree to which the observed values differ from the expected values. As noted earlier, the maximum coefficient for C with a 5×5 table is .894. Consequently, it is not surprising that, while there does appear to be a relationship between the variables, it is lower than what one might normally anticipate.

Partial Correlation (r12.3 . . . x)

Partial correlation ($r12.3 \ldots x$) is used to determine the relationship between two variables when the effects of other variables are held constant. To complete this task requires that consideration be given to the explained and unexplained variations that arise with and without the influence of the variable that is considered independent (variable X). To understand the process, suppose that a Director of Health and Physical Education is interested in knowing whether there is a relationship between final grades in social science (variable X) and health knowledge (variable Y) with age (variable Z) held constant. Once these factors are denoted in the formula, the formula appears as follows:

$$rxy.z = \frac{rxy - (rxz)(ryz)}{\sqrt{(1 - rxy^2)(1 - ryz^2)}}$$

Table 7–9 presents the data from which the calculations will be made.

Table 7–9: **Data for Computing rbis**

Subjects	X(ss)	Y(hk)	Z(age)	X^2	Y^2	Z^2	XY	XZ	YZ
D.D.	80	70	16	6400	4900	256	5600	1280	1120
A.C.	78	69	16	6084	4761	256	5382	1248	1104
F.J.	72	63	14	5184	3969	196	4536	1008	882
G.T.	73	62	14	5329	3844	196	4526	1022	868
T.W.	79	68	16	6241	4624	256	5372	1264	1088
L.P.	77	67	16	5929	4489	256	5159	1232	1072
D.S.	71	61	14	5041	3721	196	4331	994	854
M.D.	76	66	15	5776	4356	225	5016	1140	990
O.S.	74	64	14	5476	4096	196	4736	1036	896
D.A.	75	65	15	5625	4225	225	4875	1125	975

Suppose the following circumstances exist:

$Mx = 75.5$	$rxy = 0.975$
$My = 65.5$	$rxz = 0.934$
$Mz = 15.0$	$ryz = 0.934$
$\Sigma XY = 49.533$	$\sigma x = 2.872$
$\Sigma XZ = 11,349$	$\sigma y = 2.872$
$\Sigma YZ = 9,849$	$\sigma z = 0.894$

NOTE: The standard deviations of variables X and Y are identical because each distribution has the same range of nonduplicate consecutive numbers. This also accounts for the reason that the correlation between variables X and Z is the same as the correlation between variables Y and Z.

Given these circumstances, the calculation of $rxy.z$ is found as follows:

$$rxy.z = \frac{rxy - (rxz)(ryz)}{\sqrt{(1 - rxz^2)(1 - ryz^2)}}$$

$$= \frac{.975 - (.934)(.934)}{\sqrt{(1 - .934^2)(1 - .934^2)}}$$

$$= \frac{.975 - .872}{\sqrt{(1 - .872)(1 - .872)}}$$

$$= \frac{.103}{\sqrt{.016}}$$

$$= \frac{.103}{.126}$$

$$= .817$$

Findings: *When age is not held constant,* the relationship between social science (variable X) and health (variable Y) is .975. *When age is held constant,* the correlation between variables X and Y drops to .817. As indicated earlier in the chapter, age may be the common thread in many statistical relationships. Once it is held constant, the factor of age is no longer a contributing variable.

While age can be controlled by selecting from a group those students who were born at approximately the same time, this process markedly reduces the size of the sample. Since a partial correlation procedure takes *all* data into account, it is considered the preferred practice (when controls are sought).

Computer Analysis of Data

It is apparent from the illustrations of the statistical procedures in this chapter that some of them are quite labor-intensive. You are probably aware that there is software available that can expedite the analytical process (see Chapter 12, Using the Computer for Data Analysis). However, there is general agreement that one should refrain from using these programs until:

1. there is an understanding of the *type* of statistical analysis one needs to employ for his own study (for example, rank-order, product-moment, biserial *r*, and so on), and

2. the practitioner-researcher has had the opportunity to perform analyses by hand or, at the very least, has studied the processes extensively.

As a result, instructions for entering the data for processing will be become more clear, as will the output that requires interpretation.

SUMMARY

This chapter has focused on that form of descriptive investigation that utilizes correlation methods. It is a study design that enables the practitioner-researcher to assess the degree of association that exists between variables. From the simple rank-order correlation, in which pairs of data are compared on the basis of their ordered alignment, to techniques in which variables are held constant, subdivided, or combined (as is the case with multiple correlation), purposes, techniques, and interpretations have been displayed for review. In order to assist the reader, step-by-step analyses have been provided for each of the more commonly employed correlation methods. The practitioner needs only to substitute his own data for those in the illustrations.

Like Chapter 6, Survey Procedures, this chapter included templates for completing all pertinent phases of a research design. By carefully examining the displays in this chapter, the reader should be able to harness the skills to design and administer his own studies requiring correlation processes.

Although the findings of relationships between variables can be important in their own right, they can also lead to further studies affecting the process and product of education. Correlation techniques play an important role in descriptive research. It is hoped that your understanding has reached another level as a consequence of reading this chapter.

RECOMMENDED LABORATORY ASSIGNMENTS

1. Review the recommended readings.

2. Arrange to meet with fellow graduate students and colleagues in order to discuss the strategies for designing correlation research.

3. If you have not prepared a correlation research template for a problem statement, it is suggested that you do so at this time (either alone, or in collaboration with no more than two other people). All the elements of Phase 1 and Phase 2 should be addressed, including:

   a. Time schedule

   b. Tentative budget

   c. Statement of need (justification) for the study

   d. Integration of eight to ten related literature articles

   e. Statement of hypothesis

   f. List of basic assumptions

g. List of possible threats to *internal* validity, and how you would control for them

h. Identification of factors that would need to be considered to maintain *external* validity

i. Evidence that contrasting designs were examined, and the basis upon which a final determination was made

j. Definitions of important terms

k. Template that includes responses to all pertinent subproblems, as well as to the questions related to: what, where, how, organization and analysis, and conclusions

4. Working with fellow classmates or colleagues, acquire rosters of scores that can be used to calculate *and* interpret:

a. Rank-order correlation

b. Product-moment correlation

c. Biserial correlation

d. Tetrachoric correlation

e. Phi coefficient

f. Coefficient of contingency

g. Partial correlation

5. Using all pertinent data related to the correlation coefficient found in response to question 4(b), compute *and* interpret:

a. Degree of significance

b. Measurement error

c. Predicted z score

d. Coefficient of determination

6. Administer a pilot test to no fewer than ten individuals in order to compute a split-half (internal consistency) correlation. Once the coefficient has been acquired, apply the Spearman-Brown prophecy formula to the finding. Interpret the result.

7. As an alternative to question 6, attempt to administer the pilot test on two different occasions. Compute a stability coefficient, and interpret the result.

8. To the same individuals from whom you have obtained pilot test scores, administer a test for which validity has already been established. Using product-moment correlation, compute the statistical relationship between the two instruments. Interpret the results.

9. Arrange to meet with fellow graduate students, colleagues, as well as school and nonschool employees who have carried out correlation research, in order to review and discuss your research plans and the findings of your statistical analyses.

10. Describe for others the major differences in a template designed for survey research, and one designed for correlation research.

RECOMMENDED READINGS

Baumrind, D. (1973). The development of instrumental competence through socialization. In A. D. Pick (Ed.), *Minnesota Symposium on Child Psychology, 7,* 3–46. Minneapolis, MN: University of Minnesota Press.

Campbell, D. T., & Erlebacher, A. (1975). How regression artifacts in quasi-experimental evaluations can mistakenly make compensatory education look harmful. In E. L. Struening & M. Guttentag (Eds.). *Handbook of evaluation research. Vol. 1.* (pp. 597–617). Beverly Hills, CA: Sage.

Courneya, K. S., & McAuley, E. (1992, June). *Comparison of absolute versus relative value of physical activity in the prediction of intention and behavior.* Paper presented at the Annual North American Society for the Psychology of Physical Activity and Sport Conference, Pittsburgh, PA.

Draper, N. R., & Smith, H. (1981). *Applied regression analysis* (2nd ed.). New York: Wiley.

Duda, J. L. (1989). Relationship between task and ego orientation and the perceived purpose of sport among high school athletes. *Journal of Sport and Exercise Psychology, 11,* 318–335.

Freedman, D., Pisani, R., & Purves, R. (1978). *Statistics.* New York: Norton.

Gibbons, J. D. (1993). *Nonparametric measures of association.* Newbury Park, CA: Sage.

Hoover-Dempsey, K. V., Bassler, O. C., & Brissie, J. S. (1987). Parent involvement: Contributions of teacher efficacy, school socioeconomic status, and other school characteristics. *American Educational Research Journal, 24,* 417–435.

Hoover-Dempsey, K. V., Bassler, O. C., & Brissie, J. S. (1992). Explorations in parent-school relations. *The Journal of Educational Research, 85,* 287–294.

Linn, R. L. (1982). Ability testing: Individual differences, prediction, and differential prediction. In A. K. Wigdor & W. R. Gardner (Eds.). *Ability testing: Uses, consequences, and controversies. Part II.* Washington, DC: National Academic Press.

Loehlin, J. C. (1992). *Latent variable models: An introduction to factor, path, and structural analysis* (2nd ed.). Hillsdale, NJ: Lawrence Erlbaum.

Mondell, S., & Tyler, F. B. (1981). Parental competence and styles of problem-solving/play behavior with children. *Developmental Psychology, 17,* 73–78.

Nunnally, J. C. (1994). *Psychometric theory* (3rd ed.). New York: McGraw-Hill.

Pedhazur, E. J. (1982). *Multiple regression in behavioral research* (2nd ed.). New York: Holt, Rinehart & Winston.

Thompson, B. (1991). Methods, plainly speaking: A primer on the logic and use of canonical correlation analysis. *Measurement and Evaluation in Counseling and Development, 24,* 80–95.

REFERENCES

Davidoff, M. D., & Goheen, H. W. (1953). *Psychometrika, 18,* 115–121.

Garrett, H. E. (1958). *Statistics in psychology and education.* New York: Longmans, Green.

Harris, M. B. (1995). *Basic statistics for behavioral science research.* Needham Heights, MA: Allyn & Bacon.

Howell, D. C. (1982). *Statistical methods for psychology.* Boston: Duxbury Press.

Kachigan, S. K. (1986). *Statistical analysis: An interdisciplinary introduction to univariate & multivariate methods.* New York: Radius Press.

Kiess, H. O. (1989). *Statistical concepts for the behavioral sciences.* Needham Heights: MA: Allyn & Bacon.

Leedy, P. D. (1997). *Practical research: Planning and design* (6th ed.). Columbus, OH: Merrill.

CHAPTER 8

Other Descriptive Procedures

OBJECTIVES

After reading this chapter, you should be able to:

- Describe the essential procedures for conducting *qualitative* investigations.
- Distinguish between *qualitative* and *quantitative* research methods.
- Distinguish between various *purposive* samples, including: case, concept/theory-based, network, and reputational-based.
- Describe the process of *triangulation*.
- Distinguish between *descriptive, interpretive,* and *evaluative* validity.
- Distinguish between *diachronic* and *synchronic* reliability.
- Describe the purposes of and strategies for conducting *case studies*.
- Describe the role of *participant-observer*.
- Identify and discuss the functions of a *contact summary form*.
- Describe the purposes of and strategies for conducting *historical* research.
- Complete a *documentary analysis* for a topic of historical significance.

- Describe the purposes of and strategies for conducting *causal-comparative* research.
- Distinguish between *historical* and *causal-comparative* investigations.
- Distinguish between *research hypotheses, rival hypotheses,* and *research questions.*
- Describe the purposes of and strategies for conducting *philosophical* research.
- Distinguish between *epistemology* and *logic.*
- Describe the purposes of and strategies for conducting *test and measurement* research.
- Create design templates for conducting *case studies,* and *historical, causal-comparative, philosophical,* and *test and measurement* research.
- Define key terms, and answer the checkpoint questions.

KEY TERMS

Aesthetics	*Ex Post Facto Research*
Audit Trail	*External Criticism*
Case Sample	*Field Notes*
Chain of Evidence	*Frequency of Mention*
Concept/Theory-Based Sample	*Functioning of Alternatives*
Concurrent Validity	*Historical Method*
Contact Summary Sheet	*Historiography*
Content Validity	*Holistic Inquiry*
Debriefing	*Independent Variable*
Dependent Variable	*Internal Criticism*
Descriptive Validity	*Interpretive Validity*
Diachronic Reliability	*Logic*
Documentary Analysis	*Low Inference Descriptions*
Emersion	*Metaphysics*
Epistemology	*Naturalistic Setting*
Equivalence	*Network Sample*
Ethics	*Ontology*
Evaluative Validity	*Participant-Observer*

Pattern Analysis   *Research Question*

Phenomenology   *Rival Hypotheses*

Philosophical Method   *Secondary Sources*

Primary Sources   *Spearman-Brown Formula*

Qualitative Method   *Stability*

Quantitative Method   *Synchronic Reliability*

Reputational Case Sample   *Tracking*

INTRODUCTION

As you know, descriptive research encompasses those designs in which experimental treatments are *not* present. In Chapter 6, attention was given to conducting surveys, and the particulars that govern the construction and administration of open- and fixed-choice questionnaires. Chapter 7 focused upon correlation studies in which variables are analyzed in order to determine the extent to which associations exist between them. You also learned that, while there may be relationships between the variables under study in correlation research, it is *not* appropriate to attribute causes and effects to them. In this chapter, you will find reference to designs that examine causes. The chapter also addresses descriptive research methods normally unrelated to the study of causes, specifically, *philosophical* and *test and measurement* procedures.

The *case study method,* one of several approaches to *qualitative* inquiry, represents an in-depth investigation of such things as: documents; unique events, settings, or individuals. An example of the case-study approach to research is an investigation that was done on the effects of a staff development program on the professional lives of four elementary school teachers who participated in it (Kagan, Dennis, Igou, Moore, & Sparks, 1993). Each "case" was examined for common threads and uniqueness. This approach is quite prevalent when analyzing data generated from case studies. It is from the "commonalities" that inferences are drawn.

The ***historical method*** attempts to study events of the past in order to examine their causes and effects. Using **qualitative methods,** the designs are centered around the investigation of past events in order to help understand and explain the present. One such interest is frequently observed in school law in which a study of court decisions is undertaken in order to provide a better understanding of the law and legal issues, for example, sex education movement in the United States (Strong, 1972). Information from historical documents is very useful in understanding the existing status of things. One of the problems is that few people seem to be interested in studying historical documents; to infiltrate the dark and sometimes obscure sections of a library requires a great deal of dedication and commitment. Lack of interest in this form of research by greater numbers of people accounts, in part, for the fact that *history tends to repeat itself.* Why? Because we do not seem to be learning much from the mistakes of our forefathers. Evidence points to the fact that we learn by our own experiences. Does this mean that we must experience disaster firsthand before we can learn from it? Let us hope not. The section on the historical method offers step-by-step strategies for doing this very important form of research.

The *causal-comparative method,* often referred to as **ex post facto research,** begins with effects and investigates causes. While independent and dependent variables can be identified, experimental manipulation is ruled out because the treatment has already occurred. An example of such a study is one that was done to examine the effect of high school students' part-time employment on their academic achievement (Green & Jaquess, 1987). Causal-comparative studies differ from correlation studies (discussed in Chapter 7) in *two* major ways:

1. Correlation studies are *not* intended to reveal cause-and-effect relationships; causal-comparative studies are designed specifically for that purpose.

2. Correlation studies typically involve two or more variables and one group; causal-comparative studies ordinarily involve two or more groups, and one independent variable.

The ***philosophical method,*** often referred to as **phenomenology,** is a procedure for describing the various ways individuals conceptualize the world around them. As indicated in Chapter 1, Selection and Definition of a Problem, it is a process that requires critical thinking beyond the realm of fact-finding science. One such example is a study that was done by Schempp, Sparkes, and Templin (1993) in which they examined the social pressures brought to bear upon beginning teachers within their places of employment, and the teachers' strategies for dealing with these issues while advancing their own personal interests. Utilizing *qualitative* methodology, philosophical research requires interviewing subjects or analyzing their written prose in order to discover the perceptions they have about a problem that has been posed for their consideration.

The *test and measurement method* involves the creation and validation of instruments of assessment. It is a form of research that is often preliminary to investigating what is considered to be the primary problem interest. Requiring **quantitative methods,** this form of research is frequently prompted by the fact that standardized measuring instruments pertinent to a problem area do not appear to exist. As a consequence, such an instrument must be developed. In Chapter 5, Selecting Instruments of Assessment, it was made abundantly clear that the data one gathers during the course of one's study are only as good as the instruments used to generate them. Therefore, since instrumentation is a vital part of any research endeavor, quality measuring tools must be available. Test and measurement research attempts to make that possible.

This chapter presents the processes related to designing each type of research just discussed, namely, case-study, historical, causal-comparative, philosophical, as well as test and measurement research. Since the *qualitative* method is usually the dominant process for gathering and organizing information in all but causal-comparative and test and measurement research, that is the method that will be discussed here. Following a thorough discussion of the principles of qualitative research are presentations on the various designs that employ these principles.

QUALITATIVE TECHNIQUES

As McMillan and Schumacher (1997) point out, all research requires *observations* of one form or another. The key difference between qualitative and quantitative techniques is that with the former, the acquisition of data is *dependent* upon some form of observation. Further, the format for the observations is generally quite structured—that is, specific plans have been made in advance regarding how the observations will be conducted. By determining in advance the categories of behavior that will be recorded, the processes to employ when gathering the data become more clearly defined. Quite simply, *qualitative research* (frequently referred to as *ethnographic research)* involves amassing data

- from a participant's perspective,
- in a naturalistic setting,
- over an extended period of time.

Since qualitative methods require that the data be acquired by the researcher in *naturalistic* settings, a number of questions may surface about the validity, reliability, and objectivity of the researcher's findings. The two issues that seem to surface most frequently are the following:

1. Can the presence of an investigator alter the behavior of those she is attempting to study?

2. Can the opinions and other biases of the researcher influence the interpretations assigned to the findings?

In regard to whether the presence of an investigator can alter the behavior of those she is attempting to study, the answer is yes. By the **emersion** of oneself into the study environment in as *unobtrusive* a manner as possible, however, the impact of one's presence can ordinarily be *minimized*. This is often contingent upon the size of the sample. While one is unlikely to be able to factor out *all* influences one may bring to the natural setting, by being "tuned in" to the environment, one can address many of the threats to the study. In this regard, Deutscher (1973) speaks to the importance of discounting some information because of the intrusion of the investigator within the context of the behavior. If, for example, the investigator is studying classroom management strategies, the normal behavior of the teacher during the early stages of the research may be to refrain from chastising a student because she feels that it may be considered to be in bad taste. The students, themselves, may act differently than what is ordinarily the case. A principal may behave in ways that she considers to be "principal-like." However, Morris and Hurwitz (1980) point out that the researcher may be able to turn this phenomenon into an advantage if, when desiring to learn what principals consider to be principal-like behavior, she observes how principals conduct themselves when outsiders are present.

In most cases, the observations will be more valid if the researcher refrains from treating those with whom she is meeting as "research subjects." Instead, the researcher attempts to blend into the setting so that the activities that take place in her presence will not differ markedly from those that occur in her absence. This is often a product of time (Douglas, 1976), size of the group, and patience.

In regard to whether the opinions and other biases of the researcher can influence the interpretations assigned to the findings, again, the answer is *yes,* but only if she lets them. The primary objective of any form of research is to learn more about the issue under study, not to restrict the investigation to the parameters of one's own personal experiences. While personal experiences have a place in research, the researcher must not let them distort the findings. When personal reflections are included in a report, it is important to distinguish between them and the facts that were generated during the course of the observations. Among the techniques that will help to maintain *objectivity* in one's analysis are the following:

1. Use of multiple sources of information, or *triangulation* (a process that is discussed in detail later in this section)

2. Use of various methods to collect and record the data (for example, paper-pencil, audiotapes, videotapes, multiple observers)

3. Maintenance of an **audit trail** of the observation techniques that were used, as well as the materials acquired

The views of Bogdan and Biklen (1982) make it clear that qualitative studies are not "impressionistic essays" written after a short visit, and based upon casual conversations with a few people. The process requires a thoughtfully designed investigation conducted in sufficient depth and detail that those who have not experienced the setting will come to understand it. The process requires that the data acquired from the observations bear the weight of any interpretations assigned to them.

Qualitative versus Quantitative Procedures

While qualitative research focuses on words and quantitative research focuses on numbers, the distinction is greater than that. Since behavior is most often a product of the setting in which it occurs, a better understanding of why people do what they do is best acquired when one studies the context in which that behavior takes place. The employment of the methods of qualitative inquiry is based on the assumption that behavior is a product of context. Further, it should be understood that many research interests do not lend themselves to the quantitative approach alone. Merely totaling the number of times a person disrupts a classroom does not tell the entire story. What prompted the disruptive behavior on a given day? What issues exist in the child's personal life that could have impacted upon her decision to act inappropriately? How does the teacher react to the problem when it first arises? What is the reaction of other students in the class to the maladaptive behavior? What are the views of other teachers regarding that particular student's behavior in their respective classrooms? We all know that the environment has a great deal to do with how a person acts at any given time. To understand the environment leads to a better understanding of behavior, whether it is maladaptive or not. Qualitative procedures lend themselves to gaining these insights; quantitative procedures most often do not. As Shimahara (1988) points out, a primary characteristic of qualitative research is that it is designed to discover the cultural influences in human behavior. In other words, culture is the central concept in qualitative inquiry (Wax, 1993).

Figure 8–1 lists descriptors often associated with quantitative and qualitative research. Although the expressions listed are not necessarily limited to one form of research or the other, they do characterize in a *general* way the nature of these two processes.

Procedures for Conducting Qualitative Investigations

The descriptors in Figure 8–1 provide only a general flavor of the difference between quantitative and qualitative approaches to data collection and analysis. Most of them reflect the coverage provided in prior chapters. With that as background, you will now be introduced to the very heart of qualitative designs.

Acknowledging that the underlying purpose of *ethnographic inquiry* is to gain insight and understanding of the setting within which behavior occurs, and recognizing that certain strategies must be employed in order to *maximize* the opportunity to acquire information pertinent to the problem interest, it is recommended that the following guidelines be considered.

1. Start with a very general research problem. For example: "How do teachers in urban schools react to state-mandated testing?" or "What are the characteristics of those who are recipients of distinguished teaching awards?" Once the problem statement has been identified, determine the appropriate design for carrying out the study, for example, case study, correlation, experiment, survey, and so on.

Figure 8–1: **Common Descriptors Associated with Quantitative and Qualitative Research**

Quantitative Research	Qualitative Research
Control groups	Artifacts
Correlation	Context sensitivity
Data sets	Emersion
Dependent variables	Extended presence
Experimentation	Field notes
Independent variables	Naturalistic settings
Intervening variables	Nonrandom sampling
Level of confidence	Participant-observers
Moderator variables	Photographs
Questionnaires	Process examination
Statistical analysis	Tentative hypotheses
Testing	Triangulation

2. *Assuming that a* case study *is selected as the design of choice (for purposes of illustration), negotiate access to a naturalistic setting.* This can be done by adopting a role either as a *full* participant-observer or, if that is not possible, simply as an observer.

3. *Ensure that the nature of the sample you acquire as the subject of your investigation is purposeful and small.* This is necessary in order to acquire the in-depth understanding of the issue under consideration. In essence, *it is better to find out a lot about a little, than to find out a little about a lot.* Qualitative studies represent the rare exception of the usefulness of small, nonrandom samples. Among the various *purposive* sample models are the following:

- **Case samples,** in which individuals or institutions are selected because they fit a set of commonly recognized criteria—for example, teachers who are recipients of distinguished teaching awards; institutions receiving accreditation from the National Council for Teacher Education (NCATE)

- **Concept/theory-based samples,** in which individuals or institutions are selected because they are presently dealing with the issue of concern—for example, state-mandated testing; integrating sex education within the health curriculum

- **Network** (or mushroom) **samples,** in which successive individuals or groups are nominated by prior interviewees as those who would have information related to the subject—for example, a principal recommends a department head; a finance committee chair recommends the treasurer of the organization

- **Reputational-case samples,** in which knowledgeable individuals make recommendations regarding important sources of information—for example, department of education officials identify "effective" schools; the director of athletics recommends the name of one of her "effective" coaches; a teacher recommends the name of an "outstanding student," and so on

4. *Make observations within the* **naturalistic setting** *itself.* Although serving as a **participant-observer** is *not* a requisite to acquiring information that is valuable to the study, it is often a preferred practice in that, by "participating with the group," it is a bit easier to diminish the impressions people may have about you as being an "outsider."

5. *Arrange for extended engagements for on-site observations.* Information gathered over a period of time is likely to be more representative of the "real" circumstances. Further, the researcher is more likely to be considered a member of "an extended family." Unlike the survey research model described in Chapter 6, one should *not* be relying upon a "snapshot" of the situation—rather, the approach should be considered more of a "photomontage." A collection of images produced from one's emersion into the naturalistic setting will more likely provide the necessary substance for enlightened judgments.

6. *Allow research questions and hypotheses to continually evolve as data are revealed.* Unlike quantitative research in which the hypotheses are stated in *advance* of the study, ethnographic studies require that research questions (and hypotheses) be considered tentative—that is, everchanging as "new" facts come to light. In most qualitative studies, data collection and analysis go hand-in-hand. In other words, the

investigator does *not* wait until all the data are in place before she begins to inductively interpret them. As new information becomes known, new directions of inquiry begin to emerge; thus, new research questions and hypotheses are written.

> **NOTE:** For purpose of this chapter, a *research question* is a preliminary inquiry used to provide direction for evidence gathering. Its status is contingent upon the information that is uncovered, and it is always subject to revision. Also subject to revision, a *research hypothesis* is a statement of the expected results. As will be discovered later in the chapter, some descriptive investigations (such as historical, philosophical, and test and measurement research) generally rely upon research questions alone. This is because one cannot easily anticipate results until all pertinent research questions have been answered. By that time, the study is complete and there is little need to express a hypothesis for the purpose of that particular investigation.

7. *Use an approach to the research inquiry that is process-oriented, and* **holistic.** The investigator needs to examine the *totality of circumstances* underlying the behaviors that are being examined. It is important to realize that evidence of findings can arise out of many different sources, including: documents, extensive field notes, informal interviews, and observations. Use them all!

8. *Integrate the use of multiple sources of data, multiple observers, and multiple methods.* This is known as *triangulation* in that information is brought together from various perspectives in order to gain clearer insight of the nature of what is being studied. It is also important to understand that triangulation does not always lead to findings of agreement. Instead of convergence, one may find contradictions. When this occurs, it may be necessary to seek additional information sources in order to look for a **chain of evidence.** Avoid heavy reliance upon one observation method, one observer, or a single source of information. The broader the base, the more secure one can be in claiming validity for whatever interpretations are made. Other techniques for acquiring evidence of validity for qualitative investigations include the following:

- Engaging in prolonged field work
- Recording responses verbatim (as opposed to simply paraphrasing, when time and additional effort will permit otherwise)

These strategies help to address such questions as:

- Did the researcher actually observe what she thinks she observed?
- Did the researcher really "hear" the meanings that were intended?

Maxwell (1992) refers to the fact that the validity of qualitative studies arises out of several processes. Of those described, these three are considered to be most pertinent:

- **Descriptive validity,** which refers to the general accuracy of the descriptions of events
- **Interpretive validity,** which refers to the degree to which accurate interpretations are assigned to the observations. In other words, would the subjects of the investigation make the same interpretation?

- **Evaluative validity,** which refers to the extent to which judgments about the findings are legitimate

In short, when observers and the research subjects agree about the meanings of artifacts, concepts, and other pieces of evidence, validity is likely to be present in the study. (More will be said about this topic later in the chapter.)

9. *Take extensive field notes.* The descriptions that the researcher is able to make from her field notes and observations are critical to the success of any qualitative investigation; therefore, it is important that the majority of them be **low inference descriptions.** This implies that the narrative pertaining to the findings is very *literal* and that any important terminology is that which is *used* and *understood* by the research subjects themselves. The antithesis of using low inference descriptions is when the investigator uses abstract language to describe accounts of conversations and behavior of the subjects. Accounts that are verbatim are valued highly in reports of qualitative studies. When researchers are able to use direct quotations, the credibility of their accounts of the events is enhanced, particularly when interpretations are attributed to the events.

It is also important to retain personal and reflexive logs and journals in which accounts are recorded of such things as the observer's assumptions, feelings, and thoughts about the motives and rationale for the observations that are made. This is done so that personal experiences and insights can be brought to interplay with the observations.

10. *Schedule periodic debriefing with other observers.* This important "sharing" time makes it possible to learn what is known about how others are viewing the circumstances to date. Is there convergence, or are there contradictions? What new pictures are beginning to surface? Is there new evidence to be examined? Should the research questions and the hypotheses be revised?

11. *Retain all pertinent documents.* In addition, retain all other evidence and plans related to:

- what you need to know,
- where the answers will be found,
- how the answers will be found,
- procedures for organizing and analyzing the information for further use, and
- conclusions that would follow from the procedures.

This will aid the researcher immeasurably as field notes, photographs, logs, journals, and other evidence are brought to interface with the research plan.

12. *Utilize narrative reporting of the findings and conclusions.* Integrate numbers (quantitative-type information) as pertinent. When the qualitative method is employed to explain and interpret the meaning of behavior or events, any or all of the following procedures are typical of the practices recommended.

a. *Construct themes or **patterns** on the basis of the information collected.* Examine all pertinent documents, including field notes, photographs, logs, journals, and other evidence collected by the observers. From these documents, common threads and exceptions can be identified and discussed. One way to do this is to establish categories for the information. Since most case studies will generate many pages of interview and observation notes, plans should be made to order the information in a way that will encourage efficient analysis. If one supposes that there are 100 pages of notes, with 250 words on a page, it can easily be seen that 2500 words would not be conducive to easy analysis unless some form of organization (for example, a coding structure) were in place. Imagine that a case study is being done on the characteristics of those who are recipients of outstanding teaching awards. Data on this subject can be organized by the *sources* of the information, *categories* of information, or a *combination* of the two. From these data sorts, any themes or patterns that exist can become more readily apparent. If symbols or codes can be assigned meaning early in the research, they can be "attached" to the information as it is acquired.

Miles and Huberman (1994) suggest that investigators involved in case study research use a standard form to summarize data-collection events. They call the form a **contact summary sheet.** Its use not only can reveal gaps in the information, but also can suggest promising leads for further study. An adaptation of such a form is presented as Figure 8–2. You will see that critical points are noted, theme titles are assigned, and page numbers are indicated (in the event that the researcher has cause to re-examine her narrative). These and other findings recorded on such a form by you and other observers will provide a basis for uncovering patterns. By having each observer use common titles or codes, trends can be detected more readily.

b. *Attempt to interpret the social meaning of the behavior or events that occurred during the course of the observations*. Not only should the reporter reveal the context for the behaviors or events, but she should also attempt to offer their implications. However, conclusions should be considered tentative, and should be revised as new information surfaces.

c. *Analyze the relationships between the observations and any external forces that appear to be operating*. "Why did one of the teachers feel that way?" or "Why did the student threaten to leave the classroom before the period ended?" Pursuant to arriving at the findings for the study, generalizations may be speculative or even impossible to make. Remember, unlike many of the research methods described in this book, the findings of case studies are *not* generalizable. This is largely due to the:

- small sample size,
- lack of controls, and
- informality of the data-gathering processes.

With regard to the practice of measurement within the context of qualitative investigations, the investigator is the *de facto* instrument of assessment. While there is a trend toward group- or team-oriented qualitative research, most research projects are still carried out by individuals working on their own. Estimates of validity, reliability, and objectivity (discussed in Chapter 5, Selecting Instruments of Assessment) are considered a vital part of qualitative studies, as they are with any form of research. With the exception of the data generated through test and measurement research (to be discussed later in the chapter), estimates are not represented by numerical coefficients. Instead, they exist through the competence and commitment of the individuals conducting the study, and the methods they employ to address such matters as:

- comparing observations made on different occasions (**diachronic reliability**),

Figure 8–2: **Contact Summary Form**

Contact Summary

Source Name: <u>Donna Anderson</u>

Place: <u>Rounds-035</u>
Date/Time: <u>10/01/97; 0900 hrs</u>

Directions: In the space provided, record the *most important points* in the contact. Assign a *theme title* to each point, and indicate the *page number* in your notes on which that point appears.

Critical Points	Theme Title	Note Page
MS degree plus 25 hours	Credentials	1
12 years teaching experience (9 at Plymouth State College, 3 at Manchester Memorial HS), 3 years as camp director, 5 years as camp counselor, 2 years in military (corporal)	Experience	2
Majored in mathematics education, minored in special education (undergraduate); majored in administration-supervision (graduate)	Training	5
Member of Phi Delta Kappa (initiated in 1993); National Association of Mathematics Teachers (1986); Council for Exceptional Children (1988)	Memberships	7
Primary teaching interests are: introductory mathematics courses, Introduction to the Academic Community	Teaching interests	9
Aspires to move into higher-education administration; admitted into doctoral program at Columbia University (requesting sabbatical leave for Fall Semester, 1998)	Professional goals	1, 12
Became a teacher because: dad was teacher for 30 years; enjoyed working with children at camps. Feels that she can be a major influence in the lives of those she teaches	Reasons for career choice	15
Immediate family members include husband, one child, two brothers, mother, father	Family	14

Observer: Leo Sandy

- comparing observations made by two or more people of the same event (**synchronic reliability**), and

- interviewing the same individual on more than one occasion.

Other methods to help ensure consistency include the use of audio and video equipment. The value of such devices cannot be overestimated. During the course of rapid flowing conversation, it is virtually impossible to write down all verbal interactions that occurred. An audio recorder can do that. Likewise, a video recorder can "observe" things that the researcher might miss. Further, every time that the tapes are reviewed, the information presented will be exactly the same. Because of the value of such devices, the researcher should consider requesting permission to record selected observations and interviews.

At this juncture, one of the most frequently employed qualitative designs, the *case study,* will be examined.

CASE STUDY METHOD

In conjunction with selecting a problem to study, such as "What are the characteristics of those who are recipients of distinguished teaching awards?", the investigator must select an institution in which the research can take place. Is the interest of the researcher placed at the elementary, middle school / junior high, high school, or college level? An obvious criterion for making a site selection is having access to institutions within which teachers are employed who have received the award. If there is no award structure within a convenient K–12 setting, it may be necessary to move onto another environment, perhaps the college level. Once the institution is selected, it is necessary to identify those teachers who meet the criteria for the study. Once they and the criteria for their selection are known, it is necessary to arrange for information access, including documents, on-site interviews, and observations. Some of the interviews with the recipients would be one-on-one; others would be with teachers in a group. Observations would be arranged to take place in the classroom. The researcher may also want to observe the teachers as they participate in committee meetings or go to the "Academic Commons" for lunch and conversation with other faculty members. Certainly, it would be important to examine syllabi for the courses they are assigned to teach, articles or books they have written, papers they have presented, professional memberships they hold, honor societies to which they belong, and any other evidence of scholarship. The investigator may also want to meet with the direct supervisors of those teachers who meet the criteria for the study, and she would arrange interviews with students. The respective family members of the award recipients may also be valuable sources of information about hobbies and interests that may provide another perspective on the nature of those who are considered exceptional.

Since it may be possible that the members of the study group do *not* have common interests or reasons to gather together in social situations, it may be more effective to use the interview rather than the participatory approach with them. In selecting a setting for a case study, however, be mindful of the fact that, while small samples may have advantages (in terms of information access), the smaller the number of individuals who are subjects of the study, the greater the potential for the investigator's presence to cause changes in behavior. By the same token, the larger the group of subjects, the more likely it is that the researcher can remain unobtrusive. The researcher has to balance the advantages of small sample size against the threat of obtrusiveness.

The conduct of a case study will now be examined against the standard elements of a research plan discussed in earlier chapters. Assuming that Phase 1 of the research plan has been completed for the scenario: "What are the characteristics of those who are recipients of distinguished teaching awards?", the investigator is now ready to prepare the research template.

✓CHECKPOINT

For each of the following subproblems, identify what you believe would be the requisite questions for which responses must be considered in advance of carrying out the study. If necessary, refer to examples that were offered for descriptive studies in earlier chapters. Sample responses are provided at the conclusion of the exercise.

1. Permission/selection of subjects

2. Selection of instruments

3. Administration of study/collection of data

4. Analysis of data/conclusions/recommendations

Answers

Among the responses you should have considered to each of the subproblems are the following.

1. *Permission/selection of subjects*

a. What institution(s) within a selected geographical area have in their employ teachers who are recipients of distinguished teaching awards?

b. What is the identity of the teachers who are recipients of the award?

c. Do I have permission from all pertinent parties to conduct the study?

d. What sources of information pertaining to the research question are available, including:

- recipients of distinguished teaching awards,
- administrators,
- fellow teachers,
- students of those teachers who are award recipients,
- families of award recipients,
- official records, and
- personal communications?

e. What are the timelines for conducting the study?

2. *Selection of instruments*

a. What numbers of individuals do I need to assist with the observations?

b. Who would agree to serve as associate observers?

c. What responsibility would each selected observer have?

d. Have all associates been trained?

e. What recording forms will be necessary?

f. What will be the code system for **tracking** responses?

g. What technology will I need to have available and functioning?

h. Has permission has been obtained for making audio and video recordings?

i. Are recording forms and equipment available and in sufficient quantities?

3. *Administration of study/collection of data*

a. Will information from interviews, recordings, and all pertinent documents be accessed in a way to control for:
   - inadequate amounts of evidence,
   - inadequate variety of evidence, and
   - inadequate attention to discrepant findings?

b. Have all prime sources of evidence been included to a sufficient degree in the data-gathering process, including:
   - recipients of awards,
   - official records and other documents,
   - adminstrators,
   - fellow teachers,
   - students, and
   - families of recipients?

c. Are plans in place for conducting **debriefing** sessions with all associate observers?

d. Are steps in place to revise research questions (and hypotheses) should new evidence come to light?

e. Will data be sorted in a manner conducive to appropriate analysis, and in keeping with requirements for validity and reliability?

4. *Analysis of data/conclusions/recommendations*

a. What are the characteristics of those who are recipients of distinguished teaching awards as revealed through formative and summary examination of:
   - field notes,
   - observations,
   - interviews,
   - recordings, and
   - official records and personal communications?

b. What data lend themselves to quantitative analysis?

c. What statistical procedures will be appropriate given the nature of the data:

- nominal,
- ordinal,
- interval, and/or
- ratio?

d. What conclusions and interpretations are appropriate to the findings in light of data collection, and personal thoughts and experiences?

e. What follow-up studies are recommended in light of the findings, conclusions, and interpretations?

Did you come up with any other questions? Give some thought to how *all* questions, yours and those listed in the Checkpoint, would need to be addressed in terms of:

- where the answers will be found,
- how the answers will be found,
- procedures for organizing and analyzing the information for further use, and
- conclusions that would follow from the procedures and allow the researcher to proceed with the study.

It is critical that thoughtful, commonsense approaches be taken to drawing conclusions from evidence (Sadler, 1981). Be mindful of the following factors.

- First impressions. Make sure that they do *not* dominate the direction observers take in order to acquire additional information.

- Unalterable research questions and hypotheses. These can result if the investigator is too regulated by preconceived notions. Evidence may be "unconsciously" sought, obtained, and offered as fact. Be open to all sources of information, and to evidence that may discredit previous findings.

- Novelty effects. These can be disruptive in that extreme impressions or novel behavior may be assigned too much weight and importance in comparison with the ideas and facts that appear over and over again.

- Relying on memory. This can lead to gaps in the information pool. Recording *all* information will address this problem. It is very easy to be "taken up" with a particular behavior at the expense of other events in the environment.

- Terminating a study before all evidence has been examined. This relates to the "first impression" issue, but is broader. Be sure to consider all pertinent sources of information regardless of what you *think* might be said or done. Anticipation should not get in the way of observations.

Thoughtful analysis of the patterns evolving from the various data sources will lead to meaningful conclusions. While the free flow of information arising during the course of an interview may appear to have been the result of a casual research design, this is *not* the reality in quality case study investigations. Planning for circumstances that lead to the appearance of a relaxed inteview environment is often more difficult than preparing for structured experimentation. Those of you who teach or have taught know that preparing lesson plans that are designed to invoke class-room discussion is frequently more difficult than planning a lecture. In short, care-fully planned designs are critical to any successful research endeavor.

HISTORICAL METHOD

There are those who believe that historical research is little more than reading a text-book on history purchased at the local bookstore and, from that information, draw-ing a few conclusions about issues of interest. Those same individuals, it would seem, have little experience with the process of historical research. While it is true that exercising controls common to many other research designs is not possible, his-torical investigations do require thoughtful attention to data collection and analysis. The *historian* systematically locates, assesses, and interprets evidence of the past with a view toward understanding the circumstances underlying the present. From this information, it is hoped that a *new understanding* will lead to the making of more intelligent choices.

Moehlman, Van Tassel, Goetzmann, and Everett (1969) described a classification system to help organize the variety of history topics found in the literature. Specifically, the objective of this system is to provide a format for storing and retrieving the increas-ing numbers of historical documents being published in education. The authors pose eleven categories to make possible the classification of historical information:

1. Biographies relating to educational history
2. General educational history
3. History of educational legislation—for example, bonds, court cases, curriculum, equalization programs, school land boards and districts, state-supported schools and universities, and taxation
4. Historical biographies of major contributors to education
5. History of major branches of education—for example, community education, curriculum, enrollment, finance, goals, instructional methods and materials, organization and administration, personnel, and school accreditation and atten-dance laws
6. Institutional history of education—for example, colleges and universities, cor-respondence schools, elementary schools, kindergartens, secondary schools, military schools, research organizations, and vocational schools
7. Cultural history of education—for example, anthropology, ethnology, sociology, and technology
8. History of educational planning and policy
9. Historical critiques of education
10. Comparative history of international education
11. History of contemporary problems in education

Among the valuable resources available to both novice and experienced researchers is the *History of Education Quarterly* (1961 to the present). Published by the History of Education Society in cooperation with the School of Education, New York University, the *Quarterly* includes articles that cross the span of categories described by Moehlman et al. The educational historian seeking to learn more of what has been published to date, and to gain insights into the direction that future research might take, should consider beginning her search here. While there are historical studies that would not be found in this single reference, there is sufficient variety for that publication to be considered a *major* source of pertinent information. (See Chapter 1, Selection and Definition of a Problem, for other sources of information.)

While reading texts about late nineteenth century American education will provide useful information about the past, a historical study should *not* be done to find out what is already known about a topic so that it can be retold. Rather, the purpose of such a study is to explain or predict from the implications of one's findings. Further, as with other types of research, its purpose should be to examine unfamiliar information, and to use those discoveries to clarify, add, or correct what is already known. One way to examine trends in order to arrive at a concensus of evidence for selected periods of time is to use a process known as **documentary analysis.** With this technique, the investigator offers possible responses to a research question (often determined with the assistance of a jury), and then examines documents that have been identified as prime sources of information to see if the authors of those sources corroborate those suggested responses, or offer others. When it is determined that a document offers a response (whether or not it corroborates any of those suggested by the investigator), the document is noted, along with a page number where that information can be found in the prime source, on a documentary analysis form. When all documents selected as prime sources have been examined thoroughly, the investigator looks for trends on the recording form. The page numbers are recorded on the form so that the researcher can easily go back to find pertinent narrative within each of the references.

Assume that an investigator is interested in learning of the responses of eight prime sources regarding the causes of the Vietnam War. Each "cause" would be numbered down the left side of the recording form, and the eight sources would be listed across the top of the form (see Figure 8–3). An examination of the chart in Figure 8–3 shows that the cause most frequently mentioned was 4 (all *eight* references indicated that it was one of the causes of the Vietnam War). Cause 3 was the second most frequently referenced (noted in *six* of the prime sources), and cause 5 ranked third

Figure 8–3: **Recording Form for a Documentary Analysis**

				Sources				
Causes	Smith	Johnson	Anderson	Brooks	Wirble	Decotis	Smart	Carter
1	p 38	–	–	p 16	p 52	–	–	–
2	p 67	p 40	–	–	–	–	–	–
3	–	p 13	p 91	p 22	–	p 11	p 101	p 30
(4)	p 13	p 88	p 77	p 37	p 35	p 25	p 77	p 33
(5)	p 21	p 63	p 14	–	p 19	–	–	p 11

( ) = author-initiated causes

in **frequency of mention** (in that it was discussed in *five* of the prime sources). If the researcher wanted to focus on the top three causes of the Vietnam War, they would be ranked, and she would then go back to the pertinent pages within the prime sources that sited those particular causes in order to retrieve pertinent narrative. The investigator would then prepare a report to include findings, conclusions, and inferences. In addition to a *qualitative* analysis of the findings, the investigator might want to include *quantitative* backup, such as:

- the *mode* identifying the most frequent cause,
- the *percentages of attainment* for the top three causes, and
- the *chi square* value indicating whether these findings were significant when observed to expected frequencies were contrasted.

While historical research can be guided by hypotheses, the process of data collection is most often structured by the use of research questions. As these questions are addressed, commentary regarding implications and need for further inquiry is added.

One feature that makes case studies, historical research, and philosophical research different from many other forms of research is that the sources one is directed to use are often products of information and advice arising during the *course* of the investigation. Literature reviews and study procedures are woven into the same process. This is why research questions posed during the planning stages of the investigation require revision as the study unfolds. The use of research questions is important, however, not only because they provide focus to data collection, but also because they help to organize one's thoughts and direction as the study proceeds (Charles, 1995). When examining the evolution of topics for in-service programs for teachers, for example, an initial research question may be: "What provisions were made to integrate the recommendations made by teachers into the determination of meaningful themes for in-service workshops?" If, during the initial stages of the investigation, it was determined that teachers were not provided with opportunities to offer recommendations in this regard, the research question would, by necessity, have to be modified.

Another distinction is that, in the majority of survey and experimental designs, the investigator has the opportunity to use random sampling techniques in order to select representative individuals or groups. Historians, on the other hand, can examine only those persons, events, or relics for which artifacts and records remain. It is in this regard that a number of considerations must be taken into account. The study of procedures, known as **historiography,** follows an orderly sequence of events, as set out in the following text.

Selection of a Problem

Unlike many other studies, historical inquiry does not depend upon the creation of data through the use of achievement tests, questionnaires, and other instruments of assessment. The investigator is limited to whatever data are available. Hence, it is important that a problem be selected for which information is accessible. It is equally important that the topic be manageable; otherwise, the amount of data that are available on the topic may be impossible to access during the course of one's lifetime, let alone within the imposed deadlines for submitting findings and conclusions.

For those who are unaccustomed to thinking about topics suitable for historical inquiry, but who are seeking ideas, Beach (1969) suggests five general research areas that may help to provide direction and "set the wheels in motion." Within each of these areas, the author has offered topical ideas:

1. Social issues—such as absenteeism, inclusionary education, school violence, segregation, or substance abuse

2. Study of specific individuals, and educational institutions—such as Horace Mann, Montessori Schools, or the evolution of teacher-education programs leading to certification in learning disabilities within School Administrative Unit #48

3. Exploration of relationships between events—such as standardized testing *and* curriculum revision, vacancies in teaching positions *and* starting salaries, or teenage pregnancies *and* formal school health instruction

4. Synthesis of data, in which evidence of the past is merged with contemporary findings—such as national teacher-accreditation standards, school disciplinary practices, or integrated arts programs within the K–12 curriculum.

NOTE: In *quantitative* research practices, the process of integrating findings from various studies is called *meta-analysis*.

5. Reinterpretation of past events—such as incorporating the views of alumni when evaluating the appropriateness of school board practices, looking at new evidence on school-to-job transition programs for graduates with exceptionalities, or examining the views of new association members regarding program emphases of the organization

NOTE: One poignant example of reinterpreting findings of history is the recent attention being assigned to examining contemporary arguments about the Holocaust in Europe (1939–1945). While historians have provided documentation of the atrocities of the period, some individuals have made an effort to rewrite history by claiming that the Holocaust did not occur (Lipstadt, 1993).

When pursuing a topic, it is generally considered more appropriate to investigate a specific problem area with a few, clearly stated research questions (or hypotheses) than to attempt to study a broader idea, or a problem for which insufficient primary or secondary sources are available.

Preparation of a Research Plan

It is suggested that the construction of the plan follow the guidelines discussed in Chapter 3, Preparation of a Research Plan. This would include:

- Time schedule
- Tentative budget

- Statement of the problem
- Need (justification) for the study
- Review of related literature

Since the literature review and use of prime and secondary sources are processes that are connected, be mindful that consideration is given to examining all possible sources of information. To do this, the investigator should consider making plans to access:

1. oral records (through conducting interviews),
2. quantitative records (through examining such things as attendance records, budgets, and examination scores),
3. relics (through examining such things as architectural plans, buildings, furniture, instructional aids, and textbooks), and
4. written documents/records (through examining such things as administrative directives, files, journals, lesson plans, meeting minutes, memoranda, menus, newspapers, periodicals, syllabi, tests, written testimony, and yearbooks).

For obvious reasons, original documents (including written communications), relics, and reports by observers and participants of events are considered to be the most valid sources of information. Once authenticated, these are called **primary sources.**

 NOTE: It is important to understand that historical studies require that a literature search takes on a broader meaning. A challenge to the acquisition of written communications between individuals, for example, is that such pieces of information are not generally indexed by author, subject, and title within a library as would be many other pieces of evidence. As a consequence, it is often necessary to employ creative methods in order to access the information that is desired. Though painstaking, the job can generally be done by those who persist.

One example of a **secondary source** is a person who may have heard or read about the event, but did not witness it. Other examples of secondary sources are reference books (unless one is doing a historical study of reference books), newspaper accounts, and reports given by family members of witnesses. While information from such sources should not be discounted without cause, the investigator must remember that what is reported may differ from the original version (because it includes perceptions of what was read or said).

NOTE: For a discussion of *external* and *internal* criticism as they relate to the use of prime and secondary literature sources, see the text under the next heading, "Systematic Collection of the Data."

To complete Phase 1 of the research plan, the researcher needs to:

- State the research questions (or hypotheses)
- State the basic assumptions

- List possible threats to the study
- Offer testimony to the fact that design alternatives were considered
- Provide definitions of terms

Once Phase 1 of the research plan is complete, the researcher is ready to prepare the template for the study, including reference to:

1. selection of additional prime and secondary sources (not identified within the review of the literature),

2. selection of instruments, which would be the researcher and any trained assistants,

 NOTE: As with case studies, the individuals carrying out the study are the instruments of assessment.

3. administration of the study/collection of data, and

4. analysis of data/conclusions/recommendations.

After these subproblems have been addressed by way of (a) where the answers will be found, (b) how the answers will be found, (c) selecting procedures for organizing and analyzing the information for further use, and (d) identifying conclusions that would follow from the procedures and allow the researcher to proceed with the study, the researcher is in a position to move to the next step, namely, the systematic collection of the data.

Systematic Collection of the Data

When making judgments about the appropriateness of data sources, there are two forms of criticism against which those sources should be evaluated. They are called *external* (first-level) and *internal* (second-level) criticism.

External criticism refers to the *authenticity* of the evidence. Depending upon the nature of the study, it might require authentication of signatures, carbon dating of artifacts, or chemical analysis of paint. Consider that a historian may have a letter describing Montessori schools that is believed to have been written by Maria Montessori herself. Employing the process of external criticism, the researcher would investigate such things as:

1. The handwriting. Does it contain the style, grammar, spelling, and syntax quality known to be that of Maria Montessori?

2. Points of view. Are they consistent with other writings of Montessori?

3. The paper. Is it of the right age?

Once external (first-level) criticism has been established, the researcher then moves on to the next level of criticism, that is, internal (second-level) criticism.

Internal criticism addresses the *accuracy* of the information and is concerned with such things as the following.

1. Bias and motives of the author. Is there evidence that the reporter is distorting reality? While one might have originally intended to report "what was observed," there might be an embellishment of details in order to make the report more "exciting." An account of an event may have even been enhanced unintentionally. It is the task of the researcher to determine the accuracy of a report *before* it is used. Bearing witness to some of the news that is reported to the public, it is easy to see the importance of accuracy in any account of an event.

2. Consistency of the data. Do the accounts provided by one individual concur with accounts others have given of the event? The fact that there is agreement between the accounts of different individuals helps to offer evidence of validity for the statements. At the same time, however, do *not* automatically disregard a report that may appear to be in contradiction with others. Consider the observation positions that different individuals may have had of an event. It is possible for two people to witness an event and, because of where each was located, see things differently.

3. Knowledge and competence of the author. Was the individual qualified to write on the subject? Was she in a position to be aware of the facts? These are considerations that must be taken into account before assigning credibility to what has been written. Because individuals are notable authors in one discipline does not necessarily qualify them as experts in another.

4. Time delay between the occurrence of an event and the telling or writing about it. As time passes, memories can become clouded. The sooner a witness can sit down and write about what was seen, the more accurate the account is likely to be. If the witness took notes during the observation, the chances of reporting an accurate account of the event are even greater (*unless the individual was so busy taking notes that she did not see what happened*).

There are many factors that go into the evolution of good historical investigations. When, in conjunction with the principles of qualitative (and quantitative) analysis described earlier, each of them is attended to with care and diligence, there is every reason to believe that a credible report will follow.

CAUSAL-COMPARATIVE METHOD

While historical research is undertaken in order to examine the causes and effects of events from the past, causal-comparative studies begin with effects followed by an investigation of causes. In this design, attempts are made to examine whether events or circumstances that have already occurred could have produced the subsequent differences in the subjects selected for investigation. The essence of the procedure is that, upon observing that groups are different on some **dependent variable,** the investigator attempts to identify the **independent variables** that contributed to that difference. Since both the effect and probable causes have already occurred and, therefore, are investigated in retrospective, the design is referred to as *ex post facto* (Latin for "after the fact"). The circumstances are present and have *not* been arranged by the investigator.

Other than being able to take advantage of an existing opportunity, there are two reasons why the researcher may *not* have manipulated the variables.

1. It may not have been possible to manipulate the variables. Such examples include: (a) birth order, (b) employment status of parents, (c) ethnicity, (d) family income, and (e) gender.

2. It may not have been appropriate (ethical) to manipulate the variables. Such examples include: (a) behavior modification (for example, corporal punishment), (b) denying access to counseling services, (c) denying early intervention to parents of children with exceptionalities, (d) denying health care, and (e) ergogenic aids (for example, alcohol, amphetamines, nicotine).

To understand the principles of the process, consider that an instructor of a graduate course in research design has administered a diagnostic pretest on the first day of class in order to determine the extent to which students are already knowledgeable about topics normally included in the course. She feels that information gained through examining student responses will aid in the planning of upcoming lessons. Upon reviewing student answers, it is found that a group of students were able to correctly answer a significant number of the questions but, for the most part, other students appear to have had great difficulty. With the instructor's interest in determining what may have led to that difference, she poses hypotheses to test.

Unlike the nature of research hypotheses for descriptive studies that have been described to date, causal-comparative studies require that the researcher identify plausible **rival hypotheses** that might explain observed differences. Given the above scenario, some alternative hypotheses might be that students who scored well on the pretest had successfully completed:

- An *undergraduate* degree with a GPA of 3.25 or higher
- A *major* in mathematics
- A *minor* in mathematics
- A minimum of one *undergraduate* statistics course
- An *undergraduate* course in logic

During the investigation, it is discovered that each of the students who scored high in the pretest had completed an undergraduate course in logic with a grade of C or higher, whereas students who scored low in the pretest did not complete such a course. It would appear, therefore, that at least one common thread among the students who scored well was their having completed an undergraduate course in logic. While the testing of additional hypotheses would be necessary before arriving at final conclusions, the instructor could make a *tentative* recommendation that the logic course be listed as a prerequisite for enrolling in the graduate course in research design.

With the general principles underlying causal-comparative studies in mind, *quantitative* procedures that can prove helpful to arriving at findings and conclusions about effects (dependent variables) and causes (independent variables) can be examined. First, it is important to determine if the difference between the students on the dependent variable is *statistically significant* or can be attributed to *chance alone*. This requires that the investigator consider such statistics as:

1. the mean and standard deviation of the two groups (see Chapter 6, Survey Procedures), and

2. the *t* test and analysis of variance (see Chapter 9, Single-Group Designs, and Chapter 10, Two-Group Designs).

NOTE: Computational and analytical procedures will be presented in Part III, Chapters 9 and 10.

If significant differences between the two groups on the dependent variable are established, the investigator will proceed to treat the data generated from an examination of the rival hypotheses. The procedures that can be used include:

1. the percent of individuals in each group who have met the standard, per rival hypothesis (see Chapter 6, Survey Procedures); and

2. the chi square test to determine if there is a significant difference between expected and observed frequencies, per rival hypothesis (see Chapter 6, Survey Procedures).

 NOTE: An alternative process for conducting causal-comparative studies would be to form comparison groups on the basis of completing/not completing a particular experience (for example, a course in ethics), and to analyze their performances in the dependent variable. This procedure is also referred to as *ex post facto* research because both the independent and dependent variables are already in place.

The sequence of steps for designing causal-comparative research projects follows the procedures described earlier in this chapter, and in Chapter 3, Preparation of a Research Plan. Needless to say, the *tighter* the design, the *fewer* the threats to the success of the investigation.

 **CHECKPOINT**

Earlier in the chapter, a case study was selected as the design of choice for the scenario: "What are the characteristics of those who are recipients of distinguished teaching awards?" Under what conditions would causal-comparative research have been appropriate?

Answer

It would have been possible to do an *ex post facto* study with this topic if the researcher was going to limit her study to examining the independent variables that could have contributed to being selected as distinguished teachers. Once it was determined, however, that the researcher wanted to observe teaching methods, she was moving from what had already been established to an examination of *current* practices. Can one employ more than one design during the course of a study? The answer is *yes,* providing all pertinent principles for each of the designs are followed.

PHILOSOPHICAL METHOD

The most critical and far-reaching decisions made in education are based, in large part, upon philosophical considerations. Whether a practitioner is deciding upon course content, teaching methodology, curriculum reorganization, or the objectives of education, her philosophy on the matter is brought "to the table." It is *philosophy* that provides the underpinning for action. Further, it provides a method for solving problems that cannot wait for protracted experimentation. Through the avenues of critical thinking, reason is applied to the processes that govern thought and conduct. Out of deliberations, the philosophical method attaches generalizations to the findings of science. To arrive at such generalizations, the researcher employs the practice of aesthetics, epistemology, ethics, logic, and metaphysics:

1. **Aesthetics** refers to the sensitivity one has for appreciating and cultivating art and beauty.

2. **Epistemology** refers to the study of nature, sources, and limits of knowledge.

3. **Ethics** refers to a system of moral standards, values, and conduct.

4. **Logic** refers to the science of inductive and deductive reasoning, and that which describes relationships among propositions in terms of contradiction and implication.

5. **Metaphysics** is that branch of philosophy that deals with the *first* principles of things, seeks to explain the nature of being or reality **(ontology),** and is closely associated with the study of nature and knowledge **(epistemology).**

When confronted with a problem, one frequently draws from personal experiences in order to arrive at a solution. A teacher who faces a disruption in class will often choose to respond in a way that she has found to be effective in the past. We all know, however, that a behavior modification strategy that was successful with one student may not be effective with another. Hence, personal experiences do *not* always generate useful responses. When the practitioner-researcher acknowledges that this is reality, she will seek and evaluate additional information in order to acquire a basis for more thoughtful choices.

Through the work of Dewey (1933) and others, recommended steps for conducting philosophical studies have emerged. While the general procedures closely parallel those of other research designs discussed to date, there are additional thought processes that should be integrated into the Phase 1 and 2 templates (described in Chapter 3, Preparation of a Research Plan, and other sections of this book). It is in this regard that the following information is provided.

1. Upon identifying and delimiting the problem area to manageable proportions, the investigator would begin to collect available facts related to that problem. As with historical studies, this process is closely connected with the literature review (common to Phase 1 of the research plan). Considering *violence in sport* as a possible topic for philosophical investigation, the initial research questions might include the following.

a. What photographs can be found in *Sports Illustrated* that appear to glorify violence?

b. To what degree do insurance premiums change when football, lacrosse, rugby, or wrestling is added as an intramural or intercollegiate sport within a high school or college?

c. What books related to sport violence are published by Random House?

d. What published works on the effects of ergogenic aids upon human performance and aggressiveness can be found in the *Research Quarterly for Exercise and Sport* (published by the American Alliance for Health, Physical Education, Recreation and Dance)?

e. Do aggressive individuals seek to play football, or does the playing of football make individuals aggressive?

f. What is the effect of crowd noise on the incidence and intensity of spectator violence at indoor sports arenas?

g. Has the redesign of football equipment contributed to the seriousness of athletic injuries among adversaries?

2. While the researcher will start out with tentative research questions, newly acquired information will likely prompt new questions. Not only is this expected, but it is also desired because the researcher wants to update her thinking as new facts and sources of information become known.

Consider a scenario in which a teaching practitioner at a local college is interested in creating a course that would integrate various academic disciplines. Given her interest in examining the emerging force of violence upon the sport scene, the practitioner decides that she would like to develop a course that would provide for an examination of the relationship between sport and violence as examined through the fields of art, business, English, natural science, psychology, sociology, and sports medicine. The researcher elects to recruit a minimum of one interested faculty member from each of these program areas in order to form a course planning task force (jury). It is expected that each of these individuals will bring her own expertise and philosophical perspective to the debate.

a. The representative from the *art department* will be responsible for examining drawings, paintings, photographs, and sculpture for related evidence.

b. The representative from the *business department* will be responsible for examining sport marketing, trends in fan attendance, as well as implications of injuries (care, treatment, player replacement) to costs of the organization.

c. The representative from the *English department* will be responsible for examining published and unpublished documents for reference to sport violence.

d. The representative from the *natural science department* will be responsible for examining the implications of the use and abuse of chemicals and other substances by athletes.

e. The representative from the *psychology department* will be responsible for examining mental and emotional processes contributing to the individual and group behavior of athletes and fans at sporting events.

f. The representative from the *social science department* (who teaches sociology) will be responsible for examining historical and contemporary beliefs and values as they relate to violence in athletics.

g. The representative from the *health and physical education department* (who manages the athletic training/sports medicine program) will be responsible for examining the effect of equipment modifications and conditioning/training upon frequency and intensity of sport injuries.

3. As findings are gathered, they are synthesized and analyzed, and efforts are made to identify relationships between them. From these patterns, general principles are formed which, in the case of the scenario on developing a course on the topic of sport violence, provide for the integration of the findings from various fields of study. As a consequence of thoughtful deliberation of all elements pertinent to the investigation, the researcher would eventually arrive at a course title and description.

Course title: Violence in Sport: Psychosocial Implications

Description: A study of psychological and social forces that contribute to sport violence. This phenomenon will be examined from ancient civilization to contemporary amateur and professional athletics as revealed through literature, the arts, and social and natural sciences.

Described have been the considerations that make philosophical research unique from more traditional designs. For the subproblems found in Phase 2 of the research plan:

a. Permission/selection of subjects would address:

- gaining permission from pertinent parties to offer a new course,
- identifying departments appropriate for inclusion in the planning process, and
- selecting department representatives to serve as members of the jury.

b. Selection of instrument would be addressed by:

- having the jury serve as the instruments of assessment (similar to the process in historical studies).

c. Administration of study/collection of data would include the process of gathering data from prime and secondary sources, per:

- the art perspective,
- the business pespective,
- the literature perspective,
- the natural science perspective,
- the psychology perspective,
- the sociology perspective, and
- the sports medicine perspective.

d. Analysis of data/conclusions/recommendations would include:

- the application of the principles of critical thinking to the acquired data, and
- the formulation of a tentative solution—that is, the syllabus.

The findings of scientific inquiry are tempered with the judgments of critical thinking in order to arrive at a tentative solution (for example, the course syllabus). Per consideration for the scenario, as the course is taught, new findings and reflections will cause modifications in course objectives, content, and delivery. This is the essence of emerging enlightenment. The practice of science reveals new evidence; the practice of critical thinking leads to new philosophical positions. What better use can be made of philosophical inquiry than applying its principles to the process of curriculum design?

TEST AND MEASUREMENT METHOD

This form of research is used to create, validate, field-test, and revise instruments of assessment. Commonly used as a forerunner to conducting studies for which instruments are not already available, this method is very important to the gathering of information that otherwise would not be attainable. Many of the processes described in the chapter are also useful for the teacher who is interested in *revising* questions within her test. Of particular interest in this regard are *item analysis* techniques.

All forms of tests—including achievement, aptitude, attitude, interest, and intelligence—should be subjected to criticial analysis in advance of their use in data collection. Since the data that are gathered are only as good as the instruments that produce them, it is incumbent upon the practitioner-researcher to be as diligent as possible in the preparation and revision of these instruments.

While *research hypotheses* are almost always possible to create for studies of the descriptive variety, it is recommended that **research questions** be used with this method. Since validity, reliability, and objectivity are largely the product of the population samples and statistical tools used to estimate them, acceptable levels of test validity may be elusive. Therefore, preliminary data will likely cause a revision in the initial drafts of the test and, further, the research questions. Suppose, for example, that a preliminary research question was:

Does the test have estimates of **content validity?**

Subsequent to having a jury examine the test items against the objectives and table of specifications for purposes of estimating content validity, it may be determined that there would be merit in correlating that test against a test recently published by the Educational Testing Service (ETS) in Princeton, New Jersey, for which validity has already been established. The new research question might be:

Does the test have estimates of **concurrent validity?**

Like many other descriptive research models (that is, case-study, historical, and philosophical methods), test and measurement research often elicits information during the process of data collection that is best addressed by a change of focus.

In keeping with the traditions of all meaningful investigative inquiries, test and measurement research also requires that careful planning precede the actualization of the design. Pursuant to the identification of a problem interest, the researcher would attend to each of the ingredients of Phases 1 and 2 (see Chapter 3, Preparation of a Research Plan). Without repeating the details of each component, the essential elements to consider in Phase 1 are the following.

1. Time schedule
2. Tentative budget

3. Statement of the problem

4. Need (justification) for the study

5. Review of related literature

> **NOTE:** For test and measurement research, *review of the literature* would include an examination of: (a) related measuring instruments, including the processes for determining their validity and reliability, and (b) other studies that were designed to create assessment instruments.

6. Statement of the hypothesis (or, in the instance of test and measurement research, a statement of the research question)

> **NOTE:** An example of a research question for test and measurement research would be: *What evidence exists for content validity of a test designed to measure achievement in a first-year college anatomy course?*

7. Basic assumptions

8. Possible threats to the study

9. Design alternatives

10. Definitions of terms

> **NOTE:** Except as indicated, all of the considerations that are pertinent to these categories, per guidelines of Phase 1 of the research designs discussed to date, are applicable here.

When it comes to Phase 2, the nature of test and measurement research requires that very specific indicators pertinent to this particular form of investigation be addressed. Included among the important entries in the design template are the following.

1. *Permission/selection of subjects*

    a. What individuals would be available to serve as jurors to estimate the *content validity* of the testing instrument?

    b. What standardized tests exist that could serve as criteria by which *concurrent validity* can be estimated?

    c. What institutions/individuals would be willing to serve as a pilot test group for estimating the *reliability* of the testing instrument?

    d. What individuals would be available for training to serve as assistants to estimate the *objectivity* of the testing instrument?

    e. What are the timelines for conducting the study?

2. *Selection of instruments*

    a. What are the objectives of the test?

b. What categories of questions should be considered for inclusion in the test (for example, true-false, multiple-choice, matching, master list, enumeration, completion, or essay)?

c. What is the configuration of the *table of specifications?*

d. What are the tentative questions for the test?

e. What are the administrative directions for the test?

f. Has the test been prepared in keeping with the design of the study?

g. Has the cover letter for the test been prepared?

h. Have provisions been made for developing two or more forms of the test?

3. *Administration of the study/collection of data*

a. Has all pertinent information been distributed to the members of the jury in accordance with the design of the study, including: cover letter, administration directions, test objectives, table of specifications, and questions?

b. What are the estimates of the jury members regarding test *validity?*

c. Have revisions to the test been made in keeping with recommendations of the jury?

d. Does the instrument of assessment satisfy the criteria for estimates of *content* validity?

e. What are the estimates of *concurrent* validity for the test?

f. Have revisions been made to the test in response to the estimates of *concurrent* validity?

g. Does the instrument of assessment satisfy the criteria for estimates of *concurrent* validity?

h. What are the estimates of *reliability* for the test, including: **stability, equivalence** (if two forms of the test have been prepared), and internal consistency?

i. Have revisions been made to the test in response to the estimates of *reliability?*

j. Does the instrument of assessment satisfy the criteria for estimates of *reliability?*

k. What is the *measurement error* for the test?

l. Does the finding comply with recommendations, including: 100-point test (measurement error no greater than 2), or 1,000-point test (measurement error no greater than 20)?

m. What are the estimates for each item in terms of: difficulty, discrimination, and **functioning of alternatives** (in the case of multiple-choice items)?

n. What revisions are necessary in light of the findings?

o. What are the estimates of *objectivity* for the instruments of assessment?

p. What revisions are necessary in light of the findings?

q. Are steps in place to revise research objectives as new information becomes available?

4. *Analysis of data/conclusions/recommendations*

  a. Are findings of subproblem 3 sufficient to claim estimates of: validity, reliability, and objectivity?

  b. Are conditions suitable for norming the data (for example, percentiles)?

  c. Have all research objectives been addressed?

  d. What conclusions can be made about the instrument of assessment?

  e. What recommendations are appropriate to maintaining: validity, reliability, objectivity, quality of individual items (as to difficulty, discrimination, and functioning of alternatives), and norms?

In order to complete the planning template, one would respond to the questions for subproblems 1–4, in sequence, as to (a) where the answers will be found, (b) how the answers will be found, (c) procedures for organizing and analyzing the information for further use, and (d) conclusions that would follow from the procedures and allow the researcher to proceed with the study.

✓CHECKPOINT

The following questions are raised in regard to the relationship of test and measurement research to the information presented in Chapter 5, Selecting Instruments of Assessment. Correct answers are provided at the conclusion of the exercise.

1. What statistical procedure would be used to estimate the *concurrent validity* of an instrument of assessment?

2. What statistical procedures would be used to estimate the *stability* and *equivalence* of a testing instrument?

3. What statistical technique must be applied to a *split-half correlation* procedure in order to estimate the *reliability* of an entire test?

4. What is the relationship of the *measurement error* to the *reliability* of a test?

5. What distinguishes item *difficulty* from item *discrimination?*

Answers

The correct responses to the above questions are as follows.

1. One would use a *product-moment correlation* procedure. The investigator would administer the standardized test (Variable X) and the practitioner-made test (Variable Y) to the same group of individuals—thus creating pairs of scores for each subject.

2. Again, the investigator would employ *product-moment correlation* procedures. For estimating *stability,* one form of the practitioner-made test would be administered *twice* to the *same* group of individuals. The first administration of the test would be identified as Variable *X;* the second administration of the test would be identified as Variable *Y.* Estimates of *equivalence* would be determined by administering *two forms* of the test to the *same* group of individuals—that is, form *X* and form *Y.*

3. The **Spearman-Brown prophecy formula** would be administered to the results of a split-half correlation. Since the finding in the correlation analysis would represent the reliability of one-half of a test, the prophecy formula is used to estimate the reliability of the entire test.

4. The greater the reliability of a test, the less the measurement error would be. If a test has perfect reliability, there would not be any measurement error for that test at all. On the other hand, if a test lacks estimates of reliability, the measurement error would be as high as the variability of the test (that is, standard deviation).

5. *Item difficulty* represents the proportion of subjects who *got* the correct answer to a question compared with those who *attempted* to answer the question. On the other hand, *item discrimination* techniques examine the ratio between those who scored highest and lowest in the total test. If a test item is discriminating properly, the subjects who earned high scores in the test should get it correct, whereas subjects who earned low scores on the test should get the item incorrect. The important point in the analysis is: if subjects who earned low scores in the test got an item correct (where the high scorers got that same item incorrect), that item is in need of revision because it is discriminating inappropriately. In short, if an item is valid to the test, those who earn the highest total scores on that test should be more inclined to get the item correct.

If you do not remember the rationale underlying the responses to these five questions, it is recommended that you re-examine Chapter 5, Selecting Instruments of Assessment. In that chapter, you will also find pertinent formulas and procedural discussion.

SUMMARY

This chapter brought to light the purposes of and strategies for carrying out qualitative-type designs, including case-study, historical, causal-comparative, philosophical, and test and measurement research. For each of these approaches to descriptive investigations, strategies for planning design templates were presented. While each of the processes employ practices that are common to *all* qualitative designs, it should have become clear that there are techniques that are unique to each of them. Unlike the emphasis on random sampling presented in Chapter 4, Sampling Procedures, the nature of qualitative studies often requires the use of *purposive* sampling methods. This was made particularly evident when discussing case-study research in that, once a topic has been identified, the investigator must gravitate to those sites that house the information needed.

To some observers, historical and causal-comparative studies appear to have many similarities. From reading the chapter, however, it should be clear that each has a very distinct purpose. To illustrate: historical studies address the internal and external validity of prime and secondary sources in order to arrive at the causes and effects of events from the past. On the other hand, causal-comparative studies generally begin with effects, followed by an examination of possible causes.

Philosophical research is designed with the intent of attaching generalizations to the findings of science. Through the principles of aesthetics, epistemology, ethics, logic, and metaphysics, reason is applied to the processes that govern thought and conduct. While it was made clear that philosophy impacts upon all areas of the curriculum, including systems of evaluation, test and measurement research extends to the practice of utilizing specific evaluatory methods in order to create or revise these instruments.

With a knowledge of the various descriptive methods available, the researcher-practitioner is now able to make intelligent choices about the model that is most appropriate for actualizing her research interests.

RECOMMENDED LABORATORY ASSIGNMENTS

1. Review the recommended readings.

2. Arrange to meet with fellow graduate students and colleagues in order to discuss strategies for designing:

    a. Case studies

    b. Historical research

    c. Causal-comparative research

    d. Philsophical research

    e. Test and measurement research

3. Prepare a research plan for a topic suitable for examination by one of the methods identified in question 2. All of the elements of Phase 1 and Phase 2 should be addressed, including:

    a. Time schedule

    b. Tentative budget

    c. Statement of need (justification) for the study

    d. Integration of eight to ten related literature articles

    e. Statement of your research hypothesis, rival research hypotheses, and research questions

    f. List of basic assumptions

    g. List of possible threats to *internal* validity, and how you would control for them

    h. Identification of factors that would need to be considered to maintain *external* validity

    i. Evidence that contrasting designs were examined, and the basis upon which a final determination was made

    j. Definitions of important terms

    k. Template that includes responses to all pertinent subproblems, as well as to the questions related to: what, where, how, organization and analysis, and conclusions

4. For a historical issue of your choice, complete a documentary analysis using no fewer than *five* documents that have satisfied all pertinent standards of internal *and* external validity.

5. Arrange to meet with fellow graduate students, colleagues, as well as school and nonschool employees who have carried out any of the forms of descriptive investigations presented in this chapter, in order to review and discuss common interests and plans.

6. Using a research plan for a topic designed in response to the Recommended Laboratory Assignments of Chapters 6, 7, or 8, administer the study and arrange to present the findings at a professional meeting, conference, or convention.

RECOMMENDED READINGS

Asher, W., & Schusler, M. M. (1967). Students' grades and access to cars. *Journal of Educational Research, 60,* 10.

Atkinson, P., Delamont, S., & Hammersley, M. (1988). Qualitative research traditions: A British response to Jacob. *Review of Educational Research, 58,* 231–250.

Bailyn, B. (1969). The problems of the working historian. In A. S. Eisenstadt (Ed.), *The craft of American history.* New York: AHM.

Barzun, J., & Graff, H. F. (1992). *The modern researcher* (5th ed.). San Diego, CA: Harcourt-Brace Collegiate.

Beauchamp, E. R. (1987). The development of Japanese educational policy, 1945–1985. *History of Education Quarterly, 27,* 299–324.

Becker, H. S. (1958). Problems of inference and proof in participant observation. *American Sociological Review, 23,* 652–660.

Belmont, L., & Marolla, F. A. (1973). Birth order, family size, and intelligence. *Science, 182,* 1096–1101.

Benn, R. K. (1986). Factors promoting secure attachment relationships between employed mothers and their sons. *Child Development, 57,* 1224–1231.

Beringer, R. E. (1978). *Historical analysis: Contemporary approaches to Clio's craft.* Malabar, FL: R.E. Krieger.

Blase, J. J. (1988). The everyday political perspective of teachers: Vulnerability and conservatism. *Qualitative Studies in Education, I,* 125–142.

Brickman, W. W. (1982). *Educational historiography: Tradition, theory, and technique.* Cherry Hill, NJ: Emeritus.

Brooks, P. C. (1969). *Research in archives: The use of unpublished primary sources.* Chicago: University of Chicago Press.

Burstyn, J. N. (1987). History as image: Changing the lens. *History of Education Quarterly, 27,* 167–180.

Burton, O. V., & Finnegan, T. (1990). Teaching historians to use technology: Databases and computers. *International Journal of Social Education, 5,* 23–35.

Button, H. W. (1979). Creating more usable pasts: History in the study of education. *Educational Researcher, 8*(5), 3–9.

Button, H. W., & Provenzo, E. F., Jr. (1989). *History of education and culture in America* (2nd ed.). Englewood Cliffs, NJ: Prentice-Hall.

Carr, E. H. (1967). *What is history?* New York: Random House.

Chepyator-Thomson, J. R., & Ennis, C. D. (1997, March). Reproduction and resistance to the culture of feminity and masculinity in secondary school physical education. *Research Quarterly for Exercise and Sport, 68*(1), 89–99.

Clarke, C. R. (1975). *The influence of the idea of progress on the curriculum theories of experimentalism, essentialism, and reconstructionism.* Unpublished doctoral dissertation. East Tennessee State University, Johnson City, TN.

Cochran-Smith, M., & Lytle, S. L. (1990). Research on teaching and teacher research: The issues that divide. *Educational Researcher, 19*(2), 2–11.

Cohen, S. (1976). The history of the history of American education, 1900–1976: The uses of the past. *Harvard Educational Review, 46,* 298–330.

Connelly, M., & Clandinin, D. (1990). Stories of experience and narrative inquiry. *Educational Researcher, 19*(5), 2–14.

Cronbach, L. J. (1982). *Designing evaluations of educational and social programs.* San Francisco: Jossey-Bass.

Cunningham, L. J. (1987). The development and validation of a high school textbook on the ancient Chamorros of Guam. *Dissertation Abstracts International, 48*(11), 2796A. University Microfilms No. AAG88–00517.

Cunningham, L. J. (1992). *Ancient Chamorro society.* Honolulu, HI: The Bess Press.

Cutler, W. W., III. (1989). Cathedral of culture: The schoolhouse in American educational thought and practice since 1820. *History of Education Quarterly, 29,* 1–40.

Denzin, N. K., & Lincoln Y. S. (Eds.). (1994). *Handbook of qualitative research.* Thousand Oaks, CA: Sage.

Durm, M. W. (1993, Spring). An AQ is not an A is not an A: A history of grading. *The Educational Forum, 57,* 294–297.

Edson, C. H. (1986). Our past and present: Historical inquiry in education. *The Journal of Thought, 21,* 13–27.

Eliot, C. W. (1923). *Harvard memories.* Cambridge, MA: Harvard University Press.

Emerson, R. M. (Ed.). (1988). *Contemporary field research.* Prospect Heights, IL: Waveland.

Evans, V. W., & Schiller, J. (1970). How preoccupation with possible regression artifacts can lead to a faulty strategy for the evaluation of social action programs: A reply to Campbell and Erlebacher. In V. Hellmuth (Ed.), *Compensatory education: A national debate. Vol. 3: Disadvantaged Child.* New York: Brunner/Mazel.

Fetterman, D. M. (Ed.). (1988). *Qualitative approaches to evaluation in education: The silent scientific revolution.* New York: Praeger.

Floyd, W. D. (1960). *An analysis of the oral questioning activity in selected Colorado primary classrooms.* Unpublished doctoral dissertation, Colorado State College, Greeley, CO.

Gipe, J. P., & Richards, J. C. (1992). Reflective thinking and growth in novices' teaching abilities. *Journal of Educational Research, 86,* 52–57.

Goetz, J. P., & LeCompte, M. D. (1984). *Ethnography and qualitative design in educational research.* New York: Academic Press.

Green, K. E. (1992). Differing opinions on testing between preservice and inservice teachers. *Journal of Educational Research, 86,* 37–42.

Guba, E. G. (1981). Criteria for assessing the trustworthiness of naturalistic inquiries. *Educational Communication and Technology Journal, 29,* 75–91.

Hill, M. R. (1993). *Archival strategies and techniques.* Thousand Oaks, CA: Sage.

Horn, T. C. R., & Ritter, H. (1986). Interdisciplinary history: A historiographical review. *The History Teacher, 19,* 427.

Itard, J. G. (1962). *The wild boy of Aveyron.* New York: Appleton.

Jacob, E. (1988). Clarifying qualitative research: A focus on traditions. *Educational Researcher, 17,* 16–24.

Katz, M. B. (1987). *Reconstructing American education.* Cambridge, MA: Harvard University Press.

Levine, H. G. (1985). Principles of data storage and retrieval for use in qualitative evaluations. *Educational Evaluation and Policy Analysis, 7,* 169–186.

Lincoln, Y. S., & Guba, E. G. (1985). *Naturalistic inquiry.* Beverly Hills, CA: Sage.

Magnusson, D., Bergman, L. R., Rudinger, G., & Torestad, B. (Eds.). (1991). *Problems and methods in longitudinal research: Stability and change.* New York: Cambridge University Press.

Maher, C. A. (1982). Program evaluation of a special education day school for conduct problem adolescents. In E. R. House, S. Mathison, J. A. Pearsol, & H. Preskill (Eds.), *Evaluation studies review annual. Vol. 7* (pp. 406–412). Beverly Hills, CA: Sage.

McCutcheon, G. (1981). On the interpretation of classroom observations. *Educational Researcher, 10,* 5–10.

McLaughlin, M. W. (1975). *Evaluation and reform: The Elementary and Secondary Education Act of 1965/Title I.* Cambridge, MA: Ballinger.

Medley, D., & Mitzel, H. (1963). Measuring classroom behavior by systematic observation. In N. Gage (Ed.), *Handbook of research on teaching* (pp. 247–328). Chicago: Rand McNally.

Merriam, S. B. (1988). *Case study research in education.* San Francisco: Jossey-Bass.

Mischler, E. G. (1979). Meaning in context: Is there any other kind? *Harvard Educational Review, 49,* 2–10.

Nye, D. E. (1983). *The invented self: An anti-biography, from documents of Thomas A. Edison.* Odense, Denmark: Odense University Press.

Patton, M. Q. (1990). *Qualitative evaluation and research methods* (2nd ed.). Thousand Oaks, CA: Sage.

Pelto, P. J., & Pelto, G. H. (1978). *Anthropological research: The structure of inquiry* (2nd ed.). New York: Cambridge University Press.

Peterson, S. E., DeGracie, J. S., & Ayabe, C. R. (1987). A longitudinal study of the effects of retention/promotion on academic achievement. *American Educational Research Journal, 24,* 107–118.

Rist, R. C. (1980). Blitzkreig ethnography: On the transformation of a method into a movement. *Educational Researcher, 9*(2), 8–10.

Robinson-Awana, P., Kehle, T. J., & Jensen, W. R. (1986). But what about smart girls? Adolescent self-esteem and sex role perceptions as a function of academic achievement. *Journal of Educational Psychology, 78*(3), 179–183.

Rogerson, B. C. F., & Rogerson, C. H. (1939). Feeding in infancy and subsequent psychological difficulties. *Journal of Mental Science, 85,* 1163–1182.

San Miguel, G., Jr. (1986). Status of the historiography of Chicano education: A preliminary analysis. *History of Education Quarterly, 26,* 523–536.

Schatzman, L., & Strauss, A. L. (1973). *Field research: Strategies for a natural sociology.* Englewood Cliffs, NJ: Prentice-Hall.

Schooler, C. (1972). Birth order effects: Not here, not now! *Psychological Bulletin, 72,* 161–175.

Schultz, J., & Florio, S. (1979). Stop and freeze: The negotiation of social and physical space in a kindergarten/first grade classroom. *Anthropology & Education Quarterly, 10,* 166–181.

Schwandt, T. A., & Halpern, E. S. (1988). *Linking auditing and metaevaluation.* Beverly Hills, CA: Sage.

Shaffir, W. B., Stebbins, R. A., & Turowetz, A. (1980). *Field experience.* New York: St. Martin.

Siegel, K., & Tucker, P. (1985). The utilization of evaluation research: A case analysis. *Evaluation Review, 9,* 307–328.

Smallwood, M. L. (1935). *Examinations and grading systems in early American universities.* Cambridge, MA: Harvard University Press.

Smith, J. K., & Heshius, L. (1986). Closing down the conversation: The end of the quantitative-qualitative debate among educational inquirers. *Educational Researcher, 15*(1), 4–12.

Smith, M. L., & Shepard, L. A. (1988). Kindergarten readiness and retention: A qualitative study of teachers' beliefs and practices. *American Educational Research Journal, 25,* 307–333.

Spradley, J. (1980). *Participant observation.* New York: Holt, Rinehart & Winston.

Stake, R. E. (1978). The case study method in social inquiry. *Educational Researcher, 7*(2), 5–8.

Stake, R. E. (1991). Retrospective on "The countenance of educational evaluation." In M. W. McLaughlin & D. C. Phillips (Eds.), *Evaluation and education: At quarter century* (pp. 67–88). Chicago: University of Chicago Press.

Strauss, A., & Corgin, J. (1990). *Basics of qualitative research.* Thousand Oaks, CA: Sage.

Stufflebeam, D. L. (Ed.). (1991). *The personnel evaluation standards* (2nd ed.). Thousand Oaks, CA: Sage.

Thompson, B. (1994). The revised program evaluation standards and their correlation with the evaluation use literature. *Journal of Experimental Education, 63,* 54–81.

Tuckman, B. W. (1981). *Practicing history.* New York: Knopf.

Tyack, D. B. (1976). Ways of seeing: An essay on the history of compulsory schooling. *Harvard Educational Review, 46,* 55–89.

Wilson, S. (1977). The use of ethnographic techniques in educational research. *Review of Educational Research, 47,* 245–265.

Wise, L. L. (1997, April). *The fight against attrition in longitudinal research.* Paper presented at the annual meeting of the American Educational Research Association, New York.

Wolf, R. L. (1975). Trial by jury: A new evaluation method. *Phi Delta Kappan, 57,* 185–187.

Wolf, R. L. (1990). Judicial evaluation. In H. J. Walberg & G. D. Haertel (Eds.), *The international encyclopedia of educational evaluation* (pp. 79–81). New York: Pergamon.

Worthen, B. R., & Sanders, J. R. (1987). *Educational evaluation.* New York: Longman.

Wrigley, J. (1989). Do young children need intellectual stimulation? Experts' advice to parents, 1900–1985. *History of Education Quarterly, 29,* 41–76.

Yow, V. R. (1994). *Recording oral history*. Thousand Oaks, CA: Sage.

Zeichner, K., & Teitelbaum, K. (1982). Personalized and inquiry-oriented teacher education: An analysis of two approaches to the development of curriculum for field-based experience. *Journal of Education for Teaching, 8,* 95–117.

REFERENCES

Beach, M. (1969). History of education. *Review of Educational Research, 39,* 561–576.

Bogdan, R. C., & Biklen, S. K. (1982). *Qualitative research for education: An introduction to theory and methods*. Boston: Allyn & Bacon.

Charles, C. M. (1995). *Introduction to educational research* (2nd ed.). White Plains, NY: Longman.

Deutscher, I. (1973). *What we say/what we do*. Glenview, IL: Scott, Foresman.

Dewey, J. (1933). *How we think*. Boston: Raytheon Education.

Douglas, J. (1976). *Investigative social research*. Beverly Hills, CA: Sage.

Green, G., & Jaquess, S. N. (1987). The effect of part-time employment on academic achievement. *Journal of Educational Research, 80,* 325–329.

Kagan, D. M., Dennis, M. B., Igou, M., Moore, P., & Sparks, K. (1993). The experience of being a teacher in residence. *American Educational Research Journal, 30,* 426–443.

Lipstadt, D. E. (1993). *Denying the Holocaust: The growing assault on truth and memory*. New York: Free Press.

Maxwell, J. A. (1992). Understanding and validity in qualitative research. *Harvard Educational Review, 62,* 279–300.

McMillan, J. H., & Schumacher, S. (1997). *Research in education: A conceptual introduction* (4th ed.). Reading, MA: Addison-Wesley.

Miles, M. B., & Huberman, A. M. (1994). *Qualitative data analysis: An expanded sourcebook* (2nd ed.). Thousand Oaks, CA: Sage.

Moehlman, A. H., Van Tassel, D., Goetzmann, W. H., & Everett, G. D. (1969). *A guide to computer-assisted research in American education*. Austin, TX: University of Texas.

Morris, V. C., & Hurwitz, E. (1980, April). *The Heisenberg problem: How to neutralize the effect of the observer on observed phenomena*. Paper presented at the meeting of the American Educational Research Association, Boston, MA.

Sadler, D. R. (1981). Intuitive data processing as a potential source of bias in naturalistic evaluations. *Educational Evaluation and Policy Analysis, 3*(4), 25–31.

Schempp, P. G., Sparkes, A. C., & Templin, T. J. (1993). The micropolitics of teacher induction. *American Educational Research Journal, 30,* 447–472.

Shimahara, N. (1988). Anthroethnography: A methodological consideration. In R. R. Sherman & R. B. Webb (Eds.), *Qualitative research in education: Focus and methods* (pp. 76–89). New York: Falmer.

Strong, B. (1972). Ideas of early sex education movements in America, 1890–1920. *History of Education Quarterly, 13,* 139–161.

Wax, M. (1993). How culture misdirects multiculturalism. *Anthropology and Educational Quarterly, 24,* 99–115.

PART III

EXPERIMENTAL RESEARCH METHODS

CHAPTER 9

Single-Group Designs

OBJECTIVES

After reading this chapter, you should be able to:

- Define *experimental* research.
- Distinguish between *experimental* and *descriptive* research.
- Identify the conditions under which *single-group* designs are considered appropriate for use in research activities.
- Discuss the relative strengths and weaknesses of single-group research.
- Distinguish between *posttest, pretest-posttest,* and *interrupted time series* designs.
- Diagram three single-group designs.
- Describe the use of *null* and *directional* hypotheses.
- Distinguish between *one-tailed* and *two-tailed* tests.
- Distinguish between *parametric* and *nonparametric* measures.
- Distinguish between *independent* and *dependent* variables.
- Distinguish between *intervening* and *moderator* variables.

- Identify and discuss the threats to *internal* validity, including reference to those that are controlled because of nonapplicability, controlled because of the design, and uncontrolled. Discussion should include giving attention to expectancy, experimental mortality, history, instability, instrumentation, maturation, pretesting, regression, selection, and threats of interaction.
- Identify and discuss factors related to controlling for threats to *external* validity.
- Demonstrate the calculation of the *single-sample* t *test.*
- Describe sampling error, standard error of the mean, *t* ratio, critical values for *t* ratios, procedures for determining statistical significance, the difference between *Type I* and *Type II* errors, and the difference between *statistical* and *practical* significance.
- Compute statistical intervals for the .05, .02, and .01 levels of confidence.
- Demonstrate the calculation of the *nonindependent* t *test.*
- Identify and discuss the various intergroup analyses that can be conducted with interrupted time series designs.
- Discuss the interpretations that are possible from accepting or rejecting null hypotheses, and the inherent weaknesses of inferences arising out of single-group designs.
- Define the key terms, and answer the checkpoint questions.

KEY TERMS

Causes	Interrupted Time Series
Confidence Interval	Intervening Variable
Control Group	Level of Confidence
Controlled Threats	Manipulation
Criterion	Moderator Variable
Critical Values	Nonapplicable Threats
Degrees of Freedom	Nonindependent-Samples t Test
Dependent-Samples t Test	Nonparametric Statistics
Diagram	One-Tailed Test
Directional Hypotheses	Outcome
Effects	Parametric Statistics
Experiment	Person(s)
Grand Mean	Place(s)
Interaction	Population

INTRODUCTION

In Part II, Descriptive Research Methods, you were introduced to those investigative processes that are *not* governed by the utilization of treatments. Specifically, reference was made to survey, correlation, causal-comparative, and test and measurement research, as well as to case-study, historical, and philosophical research (which represent the very essence of qualitative-type investigations). It was made clear that the selection of any of these (or other) methods is contingent upon the requirements of the inquiry one wants to make. For example, if a researcher were interested in determining whether there is a relationship between the health knowledge and practice of a group of seventh-grade students, the design of choice would be correlation. However, with this particular design, one cannot attribute a specific cause (or causes) to whatever findings result. If an investigator wants to study *causes,* a correlation procedure is not the form of research to use. Essentially, what is learned from a correlation study is whether there is a relationship between the variables and, if so, to what extent. The process makes it possible for the researcher to determine whether students who demonstrated greater degrees of knowledge than their classmates, also demonstrated more acceptable behavioral practices.

 **CHECKPOINT**

Within which of the four measurement scales would the data generated by a study have to fall in order for a correlation to be conducted?

Answer

The data would have to be *ordinal, interval,* or *ratio.* If one of the distributions—for example, behavioral practices—generated only *nominal* data, correlation processes would be inappropriate. Thus, in order to carry out a correlation study, the investigator would need to use a measuring device that would do more than just record *yes* or *no* to a singular favorable or unfavorable practice. He would have to be able to rate behavioral practices in accordance with their frequency and/or quality so that the subjects of the study could be placed in some quantifiable order. This would require that clear definitions were in place that would distinguish favorable from less favorable practices. If the subjects could be ranked according to their compliance with these practices, the data would then be ordinal and, thus, subject to being analyzed through rank-order correlation processes.

NOTE: This, of course, assumes that the health knowledge test selected for use in the study was capable of generating data that were ordinal, interval, or ratio. If the health knowledge achievement test generated interval data, one would still have to employ rank-order techniques. You may remember from Chapter 7, Correlation Procedures, that both sets of data would have to be interval or ratio in order to use product-moment correlation procedures.

If, instead of doing a correlation study, an investigator wanted to determine if some of the practices currently observed among a select group of the seventh graders (referenced earlier) could be attributed to some episode or pattern of episodes in their past, the design of choice would be causal-comparative. Again, however, it is *not* experimental because, if causes can be found, they would not be the result of anything the present investigator had introduced or manipulated.

In neither the correlation nor the causal-comparative study does the researcher attempt to manipulate anything. This is the major distinction between descriptive and experimental forms of investigations. In *experimental studies,* the investigator manipulates what the subjects will experience. In effect, he attempts to determine through **manipulation** whether a particular treatment that has been imposed upon a group (or groups) of subjects will effect a change in, for example, such things as health practices, knowledge, attitudes, and so on. Experimental research is the *only* form of investigative inquiry in which the researcher has the opportunity to manipulate variables in order to study **causes** and **effects.** When intervening, related variables and threats are either eliminated or controlled, the researcher is in a position to determine whether the dependent variable is altered as a consequence of the treatment. If the findings are held to be statistically significant, they can be attributed to the manipulated variable—that is, the cause. In other words, something other than chance has prompted the change. In short, an **experiment** is a carefully planned investigation that is designed to test a hypothesis concerning the effects of one or more variables (experimental, treatment) upon another variable (dependent, outcome), when all related variables (intervening, moderator) are eliminated from the study or held constant.

Considering the scenario regarding health knowledge and practice, if the researcher wanted to determine whether integrating new approaches to knowledge instruction would have an effect upon the health practices of the seventh-grade students, he would be setting the stage for an experimental investigation. The specific processes related to forming experimental hypotheses, controlling for threats to validity, and data analysis are among the subjects of this chapter.

PURPOSE OF SINGLE-GROUP DESIGNS

While multiple-group designs (that is, two, three, or more) are considered to be more formidable than **single-group designs** because the former provide for the use of **control groups,** single-group investigations still hold a rightful place in experimental research. Not only is it occasionally impossible to gain access to more than one group at a time, but the use of single-group methods can serve as *pilots* for more sophisticated studies to follow. Among other things, it provides an opportunity for an investigator to test preliminary hypotheses, procedures, or experimental materials. For purposes of this textbook, a discussion of single-group designs is a good place to start when introducing experimental research methods. It is generally a bit easier to manage the variables for one group because there are fewer people-management problems with which to concern oneself. At the same time, however, single-group designs place limitations on the interpretations that can be made from the findings. As with all designs, there are relative strengths and weaknesses, but more will be said about this particular issue later in the chapter.

Specifically, single-group designs are created in order to enable an investigator to assess the effects of an *independent variable* upon a *dependent* (or outcome) *variable.* The independent variable, also referred to as the experimental or **treatment** variable, is that activity or procedure that is introduced into the study in order to examine the extent to which it "made a difference." In educational research, the independent variable usually manipulated for purposes of study includes such things as: (1) arrangement of a learning environment, (2) behavior modification systems, (3) ergogenic aids, (4) instructional methods, (5) size of learning group, (6) teaching materials, and (7) time of instruction.

The outcome (or **criterion**) variable is called the dependent variable because it is "dependent" upon the treatment (independent) variable. Included among the **outcome** variables that are often considered for examination in educational studies are: (1) achievement, (2) attendance, (3) attention span, (4) attitudes, (5) behavior, (6) interests, and (7) number of disciplinary actions.

Related variables fall into two distinct categories: *intervening* and *moderator*. **Intervening variables** are those that arise during the course of the study that could impact upon the findings. These would include such things as the following.

- Afternoon television specials on issues related to the topic under investigation (threat of history)
- Fire alarms, broken equipment, snow days (threats of instability)
- Subjects moving out of town and no longer available to participate in the study (threat of experimental mortality)
- **Threats of interaction** because of the existence of instability and history working together

 NOTE: An example of the interactive threat of instability and history would be if students were out of school due to snow days and, while at home, viewed afternoon television specials on issues related to the topic under investigation.

Moderator variables are those that are in place (and are capable of being identified) at the *onset* of the study and, because they are known about, can be accounted for in the design. They are called *moderator variables* because they can "moderate" (or influence) the results if thoughtful regard is not assigned to them. Examples of such threats would include:

- Age
- Birth order
- Gender
- Grade level

 NOTE: Although a member of a study group may have a birthday during the course of the investigation, that fact does not alter his chronological position with reference to the rest of the group. A student may celebrate a birthday tomorrow by turning fifteen, but he is still only one day older than today. As a matter of fact, so is everyone else.

Moderator variables are the variables which, upon examining their influence as reported in related literature, can be eliminated or controlled simply by taking an early stock of the composition of the groups. For example, age can be controlled by analyzing only the test scores for those students who satisfy a specific age requirement, such as: only those who are fourteen years old, or fifteen years old, and so on. Birth order can be controlled by analyzing only the test scores for those students who satisfy a specific birth-order requirement, such as: only first born, only second born, and so on. Gender can be controlled by considering the scores of only girls *or* boys when analyzing the test data.

In a school situation, boys or girls cannot be eliminated (literally) from the class on the basis of their age, birth order, or gender because, regardless of the study interests of the researcher, all students have the right to be there (providing that pertinent academic prerequisites are satisfied). For purposes of the investigation, however, the practitioner-researcher can choose to analyze only those data that satisfy the requirements of the design.

Grade level can be controlled by studying the effects of a treatment upon the students of only one grade level (as opposed to studying the "pooled" findings of all grades or classes in an elementary, junior high, or senior high school).

NOTE: If data from different grades are grouped in order to test the effect of a particular treatment, the findings can be misleading because, for example:

- the results for ninth graders may be low,
- the results for the eighth graders may be high, and
- the results for seventh graders may be observed as being neither high nor low.

From the average of the pooled scores, it would appear to the observer that the treatment had a similar effect across all junior high grade levels, whereas an examination of eighth- or ninth-grade scores alone would indicate that the treatment had a greater effect for them. The researcher would not know that by examining only the pooled average of the three grades. For obvious reasons, the various grade levels may respond differently to a given treatment. As a consequence, grade level should be controlled in some studies. The discussion found within the related literature (along with consideration for one's own personal experiences) can help the researcher to make a determination in this regard.

The hypotheses that are used in experimental studies are *null* or *directional*. For reasons described in Chapter 1, Selection and Definition of a Problem, it is recommended that one consider testing the *null hypothesis* on most occasions. As you may remember from previous discussion, this approach (1) implies neutrality on the part of the researcher, that is, the researcher is not casting an appearance of "favoritism" for one outcome or another, and (2) makes it less difficult to procure permission from all pertinent parties for the study. If the researcher chose to test a directional hypothesis in which it was predicted that one method of instruction was superior to another, it would be reasonable to expect that parents would balk at the idea of granting permission unless they were assured that their sons or daughters were going to be benefactors of the "superior" treatment. By testing the null hypothesis, the researcher is not implying that one treatment will generate greater results than will another. If the data generated from the investigation leads to an acceptance of the null hypothesis, that means that any observed difference can be attributed to chance alone. On the other hand, if the null hypothesis is rejected, it can be assumed (within a selected level of confidence) that something other than chance affected the results. If related intervening and moderator variables are accounted for, it is likely that the difference can be attributed to one "treatment" or the other.

NOTE: Procedures for determining which of the groups had made the greater gains will be a subject of discussion later in the chapter.

In the case of *single-group, posttest only designs,* the mean can be compared against a hypothesized value, and the null hypothesis would test the assumption that there is no difference between the two. When there are both pretest and posttest scores, the purpose of the null hypothesis would be to test that the posttest scores are *equivalent* to the pretest scores. If one were to choose to test a directional hypothesis, it could be assumed that the posttest generated higher scores than did the pretest. Unless the researcher has a strong justification for doing otherwise, however, he should test for the null hypothesis. The null hypothesis also enables the investigator to use those statistical tables of significance that are based upon tests of no preference.

Finally, *all* single-group designs follow the sequence of steps necessary to planning any form of research. This sequence includes Phase 1:

1. Statement of the problem
2. Need (justification) for the study
3. Review of related literature
4. Statement of (null or directional) hypotheses
5. Basic assumptions
6. Possible threats to the study
7. Design alternatives
8. Definitions of terms

and Phase 2:

1. Permission/selection of subjects
2. Selection of instrument
3. Administration of study/collection of data
4. Analysis of data/conclusions/recommendations

each with regard to:

- what I need to know,
- where I will find it,
- how I will find it,
- procedures for organizing the information for further use, and
- conclusions that follow from the procedures that will allow the researcher to proceed with the study.

STRATEGIES FOR CONDUCTING SINGLE-GROUP DESIGNS

There are three basic approaches to conducting single-group experimental research designs: (1) the posttest only design, (2) the pretest-posttest design, and (3) the interrupted time series design.

Posttest Only Design

Considered to be the *weakest* of all single-group designs, the **posttest only design** procedure provides for a group to be introduced to a treatment (X) and then posttested (O).

> **NOTE:** When diagraming experimental research designs of any form, the (X) *always* refers to a treatment, and the (O) *always* represents the observation. The observation is any method that is used to generate data for purposes of analysis. A common "observation" system would be the use of paper-pencil tests.

The **diagram** for a *posttest only experimental research design* would be written as:

$$X \qquad O$$

When diagraming a design, the symbols are displayed in a sequence from left to right. Thus, in this example, the first notation is the treatment (X), followed by the observation (O).

The posttest only design is considered to be the weakest of experimental designs because:

1. There is no pretest.
2. There is no control group.
3. Some of the threats to internal validity are difficult, if not impossible, to control.
4. The inferences that can be generated through statistical treatments are limited in scope.

These factors are discussed more fully in the following text.

Without measuring the group's level of performance prior to the treatment with a pretest, there is no way to know what the subjects knew at the onset of the study. Consequently, the investigator cannot determine whether there has been an improvement. Even if it is determined that the subjects of the study scored high on the posttest, it would be inappropriate to assume that the findings are totally the result of the treatment. As weak as it is, however, the process holds some merit. As you might surmise, the fact that there is a posttreatment assessment provides *some* measure of accountability.

Suppose, for example, that a group of high school seniors went to their school guidance counselor requesting that he schedule admission visits for them at five different local colleges. The guidance counselor complies and, after their visits, all of the students decide to apply to the same school. The guidance counselor might believe that the students selected the college (O) as a result of their visits (X). This may be a reasonable assumption to make. Lack of knowledge about their inclination toward any of the colleges before their visits, however, is an impediment to the making of unqualified generalizations about "cause and effect."

Without a control group, it is impossible to know whether any growth that may have occurred would have taken place anyway. A control group provides for a basis of comparison.

NOTE: As will be discussed in Chapter 10, Two-Group Designs, the investigator usually arranges for the control group to receive something other than the "new" treatment. Typically, the control group receives the "traditional" treatment (for example, instructional methods that have been used regularly). Suppose, for example, a teacher is interested in determining whether a new method that has been described in the professional literature would be as effective as the traditional method he has been using to generate achievement among his students. By administering equivalent posttests to both groups, the researcher would be able to judge the effects of the treatment (assuming that threats to internal validity, such as intervening variables, have been controlled). Without a control group, however, this determination would be difficult to make.

Although some of the *threats to internal validity* are not applicable, others would be difficult, if not impossible, to control. You may remember from discussion in Chapter 3, Preparation of a Research Plan, that thoughtful randomization will control for most threats to internal validity, including:

- History
- Selection
- Maturation
- Instrumentation
- Statistical regression
- Pretesting

This theory can be supported because of the assumption that the effects of the threats would be equally distributed between the various groups in the study during the random-sampling process. As a consequence of this expectation, and the management of moderator variables, any *posttest* differences between groups can be attributed to the treatments, and not to the effects of the threats. To clarify further, if the treatment and control groups are assumed to be influenced by threats to the same degree, it is probable that any difference in the posttest scores can be attributed to something other than those threats.

In single-group designs, however, such assumptions of threat equivalence cannot be made. Thus, it is likely that the impact of whatever threats are in existence will accompany the effect of a treatment. In this regard, there is general agreement with the work of Campbell and Stanley (1971) that, in single-group, posttest only designs, threats of *experimental mortality, history,* and *maturation* are *not* controlled; and the threats of *instrumentation, selection, **regression,*** and *pretesting* are controlled because of their irrelevance. *Expectancy, instability,* and the ***interaction*** of existing threats continue to be of concern in this design, as they are with all others.

✓CHECKPOINT

Can you relate an example that illustrates the threat of *interaction* (on the basis of information provided in Chapter 3, Preparation of a Research Plan)?

Answer

One example of interactive threats would be *maturity* and *history*. If an extended study takes place in the classroom, there is a greater chance for a subject's maturity to begin influencing the choices he makes outside the classroom, for example, home television viewing. The substantive information that is provided through selected television viewing may influence the subject's attitudes, interests, knowledge, and so on regarding topics related to the investigation.

NOTE: You may remember from discussion in Chapter 3 that random sampling will control for all threats to internal validity except *expectancy, experimental mortality,* and *instability.* Therefore, random sampling, coupled with thoughtful anticipation of the threats that are *not* controlled through the random-sampling process, should go a long way to reduce their compromising effects.

With this said, *the implications of a weak design are themselves threats to valid findings.* All researchers should consider this matter seriously as they contemplate design selection.

In the case of *threats to external validity,* the reader is reminded that making sound generalizations from one's findings is dependent upon:

1. Sampling. Without consideration for proper sampling, it is inappropriate to draw inferences to larger groups. Accordingly, the lack of a pretest and control group in the single-group, posttest only design sets the stage for not knowing whether or not the findings are a product of whatever treatment was administered, even if a decision was made during the design process of the study to randomly select an appropriately sized **sample** from a finite **population.** Hence, the researcher needs to be mindful of the grave reservations there are about generalizing to a population group any findings that may be revealed through the study.

2. Person(s). The findings can only be inferred to a population if both the sample and that population share the more selective characteristics. Since the findings are held suspect except, perhaps, for providing preliminary information, it would be considered inappropriate to draw inferences to any other **person(s)** or group (whether or not they have characteristics common with those of the sample).

3. Place(s). Since the findings of a study can only be generalized to groups who are found in similar settings, the threat is controlled providing inferences are made with **place(s)** in mind. However, because of the questionable credibility of any findings that would arise out of such a single-group design, any inferences would be subject to serious criticism.

4. Time(s). **Time(s)** refers to:
   • the time of the day or month;
   • whether the study is conducted immediately before, during, or after particularly stressful (or relaxing) events; and

• the duration of the study.

All of these factors have the potential to influence results. Therefore, when drawing inferences to other groups, reference must be made to the "time" conditions for the study.

The nature of the design in question precludes credible findings in any case. Consequently, the results should be subject to greater suspicion than the effects of threats resulting from a reader's lack of attention to sampling, persons, places, and/or times.

Because there are no pretests or control groups, the inferences that can be generated through **statistical treatments** are quite limited in scope. Since there is no pretest, it is impossible to document statistical improvements. Without a control group, there is nothing to which the researcher can compare the experimental group's posttest scores. At the same time, however, there are some basic procedures that can be applied to the data of a single group of scores that can prove to be useful. First of all, the investigator might want to employ *qualitative* methods in order to produce narrative on the circumstances surrounding the acquisition of information made possible during the conduct of the study. (For a review of such procedures, see Chapter 6, Survey Procedures.) Secondly (assuming that interval or ratio data have been generated by the instruments of assessment), it would be possible to compute such *quantitative* measures as central tendency (that is, mean, median, mode), percentiles, and variability measures (for example, standard deviation). (The processes for calculating these values were also described in Chapter 6.)

With the mean and standard deviation in hand, they could be incorporated within an *inferential* statistical procedure in order to test for statistical significance. One such measure is a *t* test, formally known as **student's *t* test,** because its creator, W. S. Gossett, wrote about it in documents that he signed, not with his own name, but just with "Student" (1908).

The formula for a **single-sample *t* test** is:

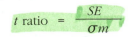

$$t \text{ ratio} = \frac{SE}{\sigma m}$$

where: *SE* = **sampling error** (or the difference between the two means)

σm = **standard error of the mean** (which represents the standard deviation of a *hypothetical* population of sample means)

NOTE: If one were going to randomly select different samples from a population, it could be expected that the averages of those distributions would vary by some amount. The standard error of the mean is a probability statistic that indicates by how much the sample means can be expected to differ if other samples from the same population were selected.

For purposes of illustration, suppose that an investigator is interested in knowing whether the arithmetic average of the posttest scores generated from his study is equivalent to the mean value that was generated from a similar study conducted in a different school district. To proceed with this analysis, the researcher would follow these steps:

Step 1. Compute the standard error of the mean (σm) by dividing the standard deviation of the scores by the square root of $N - 1$ (where N represents the number of subjects in the study group).

$$\sigma m = \frac{\sigma}{\sqrt{N - 1}}$$

Step 2. Compute the difference between the obtained mean (M) and the criterion mean (X). This is referred to as the sampling error (SE).

$$SE = M - \overline{X}$$

Step 3. Divide the sampling error (SE) by the standard error of the mean (σm). This quotient will give you the **t ratio.**

$$t \text{ ratio} = \frac{SE}{\sigma m}$$

Step 4. Refer the findings (t ratio) to a table for **critical values** for t ratios in order to determine whether the finding is significant, and can be attributed to something other than chance (see Appendix E, Critical Values for t).

Utilizing the single-sample t test, the following hypothetical set of data can be used to illustrate the test:

- A mean (M) value of 81
- A standard deviation (σ) of 10
- An $N = 26$ for a group of posttest scores
- A criterion mean ($\overline{X}$) value of 84

The researcher will plan to test the null hypothesis that the obtained and criterion mean values are equivalent. The research question is attempting to determine whether the criterion average is really greater than the obtained average, or whether the difference can be attributed to chance alone. In other words, is the researcher's group really achieving at a lower level than is the group in another school district? The researcher uses the four steps presented earlier:

1. The researcher begins by finding the standard error of the mean (σm).

$$\sigma m = \frac{\sigma}{\sqrt{N - 1}}$$

$$= \frac{10}{\sqrt{26 - 1}}$$

$$= \frac{10}{\sqrt{25}}$$

$$= \frac{10}{5}$$

$$= 2$$

2. The investigator then proceeds to find the sampling error (*SE*), which is the difference between the obtained mean (*M*) and criterion mean ($\bar{X}$) values.

$$SE = M - \bar{X}$$

$$= 81 - 84$$

$$= 3 \text{ (considered as an } absolute \text{ rather than a } relative \text{ difference)}$$

3. To obtain the *t* ratio, the investigator now divides the sampling error (*SE*) by the standard error of the mean (σm).

$$t \text{ ratio} = \frac{SE}{\sigma m}$$

$$= \frac{3}{2}$$

$$= 1.500$$

4. To determine whether the null hypothesis can be accepted or rejected for *N* – 1 **degrees of freedom** (*df*), the investigator now refers the obtained *t* ratio to an appropriate table for critical values for *t* (see Appendix E).

NOTE: You will observe in the table in Appendix E that there is reference to two-tailed and one-tailed values. Unless you have an extremely strong justification for using one-tailed values, you should use the two-tailed *t* values. The **two-tailed test** is for use with the null hypothesis. You see, with the null hypothesis, the researcher is assuming that one value is equivalent to another value. However, if in examining the table it is determined that the assumption of equivalence should be rejected, you could find that value A is greater than value B, *or* value B is greater than value A. In a **one-tailed test,** the researcher is testing a **directional hypothesis** that one value is greater than the other. If that is rejected, a hypothesis for an alternative one-tailed test must be established before proceeding.

A portion of Appendix E, Critical Values for *t,* is presented as Table 9–1. Across the top of the table are critical values for the .05, .02, and .01 **levels of confidence** (*loc*), two-tailed test. Along the left side of the table are the degrees of freedom (*df*).

NOTE: In some tables of critical *t* values, greater levels of significance are displayed, such as .001. For most educational studies, however, the .01 *loc* is considered to be sufficiently significant.

Table 9–1: **Portion of Appendix E, Critical Values for *t***

Degrees of Freedom df	Levels of Confidence (*loc*)		
	.05	.02	.01
1	12.706	31.821	63.657
2	4.303	6.965	9.925
3	3.182	4.541	5.841
4	2.776	3.747	4.604
5	2.571	3.365	4.032
–	–	–	–
–	–	–	–
–	–	–	–
–	–	–	–
–	–	–	–
21	2.080	2.518	2.831
22	2.074	2.508	2.819
23	2.069	2.500	2.807
24	2.064	2.492	2.797
25	2.060	2.485	2.787
26	2.056	2.479	2.779
27	2.052	2.473	2.771
28	2.048	2.467	2.763
29	2.045	2.462	2.756
30	2.042	2.457	2.750
–	–	–	–
–	–	–	–
–	–	–	–
–	–	–	–
–	–	–	–

Hence, with *df* = 25, *t* = 1.500, it can be seen that the value does *not equal or exceed* the .05 *loc* entry in the table. In order to be significant, the number found through the *t* ratio formula must equal or exceed 2.060, per the display in Table 9–1. As a consequence of this finding (and within the limitations of the investigation), the researcher *accepts* the null hypothesis. Any observed difference between the obtained and criterion means can be attributed to chance alone. So, while a criterion mean of 84 (generated by a study in another school) *appears* to be higher, the difference between that and the finding within the researcher's institution can be attributed to chance alone. In this instance, *P*, a symbol for significance, would be written as *P* > .05. This means that significance (the ***P value***) may be found at some level above .05. However, for the purposes of this study, knowing that particular point of significance is of no interest to the investigator.

 NOTE: The .05 level of confidence (*loc*) means that the researcher would be wrong five times out of one hundred in rejecting a null hypothesis at that level; the .02 *loc* means that the researcher would be incorrect two times out of one hundred in rejecting a null hypothesis; and so on. Normally, one is not interested in testing a null hypothesis at a point greater than the .05 *loc* (for example, .10) because one would not want to be wrong that many times (one out of ten) in rejecting a hypothesis.

If, in testing the null hypothesis, significance is found at the .05 *loc,* the researcher would then examine the column marked .02. If significance is found there and not at .01, the researcher would reject the null hypothesis at the .02 *loc*. This implies that the researcher would be wrong only two times in one hundred in making a statement of rejection. In other words, the greater the level of significance, the fewer times one will be wrong in rejecting the null hypothesis.

Another use of the standard error of the mean would be to set up **confidence intervals** in order to estimate where a criterion measure is likely to fall (for example, a mean value from a study completed in another school, a norm value on a standardized achievement test, or a minimum score being proposed for passing a course). These estimates are also ordinarily based upon the .05, .02, and .01 levels of confidence.

For example, in order to find the confidence interval for the .05 *loc*, you would look in the table for critical values for t (two-tailed test) at $N-1$ degrees of freedom (df). For the earlier problem in which the standard error of the mean (σm) was 1.500, at $df = 25$, you would look into the table (see Table 9–1) and note that for $df (N-1 = 25)$, .05 *loc*, the critical value is 2.060. Then you would multiply the standard error of the mean ($\sigma m = 1.500$) by 2.060, which equals 3.090. By subtracting ($-$) this product from and adding ($+$) it to the obtained mean ($M = 81$), you would be able to express the .05 confidence interval for estimating where other (criterion) measures are likely to fall.

What is the .05 confidence interval for an obtained mean of 81?

$$81 - 3.090 = 77.910$$

$$81 + 3.090 = 84.090$$

Referencing this finding (obtained mean = 81; criterion mean = 84), it can be seen that the criterion value of 84 falls within the range limits of the .05 confidence interval (though barely), and thus provides further testimony as to why the *null hypothesis* (of no significant difference) was accepted. In other words, 95% of the time, a criterion value will fall between the score limits of 77.910 and 84.090.

 NOTE: With *interval* or *ratio* data, the researcher has the option of using what are referred to as **parametric statistics.** This is because it can be assumed that the scores on which they are applied would be distributed as a normal, bell-shaped curve—in other words, a reflection of a "population." An example of such a statistic would be the t test (which has been the topic of discussion). **Nonparametric statistics,** such as the chi square, make no such assumption about the normalcy of distributions. This accounts for the fact that they can be used with nominal and ordinal data (see Chapter 5, Selecting Instruments of Assessment).

✓CHECKPOINT

Using the previous example, that is, data with $M = 81$, what would be the range limits for the .02 level of confidence?

Answer

The range limits for the .02 *loc* would be: 77.273–84.727. Explanation: The critical value for $df = 25$, .02 *loc* would be 2.485. By multiplying this value by the standard error of the mean ($\sigma m = 1.500$), the answer would be 3.727. This product is then subtracted from and added to the obtained mean value of 81.

While it can be seen that the investigator is able to infer *some* impressions from the findings, alternatives to the single-group, posttest only design should be considered seriously during the research design process. If a researcher selects the single-group, posttest only design, he is going to be involved in a study fraught with limitations, including the following.

1. There is no way of knowing the ability level of the subjects in advance of the treatment. Consequently, there is no way to determine improvement (because there is no pretest).

2. There is no way of knowing whether the members of the experimental group receiving the treatment would have earned the scores they did without the treatment (because there is no control group with which the findings can be compared).

3. Because of the limitations imposed by the previous two statements, many of the controls for threats to validity are compromised.

Gall, Borg, and Gall (1996), Gay (1996), and Leedy (1997) all refer to this form of design as a *one-shot experimental case study*. Not to be confused with the case study design described in Chapter 8, it is the method often equated with the mentality of "folklore." A librarian sees a group of students congregating in the library, and draws the conclusion that they are going to cause disciplinary problems; the school nurse sees children without raincoats on a cloudy day, and draws the conclusion that they do not own them; the principal makes a note that the same teachers apply for permission to attend a three-day conference each year, and concludes that they make these requests to get days off from work. Why are inferences of this sort made? Certainly, these generalizations must be held suspect. There are so many other variables that could prompt children to go to the library or to not carry raincoats, or prompt teachers to seek permission to attend conferences. See how many possibilities you can come up with—what you arrive at on a list is probably only a sample (not random sample) of possibilities.

Given what has been said about the weaknesses of the single-group, posttest only design, it would follow that it would be important to investigate other alternatives.

Early in the chapter, three forms of single-group designs were indicated. Now the second, the pretest-posttest design, will be examined.

Pretest-Posttest Design

Although one should not be overly excited about this particular method, the **pretest-posttest design** is, by at least one measure, superior to the posttest only design. First, it requires that a *pretest* be administered. This ensures that the researcher will gather pre-experiment information regarding the status of those selected for participation in the study. For reasons indicated earlier, this information is very helpful in making it possible to assign some level of credibility to the findings. At the same time, however, there is *no* control group. Again, this makes for a significant weakness in the design in that there is no way of determining whether observed gains would have occurred in absence of the treatment.

✓CHECKPOINT

Diagram a single-group, pretest-posttest design by using *X* to designate the treatment, and *0* to designate an observation.

Answer

Using *X*s and *0*s, the diagram for a pretest-posttest design would be:

$$0 \quad X \quad 0$$

Since there is a pre-experiment assessment (*pretest*), the first symbol (moving in a left-to-right direction) is *0*. The second symbol designation is an *X*, representing the treatment; and the third symbol would again be an *0*, representing the postexperiment assessment (*posttest*).

If you had any difficulty with this diagram (or fail to understand its implications), reexamine the previous section on posttest only designs.

In the single-group, pretest-posttest design, the investigator attempts to judge the success of the treatment by comparing pre- and posttest scores. Both null (two-tailed) and directional (one-tailed) hypotheses have a place in this design. The *null hypothesis* is used to infer that the posttest scores will be equivalent to the pretest scores. While this approach is possible, some argue that, because it is likely that posttest scores will improve by some amount over the pretest scores, the use of the directional hypothesis is more sensible. At the same time, however, if one were going to test the effectiveness of an experimental behavior modification system on a group of seventh-grade students, it could very well be that pretest behavior scores would be found to be superior to posttest behavior scores. In short, even if it can be predicted that students would likely exceed their pretest mean value, if they do not, the researcher should still be willing to report that fact. As stated earlier, the null hypothesis approaches the study from a position of neutrality. If the null hypothesis is accepted, any observed difference between the mean values can be attributed to chance factors. On the other hand, if the null hypothesis is rejected, something other than chance appears to be contributing to the difference.

While stronger than the single-group, posttest only design, the single-group, pretest-posttest design still contains threats to internal validity that could impact upon the findings. As long as threats are operating, assigning differences in pretest-posttest scores to a treatment will always be suspect. This is particularly so for designs in which there is no control group.

In addition to history and maturation, other threats to *internal* validity that are *not* controlled are the following:

1. Pretesting (because subjects may learn something from the pretest)

2. Instrumentation (because subjects may do better or worse on the posttest because of the lack of test reliability)

3. Regression (because, even if subject selection had nothing to do with prior assessments that were made with those individuals, it is possible, by chance alone, that they would do poorly on the pretest, thus giving them a better chance to show improvement in the posttest. Although this could also happen in the case of a control group, with a *randomly selected* control group, the principle of random sampling would assume equal distribution of "gifted" traits between the groups; thus, it is assumed that the problem will factor itself out.)

4. Expectancy, instability, and the interaction of threats that arise during the course of the investigation (all of which continue to be of concern unless monitored carefully)

With regard to the *controlled* threats to *internal* validity:

1. Experimental mortality (because of the existence of a pretest. If a subject withdraws from the study, his score on the pretest can be discarded from the data pool when comparing group pre- and posttest scores.)

2. Selection (because there is only one group. In other words, the composition of the group cannot be expected to be different than that of "another group," as there is no *other* group.)

Threats to *external* validity will always be of concern unless thoughtful attention is paid in one's report to issues of sampling, person(s), place(s), and time(s). It is critical for the reader to know the nature of those things in order to make judgments about the appropriateness of the findings to his conditions. In this design, however, there are still major concerns about any interpretations that may be assigned to the findings. Without a control group, one will never really know whether any observed gains would have occurred in the absence of the treatment.

Qualitative forms of information analysis are always possible. As far as applying quantitative statistical procedures, one can again employ measures of central tendency (that is, mean, median, mode), percentiles, and variability (for example, standard deviation) to the separate pre- and posttest distributions (assuming the existence of interval or ratio data). Unlike the instance in which there was no pretest, in this design, a comparison can be made between the pre- and postexperiment scores. One statistic for making such an analysis is the **nonindependent-samples *t* test.**

The **dependent-samples *t* test** (as it is sometimes called) is used to compare the arithmetic averages of two groups when the scores earned by particular individuals on one test can be paired with the scores of those individuals on another test. Suppose that a researcher is interested in knowing whether there is a difference between pre- and posttest scores for students who were introduced to an integrated lecture/laboratory biology class. The pretest scores can be indicated as Variable *X*; the posttest scores, Variable *Y*.

NOTE: This "pairing" would not exist if scores were generated by two different groups of individuals. In such an instance, the form of test to be used is the *independent-samples t test* (to be presented in Chapter 10, Two-Group Designs).

There are a number of procedural suggestions for computing the *t*-test ratio, but of those described in various sources (Freedman, Pisani, & Purves, 1978; Garrett, 1958; Gravetter & Wallnau, 1995; Kachigan, 1986; Mansfield, 1986; Moore & McCabe, 1993; Sirkin, 1995), the author's experience has shown the following to be among the most direct and easiest to understand. Looking at the *entire picture,* the techniques may seem ominous. To proceed, however, all one needs to do is adhere to the specific steps in the order presented. First, the formulas will be displayed, and then you will be taken through a problem.

$$t \text{ ratio} = \frac{SE}{\sigma \overline{D}}$$

where *SE* = sampling error; that is, the difference between the two means.
$\sigma \overline{D}$ = standard error of the *mean* difference, which is found by:

$$\sigma \overline{D} = \frac{\sqrt{\dfrac{\Sigma D^2 - [(\Sigma D)^2 / N]}{N - 1}}}{\sqrt{N}}$$

Table 9–2 shows the data upon which the *t*-ratio analysis for nonindependent groups will be applied. The following text illustrates the steps necessary to apply the formulas.

For the *numerator* of the formula, find the difference between the two means. The answer is:

$$SE = 75 - 60 = 15$$

For the *denominator* of the formula:

1. Find the difference between each score (*D*).
2. Sum the *D* column.

Table 9–2: **Pre- and Posttest Scores, and Score and Squared Differences, for Ten Students Introduced to an Integrated Lecture/Laboratory Biology Class**

Students	Pretest Scores X	Posttest Scores Y	Score Differences D	Squared Differences· D^2
A	63	77	14	196
B	66	76	10	100
C	59	74	15	225
D	56	78	22	484
E	64	75	11	121
F	59	80	21	441
G	58	79	21	441
H	60	66	6	36
I	64	72	8	64
J	51	73	22	484
	$M = 60$	$M = 75$	$\Sigma D = 150$	$\Sigma D^2 = 2592$

NOTE: The sum of the D column divided by N will be equivalent to the difference between the means (that is, sampling error).

3. Square the sum of the D column.

4. Divide the squared sum by N.

5. Square the differences between each score (D^2).

6. Sum the squared differences column.

7. Subtract the answer in step 4 from the answer in step 6.

8. Divide the answer in step 7 by $N - 1$.

9. Take the square root of the answer in step 8.

10. Divide the answer in step 9 by the square root of N.

In other words:

$$\sigma \overline{D} = \frac{\sqrt{\dfrac{\Sigma D^2 - [(\Sigma D)^2 / N]}{N - 1}}}{\sqrt{N}}$$

$$= \frac{\sqrt{\dfrac{2592 - [(150)^2 / 10]}{10 - 1}}}{\sqrt{10}}$$

$$= \frac{\sqrt{\dfrac{2592 - [22500 / 10]}{9}}}{\sqrt{10}}$$

$$= \sqrt{\frac{\frac{2592 - 2250}{9}}{\sqrt{10}}}$$

$$= \sqrt{\frac{\frac{342}{9}}{\sqrt{10}}}$$

$$= \frac{\sqrt{38}}{\sqrt{10}}$$

$$= \frac{6.164}{3.162}$$

$$= 1.949$$

So:

$$t \text{ ratio} = \frac{SE}{\sigma \overline{D}}$$

$$= \frac{15}{1.949}$$

$$= 7.696$$

By referring the *t* ratio (*df,* 10 − 1 = 9) to Appendix E, Critical Values for *t,* it can be determined whether the finding of *t* = 7.696 is significant. In order to be significant at the .05 *loc,* the *t* ratio would have to equal or exceed 2.262. Since it does so, the investigator then examines the value necessary for the finding to be significant at the .02 *loc.* It is significant there as well, so the .01 *loc* column is checked, and it is found that the *t* ratio is also significant at that level.

In short, the researcher has found significance at all three levels: .05, .02, and .01. With reference to the *null* hypothesis, the interpretation is made with regard to the *most* significant level only, and would read:

> Within the limitations of this investigation, the researcher rejects the null hypothesis at the .01 level of confidence (*df* = 9). It appears that something other than chance affected the difference between the means in favor of the posttest scores.

NOTE: If significance is found, the investigator examines the two means. The one that is the greater causes the researcher to draw the inference, in this case, in favor of the posttest scores. The mean for the posttest scores was 75; the mean of the pretest scores was 60.

If significance is *not* found, never accept a null hypothesis at a level of confidence. Since the value for significance was not reached, it is suspect to claim how many times one would be wrong in arriving at a finding of *no* difference.

With this said, remember the limitations that arise with an experimental design that does *not* include a control group. While statistically significant differences were found between the pretest and posttest scores, it is yet impossible to attribute, totally, that difference to the treatment (that is, the integrated lecture/laboratory biology class).

Whenever an investigator is making a determination about the significance of his findings, there is a chance that a Type I (*alpha*) or Type II (*beta*) error will be made. *A **Type I error** is one in which a null hypothesis is rejected when it should have been accepted. A **Type II error** is one in which a null hypothesis is accepted when it should have been rejected.*

Either of these errors can arise as a result of sampling errors—that is, the difference between what was found and what would have been found if the entire population had been subjected to the study. By procuring as large a representative sample as possible, it is more likely that critical characteristics of the population will be represented within those comprising the sample. As a consequence, it is *less* likely that a Type I or Type II error will be made. Of course, one is never sure unless the entire population is selected for the study. In this case, there would be no inferential errors because the researcher has at hand the facts about the population.

Further, one should avoid setting too high a restriction on the level of confidence that is tested. For example, if the researcher begins by looking for significance at the .01 *loc,* it is more likely that a null hypothesis would be accepted (because significance at the .01 level of confidence is harder to obtain, since it requires a higher statistical ratio than, for example, the .02 level of confidence). Thus, a Type II error is likely to be in the making. On the other hand, if one tests the null hypothesis at the .05 level of confidence only, the null hypothesis is more likely to be rejected, and a Type I error may result.

In short, the researcher should:

1. have as large a sample as possible, and

2. if significance is found at the .05 level of confidence, proceed to check for greater levels of significance, that is, .02, .01, and so on.

It is generally considered to be a more serious error if one rejects a null hypothesis when it should have been accepted. Recommendations arising out of findings that reject status quo might bring about serious implications on budget, personnel, and programs. This leads to a matter of the relationship of **practical significance** to **statistical significance.** For example, an investigator might deduce, from a finding of statistical preference for using integrated computer systems in his class, that new computers should be purchased for the entire department. The cost of purchasing additional computers could detract from essential purchases in other areas. So, where there may have been *statistical* significance, the *practicality* of implementing the findings is lacking. This argues for the use of **replication studies** in order to see whether similar results occur. As findings repeat themselves, there is stronger evidence for making generalizations.

Interrupted Time Series Design

An elaboration of the single-group, pretest-posttest design, the **interrupted time series** design model provides for a group to be:

1. repeatedly pretested,
2. exposed to a treatment, and
3. repeatedly posttested.

In effect, baseline data are established through the administration of a series of pretests and, following the treatment, a series of posttests. If a group scores approximately the same on each of the pretests and then, after the treatment, improves significantly on the posttests, the researcher has grounds for more confidence in the effectiveness of that treatment.

The diagram for the interrupted time series design is shown as follows:

$$O \quad O \quad O \quad X \quad O \quad O \quad O$$

 NOTE: It should be understood that there is no *magic* number of pre- and posttests, but usually one will find between two and four of each.

Considered to be stronger than the two previous single-group designs discussed in this chapter, there are still threats to *internal* validity with which the investigator should be concerned. In addition to expectancy and instability:

1. History and maturation are still troublesome because something could happen between the final pretest and the initial posttest that may not be accounted for by the treatment.
2. Instrumentation, while not controlled totally, can be managed by utilizing equivalent instruments of assessment throughout the study. If the difficulty of the instruments varies from pretest to pretest, pretest to posttest, or posttest to posttest, instrumentation would loom as a major threat to the internal validity of the study.
3. Pretesting can be a problem because if one instrument has the potential to interact with the experiment itself, more than one pretest can only make matters worse.
4. Interaction will continue to be a threat if any two or more of the other threats are operating within the study, for example, history and maturation.

Threats to *internal* validity that are controlled include:

1. Experimental mortality (because, like the pretest-posttest design discussed earlier, the pretest allows for excluding any reference to a particular individual's score should he elect to withdraw during the course of the study)
2. Regression (because multiple pretests allow for the study group to demonstrate "competence" levels on more than one occasion)
3. Selection (because it is *not* a factor in single-group designs; since there is no control group, there is no opportunity for the experimental group to demonstrate higher or lower scores than its counterpart)

In addition, threats to *external* validity are still of concern, and should be addressed by applying the principles described earlier in this chapter; in Part II, Descriptive Research Methods; and in Chapter 3, Preparation of a Research Plan.

While it can be expected that the findings are more credible than those of previous single-group designs discussed in this chapter, they are still subject of concern because of the lack of a control group. Again, it is possible that the same results would emerge even without the administration of the treatment. It is true that growth could occur in absence of a treatment whether the investigator is using a control group or not, but with a control group, it is easier to make that determination.

With respect to analysis of the data, one always has the option of approaching the information *qualitatively*—that is, to use narrative as a way of describing essential findings. As you may remember from Chapter 6, qualitative descriptions can go a long way to supplement numerical accounts of events. They can provide an enhanced perspective of one's findings. In the case of interrupted time series designs, one can also find the arithmetic average of each of the pretest and posttest scores (assuming the presence of interval or ratio data). To these findings, one can then administer a nonindependent *t* test.

Assuming that there are three pretests and three posttests in the design, as per:

$$O_1 \quad O_2 \quad O_3 \quad X \quad O_4 \quad O_5 \quad O_6$$

the investigator has a number of *quantitative* options. Among the statistical analyses that can be made would be to examine:

1. The sampling error of one *pretest* group mean to another *pretest* group mean; for example:

$$M_1 \; - \; M_2$$
$$M_1 \; - \; M_3$$
$$M_2 \; - \; M_3$$

NOTE: Through the testing of the null hypothesis, the researcher is attempting to determine whether any differences that can be observed in pretesting performances can be attributed to chance alone.

2. The sampling error of the *posttest* group means to each other; for example:

$$M_4 \; - \; M_5$$
$$M_4 \; - \; M_6$$
$$M_5 \; - \; M_6$$

NOTE: The investigator will be able to use the findings to determine whether any observed differences between the posttest means can be attributed to chance.

3. The sampling error of *pretest* group means to *posttest* group means; for example:

$$M_1 \; - \; M_4$$
$$M_1 \; - \; M_5$$

$$M_1 - M_6$$
$$M_2 - M_4$$
$$M_2 - M_5$$
$$M_2 - M_6$$
$$M_3 - M_4$$
$$M_3 - M_5$$
$$M_3 - M_6$$

 NOTE: Though cumbersome as the procedure appears to be, by examining the sampling error of each pretest-to-posttest average, the researcher will be able to determine whether there are *any* posttest means that statistically differ from *any* pretest means.

4. The *final pretest* mean to the *initial posttest* mean.

$$M_3 - M_4$$

 NOTE: By examining the sampling error between the final pretest and initial posttest mean scores, the researcher is attempting to test for a direct cause-and-effect relationship without the contamination of time. For reasons explained previously, however, the fact that there is no control group limits the inferences one might make about any direct relationships between the two values.

5. The **grand mean** of the *pretests* to the *grand mean* of the *posttests*.

$$\overline{M} - \overline{M}$$

 NOTE: By using the grand mean (that is, average of the means) of the pretests and posttests, the researcher is attempting to factor out (control for) the influence of extreme mean values.

While there are other combinations of *t*-test analyses that can be considered, such as comparing the *highest pretest* mean with the *highest posttest* mean, the examples provided are illustrative of the kinds of *between* two-group analyses that can be made.

In addition to the application of the mean and nonindependent *t* test to the scenario, one can also calculate the following for each pretest and posttest:

1. Median

2. Mode

3. Standard deviation

4. Percentiles

Although the interrupted time series design has its inherent weaknesses, it is generally considered in a more favorable light than are single-group, posttest only and pretest-posttest research designs.

SINGLE-GROUP DESIGN PRACTICUM

Assume that a practitioner/researcher is interested in determining whether the integration of guest speakers into a high school civics class has an effect upon student achievement. Since there is only one class section in the relatively small high school (in which the investigator is employed), he is unable to acquire a simultaneous control group—that is, one that is *external* to his own class. The group to participate in the study is classified as a nonrandomized, intact, convenience sample (see Chapter 4, Sampling Procedures). Students are assigned to be in the class on the basis of their attaining junior status within the high school.

Once consideration is given to the various steps implicit to designing the research (that is, Phase 1 and Phase 2), the investigator is ready to proceed with the study. Early in the term, data from a pretest are reviewed in order to establish a benchmark for initial, pre-experimental levels of knowledge.

> **NOTE:** The final examination in civics class for the (immediately) preceding marking period can serve as the pretest for a study beginning at the onset of the current marking period. A flaw in this procedure would be if the final examination for one marking period immediately preceded a vacation. For obvious reasons, information learned or forgotten during an extended time gap could contaminate the results (for example, threats of history and maturation).

After monitoring the treatment through the course of the marking period, the investigator is now ready to administer the posttest. It is from the data generated from that and the pretest that analyses can be made.

While standard central tendency, percentile, and variability measurements can be calculated for each of the distributions, these analyses alone will not test whether or not any differences that may be observed between the pre- and posttests can be attributed to something other than chance. Yes, one may *observe* a difference in arithmetic averages between the two tests, but a question remains: *Is that difference a chance difference?*

As indicated earlier in the chapter, one form of analysis that can be administered in order to examine the observed sampling differences between two means is the *t* test. Given that the pre- and posttest data have been generated by a *single* group of people, the nonindependent, or **related-samples, *t* test** must be used. If the findings are significant in favor of the posttest scores, the researcher would be in a position to recommend the use of integrated lecturers in subsequent civics classes.

✓CHECKPOINT

In order to measure your understanding of some of the more salient points presented in the chapter, you are requested to respond to each of the following questions in light of the scenario regarding integrated guest speakers in a high school civics class.

1. What is the identity of the research design?
2. Diagram that design.
3. State a null hypothesis for the study.
4. What threats to *internal* validity are either controlled by the design, or are **nonapplicable threats?**
5. What threats to *internal* validity are *not* controlled by the design?
6. What is a major limitation to any findings that would be offered in evidence of statistical difference between the two means?

Answers

1. As described, this study would be a *single-group, pretest-posttest design*.
2. The diagram for the study would be:

$$0 \quad X \quad 0$$

3. The *null hypothesis* for this study would be:

> There is no difference between the pre- and posttest achievement scores of students who are enrolled in a guest speaker–integrated high school civics class.

4. The **controlled threats** to *internal* validity are:
   a. Experimental mortality
   b. Selection
5. The **uncontrolled threats** to *internal* validity are:
   a. Expectancy
   b. History
   c. Instability
   d. Instrumentation
   e. Maturation
   f. Pretesting
   g. Regression
   h. Interaction of two or more of the above
6. Regardless of the significance that may be attached to pre- and posttest differences, the fact that there is *no control group* makes for a major limitation to any inferences that one might want to make.

If you had difficulty responding to any of these items, or if you do not understand the rationale underlying the correct answers, it is suggested that you reread the material in this chapter.

ANALYZING DATA

Because of the weaknesses of single-group experimental designs, it is important to remember that there will always be limitations placed on the interpretations that arise out of the findings. Pretest-posttest designs are stronger than posttest only designs, but still lack a control group. As a consequence, one is never sure that the findings that were generated are a consequence of the treatment. It is possible that growth could have occurred in spite of the treatment.

With any group of data that is *interval* in nature, one can find the mean and standard deviation. When there are two means, it is possible to administer a *t* test. If the groups generating the two means are related, as is the case with single-group designs, the form of *t* test that must be used is the *nonindependent* model.

For scenarios provided in this chapter, it was assumed that the data were interval. If, on the other hand, the data were *nominal,* the mean, median, standard deviation, and nonindependent *t* test would not have been appropriate. In this case, such analyses as the mode and percentages of attainment could be calculated, as could a chi square test (see Chapter 6, Survey Procedures).

If the data were *ordinal,* one could add the median, percentiles, and rank-order correlation to the list. *Interval* data provide for even more options, including product-moment correlation.

There are many other statistical procedures that can be used with single- or multiple-group designs that are not within the scope of this textbook. One of the additions that will be made to the quantitative methods described in the chapters to date, however, is *analysis of variance* (ANOVA). This parametric procedure utilizes the *F* test to determine the statistical differences between *two or more* means, and examines them simultaneously. Although the *t* test cannot be used with more than two groups at a time, ANOVA can be so used. And, while it is considered appropriate for use with interval or ratio data generated from single-group designs (for example, pretest-posttest or interrupted time series designs), its introduction will be made in Chapter 10, Two-Group Designs. In addition, the reader will find reference to the *independent t* test. This particular form of *t* test is used with unrelated groups.

SUMMARY

In this chapter, you were introduced to the merits of single-group designs. It should be apparent that, while there are reasons why a researcher may choose to employ such procedures, they are relatively weak. The posttest only design does not provide for pretest measures or a control group. While a pretest-posttest design does provide for pre-experimental measures, a control group is still lacking; thus, it is inappropriate to align heavy significance to any growth that may be observed. The group may have improved for a variety of reasons, none of which were part of the treatment.

Of the single-group procedures, the one that has the most "vigor" is the interrupted time series design. Its strength comes from the fact that there are multiple pre- and posttests that provide for measures of the extent to which data are stable. Again, however, there is no control group, so the inferences one can make are limited.

While some of the threats to *internal* validity are controlled because they are not applicable to single-group designs, there are others that require thoughtful attention by the investigator as Phase 1 and Phase 2 of his research design begin to unfold (see Figure 9–1). Anticipation and planning go a long way in controlling for these problems. Like all studies, descriptive or experimental, threats to *external* validity will be present and unaccounted for unless clear descriptions of sampling, person(s), place(s), and time(s) are presented in the report, and considered by the readers for relevance to their own unique settings.

In addition to *descriptive* statistics (for example, mean, median, mode, percentiles, and standard deviation), the *t* test (an *inferential* statistic) for nonindependent groups was introduced. Like the chi square (described in Chapter 6, Survey Procedures), the *t* test allows the researcher to test the statistical significance of findings and, as a consequence, draw inferences about the influence of chance. Although directional hypotheses can be used with experimental designs, testing null hypotheses is preferred. The rationale for this preference is that through the use of statistical tests of significance, one can then accept or reject the null hypothesis in light of the critical values found in standardized tables (for example, critical values for *t* ratios). If the null hypothesis is rejected, significance can be reported at the .05, .02, and .01 (or .001) levels of confidence.

Single-group designs have many limitations but can provide useful information. They also can be considered as precursors to studies requiring more stringent rules. Chapter 10, Two-Group Designs, presents some of the stronger alternatives.

 # RECOMMENDED LABORATORY ASSIGNMENTS

1. Review the recommended readings.

2. Arrange to meet with fellow graduate students and colleagues in order to discuss the advantages and disadvantages of single-group research designs.

Figure 9–1: **Summary of Indicators as to Whether Threats to Internal Validity Are Controlled or Uncontrolled**

Threats to Internal Validity	Single-Group Designs		
	Posttest Only	Pretest-Posttest	Interrupted Time Series
Expectancy	No	No	No
Experimental mortality	No	Yes	Yes
History	No	No	No
Instability	No	No	No
Instrumentation	Yes	No	No
Maturation	No	No	No
Pretesting	Yes	No	No
Regression	Yes	No	Yes
Selection	Yes	Yes	Yes
Threats of interaction	No	No	No

3. Through a collaboration with no more than three individuals, arrive at a roster of scores for which one would be able to compute:

   a. Single-sample *t* test

   b. Intervals for the .05, .02, and .01 levels of confidence

4. Working independently, compute findings (using a single-sample *t* test), and test the null hypothesis against the table of critical values for *t* ratios.

5. Compare results and, where discrepancies occur, determine their source(s), and discuss possible inferences (while accounting for threats to *internal* validity).

6. Through a collaboration with the same (or different) individuals (question 3), arrive at a pair of scores for a group of no fewer than ten individuals.

7. Working independently, administer a nonindependent samples *t* test to the data (question 6) and, testing the null hypothesis, refer the findings to a table on critical values for *t* ratios. Interpret the results with reference to pertinent threats to *internal* validity.

8. Discuss with fellow graduate students and colleagues the findings and interpretations arising out of question 7.

9. Design an *interrupted time series* project for a *setting* and *topic* of your choice. In the design, specific plans should be prepared to address, for Phase 1:

   a. Statement of the problem

   b. Need (justification) for the study

   c. Review of related literature

   d. Statement of null hypothesis

   e. Basic assumptions

   f. Possible threats to the study

   g. Design alternatives

   h. Definitions of terms

and for Phase 2:

   a. Permission/selection of subjects

   b. Selection of instrument

   c. Administration of study/collection of data

   d. Analysis of data/conclusions/recommendations

each with regard to:

- What I need to know
- Where I will find it
- How I will find it
- Procedures for organizing the information for further use
- Conclusions that would follow from the procedures and allow the researcher to proceed

10. Administer the study designed in response to question 9, analyze the results, test for significance, and interpret the findings.

11. Arrange to meet with fellow graduate students, colleagues, as well as school and nonschool employees in order to review and discuss your findings and interpretations.

12. Examine Chapter 13, Preparing the Research Report, and using guidelines provided therein, prepare a manuscript suitable for formal presentation that would reflect the study design, findings, and interpretations.

RECOMMENDED READINGS

Barlow, D. H., & Hersen, M. (1992). *Single-case experimental designs: Strategies for studying behavior change* (2nd ed.). Needham Heights, MA: Allyn & Bacon.

Brase, C. H., & Brase, C. P. (1991). *Understandable statistics: Concepts and methods* (4th ed.). Lexington, MA: D.C. Heath.

Cook, T. D., & Campbell, D. T. (1979). *Quasi-experimentation: Design and analysis issues for field settings*. Chicago: Rand McNally.

Gibbons, J. D. (1993). *Nonparametric statistics: An introduction*. Newbury Park, CA: Sage.

Kazdin, A. E. (1982). *Single case research designs: Methods for clinical and applied settings*. New York: Oxford University Press.

Kraemer, H. C., & Thielman, S. (1987). *How many subjects? Statistical power analysis in research*. Newbury Park, CA: Sage.

Semel, E. M., & Wiig, E. H. (1981). Semel Auditory Processing Program: Training effects *among* children with language-learning disabilities. *Journal of Learning Disabilities, 4,* 192–196.

Shaver, J. P. (1993). What statistical significance testing is, and what it is not. *Journal of Experimental Education, 61*(4), 293–316.

Siegel, S. (1956). *Nonparametric statistics for the behavior sciences*. New York: McGraw-Hill.

Zuckerman, M., Hodgins, H. S., Zuckerman, A., & Rosenthal, R. (1993). Contemporary issues in the analysis of data: A survey of 551 psychologists. *Psychological Science, 4*(1), 49–53.

REFERENCES

Campbell, D. T., & Stanley, J. C. (1971). *Experimental and quasi-experimental designs for research*. Chicago: Rand McNally.

Freedman, D., Pisani, R., & Purves, R. (1978). *Statistics*. New York: W.W. Norton.

Gall, M. D., Borg, W. R., & Gall, J. P. (1996). *Educational research: An introduction* (6th ed.). White Plains, NY: Longman.

Garrett, H. E. (1958). *Statistics in psychology and education*. New York: Longmans, Green and Co., Inc.

Gay, L. R. (1996). *Educational research: Competencies for analysis and application* (5th ed.). Englewood Cliffs, NJ: Prentice-Hall.

Gravetter, F. J., & Wallnau, L. B. (1995). *Essentials of statistics for the behavioral sciences* (2nd ed.). Minneapolis, MN: West.

Kachigan, S. K. (1986). *Statistical analysis: An interdisciplinary introduction to univariate & multivariate methods*. New York: Radius Press.

Leedy, P. D. (1997). *Practical research: Planning and design* (6th ed.). Columbus, OH: Merrill.

Mansfield, E. (1986). *Basic statistics: With applications.* New York: W.W. Norton.

Moore, D. S., & McCabe, G. P. (1993). *Introduction to the practice of statistics* (2nd ed.). New York: W.H. Freeman.

Sirkin, R. M. (1995). *Statistics for the social sciences.* Thousand Oaks, CA: Sage.

"Student" (1908). The probable error of the mean. *Biometrika, 6,* 1.

CHAPTER 10

Two-Group Designs

OBJECTIVES

After reading this chapter, you should be able to:

- Distinguish between Phase 1 and Phase 2 of a research plan.
- Distinguish between *single-* and *two-group* experimental designs.
- Distinguish between *quasi-experimental* and *experimental* research.
- Discuss the relationship between treatment *fidelity* and research *protocol*.
- Describe the *structure* and *function* of nonequivalent control-group designs.
- Describe the *structure* and *function* of randomized control-group designs.
- Distinguish between *randomization* and *random assignment*.
- Describe the process for assigning treatments to groups.
- Distinguish between the *null hypothesis* and *homogeneity of variance*.
- Distinguish between *independent* and *dependent* variables.
- Provide examples of independent variables.

- Provide examples of dependent variables.

- Distinguish between *intervening* and *moderator* variables.

- Provide examples of intervening variables.

- Provide examples of moderator variables.

- Describe threats to *internal* validity that are *uncontrolled* because of (1) posttest only nonequivalent control-group designs, (2) pretest-posttest nonequivalent control-group designs, (3) randomized posttest only control-group designs, and (4) randomized pretest-posttest control-group designs.

- Describe *selection bias* and (1) history, (2) maturation, (3) pretesting, and (4) regression.

- Provide research diagrams for (1) posttest only nonequivalent control-group designs, (2) pretest-posttest nonequivalent control-group designs, (3) randomized posttest only control-group designs, and (4) randomized pretest-posttest control-group designs.

- Describe processes for (1) matching subjects on the basis of their pretest scores, and (2) placing them into groups.

- Describe the relationship between a *t test* and *analysis of variance*.

- Demonstrate the calculation of an independent-samples *t* test (with both *deviation* and *raw-score* formulas).

- Interpret the table of critical values for *t*.

- Distinguish between *dependent-* and *independent-samples t tests*.

- Demonstrate and discuss the calculation of a one-way analysis of variance with regard to each of the following: (1) grand sum of X, (2) grand sum of X^2, (3) total sum of squares, (4) between sum of squares, (5) within sum of squares, (6) between mean squares, (7) within mean squares, and (8) F ratio.

- Interpret the table of critical values for F.

- Identify and discuss the various *within* and *between* group analyses that can be conducted with t and F tests.

- Contrast the interpretations that are possible from accepting and rejecting a null hypothesis, and the inherent weaknesses of inferences arising out of nonequivalent and randomized control-group designs.

- Distinguish between *Solomon four-group* and *counterbalanced control-group* designs.

- Describe interrupted time series control-group designs.

- Describe multiple pretest control-group designs (with posttest).

- Describe multiple posttest control-group designs (with pretest).

- Distinguish between (1) ANCOVA and MANCOVA, and (2) factorial MANCOVA and factorial MANCOVA with repeated measures.

- Define key terms, and answer the checkpoint questions.

KEY TERMS

Alternative Treatment

Analysis of Covariance

Analysis of Variance

Comparative-Group Designs

Control-Group Designs

Counterbalanced Control-Group Designs

Covariate

Criterion Variable

Critical Values for F

Critical Values for t

Denominator

Descriptive Statistics

Deviation Formulas

F *Ratio*

F *Test*

Factorial MANCOVA

Factorial MANCOVA with Repeated Measures

Homogeneity of Variance

Independent-Group Designs

Independent-Samples t *Test*

Inferential Statistics

Interaction

Interrupted Time Series Control-Group Design

Matched Groups

Mortality

Multiple Posttest Control-Group Design (with Pretest)

Multiple Pretest Control-Group Design (with Posttest)

Multivariate Analysis of Covariance

Nonequivalent Groups

Numerator

Outcome Variable

Posttest

Posttest Only Nonequivalent Control-Group Designs

Pretest

Pretest-Posttest Nonequivalent Control-Group Designs

Protocol

Pseudoreplication Study

Quasi-Experimental Designs

Random Assignment

Randomization

Randomized Posttest Only Control-Group Designs

Randomized Pretest-Posttest Control-Group Designs

Raw Score Formulas

Research Diagrams

Treatment Fidelity

INTRODUCTION

The purpose of Chapter 9 was to introduce the reader to experimental research and, more specifically, to the techniques associated with the design and analysis of single-group investigations. Although there are many process weaknesses inherent in such designs, they do provide some structure for conducting investigations that, otherwise, may not be thoughtfully pursued. Since the practitioner/researcher should always be seeking to find better ways to solve educational problems, this chapter presents a refinement of the aforementioned procedures. To be specific, it presents those designs that utilize *comparative (nonequivalent)* or *control* groups. As you know, a major encumbrance that accompanies designs in which there is but one group is that they do not enable the researcher to isolate the treatment as the sole source of change. Because of various uncontrolled threats to internal validity, investigators are forced to consider that the findings may have occurred regardless of the imposed treatment.

Both nonequivalent and control-group studies involve a minimum of two groups. One of the groups receives a new (or unusual) treatment, while the other receives the traditional (or alternative) treatment. Following a predetermined period of time, both groups are posttested.

Nonequivalent group research is different from **control-group designs** in that the membership of the former has *not* been selected through the process of **randomization.** In many schools, the "luxury" of randomly assigning students to classes does not exist, so investigations of class activity are usually carried out with *intact* (rather than random) groups.

This chapter begins with a discussion of the purposes and strategies for conducting nonequivalent control-group designs. This is accompanied by a demonstration of appropriate statistical procedures that can be used with the data generated through such processes. The chapter then proceeds to randomized control-group research, a practicum, and discussion of alternative analytical procedures.

NONEQUIVALENT CONTROL-GROUP DESIGNS

From discussion in Chapter 9, Single-Group Designs, it should be clear that there are many threats to the internal validity of studies in which one group is the target of an investigation. As a consequence, their employment should be avoided unless the use of more than one group is impossible to arrange.

On the other hand, **comparative-group designs** are conducted in a way that allows two or more intact groups to be studied. As indicated in the introduction, one group is usually administered a "new" treatment, while the group used for purposes of comparison receives the "traditional," or **alternative, treatment.** In this design, the subjects are not randomly assigned to the groups; however, the researcher should attempt to assign the treatment at random. By tossing a coin, for which it has been predetermined that:

- Heads = new treatment, and
- Tails = traditional treatment,

and, on the display of the coin:

- Group 1 will be given its assignment, and
- Group 2 will receive the alternative,

some degree of randomness has been employed.

Posttest only nonequivalent control-group designs do not employ pre-experiment measurements, and are diagrammed as follows:

$$\frac{X \quad O}{O}$$

or

$$\frac{X_1 \quad O}{X_2 \quad O}$$

NOTE: You may remember from Chapter 9, Single-Group Designs, that the diagram is read from left to right. *X* signifies a treatment, *O* signifies the observation. The first row displays the treatment and posttest for one group (for example, Group 1); beneath the broken line is the comparison group that does *not* receive the new treatment. The broken line between the two groups indicates that they were in place (that is, static), and *not* determined by random assignment.

The characteristics of experimental research described in Chapter 9 that are common to both nonequivalent control-group and randomized control-group designs include the following:

1. The treatment, or experimental, variable is considered to be the *independent* variable.

2. The **outcome, or criterion, variable** is considered to be the *dependent* variable.

3. Intervening variables are those that arise during the course of the investigation.

4. Moderator variables are those that are in place at the beginning of the study and, by introducing controls into the design, could ordinarily be eliminated, or at least managed, with proper planning.

5. The null form of hypothesis is preferred for testing.

6. The research design plan should follow the guidelines of Phase 1 and Phase 2.

✓CHECKPOINT

Take this time to review the six factors just listed. You are asked to respond to each of the following items from your memory of Chapter 9, Single-Group Designs.

1. Identify five examples of what could constitute *treatment* (independent) variables.

2. Identify five examples of what could constitute *outcome* (dependent) variables.

3. Identify three examples of what could constitute *intervening* variables.

4. Identify three examples of what could constitute *moderator* variables.

5. Why should a researcher test the *null* hypothesis?

6. Identify the eight elements of Phase 1 of a research design.

7. Identify the four subproblems found in a research design template (Phase 2), and the five guiding questions common to each of them.

Answers

Examine each of the following responses. If you were able to arrive at similar answers on the basis of memory alone, you did extremely well. If not, you should consider reviewing pertinent sections of Chapter 9 again.

Suggested answers to the above items are as follows:

1. Examples of treatment (independent) variables would include:

    a. Arrangement of a learning environment

    b. Behavior modification systems

    c. Ergogenic aids

    d. Instructional methods

    e. Size of learning group

    f. Teaching materials

    g. Time of instruction

2. Examples of outcome (dependent) variables would include:

    a. Achievement

    b. Attendance

    c. Attention span

    d. Attitudes

    e. Behavior

    f. Interests

    g. Number of disciplinary actions

3. Examples of intervening variables would include:

    a. Afternoon television specials on issues related to the topic under investigation (threat of history)

    b. Fire alarms, broken equipment, snow days (threats of instability)

    c. Subjects moving out of town and no longer available to participate in the study (threat of experimental mortality)

    d. Threats of interaction because of the existence of two or more intervening variables working together

4. Examples of moderator variables would include:

    a. Age

    b. Birth order

    c. Gender

    d. Grade level

5. The null hypothesis should be tested because:

    a. of the importance of the presence of neutrality on the part of the researcher.

    b. it facilitates the procurement of permission from authorities for conducting the research.

6. The eight elements of Phase 1 of a research design are:

    a. Statement of the problem

    b. Need (justification) for the study

    c. Review of related literature

    d. Statement of null hypothesis

    e. Basic assumptions

    f. Possible threats to the study

    g. Design alternatives

    h. Definitions of terms

7. The four subproblems found in a research design template (Phase 2) are:

    a. Permission/selection of subjects

    b. Selection of instrument

    c. Administration of study/collection of data

    d. Analysis of data/conclusions/recommendations

The five guiding questions common to each of the subproblems are:

- What I need to know
- Where I will find it
- How I will find it
- Procedures for organizing the information for further use
- Conclusions that would follow from the procedures that would allow the researcher to proceed with the study

---

Speaking of intervening variables (threats to the *internal* validity of the study), posttest only, nonequivalent control-group investigations have a number of threats to internal validity that are *not* controlled by the design. In addition to expectancy and instability, other threats to *internal validity* are:

1. Selection and history. Because random assignments of individuals to groups did not take place, individuals in one group may be more susceptible to enlightenment by environmental circumstances than are their counterparts. To the extent that events "external" to the experiment relate to the dependent variable, **posttest** scores could be affected.

2. Selection and maturation. These are threats because any posttest differences that are revealed upon the conclusion of the study may be due to group differences rather than the effect of a treatment, since the members of the groups were not determined on the basis of random selection.

3. Experimental **mortality.** This is a threat because there is no **pretest.** If someone withdraws from the study, there is no information in hand about that particular individual.

With regard to the threats to *internal validity* that are controlled, because there is no pretest, there is:

1. Pretesting

2. Instrumentation

3. Regression

NOTE: You can see that there are advantages and disadvantages of pretests. As a researcher, a decision to pretest must be made on the basis of the "lesser of two evils." While a pretest may cause potential threats to surface, the data will provide indicators of initial levels of performance which, for purposes of one's study, may be particularly valuable.

In addition to employing qualitative forms of analyses (see Chapter 6, Survey Procedures), one can employ such **descriptive statistics** as the mean, median, and mode (that is, measures of central tendency), percentiles, and the standard deviation (for example, measure of variability) to each of the posttest distributions. Further, the investigator could administer an **independent-samples *t* test.** As an **inferential statistic,** such would enable the user to test the null hypothesis that the posttest means of the two groups are equivalent and, on the basis of the findings, make qualified deductions.

NOTE: The expression *qualified deductions* is used because neither random sampling nor pretesting are part of this form of research design.

The independent-samples form of *t* test would be used because the members of the groups have not been paired in any way. If they had been paired, this would be called a paired- or **matched-group** design, rather than a nonequivalent control-group design.

NOTE: If there were more than two means for which the investigator was interested in simultaneously testing the null hypothesis, she would not use the *t* test. Rather, the researcher would employ such a measure as **analysis of variance** (ANOVA). You may remember from Chapter 9, Single-Group Designs, that ANOVA can be used with two or more means.

The independent-samples *t* test is appropriate for use when:

1. the members of the groups have *not* been paired in any way,

2. a large number of individuals have been sampled from a population and randomly assigned to one group *or* another, and

3. the means have been generated from groups of *unequal* size.

NOTE: If the members of a sample had been paired in advance of their assignment to groups, these groups would be of equal size. If the groups are matched, the researcher would employ the dependent-samples *t* test (described in Chapter 9, Single-Group Designs).

The **raw score formula** for the independent-samples *t* test is:

$$t\ \text{ratio} = \frac{SE}{\sqrt{\left[\dfrac{\Sigma X_1^2 - [(\Sigma X_1)^2 / N_1] + \Sigma X_2^2 - [(\Sigma X_2)^2 / N_2]}{N_1 + N_2 - 2}\right]\left(\dfrac{1}{N_1} + \dfrac{1}{N_2}\right)}}$$

where SE = sampling error; that is, the difference between the two means.

ΣX_1^2 = sum of squared scores for Group 1.

$(\Sigma X_1)^2$ = sum of scores for Group 1, squared.

N_1 = size of Group 1.

ΣX_2^2 = sum of squared scores for Group 2.

$(\Sigma X_2)^2$ = sum of scores for Group 2, squared.

N_2 = size of Group 2.

Consider a scenario in which an instructor of two eighth-grade Algebra I classes decides that he would like to compare the effects of weekly classroom quizzes to weekly written homework assignments upon student performance in a comprehensive term examination. Since class enrollments are predetermined, no randomization is possible except for determining which of the two groups will receive the weekly quizzes. While there are no pretests, the researcher assumes that the groups are fairly equal at the onset of the study because this is the first algebra class for any of the students in either group. Agreement has been reached with the department chair that all instruction and normal evaluatory processes will remain the same except for the scheduling of weekly quizzes and written homework.

Table 10–1 presents the data generated from the Algebra I term comprehensive examination. The following text will take you through the steps necessary to apply the *t* ratio formula for **independent-group designs.**

For the **numerator** of the formula, compute the sampling error by the following procedure:

1. Find the mean (*M*) of Group 1.

$$M_1 = \Sigma X / N$$

$$= 643/10$$

$$= 64.3$$

Table 10–1: **Posttest and Squared Posttest Scores of Two Groups of Ten Subjects in an Algebra I Term Examination**

| Group 1 | | Group 2 | |
X_1	X_1^2	X_2	X_2^2
77	5929	38	1444
76	5776	40	1600
74	5476	55	3025
70	4900	70	4900
68	4624	72	5184
65	4225	80	6400
60	3600	90	8100
58	3364	97	9409
55	3025	98	9604
40	1600	100	10000
$\Sigma X_1 = 643$	$\Sigma X_1^2 = 42519$	$\Sigma X_2 = 740$	$\Sigma X_2^2 = 59666$

2. Find the mean (*M*) of Group 2.

$$M_2 = \Sigma X / N$$
$$= 740/10$$
$$= 74.0$$

3. Find the difference between the two means (*SE*).

$$SE = M - M$$
$$= 74.0 - 64.3$$
$$= 9.7$$

 NOTE: Since sampling error (*SE*) can be described as an *absolute* (rather than *relative*) value, subtract the mean with the lower value from the mean with the higher value.

For the **denominator** of the formula:

1. Square the sum of the raw scores for Group 1.
2. Divide this squared value by the number of scores in Group 1.
3. Square each raw score in Group 1.
4. Sum these squares.
5. Subtract the quotient found in step 2 from the sum of the squared scores found in step 4.
6. Square the sum of the raw scores for Group 2.

7. Divide this squared value by the number of scores in Group 2.

8. Square each raw score in Group 2.

9. Sum these squares.

10. Subtract the quotient found in step 7 from the sum of the squared scores found in step 9.

11. Sum the two numbers found in step 5 and step 10.

12. Divide the sum found in step 11 by the total number of scores minus 2.

13. Divide the number 1 by the number of scores in Group 1.

14. Divide the number 1 by the number of scores in Group 2.

15. Sum the values found in step 13 and step 14.

16. Multiply the sum found in step 15 by the quotient found in step 12.

17. Find the square root of the answer found in step 16. This will give you the denominator.

The t ratio can now be found by dividing the numerator by the denominator. In other words:

$$t \text{ ratio} = \frac{SE}{\sqrt{\left[\dfrac{\Sigma X_1^2 - [(\Sigma X_1)^2 / N_1] + \Sigma X_2^2 - [(\Sigma X_2)^2 / N_2]}{N_1 + N_2 - 2}\right]\left(\dfrac{1}{N_1} + \dfrac{1}{N_2}\right)}}$$

$$= \frac{9.7}{\sqrt{\left[\dfrac{42519 - [413449/10] + 59666 - [547600/10]}{10 + 10 - 2}\right]\left(\dfrac{1}{10} + \dfrac{1}{10}\right)}}$$

$$= \frac{9.7}{\sqrt{\left[\dfrac{[42519 - 41344.9] + [59666 - 54760]}{18}\right](.1 + .1)}}$$

$$= \frac{9.7}{\sqrt{\left[\dfrac{1174.1 + 4906}{18}\right](.2)}}$$

$$= \frac{9.7}{\sqrt{\left[\dfrac{6080.1}{18}\right](.2)}}$$

$$= \frac{9.7}{\sqrt{[337.783](.2)}}$$

$$= \frac{9.7}{\sqrt{67.556}}$$

$$= \frac{9.7}{8.219}$$

$$= 1.180$$

By referring the t ratio (df, $20 - 2 = 18$) to Appendix E, **Critical Values for t,** it can be determined whether the finding of $t = 1.180$ is significant. In order to be significant at the .05 *loc,* the t ratio would have to equal or exceed 2.101. It does not, so the investigator would *accept* the null hypothesis that any observed difference that appears to exist between the two mean values can be attributed to chance alone.

> **NOTE:** If one were testing a *directional* hypothesis that mean 2 was greater than mean 1 (one-tailed test), significance would be found at the .05 level of confidence (*loc*). While the one-tailed test is a weaker test than the two-tailed test, the investigator might want to indicate that significance was found at that particular *loc*. It is important, however, that any statement of significance for a one-tailed test be qualified by saying: Significance was found at the .05 *loc* in favor of Group 2 (one-tailed test).

An alternative to the raw score technique for computing t ratios is through what is referred to as a **deviation formula.** If properly executed, either will provide identical answers. The selection of a raw score or deviation method is a matter of personal preference. Using this alternative, and the values from Table 10–1, the calculation of a t ratio would be as follows (see Table 10–2).

Table 10–2: **Data for Calculating t Ratio Using Deviation Procedures**

Group 1	d_1	$d_1{}^2$	Group 2	d_2	$d_2{}^2$
77	12.7	161.29	38	36	1296
76	11.7	136.89	40	34	1156
74	9.7	94.09	55	19	361
70	5.7	32.49	70	4	16
68	3.7	13.69	72	2	4
65	0.7	00.49	80	6	36
60	4.3	18.49	90	16	256
58	6.3	39.67	97	23	529
55	9.3	86.49	98	24	576
40	24.3	590.49	100	26	676
$M = 64.3$		$\Sigma d_1{}^2 = 1174.10$	$M = 74.0$		$\Sigma d_2{}^2 = 4906.00$

The deviation formula for calculating a *t* ratio is:

$$t \text{ ratio} = \frac{SE}{\sqrt{\left(\dfrac{\Sigma d_1^2 + \Sigma d_2^2}{N_1 + N_2 - 2}\right)\left(\dfrac{1}{N_1} + \dfrac{1}{N_2}\right)}}$$

To proceed, one would take the following steps:

1. Find the mean (*M*) of Group 1.
2. For Group 1, find the deviation (*d*) of each score from the mean.
3. Square the deviation of each score found in step 2.
4. Sum the squared deviations (Σd_1^2) found in step 3.
5. Find the mean (*M*) of Group 2.
6. For Group 2, find the deviation (*d*) of each score from the mean.
7. Square the deviation of each score found in step 6.
8. Sum the squared deviations (Σd_2^2) found in step 7.

The values are then entered within the deviation formula as follows:

$$t \text{ ratio} = \frac{SE}{\sqrt{\left(\dfrac{\Sigma d_1^2 + \Sigma d_2^2}{N_1 + N_2 - 2}\right)\left(\dfrac{1}{N_1} + \dfrac{1}{N_2}\right)}}$$

 NOTE: The sampling error (*SE*) is found the same way as it has been in the past: the mean with the lower value is subtracted from the mean with the higher value.

$$= \frac{9.7}{\sqrt{\left(\dfrac{1174.10 + 4906.00}{10 + 10 - 2}\right)(.1 + .1)}}$$

$$= \frac{9.7}{\sqrt{\left(\dfrac{6080.10}{18}\right)(.20)}}$$

$$= \frac{9.7}{\sqrt{(337.783)\,(.20)}}$$

$$= \frac{9.7}{\sqrt{67.556}}$$

$$= \frac{9.7}{8.219}$$

$$= 1.180$$

As you can see, the t ratio of 1.180, as calculated via the deviation method, is exactly what was found when using the raw-score technique.

NOTE: Now that the deviation method for making computations has been introduced, a description of its use when calculating the standard deviation (σ) should be of interest. You may remember from Chapter 6, Survey Procedures, that the raw score method for calculating σ was:

$$\sqrt{\frac{\Sigma X^2}{N} - M^2}$$

Well, the deviation formula for computing σ is:

$$\sqrt{\frac{\Sigma d^2}{N}}$$

The difference in the two approaches arises from the fact that in the deviation technique, the variation of each score from the mean comes *before* entering the values into the formula. Using the raw score technique, the deviation of the scores from the mean comes *after* entering the values into the formula. You will find additional reference to this point when analysis of variance (ANOVA) is presented later in the chapter.

Using the scores from Table 6–4 in Chapter 6, the standard deviation will now be computed using the *deviation* formula, and the answer will be compared to that found in Chapter 6 for the same set of numbers (see Table 10–3). The calculations for the standard deviation (using the deviation formula) would be as follows:

1. Find the mean of the scores by:

$$M = \frac{\Sigma X}{N}$$

$$= \frac{421}{10}$$

$$= 42.1$$

2. Find the deviation of each score from the mean by subtracting it from the mean. For example, the score ($X = 50$) deviates from the mean ($M = 42.1$) by 7.9.

3. Square each deviation from the mean. Remember, a minus (–) *times* a minus (–) equals a plus (+). In other words, all squared deviation values will be positive numbers. For example, the squared deviation of $d = -1.1$ is $d^2 = +1.21$.

Table 10–3: **Scores of Ten Students, Deviations, and Squared Deviations from the Mean**

Students	Scores	d	d²
A	50	7.9	62.41
B	48	5.9	34.81
C	46	3.9	15.21
D	44	1.9	3.61
E	43	.9	.81
F	41	−1.1	1.21
G	39	−3.1	9.61
H	38	−4.1	16.81
I	37	−5.1	26.01
J	35	−7.1	50.41
			$\Sigma d^2 = 220.90$

4. Sum the squared deviations.

5. Divide the answer in step 4 by N (in this case, 10).

6. Compute the square root of the response found in step 5. The acquired value will be the standard deviation of the numbers.

For the scores in Table 10–3, the standard deviation is found as follows:

$$SD = \sqrt{\frac{\Sigma d^2}{N}}$$

$$= \sqrt{\frac{220.90}{10}}$$

$$= \sqrt{22.09}$$

$$= 4.70$$

As you can see, the answer is exactly the same as that found in Chapter 6, Survey Procedures.

In determining which form of calculation to use, in general, if the mean leads to a *whole* number, the *deviation* method is preferred. On the other hand, if the mean is *not* a whole number (for example, $M = 42.1$), the raw score method seems to be more efficient.

NOTE: Remember, when the standard deviation is used to describe, rather than infer, variability to a larger population, use N (not $N - 1$) in the denominator.

CHECKPOINT

To test your understanding of the use of these formulas, calculate the standard deviation (utilizing the *deviation* formula) for the scores in Group 2 (Table 10–2). You will note that the Σd^2 has already been calculated (that is, 4906.00).

Answer

The answer to the value of the standard deviation (σ) for the Group 2 scores in Table 10–2 is 22.14 (using the deviation method), per the following procedures:

$$SD = \sqrt{\frac{\Sigma d^2}{N}}$$

$$= \sqrt{\frac{4906.00}{10}}$$

$$= \sqrt{490.6}$$

$$= 22.14$$

CHECKPOINT

Now, to determine if this answer is correct, compute the standard deviation for the same set of numbers (that is, Table 10–2, Group 2) utilizing the *raw score* formula.

Answer

The answer to the value of the standard deviation (σ) for Group 2 scores in Table 10–2 is 22.14 (using the raw score method), per the following procedures:

1. Square each score (for example, the square of the score 38 is 1444; the square of the score 40 is 1600, and so on).
2. Sum the squared scores and divide by N.
3. Square the mean (arithmetic average).
4. Subtract the squared mean value from the average of the squared scores.
5. Compute the square root. This will generate the standard deviation.

You are referred to the data in Table 10–4 for scores from which the standard deviation (raw score method) will now be found. Applying the raw score formula to the data in Table 10–4, the standard deviation is computed as follows:

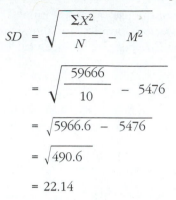

$$SD = \sqrt{\frac{\Sigma X^2}{N} - M^2}$$

$$= \sqrt{\frac{59666}{10} - 5476}$$

$$= \sqrt{5966.6 - 5476}$$

$$= \sqrt{490.6}$$

$$= 22.14$$

The answers are in total agreement. It can be seen that one can compute the standard deviation by either the *deviation* or *raw score* techniques, and arrive at the same values.

Like single-group studies, posttest only nonequivalent control-group designs are quite frequently used in exploratory studies. For example, early in the fall semester, the author of this text was interested in knowing whether increasing the hours of observations in out-of-school settings would have an effect upon understanding of key concepts in the course "Learning Environments for Exceptional Children." So, for one of the sections in the course, he assigned forty hours of observation; the other section was assigned the traditional twenty hours (supplemented by disability simulations). At the conclusion of the semester, group performance was compared on final examinations by way of an independent *t* test. It was observed that there was no significant difference in the arithmetic averages of the two groups. While requiring increased hours of observation in integrated classrooms may provide students with additional

Table 10–4: **Scores and Squared Scores for Ten Students**

Scores (X)	Squared Scores (X²)
38	1444
40	1600
55	3025
70	4900
72	5184
80	6400
90	8100
97	9409
98	9604
100	10000
	$\Sigma X^2 = 59666$

insights on teaching strategies, it did not appear to influence achievement as measured by the questions on the examination. The question remaining, however, is whether increasing the required observation time to only twenty-five or thirty (instead of forty) hours would have produced the same results. Perhaps there is a saturation point above which additional hours may reinforce, but not increase, knowledge and understanding. In order to make this determination, a more formal study (with integrated disability simulations) was designed for the following semester.

Pretest-posttest nonequivalent control-group designs are stronger than posttest only designs because they provide for the formal acquisition of information about the groups in advance of administering the treatments. The diagram for pretest-posttest nonequivalent control-group designs is:

$$\frac{O \quad X \quad O}{O \qquad\quad O}$$

or

$$\frac{O \quad X_1 \quad O}{O \quad X_2 \quad O}$$

The broken line indicates that the groups were intact at the onset of the study. While individuals are *not* assigned to groups at random, it would make the design more viable if groups were at least assigned the treatment at random. By having pretest information, it would be possible for the investigator to test the null hypothesis that the pretest means are alike. This could be accomplished through the use of an independent-sample *t* test. If the null hypothesis is accepted, this would give the researcher cause to believe that the groups were reasonably similar at pretreatment.

It is only by comparing the pretest scores of the two groups that one can hope to rule out initial selection difference as a threat to internal validity. If the two groups perform similarly at the onset of the study, but differently following the treatment, selection bias is reduced, and the researcher is more justified in attributing a finding to the treatment. Without a pretest, the investigator lacks evidence for eliminating the possibility that observed differences on the posttest could have occurred regardless of treatment intervention. Of course, if the test used to measure pretreatment information is ill-prepared and relates only remotely to the dependent variable, the apparent pre-experiment similarity of the groups will be meaningless to the purpose of the investigation. Although a number of measures may be administered before a study begins, the term *pretest* ordinarily refers to a test of the *dependent* variable.

With regard to the threats to *internal* validity, if the pretest results reveal similar performance levels against the dependent variable, all threats to internal validity are accounted for except:

1. Expectancy
2. Instability
3. Interaction of:
   a. Selection bias and history
   b. Selection bias and maturation

      c. Selection bias and pretesting

      d. Selection bias and regression

The **interaction** threats are discussed in more detail in the following text.

Selection bias and history. Even though the groups are shown to be alike on a pretest measure, the members of one group may be more "tuned in" to events around them than is the case with the second group. As a consequence, that group is more likely to be influenced by events not controlled by the design. If these events relate to the treatment, posttest results are likely to be affected. If the groups had been randomly selected, it could be assumed that the quality of being responsive to the environment would have been distributed to both groups in equal amounts.

Selection bias and maturation. Earlier it was stated that selection would be addressed by determining through a pretest that the two groups were alike at the beginning of the study. If that is shown to be a reality, it is likely that the members of both groups would have equal opportunity to mature. However, this assumption is based on the premise that both groups are equivalent as far as their susceptibility to maturation is concerned. Unlike random sampling in which the presumption of equal distribution of traits in both groups can be made, it is unlikely that any pretest could measure for all factors contributing to maturation.

Selection bias and pretesting. Even though it may be determined that both groups demonstrated similar performances on the pretest, lack of random assignment of individuals to the two groups could mean that individuals in one group have qualities that cause them to react differently to pretesting information. This could result in a contamination of the findings.

Selection bias and regression. If the two groups had been selected at random, it could be assumed that the characteristics leading to possible regression in one of the groups would be present in the other, thus factoring each other out. In nonequivalent control-group designs, however, such a presumption is inappropriate.

 NOTE: It may appear ironic that single-group designs, as weak as they are, do *not* have selection as a threat to their internal validity. This is because they lack comparative groups. However, the fact that there is no basis for comparison leads to a weakness in the design that transcends the problem of selection. The interactive threat caused by selection bias becomes a matter of concern when the design provides for more than one group, and the composition of these groups is not made on the basis of random selection.

Threats to *internal* validity that are controlled are experimental mortality and instrumentation. *Experimental mortality* is controlled because if a subject withdraws from the study, pre-experiment information is available about that individual. In other words, the researcher would know what she was losing. If that person's counterpart can be identified through an examination of the pretest scores that were generated by the comparison group, her posttest data can be excluded from the analysis. In effect, this process provides for a mechanical re-equalizing of the two groups. *Instrumentation* is controlled if equivalent instruments are used with both groups during the course of the investigation. If the testing instrument administered to one of the groups is more difficult than that administered to the other, one would expect scores to differ. Under these conditions, any effect thought to be attributable to the treatment would have to be discounted.

✔CHECKPOINT

If it is found that there is a statistical difference between the two pretest means, what threat or threats to internal validity would be controlled?

Answer

If the means of the two groups are shown to be statistically different on the pretest, the *only* threat to internal validity that is controlled is *experimental mortality,* for the following reasons.

1. Expectancy remains a threat (under all conditions) unless the investigator monitors any personal bias she may have so that it does not reveal itself in any way during the course of the study.

2. History remains a threat because the members of one of the groups may be more or less responsive to events in the environment than are the members of the other group. The fact that it is known that the groups are *unequal* at the beginning of the study makes matters worse.

3. Instability remains a threat because of chance factors arising during the study. There is no way of knowing in advance whether an event (such as a fire alarm going off) will take place during one of the group sessions.

4. Instrumentation is a threat, since one of the groups may have had a lower average because the instruments were not equivalent in difficulty.

5. Maturation remains a threat because individuals in one group may be more susceptible to mature than are those in the other group. The fact that the groups generated means that were statistically different could be accounted for by the fact that one of the groups was already more "mature."

6. Pretesting remains a threat because the two groups may differ in the degree to which they profit from being exposed to the content of the pretest.

7. Regression continues to be a threat because the group with the lower arithmetic average has more room to improve in the posttest. To offer an illustration that points to this issue: If one of the groups had scored an average of 90 out of 100 possible points in the pretest, it could only improve by 10 points in a 100-point posttest. If the other group had scored an average of 50 out of 100 possible points in the pretest, it would have the potential to improve by 50 points on an equivalent posttest. If the investigator were interested in assessing rate of change between pre- and posttest scores, the group with the lower initial average would have the best chance to demonstrate improvement.

8. Selection has become an implicit threat to the internal validity of the study because it has been determined by the pretest that the groups *are*

different at onset. For obvious reasons, it would be difficult to attribute any observed posttest differences to the treatment.

9. Interaction of threats exists as a possibility whenever there are two or more uncontrolled threats present.

Assume that a principal is interested in knowing whether student achievement is influenced by the presence of paraeducators in the classroom. At the beginning of the school year, and before any paraeducators have been hired, student academic records are reviewed for those classes that meet the criteria for additional staffing. On the basis of budget limitations, only fifty percent of the number of paraeducators that would be desirable can be hired. It is determined by the principal that the teachers who have the most teaching experience will be assigned these aides. At the end of the school year, the achievement scores of students in classes with and without paraeducators are compared. The independent-sample t test is employed to test the mean between the two nonequivalent groups.

✓CHECKPOINT

Given pertinent information regarding the above scenario, compute an independent-sample t test, and respond to the six questions that follow.

Group 1	Group 2
No Paraeducators	*Paraeducators*
$N_1 = 10$	$N_2 = 10$
$\Sigma d_1^2 = 124$	$\Sigma d_2^2 = 348$
$M_1 = 81$	$M_2 = 87$

1. What is the t ratio for the above data?

2. What are the degrees of freedom?

3. Is the t ratio significant at the .05 *loc* (two-tailed test)? Yes or No

4. Is the t ratio significant at the .02 *loc* (two-tailed test)? Yes or No

5. Is the t ratio significant at the .01 *loc* (two-tailed test)? Yes or No

6. In regard to the null hypothesis, my interpretation of the finding is: _____.

Answers

The answers to the above six questions are as follows:

1. The t ratio is 2.621, per:

$$t \text{ ratio} = \frac{SE}{\sqrt{\left(\dfrac{\Sigma d_1^2 + \Sigma d_2^2}{N_1 + N_2 - 2}\right)\left(\dfrac{1}{N_1} + \dfrac{1}{N_2}\right)}}$$

$$= \frac{6}{\sqrt{\left(\dfrac{124 + 348}{10 + 10 - 2}\right)(.1 + .1)}}$$

$$= \frac{6}{\sqrt{\left(\dfrac{472}{18}\right)(.2)}}$$

$$= \frac{6}{\sqrt{(26.222)\quad(.2)}}$$

$$= \frac{6}{\sqrt{5.244}}$$

$$= \frac{6}{2.289}$$

$$= 2.621$$

2. The degrees of freedom = 18 (*df* = 10 + 10 − 2).

3. *Yes,* the findings are significant at the .05 *loc*. To be significant at the .05 *loc,* the *t* ratio had to equal or exceed 2.101.

4. *Yes,* the findings are significant at the .02 *loc*. To be significant at the .02 *loc,* the *t* ratio had to equal or exceed 2.552.

5. *No,* the findings are not significant at the .01 *loc*. To be significant at the .01 *loc,* the *t* ratio had to equal or exceed 2.878.

6. In regard to the null hypothesis, the correct interpretation of the finding is:

> Within the limitations of the investigation, this researcher rejects the null hypothesis at the .02 level of confidence. It appears that something other than chance affected the findings in favor of Group 2.

Although there are many threats to the study because of the lack of randomized groups, the classes in which paraeducators were assigned appeared to benefit by their presence. However, among the factors that could have had a bearing on the results is that the teachers who were assigned the paraeducators had more experience than the other teachers selected for the study. Therefore, before any general inferences could be made from the statistical significance of the findings, it would be important to determine the levels of student achievement in the classes taught by more and less experienced teachers in prior academic years. This information should be sought by the investigator during the creation of Phase 1 and Phase 2 of her research plan. By knowing this in advance of carrying out the study, greater credibility can be attached to any inferences that are deduced from the findings.

Practitioner/researchers often select nonequivalent control-group **(quasi-experimental)** designs because:

1. intact, comparative groups are already convenient and in place (acknowledging that assignments of individuals to groups have been made without the application of randomization procedures).

2. of their value as preliminary studies for more sophisticated designs to follow.

This leads to what are referred to as *true* experimental designs; that is, designs that require the selection and assignment of subjects on the basis of strict adherence to randomization procedures.

RANDOMIZED CONTROL-GROUP DESIGNS

A control group is a group of subjects whose experiences and selection are identical in every way possible to the experimental (treatment) group except that its members do not receive the treatment (that is, the independent variable is absent). All of the *true* experimental designs have one characteristic in common that is not present in the others—that is, random selection and assignment of individuals to groups.

The first of these designs to be studied in this chapter is the **randomized posttest only control-group design,** which has as its **research diagram:**

$$R \quad X \quad O$$
$$O$$

 NOTE: The investigator may choose to designate X_2 as the control group. In other words, the *traditional treatment* is the control. Hence:

$$R \quad X_1 \quad O$$
$$R \quad X_2 \quad O$$

Individuals are randomly assigned to one of two groups. One of the groups is subjected to a *new* or *unusual* treatment, and then both groups are posttested. The scores of the posttests are then compared to determine the effectiveness of the treatment.

Random assignment and the presence of a control group serve to control for all sources of threats to internal validity, except: expectancy, instability, and experimental mortality. Expectancy remains as a threat because the researcher may have an uncontrolled bias (Rosenthal, 1976); instability is a threat because of the fact that chance factors may arise without warning during the course of the study

(Borg, 1984); and experimental mortality is a threat because of the fact that there is no pretest information on the subjects (Jurs & Glass, 1971). If all subjects remain during the study, the researcher would report that, while experimental mortality was a threat, it did not materialize because the composition of the groups remained unchanged from pretest to posttest. Depending upon circumstances, the same could be said about expectancy and instability.

> **NOTE:** The posttest only design can be very effective if the probability of differential mortality is low—that is, if the chances of losing unequal numbers or quality of subjects are virtually nonexistent. For obvious reasons, the shorter the study, the less is the probability that the composition of the groups will change.

There are various ways to arrange for the random assignment of subjects to the experimental and control groups. Among the most common are the following.

1. A random sample of subjects is selected from a finite population. The first one-half of the desired sample size selected is assigned to one group; the second one-half of the desired number is assigned to the other (see Chapter 4, Sampling Procedures). By a toss of a coin, the experimental treatment is then assigned to one of the groups. This is not as desirable a procedure because, once the size of Group 1 is determined, the remaining individuals who are selected can only be placed in Group 2. This is addressed in part, however, by refraining from assigning treatments to groups until after their memberships are determined.

2. A random sample of subjects is selected from a finite population. After the sample of a desired size is procured, the members of that group are renumbered—that is, if the sample size is 100, each member is assigned a number in order from 00–99. The researcher then returns to a table of random numbers (or raffle box) and makes a selection of the first fifty. They are assigned to one group, and the remaining fifty are assigned automatically to the other group. (In this procedure, each member of the population has an equal and independent opportunity to be selected for Group 1.) The experimental treatment is then assigned to one of the groups by a toss of a coin.

3. A random sample of subjects is selected from a finite population by placing the first person selected into Group 1, the second person selected into Group 2, the third person selected into Group 3, the fourth selected into Group 4, and so on. This is done until the desired sample (group) size is reached. (This process relates to example 1 in that the *odd-even* assignment of individuals to one group or the other is *arranged* in advance of their selection. Again, however, this is addressed in part by assigning treatments after group selections have been made.) By tossing a coin, a decision is made about which of the groups will receive the treatment.

4. In a study in which the entire finite population is going to be used, each member is assigned a number from 00–n. The first one-half of the individuals who are selected will be assigned to one group; the other one-half of the population is assigned automatically to the other group. (Again, each member of the finite population has an equal and independent opportunity to be selected for Group 1 and, by virtue of chance selections, those who are not placed in Group 1 will be in Group 2.) By toss of a coin, a decision is then made about which group will receive the treatment.

5. In a study in which the entire finite population is going to be used, each member is again assigned a number from 00–n. The first individual selected will be assigned to Group 1, the second individual selected will be assigned to Group 2, the third individual will be in Group 1, the fourth in Group 2, and so on, until both groups are formed. Like example 3, this method predetermines the groups to which succeeding individuals will be assigned. However, if the investigator then proceeds to toss a coin in order to determine the group that will receive the treatment, selection weaknesses are less problematic.

NOTE: It may be possible that a principal of a given school would not be interested in having one group of subjects (for example, a class of fifth graders) treated differently than another (for example, another class of fifth graders). If this is the case, it may be necessary to seek the services of a different school in order to procure one of the groups. (While classroom teachers normally enjoy the privilege of academic freedom when it comes to teaching methods, when a teacher/researcher wants to experiment with *new* materials, administrators may not be as liberal in their thinking.) Very often, a principal of a school wants her students to be treated the same. (After all, to some extent, that is a worthy goal.) Again, this speaks to the importance of maintaining neutrality during the design and administration of the research. If the investigator knows that using certain materials with an experimental group will generate greater results than will the use of traditional materials by the control group, it is a matter of *ethics* that the researcher *not* go forward with the research. One should never knowingly expose a group of subjects to an inferior treatment (in the name of research) in order to promote a cause.

Randomization is the employment of a sampling procedure (for example, simple, stratified, or cluster) that ensures that every individual in a finite group of individuals has an equal and independent opportunity to be selected for participation in the study. Remember that the larger the size of the sample, the greater the chance that population characteristics will be present.

Random assignment refers to the fact that each sampling unit, whether it be age, gender, student, classroom, grade level, department, family size, employment status, trained or untrained, graduate or nongraduate, school district, and so on, has an equal chance of being assigned to one group or another. Random assignment of units to groups is the best technique available in the posttest only control group design to ensure equality of the groups at the onset of the study.

Suppose that an investigator is interested in learning whether achievement on tasks requiring multiple intelligences (Gardner, 1993), is affected by exposure to an integrated artists-in-residence program. One group of eighth-grade students is selected at random from each of two equivalent middle schools. With endorsement from all pertinent authorities, a toss of a coin determines that Group 1 will receive the treatment (that is, integrated artists-in-residence program). Upon the completion of the term (per study design), identical posttests are administered to both groups.

Since the treatment (in this illustration) is being administered in a setting without the presence of the investigator, it will be necessary for the practitioner/experimenter in that school to comply with the **protocol** specified by the investigator in her design. Failure to do so will influence what is referred to as **treatment fidelity**— that is, the extent to which the administration of a study is in compliance with the protocol of the investigator's research design. Failure to follow the exact procedures specified by the investigator for administering the treatment (or control, for that matter) causes a bias and reduces the credibility of interpretations that attempt to assign cause to the findings. Investigators should make it a point to check on the extent to which fidelity has been maintained (Barber, 1973). In a study of twenty-two reports of teaching-methods research in which making such a check would have been appropriate, it was found that less than fifty percent ($N = 9$) reported that it was actually done (Shaver, 1983).

 NOTE: Whenever individuals other than the writer of the research design are going to be involved in the administration of any part of the study, it is important that research *protocol* is explained and understood. This holds true whether the study is being done by different teacher/researchers within or between schools.

Although a t test for independent samples would provide suitable analyses of the posttest scores (assuming the presence of interval or ratio data), for purposes of illustration, this writer is going to introduce *analysis of variance (ANOVA),* otherwise known as the **F test.** As you may remember from previous discussion, ANOVA enables the researcher to draw inferences about the differences in the means of two or more groups. In fact, if there were only two groups to be compared, both the t test for independent samples and a one-way analysis of variance would lead to identical conclusions.

 NOTE: A one-way *ANOVA* is used when there is but *one* treatment upon which analyses are to be made.

Using the data from Table 10–5, the steps leading to a determination of whether a statistical difference exists between the two means can be shown. For purposes of this illustration, the *raw score* method will be used.

Applying the raw score formula for analysis of variance (ANOVA), one would use the following steps:

1. Find the ΣX and ΣX^2 for Group 1 and Group 2.

$$\text{Group 1: } \Sigma X = 72 \qquad \text{Group 2: } \Sigma X = 50$$
$$\Sigma X^2 = 742 \qquad\qquad \Sigma X^2 = 324$$

 NOTE: Values will be truncated at three places throughout the calculations because the F distribution (Appendix F, Critical Values for F) is displayed as three places.

2. Find the *grand* sum of X by adding 72 and 50: $72 + 50 = 122$.

Table 10-5: **Scores and Squared Scores for Two Independent Groups of Subjects Generated from Equivalent Posttests to Measure the Effect of Participation in an Artists-in-Residence Program**

Group 1		Group 2	
X_1	X_1^2	X_2	X_2^2
10	100	3	9
16	256	6	36
5	25	2	4
6	36	3	9
12	144	7	49
8	64	6	36
9	81	10	100
6	36	1	1
		8	64
		4	16
$\Sigma X_1 = 72$	$\Sigma X_1^2 = 742$	$\Sigma X_2 = 50$	$\Sigma X_2^2 = 324$

3. Find the *grand* sum of X^2 by adding 742 and 324: 742 + 324 = 1066.

4. Find SS_T (total sum of squares) by:

$$\text{Grand sum of } X^2 - \frac{(\text{Grand sum of } X)^2}{\text{Total } N}$$

$$= 1066 - \frac{(122)^2}{18}$$

$$= 1066 - 826.888$$

$$= 239.112$$

5. Find SS_B (between sum of squares) by:

$$= \frac{(\Sigma X)^2}{N_1} + \frac{(\Sigma X)^2}{N_2} - C$$

NOTE: C constitutes a correction because the raw score formula is being used. You may remember that the same principle was applied when using the raw score to find the standard deviation, per:

$$\sqrt{\frac{\Sigma X^2}{N} - M^2}$$

In step 5 of ANOVA:

$$C = \frac{(\text{Grand sum of } X)^2}{\text{Total } N}$$

which is shown in step 4.

$$= \frac{(72)^2}{8} + \frac{(50)^2}{10} - 826.888$$

$$= \frac{5184}{8} + \frac{2500}{10} - 826.888$$

$$= 648 + 250 - 826.888$$

$$= 898 - 826.888$$

$$= 71.112$$

6. Find SS_W (within sum of squares) by:

$$= SS_T - SS_B$$

$$= 239.112 - 71.112$$

$$= 168.000$$

7. Find MS_B (between mean squares) by:

$$= \frac{SS_B}{K - 1}$$

 NOTE: K equals the number of groups. In this scenario, $K = 2$.

$$= \frac{71.112}{2 - 1}$$

$$= \frac{71.112}{1}$$

$$= 71.112$$

8. Find MS_W (within mean squares) by:

$$= \frac{SS_W}{N - K}$$

NOTE: N equals the total number of subjects. In this scenario, $N = 18$.

$$= \frac{168}{18 - 2}$$

$$= \frac{168}{16}$$

$$= 10.500$$

9. Find the **F ratio** by:

$$= \frac{MS_B}{MS_W}$$

$$= \frac{71.112}{10.500}$$

$$= 6.772$$

By referring the F ratio (df with $K - 1$ as numerator, and $N - K$ as denominator) to Appendix F **(Critical Values for F),** it can be determined whether the finding of $F = 6.772$ is significant. In order to be significant at the .05 *loc,* the F ratio would have to equal or exceed 4.494.

NOTE: To use the critical values for F table (Appendix F), go to the top of the page, at column 1 (because of $K = 2 - 1 = 1$). This is the *numerator.* Now go to the left side of the page, at row 16 (because of $N - K = 18 - 2 = 16$). This is the *denominator.* Where these points intersect in the table is where you will find the critical value that must be equaled or exceeded in order for significance to be established.

Since the earned value of 6.772 *does* equal or exceed 4.494, the investigator would now refer to the next level of significance (that is, in Critical Values for F, Appendix F). Per display, the next critical level would be .01.

✓CHECKPOINT

What is the critical value for F in order to find significance at the .01 level of confidence ($df = 1,16$)?

Answer

The answer is 8.531. Since the earned F ratio of 6.772 does not equal or exceed the table requirement, the most that can be said with the information available is that:

Within the limitations of the investigation, this researcher rejects the null hypothesis at the .05 level of confidence. It appears that something other than chance affected the findings in favor of Group 1.

✓CHECKPOINT

Why did it appear to the investigator that the finding is in favor of Group 1?

Answer

The answer is: Group 1 had the higher mean value. This can be determined by going back to the original set of data and examining the arithmetic averages of Group 1 and Group 2. Group 1 had a mean of 72; Group 2 had a mean of 50.

If there were more than two groups, it would be more problematic to make such a judgment on the basis of observation alone. In order to make this determination, the *Scheffe test* is used. (It will be presented in Chapter 11, Other Experimental Procedures.)

NOTE: The reader will often find the expression **homogeneity of variance** instead of *null hypothesis* in literature that references the use of analysis of variance (ANOVA). This is because investigators are technically testing the hypothesis that there are equal variances for the populations from which the samples came. Do not be confused by the terminology. If homogeneity of variance is rejected, it means the same as rejecting the null hypothesis—that is, the researcher is claiming that something other than chance affected the "hypothesis of no difference," and she would have to offer support for that statement by referencing a level of confidence.

Earlier in the chapter, it was said that random assignment is the best technique available in the posttest only control-group design to ensure equality of the groups at the onset of the study. This leads to another design that takes the presumption of pre-experiment equality to a higher level—that is, the randomized, pretest-posttest control-group design.

The **randomized pretest-posttest control-group design** is diagrammed as:

$$R \quad O \quad X \quad O$$

$$R \quad O \quad \quad O$$

or

$$R \quad O \quad X_1 \quad O$$

$$R \quad O \quad X_2 \quad O$$

In this design, individuals are randomly assigned to one of two groups, and the two groups are then pretested on the dependent variable; one of the groups receives a new treatment, and then both groups are posttested. Scores on the posttest are then compared in order to determine treatment effectiveness. Because of random assignment, a pretest, and a control group, all threats to internal validity are controlled except for expectancy and instability. Unlike the randomized posttest only control-group design, this plan will control for experimental mortality.

✓ CHECKPOINT

Why is experimental mortality controlled for in the randomized, pretest-posttest control-group design?

Answer

The answer is: Valid pretests provide investigators with information on the subjects with regard to the dependent variable. As indicated earlier, if a subject withdraws from the study, the researcher knows what she is losing. Because both groups are receiving pretests, should an individual withdraw from the study, her counterpart can be determined in the opposite group so that the posttest score for that person can be omitted from any final analysis.

While a pretest can provide subjects with information that could compromise the *effect* of the treatment, its use does control for mortality. The researcher has to make a decision about the "lesser of two evils." Of course, with a study that is not too long, the chances of experimental mortality becoming actualized are virtually nonexistent. In short, suppose that a researcher were faced with the following dilemma:

1. The study is going to last an entire academic semester (that is, sixteen weeks).
2. The acquisition of pretest information is important (for example, present level of student behavior).
3. The treatment (for example, behavior modification) is designed to address student behavior.

The researcher would be better off to subject the study to a threat of experimental mortality. At the same time, however, there are even designs to deal with this problem.

Although a thorough analysis is beyond the scope of this chapter, the *Solomon four-group design* involves the random assignment of subjects to one of four groups. In this plan, two of the groups receive pretests, and the other two groups do not. One of the *pretested* and one of the *unpretested* groups receive the treatment. As a culmination to the study, all four groups receive equivalent posttests. One of the weaknesses of this design is the need for more subjects (perhaps twice as many); as you well know, subjects may be difficult to acquire. The design, however, enables the researcher to assess for factors related to experimental mortality and pretesting.

The design for the Solomon four-group study would be diagrammed as:

$$
\begin{array}{cccc}
R & O & X & O \\
R & O &   & O \\
R &   & X & O \\
R &   &   & O \\
\end{array}
$$

As you can see, this design is a combination of:

1. the randomized pretest-posttest control-group design, and

2. the randomized posttest only control-group design.

Speaking of possible variations of typical *two-group* plans, there are several other designs of which the reader should be aware. Among the most common are the following.

1. Counterbalanced control-group design. In this plan, each of the groups receive a new or traditional treatment, but in a different order. While there can be two or more groups in a **counterbalanced control-group design,** one major condition to its use is that there cannot be more treatments than there are groups. An example of a typical counterbalanced control-group design would be where Group 1 receives Treatment 1; Group 2 receives Treatment 2; then, both groups are posttested. Following the posttest, Group 1 would then receive Treatment 2, and Group 2 would receive Treatment 1. Both groups would then be posttested again. Each row represents a **pseudoreplication** of the study—*pseudo* because of the possible multiple-treatment interference on the second round of treatments. The diagram of the counterbalanced control-group design would be:

$$
\begin{array}{cccc}
X_1 & O & X_2 & O \\
X_2 & O & X_1 & O \\
\end{array}
$$

With regard to the use of this design, it is important to note that:

1. its use most frequently comes into play with intact groups, and when a pretest is not feasible, and

2. a major weakness of this design is the potential for cumulative treatment effects. This can occur any time a single group receives more than one treatment. Thus, this design is most appropriate when exposure to one treatment will not affect the potential influence of the other.

An example of a study that would be suitable for such a design would be one in which the investigator is interested in knowing whether one form of question is as effective as another in assessing acquisition of a specific body of knowledge. Consider, for example, that a teacher of a second-year course in aeronautics randomly divides her homogeneous class into *two* groups for the purpose of testing. For the first half of a timed, unit examination, one group is administered completion and essay questions (Treatment 1). Meanwhile, the second group is administered a series of multiple-choice questions (Treatment 2) on the same material. When the time limit is reached for the first half of the class period, test papers are turned in, and the treatments (that is, form of question) are immediately reversed (with no intervening questions or discussion). The identical questions are administered during both halves of the class period. In this design, the independent variable is the question type, and the dependent variable is the test score.

2. *Multiple pretest control-group design (with posttest).* As you may surmise from the title of the design, the researcher administers two or more pretests. This procedure is followed in order to assess the extent to which scores are stable in the pre-experiment observations (see Chapter 9, Single-Group Designs). The diagram for the **multiple pretest control-group design (with posttest)** is:

$$
\begin{array}{ccccc}
O & O & O & X & O \\
O & O & O & & O
\end{array}
$$

or

$$
\begin{array}{ccccc}
O & O & O & X_1 & O \\
O & O & O & X_2 & O
\end{array}
$$

3. *Multiple posttest control-group design (with pretest).* This design provides for two or more posttest measurements. The **multiple posttest control-group design (with pretest)** is often used in order to assess the degree to which retention of knowledge declines between initial and subsequent posttests. Investigators may be interested in knowing whether findings of the initial posttest scores for both groups remain unchanged through a series of posttest measures. The diagram of this design would be:

$$
\begin{array}{ccccc}
O & X & O & O & O \\
O & & O & O & O
\end{array}
$$

or

$$
\begin{array}{ccccc}
O & X_1 & O & O & O \\
O & X_2 & O & O & O
\end{array}
$$

4. *Interrupted time series control-group design.* This plan provides for the utilization of a control group for what was introduced in Chapter 9 as a single-group interrupted time series design. The advantage of the control group over any single-group design is that it provides more credibility to any interpretation that is assigned to the findings. Once groups are established, the treatment is randomly assigned to one of them. The diagram for the **interrupted time series control-group design** is:

$$
\begin{array}{ccccccc}
O & O & O & X & O & O & O \\
O & O & O & & O & O & O
\end{array}
$$

or

$$
\begin{array}{ccccccc}
O & O & O & X_1 & O & O & O \\
O & O & O & X_2 & O & O & O
\end{array}
$$

NOTE: Although three pretests and three posttests were diagrammed for the interrupted time series control-group designs described, it could just as easily have been two, four, and so on. Except for the effects of pretesting upon threats to internal validity, there is no specific number that is recommended, although the range is generally between two and four.

5. Pretest, matched, randomized, posttest, control-group design. This design is based upon the intent of the investigator to equate groups of subjects on one or more variables that have been selected on the basis of their relationship to the dependent variable. (As you would suspect, the more variables that one is trying to match, the more difficult is the process.)

The procedure entails administering a pretest to a finite population or its representative sample. On the basis of attained scores, pairs of individuals are identified, and each is randomly (R) assigned to one of two groups. Since it may be impossible to find exact matches, except for such things as gender, the researcher may decide (for the purpose of the study) that scores within ten points of each other shall constitute a match (m). If an individual does not fall within the range considered to be an acceptable match with any other individual's score, both persons would be excluded from the study.

While perfect matching would be the optimum objective in matched, control-group designs, it is likely that such a case would never occur unless the population that was initially tested is very large. At the same time, if the range for an acceptable match of scores is too large, the value of this design is compromised. The diagram for this design would be:

$$O \quad m \quad R \quad X \quad O$$
$$O \quad m \quad R \qquad\;\; O$$

$$\text{or}$$

$$O \quad m \quad R \quad X_1 \quad O$$
$$O \quad m \quad R \quad X_2 \quad O$$

There are many combinations of designs that can be tailored to the requirements of a study. The task for the investigator is to plan for the best design possible that will address the research problem. When considering the options available, thoughtful consideration to the control for threats to the internal (and external) validity of the study will set the stage for generating findings from which meaningful inferences can be made.

CONTROL-GROUP DESIGN PRACTICUM

Assume that a third-grade teacher is interested in studying the effect of flash cards (Dolch, 1951) upon sight word recognition (Skinner, Smith, & McLean, 1994). Twenty-four students who are found to score one year or more below grade level on a standardized reading test are randomly assigned to one of two groups. Based upon the toss of a coin, the treatment (that is, use of flash cards) is assigned to Group 1. Upon the conclusion of the treatment period, both groups of students are administered an identical posttest, and Group 1 is found to have the higher arithmetic average.

NOTE: The parents of one of the students moves to another state, so their daughter (who was in Group 2) withdraws from the study. Since an examination of her pretest score reveals that she scored at average of the group, the threat of experimental mortality is not seen to be a source of concern.

Prior to commencing the study, all elements of Phase 1 and Phase 2 were addressed thoroughly. The elements addressed in Phase 1 were:

1. Statement of the problem

2. Need (justification) for the study

3. Review of related literature

4. Statement of the null hypothesis

5. Basic assumptions

6. Possible threats to the study

7. Design alternatives

8. Definitions of terms

In Phase 2, the following elements were addressed:

1. Permission/selection of subjects

2. Selection of instrument

3. Administration of study/collection of data

4. Analysis of data/conclusions/recommendations

Each of these elements was addressed with regard to what I need to know, including:

1. Selection of subjects:
   - Procurement of permission from administrators and other appropriate individuals in writing
   - Names of all grade 3 students who scored one year or more *below* grade level on pretest
   - Names of those who will be in each group
   - Identity of the group that will receive the treatment

2. Selection of instrument:
   - Name of a valid test that will measure reading ability
   - Availability of selected instrument at appropriate times, and in sufficient quantities

3. Administration of study/collection of data:
   - That plans have been made to carry out the study in a manner that will maximize the control for threats to internal validity: history, selection, maturation, instrumentation, regression, mortality, pretesting, instability, and expectancy

- Whether the best possible design for the study has been determined
- Whether pretests have been administered, and data collected/made ready for analysis
- Whether protocol for experimental and control groups has been followed
- Whether posttests have been administered, and data collected/made ready for analysis

4. Analysis of data/conclusions/recommendations:
   - Pretest reading ability scores
   - Posttest reading ability scores
   - Statistical treatments that are appropriate for use
   - Conclusions that can arise from the findings
   - Recommendations, appropriate to the findings and conclusions, that are capable of being generated

Due consideration to these issues was given through acquiring responses to: where I will find it, how I will find it, what needs to be done to organize and analyze the information, and what conclusions would follow from the procedures that would allow the researcher to proceed with the study. It is from this planning that:

- Permission has been granted.
- Research design (and protocol) is established.

 NOTE: It has been determined that the design for the study will be a pretest, randomized, posttest, control-group design, the diagram of which is:

$$O \quad R \quad X \quad O$$
$$O \quad R \qquad O$$

- Tests have been determined.
- Students have been selected.
- Study has been administered.
- Data have been collected.
- Data have been prepared for analysis.

On the basis of the design alone (that is, use of pretests, randomization, and control groups), all threats to internal validity have been controlled except for expectancy and instability. In this regard, the researcher has made every effort to control for potential bias (expectancy), and has planned for contingencies (instability) that may arise during the course of the study.

From prior discussion you know that, while standard central tendency, percentile, and variability measurements could be calculated for the pre- and posttest data distributions, they alone will not make it possible for inferences to be drawn between any observed within and between group differences. Thus, one may consider computing a *t* test for independent samples, or a one-way analysis of variance.

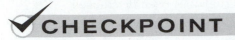

CHECKPOINT

Why would an *independent* rather than a *nonindependent t* test be used?

Answer

The answer is: Although individuals have been randomly assigned to one group or another, pairs of individuals having common or related scores were *not matched* before randomization took place.

CHECKPOINT

Given the following information, compute ANOVA, and interpret the findings in relationship to the null hypothesis.

$$SS_T = 280$$
$$SS_B = 70$$
$$K = 2$$
$$N = 23$$

Answers

The answers are as follows:

Entering the hierarchy of procedures for calculating ANOVA at step 6:

$$SS_W = SS_T - SS_B$$
$$= 280 - 70$$
$$= 210.000$$

 NOTE: The user of the formula enters the sequence of ANOVA procedures at step 6 because total sum of squares *and* between sum of squares were provided.

Steps 7, 8, and 9 are as follows:

Step 7.
$$MS_B = \frac{SS_B}{K - 1}$$
$$= \frac{70}{1}$$
$$= 70.000$$

Step 8.
$$MS_W = \frac{SS_W}{N - K}$$

$$= \frac{210.000}{23 - 2}$$

$$= \frac{210.000}{21}$$

$$= 10.000$$

Step 9.
$$F \text{ ratio} = \frac{MS_B}{MS_W}$$

$$= \frac{70.000}{10.000}$$

$$= 7.000$$

For significance to exist at the .05 level of confidence ($df = 1,21$), the obtained F ratio would have to equal or exceed 4.325. The obtained value of 7.000 is held to be significant at the .05 level of confidence.

In order to be significant at the .01 level of confidence ($df = 1,21$), the obtained finding would have to equal or exceed 8.017. The obtained value of 7.000 does *not* reach that value. Hence, with regard to the null hypothesis (or homogeneity of variance), the interpretation would be:

> Within the limitations of the investigation, this researcher rejects the null hypothesis at the .05 *loc* ($df = 1,21$). It appears that something other than chance affected the findings in favor of Group 1 (that is, the group that had the use of flash cards).

NOTE: The findings were in favor of Group 1 because it was stated in the scenario that "based upon the toss of a coin, the treatment (that is, the use of flash cards) is assigned to Group 1," and further, it was stated that Group 1 was "found to have the greater arithmetic average."

ANALYZING DATA

Since there were pretest scores, the investigator may believe it important to account for any initial differences between the two groups that may bring influence upon the dependent variable. Since both groups shared common characteristics at the onset of the study insofar as reading level is concerned, there may yet be a **covariate** (for example, time spent in direct reading) that is contributing to the observed differences in posttest reading scores. An **analysis of covariance** *(ANCOVA)* can be used to statistically adjust any effects the covariate may have had on the differences between the posttest scores.

To take this principle a bit further, it may have been one's personal experience or, perhaps, discovered in related literature that factors other than *time spent in direct reading* can also influence reading scores. For example, in a review of the related literature section of Phase 1 of her research plan, Dyke (1996) reported that:

- time spent in direct reading (Haynes & Jenkins, 1986),
- time in reading instruction (Nessel & Jones, 1981), and
- time spent with tutors (Cochran, Feng, Cartledge, & Hamilton, 1993),

all had the potential to influence reading abilities. Knowing this, the investigator may want to take these factors into account when selecting statistical treatments for the data. For example, **multivariate analysis of covariance** *(MANCOVA)* could be used with pretest scores on all three measures as covariates, with flash cards as the independent variable, and posttest scores as the dependent variable. Add age as another factor, and one may want to employ a factorial MANCOVA. As Harris (1995) points out, if an investigator were to add follow-up measures taken when students enter the fourth and fifth grades, she could use a factorial MANCOVA with repeated measures.

As you can see, there are numerous statistical systems that can be employed in order to refine analytical procedures. Although these techniques (for example, ANCOVA, MANCOVA, **factorial MANCOVA,** and **factorial MANCOVA with repeated measures)** are discussed more appropriately in textbooks on advanced statistics, their general use and importance warranted some introduction here. For examples of such sources, refer to the Recommended Readings section offered at the end of this chapter.

SUMMARY

In this chapter, you have been introduced to a variety of two-group research designs. While nonequivalent group studies have merit in situations in which randomization is not possible, more refined techniques are possible. Randomized control-group designs with pre- and posttest measures address all threats to internal validity except *expectancy* and *instability*. With regard to these threats, thoughtful investigators should be able to manage their own bias and that of their associates by following design *protocol*. By anticipating contingencies that may arise during the study, plans can be made to reduce their impact (for example, alternative testing sessions, makeup days, and so on). Remember, threats to internal validity are just that—*threats,* nothing more (unless weak designs, carelessness, or pure chance invoke their presence). Several alternatives to the traditional nonequivalent and randomized control-group designs were also described as ways to address unique research interests.

Both the *t test* and *analysis of variance* enable the researcher to test hypotheses regarding observed differences within and between groups (that is, pretest to pretest, pretest to posttest, and posttest to posttest). From a determination of whether significance levels are reached, the investigator proceeds to accept or reject the null hypothesis and, if rejected, states a level of confidence.

In conclusion, two-group designs that employ random sampling, random assignment, and pretesting will control for most threats to internal validity that are frequently actualized by alternative research methods. Through proper planning, adherence to protocol, and the use of sound statistical procedures, the investigator should find it possible to deduce inferences that equate findings with causes. Threats to external validity will also be managed if reports on results include references to sampling, person(s), place(s), and time(s), per Chapter 3, Preparation of a Research Plan.

In addition to what has been presented to date in Part III of this text, Chapter 11, Other Experimental Procedures, will provide information on other research designs and data treatment systems which, collectively, should arm teachers, administrators, guidance counselors, and others with all the tools they need to carry out their important role as practitioner/researchers.

RECOMMENDED LABORATORY ASSIGNMENTS

1. Review the recommended readings.

2. Arrange to meet with fellow graduate students and colleagues in order to discuss the advantages and disadvantages of nonequivalent and randomized control-group designs.

3. Through a collaboration with no more than three individuals, create scores for an nonequivalent posttest only control-group design (in which Group 1 receives the new treatment).

4. Working independently, analyze the data utilizing an independent-samples *t* test, and for the findings, examine and interpret the null hypothesis at the .05, .02, and .01 levels of confidence.

5. Compare results, and where discrepancies are found to occur, determine their sources and discuss possible inferences (while accounting for threats to internal validity).

6. Design a randomized posttest only control-group project for an intact setting and topic of your choice. In the design, specific plans should be prepared for Phase 1:

a. Statement of the problem

b. Need (justification) for the study

c. Review of related literature

d. Statement of null hypothesis

e. Basic assumptions

f. Possible threats to the study

g. Design alternatives

h. Definitions of terms

and for Phase 2:

a. Permission/selection of subjects

b. Selection of instrument

c. Administration of study/collection of data

d. Analysis of data/conclusions/recommendations

each with regard to:

- What I need to know
- Where I will find it
- How I will find it
- Procedures for organizing the information for further use
- Conclusions that would follow from the procedures and allow the researcher to proceed

7. Administer the study designed in response to question 6, analyze the data using a one-way analysis of variance, test for significance, and interpret the findings.

8. Arrange to meet with fellow graduate students, colleagues, as well as school and nonschool employees in order to review and discuss your findings and interpretations.

9. Examine Chapter 13, Preparing the Research Report, and using the guidelines provided therein, prepare a manuscript suitable for formal presentation that would reflect the study design, findings, and interpretations.

10. Through a collaboration with no more than three individuals, identify three research topics for each of the following designs:

   a. Counterbalanced control-group design

   b. Multiple pretest control-group design (with posttest)

   c. Multiple posttest control-group design (with pretest)

   d. Interrupted time series control-group design

   e. Pretest, matched, randomized, posttest control-group design

11. Extending the table provided in the summary section of Chapter 9, Single-Group Designs, add notations of *Yes* or *No* to indicate whether threats to *internal* validity are controlled for in each of the following:

   a. Nonequivalent posttest only control-group design

   b. Nonequivalent pretest-posttest control-group design

   c. Randomized posttest only control-group design

   d. Randomized pretest-posttest control-group design

12. Identify and discuss the following diagrams:

   a. X O
                   O

   b. O X O

   c. $\underline{O \quad X \quad O}$
       O O

   d. R O X O
       R O O

   e. R X O
       R O

RECOMMENDED READINGS

Achen, C. H. (1986). *The statistical analysis of quasi-experiments*. Berkeley, CA: University of California Press.

Agnew, N. M., & Pyke, S. W. (1987). *The science game: An introduction to research in the behavioral sciences* (4th ed.). Englewood Cliffs, NJ: Prentice-Hall.

Anderson, B. F. (1971). *The psychology experiment* (2nd ed.). Belmont, CA: Brooks/Cole.

Barber, T. X., Forgione, A., Chaves, J. F., Calverley, D. S., McPeake, J. D., & Bowen, B. (1969). Five attempts to replicate the experimenter bias effect. *Journal of Consulting and Clinical Psychology, 33,* 1–6.

Barber, T. X., & Silver, M. J. (1968). Fact, fiction, and the experimenter bias effect. *Psychological Bulletin Monograph, 70*(6, Pt. 2), 1–19.

Benjafield, J. G. (1994). *Thinking critically about research methods*. Needham Heights, MA: Allyn & Bacon.

Bracht, G. H., & Glass, G. V. (1968). The external validity of experiments. *American Educational Research Journal, 5,* 437–474.

Campbell, D. T., & Stanley, J. C. (1966). *Experimental and quasi-experimental designs for research*. Chicago: Rand McNally.

Carnahan, H., Vandervoort, A. A., & Swanson, L. R. (1996, September). The influence of summary knowledge of results and aging on motor learning. *Research Quarterly for Exercise and Sport, 67*(3), 280–287.

Chambers, W. V. (1986). Inferring causality from corresponding variances. *Perceptual and Motor Skills, 63,* 475–478.

Cook, D. L. (1967). *The impact of the Hawthorne effect in experimental designs in educational research* (Cooperative Research Project No. 1757). Washington, DC: U.S. Office of Education.

Cook, T. D., & Campbell, D. T. (1979). *Quasi-experimentation: Design and analysis issues for field settings*. Chicago: Rand McNally.

Cross, L. H., & Cross, G. M. (1981). Teachers evaluative comments and pupil perception of control. *Journal of Experimental Education, 49,* 68–71.

Edwards, R. (1988). The effects of performance standards on behavior patterns and motor skill achievement in children. *Journal of Teaching in Physical Education, 7,* 90–102.

Fitz-Gibbon, C. T., & Morris, L. L. (1987). *How to design a program evaluation* (2nd ed.). Newbury Park, CA: Sage.

Friedman, H. (1987). Repeat examinations in introductory statistics courses. *Teaching of Psychology, 14,* 20–23.

Gay, L. R. (1980). The comparative effects of multiple-choice versus short-answer tests on retention. *Journal of Educational Measurement, 17,* 45–50.

Glass, G. V. (1988). Quasi-experiments: The case of interrupted time series. In R. M. Jaeger (Ed.), *Complementary methods for research in education* (pp. 445–464). Washington, DC: American Educational Research Association.

Glass, G. V., Wilson, V. L., & Gottman, J. M. (1975). *Design and analysis of time-series experiments*. Boulder, CO: Colorado University Press.

Harris, R. J. (1994). *ANOVA: An analysis of variance primer*. Itasca, IL: F.E. Peacock.

Helm, C. M., & Burkett, C. W. (1989). Effects of computer-assisted telecommunications on school attendance. *Journal of Educational Research, 82,* 362–365.

Howell, D. C. (1987). *Statistical methods for psychology* (2nd ed.). Boston: Duxbury Press.

Howell, M. B. (1995). *Basic statistics for behavioral science research*. Needham Heights, MA: Allyn & Bacon.

Johnson, N., Johnson, J., & Yates, C. (1981). A six-month follow-up on the effects of the Vocational Exploration Group on career maturity. *Journal of Counseling Psychology, 28,* 70–71.

Keppel, G., & Zedeck, S. (1989). *Data analysis for research designs: Analysis of variance and multiple regression/correlation approaches*. New York: W.H. Freeman.

Kratochwill, T. R. (1992). Single-case research design and analysis: An overview. In T. R. Kratochwill & J. R. Levin (Eds.), *Single-case research design and analysis* (pp. 1–14). Hillsdale, NJ: Lawrence Erlbaum.

Linn, R. L. (1986). Quantitative methods in research on teaching. In M. C. Wittrock (Ed.), *Handbook of research on teaching* (3rd ed., pp. 92–118). New York: Macmillan.

Lockmiller, P., & DiNello, M. C. (1970). Words in color versus a basal reader program with retarded readers in grade 2. *Journal of Educational Research, 63,* 330–334.

Morris, C. N., & Rolph, J. E. (1981). *Introduction to data analysis and statistical inference*. Englewood Cliffs, NJ: Prentice-Hall.

Pillemer, D. B. (1991). One-tailed vs. two-tailed hypothesis tests in contemporary educational research. *Educational Researcher, 20*(9), 13–17.

Popham, W. J., & Sirotnik, K. A. (1992). *Understanding statistics in education*. Itasca, IL: F.E. Peacock.

Rivera, E., & Omizo, M. M. (1980). The effects of relaxation and biofeedback on attention to task and impulsivity among male hyperactive children. *Exceptional Child, 27,* 41–51.

Rosenthal, R., & Fode, K. L. (1961). The problem of experimenter outcome-bias. In D. P. Ray (Ed.), *Series research in social psychology* (Symposia Studies Series, No. 8). Washington, DC: National Institute of Social and Behavioral Science.

Rosnow, R. L., & Rosenthal, R. (1989). Statistical procedures and the justification of knowledge in psychological science. *American Psychologist, 44*(10), 1276–1284.

Saretsky, G. (1972). The OEO P.C. experiment and the John Henry effect. *Phi Delta Kappan, 53,* 579–581.

Schneider, A. L., & Darcy, R. E. (1984). Policy implications of using significance tests in evaluation research. *Evaluation Review, 8*(4), 573–582.

Shaver, J. P. (1985). Chance and nonsense: A conversation about interpreting tests of statistical significance, part 1. *Phi Delta Kappan, 67*(1), 57–60.

Shulman, L. S. (1986). Paradigms and research programs in the study of teaching: A contemporary perspective. In M. Wittrock (Ed.), *Handbook of research on teaching* (3rd ed., pp. 3–36). New York: Macmillan.

Thompson, B. (1989a). Asking "what if" questions about significance tests. *Measurement and Evaluation in Counseling and Development, 22,* 66–68.

Thompson, B. (1989b). Statistical significance, result importance, and result generalizability: Three noteworthy but somewhat different issues. *Measurement and Evaluation in Counseling and Development, 22,* 2–6.

Thompson, B. (1992). Misuse of ANCOVA and related "statistical control" procedures. *Reading Psychology: An International Quarterly, 13,* iii–xviii.

Thompson, B. (1993). The use of statistical significance tests in research: Bootstrap and other alternatives. *Journal of Experimental Education, 61*(4), 361–377.

Wielkiewicz, R. J. (1986). *Behavior management in the schools: Principles and procedures*. Elmsford, NY: Pergamon.

Wilson, V. L., & Putnam, R. R. (1982). A meta-analysis of pretest sensitization effects in experimental design. *American Educational Research Journal, 19,* 249–258.

Windle, C. (1954). Test-retest effects in personality questionnaires. *Educational and Psychological Measurement, 14,* 617–633.

Woodward, J., & Baxter, J. (1997, Spring). The effects of an innovative approach to mathematics on academically low-achieving students in inclusive settings. *Exceptional Children, 63*(3), 373–388.

REFERENCES

Barber, T. (1973). Pitfalls in research: Nine investigator and experimenter effects. In R. M. W. Travers (Ed.), *Second handbook of research on teaching* (pp. 382–404). Chicago: Rand McNally.

Borg, W. (1984). Dealing with threats to internal validity that randomization does not rule out. *Educational Researcher, 13*(10), 11–14.

Cochran, L., Feng, H., Cartledge, G., & Hamilton, S. (1993). The effects of cross-age tutoring on the academic achievement, social behaviors, and self-perceptions of low-achieving African-American males with behavioral disorders. *Behavioral Disorders, 18*(4), 292–302.

Dolch, E. (1951). *Psychology and teaching of reading.* Westport, CT: Greenwood Press.

Dyke, W. S. (1996, July). *A project to study the effectiveness of the flash card method of sight word instruction with third grade students one or more years below grade level in reading: A graduate research proposal.* Unpublished document, Department of Education, Plymouth State College, Plymouth, NH.

Gardner, H. (1993). *Multiple intelligences: The theory in practice.* New York: Basic Books.

Harris, M. B. (1995). *Basic statistics for behavioral science research.* Needham Heights, MA: Allyn & Bacon.

Haynes, M., & Jenkins, J. (1986). Reading instruction in special education resource rooms. *American Educational Research Journal, 23*(2), 161–190.

Jurs, S. G., & Glass, G. V. (1971). The effect of experimental mortality on the internal and external validity of the randomized comparative experiment. *Journal of Experimental Education, 40,* 62–66.

Nessel, D., & Jones, M. (1981). *The language-experience approach to reading.* New York: Columbia Teachers College Press.

Rosenthal, R. (1976). *Experimenter effects in behavioral research.* New York: Irvington.

Shaver, J. P. (1983). The verification of independent variables in teaching methods research. *Educational Researcher, 12*(8), 3–9.

Skinner, C., Smith, E., & McLean, J. (1994). The effects of intertrial interval duration of sight-word learning rates in children with behavioral disorders. *Behavioral Disorders, 19*(2), 98–107.

CHAPTER 11

Other Experimental Procedures

OBJECTIVES

After reading this chapter, you should be able to:

- Distinguish between a *constant* and a *variable*.
- Distinguish between *single-subject* and *single-group* research.
- Distinguish between *multiple-baseline* and *multiple-group* designs.
- Identify and discuss three basic forms of multiple-baseline research.
- Describe the *structure* and *function* of alternating-treatment designs.
- Describe the *structure* and *function* of cohort designs.
- Describe the *structure* and *function* of 2×2, 2×3, 3×2, and 3×3 factorial designs.
- Diagram A-B single-subject designs, A-B-A single-subject designs, A-B-A-B single-subject designs, $A-B_1-B_2$ single-subject designs, alternating-treatment designs, cohort designs, and multiple-group designs, including: posttest only (two treatment) intact control-group; pretest, posttest (two treatment) intact control-group; and randomized, pretest-posttest (two treatment) control-group.
- Discuss the *ceiling effect* in pretest-posttest research.

- Discuss the advantages of *randomization* with regard to threats to internal validity.
- Discuss the advantages and disadvantages of *pretests* in a research design.
- Demonstrate the *deviation* method for calculating a one-way analysis of variance, including: within group sum of squared deviations, between group sum of squared deviations, total sum of squared deviations, between mean squares, within mean squares, and *F* ratio.
- Discuss the relevance of the *Scheffe test,* and demonstrate its calculation.
- Interpret critical values of *F.*
- Discuss the relevance of *truncation* to the calculation of critical values.
- Identify five alternatives to the *Scheffe test* for computing individual comparisons in analysis of variance.
- Distinguish between a *one-way analysis of variance* and the *Kruskal-Wallis* H *test*.
- Distinguish between a *nonindependent* t *test* and the *Wilcoxon test.*
- Discuss the purpose of *meta-analysis,* and demonstrate the calculation of effect size (*ES*) for experimental and correlation studies.
- Distinguish between *weighted* and *unweighted* averages.
- Define key terms, and answer checkpoint questions.

KEY TERMS

A-B-A-B Design

A-B-A Design

A-B Design

Alternating-Treatment Designs

Attribute-Treatment Interaction Research

Baseline Phase

Between Group Sum of Squared Deviations

Between Mean Squares

Ceiling Effect

Cohort Designs

Deviation Method for Computing ANOVA

Effect Size

Factorial Designs

Grand Sum of Squared Deviations

Interactive Effect

K – 1

Main Effect

Meta-Analysis

Multiple-Baseline Designs

Multiple-Group Designs

N – K

Repeated Measures

Scheffe Test

Score Stability

INTRODUCTION

In Chapter 9, Single-Group Designs, you were introduced to those techniques basic to the implementation of studies in which investigators attempt to test the effects of a treatment upon a dependent variable (without the benefit of comparison groups). It was pointed out that, while this form of study has value at the level of a preliminary inquiry, one must be cautious when attempting to attach specific causes to findings, since numerous threats to internal validity are in operation.

NOTE: *Selection* was the single threat to internal validity for which controls were present in all three designs introduced within Chapter 9 (see Figure 9–1).

Further, the external validity of single-group designs is quite limited. The generalizability of the results of one's study is increased, for the most part, by its replication or comparison (for example, meta-analysis) with studies of other subjects at different times and places. At the same time, this is a very important level of inquiry because, as Spanier (1997) states, preliminary studies often determine what gets funded, what topics of investigation get pursued in detail, and what the *hot* approach is to the study of a problem.

NOTE: Based on its own merits, a nonreplicated single-group study offers little credibility to inferences that are predicated on an observed change in a posttest measure.

In order to describe procedures appropriate to comparative-group studies, Chapter 10, Two-Group Designs, was presented. Both single- and two-group experiments can be designed with and without *randomization*. But because a two-group design distinguishes itself by having a comparison group, the investigator is in a better position to draw valid inferences from the findings. In this regard, it was pointed out why fewer threats to internal validity are present when both randomization and *control groups* exist. When pretest measures are taken, all threats to internal validity are addressed except for expectation and instability.

With this review as background, this chapter presents alternatives to the traditional pre- and posttest, single- and two-group models. Having had an introduction in Chapter 9 to such procedures as counterbalanced control-group, interrupted time series, multiple pretest (with posttest), and multiple posttest (with pretest) designs, it can readily be seen that the form a design takes is limited only by one's imagination and the practicality of its application. Add to that the principle of multiple-group designs, and even more credibility can be assigned to the inferences arising out of one's observations. As this chapter unfolds, you will see a sample of the numerous design variations that are possible—each with its own character and purpose.

Upon completion of Part III, Experimental Research Methods, readers should know which designs to select in order to meet their specific research goals. To that end, this chapter will add to current levels of knowledge by presenting, in order:

1. Single-subject designs
2. Multiple-baseline designs
3. Alternating-treatment designs
4. Cohort designs
5. Multiple-group designs
6. Factorial designs

There are standards of adequacy for all single-group, quasi-experimental, and true experimental designs. This also holds true with regard to the selection and administration of statistical treatments appropriate to data analysis. Integrated into the discussion, therefore, will be reference to various statistical procedures, including: **deviation method for computing analysis of variance (ANOVA), Scheffe test,** and **meta-analysis.**

SINGLE-SUBJECT DESIGNS

Not to be confused with descriptive case studies, the **single-subject designs** presented in this chapter refer to those studies that include the administration of the treatments, and at least one *posttest* to a single individual. A process frequently observed in clinical environments, its emergence in educational settings speaks to the value it appears to have with such topics as behavior management. For the most part, the primary focus in such studies relates to their ability to monitor the behavioral change of specific subjects, rather than to the generation of inferences for use by the population at large. On the other hand, common findings arising out of *replication studies* with multiple numbers of individuals may lead to externally valid generalizations that are applicable to additional settings.

As with time series research introduced in Chapter 9, Single-Group Designs, pretest performance is assessed a number of times in order to establish a baseline. In the process, an establishment of a behavior trend is identified as it actually occurs without an intervention (that is, the treatment). There are no specific numbers of pretests that are recommended, except to say that they should be sufficient in number to ensure that **score stability** has an opportunity to be demonstrated. Once the subject's behavior appears to be consistent, a treatment is introduced. During the **treatment phase,** a predetermined number of measurements are made. That number varies from study to study. While the basic **A-B design** diagram for single-subject research is:

$$/\underline{\overset{O\ O\ O}{\text{A}}}//\underline{\overset{X\ O\ X\ O\ X\ O}{\text{B}}}/$$

Baseline Phase   Treatment Phase

by adding a *second* **baseline phase** to the A-B design, the design becomes stronger. Symbolized as A-B-A, the diagram would read:

$$/\underline{\overset{O\ O\ O}{\text{A}}}//\underline{\overset{X\ O\ X\ O\ X\ O}{\text{B}}}//\underline{\overset{O\ O\ O}{\text{A}}}/$$

Baseline Phase   Treatment Phase   Baseline Phase

This design is stronger because if:

- behavior is observed to be stable during the baseline phase,
- behavior is observed to change and becomes stable during the treatment phase, and
- when the treatment phase ends, the behavior reverts to original baseline levels,

then it can be assumed that the behavior change is a result of the treatment. If the baseline phase was *not* repeated, the investigator could not be certain that any observed change was due to the treatment. For example, something may have occurred in the subject's personal life that caused the "improved" behavior. If that behavior remained the same during the second baseline phase, one's attempt to attribute the results to the treatment would likely be held suspect.

To view an example of how data might be portrayed from the results of an A-B-A study, consider Figure 11–1.

The internal validity of the **A-B-A design** is superior to the A-B design. With the A-B design, improvements may be observed pursuant to the transition from baseline (**A**) to treatment (**B**), but there is no provision for observing behavior after that time. On the other hand, consider that changes have been observed throughout the phases of the A-B-A design. It is unreasonable to believe that improvement in behavior during movement from (**A**) to (**B**) and regression of behavior from (**B**) to (**A**) were both a product of coincidence. Without the design that includes a second baseline, the investigator would not be able to make a determination of change.

Since the subject is compared against himself through the A-B-A design process, most threats to internal validity are controlled, including: experimental mortality, history and maturation (because of the multiple observations during the treatment phase of the study), instrumentation (assuming that the multiple observation systems are valid and consistent), regression, and selection. Threats that are *not* controlled by the design are: expectancy, instability, pretesting, and possible interaction should two or more threats become actualized during the study.

Some of the variations in the basic A-B and A-B-A designs are the following.

1. Adding an additional treatment as a supplement to the original treatment. For example, after two or three observations during the experimental phase, it might be noted by the investigator that insufficient changes in behavior are being made. He

Figure 11-1: **Results of a Sample A-B-A Study**

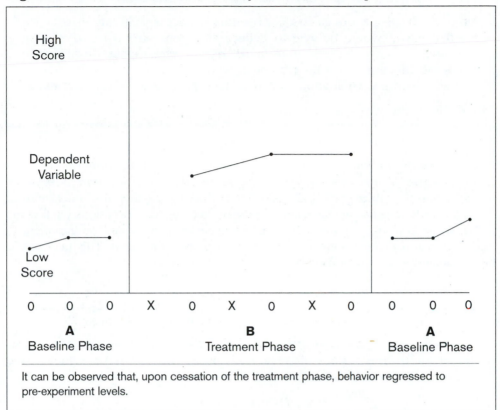

It can be observed that, upon cessation of the treatment phase, behavior regressed to pre-experiment levels.

may choose to introduce a second, complementary treatment in order to determine if that addition makes a difference. A diagram showing the introduction of a supplement would be:

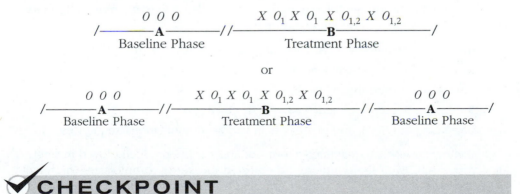

or

 CHECKPOINT

What would be the *major* weakness of a B-A-B design?

Answer

Although the B-A-B design has *not* been introduced specifically, it is anticipated that you would be able to deduce a response from past discussion of various designs. The lack of an initial baseline phase makes it difficult to assess the effectiveness of the treatment. Without knowing levels of behavior in advance of the application of a treatment, judging its effects is virtually impossible.

2. Adding an additional treatment phase in order to address an ethical concern that could arise in a situation in which the treatment phase was found to influence behavior in a positive way. This alternative would also strengthen the conclusions of the study if they were demonstrated to exist on two separate occasions (Hall et al., 1971). If the behavior regressed to initial baseline levels, it would be important to have the treatment reconstituted (perhaps on a permanent basis). This plan would be designated as an **A-B-A-B design** and would be diagramed as:

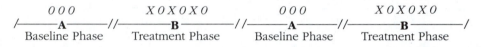

3. Introducing a revised treatment following the initial treatment phase. This would replace the postbaseline phase normally present in the A-B-A design. Referred to as a reversal design (A-B-B), it would be diagramed as:

$$/\text{———}\underset{\text{Baseline Phase}}{\overset{0\ 0\ 0}{A}}\text{———}//\text{———}\underset{\text{Treatment Phase}}{\overset{X_1\ 0\ X_1\ 0\ X_1\ 0}{B_1}}\text{———}//\text{———}\underset{\text{Treatment Phase}}{\overset{X_2\ 0\ X_2\ 0\ X_2\ 0}{B_2}}\text{———}/$$

An example of the use of this design would be in a case where treatment (B_1) was a form of differential reinforcement designed for students whose social behavior was *appropriate* to grade level (Kirk, Gallagher, & Anastasiow, 1997), and treatment (B_2) was differential reinforcement designed for behavior that was *inappropriate* to grade level. And, of course, this design could be augmented by:

- Adding a baseline phase (**A**) following the alternative treatment (B_2)
- Revisiting the initial treatment (B_1)
- Introducing a third treatment (B_3)
- Combining treatments, that is, ($B_{1,2}$), ($B_{1,3}$), ($B_{2,3}$)
- Alternating baselines and treatments in various combinations/sequences

Qualitative rather than quantitative forms of analysis are often employed in single-subject research. Even though there are repeated measures, sample sizes this small make any statistical significance rather meaningless in terms of its generalizability. If consistency is shown through replication studies, however, one can begin to attribute value to the treatment systems, and draw inferences to larger groups. In short, single-subject research involves using:

1. Valid criteria for what constitutes appropriate and inappropriate behavior (Wood, 1982)

2. Valid and consistent (reliable) assessment systems at each point of measurement (Bijou, Peterson, & Ault, 1968; Wiseman, 1982; Wiseman, 1994)

3. Visual inspection and recording of events against valid performance criteria (Walker & Fabre, 1987)

4. Techniques appropriate to calculating:

   a. Measures of central tendency and variability for each phase

   b. *t* test or analysis of variance (ANOVA) within and between baseline and treatment phases in order to establish database for replication studies and meta-analysis

5. Qualitative analysis (see Part II, Descriptive Research Methods), supplemented by quantitative findings in order to plot graphs, prepare charts, and make interpretations.

MULTIPLE-BASELINE DESIGNS

Used when the only alternative would be the basic A-B design, **multiple-baseline designs** are used when it would be unethical, or impossible, to reverse or withdraw the treatment without its cumulative effects being present in subsequent measures. The effects of many behavior programs will linger in spite of treatment withdrawal. As a matter of fact, this would be desirable in most real-life situations. After all, the purpose of behavior modification systems is to cause (or help cause) permanent, positive behaviors. The value of multiple-baseline research is to see which of the modification systems will elicit the more favorable results. To the extent that the treatments can be isolated or combined (through planning), the virtue of the selected design becomes assured.

There are three basic forms of multiple-baseline research:

1. Across behaviors

2. Across subjects

3. Across settings

As an alternative to collecting baseline data for one target behavior, for one subject, or within one particular setting, the investigator can design the research in a way that will examine the effectiveness of several behaviors for one subject, one behavior for several subjects, or one subject in several settings. The researcher continues a systematic application of the treatment to each behavior, subject, or setting (one at a time). If, upon visual inspection of the findings, he finds that the behavior improves only after the treatment is introduced, the researcher can assume that the treatment is the cause of the change (see Figure 11–2). By visual inspection of the information presented in Figure 11–2, it can be seen that scores are *high* when treatments are *present* in the behavior, subjects, and settings, and *low* when treatment is *absent*.

Figure 11-2: **Influence of Treatment upon Behaviors, Subjects, and Settings in a Multiple-baseline Design**

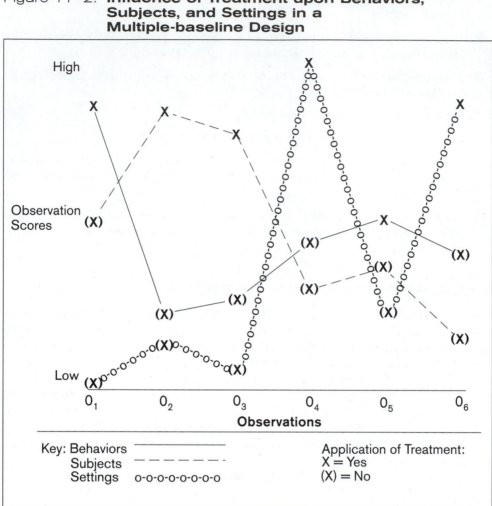

ALTERNATING-TREATMENT DESIGNS

While alternating treatments are usually thought of within the context of comparative-*group* designs, **alternating-treatment designs** can also be administered to single subjects. In fact, they are more appropriate there if one wants to test the significance of their application upon a single subject. This is because the findings of groups within group contexts may have little to do with the results that would be found with the same treatments in single-subject contexts.

This design involves the alternation of treatments at fixed or random intervals. For example, if a student with behavior problems was to visit with a counselor every Monday, some Mondays he would receive one treatment (for example, aversive conditioning), and on other Mondays, another treatment (for example, differential reinforcement). Using the symbols X_1 and X_2 to represent the two treatments, the alternating-treatment design could be displayed as:

$$X_1 - X_2 - X_1 - X_2 - X_1 - X_2 - X_1 - X_2$$

Or, to avoid a possible threat to internal validity caused by a fixed *ordering* of events, one might assign treatments X_1 and X_2 on a random basis, such as:

$$X_1 - X_2 - X_2 - X_1 - X_2 - X_1 - X_1 - X_2$$

Figure 11–3 offers a display of fictitious data arising out of the random administration of aversive conditioning (X_1) and differential reinforcement (X_2). It can been seen that the observation scores are consistently higher when X_1 (aversive conditioning) is employed.

> **NOTE:** A baseline phase is considered to be unnecessary in this design because the investigator is not attempting to determine whether a treatment is equivalent (or better) than no treatment but, rather, whether one treatment is equivalent (or better) than another treatment.

There may be instances in which the investigator is interested in testing the equivalence of a treatment to *no* treatment. In this case, the design would be arranged to provide for alternating a treatment (X_1) with no treatment (X_0), such as:

$$X_1 - X_0 - X_0 - X_1 - X_0 - X_1 - X_1 - X_0$$

> **NOTE:** The observations of the effect of the treatment are occurring in conjunction with the administration of the treatment itself.

Figure 11–3: **Example of Alternating-Treatment Design Comparing Aversive Conditioning (X_1) and Differential Reinforcement (X_2)**

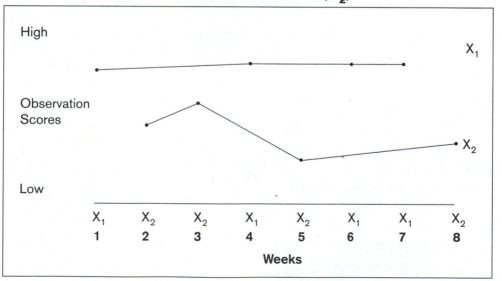

Analysis of the findings arising from such studies is normally through visual inspection. At the same time, with a sufficient number of treatment/observations, the researcher could choose to *compare* the *averages* of X_1 and X_0 (or, in the situation described in Figure 11–3, X_1 and X_2) through descriptive or inferential statistics. Remember, however, unless analyses are made of *grand* means and variances generated through replication (or comparison) studies, inferences would be quite *mean*ingless.

COHORT DESIGNS

The term *cohort* refers to successive groups of individuals who follow each other through an institution. An institution could be defined as: tenth-grade high school students, first-year college students, a cross-country team, recruits at a basic training center, and so on. To activate a **cohort design,** one group of individuals would be tested without their being exposed to a treatment, and their counterparts would be introduced to a treatment and posttested. Comparisons would then be made between the two groups of scores.

The diagram for a *basic* cohort design would be:

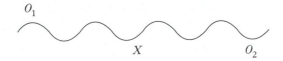

The wavy line represents the fact that the study is being done with cohort groups. As you would expect, this design can be enhanced by adding observations, and varying treatments and schedules.

An alternative to this basic design is called *cohort longitudinal research,* in which changes in a specific population are studied over time by selecting a different sample at each data-collection point. An application of this design would be for the researcher to assess different samples of subjects over subsequent semesters who have been exposed to a particular course. Each sample, therefore, becomes a cohort of the other.

Consider that an undergraduate studies committee within a college is designing a course, tentatively entitled "Introduction to the Academic Community," that will be required of all newly admitted students in their first semester, and include such topics as:

1. Academic responsibility

2. Athletics: intercollegiate and intramural

3. Residential living

4. Role and location of:

    a. Academic support services

    b. Campus security

    c. Career development office

    d. College writing center

    e. Computer services

  f. Counseling and human relations center

  g. Infirmary and health services

  h. Library, media services, and microcomputer labs

  i. Math activities center

  j. Registrar

  k. Women's services and gender resource center

 5. Study habits, including:

  a. Note taking, preparing for examinations, and writing papers

  b. Balancing academic requirements, social activities, and work responsibilities

Since the course will not be ready for implementation until the following year, it is decided to use the present first-year students as a cohort. Their first-semester grade-point averages are recorded and held for comparison with the grade-point averages of next year's students who complete the course. The college administration is interested in determining whether the successful completion of that course has any effect on the achievement levels of students upon the completion of their first semester in college. Since the range of ability levels for each class has remained relatively constant for three years previous (as measured by SAT scores and class rankings), it is expected that, without a change in admission standards, the population of students will likely remain similar during the period of the study. For cohort designs to be valid, the groups under study should share common characteristics at the onset of the investigation.

 Graphic representations of sample findings generated from a study similar to this one can be found in Figures 11–4, 11–5, and 11–6. Figure 11–4 describes a situation

Figure 11–4: **Sample Results Implying Improvement on Achievement Scores Arising from Treatment**

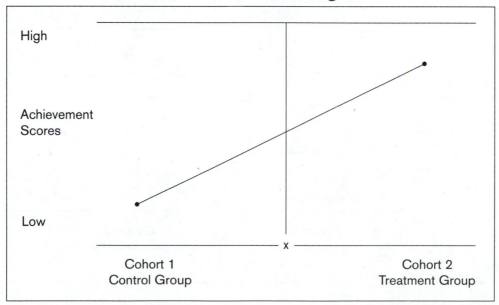

Figure 11–5: **Sample Results Implying That Improvement on Achievement Scores Was Temporary**

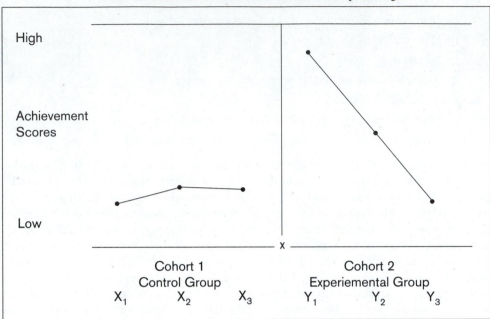

Figure 11–6: **Sample Results Demonstrating Stability in Experimental Group Measures**

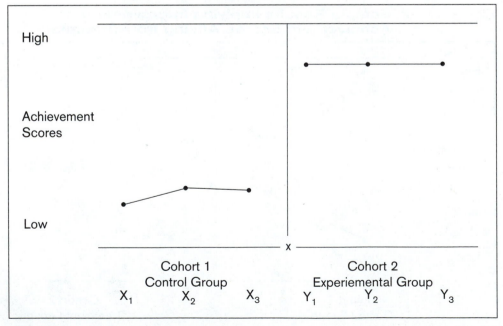

in which the findings *suggest* that an improvement occurred as the result of the treatment. Figure 11–5 displays findings that indicate that the improvement from the treatment was only temporary, although information would not have been made known unless there were **repeated measures** built into the cohort design. The display in Figure 11–6 provides evidence that is more persuasive regarding the improvement in achievement scores from the control to the experimental group.

✓CHECKPOINT

What two factors would lead a reader of Figure 11–6 to support the contention that the change in achievement scores can be attributed to the treatment?

Answer

The answer to the above question is:

1. There were repeated measures.
2. Stability in subject performance was demonstrated, which would lead the investigator to rule out the threat of instability during the treatment phase of the study.

At the same time, however, there are numerous reasons why posttest scores may differ between cohort groups for reasons other than the treatment. For one thing, it would be inappropriate to assume that the treatment caused a difference if students had various abilities at onset of the study. Therefore, it is important that all reasonable efforts be made to ensure that cohort groups are equivalent on matters related to the dependent variable.

✓CHECKPOINT

With reference to the scenario on grade-point averages and instructional methods, what are some of the factors that could influence grade-point averages for reasons *other* than:

1. initiating a study that involves groups of varying abilities, or
2. completing a course in "Introduction to the Academic Community"?

Answers

There are many possible responses that could be given to this question. Among those that stand out, however, are the following:

1. Motivation levels of students (students who are more motivated to achieve are more likely to do so)
2. Difficulty levels of courses taken during the first semester
3. Quality of instruction between courses and sections of courses
4. Grading practices
5. *Knowing* versus *applying* the information gained from the course "Introduction to the Academic Community"

MULTIPLE-GROUP DESIGNS

This model of research is selected when investigators are interested in administering two or more treatments while maintaining a control group. This is also known as a one-variable, multiple-condition design. The "one-variable" designation indicates that the groups differ on only one variable—the type of the treatment each receives.

Consider an example of a **multiple-group design** in which three sections of students are enrolled in a first-year chemistry class. While students are assigned to class on the basis of convenience, treatments are assigned at random. One group will receive the traditional lecture course, with a separate laboratory period. The experiment (X_1) group will receive an integrated lecture-laboratory class, and the experiment (X_2) group will be in a class in which the use of computer software accompanies the integrated lecture-laboratory format. The same instructor is teaching all three classes, which reduces the chances of compromising research *protocol*.

Without a pretest, the diagram would read as:

$$
\begin{array}{cc}
X_1 & O \\
\hline
X_2 & O \\
\hline
& O
\end{array}
$$

If a pretest *and* posttest were to be administered, the diagram would be described as follows:

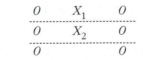

If the population of students who were required to take the chemistry course had been randomly assigned to each of the three groups, the design would be:

$$
\begin{array}{cccc}
R & O & X_1 & O \\
R & O & X_2 & O \\
R & O & & O
\end{array}
$$

On the other hand, if there was *no* pretest following the randomization, the design would be described as:

$$
\begin{array}{ccc}
R & X_1 & 0 \\
R & X_2 & 0 \\
R & & 0
\end{array}
$$

✓ CHECKPOINT

1. What would be the names of the designs for the following?
   a. No randomization or pretest
   b. Randomization with a pretest and posttest
2. Is there an advantage to using one of these designs over using the other?
3. What statistical treatments could be applied to the data generated from such studies?

Answers

The answers to the above items would be:

1. Names of designs:
   a. Posttest only (two-treatment) intact control-group design.
   b. Randomized, pretest-posttest (two-treatment) control-group design.

    NOTE: Instead of using the expression *two-treatment,* it would be equally appropriate to say "two-experiment." It would be important to reference one or the other because, without seeing a diagram, an individual would not know that there were two different groups receiving alternate treatments. Likewise, without seeing a diagram, one would not necessarily know that it was an intact design, unless you said so. The mere absence of the expression *randomized* may not "ring a bell" with the reader. Without being unnecessarily verbose, the description should be clearly expressed in a way that all will understand.

2. There is an advantage to employing a randomized, pretest-posttest (two-treatment) control-group design because:
   a. the randomization makes it possible to assume the existence of an equal distribution of character traits throughout the three groups. The larger the sample, the greater the probability that equal distributions of traits will occur.
   b. pretesting enables the researcher to assess pre-experiment knowledge levels (and not leave it to chance that randomization will cause knowledge levels to be disbursed in equal amounts between the groups). While using such tests may introduce the threat of pretesting, the investigator has to weigh the advantages versus the disadvantages of

doing so. As indicated earlier, if evidence from related studies shows that the presence of pre-experiment testing is likely to compromise the valid measure of treatment effects, it should probably be avoided (at the risk of introducing the threat of experimental mortality).

c. with the possible exception of experimental mortality, all threats to internal validity are controlled except for expectancy (which can be controlled through the practice of objectivity by the investigator, that is, following experiment protocol), and chance episodes that may arise during the course of the study to one group or another (instability). In this regard, if the principal of the school calls for a special assembly for one of the class periods, it would be unlikely that the same event would be called for when each of the other two classes was meeting. Although that *one* circumstance may not cause a major disruption to what would have happened anyway, the investigator could not be sure. At the same time, however, should a *series* of such chance events happen to one of the groups during the course of a study, the investigator would have reason to believe that threats of instability were present.

3. The statistical treatments that could be applied are:

   a. analysis of variance (ANOVA) between posttests in the posttest only design,

   b. analysis of variance (ANOVA) between pretests in the pretest-posttest design,

   c. nonindependent *t* tests between pretests and posttests within each group (if ANOVA between pretests demonstrates equivalence—in other words, that the null hypothesis (homogeneity of variance) was accepted, and

   d. analysis of covariance (ANCOVA) if statistically significant differences exist between the pretest measures of the three groups.

NOTE: When inferring the findings of this study to subsequent chemistry classes, it is important to realize that *reasonable* disruptions to planned activities can be considered a matter of course for this year, next year, or years to follow. The inferential statistics that one uses take elements of chance into account. For example, when an investigator rejects a null hypothesis at the .05 (or 5%) level of confidence, he is implying that, due to chance factors, he will be wrong five times out of one hundred in making such a statement. On the other hand, if the investigator rejects a null hypothesis at the .01 *loc,* he would be incorrect but one time out of one hundred (on the basis of probability alone). Thus, more credence can be placed on a finding that demonstrates significance when, on the basis of probability alone, the researcher will be wrong fewer times.

If the experiment was removed from the school and conducted in a building without principals (not principle*s*), the only generalizations that could be made would be to those students who take chemistry in similar settings. While statistical significance showing preference for one treatment over another may exist, it would not be of *practical* significance. (You are reminded of the difference between *statistical* and *practical* significance discussed in Chapter 9, Single-Group Designs.) The importance of studies in true-to-life settings rests with the fact that the findings of such studies can then be inferred to other true-to-life settings.

FACTORIAL DESIGNS

Per previous discussion, it is unrealistic to expect that experiments in educational settings can be administered in complete isolation. There are numerous variables that have the potential to impact upon outcomes. Take, for example, a study on the effectiveness of interactive television upon academic achievement. Although it might be found that the mean achievement score improved over pre-experiment levels, its effect may *not* have been the same for all students who took part in the study. Its positive influence may be more evident among those who have had high grade-point averages (GPAs), but the researcher would not know that unless factors such as prior academic averages were isolated. Thus, we have the purpose of **factorial designs.**

The term *factor* means that there will be more than one independent variable accounted for in the design. In the illustration regarding teaching method (that is, interactive television), the teaching method is one factor and GPA is another factor. A *factorial experiment* is one in which the investigator attempts to determine the effect of two or more experimental variables (for example, teaching method and GPA), both alone and in combination, upon a dependent variable (for example, achievement). The effect of each independent variable upon the dependent variable is called a **main effect.** The **interactive effect** is so named because it considers the *interaction* of the effects of two (or more) independent variables upon the dependent variable.

The basic form of factorial design is the 2 × 2 experiment. This refers to the fact that two variations of one factor (X_1 and X_2) and two variations of another factor (Y_1 and Y_2) are manipulated simultaneously. By examining Figure 11–7, it can be seen that there are four groups in a 2 × 2 factorial design. One factor, instructional method, has two levels: interactive television (ITV) and no interactive television (NITV). Similarly, grade-point average (GPA) has two levels: high (HGPA) and low (LGPA).

In 2 × 2 factorial design studies, there is ordinarily a manipulated (experimental) variable, and a nonmanipulated (control) variable. In Figure 11–7, the manipulated variable would be instructional method, and the control variable would be grade-point average. Ordinarily, control variables would include such traits as aptitude, gender, height, weight, and so on.

Considering grade-point average as the control variable and dividing it further, into three categories instead of two (Figure 11–8), the study would be diagramed as a 2 × 3 (not 3 × 2) factorial design. The reason for this is that the manipulated (experimental) variable is traditionally indicated first. However, increasing the number of cells in a factorial study raises another consideration. For example, given a finite

Figure 11–7: **An Example of a Layout for a Basic 2 x 2 Factorial Design**

		ITV	NITV
GPA	High (HGPA)	Group 1	Group 2
	Low (LGPA)	Group 3	Group 4

Figure 11–8: **An Example of a Layout for a 2 x 3 Factorial Design**

		ITV	NITV
	High (HGPA)	Group 1	Group 2
GPA	Medium (MGPA)	Group 3	Group 4
	Low (LGPA)	Group 5	Group 6

population (or sample) size, the greater the number of groups, the smaller the number of persons that would be available for assignment to each group. In this regard, Gay (1996) recommends that there should be at least fifteen subjects in each of the cells in order for a factorial design to be effective. If these recommendations are followed, the investigator should have a minimum of sixty individuals in a 2 × 2 design. On the other hand, a 2 × 3 design would require ninety subjects. Therefore, if the size of the research target group were less than ninety, attempting to use a 2 × 3 design could invoke limitations on any inferences one would hope to make. Again, however, the researcher needs to weigh the importance of cell division against the number of subjects that are available. If the researcher does not delineate the number of cells in a way that best defines the variables, there would be inherent weaknesses in the study regardless of the number of individuals in each group. It is to this issue that the investigator has to exercise informed judgment.

If, in addition to having three divisions of the GPA variable, the category of instructional method was also divided into three groups (namely, ITV, NITV, and a combination designated as ITV/NITV), the study would be diagrammed as a 3 × 3 factorial design (see Figure 11–9).

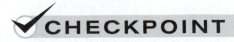

CHECKPOINT

What would be the recommended minimum sample size for a 3 × 3 factorial design?

Figure 11–9: **An Example of a Layout for a 3 x 3 Factorial Design**

		ITV	NITV	ITV/NITV
	High (HGPA)	Group 1	Group 2	Group 3
GPA	Medium (MGPA)	Group 4	Group 5	Group 6
	Low (LGPA)	Group 7	Group 8	Group 9

Answer

The answer is 135, determined by the recommendation that there be fifteen subjects in each of nine cells.

In order to relate the basic 2 × 2 factorial design to an outcome, you are referred to Figure 11–10. It can be seen that those with a high GPA who were taught with the traditional teaching method (NITV), referred to as Method B, had an average posttest score of 70. Those with a low GPA also scored higher posttest scores when they were taught with the traditional method (NITV).

The grand averages of the means for each row are found at the right side of the chart. The grand averages of the means for each column are found at the lower horizontal axis of the chart. Method B was better for students with high GPAs. It can be noted that Method B was also better for students with low GPAs. Thus, traditional instruction methods appeared to generate higher achievement scores, regardless of grade-point averages. This indicates that there was no interaction between teaching methods and GPAs (see Figure 11–11).

Figure 11–10: **Sample Means and Grand Means for 2 x 2 Factorial Experiment on Teaching Methods and GPA**

		Method A ITV	Method B NITV	Grand Mean
	High (HGPA)	50	70	60
GPA	Low (LGPA)	30	50	40
	Grand Mean	40	60	

Figure 11–11: **Demonstration of <u>No</u> Interactions Between Variables**

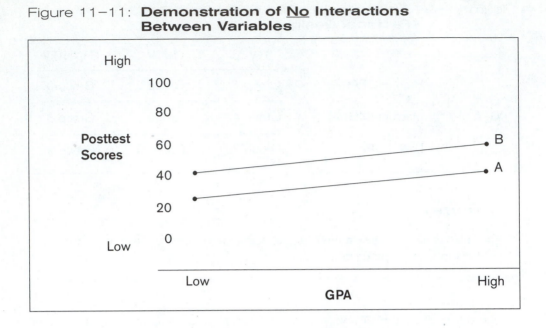

Suppose that, upon examination of the cells, it was discovered that the average score for those with high GPAs was 70 for Method A and 50 for Method B; in other words, suppose that the *mean scores were reversed* (see Figure 11–12). In this case, the investigator would find an *interaction* between the variables (see Figure 11–13). When the regression lines cross, as they do in Figure 11–13, interaction is present. By using a factorial design, it can be observed that interaction exists between the variables when each of the methods is differentially effective depending upon the grade-point averages of the students. By observing the fact that interaction is present, detailed examination of entries within the cells will provide a basis for interpretation.

Should the investigator desire to test for the significance of the findings, however, a factorial (or multifactor) analysis of variance could be used to investigate the

Figure 11–12: **Sample Means and Grand Means for 2 x 2 Factorial Experiment on Teaching Methods and GPA (Alternative Profile to Figure 11–10)**

		Method A ITV	Method B NITV	Grand Mean
GPA	High	70	50	60
	Low	30	50	40
	Grand Mean	50	50	

Figure 11–13: **Demonstration of Interactions Between Variables**

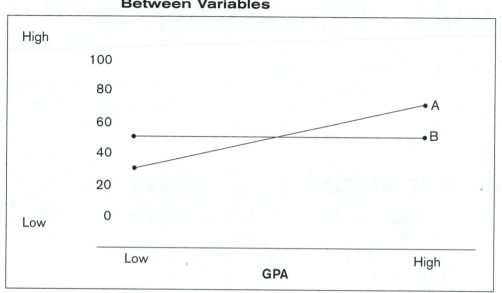

independent variables, as well as the interaction between them. This form of statistical treatment will generate an F ratio for each experimental variable, and one for each interaction. Using the data from Figure 11–7, for example, there would be three F ratios. There would be one for the manipulated variable (method of instruction), one for the control variable (grade-point average), and one for the interaction between grade teaching method and grade-point average. Further discussion of factorial analysis of variance procedures is beyond the scope of this book, but the reader is referred to the Recommended Readings section at the end of this chapter.

To further understand the use of factorial design procedures, you should know something about **attribute-treatment interaction research** (ATI). As you well know, students within a class are likely to have different aptitudes, interests, and learning styles. To the extent that instructional methods match these particular characteristics, the more likely it is that student learning will occur. Attribute-treatment interaction research attempts to examine whether the effects of various teaching methods are influenced by such attributes. In short, this form of inquiry attempts to examine the interaction of these characteristics with instructional methods. In this process, it is *not* assumed that students with certain characteristics are more effective learners or that one instructional method is better than the other. This research is based upon the assumption that instructional methods and student attributes can interact in ways that have a bearing upon learning, and that these ways are capable of being identified.

RESEARCH PRACTICUM

A superintendent of schools is interested in determining the effectiveness of peer mentoring and team meetings upon the social adjustment of first-year teachers. A population of twelve beginning teachers is divided at random into three different groups of four teachers each. Once the groups are established, treatments are randomly assigned to them. As a result, it is determined that:

1. Group 1 will engage in team meetings,
2. Group 2 will receive peer mentoring, and
3. Group 3 will be the control group—that is, its membership will engage in traditional orientation sessions but will *not* participate in special team meetings or receive peer mentoring.

✔CHECKPOINT

Before moving on with the scenario, attempt to respond to each of the following questions:

1. What is the name of the design being described in the narrative?
2. What would be the diagram for this design?

Answers

Given what was expressed in the narrative, the answers to these questions are:

1. The name of the design would be a *randomized (two-treatment) posttest only control-group design*.
2. The diagram for this design would be:

$$R \quad X_1 \quad O$$
$$R \quad X_2 \quad O$$
$$R \qquad\quad\ O$$

✔CHECKPOINT

What threats to internal validity would be of concern in the design selected for the study on the effectiveness of peer mentoring and team meetings?

Answers

The threats that are *uncontrolled* by the randomized (two-treatment) posttest only control-group design would be:

1. expectancy,

2. instability, and

3. experimental mortality.

Within the Phase 1 and Phase 2 planning stages of the study on peer mentoring and team meetings, specific protocols are prepared for both treatments.

> **NOTE:** The research topic, experimental protocols, and those designated to serve as research associates have been approved by the school board of the school administrative unit, and other pertinent parties. Although the study group is rather small, it is believed that the findings will serve a valuable preliminary function for the school district, as well as provide replication evidence for similar studies being carried out in other school districts throughout the state.

Neither the investigator nor the project associates (that is, mentors and team meeting designees) know the specific assignments of those associates until sealed envelopes prepared by the administrative assistant are opened. This takes place on Monday of the *first* full week of classes, and the two treatments are scheduled to begin on Monday of the *second* full week of classes. During the course of the investigation, protocols are monitored, and biweekly conferences between the superintendent/researcher and his associates are conducted. Upon the conclusion of the study period, equivalent forms of standardized social adjustment scales are administered to the twelve teachers.

> **NOTE:** All beginning teachers who began the study completed it. Thus, experimental mortality as a threat did not materialize. To the best of the investigator's knowledge, all protocols were followed (which controlled for expectancy), and no unusual events arose with any one of the groups during the course of the study that would tend to actualize the threat of instability. In short, the prevailing circumstances might be summed up by the phrase: *Chance favors the prepared mind.*

Given the nature of the design, and the fact that interval data were generated by the test on social adjustment, it was decided that analysis of variance (ANOVA) would be used to test the null hypothesis.

✓CHECKPOINT

What is the name of the *alternative* to the null hypothesis when one is employing ANOVA?

Answer

The alternative is called *homogeneity of variance.*

Earlier in the chapter, it was indicated that the process for computing ANOVA would be demonstrated using the *deviation* method. Since only twenty-five percent of the one-hundred-point instrument used in the study had been offered by the test publisher as having been validated to measure social adjustment *in school settings,* only the earned points for those questions will be used in the analysis. The data in Table 11–1 will serve as a backdrop for procedures to follow.

Applying the *deviation* formula for analysis of variance (ANOVA), one would employ the following steps:

1. Find the sum and mean of the scores for each distribution (see Table 11–1).

2. Find the grand mean, weighted according to group size, by dividing the summed products by N (the total number of scores), per:

$$\text{Grand Mean} = \frac{4(14) + 4(20) + 4(11)}{12}$$

$$= \frac{56 + 80 + 44}{12}$$

$$= \frac{180}{12}$$

$$= 15$$

 NOTE: When group sizes are identical, the grand mean can be found by simply adding the group means together, and dividing by

Table 11–1: **Scores Generated from Three Equivalent Posttests to Measure Social Adjustment in a School Setting**

Team Meetings Group X_1	Peer Mentoring Group X_2	Control Group X_3
6	24	13
14	16	12
19	20	9
17	20	10
$\Sigma X_1 = 56$	$\Sigma X_2 = 80$	$\Sigma X_3 = 44$
$M_1 = 14$	$M_2 = 20$	$M_3 = 11$

the number of groups. For example, in the above illustration, the grand mean is found as follows:

$$\text{Grand Mean} = \frac{14 + 20 + 11}{3}$$

$$= \frac{45}{3}$$

$$= 15$$

3. Find SS_W **(within group sum of squared deviations)** for each group, per:

$$\begin{aligned}
SS_W \text{ for Group } X_1 &= (6 - 14)^2 + (14 - 14)^2 + (19 - 14)^2 + (17 - 14)^2 \\
&= 64 + 0 + 25 + 9 \\
&= 98.000 \\
SS_W \text{ for Group } X_2 &= (24 - 20)^2 + (16 - 20)^2 + (20 - 20)^2 + (20 - 20)^2 \\
&= 16 + 16 + 0 + 0 \\
&= 32.000 \\
SS_W \text{ for Group } X_3 &= (13 - 11)^2 + (12 - 11)^2 + (9 - 11)^2 + (10 - 11)^2 \\
&= 4 + 1 + 4 + 1 \\
&= 10.000
\end{aligned}$$

Pooling **grand sum of squared deviations** *within* groups by:

$$\begin{aligned}
SS_W \text{ for all groups} &= 98.000 + 32.000 + 10.000 \\
&= 140.000
\end{aligned}$$

 NOTE: Values will be **truncated** at three places throughout the calculations because the *F* distribution (Appendix F, Critical Values for *F*) is displayed as three places.

4. Find SS_B **(between group sum of squared deviations),** weighted by group sample size, by:

$$\begin{aligned}
SS_B &= 4(14 - 15)^2 + 4(20 - 15)^2 + 4(11 - 15)^2 \\
&= 4(1) + 4(25) + 4(16) \\
&= 4 + 100 + 64 \\
&= 168.000
\end{aligned}$$

5. Find SS_T **(total sum of squared deviations)** by:

$$\begin{aligned}
SS_T &= (6 - 15)^2 + (14 - 15)^2 + (19 - 15)^2 + (17 - 15)^2 + \\
&\quad (24 - 15)^2 + (16 - 15)^2 + (20 - 15)^2 + (20 - 15)^2 + \\
&\quad (13 - 15)^2 + (12 - 15)^2 + (9 - 15)^2 + (10 - 15)^2 \\
&= (9)^2 + (1)^2 + (4)^2 + (2)^2 + \\
&\quad (9)^2 + (1)^2 + (5)^2 + (5)^2 + \\
&\quad (2)^2 + (3)^2 + (6)^2 + (5)^2 \\
&= 81 + 1 + 16 + 4 + \\
&\quad 81 + 1 + 25 + 25 + \\
&\quad 4 + 9 + 36 + 25 \\
&= 102 + 132 + 74 \\
&= 308.000
\end{aligned}$$

6. Find MS_B **(between mean squares)** by:

$$MS_B = \frac{SS_B}{K-1}$$

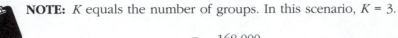 **NOTE:** K equals the number of groups. In this scenario, $K = 3$.

$$= \frac{168.000}{2}$$

$$= 84.000$$

7. Find MS_W **(within mean squares)** by:

$$MS_W = \frac{SS_W}{N-K}$$

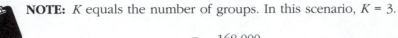 **NOTE:** N equals the total number of subjects. In this scenario, $N = 12$.

$$= \frac{140.000}{12-3}$$

$$= \frac{140.00}{9}$$

$$= 15.555$$

8. Find the F ratio by:

$$F \text{ ratio} = \frac{MS_B}{MS_W}$$

$$= \frac{84.000}{15.555}$$

$$= 5.400$$

By referring the F ratio (df with **$K-1$** as numerator, and **$N-K$** as denominator) to Appendix F (Critical Values for F), it can be determined whether the finding of $F = 5.400$ ($df = 2,9$) is significant. In order to be significant at the .05 *loc*, the F ratio would have to equal or exceed 4.256. Since the obtained value of 5.400 does equal or exceed 4.256, the investigator would now refer to the next level of significance (that is, in Critical Values for F, Appendix F). Per display, the next critical value would be .01. Since F ratio = 5.400 does not reach 8.022 (at .01 *loc*), the most that can be said with the information available is that:

> Within the limitations of the investigation, this researcher rejects the null hypothesis at the .05 level of confidence ($df = 2,9$). It appears that something other than chance has affected the within to between group variances.

At this point, a few observations need to be made. First, the total sum of squared deviations—that is SS_T (found in step 5, above)—should be the sum of SS_B and SS_W

(see Table 11–2). Given the fact that the sum of 308.000 (reported in Table 11–2) is the answer reported in step 5, one might suggest that to go through those somewhat tedious calculations is an unnecessary activity. Why not simply compute the *between* and *within* sum of squares, and be done with it? The reason is that, because there are numerous steps, there are many places where an error may be made. By carrying out the steps as indicated, there is a built–in check for errors.

Second, the *F* ratio can be calculated directly from a table (see Table 11–2), as a substitute for steps 6–10, above. This is explained as follows:

a. By dividing SS_B by the numerator $(K - 1)$ degrees of freedom, one will have MS_B (between mean squares), which is the numerator in the *F* ratio formula:

$$168.000/2 = 84.000$$

b. By dividing SS_W by the denominator $(N - K)$ degrees of freedom, one will have MS_W (within mean squares), which is the denominator in the *F* ratio formula:

$$140.000/9 = 15.555$$

c. By dividing MS_B by MS_W (values for which are found in the "Variance Estimate" column), the *F* test value is obtained:

$$84.000/15.555 = 5.400$$

Third, it would appear, on the basis of observation alone, that the significance of the findings would be in favor of Group X_2—that is, the group with the higher mean. If there were but two distributions of scores, that would be the way that a significant *F* value would be interpreted. If significance is found *within* and *between* the distributions of *more than two* groups of subjects, however, an additional statistical analysis must be made. Although there are a number of such tests designed for that purpose (see the section entitled "Analyzing Data" offered later in this chapter), the process that is considered to be among the favored is the *Scheffe test*. This technique, referred to as a *post hoc comparison,* is described as follows.

Table 11–2: **Summary Analysis of Variance**

Source of Variation	Sum of Squared Deviations	df	Variance Estimate	F Ratio
SS_B	168.000	2	84.000	
				5.400
SS_W	140.000	9	15.555	
Total:	308.000			
				$p < .05$ (2,9)

p = significance
(2,9) = numerator and denominator degrees of freedom

In the example of the study by the superintendent of schools, the only finding from the *F* test was that, somewhere, there was at least one significant difference between the groups.

 NOTE: If the null hypothesis had been accepted, there would be no finding of significance, and as a consequence, there would be little need to pursue a "source of difference."

The Scheffe test involves an analysis of comparisons between means of each of the distributions in a study. Examining the following formula, it can be observed that most of the information has been acquired through the use of ANOVA.

$$F = \frac{(M - M)^2}{MS_W \left(\frac{1}{N} + \frac{1}{N} \right) (K - 1)}$$

where $(M - M)^2$ = squared difference between the two means being compared.
MS_W = within mean squares (calculated through process of ANOVA).
N = number of subjects in the groups being compared.
K = total number of groups.

To compare distribution X_1 with distribution X_2, the following calculations are made:

$$F = \frac{(M_1 - M_2)^2}{MS_W \left(\frac{1}{N_1} + \frac{1}{N_2} \right) (K - 1)}$$

$$= \frac{(14 - 20)^2}{15.555 \ (\frac{1}{4} + \frac{1}{4}) \ (2)}$$

$$= \frac{(-6)^2}{15.555 \ (\frac{2}{4}) \ (2)}$$

$$= \frac{36}{15.555 \ (.5) \ (2)}$$

$$= \frac{36}{15.555 \ (1)}$$

$$= \frac{36}{15.555}$$

$$= 2.314$$

Given that the *F* ratio required for significance at the .05 *loc* (*df* = 2,9) is 4.256 (see Appendix F, Critical Values for *F*), it can be concluded that the observed finding is *not* held to be significant. In other words, there is *no* significant difference between M_1 and M_2.

 NOTE: With a visual inspection alone (Table 11–1), it would appear as if there would have been a significant difference between M_1 and M_2. You see, the observed difference between those two means can be attributed to chance alone. *Voila,* the value of further analysis.

To compare distribution X_1 with distribution X_3, the following calculations are made:

$$F = \frac{(M_1 - M_3)^2}{MS_W \left(\frac{1}{N_1} + \frac{1}{N_3}\right)(K - 1)}$$

$$= \frac{(14 - 11)^2}{15.555\ (\frac{1}{4} + \frac{1}{4})\ (2)}$$

$$= \frac{(3)^2}{15.555\ (\frac{2}{4})\ (2)}$$

$$= \frac{9}{15.555\ (1)}$$

$$= \frac{9}{15.555}$$

$$= .578$$

Given that the *F* ratio required for significance at the .05 *loc* (*df* = 2,9) is 4.256 (see Appendix F, Critical Values for *F*), it can be concluded that the observed finding is *not* held to be significant. In other words, there is *no* significant difference between M_1 and M_3.

To compare distribution X_2 with distribution X_3, the following calculations are made:

$$F = \frac{(M_2 - M_3)^2}{MS_W \left(\frac{1}{N_2} + \frac{1}{N_3}\right)(K - 1)}$$

$$= \frac{(20 - 11)^2}{15.555\ (\frac{1}{4} + \frac{1}{4})\ (2)}$$

$$= \frac{(9)^2}{15.555\ (\frac{2}{4})\ (2)}$$

$$= \frac{81}{15.555\ (.5)\ (2)}$$

$$= \frac{81}{15.555\ (1)}$$

$$= \frac{81}{15.555}$$

$$= 5.207$$

The critical value for F (df = 2,9) at the .05 level of confidence is 4.256 (see Appendix F, Critical Values for F). Thus, it can be concluded that the observed difference is held to be significant at $p < .05$ *loc.*

✓ CHECKPOINT

Is the finding for the X_2 and X_3 comparison significant at the .01 level of confidence (df = 2,9)?

Answer

As to whether the finding is significant at the .01 level of confidence, the answer is *no*. In order to be significant with df = 2,9, the observed F ratio would have to equal or exceed 8.022; hence, we would *reject* the null hypothesis at the .05 level of confidence. It appears that something other than chance affected the two distributions in favor of Group X_2, peer mentoring (see Table 11–1).

With regard to this matter of peer mentoring and team meetings, the response that would be sent to the state board of education would note the fact that, of the three approaches to addressing social adjustment in a school setting, the *most* effective was peer mentoring. Since this study consisted of a relatively small number of subjects, it would be recommended that a *meta-analysis* be conducted to include the investigations on related issues being reported by other districts in the state.

Meta-Analysis

To this point in Part III, Experimental Research Methods, reference has been made to various techniques for analyzing the results of experimental studies. In many of the investigations that practitioner-researchers will do, however, group sizes will be small. Regardless of that possibility, a good research design will generate findings that will provide very valuable information, particularly that which can be used in local educational settings. When random samples are selected from populations for such studies, the findings will become more generalizable (not to mention the controls that will be in place for addressing most threats to internal validity). The larger the sample, the greater the chance that the results, in fact, would be indicative of what would have been found if the entire population had participated in the investigation.

Since there are many independent studies that may have been completed (or are in process) dealing with the same research problem, meta-analysis procedures become more attractive. They make it possible to incorporate the results of such studies by producing a numerical value that expresses the "average" result. Those who have experience with literature reviews know that it is likely that, for any given topic, numerous variables could be controlled, factored out, used as treatments, or targeted for study. Traditional attempts for dealing with these issues have generally been a matter of looking for studies with common threads, collating the commonalities, and, while noting the number of studies in which a variable *was* or *was not* significant, arriving at conclusions.

While there is some merit in approaching studies in this way, there are limitations. For one, there can be a great deal of **subjectivity** in determining which studies should be included in the analysis. It is very important that specific criteria be identified and followed when making the selections. One example of a study in which painstaking efforts were made to bring objectivity into the process was published by Payne and Morrow (1993). In preparing criteria for their study dealing with exercise and maximum oxygen uptake in children, they conducted three online computer searches: ERIC, Medline, and SPORT Database. Sources were screened and reference lists were cross-checked in order to identify additional sources. All related manuscripts were examined in order to finalize the general criteria for inclusion that had originally been established for the library search. As a result of these efforts, the final selection criteria included the following:

1. Studies must have sought to examine the effects of physical training on oxygen utilization.

2. Studies must have been conducted with "typical" individuals, rather than with those with asthma, heart conditions, and so on.

3. Standard measurements of maximum oxygen utilization (employing open-circuit spirometry) must have been taken while subjects were using either a treadmill or cycle ergometer. (No studies were included that employed oxygen use *predictions* based on distance, time, or heart rate.)

4. Research must have been done on subjects *under* the age of fourteen.

5. Means, standard deviations, and *N* values must have been reported for *both* the control and the experimental groups.

 NOTE: Meta-analysts may also want to include in their selection criteria (1) the nature of the design (for example, posttest only, pretest-posttest); (2) whether groups were intact, randomized, and so on; and (3) depending upon the nature of the study, environmental conditions.

Twenty-eight of sixty-nine studies (40.5%) examined by Payne and Morrow met all criteria and, thus, were maintained for subsequent analysis.

With that as background, the specific analytical procedures for meta-analysis will be examined. Pioneered by Glass (1976), and further refined by Hedges and Olkin (1985), the key feature of meta-analysis (*meta* is a Greek prefix that means "beyond") is that it goes *beyond* an initial analysis or investigation. With meta-analysis, the researcher translates the results of each study into what is referred to as an **effect size** (*ES*). The *ES* (often symbolized as Δ) is a procedure for describing, in *standard score* form, the difference between the experimental (M_E) and control (M_C) group averages, divided by the standard deviation of the control group (SD_C). The formula is displayed as:

$$ES = \frac{M_E - M_C}{SD_C}$$

where M_E = the mean of the scores for the experimental group.
  M_C = the mean of the scores for the control group.
  SD_C = the standard deviation (σ) of the scores for the control group.

 NOTE: The process should remind you of the single-sample *t* test described in Chapter 9, Single-Group Designs. You may remember that it is used when a researcher is interested in knowing how an obtained mean compares with a mean generated from a similar study conducted in a different school district. The only observable differences in the formula are (1) the numerator (*SE*) was described as an absolute rather than a relative value, and (2) the denominator was described as a standard error of the mean rather than the standard deviation.

After *ES* has been calculated for each of the studies, the values are averaged. The cumulative effect size (ES_C) results are indicated by one number that summarizes the effects.

To initiate an illustration of the procedure, refer to Table 11–3 for the set of values that is used as a foundation for the following calculations:

For Group 1:

$$\frac{70 - 65}{5} = 1.000$$

For Group 2:

$$\frac{43 - 43}{5} = 0.000$$

For Group 3:

$$\frac{62 - 61}{4} = 0.250$$

By summing the individual effect sizes (*ES*), and dividing by the number of groups, the cumulative effect size is obtained:

Table 11–3: **Sample Sizes (*N*), Means, Standard Deviations, and Effect Sizes for Three Studies on School-to-Work Programs**

		N	M	Standard Deviation	ES
Group 1	Experimental	10	70	6	1.000
	Control	10	65	5	
Group 2	Experimental	10	43	4	0.000
	Control	10	43	5	
Group 3	Experimental	10	62	5	0.250
	Control	10	61	4	
					$ES_C = 0.416$

$$ES_C = \frac{1.250}{3}$$

$$= .416$$

As indicated earlier, effect sizes (*ES*) are standard scores. While there are various categories of standard scores, this standard score is equivalent to a *z* score, in which *M* = 0.0 and *SD* = 1.0, with an approximate range from -3.00 to +3.00 (see Appendix G, Standard Score Conversion Table). If ES_C = 0.0, it means that, on the average, the experimental and control groups were near equivalent. If the combined *ES* is a *positive* number, it means that, on average, the experimental groups did better with regard to the dependent variables.

✓CHECKPOINT

Why does a combined *ES* value that is *positive* indicate that, on the average, the experimental groups did better than the control groups in the related studies?

Answer

The reason is because in the formula for computing *ES,* the control group mean is *always* subtracted from the experimental group mean, per:

$$ES_E - ES_C$$

As a consequence, whenever the mean of the experimental group is *higher* than the mean of the control group, the *positive* number will be in favor of the experimental group.

If, on the other hand, the combined *ES* is negative, it would indicate that, on average, the control group did better than the experimental group. In the example from Table 11–3, ES_C = .416 means that, on average, the experimental groups performed at a higher level than the control groups by .416.

 NOTE: With regard to Appendix G, Standard Score Conversion Table, a combined effect size of .416 means that the experimental groups, on average, scored .416 standard deviations above the control group (per meta-analysis) in the study under consideration. Remember, the mean and standard deviation of a *z* score distribution are 0.0 and 1.0, respectively.

Although there are no hard-and-fast rules with regard to how high a combined *ES* has to be in order to reject a hypothesis of no difference (that is, null hypothesis), Hedges and Olkin (1985) suggest a combined effect size of:

- up to .20 for a finding of small significance,
- .21 to .79 for a finding of medium significance, and
- .80 and up, for a finding of large significance.

To illustrate the implications of findings from a meta-analysis of studies examining alternative teaching methods, Walberg (1984) reported an effect size of .76 for studies on cooperative learning. It appears, therefore, that this form of teaching strategy is very effective. Meta-analysis was able to provide a form of evidence that more traditional searches of the literature on teaching methods would not have been able to provide. While it is not a panacea when it comes to data analysis, it is considered a marked improvement over what has often been done to summarize findings of independent experiments.

As more and more independent studies are done on related topics, there will be an increased need for the use of meta-analysis procedures because (1) they tend to balance out errors of measurement, such as those arising from threats to internal validity (that is, expectancy, experimental mortality, history, instability, instrumentation, maturation, pretesting, regression, selection, and interaction); and (2) they provide for greater generalizability (that is, external validity) because of the increased heterogeneity of subjects and contexts. Factors unique to a particular experiment will be subsumed within the effect size (*ES*) of the combined findings.

ANALYZING DATA

After reading this far in Part III, Experimental Research Methods (Chapters 9, 10, and 11), it should be clear that there are research designs for any study question one may have in mind to investigate. Whether one's topic requires a more traditional model, such as a pretest-posttest control-group design, or a combination of that and repeated measures, there are methods which, if thoughtfully selected, will provide the kind of structure necessary to effective measurement. To this end, every characteristic that is measured within research is classified as either a *constant* or a *variable*.

A *constant* is something that is common to all individuals or groups of individuals selected for participation in a study. To illustrate, if an investigator is interested in conducting a study in a particular junior-high school, *grade level* would be a constant. If one were studying *only* girls within the eighth grade of that school, both *gender* and *grade level* would be constants. As you would expect, gender and grade level may be constants in one study, but not be considered constants in another. In other words, if the researcher were studying *all* students (boys and girls) in the eighth grade, gender would not be a constant.

Although every investigation has something that is held constant, a constant is not ordinarily the thing that is subject to statistical analysis. On the contrary, statistical analyses focus primarily on variables, the values of which tend to vary across the subjects within a particular study. Statistical analyses may reveal that the observed differences in these values may be the product of chance, or it may be found that these differences are statistically significant. In either instance, the use of statistics enables the researcher to make such determinations within the limitations of his particular study. Practitioner-researchers may find it possible to study an entire population, in which case they may use inferential statistics to describe the character of that population, and to draw inferences about others like it. Or the study group may be a random sample of a population in which the inferential statistics are used with the data arising from the sample to be able to infer about that population. Further, inferential statistics may be used with data generated from an intact group (for example, tenth-grade geography) in order to draw inferences about tenth-grade geography classes that will be scheduled in a subsequent semester. Regardless of the size or nature of the study group, it is critical that the investigator select statistical procedures that are appropriate to his design, study group, and the data. To a great extent, it is in this regard that Chapter 9, Single-Group Designs, Chapter 10, Two-Group Designs, and this chapter, Other Experimental Procedures, have been written.

Upon a thorough study of Part III, you will be familiar with a sufficient number of experimental designs and statistical procedures to enable you to analyze and interpret data that will arise from most experimental studies that one would hope to conduct—whether they be yours or those of others. At the same time, however, it should be understood fully that there are statistical methods (other than those presented in this book) which, depending upon the particuliarities of one's study, would be appropriate to consider for use. While it would not be feasible to include all possible statistical designs in a single book, it needs to be said that if you understand the processes described here, you are well on your way to understanding the procedures for employing virtually any statistical tool available. At the very least, you would know how to follow the steps to complete the analysis.

Although the *Scheffe test* for computing individual comparisons in an analysis of variance is among those most frequently used for that purpose, there are alternatives, namely:

- Bonferroni significant difference test,
- Duncan's multiple-range test,
- Dunnett's test,
- Fisher's significant difference test,
- Neuman-Keuls test,
- Protected *t* test, and

- Tukey's significant difference test.

If you are interested in finding out more about the particulars of these alternative techniques, refer to the Recommended Readings section provided at the end of this chapter.

You will remember that data must be interval or ratio before an analysis of variance (ANOVA) can be used. However, although not described in this book, there are alternatives to ANOVA when data are ordinal. It may be useful for you to be aware of a few of the alternatives in the event that a multiple-group study you are contemplating would generate *nonparametric* (that is, ordinal) data. One nonparametric equivalent of a one-way analysis of variance is the Kruskal-Wallis *H* test. An example of a nonparametric test for ordinal data that is equivalent to a matched-pair non-independent *t* test is the Wilcoxon test. When there are two treatment groups and *multiple outcome* variables, an example of a multivariate equivalent of a *t* test is Hotelling's *T*.

One of the major topics of this chapter was single-subject research. Whether statistical tests should be employed in single-subject research will continue to be a controversial issue for some time to come. While their future is uncertain, one important prerequisite to their selection in any set of circumstances, according to Kazdin (1992), is the use of reasoned judgment. The employment of statistical analyses should be thought of as a tool to assist, rather than replace, the commonsense approach to information analysis.

In the absence of the feasibility for conducting multiple-group designs in some school settings, single-group research will (and should) continue to flourish. It is largely because of the presence of single-group research that meta-analysis has surfaced as a way of examining related literature. Although there has been some debate about whether meta-analyses should be conducted with *all* studies, regardless of the design (Joyce, 1987), or only with those studies selected as representative of *best evidence* (Slavin, 1986), the employment of carefully developed selection criteria should help to combat the reservations people have about their use.

In addition to employing meta-analyses with experimental designs, the process has also been extended for use with correlation studies in which the coefficients are summed and averaged. For an illustration of the process, refer to Table 11–4.

One of the criticisms, however, of a *flat* average is that the calculations assume equal weighting. In other words, the finding of a study in which $df = 70$ should have greater influence in the overall average than a correlation study in which $df = 13$. To address this criticism, one could weight the studies, per *df,* by the following steps:

1. Multiply each *r* by *df*:

$$r = .62 \ (df = 20) = 12.400$$
$$r = .71 \ (df = 13) = 9.230$$
$$r = .80 \ (df = 70) = 56.000$$

2. Sum the products:

$$12.400 + 9.230 + 56.000 = 77.630$$

Table 11-4: **Coefficients (*r*) and Degrees of Freedom (*df*) for Three Correlation Studies on Health Knowledge and Practice**

	Studies		
	1	2	3
r	.620	.710	.800
df	20	13	70
$M_r = .710$			

Note: By summing the three correlation coefficients, and dividing by three (number of groups), the mean correlation coefficient $(M_r) = .710$.

3. Divide the sum by total *df*:

$$\frac{77.630}{103} = .753$$

The **weighted average** of the correlation coefficients is .753. This value takes into account the number of pairs of subjects in each study.

NOTE: The topic of weighted *N* values was referenced earlier in the chapter, per calculation of analysis of variance (ANOVA), both in step 2 and step 4.

In a report of any findings, it should be made as clear as possible to the reader such things as:

1. whether findings are significant (*p*) and, if so, at what level of confidence (*loc*);

2. the degrees of freedom (*df*) that were used when testing critical values; and

3. if applicable, whether values have been weighted.

With regard to the matter on conducting meta-analyses with correlation study coefficients, the closer the combined *r* is to +1.00 or -1.00, the stronger the relationship between the two variables. The investigator can also make a determination about whether the findings are significant (per *df*) by referring to Appendix D, Critical Values for *r*. The interpretation of significance remains the same whether or not the coefficient represents a combined average (see Chapter 7, Correlation Procedures).

Another criticism that is frequently made is related to the use of "gain" scores as a basis for determining treatment effects (Deiderich, 1956). A gain score is found by subtracting a pretest from a posttest value. For example, if a subject's initial score was a sixty (out of one hundred possible points), and his posttest score was seventy (out of one hundred possible points), his gain score would be ten. To illustrate the problem, if a researcher averaged the gain scores for the members of each of two groups at the conclusion of the study, he might *not* find a significant difference (and accept the null hypothesis), but one of the groups might have scored high on the pretest and, thus, had less room for positive change. The condition of having earned near maximum on a pretest is referred to as the **ceiling effect**. Initial scores that are high (or low) may also actualize statistical regression as a threat to internal validity.

Many times the problem associated with the employment of statistics is not a matter of whether they are appropriate to use as tools but, rather, whether the right statistical tool (from options available) has been selected for the job. This holds true whether one is deciding on the issue of weighted versus unweighted averages, a *t* test for independent or nonindependent groups, a Scheffe test (or alternatives) for computing individual comparisons in analysis of variance, or meta-analysis. There is nothing inherently incorrect with any of these procedures (if properly used) that would lead to erroneous conclusions. A thoughtful match between the research design and the appropriate analytical tool, be it qualitative or quantitative, will lead to conclusions that are based on best evidence. It is hoped that all practitioner-researchers will assign thoughtful regard to the alternatives available.

SUMMARY

In experimental (or descriptive) studies, an investigator does *not* select a design that he desires to use and then decide upon a topic that meets the criteria of that design. Instead, a topic is chosen first, and then the procedures that will best provide for its investigation are selected. The researcher has the responsibility to find and employ the best design possible. In this chapter, you were introduced to a number of designs, including single-subject, multiple-baseline, alternating-treatment, cohort, multiple-group, and factorial designs. Each has its place, depending upon the purpose of the inquiry, the character and size of the study group, and the number of controls and treatments the investigator wants to impose for examination. For these designs, both structure and function were described, diagrams were presented, and relative strengths and weaknesses were discussed.

In conjunction with the presentation of various research designs, the chapter also provided illustrations of pertinent statistical procedures. Specifically, reference was made to:

1. the deviation method for computing analysis of variance (ANOVA);
2. the Scheffe test, when three or more groups are in the study and homogeneity of variance has been rejected;
3. meta-analysis with both experimental and correlation studies, and
4. weighted and unweighted averages.

Typical of the type of question one should be able to answer upon reading the chapter is:

> Under what conditions would an investigator choose a factorial design instead of a single-variable experiment?

To illustrate the point of the question: If a posttest only control-group design was selected to study the effects of interactive television upon achievement (a topic referenced earlier in the chapter), the two groups would consist of students with different grade-point averages. Without factoring GPA into the inquiry, one would never know whether findings would hold true for those with high, or low, averages. It is to an issue such as this that consideration must be given when selecting from among the designs available.

There are a number of mistakes that occasionally are made when conducting experiments. Among the most frequent are the following:

1. Failing to examine the literature in order to discover factors that other researchers considered (or recommended) when conducting studies on similar topics

2. Selecting a study group because it is convenient when, with a little more effort, randomization would have been possible

3. Failing to randomly assign individuals to groups, and groups to treatments

4. Failing to establish designs that will control for threats to validity

5. Failing to follow established protocol for the study

6. Using instruments of assessment that lack evidence for validity, reliability, and objectivity

7. Selecting analytical methods that are inappropriate to the design or the data scales (that is, nominal, ordinal, interval, or ratio) generated by the instrument

8. Failing to interpret findings appropriately—that is, rejecting a null hypothesis when it should have been accepted (Type I error), or accepting a null hypothesis when it should have been rejected (Type II error)

9. Drawing inferences that are inappropriate to the findings

10. Failing to include in one's report all pertinent elements of the design, including sample, person(s), place(s), and time(s)

It is anticipated that thoughtful readers of the chapters found in Part III, Experimental Research Methods, will be in a position to avoid pitfalls common to all too many investigations. Classroom teachers, administrators, school counselors, and others who are seeking or practicing their careers in the helping professions need only to consider the problems that are present in our schools to realize the importance of selecting and implementing designs of quality. Positive effects do occur when educators are willing to integrate their complementary role as researchers (Mohr & MacLean, 1987). As Copper (1991) points out, on-site research can cause such things as:

- lesson design and curriculum development to unfold as teachers investigate why some lessons are more effective than others,

- administrators to learn whether participatory agenda planning (for faculty meetings) affects the morale of teachers, and

- school counselors to learn of the effectiveness of various intervention techniques upon truancy.

As indicated earlier in this book, no one is better informed about the nature of problems in our schools than are the individuals who are employed there. When school practitioners accept the fact that education is a research-based discipline, a revolution that will make schools what they need to be will certainly follow.

RECOMMENDED LABORATORY ASSIGNMENTS

1. Review the Recommended Readings.

2. Arrange to meet with fellow graduate students and colleagues in order to discuss the advantages and disadvantages of the following:

a. Single-subject designs

b. Multiple-baseline designs

c. Alternating-treatment designs

d. Cohort designs

e. Multiple-group designs

f. Factorial designs

3. Through a collaboration with no more than three individuals, complete the following.

a. Identify a topic that could be studied experimentally.

b. Create a research plan that will include comprehensive responses to the subproblems of Phase 1:

- Statement of the problem
- Need (justification) for the study
- Review of related literature
- Statement of null hypothesis (or homogeneity of variance)
- Basic assumptions
- Possible threats to the study
- Design alternatives
- Definitions of terms

and to the subproblems of Phase 2:

- Permission/selection of subjects
- Selection of instrument
- Administration of study/collection of data
- Analysis of data/conclusions/recommendations

each with regard to:

- What I need to know
- Where I will find it
- How I will find it
- Procedures for organizing the information for further use
- Conclusions that would follow from the procedures and allow the researcher to proceed

c. Administer the study, analyze the data using appropriate statistical procedures, test for significance at pertinent levels of confidence, and interpret the findings.

d. Examine Chapter 13, Preparing the Research Report, and using the guidelines provided therein, prepare a manuscript suitable for formal presentation that would reflect the study design, findings, and interpretations.

e. Arrange to meet with fellow graduate students, colleagues, as well as school and nonschool employees in order to review and discuss the findings, interpretations, as well as reactions to your collaborative efforts.

4. Extend the table created in response to Recommended Laboratory Assignment 11 in Chapter 10, Two-Group Designs, by adding notations of *Yes* or *No* to indicate whether threats to internal validity are controlled in each of the designs referenced in assignment 2, above.

5. Prepare at least one research diagram for each of the following:

a. A-B-A design

b. Alternating-treatment design

c. Cohort design

6. Create criteria for a meta-analysis of an experimental topic of your choice.

7. Utilizing the criteria prepared in response to assignment 6, complete a meta-analysis for no fewer than five articles, and arrange to present findings to fellow graduate students and colleagues.

RECOMMENDED READINGS

Abrami, P. C., Cohen, P. A., & d'Apollonia, S. (1988). Implementation problems in meta-analysis. *Review of Educational Research, 58,* 151–179.

Asher, J. W. (1990). Educational psychology, research methodology, and meta-analysis. *Educational Psychologist, 25,* 143–158.

Ayllon, T., & Roberts, M. D. (1974). Eliminating discipline problems by strengthening academic performance. *Journal of Applied Behavior Analysis, 7,* 71–76.

Barlow, D. H., & Hersen, M. (1992). *Single-case experimental designs: Strategies for studying behavior change* (Rev. 2nd ed.). Needham Heights, MA: Allyn & Bacon.

Bass, R. F. (1987). The generality, analysis, and assessment of single-subject data. *Psychology in the Schools, 24,* 97–104.

Blough, P. M. (1983). Local contrast in multiple schedules: The effect of stimulus discriminability. *Journal of the Experimental Analysis of Behavior, 39,* 427–437.

Chan, K. S., & Cole, P. G. (1987). An aptitude-treatment interaction in a mastery learning model of instruction. *Journal of Experimental Education, 55,* 189–200.

Cooper, H. (1984). *The integrative research review: A systematic approach.* Newbury Park, CA: Sage.

Couch, J. V. (1982). *Fundamentals of statistics for the behavioral sciences.* New York: St. Martin's Press.

DeProspero, A., & Cohen, S. (1979). Inconsistent visual analyses of intrasubject data. *Journal of Applied Behavior Analysis, 12,* 573–579.

Glass, G. V., McGaw, B., & Smith, M. L. (1981). *Meta-analysis in social research.* Newbury Park, CA: Sage.

Glass, G. V., Wilson, V. L., & Gottman, J. M. (1975). *Design and analysis of time-series experiments.* Boulder: Colorado University Press.

Greenwald, A. G. (1975). Consequences of prejudice against the null hypothesis. *Psychological Bulletin, 82*(1), 1–20.

Grejda, G. F., & Hannafin, M. J. (1992). Effects of word processing on sixth graders' holistic writing and revisions. *The Journal of Educational Research, 85,* 144–149.

Gupta, J. K., Srivastava, A. B. L., & Sharma, K. K. (1988). On the optimum predictive potential of change measures. *Journal of Experimental Education, 56,* 124–128.

Harris, M. B. (1995). *Basic statistics for behavioral science research.* Needham Heights, MA: Allyn & Bacon.

Hedges, I. V. (1986). Issues in meta-analysis. In E. Z. Rothkopf, *Review of research in education. Vol. 13* (pp. 353–398). Washington, DC: American Educational Research Association.

Hyde, J. S., Fennema, E., & Lamon, S. J. (1990). Gender differences in mathematics performance: A meta-analysis. *Psychological Bulletin, 107*(2), 139–155.

Hyde, J. S., & Linn, M. C. (1988). Gender differences in verbal ability: A meta-analysis. *Psychological Bulletin, 104*(1), 53–69.

Jackson, G. B. (1980). Methods for integrative reviews. *Review of Educational Research, 9*(3), 438–460.

Johnson, N., Johnson, J., & Yates, C. (1981). A six-month follow-up on the effects of the Vocational Exploration Group on career maturity. *Journal of Counseling Psychology, 28,* 70–71.

Jones, R. R., Vaught, R. S., & Weinrott, M. (1978). Time-series analysis in operant research. *Journal of Applied Behavior Analysis, 11,* 277–283.

Kazdin, A. E. (1977). Assessing the clinical or applied importance of behavior change through social validation. *Behavior Modification, 1,* 427–452.

Keppel, G., & Zedeck, S. (1989). *Data analysis for research designs: Analysis of variance and multiple regression/correlation approaches.* New York: W.H. Freeman.

Kiess, H. O. (1989). *Statistical concepts for the behavioral sciences.* Needham Heights, MA: Allyn & Bacon.

Kratochwill, T. R., & Levin, J. R. (Eds.). (1992). *Single-case research design and analysis.* Hillsdale, NJ: Lawrence Erlbaum.

Kromrey, J. D. (1993). Ethics and data analysis. *Educational Researcher, 22*(4), 24–27.

Lancioni, G. E. (1982). Normal children as tutors to teach social responses to withdrawn mentally retarded schoolmates: Training, maintenance, and generalization. *Journal of Applied Behavior Analysis, 15,* 17–40.

Lauer, J. M., & Asher, J. W. (1988). *Composition research: Empirical designs.* New York: Oxford University Press.

Leitenberg, H. (1973). The use of single-case methodology in psychotherapy research. *Journal of Abnormal Psychology, 82,* 87–101.

Light, R. J., & Pillemer, D. B. (1984). *Summing up: The science of reviewing research.* Cambridge, MA: Harvard University Press.

Linn, R. L. (1986). Quantitative methods in research on teaching. In M. C. Wittrock (Ed.). *Handbook of research on teaching* (3rd ed., pp. 92–118). New York: Macmillan.

Matson, J. L., & Adkins, J. (1980). A self-instructional social skills training program for mentally retarded persons. *Mental Retardation, 18*(5), 245–248.

Meyer, M. M., Linville, M. E., & Rees, G. (1993, Spring). The development of a positive self-concept in preservice teachers. *Action in Teacher Education, XV*(1), 30–35.

Moore, D. S., & McCabe, G. P. (1993). *Introduction to the practice of statistics* (2nd ed.). New York: W.H. Freeman.

Patel, H. I. (1983). Use of baseline measurements in two-period crossover designs in clinical trials. *Communications in Statistics, Theory and Methods, 12,* 2693–2712.

Popham, W. J., & Sirotnik, K. A. (1992). *Understanding statistics in education*. Itasca, IL: F.E. Peacock.

Rosenthal, R. (1984). *Meta-analytic procedures for social science research*. Newbury Park, CA: Sage.

Ryan, A. W. (1991). Meta-analysis of achievement effects of microcomputer applications in elementary schools. *Educational Administration Quarterly, 27,* 161–184.

Samson, G. E., Strykowski, B., Weinstein, T., & Walberg, H. J. (1987). The effects of teacher question levels on student achievement: A quantitative synthesis. *Journal of Educational Research, 80*(5), 290–295.

Saunders, W. L., & Jesunathadas, J. (1988). The effect of task content upon proportional reasoning. *Journal of Research in Science Teaching, 25,* 59–67.

Scruggs, T. E., Mastropieri, M. A., & Casto, G. (1987). The quantitative synthesis of single-subject research: Methodology and validation. *Remedial and Special Education, 8,* 24–33.

Sharpley, C. F. (1986). Some arguments against analyzing client change graphically. *Journal of Counseling and Development, 65,* 156–159.

Slavin, R. E. (1984). Meta-analysis in education: How has it been used? *Educational Researcher, 13*(8), 6–15.

Solomon, R. I. (1949). An extension of control group design. *Psychological Bulletin, 46,* 137–150.

Stern, G. W., Fowler, S. A., & Kohler, F. W. (1988). A comparison of two intervention roles: Peer monitor and point earner. *Journal of Applied Behavior Analysis, 21,* 103–109.

Tobias, S. (1976). Achievement-treatment interactions. *Review of Educational Research, 46,* 61–74.

van der Mars, H. (1987). Effects of audiocueing on teacher verbal praise of students' managerial and transitional task performance. *Journal of Teaching in Physical Education, 6,* 157–165.

Vaughn, V. L., Feldhusen, J. F., & Asher, J. W. (1991). Meta-analyses and review of research in pull-out programs in gifted education. *Gifted Child Quarterly,* 92–98.

Walberg, H. J. (1986). Synthesis of research on teaching. In M. C. Wittrock (Ed.), *Handbook of research on teaching* (3rd ed.). New York: Macmillan.

Walker, H. M., & Buckley, N. K. (1968). The use of positive reinforcement in conditioning-attending behavior. *Journal of Applied Behavior Analysis, 1,* 245–250.

Willig, A. C. (1985). A meta-analysis of selected studies on the effectiveness of bilingual education. *Review of Educational Research, 55*(3), 269–317.

Witte, R. S. (1989). *Statistics* (3rd ed.). New York: Holt, Rinehart & Winston.

REFERENCES

Bijou, S. W., Peterson, R. F., & Ault, M. H. (1968). A method to integrate descriptive and experimental field studies at the level of data and empirical concepts. *Journal of Applied Behavior Analysis, 1,* 175–191.

Copper, L. R. (1991, Summer). Teachers as researchers. *Kappa Delta Pi Record, 27*(4), 115–117.

Deiderich, P. B. (1956). Pitfalls in the measurement of gains in achievement. *School Review, 64,* 59–63.

Gay, L. R. (1996). *Educational research: Competencies for analysis and application* (5th ed.). Englewood Cliffs, NJ: Prentice-Hall.

Glass, G. V. (1976). Primary, secondary, and meta-analysis of research. *Educational Researcher, 5,* 3–8.

Hall, R. V., Fox, R., Willard, D., Goldsmith, L., Emerson, M., Owen, M., Davis, F., & Porcia, E. (1971). The teacher as observer and experimenter in the modification of disputing and talking-out behaviors. *Journal of Applied Behavior Analysis, 4,* 141–149.

Hedges, I. V., & Olkin, I. (1985). *Statistical methods for meta-analysis.* Orlando, FL: Academic Press.

Joyce, B. (1987). A rigorous yet delicate touch: A response to Slavin's proposal for "best evidence" reviews. *Educational Researcher, 16*(4), 12–16.

Kazdin, A. E. (1992). Statistical analyses for single-case experimental designs. In D. H. Barlow & M. Hersen, *Single-case experimental designs: Strategies for studying behavior change* (Rev. 2nd ed., pp. 285–324). Needham Heights, MA: Allyn & Bacon.

Kirk, S. A., Gallagher, J. J., & Anastasiow, N. J. (1997). *Educating exceptional children* (8th ed.). Boston: Houghton Mifflin.

Mohr, M., & MacLean, M. (1987). *Working together: A guide for teacher-researchers.* Urbana, IL: National Council of Teachers of English.

Payne, V. G., & Morrow, J. R., Jr. (1993, September). Exercise and VO in children: A meta-analysis. *Research Quarterly for Exercise and Sport, 64*(3), 305–313.

Slavin, R. E. (1986). Best evidence synthesis: An alternative to meta-analysis and traditional reviews. *Educational Researcher, 15,* 5–11.

Spanier, B. (1997, Spring). Sexism and scientific research. *National Forum: The Phi Kappa Phi Journal, 77*(2), 26–30.

Walberg, H. J. (1984). Improving the productivity of America's schools. *Educational Leadership, 41*(8), 19–27.

Walker, H., & Fabre, T. (1987). Assessment of behavior disorders in the school setting: Issues, problems, and strategies revisited. In N. Harring (Ed.), *Assessing and managing behavior disorders* (pp. 198–234). Seattle, WA: University of Washington Press.

Wiseman, D. C. (1982). *A practical approach to adapted physical education.* Reading, MA: Addison-Wesley.

Wiseman, D. C. (1994). *Physical education for exceptional students: Theory to practice.* Albany, NY: Delmar.

Wood, F. (1982). Defining disturbing, disordered, and disturbed behavior. In F. Wood & K. Laken (Eds.), *Disturbing, disoriented, or disturbed?* Reston, VA: Council for Exceptional Children.

POSTANALYTICAL CONSIDERATIONS

CHAPTER 12

Using the Computer for Data Analysis

OBJECTIVES

After reading this chapter, you should be able to:

- Discuss the evolution of the *Internet* and the common communication options it provides, including: Archie and Ftp, Gopher, Telnet, Veronica, WAIS, and WWW.

- Distinguish between the *mainframe* and *personal computers*.

- Describe the various ways in which microcomputers have impacted upon the schools.

- Distinguish between *hardware* and *software*.

- Distinguish between bits and bytes, CPU and CP/M, dot matrix and laser printers, RAM and ROM, and personal computers and terminals.

- Describe the functions of a database, disk drive, disk operating system, modem, mouse, RF modulator, and voice synthesizer.

- Identify and discuss no fewer than ten software modules that are available for data analysis.

- Identify sixteen analytical procedures (described in Parts II and III of this book) that are available through the Statistical Products and Service Solutions (SPSS).

- Distinguish between a *database management system* and a *spreadsheet program*.
- Identify and discuss criteria for selecting hardware.
- Identify and discuss criteria for selecting software.
- Define and discuss baud rate, booting, formatting, and interfacing.
- Discuss the function of a *text editor*.
- Demonstrate the *coding* of data for subsequent entry into a computer.
- Discuss the function of *program commands*.
- Interpret a sample hardcopy display of a Pearson correlation coefficient.
- Define key terms, and answer the checkpoint questions.

KEY TERMS

Archie

Baud Rate

Bit

Boot

Byte

Central Processing Unit (CPU)

Coding

Computer-Assisted Instruction (CAI)

Computer-Managed Concept Instruction (CMCI)

Computer-Managed Drill and Practice (CMDP)

Computer-Managed Instruction (CMI)

Computer-Managed Problem Solving (CMPS)

Computer-Managed Simulation (CMS)

Computer-Managed Tutorial (CMT)

Control Program for Microcomputers (CP/M)

Correlation Command

Data Analysis

Database

Database Management System (DMS)

Data List Command

Disk Drive

Disk Operating System (DOS)

Display

Dot Matrix Printer

E-mail

File Transfer Protocol (Ftp)

Formatting

Gopher

Hardware

Interface

Internet

Kurzweil Reading Machine

Laser Printer

Mailing List

Mainframe	*Statistics Command*
Microcomputer	*Telnet*
Modem	*Terminal*
Mouse	*Title Command*
Newsgroup	*User-Managed Problem Solving (UMPS)*
Optical Mark Reader (OMR)	
Random Access Memory (RAM)	*Veronica*
Read Only Memory (ROM)	*Voice Synthesizer*
RF Modulator	*Wide Area Information Service (WAIS)*
Software	
Spreadsheet	*Word Processing*
Statistical Products and Service Solutions (SPSS)	*World Wide Web (WWW)*

INTRODUCTION

When computers entered the market, they were classified along a continuum of **microcomputers,** minicomputers, and **mainframes.** Originally categorized on the basis of such things as processing power and size of internal memory, the present distinctions between them are less clear. Full realization of the capabilities of *micros* is yet to be demonstrated but is in the realm of speculation. "The future isn't what it used to be," a quote attributed to both the writer Arthur C. Clarke and the poet Paul Valery, is as applicable today as it has been at any time in recent history. Consider, for example, a few of the ways in which microcomputers (*micros*) have begun to impact upon schools.

1. Assistive devices for those with disabilities, namely:

    a. Students with physical impairments: head pointers, manual pointers, joysticks, light pens, and rocking levers for use when responding to questions and other stimuli

    b. Students with visual impairments: **Kurzweil reading machine,** which uses an electronic scanner with a speech synthesizer to read printed material aloud (Otto, 1989)

    c. Students with hearing impairments: *Baudot* system [related to *baud,* in **baud rate** (see Figure 12–1)], which translates characters into electronic code, and provides for those who are hearing-impaired to "hook up" to computer information networks and simultaneously communicate with others who are using teletypewriters

2. Use of **software** for administrative budgeting, scheduling of classes, record keeping, and word processing

3. **Computer-assisted instruction (CAI),** which augments teaching through the use of computer-aided strategies in the areas of drill and practice, simulation techniques, and tutorials, including:

   a. **Computer-Managed Concept Instruction (CMCI),** which instructs the learner through individualized sequencing, using the *branching* capabilities of the microcomputer

   b. **Computer-Managed Drill and Practice (CMDP),** which reinforces information previously learned

   c. **Computer-Managed Problem Solving (CMPS),** which places the learner in situations to solve problems and to receive appropriate consequences

   d. **Computer-Managed Simulation (CMS),** which places the learner in situations that replicate original situations

   e. **Computer-Managed Tutorial (CMT),** which presents information already taught in the classroom, but which has to be broken into smaller steps or presented at a lower conceptual or reading level

   f. **User-Managed Problem Solving (UMPS),** which develops and programs software using methods appropriate to individual technical knowledge and ability

4. **Computer-Managed Instruction (CMI),** which makes use of the computer as a diagnostic, prescriptive, and organizational tool to gather, store, manipulate, analyze, and report information relative to the student and the curriculum

5. Information retrieval through such processes as E-mail, ERIC, and PsycLit

In Chapter 1, Selection and Definition of a Problem, information was presented on accessing information through such sources as the Educational Resources Information Center (ERIC). Both ERIC and PsycLit collect the findings of educational and psychological research, respectively, from wherever they originate, and index and store them with a view toward making the information available to interested individuals. Computers play a significant role in accessing information made available through these sources.

Comprised of independent networks connected together, the *Internet* began as an experiment in the 1960s by the United States Defense Department's Advanced Research Projects Agency (ARPA). Its scientists, working on assorted government and military projects, were trying to find a way to use computers in order to communicate with one another and, in so doing, to establish a system that could keep functioning even if individual sites could no longer operate because of a nuclear disaster (Bradley, 1995). ARPAnet, the original network system, then expanded to include colleges and universities. It was through experimentation conducted by faculty and students that separate networks, such as UUCP (UNIX-TO-UNIX CoPy) and bitnet (*because it's time network*) were created. In the 1980s, work of the National Science Foundation (NSF), with its computer system, led to what is now, in fact, a network of networks. In its current state, the **Internet** (*interworking networks*) provides practitioner-researchers with numerous communication options, including:

1. **Archie** and **File Transfer Protocol (Ftp),** for use when one wants to transfer in files from a remote computer. Through the Archie server, the investigator can search worldwide sites for program files and, with Ftp, transfer them in.

2. **E-mail,** an electronic mailing service that enables individuals to communicate with other users all over the world.

3. **Gopher,** which is used to *tunnel* through Internet in search of specific files, and present what it finds in menu form.

4. **Mailing Lists,** which provide for messages to be sent directly to one's electronic address. They are similar to newsgroups except that messages come to the *addressee* rather than to the *group*.

5. **Newsgroups,** which are comprised of individuals who share specific interests. Users can choose to offer information to the group, or simply "listen in." They are similar to what are referred to in other systems as BSSs (bulletin board systems) or SIGs (special interest groups).

6. **Telnet,** which provides the capability for those with accounts to *login* to remote systems (for example, with your home or business computers when you are traveling, or with the computers of business and government).

7. **Veronica,** which enables the user to locate files from a master index that lists topic titles from all over the Net.

8. **Wide Area Information Service (WAIS),** which enables users to search indexes of databases in the Net for *content* rather than simply *titles* (as Archie and Veronica do).

9. **World Wide Web (WWW),** which, using buttons or words displayed on the screen, provides users with the capability to navigate from one point to another as they search for new information. In addition to *Microsoft Navigator* and *Netscape,* one of the primary programs within WWW is called *Mosaic*. Developed by the National Center for Supercomputing Applications (NCSA), versions of *Mosaic* are currently available for use in a number of systems, including Macintosh, Windows, and X-Windows.

Each of these access routes through the computer makes it possible for the practitioner-researcher to have global information at her fingertips. Although computers serve a major function in information retrieval, they are not limited to that purpose.

✓CHECKPOINT

What is the difference between the wide area information service (WAIS) and either Archie or Veronica?

Answer

The wide area information service (WAIS) enables users to access indexes of the databases in the Internet for *content*. Both Archie and Veronica search indexes in the Net for *titles*.

A second major capability of computers is that of **word processing.** *Micros* enable researchers to store, edit, revise, and reformat text without retyping entire documents.

 NOTE: Something to which many of the author's colleagues will attest, is that it was not too long ago that copies of 150–300 page dissertations were typed between pages of carbon paper. It seems that we were born too early.

Selecting the word processing software that is *best* depends upon the computer and printer available to you. Further, if one is going to use other tools, such as electronic dictionaries, file management programs, and spreadsheets, the processor should be able to create files that can be moved to disk and read by these other programs. In other words, it is important that the program that is selected will meet all pertinent needs. Further reference to word processing will be included in Chapter 13, Preparing the Research Report.

To date, the computer has been discussed as a tool for:

1. conducting information searches, and

2. word processing.

The third primary use of the computer to the practitioner-researcher is in the area of **data analysis.** Prerequisite to their use for this purpose, however, is that the investigator know enough about the statistical processes available to know which of them is appropriate to the problem at hand. Over and over again the author's experience has revealed that, when graduate students first perform analyses by hand, they have a better understanding of the results than is the case when, initially, they learn to rely upon the use of a computer. For example, if several chi square measures have been computed with paper and pencil (perhaps with the assistance of a simple calculator), students then have the knowledge and understanding necessary to effectively gravitate to the computer in order to compute subsequent chi square analyses.

The computer can be used to calculate the results, but the researcher must be able to describe what these results mean. Investigators must also be mindful of accuracy when entering the data. An expression often used by programmers, *garbage in, garbage out,* applies to anyone who is in a position to enter data into a computer (or, for that matter, a calculator). For example, if a computer is instructed to compute an ANOVA for distributions of *ordinal* data, it will *not* know of your theoretical error and will proceed to perform the analysis regardless.

All of the statistical procedures detailed in Part II, Descriptive Research Methods, and Part III, Experimental Research Methods, can be performed by computer. With that as introduction, this chapter will move into a discussion of computerized data analysis. The topics that will be covered in the remainder of the chapter are selecting hardware and software, statistical packages, formatting, and computer practicum.

SELECTING HARDWARE AND SOFTWARE

As equipment improves, so does the software (the programs that are written for the computer). Emerging from the *hyperbole* of advancing technology is the choice researchers must make about the **hardware** and software that should be purchased. For a partial list of terms that an investigator should know as she endures the vernacular of the computer trade, see Figure 12–1. Although the list in that figure is not exhaustive, a knowledge of the terms in the list will arm you with some of the jargon that will be commonly used when you are "interfacing" with representatives of the computer industry.

With regard to making purchasing decisions, the questions that should be addressed when choosing computer *hardware* include the following.

1. What is the history of reliability for the machine?

2. What is the nature of the guarantee?

3. Are manufacturer's representatives conveniently located and reliable in repairing malfunctions?

4. Are adequate peripherals and special equipment available to meet the needs of the practitioner-researcher?

5. Are features (for example, external ports, memory, peripherals, and so on) available at minimum cost?

6. Will the machine interface with other machines for generalizable applications (for example, hookups, language, and so on)?

7. Is the operating and programmable language easy to learn and compatible with other machines in the workplace?

8. Is the machine easy to load and initiate operation?

9. Are adequate operating manuals and training available for the practitioner-researcher (or other primary users)?

10. Is unit self-contained—that is, relatively free of connectives, ribbons, and wires?

Figure 12–1: **Selected Glossary of Computer Terminology**

Terms	Definitions
Baud Rate	Rate (in bits per second) of reception or transmission of information between computers or between terminals and computers.
Bit	A term derived from the words *binary digit,* the single digit of a binary number, either 0 or 1.
Boot	The process of loading or transferring information from a disk (or other source) into the computer via the disk drive.
Bytes	The smallest meaningful memory units of a computer. The number of bytes available for storage is usually expressed in: 1. thousands, or *kilobytes;* thus, 16K refers to 16,000 bytes of available memory, 32K refers to 32,000 bytes, and so on; or 2. millions, or *megabytes;* thus, 16MB refers to 16,000,000 bytes of available memory, and so on.
Central Processing Unit (CPU)	The part of the computer that does the computing.
Control Program for Microcomputers	CP/M is an operating system program (developed by Digital Research Corporation) that enables different brands of microcomputers to share software.
Database	A software program that converts a computer system into a tool for organizing, storing, and printing out information. The term is also used to refer to the tool that is created when a database program is loaded into a computer.
Disk Drive	The piece of computer equipment that allows the computer to receive information stored on disks and to store information on disks. The computer, via the disk drives, reads material off disks and writes on those disks much like a cassette player tapes music on a cassette.
Disk Operating System	DOS enables the computer to control and communicate with one or more disk drives.
Dot Matrix Printer	A printer that uses a series of electrically hammered pins to create characters composed of a pattern of dots.
Formatted Disk	A disk that has its magnetic field rearranged on a particular computer, so that it is receptive to receiving files created on that computer. A blank disk needs to be formatted before it can receive information from a computer or give information to that computer. Since each computer (for example, Apple, IBM, and so on) formats a disk in its own particular way, a disk that has been formatted on an Apple will have to be reformatted

Figure 12–1: **Selected Glossary of Computer Terminology (continued)**

	on an IBM before it can store IBM files. If a double-sided disk is to be used on both sides on the Apple, it must be formatted and notched on both sides.
Hardware	The physical components of the computer system, including computer, disk drives, keyboard, monitor, and printer.
Interface	The relationship, boundary, or overlap between systems or system components; a device that facilitates that relationship.
Laser Printer	A printer that transfers information to hard copy by employing a ruby laser to burn the characters onto the surface of the paper.
Mainframe	A centralized computer that handles the processing needs of a large number of individuals at a facility (for example, college, hospital, military installation, and so on).
Microcomputer	A self-contained personal computer (PC) that sits on a desk; designed to be used by one person at a time.
Modem	A device that allows a telephone hookup of a smaller computer or remote terminal to another computer. Information is transmitted through telephone lines between the machines.
Mouse	A handheld device connected to the input port of a computer which, by moving it across a flat surface, controls a pointer on the screen that selects functions or options.
Random Access Memory	RAM refers to the internal space (or memory) the computer allocates for temporary storage of information (which will be erased if power to the computer system is interrupted). Material created in RAM may be permanently stored on a disk.
Read Only Memory	ROM refers to the computer's permanent built-in memory that contains the basic instructions that enable programs to be written and executed.
RF Modulator	A device employed to convert the video signal from the computer to a radio frequency (RF) signal that can be received by a standard television set.
Software	The programs that control the operations of the computer. Examples include word processor, data analysis, and educational programs.
Terminal	A device that functions as a communication tool for a mainframe computer. It consists of a keyboard (for input) and a monitor (for output).
Voice Synthesizer	A process by which a computer converts an electronic code into sounds recognizable as words.

11. What is the basic cost of the machine compared with others on the market with similar features?

Included among the concerns one should have when selecting *software* are the following.

1. Is the program (for example, data analysis) going to meet the needs of the investigator in terms of the analytical functions that are required?

2. Is the program compatible with the computer hardware and peripherals?

3. Is the program "glitch free" so that it will *not* require reprogramming to operate?

4. Are there add-on modules?

5. Are supplemental materials available?

6. Are functions menu-driven (for example, user-friendly)?

7. Are hard-copy printouts of records easily attainable?

8. Does the software have branching feedback and reinforcement functions?

9. Are records retained automatically?

10. Does it enable researchers to execute optional control over entered data?

11. Is field-test information on use with various populations available?

12. Is the cost of the software within budget?

In addition to making decisions on hard- and software purchases, investigators frequently attempt to find ways to integrate the systems that they have. The importance of being able to integrate hardware, however, is not a product of recent years. A major project was undertaken by a colleague of the author's some time ago (Otto, 1989). He had finished editing an anthology of philosophy papers and mailed it off to Reidel Press in The Netherlands. The book, called *Perspectives on Mind,* was a massive undertaking in several ways. It involved coordinating and editing the work of twenty-eight authors with extremely varied philosophical perspectives and writing styles, and required the editorial writing of "unifying commentary" around each paper. And, as if the challenges having to do with content of the book were not sufficiently formidable, it was agreed to send the publisher a "camera-ready" manuscript. This meant that Otto had to produce pages, per specifications, that could be photographed and printed directly (without typesetting by the publisher). The first step was to get all the original papers typed on an available DECmate II word processor in the most expedient way possible. What came to be selected for this task was a Kurzweil reader for the blind.

A few years earlier, an electronic marvel had been donated to Plymouth State College. Intended for use by those who are visually impaired, the Kurzweil machine is an "omni-font" reader—that is, it "learns" to read any style of type (providing the print is clear and uniform). Of particular value to the visually impaired, is that the machine is programed to *scan* printed documents and to *read* them aloud.

 NOTE: The Kurzweil reader was not designed for data entry, although the Kurzweil company subsequently built and marketed omni-font data entry machines.

Coincidental with the time of Otto's interest in finding a way to do electronic data entry for the anthology, it was discovered that the college's Kurzweil reader could also double as a data-entry machine. Instructions were procured from the Kurzweil company on how to configure a cable that would connect the reading machine to the DECmate microcomputer. Directions in hand, the Office of Computer Services quickly tailored one to do the job. Since the reader could only transmit the words electronically as fast as it could speak them, the "voice" was set to the lowest volume and the greatest speed. The machine *muttered* its way through page after page of philosophical text (ironically, a text dealing with the possibility of machine intelligence), simultaneously dumping it onto DECmate floppy disks.

The task complete, the manuscript was sent off to the publisher in a timely fashion. Much human effort had been preserved through the collaboration of two independent hardware systems. More important, a creative process of integration was introduced to solve a problem.

In the 1980s, microcomputers were also beginning to assume greater roles within the laboratory portion of college psychology classes, particularly with regard to online data collection. In the simplest cases, stimulus materials (for instance, verbal items to be memorized) could be displayed on monitors and individual responses collected through the keyboard. In those cases where precise durations of stimuli were required, or response latencies had to be timed, researchers were using real-time clock boards that maintained time to the nearest millisecond. However, the situation became more complex in developmental, animal, or physiological research because data had to be *input* through some interface or analog-to-digital device. Kulig (1989) interfaced several operant learning chambers for use in his course entitled "Learning," and used Apple II and IBM PC microcomputers. Both were tailor-made for laboratory interfacing, since their pop-top "open architecture" permitted flexibility and experimenter control in interfacing the computer to the "real world."

Before describing the system, it would be useful to define a few phenomena from the laboratory portion of that course which students regularly encountered. In an operant chamber, rats are trained to press levers (bars) to obtain food reward. Once the rats are bar pressing, a variety of manipulations can be introduced to study their effects upon learning processes. The most common manipulations studied in introductory courses in "Learning" are "schedules of reinforcement," since the behavior of animals changes under different schedules. In *ratio* schedules, the animal must press a lever some number of times for each reward. The number of bar presses required for reward can be fixed, or can vary randomly around a mean value. A "variable ratio 10" schedule, for instance, means that the number of bar presses required for each food pellet varies but, in the long run, converges on the expected value of 10.

NOTE: Variable ratio schedules are in effect in human gambling and lottery situations, since the number of responses (pulling the lever or buying a ticket) required for monetary reward varies randomly from an expected value predetermined by gambling and lottery officials. Variable ratio schedules produce the highest response rate as well as the greatest resistance to extinction (that is, stopping when the reward is removed) in both humans and animals.

Interval differ from *ratio* schedules in that, in the former, a reward is delivered for the *first* response occurring after a time period but, again, may be fixed or variable around an average value. In a *fixed* interval schedule, animals learn to withhold their responses until the interval nears its end, while a *variable* interval schedule produces a slow, steady response rate.

In the laboratory, Kulig interfaced an Apple II with a Med Associates LVB to train as well as maintain several animals on various schedules, simultaneously and all online. He had one animal on a *fixed* interval schedule, a second on a *variable* interval schedule, and a third on *continuous* reinforcement. The levers from the chambers acted as switches that delivered ground input to the interface inputs.

NOTE: Note: The software used a PEEK command to sample the memory address of the interface. When the returned value exceeded zero, he had a bar press. (If more than one animal pressed a bar at the same time, the returned value was decoded in software to determine which levers had been pressed.) Delivering food pellets was done by POKEing the address of the interface that controlled power for the pellet dispensers.

Dealing with the various schedules was a simple BASIC "language" problem, specifically:

1. For *ratio* schedules, one would simply increment a counter for all those animals on ratio schedules, and compare the count with the number required for reinforcement. For *variable* ratios, the investigator used the expression INT (RND(1) * 2 * N + .5), where RND is random between zero and one, to generate a variable number that converges upon *N* over a long series of numbers.

2. For *interval* schedules, the investigator used a Mountain Hardware real-time clock that is able to maintain millisecond accuracy time independent of the computer and accessed as a string variable through an IN# <slot> command. Variable *interval* times were generated with RND statements.

As a consequence of the experience, it was realized that even those with rather modest BASIC and technical skills would be able to get similar interfaces up and running inexpensively. But, in response to expressed needs, manufacturers are now providing interface hard- and software systems. Further, peripheral single-board computers with their own RAM/EPROM currently exist that can interface to the "real world." Inspired by competition between manufacturers, turn-key hardware/software enhancements for school laboratories are upon us.

With the early call for compatibility between hard- and software systems, it was but a matter of time before significant improvements were advanced. A perusal of industry catalogs from month to month will reveal the extent to which cyberspace-like technology is changing. The challenge for all of us is to stay current with these advancements. Indeed, "the future isn't what it used to be."

STATISTICAL PACKAGES

For many studies, the simple, inexpensive, handheld calculator that costs less than $10 will continue to be the tool of choice for some investigators. This is particularly so when sample sizes are relatively small and the computation requirements are minor (such as means, percentiles, and square roots). As confidence is acquired and the requirements for analysis become more demanding, one may elect to move toward a more sophisticated model. For under $40–50, one can find programmable calculators that, in addition to the aforementioned capabilities, will make such statistical computations as standard deviation and regression. Information can also be stored within these devices for subsequent use.

When the nature of the investigation requires analyses that are more complex, however, the use of a computer becomes imperative. In this regard, researchers will select either a mainframe or personal computer (PC).

Mainframe computers are very large, handle data quickly, and are capable of processing and storing large quantities of data simultaneously. However, unless the research offers the potential for numerous subjects to be entering responses from various terminals at the same time, the latter feature is not particularly important. If you are a student of, or employed by, a college or university, you will likely have a choice between a mainframe and a personal computer. Others will probably prefer to use personal computers. For one thing, PCs are readily available for use within the home and the office, or while traveling.

One of the things that computers can do *best* is handle large quantities of numbers. This is what makes them ideal for analyzing volumes of data produced by research. Values can be analyzed, sorted, graphed, printed, and manipulated in any number of ways. All the computer needs is for you to give it directions. That is the one thing that computers cannot yet do. They cannot make decisions about what analyses to apply. A computer must have a program that will guide it through the operations. It does not know whether designated columns consist of attitude, bowling, height, weight, or situp scores. All it does is respond to the commands that tell it what to do. This is why it is important for the investigator to know enough about the procedure to understand what the computer is doing, and to have a general idea about what the findings should be. With recent technological advances, a personal computer has the capability to serve most requirements, including those of listing, ordering, and analyzing data.

A **database management system (DMS)** provides formats for organizing information. These systems can alphabetize, arrange scores in order, as well as select and print records. In addition, they can easily be integrated with word processing programs. This feature is particularly valued for *qualitative* analyses and general report writing (see Chapter 13, Preparing the Research Report).

In addition to performing information organization functions, **spreadsheet** programs are able to complete more advanced mathematical calculations. An advantage of the electronic spread sheet is that, should a researcher *enter* a revised set of data for a subject, not only will that individual's original score be corrected, the group average and other statistical findings that depend upon that entry will be recalculated as well.

When practitioner-researchers are conducting investigations in the classroom, they may want to combine database management systems, electronic spreadsheets, and statistical programs through a single entry. With programs such as *Systat,* the investigator can enter data, select from among various options, and, based upon those selections, have analyses carried out. She can then electronically transfer the results to graphics and word processing programs.

There are numerous packages on the market that will perform these functions. For the most part, it is a matter of compatibility and familiarity that will govern the statistics program one will choose. While the systems described here have the capability to treat data in a variety of ways, they are somewhat limited in the scope of the functions that some researchers would hope to have performed. In this regard, one might look to one of the comprehensive statistical packages.

One of the most popular and available is **Statistical Products and Service Solutions (SPSS).** Used with mainframe and IBM-compatible personal computers, it does not depend on the user having prior knowledge of programming or an extensive background in mathematics. Containing statistical analyses that range from the very basic to the complex, SPSS requires only that one follow the instructions provided within the manuals accompanying the software. The following is a partial listing of modules, with corresponding *websites,* that are currently available:

1. SPSS Professional Statistics
   - http://www.spss.com/software/spss/base/pro1.htm
   - Includes nonlinear regression, logistic, and other advanced regression techniques, including weighted least squares and two-stage least squares.

2. SPSS Advanced Statistics
   - http://www.spss.com/software/spss/base/Win75/advspec.html
   - Includes multivariate techniques: variance component analysis, GLM, Kaplan-Meier estimation, Cox regression, life table analyses, hiloglinear, and a matrix language.

3. SPSS Tables
   - http://www.spss.com/software/spss/base/table1.htm
   - Includes complex stub-and-banner tables, contingency tables, and multiple-response data displays. This module provides over thirty-five statistical procedures that can be calculated within tables automatically.

4. SPSS Trends
   - http://www.spss.com/software/spss/base/trend1.htm
   - Includes forecasting with time-series analyses: multiple curve-fitting and smoothing models and methods for estimating autoregressive functions. ARIMA modeling techniques are presented, including X11ARIMA and four other estimation procedures.

5. SPSS Categories
   - http://www.spss.com/software/spss/base/cat1.htm
   - Includes processes for analyzing categorical data, and measuring preferences. Performs conjoint analysis and optimal scaling, including correspondence analysis.

6. SPSS CHAID
   - http://www.spss.com/software/spss/base/chaid1.htm
   - Automatically segments a population into subgroups sharing similar characteristics and presents them in a *tree* diagram. Develops predictive models and screens out extraneous predictor variables.

7. SPSS Exact Tests
   - http://www.spss.com/software/spss/base/exact1.htm
   - More than thirty exact tests cover the entire spectrum of nonparametric and categorical data problems for small or large data sets. They include one-sample, two-sample, and K-sample tests on independent or related samples, goodness-of-fit tests, tests of independence in RxC contingency tables, and tests on measures of association.

8. SPSS Missing Value Analysis
   - http://www/spss.com/software/spss/base/mva1.htm
   - Includes statistical algorithms that let the user estimate summary statistics and impute missing values. MVA makes it possible to examine data from several angles by using six diagnostic reports that uncover missing data patterns.

9. SPSS Amos
   - http://www.spss.com/software/spss/base/Amos/amos1.htm
   - Includes a statistical program for mean and covariance structure modeling.

Modules are also available for graphics (SPSS Diamond) and sample-size analysis (SamplePower). These and the nine modules described above are for SPSS 7.5 for Windows. The minimum requirement for using the modules is a 486 IBM-compatible computer, with a recommended RAM of 16 MB.

NOTE: With the exception of SPSS Amos, SPSS CHAID, and SPSS Diamond, the programs are also available on CD-ROM.

Intended as illustrative of what is available in the software market, the reader should find solace in knowing that she should be able to find virtually any statistic that is needed in order to solve a research problem. With regard to the statistics introduced within Parts II and III of this book, the following are found within these or alternative SPSS software packages that are available:

1. Frequency distributions
2. Graphics
3. Measures of central tendency (that is, mean, median, and mode)
4. Percentiles
5. Measures of variability (for example, standard deviation)
6. Confidence intervals
7. Chi square
8. Pearson product-moment correlation
9. Regression
10. Coefficient of contingency
11. Phi coefficient
12. Student's *t* test
13. Analysis of variance

14. Scheffe test

15. Factor analysis

16. Time series analysis

In addition, SPSS software is being upgraded regularly to:

1. Refine the programs and make them more efficient, and

2. Include statistical procedures not included in the above lists.

Although improvement in present status is always desirable, packages in production by SPSS and other software manufacturers currently address the analytical requirements appropriate to studies with which most researchers are going to be involved. To find out more about the various statistical packages/programs that are available and, specifically, what these packages have to offer, it is recommended that you refer to:

1. The Recommended Readings found at the end of this chapter

2. Specialists found within computer departments of schools and colleges

3. Representatives of software manufacturers

4. The mailing address reported in Figure 12–2

Regardless of the software that the investigator eventually decides to employ, it is necessary that her data be arranged in some systematic format. While there are statistical packages that allow more latitude than do others, some degree of formatting is required. It is to this end that the following section is devoted.

FORMATTING

In advance of collecting the actual data, it is very important that a suitable recording form be prepared (see Chapter 5, Selecting Instruments of Assessment, and Chapter 6, Survey Procedures). With some instruments, the subject *and* the investigator will enter the information. Others will require that the investigator *or* the subject enter the information. Regardless of the individuals responsible, it is important that the responses be recorded in a way that can be easily entered into a computer. Whether this will occur, however, is largely a function of the form itself. For example, if the instrument employs fixed-choice items, the scorer will have a much easier time

Figure 12–2: **Mailing address for SPSS Statistical Software**

Software Company	Address
Statistical Products and Service Solutions (SPSS)	SPSS, Incorporated 444 North Michigan Avenue Chicago, Illinois 60611-3962 Telephone: (800) 543-5815 FAX: (800) 841-0064

coding the responses for computer entry than would be the case if the questions were open-ended. For an illustration of both types of items, refer to Chapter 6 and the following:

- *Fixed-choice item:*

    Directions. *Place a check mark in the space provided to the left of the descriptor that you believe is the <u>most important</u> personal characteristic of a teacher.*

    ____ Appreciative
    ____ Considerate
    ____ Relaxed
    ____ Systematic

- *Open-ended item:*

    Directions: *In the space below, indicate what you believe is the <u>most important</u> personal characteristic of a teacher.*

    _____
    _____
    _____
    _____

Although open-ended items have their appropriate place in research, they do not lend themselves to "ease of analysis." Further, with fixed-choice items, the investigator can test the perception of the subjects within the parameters of specific descriptors. In the open-ended item above, subjects would respond to the question without knowledge of those parameters.

 NOTE: As an alternative to entering the data into a computer via a keyboard, the investigator may want to direct the subjects to enter their responses directly onto answer sheets that can be "read" by a scanner (for example, a Scantron machine). An **optical mark reader (OMR),** however, requires fixed-choice responses.

In the instance of the item on personal characteristics of teachers, the investigator would assign a number (1, 2, 3, or 4), in order, to each alternative. The subjects would make their selection and, using a soft-lead pencil, so indicate by filling in a corresponding space on a computerized answer sheet. In preparing alternatives, however, be sure their number does not exceed the number of spaces, per item, that are allocated on the answer sheet.

When contemplating the method one wants to use to analyze data, it is important to recognize that a statistical program is nothing more than a tool. The investigator communicates with this tool by way of commands. Simply stated, a *command* is a word or group of words to which the program will react. If a computer is going to be used for data analysis, the researcher will be required to make use of a *text editor*. An editor is a program that lets the user create or modify files, and store new files containing the modified data. When an investigator enters data into the computer herself, the editor is used with the data files. An editor is a basic tool for working with the files. It is important that you learn how to use it. If an editor does *not* exist with the command file, one must be created before a statistical analysis can be undertaken.

> **NOTE:** Statistical Products and Service Solutions (SPSS) has an editor that is used with its command files. The command files contain the directions on how to analyze the data.

When **formatting** the information for data entry, it is very important that the investigator consider the following guidelines:

1. Place the subject identification number (ID) at the beginning of each line.

2. Line data up so that the identified categories of information will always appear in the same position on each line.

3. Never place the data for more than one subject on the same line.

4. Save the data frequently.

In Figure 12–3, you will find data for a single subject who is participating in a study on the relationship between Standardized Writing Test (SWT) and Department Writing Assessment (DWA) scores (Richey, 1997). In Figure 12–4, you will find a **coding** of that data for subsequent entry into a computer.

Each statistical package has various commands that must be followed in order to utilize its program. Assuming that an SPSS program were going to be used to analyze the standardized (SWT) and department (DWA) writing assessment scores, the following commands would be among those that the investigator would need to use in order to initiate and complete the analytical transaction:

- **Title command**—assigns a label that will be placed at the top of each printed output page. A title is an important reference point in that the investigator may want to refer back to the data set in order to introduce additions or deletions or to "request" alternative analyses.

- **Data List command**—attaches a label designation to each variable, and tells the computer in which column to find it.

- **Correlation command**—tells the computer that the investigator wants to calculate a Pearson product-moment correlation coefficient.

- **Statistics command**—allows the investigator to identify other analyses that she wants the computer to calculate while it is processing the correlation coefficient that has been requested.

Once the information file is complete and carefully entered, the data are now ready to be analyzed. It is important that all entries be checked thoroughly. As indicated earlier, the computer will not be able to determine whether the number 02 was entered for a male subject (when it should have been 01). The computer will simply proceed to run the analysis whether the entries were right or wrong.

In summary:

1. Create a file that contains the data you want to analyze (see Table 12–1 in the "Computer Practicum" section of this chapter).

2. Create a command file that gives the computer directions for data analysis.

Figure 12–3: **Profile of Sample Subject in Study on College Writing Assessment Program**

1. Subject Number

$$\underline{0\ \ 0\ \ 0\ \ 1}$$

2. Date of Birth

$$\underline{0\ 2}\quad\quad\underline{2\ 8}\quad\quad\underline{1\ 9\ 8\ 0}$$

Numerical Equivalents of Months:

January	01	July	07
February	02	August	08
March	03	September	09
April	04	October	10
May	05	November	11
June	06	December	12

3. Gender

$$\underline{0\ 1}$$

Male	01
Female	02

4. Graduating Class

$$\underline{0\ 2}$$

Class of 2001	01
Class of 2002	02
Class of 2003	03
Class of 2004	04

4. Academic Major

$$\underline{0\ 3}$$

*Art	01	*Music	09
Business	02	*Natural Science	10
*Childhood Studies	03	Philosophy	11
Computer Science	04	*Physical Education	12
*English	05	Psychology	13
*Foreign Languages	06	Recreation	14
*Health	07	*Social Science	15
*Mathematics	08	Undecided	16

*Teacher-education programs

5. SWT Score

$$\underline{4\ 0}$$

Score range: 00–50

6. DWA Score

$$\underline{2\ 7}$$

Score range: 00–32

Figure 12–4: **Coded Data Ready for Computer Entry**

0001 02281980 1 0203 4027	. . . for the subject described in Figure 12–3.
0002 12101979 2 0207 3825	. . . for the second subject, a female, born on December 10, 1979, scheduled to graduate in the year 2002 with a major in health. Her SWT score was 38, and the DWA score was 25.
. . . and so on for all the other subjects in the study.	

3. Instruct the computer to run the program.

4. Review the output *listing* created by the entry of the data, commands, and analysis. This can be observed on the terminal screen or on a printout. Such an examination will enable the investigator to note errors that may need correction. While some errors may be obscured by the summary information that is provided, others are more readily detectable. If there have been no input errors, if commands were written appropriately for the analyses that were desired, there should not be any problems (short of a computer virus or electronic breakdown).

✓CHECKPOINT

Using the information in Figure 12–3, read the following number codes:

0003 04071978 2 0310 4120

Answer

The code numbers would be read as: This is the third entry line for a female subject born on April 7, 1978, who expects to graduate in 2003 with a major in natural science. Her SWT score was 41, and her DWA score was 20.

If you were able to recognize all of the elements, congratulations are due. It appears that you are ready to proceed. On the other hand, if you made two or more errors, it is recommended that you go back to Figure 12–3 to see if you can account for them.

 NOTE: It was not necessary that you identified the individual elements in the same order as that presented in the answer. That order is a logical order, however, in that the information is presented in an order that corresponds with the order of the codes.

Whenever you are determining the number of code columns for a particular variable, be sure to have a sufficient number of them to account for the *total* number of possibilities. In other words, if there were going to be more than 9,999 subjects, having but *four* subject columns would not be sufficient. Instead of leaving spaces between selected data columns (as is indicated earlier), Vockell and Asher (1995) suggest inserting zeros. They feel that, with the additional zeros, it is more likely that the assigned values for each subject will be aligned appropriately and lead to fewer errors when data are entered into the computer. The writer of this book feels that, by leaving the spaces, it is easier to track the *clusters* of numbers as they are being "typed" into the computer. Whichever model one elects to follow, exercising care during data entry is critical. If errors are made, any result that the computer offers will also be incorrect, as will the conclusions and inferences that follow.

Now it is time to apply the principles introduced in this chapter to a sample research practicum.

COMPUTER PRACTICUM

For the scenario that follows, it should be assumed by the reader that all pertinent elements of Phase 1 and Phase 2 of the research design have been completed.

Topic: Writing Assessment

With consideration to improving student writing as an overriding goal, the immediate research objective of the Department of Education is threefold, namely:

1. to assess the writing abilities of teacher-education candidates as measured by a writing assessment instrument that has been developed by the Department of Education, hereafter referred to as the DWA;

2. to assess the results of a standardized writing test (SWT) that is required of all students as a condition of admission; and

3. to correlate the results using appropriate analytical techniques.

In addition to assisting the Department of Education to get a clearer picture of student writing in order to more intelligently plan course requirements, any relationship that is revealed between the DWA and the SWT scores will contribute to the evidence useful in determining whether it continues to be necessary to require teacher-education candidates to take the departmental writing examination.

The standardized writing test (SWT), scored by a jury of "experts" selected by its publisher, is graded within a range of 00–50. The department writing assessment instrument (DWA) is scored analytically by selected members of the Department Writing Assessment Committee, and is graded within a range of 00–32 (see Figure 12–5).

Permission has been granted from students and administrators to:

1. access the scores of the SWT for all incoming students, and

2. administer the DWA to all first-year students.

It has been decided that an SPSS 7.5 for Windows (microcomputer) program will be used to analyze the data. Pursuant to specifications, pertinent commands are given

Figure 12–5: **Sample Writing Assessment Rubric**

PLYMOUTH STATE COLLEGE
Department of Education
Writing Assessment for First-Year Students

Name: _____ Date: _____

SNN: _____/ _____/ _____

Your writing assessment essay has been evaluated by faculty in the Department of Education. The grids below will help you to identify your writing strengths and your challenge areas. Your writing was scored by *two* different faculty members (selected at random). The total score for each assessment is provided below the corresponding grids, and is based upon the following four elements:

I = Idea development
O = Organization
E = Expression (sentence variety and vocabulary)
M = Mechanics (spelling, punctuation, capitalization, sentence structure, usage)

	4	3	2	1			4	3	2	1
I						I				
O						O				
E						E				
M						M				

Score:____   Score:____

Combined Score: _____

To determine your total assessment score, combine the two scores from the above grids. Find your score in the ranges listed below and follow the directions in the *You must register for* column.

If your *combined score* is:	You *must* register for:
0–18	EN120, English Composition, Sections 14 or 15 (Education faculty signature required). Note: (1) Do *not* register for RL 210, Language Arts and Literature. (2) It is *required* that you use the Reading and Writing Lab.
19–25	EN120, English Composition, Sections *other than* 14 and 15. RL210, Language Arts and Literature. Note: It is *suggested* that you use the Reading and Writing Lab.
26–32	EN120, English Composition, Sections *other than* 14 and 15. RL210, Language Arts and Literature.

Adapted with permission of the Department of Education Writing Assessment Committee, Plymouth State College.

to *correlate* the SWT and DWA for students who are majoring in *childhood studies.* The findings for this relationship are displayed as Table 12–1.

NOTE: "." is printed because, as SWT is correlated with SWT, and DWA is correlated with DWA, a perfect positive relationship is automatic. After all, each pair represents the *same* set of scores. The computer reads this circumstance as an impossible format for a calculation.

The **display** in Table 12–1 is a *sample* matrix wherein each cell of the table has three numbers. The first is the value of the coefficient (*r*), the second is the number (*N*) to calculate it, and the third is the observed significance level (*P* or *p*). Since the observed *p* is lower than .05 (you will remember earlier reference to .05 level of confidence), the investigator accepts the hypothesis that there is a linear relationship between the two variables. If the researcher does *not* know in advance whether the pair of variables are positively or negatively related, she should use a two-tailed test. When the coefficient is a large positive or a large negative value, a finding of significance (*p*) for linearity would ordinarily follow.

NOTE: When using the SPSS PEARSON CORR command, if the investigator does not specify that a two-tailed test is desired, she will automatically get a one-tailed test analysis.

There are other correlation analyses that could be conducted with the profile presented in Figure 12–3. Among these are the following:

1. A correlation between SWT and DWA for *all* students
2. A correlation between SWT and DWA for students enrolled in teacher-education programs

Table 12–1: **Sample Correlation Display for SWT and DWA Scores Generated by One Hundred and Ten Childhood Studies Majors**

FILE: 1997 Writing Assessment
PEARSON CORRELATION COEFFICIENTS

	SWT	DWA
SWT	1.0000 (110) P = .	.7485 (110) P = .000
DWA	.7485 (110) P = .000	1.0000 (110) P = .

(COEFFICIENT / (CASES) / 2-TAILED SIG)
"." It is PRINTED IF A COEFFICIENT CANNOT BE COMPUTED

3. A *biserial* correlation between gender and total scores of SWT

4. A *biserial* correlation between gender and total scores of DWA

5. A *tetrachoric* correlation between SWT scores (29 and below, 30 or higher) and DWA scores (18 and below, 19 or higher) for students who are majoring in childhood studies

CHECKPOINT

Identify five other examples of *tetrachoric* correlations that could be computed with the data presented. Should you feel it necessary to review the characteristics and requirements of tetrachoric procedures, see Chapter 7, Correlation Procedures.

Answers

While there are a number of possible tetrachoric analyses that could be computed with these data, the following are offered as illustrative of possibilities:

1. SWT scores (29 and below, 30 or higher) and DWA scores (18 and below, 19 or higher) for *all* students

2. SWT scores (29 and below, 30 or higher) and DWA scores (18 and below, 19 or higher) for students who are enrolled in teacher-education programs

3. SWT scores (29 and below, 30 or higher) for all students, and those enrolled in teacher-education programs

4. DWA scores (18 and below, 19 or higher) for all students, and those enrolled in teacher-education programs

5. Students who *are* and *are not* childhood studies majors, and SWT scores (29 and below, 30 or higher)

6. Students who *are* and *are not* childhood studies majors, and DWA scores (18 and below, 19 or higher)

7. Students who *are* and *are not* graduating, and SWT scores (29 and below, 30 or higher)

8. Students who *are* and *are not* graduating, and DWA scores (18 and below, 19 or higher)

From what you have read in Part II, Descriptive Research Methods, and Part III, Experimental Research Methods, you know that there are analyses other than correlations that can be applied to the data described in the scenario of this chapter. The discussion in this section will end here, however, and you are referred to the Recommended Laboratory Assignments (specifically, question 15) following the Summary in this chapter.

SUMMARY

From conducting information searches and word processing, to the complexities of information analysis, computer programs are available that can add to the efficiency of the investigative process. In particular, this chapter was written to assign emphasis to but one of these functions—that is, electronic data analysis. To do so, however, required brief reference to the evolution of events that contributed so markedly to the computer systems we currently enjoy.

A difficult task for all of us is to be in a position to make informed selections from the many rosters of soft- and hardware options available. To understand the match between the alternatives and what is needed, will continue to require a great deal of our attention and the attention of those who are advising us. In order to introduce information pertinent to the selection and use of computers, reference in this chapter was made to: terminology, purchasing criteria, system interfacing, statistical packages, formatting, the structure and function of representative commands, and a computer practicum.

To identify and discuss the many upgraded soft- and hardware packages entering the market on a monthly (if not weekly) basis, however, would prohibit closure. For more information, you are encouraged to examine the Recommended Readings at the end of the chapter, to talk with soft- and hardware specialists who are eager to represent the particulars of their products, and to meet with other practitioner-researchers who are qualified to make serious recommendations of their own.

With the complexities implicit to higher levels of data analysis, investigators may have to accept on faith that the formulas and computer programs do produce accurate results. The major role of the investigator is to establish and follow designs and protocol that will lead to an information base that is accurate, representative, and conducive to appropriate analytical treatment.

Part IV of this book, Postanalytical Considerations, is dedicated to addressing the results that emerge from one's study. The relevance of those results is limited, however, to the validity of all pertinent processes leading to the findings. It is for this reason that this chapter has been included within this part of the book. The next chapter proceeds to the next step in the hierarchy of events leading to the actual dissemination of results—that is, preparation of the research report.

 RECOMMENDED LABORATORY ASSIGNMENTS

1. Review the recommended readings.

2. Arrange to meet with fellow graduate students and colleagues in order to discuss mutual and unique experiences with the Internet.

3. Of the following systems, acquire user-friendly competence with any of them you have not accessed:

  a. Archie and Ftp

  b. Gopher

  c. Veronica

  d. WAIS

  e. WWW

4. Arrange to meet with representatives of the soft- and hardware industries in order to discuss their recommendations in regard to your specific needs and interests. Include in your discussion such topics as the following:

   a. Compatibility/interfacing

   b. Baud rates

   c. Bytes

   d. Disk operating systems

   e. Formatting

   f. Modems

   g. Random access memory

   h. Read only memory

   Also, request to have demonstrations of statistical software packages, including no fewer than two produced by SPSS—that is, SPSS 7.5 for Windows (Microcomputers) and SPSSX (Mainframes).

5. Write to soft- and hardware distributors, and request that they put you on their mailing lists for catalogs and other literature.

6. Arrange to meet with a representative of the Computer Services Department of a local college, university, or other institution in order to see (and hear explanations of) its mainframe.

7. Make arrangements to access a *newsgroup* consisting of members having similar teaching, administration, or school counseling interests.

8. Acquire E-mail addresses from various professional colleagues, and arrange to communicate with them on topics of mutual concern.

9. A survey was conducted of fourth-year college students in order to examine their perceptions of the high school core requirement most valuable in preparing them for their college major. The four courses comprising the core are: English, Mathematics, Natural Science, and Social Science. Table 12–2 contains the responses from five of the candidates who participated in the investigation.

   a. Determine how you would code each of the variables.

   b. Using your coding scheme, code the data in the table.

Table 12–2: **Candidate Responses**

Subject	Gender	College	Preferred Major	Course
Johnson	Female	Northeastern	Teaching	Mathematics
Smith	Male	PSC	Business	Social Science
Anderson	Male	UNH	Liberal Arts	English
Wiseman	Female	Indiana	Teaching	English
Brooke	Female	Dartmouth	Business	Natural Science

10. Devise coding systems for each of the following:

    a. Number of credits completed at the conclusion of the junior year of high school

    b. Number of credits to complete a college major (B.A.) in English

    c. Number of points made in one game by starting players on a women's high school basketball team

    d. Favorite teacher in high school

    e. Number of prime sources used in a historical study on Montessori schools

11. Arrange to meet with fellow graduate students, colleagues, as well as school and nonschool employees in order to complete the following:

    a. Discuss the coding system arrived at in response to question 9.

    b. Determine if refinements need be made and, if so, revise the code plan.

    c. Determine the appropriate statistical measures to apply to the data.

    d. Analyze the findings with the use of a calculator only.

    e. Select a software package that would be appropriate to the analyses you would want to make.

    f. Run the analyses, and compare the results with those obtained with a calculator in (d), above.

12. If there are discrepancies in the answers to questions 11(d) and 11(f), track and account for the source of the errors.

13. Arrange to visit an institution that has a Kurzweil reading machine. Request that a demonstration of the unit be provided for you.

14. For the data-analysis items in the Recommended Laboratory Assignments proposed in previous chapters, arrange to have the same data analyzed through appropriate statistical software, and compare the results. Include in your analyses the following:

    a. Chapter 6, Survey Procedures, question 4

    b. Chapter 7, Correlation Procedures, question 4

    c. Chapter 9, Single-Group Designs, questions 4 and 7

    d. Chapter 10, Two-Group Designs, question 4

    e. Chapter 11, Other Experimental Procedures, question 3(c)

15. Arrange to meet with fellow graduate students and colleagues in order to discuss alternatives to a correlation procedure for analyzing the data for the scenario of this chapter. Include in your discussion the merits of each of the following:

    a. Measures of central tendency (that is, mean, median, mode)

    b. Measures of variability (for example, standard deviation)

    c. Nonindependent *t* test

    d. ANOVA

16. Arrange to meet with fellow graduate students and colleagues in order to collaborate on a research project that would include the planning stages of Phase

1 and Phase 2; then, administer the study, complete a data analysis (employing appropriate software), prepare your report (refer to Chapter 13, Preparing the Research Report), and make a formal presentation at a conference or some other professional meeting.

 # RECOMMENDED READINGS

Capron, H. L. (1996). *Computers: Tools for an information age* (4th ed.). Reading, MA: Benjamin/Cummings.

Christian, K. (1994). *How Windows work.* Emeryville, CA: Ziff-Davis Press.

Decker, R., & Hirshfield, S. (1995). *The object concept.* Boston, MA: PWS.

Dvorak, J. C. (1994). *Dvorak predicts.* Berkeley, CA: Osborne McGraw-Hill.

Engst, A. C., Low, C. S., & Simm, M. A. (1995). *Internet starter kit for Windows* (2nd ed.). Indianapolis, IN: Hayden.

Frisbie, L. H. (1992). *STATPAK: Some common educational statistics* [Computer software]. Columbus, OH: Merrill.

Gates, B. (1995). *The road ahead.* New York: Penguin.

Gookin, D. (1993). *DOS for dummies* (2nd ed.). San Mateo, CA: IDG Books Wordwide.

Graur, R. T., & Barber, M. (1996). *Essentials of Windows '95: And essential computing concepts.* Saddle River, NJ; Prentice-Hall.

Huff, C., & Finholt, T. (Eds.). (1994). *Social issues in computing: Putting computing in its place.* New York: McGraw-Hill.

Kearsley, G., Hunter, B., & Furlong, M. (1992). *We teach with technology: New visions for education.* Wilsonville, OR: Franklin, Beedle.

Kiesler, S., Siegel, J., & McGuire, T. W. (1984). Social psychological aspects of computer-mediated communication. *American Psychologist, 39,* 1123–1134.

Lillie, D. L., Hannum, W. H., & Stuck, G. B. (1989). *Computers and effective instruction: Using computers and software in the classroom.* New York: Longman.

Magid, L. J. (1993). *The little PC book.* Berkeley, CA: Peachpit Press.

Marvasti, F. (1989). *PC-statistics: Version 2.1.* Wilsonville, OR: Franklin, Beedle.

Miller, H. (1988). *An administrator's manual for the use of microcomputers in the schools.* Saddle River, NJ: Prentice-Hall.

Nelson, K. N., & Pechar, G. S. (1995, March). *Computer-supported laboratory exercises for physical fitness assessment.* Paper presented at the Annual Eastern District Association of the American Alliance for Health, Physical Education, Recreation and Dance Convention, Springfield, MA.

Nogales, P. D., & McAllister, C. H. (1992). *AppleWorks for teachers.* Wilsonville, OR: Franklin, Beedle.

Norusis, M. J. (1987). *The SPSS guide to data analysis for SPSS-X.* Chicago, IL: SPSS.

Norusis, M. J. (1997). *The SPSS 7.5 guide to data analysis.* Chicago, IL: SPSS.

Potter, B., Maxwell, T., & Scott, B. (1993). *Visual Basic superbible* (2nd ed.). Corte Madera, CA: The Waite Group.

Schneider, G. M., & Gersting, J. L. (1995). *An invitation to computer science.* St Paul, MN: West.

Weitzman, E. A., & Miles, M. B. (1995). *Computer programs for qualitative data analysis: A software sourcebook.* Thousand Oaks, CA: Sage.

Weizenbaum, J. (1976). Computer power and human reason: From judgment to calculation. San Francisco, CA: Freeman.

Weverka, P. (1996). *Word 97 for Windows.* Foster City, CA: IDG Books.

REFERENCES

Bradley, J. C. (1995). *A quick guide to the Internet.* Boston, MA: ITP.

Kulig, J. (1989, Spring). Computers in the lab. *Computing at PSC, 1*(3), 2–5.

Otto, K. (1989, Spring). Technology and the anthology. *Computing at PSC, 1*(3), 6–7.

Richey, G. (1997, June). *A project to determine concurrent validity for the Plymouth State College Department of Education writing assessment: A proposal.* Unpublished document, Department of Education, Plymouth State College, Plymouth, NH.

Vockell, E. L., & Asher, J. W. (1995). *Educational research* (2nd ed.). Columbus, OH: Merrill.

CHAPTER 13

Preparing the Research Report

OBJECTIVES

After reading this chapter, you should be able to:

- Distinguish between the *format* and *style* of a written document.
- Identify no fewer than five references on format and style that are frequently used by colleges, universities, and journal publishers.
- Demonstrate familiarity with the *Publication Manual of the American Psychological Association.*
- Distinguish between *mechanical* and *conventional* practices with regard to the writing of reports.
- Distinguish between and provide illustrations for: sentence *coordination* and *subordination;* mixed sentence *structure* and *parallelism; adverbs* and *adjectives;* pronoun *agreement* and *clarity; subjective, objective,* and *passive* case; *passive* and *active* voice; *definitive* and *tentative* statements; *five* headings of manuscripts, per recommendations of APA; *bar graphs* and *histograms;* and *index* and *vita sheet.*

- Demonstrate appropriate APA-style reference citations for journal articles, books, references to an article within a book, ERIC documents, unpublished papers presented at conferences, and CD-ROM abstracts.
- Discuss the purpose of placing *key terms* at the beginning of a document.
- Identify and discuss the major components of a research report.
- Distinguish between topical headings for a journal article and a thesis.
- Identify and discuss the three major divisions of a graduate thesis or dissertation.
- Discuss the *structure* and *function* of an abstract.
- Discuss the composition of each of the following: title page, acceptance page, acknowledgment page, table of contents, list of tables, and list of figures.
- Discuss the composition of a research report, as it relates to each of the following: introduction, methods, findings, conclusions, and references.
- Identify and discuss the categories of information suitable for placement in an appendix.
- Discuss no fewer than ten factors that should be addressed when contemplating the publication of a research paper.
- Identify and discuss no fewer than six reasons why manuscripts are rejected for publication.
- Discuss no fewer than five reasons why delays exist between the acceptance of manuscripts and their actual publication.
- Define key terms, and answer the checkpoint questions.

KEY TERMS

Acceptance Page

Acknowledgment Page

Adjective

Adverb

Ampersand

Article Citation

Bar Graph

Bibliography

Body of the Report

Book Citation

Capitalization

Chapter Headings

Conclusions

Conventional Practice

Coordination

Definitive Statements

Direct Object

Discussion

Essential Definitions

Findings

INTRODUCTION

A research project is incomplete until the investigator communicates the procedures, findings, and implications of work accomplished. This requires that as much care go into the writing of the report as went into the design and administration of the research. For many, however, writing research is not an easy chore because it requires a transition from a literary writing style to a scientific writing style—a style that requires specificity and documentation. Because the investigator is integrating the ideas and findings emerging from other studies, the process becomes somewhat more complex. Since the writer will be drawing on the work of others (that is, related literature), the contributions of those individuals must be made known. One of the last things that a writer of research wants to do is engage in the practice of **plagiarism**—that is, to take another's work and pass it off as one's own. Not only is this illegal and unethical, but it also denies the readers of the report an opportunity to learn of other sources of information. One of the significant features of a research report is that it provides bibliographical information about related studies. The document that is produced should serve as a good reference source for other practitioner-researchers. But there are additional characteristics that also make for a quality research report.

While organization, expression, and good mechanics are essential for any form of writing, good research reports must also be precise. Writers of these reports should remember that those engaged in literature searches are attempting to get the facts (without being overwhelmed with *blaviation*).

NOTE: A coined expression, *blaviation* refers to a situation in which a writer of a research proposal or report uses multiple paragraphs to say what could have been said in a sentence or two. In short, a "statement of the problem" should not be written as would be a composition. Such practice may be construed as a measure of the researcher's lack of understanding about the nature of the specific problem.

Recently, the results of a bad writing contest held in Christchurch, New Zealand, were reported to a number of newspapers around the country via *The Associated Press* (Lilley, 1997). In reporting their selections, the judges said that reading one of the documents, in particular, "was like swimming through cold porridge." Here it is, the winner—or loser—of the academic bad writing contest:

> The visual is essentially pornographic, which is to say that it has its end in rapt, mindless fascination; thinking about its attributes becomes an adjunct to that, if it is unwilling to betray its object; while the most austere films necessarily draw their energy from the attempt to repress their own excess (rather than from the more thankless effort to discipline the viewer) (p 7A).

The researcher must be mindful of the fact that he is reporting something, *not* producing a document in the style of creative writing or a position paper. Each of these has its place, but *not* in a research report.

> **NOTE:** The author is reminded of an early draft of chapter one of his doctoral dissertation in which he wrote of the need to *satiate the needs of the populous.* Upon reading the statement, his Committee Chair asked him exactly what he meant. The author responded, *"to satisfy the needs of the public."* The Chair said, "Well, why don't you say so? After all, one can drive from Indiana to Florida by way of Canada. Isn't it a great deal more efficient, however, to head South?" The author got the message.

Another issue for consideration is that the writer needs to take into account the audience for whom he is preparing the report. How much detail does the presentation require? Is the final paper going to be presented to a department head, principal, school board, or convention delegates? Is the report going to be written as a manuscript for submission to an editorial board of a journal? Or is the work in response to the requirements of completing a graduate thesis or dissertation? This is not to say that one category is more or less important than another. Though the depth of the exposition may vary, the same standards of scholarship should be applied to all research documents (regardless of the audience). If a paper is very sloppy in appearance, the reader will likely believe that the content was derived in a similar fashion. In fact, it is not uncommon for potential publishers to give up reading your document if such circumstances are present. The content, therefore, does not even have the opportunity to be examined. (More will be said about this issue in the section entitled "Writing for Publications," presented just prior to the Summary at the end of this chapter.)

In addition to maintaining general professional standards, however, the writer may have to comply with the specific submission requirements of the journal or college/university. For example, some organizations require that documents be submitted in accordance with the guidelines of the *Publication Manual of the American Psychological Association* (American Psychological Association, 1994); Campbell, Ballou, and Slade (1990); the *Chicago Manual of Style* (1993); Dugdale (1967); Modern Language Association of America (Gibaldi & Achtert, 1988); or Turabian (1987). It is important, therefore, that the investigator become familiar with the specifics of the appropriate set of requirements before getting started. While there are generic standards common to all, most of the guidelines have procedural requirements that are unique to themselves. Regardless of the **format** and **style** one is required (or elects) to use, however, the *categories* of what is to be included almost never vary.

Given the importance of the above areas to a successful research report, this chapter provides an overview of each, beginning with format and style. In sequence, this is followed by general rules for writing and processing a research document, categories of research reports, and writing for publication.

FORMAT AND STYLE

All too many investigators appear to avert the importance of *format* and *style* in the writing of their reports. While they are willing to attach full significance to design, administration, and findings, they do not give equal emphasis to the matter of reporting. Most research reports consistently follow the format of one set of guidelines or another, such as those identified within the Introduction portion of this chapter. Specifically, *format* refers to the pattern of arrangement and organization of the report. *Style,* on the other hand, refers to the rules of mechanics, including: capitalization, punctuation, sentence structure, spelling, and word usage.

The researcher's report is an integral part of the whole project and must be attended to carefully. Only when the findings are adequately communicated to others has a contribution been made to the field. This chapter begins with the very foundation of writing, that is, with the basic mechanical issues of writing.

Basic Mechanical Issues

Spelling. There is little excuse for a **spelling** error in a research report. A writer should always have access to a dictionary. Although "typographical" errors may surface, careful proofreading will make it possible to attend to those as well.

NOTE: Have more than one person read a draft of your paper. Since the writer is intimately familiar with the contents of the paper, there is a tendency to "see" the concept rather than the sentence. One thing that can be done to encourage the reader to read one word at a time is to read a sentence backwards. This forces each word to be examined, one at a time. This will *not* provide meaning to a sentence, but it will uncover spelling errors.

The citations of references and the dates of publications should also be carefully scrutinized. All too frequently, the author has read manuscripts in which the date entry in the body of the paper does not match the date entry in the reference section. While proofreading a particular page may not uncover such errors, simultaneously proofing the entry of the name/date in the body of the paper *and* in the reference list will most likely uncover such mistakes. Remember, the reference citations are for the reader, *not* the writer. If names are misspelled and publication dates are inaccurate, the reader is certain to find it more difficult than necessary to track down the source. Unfortunately, many readers of research reports have come to experience that frustration.

A **thesaurus** is another valuable tool for writers. What is another name for thesaurus? As most of you know, a thesaurus is a collection of antonyms and synonyms. The thesaurus is very helpful to writers in their efforts to avoid using the same word over and over again (for example, accordingly, conformably).

NOTE: A thesaurus is also a categorized index of terms for use in information retrieval (for example, see the reference to the ERIC system in Chapter 1, Selection and Definition of a Problem).

Punctuation. In addition to separating sentences and sentence elements, punctuation helps to make the meaning of the sentences clearer. Riebel (1972) referred to it as "gestures in writing." Note the influence of **punctuation** in the meaning of the following sentence:

> *Example 1:* Dr. Wiseman says the author of the article missed the point.
> *Example 2:* Dr. Wiseman, says the author of the article, missed the point.

It can be seen that the use of two commas brings completely different meaning to the sentence. Although one should not go overboard with "gestural" punctuation, it is important that proper meaning be attached to sentences that are used in reports. As is the case with proofreading for spelling and typographical errors, additional readers might be able to point out areas that could be clarified through the use of punctuation.

Capitalization. Standard rules for **capitalization** of letters hold as true in research reports as they do in any scholarly work (for example, beginning a sentence, proper **nouns,** and so on). The question of whether or not to capitalize appears to cause the most problems for writers of research when it comes to preparing **reference** lists or **bibliographies.** Which of the following two **book citations** would be correct?

> *Example 1:* Huck, S. W., & Cormier, W. H. (1996). *Reading statistics and research.* New York: HarperCollins.
> *Example 2:* Huck, Schuyler W., and William H. Cormier. *Reading Statistics and Research.* New York: HarperCollins, 1996.

In Example 1, only the first letter of the first word in the book title is capitalized; whereas in Example 2, all words (except the article *and*) are capitalized. Further, Example 2 differs from Example 1 in that (a) *given names* are provided, (b) the position of the *sur-* and *given names* of the second author is reversed, and (c) the date is entered at the end of the citation. Both systems are correct, depending upon the manual of form and style that is being followed. Example 1 is using the style of the *Publication Manual of the American Psychological Association* (1994), and Example 2 is using Modern Language Association (MLA) style (Gibaldi and Achtert, 1988). As indicated earlier, be sure that you are familiar with the appropriate **form** for your report, and follow it carefully.

Sentence Structure. Effective **sentence structure** gives consideration to such things as the following.

  1. Coordination and subordination. When combining ideas in a single sentence, **coordination** is demonstrated by:

> Dr. Brown is *no longer publishing articles,* but he *is presenting at conferences.*

Both *no longer publishing articles* and *is presenting at conferences* are receiving *equal* emphasis. On the other hand, if one wanted to stress Dr. Brown's contributions at conventions, thus creating *unequal* emphasis, **subordination** could be used:

> *Though* Dr. Brown is no longer publishing articles, he is presenting at conferences.

This places *no longer publishing articles* in a subordinate position to *is presenting at conferences*.

2. Mixed constructions. This refers to parts of a sentence that do not fit together. For example, the following sentence contains **mixed construction:**

> Although James Vittum is a conscientious research associate, but additional training would increase his technical skills.

The *although* clause is subordinate, so it cannot be linked to an independent clause with the coordinating conjunction *but*. Instead, the sentence should be:

> Although James Vittum is a conscientious research associate, additional training would increase his technical skills.

3. Parallelism. This concept refers to maintaining balance between parallel ideas. For example, the following sentence lacks **parallelism:**

> As Donna began to prepare the manuscript, she discovered the word processor wasn't working properly.

Donna did not discover the word processor; she discovered that the word processor was not working properly. Instead, the sentence should be:

> As Donna began to prepare the manuscript, she discovered *that* the word processor wasn't working properly.

4. Modifiers. A **modifier** is a word, phrase, or clause (for example, an adjective or adverb) that limits the meaning of another word or phrase. In this regard, the modifiers should point clearly to the words they modify. For example:

> The researcher will *only* need to have one placebo tablet per subject.

This sentence could be improved by saying:

> The researcher will need to have *only* one placebo tablet per subject.

The modifier should be placed as close as possible to the word it modifies. In the first example, the word *only* appeared to modify the word *need* instead of the word *one*.

5. Sentence variety. The writer should attempt to use a combination of *simple* and *compound* sentences within paragraphs, and not rely too heavily on one form or another. As Hacker (1992) points out, too heavy a reliance on one form or another tends to produce an effect that is both choppy and monotonous. An example of **sentence variety** within a paragraph is presented in the following illustration:

> An ordinal scale, as its name implies, includes order—the first important feature of a real-number system. Neither distance nor origin is known, which means that in an ordinal scale we know only that a 5

is larger than a 4, but we do not know how much the difference is or to what these values refer. An interval scale includes both order and distance features. The only feature missing is the origin.

6. *Subject-verb agreement.* A singular subject needs a singular verb. Plural subjects need plural verbs. For example, the following phrases are examples of **subject-verb agreement:**

> The investigator *is* . . .
> The subjects *are* . . .

7. *Pronoun agreement.* For example, in the following phrases, **pronoun agreement** is demonstrated with singular and plural pronouns:

> The investigator completed *his* study . . .
> The subjects completed *their* questionnaires . . .

8. *Pronoun clarity.* For example, the following sentence lacks **pronoun clarity:**

> When Alan set the oxygen analyzer on the table, it broke.

What broke, the oxygen analyzer or the table? The meaning would be clearer if the sentence read:

> When Alan set the oxygen analyzer on the table, the oxygen analyzer broke.

9. *Pronoun case.* A pronoun that functions as a **subject** or **subject complement** should be presented in the **subjective case;** one that functions as an object should appear in the **objective case;** and one that functions as a possessive should be in the **possessive case.** Examples of words expressing **pronoun case** are presented in Figure 13–1. Examples of sentences related to the *subject/subject complement* case are:

> *Subject:* John and *he* wrote the article.
> *Subject complement:* The publisher announced that the writers of the article were John and *he.*

Examples of sentences related to the *objective* case are:

> **Direct object:** Cindy found the article and brought *it* home.
> **Indirect object:** Cindy gave *me* a copy of the article.
> *Object of a preposition:* Steve wondered if the article was for *him.*

When a **pronoun** modifies a **gerund** or a gerund phrase, it should appear in the *possessive* case (see Figure 13–1).

 NOTE: A *gerund* is a **verb** form ending in -ing that has all the uses of a noun but retains certain syntactic characteristics of the verb, such as the ability to take an object or an adverbial modifier (for example, *writing* in "*writing* is his only form of relaxation").

Figure 13–1: **Pronouns in the Subjective, Objective, and Possessive Case**

Subjective Case	Objective Case	Possessive Case
I	me	my
we	us	our
you	you	your
he/she/it	him/her/it	his/her/its
they	them	their

An example of incorrect use of a possessive case to modify a gerund is:

> The President and the Dean of the College always respected *us* collaborating on research projects.

The sentence should be written as:

> The President and the Dean of the College always respected *our* collaborating on research projects.

The second example is correct because the possessive pronoun *our* modifies the gerund *collaborating*.

   10. Adjectives and adverbs. **Adjectives** modify nouns or pronouns; **adverbs** modify verbs, adjectives, or other adverbs. For example, this sentence is incorrect:

> The research protocol worked out *perfect* for everyone.

The sentence should be written as:

> The research protocol worked out *perfectly* for everyone.

Although many adjectives change to adverbs by adding *-ly* (for example, *quick* to *quickly*), some adjectives end in *-ly* on their own (for example, *friendly*). On the other hand, some adverbs (for example, *always, never*) do not end in *-ly*.

Usage. Attempt to blend the terminology of the topic with the vocabulary of those for whom you are preparing your report. The language that one would use in a report being submitted for publication in a professional journal might be quite different than that one would use if the report were being prepared for presentation to town citizens (for example, the school board). If the people whom you address do not understand you, the presentation will be a useless exercise, and you may even alienate your audience. Remember, we do not want to "satiate the needs of the populous"; instead, we want to "satisfy the needs of the public."

   If reference to technical expressions (for example, *level of confidence, null hypothesis, statistical significance,* and so on) is important to the presentation, you may need to provide editorial comment or offer substitute language. For example, in a report that is being made to a school board,

1. Instead of *level of confidence,* one might say, "the degree to which I can be certain."

2. Instead of *null hypothesis,* one might substitute, "there is no difference."

> **NOTE:** If the findings are such that the null hypothesis is rejected, instead of saying, "I reject the null hypothesis that there is no difference," it might be clearer to say, "there appears to be a difference." Those with a research background would know what rejecting the null hypothesis means, but to someone who is unfamiliar with the jargon, it can be quite confusing.

3. Instead of *statistical significance,* one might say, "it appears that something other than just chance affected the results."

In addition to examining how other studies have been described in the related literature, consider referring to some of the various manuals on writing that are available. If you are still uncertain about how to best present your information, check with the faculty of your local high school or college English departments. This book is not intended to be a manual on writing. It is hoped, however, that this brief review will foster appropriate levels of attention to writing and its consequences.

Conventional Practices

Conventional practice requires clear and succinct titles, headings, and subheadings; proper sequencing of topics; and consistency of expression. The following are some of the elements to be taken into consideration.

1. Person. Studies are ordinarily in the **third person** (for example, *"the writer"* or *"the investigator"* rather than *"I did . . ."* or *"my* findings indicate that . . .").

2. Voice. Studies are primarily in the **passive voice.** It is recommended that one say "it was found that" (passive voice) or "the findings seem to indicate that" (passive voice) rather than "the writer found that" (active voice) or "the investigator concludes that" (active voice).

3. Tense. Usually the **past tense** is used. In other words, the report will state what:

- The problem *was.* . . .
- The related literature *showed.* . . .
- Procedures *were taken.* . . .
- The data *revealed.* . . .

> **NOTE:** Exceptions to using past tense in the report may exist. For example, in the *introduction,* the investigator may suggest that "practitioners *are* still seeking answers to . . .," and in the *conclusion,* the investigator may suggest that "additional studies *are* recommended."

4. Definitive statements. **Definitive statements** are used when describing such things as: (a) statement of the problem; (b) character of sample, person(s), place(s), time(s); and (c) procedures for gathering and analyzing data.

5. Tentative interpretations. **Tentative interpretations** are used when reporting **conclusions.** Although one should be definitive when identifying the statistical findings (for example, numerical values of the mean, standard deviation, chi square, *r, t, F* tests, and so on), it is inappropriate to apply *interpretations* to statistical findings in that way. Interpretations are neither definite nor absolute. The following is an example of how the investigator might deal with this issue:

> (Within the **limitations** of the investigation), this investigator rejects homogeneity of variance, where: $F(3,390) = 4.12$, $p < .01$. Therefore, it *appears* that something other than chance has affected the findings.

In this example, *definitive* statements are made in regard to the numerical findings, but the interpretation of those findings is made using *tentative* statements. You will remember from prior examples in the book that the expression *it appears that* was used regularly when interpretations of the findings were being offered. The statement *Within the limitations of the investigation* was also included as a prelude to any interpretations.

While the proper use of language is a condition implicit to any form of writing, the specific format in which a report will appear is contingent upon the style manual selected for use. Most colleges and professional journal publishers have either created their own or adopted one for use. Of the various guidelines that are available (see the Introduction in this chapter), the ones that seem to be adopted with increasing frequency are those published by the American Psychological Association (APA). The following are the categories for which specific standards exist in the *Publication Manual of the American Psychological Association:*

1. Content and organization of a manuscript.
2. Expression of ideas, including writing style, grammar, and guidelines to reduce bias in language.
3. APA editorial style, including punctuation, spelling, capitalization, italics, abbreviations, headings and series, quotations, numbers, metrication, statistical and mathematical copy, tables, figures, footnotes and notes, appendixes, reference citations in text, and reference list.
4. Manuscript preparation, including author's responsibilities, general instructions for preparing the paper manuscript, and instructions for typing the parts of a manuscript.
5. Manuscript acceptance and production, including transmitting the accepted manuscript for production, reviewing the copyedited manuscript, proofreading, and after the article is published.

For each of these topics, the *APA* manual presents carefully prescribed procedures within numbered reference sections. Were one to examine alternative manuals, one would see that formats and styles are very similar. At the same time, there are features that distinguish each manual from the others. Since many colleges, universities, and journal publishers appear to be employing the *APA* guidelines, it would seem appropriate to describe some of the *APA*'s more important standards. The following text is a discussion of three of these guidelines (corresponding *APA* reference numbers are provided):

1. Organizing a Manuscript with Headings (section 3.30),
2. Reference Citations in Text (sections 3.94 to 3.103), and
3. Elements and Examples of References in APA Style (Appendix 3-A).

When organizing a manuscript, headings provide a very useful function in identifying equal and subordinate topics of discussion. They also help to provide structure for the paper. Categories of equal importance will all have the same level of heading. In *APA,* there are five different levels (see Figure 13—2).

NOTE: According to *APA,* Level 5 is the *centered uppercase heading.* The remaining levels (Levels 1–4) are presented in sequence, as indicated.

With regard to citing references within the body of the manuscript, *APA* recommends the author-date method. It is from these brief citations that the readers will be able to find the entire reference in the alphabetical listing of sources in the reference section of the paper, article, or book. The ways that one might make such a citation include:

- Heuser (1997) compared time-on-task scores . . .
- In a recent study of time-on-task scores (Heuser, 1997), . . .
- In a recent study of time-on-task scores, Heuser (1997) . . .
- In 1997, Heuser compared time-on-task scores and . . .

As indicated earlier in the chapter, it is very important that a specific match can be found between what is cited in the body of the paper and what is recorded in the reference list.

NOTE: A *reference list* includes only those sources specifically "introduced" within the body of the paper. A *bibliography,* on the other hand, includes sources that one used for background reading or recommendations for further reading.

The most important function of a reference list is that it provides "leads" to related studies. As a consequence, its accuracy should be of paramount concern. In order to

Figure 13–2: **APA Guidelines for Headings Within a Manuscript**

Level 5	CENTERED UPPERCASE HEADING
Level 1	Centered Uppercase and Lowercase Heading
Level 2	Centered, Underlined, Uppercase and Lowercase Heading
Level 3	Flush Left, Underlined, Uppercase and Lowercase Side Heading
Level 4	Indented, underlined, lowercase paragraph heading ending with a period.

©1994 by the American Psycological Assn. Reprinted by permission. Use of any other material without the express written permission of the APA is strictly prohibited.

provide consistency within and between the various sources of information, the *APA* guidelines provide that most entries include four elements. In sequence, these are:

1. author,

2. year of publication,

3. title, and

4. publishing information.

All of these elements provide specific information for library searches. Following are examples of six categories of references.

1. Journal article, two authors, journal paginated by issue.

> Klimoski, R., & Palmer, S. (1993). The ADA and the hiring process in organizations. <u>Consulting Psychology Journal: Practice and Research, 45</u>(2), 10–36.

In this **article citation,** observe that:

a. an **ampersand** (*&* instead of the word *and*) is used after the comma between the two authors. With more than two authors, the *&* would appear after the comma between the names of the last two authors only (for example, Johnson, W. B., Smith, J. A., & Aguiar, J.).

b. capital letters are used only with (1) the first letter of the first word, *and* (2) any proper nouns in the title of the article.

c. letters *and* spaces are <u>underlined</u> within the title of the article and the volume number of the journal.

d. page numbers are not preceded by *p* or *pp*.

e. a period concludes the entry.

2. Book, second edition.

> Hittleman, D. R., & Simon, A. J. (1997). <u>Interpreting educational research: An introduction for consumers of research</u> (2nd ed.). Columbus, OH: Merrill.

In this entry, observe that:

a. the same guidelines apply for the use of an ampersand in books as in journals.

b. the same guidelines apply with regard to the use of capital letters for book titles and titles of articles. Treat the first word after the colon as the first word in the title.

c. letters *and* spaces are <u>underlined</u> within the title of the book.

d. the place of publication precedes the name of the publisher, and they are separated by a colon.

e. a period concludes the entry.

3. An article or chapter in an edited book.

> Massaro, D. (1992). Broadening the domain of the fuzzy logical model of perception. In H. L. Pick, Jr., P. van den Broek, & D. C. Knill (Eds.), <u>Cognition: Conceptual and methodological issues</u> (pp. 51–84). Washington, DC: American Psychological Association.

In this entry, observe that:

a. the use of the ampersand remains the same as with references to articles and books.

b. an abbreviation for *editors* appears in parentheses after their names.

c. the spaces and letters in the title of the main source are <u>underlined</u>.

d. page numbers in which the elements of the article (or chapter) can be found are indicated after the source. Note that *pp* is included.

e. the place of **publication** precedes the name of the publisher, as it does in a book citation.

f. a period concludes the entry.

4. Report available from the Educational Resources Information Center *(ERIC).*

> Mead, J. V. (1992). <u>Looking at old photographs: Investigating the teacher tales that novice teachers bring with them</u> (Report No. NCRTL-RR-92-4). East Lansing, MI: National Center for Research on Teacher Learning. (ERIC Document Reproduction Service No. ED 346 082)

In this entry, observe that:

a. capital letters are used only with the first letter of the first word, and the initial letter of the first word following the colon. (The first letter of proper nouns would also be capitalized.)

b. the spaces and letters of the report title are <u>underlined</u>.

c. the report number is in parentheses.

d. the place of publication precedes the name of the publisher.

e. the ERIC Document Reproduction Service Number is in parentheses. Note the space between the first three digits and the last three digits.

f. a period is *not* used at the conclusion of the entry.

5. Unpublished paper presented at a meeting.

> Wiseman, D. C. (1991, March). <u>The values and visions of Minnie Lynn: A tribute to a quintessential professional.</u> Paper presented at the meeting of the Eastern District Association of the American Alliance for Health, Physical Education, Recreation and Dance, Newport, RI.

In this entry, observe that:

a. the month accompanies and follows the year of the presentation.

b. the first letters of proper names are capitalized, as are the first letter of the first word of the title and the initial letter of the first word following the colon.

c. the spaces and letters of the title are <u>underlined</u>.

d. a period concludes the entry.

6. Abstract on CD-ROM.

> Meyer, A. S., & Bock, K. (1992). The tip-of-the-tongue phenomenon: Blocking or partial activation? [CD-ROM]. <u>Memory & Cognition, 20,</u> 715–726. Abstract from: SilverPlatter File: PsycLIT Item: 80-16351

In this entry, observe that:

    a. the use of an ampersand remains the same as with earlier examples.

    b. the use of capital letters remains the same as with earlier examples.

    c. reference to CD-ROM is made in brackets (not parentheses).

    d. spaces and letters of the title and volume number are <u>underlined</u>, as with earlier examples.

    e. page numbers are not preceded by *p* or *pp*.

    f. a period is *not* used at the conclusion of the entry.

✓ CHECKPOINT

What is the major difference between a *reference list* and a *bibliography?*

Answer

The *primary* distinction between a reference list and a bibliography is that:

1. a *reference list* includes *only* those sources specifically introduced within the body of the paper, whereas

2. a *bibliography* includes sources introduced within the body of the paper *and* sources used for background reading or recommended for further reading.

Acknowledging that there are many other categories of sources, the previous discussion of six categories of references should provide some insight into the formatting of information that is to be found within the *Publication Manual of the American Psychological Association.* It can be seen that there are many similarities in the way entries are made whether referencing journals, books, elements of an edited book, reports from ERIC, unpublished papers, or abstracts on CD-ROM. As a consequence, once the principles are understood, it becomes very easy to comply with the recommended guidelines.

Whether preparing the results of your research for presentation at a meeting or for publication, the format is essentially the same. Although there may be some variation, depending upon the specific requirements of the host, the *general* outline will be likely to include:

1. The *title.*

2. An *abstract.*

3. *Key terms.*

4. The *introduction,* including (a) statement of the problem, (b) review of the literature, and (c) statement of the hypotheses/research questions.

5. A description of *methods,* including (a) selection of subjects (with *Subjects* as the subhead), (b) instrumentation (with *Instrumentation, Materials,* or *Measures* as the subhead), and (c) administration of the study and collection of data (with *Procedures* as the subhead).

6. A description of the *findings,* including (a) data analyses, and tests of significance (if applicable); (b) figure and table summaries; and (c) relationship to hypotheses/research questions, and findings of related literature.

7. A description of *conclusions,* including (a) investigator's interpretations, (b) **implications,** and (c) **recommendations** for future study.

8. *References.*

NOTE: Given the fact that many of those who attend research sessions are expected to be familiar with related literature and instrumentation, some presenters choose to categorize their presentations according to:

- **Statement of hypothesis**
- Brief description of procedures
- Findings, conclusions, and implications

The relationship of this outline to the elements of a graduate thesis or dissertation will be discussed in the section entitled "Categories of Research Reports," presented later in the chapter. At this juncture, the discussion turns to general rules for *writing* and *processing* a research document.

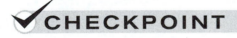

✓CHECKPOINT

What is the distinction between the *format* and *style* of a research paper?

Answer

The difference between *format* and *style* is that:

1. *format* refers to the pattern of *arrangement* and *organization* of a report, and

2. *style* refers to the *rules of mechanics,* including: capitalization, punctuation, sentence structure, spelling, and **word usage.**

WRITING AND PROCESSING A RESEARCH DOCUMENT

As indicated earlier, the topics and order of a final report almost never vary. Since conventional practices tend to shape the design of research reports, most reports contain exactly the same components. Further, many of these components have cause to be *integrated* during the report-writing process. This is where computer database management systems can be of great assistance. As indicated in Chapter 12, Using the Computer for Data Analysis, database programs enable one to alphabetize, arrange scores in order, select records, and integrate the results with word processing programs.

If other tools are going to be used (such as electronic dictionaries, file management programs, and spreadsheets), your word processor should be able to create files that can be read by these other programs. Similarly, if you intend to use a word processor at home to create text that will be printed by a word processor at your place of employment, both systems must be able to read the text file. As practitioner/researchers become more proficient in the use of word processors, they may want to advance to more powerful programs. The real investment in any processor is not so much in the program itself, but in the library of text files that will have been created. Once prepared, they can be brought to the "next level."

The most common function of personal computers (PCs) is word processing. In addition to being able to revise, format, and print documents, users can delete individual letters, sentences, and entire passages; move pieces of text from one place to another; conduct spellchecks; integrate information with that of other systems; and print. When one considers how long it takes to conduct these tasks with a regular typewriter and dictionary, it is easy to admire those who use such items to produce so many professional-appearing documents.

There are even programs on the market that will actually guide the user through the various stages of production. For example, the American Psychological Association has developed software that will produce a report that satisfies all *APA* formatting requirements. Among other features, the program will arrange for: (1) all sections of the report to be placed in the correct order, and (2) reference list citations to be formatted for documents that have been introduced within the body of the paper.

Another program particularly useful to report preparation is **WordPerfect** for Windows. In addition to standard features of creating, editing, and printing documents, it provides programs that will allow users to customize its interface capabilities to their particular needs. Although these and other features are beyond the scope of this chapter, it should be said that those who are able to use and integrate database management and word processing systems will be a step ahead of many others in regard to the efficient production of research reports. Find the software packages that will suit your needs, and practice using them.

Whether using a **word processor** (with integrated software capabilities) or a standard typewriter, the same expectations for product quality will apply. In this regard, there are certain considerations that should be given to assigning content to the various sections within the research report.

Title and Title Page

Given the recommended length of a **title** (ten to twelve words), it would seem that deciding upon what should be included would be a rather simple task. On the contrary, it is one of the most difficult ten- to twelve-word statements that you will ever have to write. At the same time, it is among the most important. It is on the basis of the title that others will be making determinations about the appropriateness of the investigation to their own study interests.

NOTE: In a survey of 42 journals in which the words in the titles of 152 research articles (in mathematics education) were counted, it was found that the median number of words in each title was 11 (Pyrczak & Bruce, 1992). Titles of graduate theses and dissertations are frequently longer than those of journal articles.

A title should be a concise statement of the main topic, and if only a small number of variables are being examined, the title should name those variables. For example, if the variables are *grades* and *attendance,* the title might be:

> The Relationship Between Grades and Attendance

NOTE: The title is not a complete sentence and does not end with punctuation (that is, a period). Both of these characteristics are common to titles of reports.

If many variables are examined, only *categories* of variables should be identified. Suppose, for example, that an investigator is examining the effects of a new dress code upon the attitudes of students with regard to differences in gender, grade level, and socioeconomic status. Because there are too many variables to cite in a title, they can be grouped within categories. For example, the title might be:

> Effects of Dress Codes upon Student Attitudes with Reference to
> Selected Demographic Variables

Since the title is likely to be indexed in various reference sources, avoid words that may be misleading. Remember that those doing the indexing will select what they believe are appropriate words to use. To the greatest extent possible, the *writer* should be making this decision by having a title that can be easily reduced for editorial purposes and easily converted to a **running head** for publication purposes.

NOTE: If used, a *running head* is placed at the top of each page of a published article in order to identify the topic for the reader. According to the *American Psychological Association* (1994), it should consist of no more than fifty characters (including letters, spaces between the words, and punctuation).

There is no need to begin the title with such expressions as:

- A Critical Evaluation of . . .
- A Study of . . .
- An Experimental Investigation of . . .

These expressions only add to the length of the title and serve no useful purpose. Fully explanatory when existing alone, the title should (1) inform readers about the study, (2) represent content for use by various abstracting services (for example, ERIC, Psyclit, and so on), and (3) indicate what was studied, *not* the results of the study. To illustrate this point, a title pertaining to a study on gender and motor fitness should be written as:

Gender Differences on a Motor Fitness Test Battery

This title would be more appropriate than:

Girls Score Higher than Boys on All Motor Fitness Tests Except Foot-Eye Coordination

As you can see, it is very important that thoughtful consideration be given to assigning titles to investigations. As short as they are, they have a great deal to say about the essence of one's study.

In addition to including the title of one's research, a **title page** will normally include (1) author's name, (2) institutional affiliation, and (3) date. An example of a title page for a graduate research paper is displayed as Figure 13–3. Note that Level 5 (per *APA* guidelines) is used for the title. The remaining entries on the title page are displayed per Level 1. Also observe that the **inverted pyramid** style is used with the institutional affiliation and date. If the title of the work consisted of more than one line, that, too, would be displayed as an inverted pyramid. Colleges, universities, and editorial boards of professional journals may have their own preferences about the design of title pages. Be sure that you are familiar with their specific requirements.

On the title page, the approximate distance from the top of the page to the title is eight spaces. From the last line of the title to the word *By,* the distance is seven spaces, followed by a double space to the author's name. The last line of the institutional affiliation and date are approximately one inch from the bottom of the page.

Abstract

An abstract is a comprehensive, self-contained **summary** of an investigation that is placed in advance of the introduction to a journal article, graduate thesis, or dissertation. Although one will find a variation in the length of abstracts, journal publishers often limit their length to one hundred and twenty to one hundred and fifty words. Colleges and universities normally set their maximum according to the guidelines of *Dissertation Abstracts International (DAI).* Considered to be the most important single paragraph in your research report, the abstract should address the:

1. statement of the problem,
2. procedures,
3. number and kind of subjects,
4. instrumentation,
5. results (with reference to statistical significance, if applicable), and
6. conclusions.

It is important to remember that nothing should appear in the abstract that has not been discussed in the full body of the report. To avoid confusion on the part of the reader, be sure to use complete terms rather than abbreviations and acronyms. In addition, it is helpful to those doing computer searches if you integrate important **key terms.** Most reviewers of the literature will have their initial contact with the article you have written by accessing and reading your abstract. Though remaining

Figure 13–3: **Suggested Format for Title Page**

INTERACTIVE MULTIMEDIA AND ACHIEVEMENT

By

Tobi A. Pfenninger

Submitted in Partial Fulfillment of the Requirements
of the Course, Research Design
Department of Education
May, 1997

nonevaluative, the abstract *must* contain all substantive elements in order to enable the reader to make an intelligent decision about whether the full article is appropriate for his use.

In the following text, you will find two illustrations of abstracts. Without ready access to the articles these abstracts represent, you will be unable to evaluate their validity. At the same time, however, you will see that each contains the components that are considered important in determining relevance to one's own subject of inquiry. The first abstract describes a survey; the second abstract describes an experimental study. The first abstract reads as follows:

Abstract 1

This study was designed to determine (a) the demographic characteristics and responsibilities of educational sign language interpreters within the K–12 public school system in the United States; (b) the mode of communication they use most frequently; and (c) their education and certification levels. Surveys were completed by 222 educational sign language interpreters in three states. Results showed the lack of certification and adequate training for the majority of respondents, as well as inadequate minority/gender representation, among other concerns. The study raised questions about the dependence of students who are deaf or hard of hearing on the educational interpreter support system. Recommendations for educational practice are presented (Jones, Clark, & Soltz, 1997, p. 257).

If you were designing a study related to the effectiveness of sign language interpreters in generating achievement among students with hearing impairments, would this be a study you would want to examine in detail? With the exception of the reference list the article would provide, it would appear that this article deals primarily with certification, demographics, mode of communication, and training. If you were interested in assessing achievement, this study would *not* appear to be helpful. The reference list, however, may provide leads on studies that do address issues of student achievement.

✓CHECKPOINT

Given Abstract 1, assign what you believe would be an appropriate title for the study.

Answer

The title you gave may be appropriate, but here is the *actual* title as it appeared for that article:

Characteristics and Practices of Sign Language Interpreters in Inclusive Education Programs

The second illustration of an abstract, which describes an experimental study, reads as follows:

Abstract 2

This study examined the effects of practice schedule manipulations implemented in an instructional setting on the performance and learning of low- and high-skilled students. College undergraduates ($N = 83$) enrolled in 5 tennis classes completed a pretest on the forehand strokes, practiced these skills under a blocked or alternating schedule, and then completed a posttest. Results indicated that practice schedule effects on learning were influenced by student ability. Low-skilled students assigned to the blocked schedule had higher posttest scores than those assigned to the alternating schedule, whereas no significant differences were found for high-skilled students. These findings are discussed in relation to previous applied and laboratory-based findings and as a means for manipulating practice difficulty in teaching physical education (Hebert, Landin, & Solmon, 1996, p. 52).

The following Checkpoint questions refer to this abstract.

CHECKPOINT

Assuming that you were a tennis instructor, and you were interested in obtaining the entire article:

1. How would you go about finding the article?
2. What questions would you ask about the design of the study?

Answers

The following represent suggested answers to the two questions raised above:

1. The title of the article, for which the abstract is written, can be found in the References section of this chapter. To determine the availability of the article, you could do such things as:

   a. check the periodical holdings list found in a public or college/university library. If the journal is cited there, it means that the library has it in a hard copy and/or microfilm (or microfiche) version(s).

   b. speak with the circulation or reference librarians in order to arrange interlibrary loan of the article.

   c. check with faculty/coaches in order to see if they have personal copies of the article that they would be willing to loan to you.

   d. contact the publisher or author of the journal article in order to make arrangements to obtain a copy.

2. The questions that you might ask about the design of the study could relate to:

    a. definitions of low- and high-skilled students.

    b. definitions of block and alternating schedules.

    c. whether individuals and treatments were assigned at random.

    d. whether groups were equivalent at the onset of the study.

    e. what statistical tests were used with the data.

    f. what constituted statistical significance for the posttest scores of low-skilled students.

Difficult as they may be to write, abstracts provide the link between the reader and the research report itself. Prepare them as carefully as you can. There is the potential for a great deal to be said in the one hundred and twenty to one hundred and fifty words available to you.

Key Terms or Essential Definitions

Key terms, or **essential definitions,** are words or expressions that are vital to the study and require definition because (1) they are likely to be new or generally unfamiliar to the prospective readers, or (2) they may have more than one definition, depending upon the context within which they are being used. It is important that everyone be "on the same page" when it comes to knowing how the writer defines the important terms being used in the study. In particular, definitions should be offered for each of the variables in the hypothesis, purpose, or research question.

 NOTE: If the investigator employed a published instrument in the study, the variable(s) being measured may be operationally defined by citing the reference for it.

As indicated in Chapter 3, Preparation of a Research Plan, it is helpful to define the key terms early. As with the reading of any document, knowing the definitions of unfamiliar terms in advance of their appearance in the narrative can facilitate contextual understanding. In formal reports, such as graduate theses and dissertations, a section entitled *Essential Definitions* is normally set aside very early in the document. (For reference to its specific placement, refer to the section entitled "Categories of Research Reports," presented later in this chapter.)

Following are examples of the terms that should be considered for definition in the articles represented by the abstracts presented earlier:

- Abstract 1
  — Adequate training
  — Minority/gender groups
  — Sign language interpreters
  — Three states (that were included in the study)

- Abstract 2
  — Alternating schedule
  — Applied- and laboratory-based findings
  — Blocked schedule
  — Instructional setting
  — Low- and high-skilled students
  — Manipulations
  — Posttest elements
  — Pretest elements
  — Statistical significance

When establishing the roster of terms to define, put yourself in the place of potential readers. Remember, you are intimately familiar with the language and context. Potential readers may not be as familiar with the words you are using. If a reader continually comes across terms with which he is unfamiliar, it would not be surprising to learn that the article had been set aside. Ask fellow graduate students and colleagues to review your manuscript, and have them suggest terms that need defining. This can be very helpful in making appropriate decisions about what should be included.

Introduction

The purpose of the **introduction** section of a research report is to introduce the problem area, provide a **review of related literature,** and offer the hypotheses or research questions for testing. It is also an opportunity for the investigator to establish the significance of the problem (that is, need for the study) and to offer his own particular perspectives about its relevance.

While graduate schools may require that separate chapters be prepared for the introduction and literature review elements of a thesis or dissertation, in a journal article, the introduction and review are almost always integrated.

When writing the introduction, begin by describing the problem area, followed by its purpose and importance. Gradually begin to integrate related literature.

 NOTE: The related literature should not be presented in the form of an annotated list. Instead, it should be presented like an essay. When the findings of related studies are similar, group them together. In general, those studies having *least* relationship to the topic should be discussed first. (Think in terms of an *inverted pyramid* in which the related research *most* similar to the topic would be discussed just prior to the statement of the hypothesis.)

The introduction section is brought to closure by stating the hypotheses or research questions for the study. The section should provide answers to each of the following questions:

1. What is the problem under investigation?
2. Why is the topic important to study?

3. What does the related literature have to offer in regard to the topic?

4. What are the hypotheses/research questions?

In Chapter 3, Preparation of a Research Plan, each of these issues was discussed in detail. By examining the material presented there, as well as the various illustrations provided throughout the book, you should be in a position to prepare introductions of substance.

Methods

Upon completing the introduction, the reader is in a position to advance directly into the next section of the report, *Methods*. Stated in *past* tense, the information presented in the **methods** section should be in sufficient detail to enable the reader to replicate the study (assuming access to materials and subjects).

In the methods section, the information is ordinarily presented within one of three subsections, namely: subjects, instrumentation (or materials), and procedures.

Subjects. The selection of the sample, and its size and character, should be evident. For example,

> The subjects participating in the study were a population of 110 college, first-year students who completed a standardized writing test (SWT). The study group consisted of 60 (54.5%) females and 50 (45.5%) males. The mean combined SAT scores was 1450, and the majority of the participants were Caucasian (97.3%).

While there may be other idiosyncrasies within the membership (for example, socioeconomic background, ranking in high school, and so on), only those factors accounted for in this particular investigation should be referenced. To clarify the matter, some writers would add to the above statement a comment such as: "No other demographic features were taken into account."

If there was attrition, the number of subjects who withdrew, and the reasons (if known) for their withdrawal, should be indicated. If pertinent to the nature of the study, it would also be advisable to provide information about those particular individuals.

Instrumentation or Materials. If practitioner-made instruments were used, evidence of validity, reliability, and objectivity (if pertinent) should be provided. If a jury was used to test for content or construct validity, describe their qualifications. If concurrent or predictive validity was established, provide statistical evidence. Any pilot study (or focus) groups that were used should also be described (for example, size and relationship to the character of the group for which the instrument was designed). This section will also include the operational definitions for the variables being assessed (if such has not been provided earlier under *Key Terms*).

If a standardized (commercially made) instrument was used, its title, format, traits that it was designed to measure, evidence of validation, and range of score values possible should be provided. The source (including name and address of publisher) of the instrument will also be indicated.

If any additional equipment was used, it too should be identified and described. This would include such things as: computers, optical scanning devices, oxygen analyzers, and treadmills. If pertinent, evidence of equipment calibration should be provided. For example, is the treadmill *actually* inclined at 5.0 degrees when the indicator *claims* that it is?

Procedures. Describe the **procedures** for obtaining permission for the study. From whom was permission granted? If subjects were underage, were parents/guardians contacted? Was the initial contact by telephone or letter? Was use made of a self-addressed postal card? Was permission granted in writing?

Describe *when* and *where* the study was administered and the data were collected. Was the study conducted during the school day? Were the subjects on-site (for example, ethnographic investigation)? Was the study conducted at the site of the investigator's place of employment?

If research assistants were used in the study, were they trained? If so, how? On what basis were they selected? What specific roles did they play?

Describe the procedures for collecting data. Did the researcher use a mailed questionnaire, telephone questionnaire, or interview? How was anonymity assured? Did participants enter their responses on a computer?

If the research was experimental:

1. Identify the design. If reference was not made to the specifics of the design in the introduction, it should be done here. Depending upon the audience for whom the report is being written, it may also be helpful to include diagrams (see Part III, Experimental Research Methods).

2. Describe how (and on what basis) you went about selecting your sample and assigning subjects and treatments to groups. Was there more than one treatment group? Was there a control group? Did the control group receive the "traditional" treatment?

3. Was there a pretest? Was the pretest identical or equivalent to the posttest? Did each group receive identical or equivalent pretests? Were posttests equivalent or identical?

4. Describe, in detail, the nature of the treatment. For example, if subjects were required to learn a computer key pressing task, a typical trial should be reviewed. If there were various phases to the experiment (for example, two phases—acquisition and retention), each should be described. If a study were designed to investigate the effect of workshops upon teacher attitudes, it would be important to identify the workshop topics. Was it a study on teaching methods? Describe those methods.

5. Describe the length of the study. Was it conducted over a marking period, a semester, a school year, or over the summer months?

Each of the elements in the *Procedures* section assists in contributing evidence for both the internal and the external validity of the study.

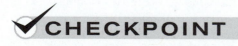

CHECKPOINT

What four factors provide evidence for the *external* validity of a study?

Answer

The answer is:

1. Sample

2. Person(s)

3. Place(s)

4. Time(s)

If you did not remember these four components, it is suggested that you go back and review pertinent sections of Chapter 3, Preparation of a Research Plan.

To this point in your report, each component would have been planned for in Phase 1 and Phase 2 of your research design. If the plan was thoughtfully prepared, most of what can be reported involves merely translating to past tense what was said in response to:

- What I need to know
- Where I will find it
- How I will find it
- Procedures for organizing the information for further use

It is from the organization and analysis of the information acquired that the next section of the report is written.

Findings or Results

Not only does the reader expect to find statements of results for the study, he should also expect to find evidence for the statements that are made. Where applicable, this would include reference to statistical significance. The **findings,** or **results,** section should be organized around the hypothesis (or research question) for the investigation. Should there be more than one hypothesis, it is appropriate to respond to each, in order. (To make it easier for the reader, some investigators use a numbering system to distinguish one hypothesis or research question from another.)

Because the results of an investigation are frequently a product of statistical analysis, the specific mathematical measures that were used should be identified. It is not necessary to show the formulas, but it is important that the statistics be named. If *descriptive* statistics have been computed, they should be identified first. Any categorical data (for example, **percentages**) would follow. Although measures of central tendency (that is, mean, median, and mode) and categorical data will *not* reveal statistical differences between groups in the study, they will provide average performance and relative status *within* groups. The next category of statistics to report would be those that are *inferential* in nature.

It is often helpful to display information in graphic form in order to reduce confusion that might arise from attempts to provide narrative explanations. Any narrative that introduces or discusses the **graph** is usually limited to an overview. For an example of an ANOVA summary table, refer to Table 11–2 in Chapter 11. In some instances, you may simply want to display descriptive data through such means as a **polygon** (Figure 11–2), **bar graph** (Figure 13–4), or **histogram** (Figure 13–5).

To introduce and provide an overview of the graph in Figure 13–4, the investigator might say, "Of the five institutions in the study, Institution 5 scored the greatest percentage of attainment with 80.5%. Attaining the lowest percentage of attainment (20.0%) was Institution 2. It can also be observed that the majority of the institutions (*N* = 3) scored above 50.0%."

Figure 13–4: **Sample Bar Graph Representing Rankings and Percentages of Attainment for Five Institutions**

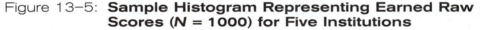

Institution Number	Rank	Percent	Percentage of Attainment
			0 20 40 60 80 100
5	1	80.5	//
3	2	70.0	/////////////////////////////////
1	3	60.0	//////////////////////////
4	4	40.0	//////////////////
2	5	20.0	//////////

Figure 13–5: **Sample Histogram Representing Earned Raw Scores (*N* = 1000) for Five Institutions**

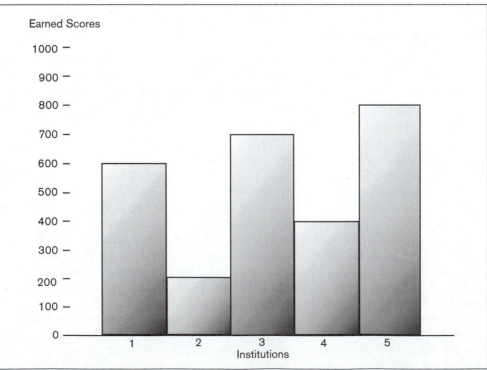

Though not limited to the display of percentages, a bar graph is frequently used for that purpose. With a larger number of groups, it may be desirable to delineate the percentage display by providing for intervals of 5% or 10%, rather than 20% (as is shown in Figure 13–4).

As another way of presenting descriptive data, histograms are often used to display the **raw score** values for the subjects. The histogram is essentially the same as the bar graph except that, in the latter, vertical bars replace horizontal bars. Figure 13–5 shows the raw score equivalents of the percentages of attainment displayed in Figure 13–4. To avoid distortions, it is important to begin with a zero on the vertical (Y) axis, and to make each line proportional to that of the others. Be sure that the labels of the graphs are clear or they, too, may cause confusion for the reader.

When using statistical symbols, they should be *italicized* or <u>underlined</u>. If the investigator is reporting upon qualitative results, the discussion should reveal major trends and themes. Organizing the information through the use of subheads may be helpful to the reader as he sorts out the findings.

Once the findings are reported, the next step is to offer discussion, which includes implications and recommendations. In a brief report, it may be more feasible to integrate the findings and implications within one section. Often, however, it makes it easier for the reader to "focus" if a separate section is provided.

Discussion

In the **discussion** section of the report, the investigator presents the conclusions of the study. This is where the author brings his own meaning to the results. It is in this section where conclusions are drawn, implications are presented, and recommendations for further study are made. If there were assumptions established during the planning stages of the research (that is, Phase 1 and Phase 2) that were not satisfied, the limitations imposed by these conditions should be described.

When summarizing the investigation, it is important that the writer make specific reference to:

1. the highlights of the study (including documentation of limitations caused by the actualization of threats to its validity),
2. the relationship of the findings to the hypotheses or research questions,
3. the relationship of the findings to those of the related literature discussed earlier in the report,
4. the implications of the findings to present or future educational practices, and
5. recommendations for future research.

It is important to remember that the results of any study are the product of the investigator, the design, and the subjects. If the investigator is biased or unprepared, if the design protocol is flawed, or if the subjects are not characteristic of the population that they are intended to represent, the validity of any conclusions and inferences that are attached to the findings will be in serious question. As has been suggested throughout the book:

1. Be thoughtful in your planning.
2. Be deliberate in your presentation.

3. Be objective in your analysis.

Immediately following the discussion portion of the report will be the investigator's list of references. Earlier in the chapter, the requirements of such a list were presented. Be sure that you follow all guidelines of the *manual of form and style* for which you are responsible.

Much of what has been presented in this section relates to the requirements of both journal publishers and graduate theses and dissertations. The major distinction is in regard to the arrangement of headings. This difference is examined in the section ahead.

CATEGORIES OF RESEARCH REPORTS

The emphasis in this portion of the chapter is on the report layout generally expected of those who are completing graduate theses or dissertations. As elements are introduced beyond what is normally included in a journal article or paper, clarification will be offered. As a frame of reference for the distinctions that are presented, refer to Figure 13–6 for a summary display of **topical headings** previously introduced.

Figure 13–6: **Sample Format for Journal Articles and Papers**

Topical Headings
   Title
   Abstract
   Key Terms
   Introduction
      –Statement of the Problem
      –Need for the Study
      –Review of Related Literature
      –Statement of Hypotheses or Research Questions
   *Methods
      –Subjects
      –Instrumentation
      –Procedures
   Findings
      –Organized by Hypotheses or Research Questions
      –Include Analyses, and Tests of Significance (if pertinent)
      –Summarize Results (using graphics, as appropriate)
      –Test Hypotheses, or Respond to Research Questions
   *Discussion
      –Conclusions
      –Implications
      –Recommendations
   References

                                          *Subhead titles are recommended

The features that distinguish the layout of a thesis or dissertation from other papers are quite specific. Although there may be some variance between graduate schools in regard to the terminology assigned to the headings, the general formats are quite similar and consist of three main parts: the **prefatory section,** the **body of the report,** and the appended section.

Prefatory Section

The prefatory section consists of the following components: title page, acceptance page, acknowledgment page, table of contents, list of tables, list of figures, and abstract.

Title Page. A discussion of the title page was offered earlier in the chapter. A sample of such a page was offered as Figure 13–3. As indicated, however, your institution may have a specific requirement of its own. Be sure that you are familiar with any related requirement.

Acceptance Page. This is where the members of the thesis (or dissertation) committee record their signatures. These signatures are placed in the appropriate spaces on the occasion of the committee's acceptance (approval) of the document and its contents. An example of an **acceptance page** is displayed in Figure 13–7.

Acknowledgment Page. On this page, the writer has the opportunity to express appreciation to those individuals who were particularly helpful in guiding, and providing support for, the work that was done. Acknowledgment is not limited to committee members, those who were prime sources of information, and research subjects, but can include family members as well. Those of you who have worked on projects of any magnitude well appreciate the importance of support that comes from immediate and extended family members. Figure 13–8 provides an example of an **acknowledgment page.**

Table of Contents. This portion of the prefatory section provides an outline of the research report and indicates the page upon which each major heading (that is, chapter) and subheading begins.

 NOTE: Theses and dissertations are arranged as chapters. For example, Chapter 1 would be *Introduction,* Chapter 2, *Review of Related Literature,* and so on. More will be said about this later.

For a portion of a **table of contents,** see the example in Figure 13–9. Note that the appended material, including the *Bibliography,* would also be included within the *Table of Contents.*

List of Tables. This section includes the identification of each table that is presented within the document. Beginning on a new page, the **list of tables** provides the number and title of each table, along with the corresponding page in the document where that table can be found. An abbreviated illustration of such a list is found in Figure 13–10.

Figure 13–7: **Sample Acceptance Page**

Accepted by the Faculty of the Department of
Education, Plymouth State College, in Partial Fulfillment
of the Requirements for the Degree of Master of Education.

_____
Director of Thesis

Committee Members: _____

_____

_____

Figure 13–8: **Sample Acknowledgment Page**

It would have been impossible to have completed this study without the advice, cooperation, and patience of many people. The writer would like to take this opportunity to express his appreciation to the following individuals and groups for their assistance:

Dr. John B. Daugherty, dissertation director, who gave of his time and counsel throughout the study's completion, and Dr. Evelyn A. Davies and Dr. Donald J. Ludwig for their many helpful suggestions.

The writer is particularly grateful to Dr. Karl W. Bookwalter, who not only provided the score cards and other valuable source materials, but also gave unselfishly of his time and wisdom to aid in the conduct of this study.

The heads of the departments and directors of physical education in the colleges and universities in New England for cooperating in making their institutions available for evaluation, and for granting time for personal interviews.

To my wife, Bonnie, son, Mark, and daughters, Lori and Kathleen, for their understanding while this study was being conducted.

D.C.W.

Figure 13–9: **Portion of Sample Table of Contents**

Figure 13–10: **Portion of a List of Tables**

List of Figures. Beginning on a separate page, and immediately following the list of tables, is the **list of figures.** Each figure is indicated on the list by number, along with pages where the respective figures can be found. An abbreviated list of figures can be found in Figure 13–11.

Abstract. As indicated earlier in the chapter, an *abstract* is a summary of the salient elements of the report. Since it is limited in length, thoughtful attention must be given to ensuring that it is written in a way that best represents the contents of the study. For a review of pertinent considerations, refer to the section entitled "Writing and Processing a Research Document," presented earlier in the chapter.

Figure 13–11: **Portion of a List of Figures**

Body of the Report

As indicated earlier, the second section of a thesis or dissertation is the body of the report. In Figure 13–9, you were provided with a sample table of contents for what would be found in that section. Each chapter begins on a new page. Depending upon the requirements of a particular institution, however, the titles of the **chapter headings** (and subheadings) may vary slightly. Further, some institutions may direct their students to include the review of the literature within Chapter 1, *Introduction*. Regardless of the label and placement of the information, adequate attention is expected to be given to each of the topics.

Appended Section

The third part of the research document is known as the appended section. In order, this part of the document would include the following elements: references (or bibliography), appendices, index, and vita.

References or Bibliography. Remember that the distinction between *references* and *bibliography* is that in the former, only those documents specifically introduced within the body of the report are listed. The bibliography, on the other hand, includes those references as well as references that were used as sources of background information or are recommended for further reading. In each case, the list of sources is alphabetized and cited in accordance with the recommended manual of form and style.

Appendices. Entries suitable for an appendix are either too lengthy or not of sufficient importance to be included in the body of the report. Whenever supportive documents are provided in the appendix, however, they should be introduced within the main part of the document. Examples of appended items include such things as:

- Form letters
- Questionnaires
- Recording forms
- Raw data
- Data analysis sheets

Each appendix is assigned a letter, such as Appendix A, Appendix B, and so on, and each of them begins on a new page. Some institutions require that a title page be included for each of the appendices; others may require a single title page to introduce the appendix section of the document.

Index. Not ordinarily included within research reports, the presence of an index does provide for topics of importance to be alphabetized and paginated for easy reference. As would be expected, the value of an **index** increases in direct proportion to the length of the document.

Vita. The final page in the thesis or dissertation, a **vita** sheet provides an opportunity for the writer to describe those professional experiences that have contributed to his qualifications for conducting the research. Typical of the inclusions one finds in this brief (normally one-page) *autobiography* are:

- Formal education, including degrees earned
- Related work experience
- Publications
- Professional memberships

Having addressed the items appropriate for inclusion in the various sections of research reports, this chapter now addresses factors that should be taken into account when seeking to *publish* one's work.

WRITING FOR PUBLICATION

A number of motives can inspire an individual to do research. Many of these have been expressed or implied in earlier chapters. Teaching practitioners may want to contrast their current teaching methods with those espoused within some of the professional journals they have been reading. Principals may want to survey recent high school graduates in order to ascertain their levels of satisfaction with the education they received. Guidance personnel may be interested in finding more effective ways to counsel students about contemporary career opportunities. School board members may want to determine the best way to recruit outstanding teachers to their school systems. The list goes on.

For answers to these and other questions, practitioners meet with colleagues, attend conferences, read professional journals, and conduct their own research. It is to the last of these processes that this book has been dedicated. In addition to increasing one's own level of understanding, however, the findings of research provide a foundation for increasing the knowledge base of others.

Among the various ways that research can be disseminated is through publication. But many of those who are just beginning to acquire publication interests perceive themselves as being incapable of preparing manuscripts in a fashion that would be of interest to editorial boards. Further, "Who would be interested in what *I* would have to say?" Often, these same individuals are under the impression that their ideas must have been investigated many times (by others) in the past.

 NOTE: It would seem that the author represents a classic example of this. Nearly thirty-five years ago, he received his first college teaching job, and part of his assignment was the coaching of tennis. Two years later, the department purchased a video camera, recorder, and monitor. The author decided to conduct an informal research project with the use of this "new" equipment. The purpose was to determine if video feedback would have an effect upon player performance.

During each practice session, time was set aside for recording and reviewing. Players had the opportunity to examine their own performance with and without verbal cues. The results appeared to be beneficial in that the team won three consecutive conference championships, going undefeated in the third year. Granted, there were no tight controls over the many variables that could have influenced individual and team performance. Perhaps they would have won the championships regardless of video feedback. One thing appears certain, however—the video machine did not seem to hurt.

The author thought of writing up the results to see if they might get published, but decided against it. He was young, rather inexperienced, and after all, others must have used such a device to assist with their coaching in the past. The year was 1966. Approximately *six* years later, the author was perusing a coaching journal and came across an article written by a coach on the topic: *A Teaching Innovation: The Use of Video Feedback in the Coaching of Tennis*. The author learned his lesson.

In order to assist you in getting *your* research published, consider the following suggestions.

1. Keep on top of the current literature in the field. Look for advanced themes. Quite frequently, editorial boards will announce themes for upcoming journals.

2. Share your ideas with colleagues. Perhaps others would like to collaborate on a project with you.

3. Begin with local *or* regional *journals*. In a recent article, entitled *Writing for Publication: Some Perennial Mistakes* (Henson, 1997), it was stated that: "One of the most common mistakes writers make is failing to resist the urge to send their manuscripts to the most prestigious and best-known journals, ignoring the less widely circulated journals" (p. 781). Henson goes on to say that, by ignoring the less-known journals, one limits the potential target audience. In a 1995–1996 survey of "prominent" journals, Henson discovered that more than half (53.8%) had fewer than five thousand subscribers.

4. Read several issues of the journal in order to become familiar with content and style. Become knowledgeable about its "Guidelines for Contributors." An example of the seriousness with which you should consider this issue is found in a statement that was made in the journal *Research Quarterly for Exercise and Sport* (Magill, 1996): "Manuscripts deviating from the recommended format will neither be reviewed nor returned" (n.p.).

5. When considering the length of an article, account for the probability that the number of pages in your manuscript will be reduced by nearly twenty-five to thirty percent when it appears in print (due to different font size). In other words, a manuscript containing twenty-five pages will cover approximately eighteen pages in a journal. At the same time, resist the tendency to write too lengthy an article.

6. Be sure that all appropriate steps have been taken to obtain informed consent from any human subjects participating in the study. Publishers may expect you to provide evidence in this regard.

7. The author is ultimately responsible for the manuscript in all respects: content, format, and style. Whether or not a separate typist has been recruited to prepare the document, the author remains accountable. The only way to be certain that errors do not exist is to carefully examine every feature of the document.

8. Submit the manuscript to only one *journal publisher at a time.* For ethical and copyright reasons, the author should wait until a publishing decision has been made before other avenues of publication are considered.

9. Submit the article in an attractive *fashion.* Although the guidelines furnished by the publisher will provide very specific format and style information, the author can take additional steps by carefully packaging whatever is submitted. Include a stamped, self-addressed envelope for returning the article should the publisher (that is, the editorial board) decide against publishing it. Should this occur, however, do *not* be discouraged. Many authors have experienced the return of their articles. There may be any number of reasons why the article is not considered suitable at a particular time. Among the most common reasons for rejecting manuscripts are the following.

- The article is too long.
- The article does not satisfy theme requirements.
- An abundance of articles have recently been published on the topic.
- The author did not follow the recommended format and style.
- The investigator employed a faulty research or statistical design.
- The article generally lacks quality.

 NOTE: Upon returning the article, the publisher may offer suggestions for revision. Take those to heart, and try again.

10. Once the manuscript has been accepted, do not be impatient for it to appear in print. Actual publication may take longer than one would think. Given the expressed interest on the part of readers to know the time delay between the acceptance and printing of articles, a number of publishers are now including submission, revision, and acceptance dates with the article. This enables the reader to know if the information is current. To illustrate the point, you are referred to Table 13–1, in which the submission and acceptance dates have been recorded for eight articles that appeared in the Spring 1997 edition of *Exceptional Children*. While it is a small sample size, the number does represent the population of articles in that one edition. It can be seen that, on average, it took 6.625 months for a manuscript to be accepted. From the time it was submitted, it took an average of 16.375 months for the article to appear in print.

Once accepted, there are a number of reasons why there may be delays in bringing the article to print, including:

1. The backlog of accepted articles
2. The frequency with which the journal is published (for example, monthly, quarterly, and so on)

Table 13–1: **Submission and Acceptance Dates for Eight Articles Published in the Spring 1997 Edition of *Exceptional Children***

Article Number	Submission Date	Acceptance Date	Months to Accept	Months to Print
1	January 1996	April 1996	3	14
2	October 1995	May 1996	7	17
3	September 1995	May 1996	8	18
4	November 1995	April 1996	5	16
5	September 1995	May 1996	8	18
6	January 1996	June 1996	5	14
7	January 1996	June 1996	5	14
8	July 1995	July 1996	12	20
			$M = 6.625$	$M = 16.375$

3. The length of the article in regard to space available

4. The number of articles that ordinarily appear in an issue

5. Whether the publisher will hold the article until there enough to form a "theme" issue.

In short, your time will come. Be persistent, as it is very important that information pertaining to your study has the opportunity to be shared with the largest audience possible.

SUMMARY

Once the investigator has gathered and analyzed the information, the next step in the research process is to communicate the results. To do this successfully requires attention to *mechanical* as well as *conventional* details. While the manuals of form and style may require different organizational structures, the elements of all reports are essentially the same. This holds true whether a document is being prepared in response to a graduate thesis requirement, or to a call for papers at a regional conference. From the prefatory to the appended sections of the report, as much attention must be given to spelling, punctuation, and sentence structure as is assigned to the objective reporting of content. In this regard, optimum standards of scholarship should be maintained from the processing of an idea to the processing of the results. If a solid foundation for the study was established at onset, not only is the task of writing the report less formidable, it can be something one looks forward to with eager anticipation.

The primary function of research activity is to discover, confirm, and communicate new knowledge. Formal procedures have been developed for preparing theses, journal articles, and papers. Mastering and employing these techniques will aid practitioner/researchers in communicating the results of their investigative efforts. With the present and anticipated features of integrated word processing and database management systems, the prospects for preparing professional-quality documents are even greater.

RECOMMENDED LABORATORY ASSIGNMENTS

1. Review the recommended readings.

2. Review the *format* and *style* of journals that are published within your professional field(s) of interest. Study the "Guidelines for Contributors."

3. Thoroughly examine the *manual of form and style* recommended for use by the publishers of those journals referenced in assignment 2, above.

4. Employing an appropriate *manual of form and style,* draft a report of a descriptive *or* experimental research project that was designed and administered in response to recommended assignments of earlier chapters. As you prepare the draft, assign appropriate consideration to each of the following categories:

   a. Key terms

   b. Introduction, including (1) statement of the problem, (2) need for the study, (3) review of related literature, and (4) statement of hypotheses or research questions

   c. Methods, including (1) subjects, (2) instrumentation, and (3) procedures

   d. Findings

   e. Discussion, including (1) conclusions, (2) implications, and (3) recommendations

5. Arrange a meeting with fellow graduate students, colleagues, and school and nonschool employees in order to review the content, format, and style of the draft prepared in response to assignment 4, above.

6. Revise the initial draft (per recommendations above). Continue to assign attention to word capitalization, punctuation, sentence structure, spelling, and word usage.

7. Prepare an abstract (in accordance with guidelines presented in the chapter).

8. Acquire the assistance of others to help evaluate the abstract against the content of the final draft in order to ensure that all critical information has been included.

9. In accordance with all pertinent "Guidelines for Contributors," submit the manuscript of the report to one of the journals referenced in assignment 2, above.

10. Arrange to meet with fellow graduate students, colleagues, as well as school and nonschool personnel in order to discuss current and future research and publishing interests.

RECOMMENDED READINGS

Balian, E. S. (1994). *The graduate research guidebook: A practical approach to doctoral-master's research.* Lanham, MD: University Press of America.

Barkley, W. R. (Ed.). (1981). *Manual for authors and editors: Editorial style and manuscript preparation.* East Norwalk, CT: Appleton & Lange.

Barzun, J. (1985). *On writing, editing and publishing: Essays explicative and hortatory* (2nd ed.). Chicago: University of Chicago Press.

Barzun, J. (1994). *Simple and direct: A rhetoric for writers*. Chicago: University of Chicago Press.

Becker, H. (1986). *Writing for social scientists*. Chicago: University of Chicago Press.

Boice, R. (1993). Writing blocks and tacit knowledge. *Journal of Higher Education, 64*(1), 19–54.

Boice, R. (1995). Writerly rules for teachers. *Journal of Higher Education, 66*(1), 32–60.

Cabell, D. (Ed.). (1995). *Cabell's directory of publishing opportunities in education* (4th ed.). Beaumont, TX: Cabell.

Day, R. A. (1994). *How to write and publish a scientific paper* (4th ed.). Phoenix, AZ: Oryx.

Evans, D. (1996). *How to write a better thesis or report*. Concord, NH: Paul & Co.

Flesch, R., & Lass, A. H. (1989). *A new guide to better writing*. New York: Warner Books.

Ford, J. E. (Ed.). (1995). *Teaching the research paper: From theory to practice, from research to writing*. Metuchen, NJ: Scarecrow.

Freed, M. N., Hess, R. K., & Ryan, J. M. (1990). *The educator's desk reference*. New York: Macmillan.

Gebremedhin, T. G., & Tweeten, L. G. (1994). *Research methods and communication in the social sciences*. Westport, CT: Praeger.

Gopen, G. D., & Swan, J. A. (1990). The science of scientific writing. *American Scientist, 78,* 550–558.

Haensly, P. A., Lupkowski, A. E., & McNamara, J. F. (1987). The chart essay: A strategy for communicating research findings to policymakers and practitioners. *Educational Evaluation and Policy Analysis, 9,* 63–75.

Hegde, M. N. (1993). *A coursebook on scientific and professional writing in speech-language pathology*. San Diego, CA: Singular.

Henson, K. T. (1995). *The art of writing for publication*. Needham Heights, MA: Allyn & Bacon.

Hult, C. A. (1995). *Researching and writing in sciences and technology*. Needham Heights, MA: Allyn & Bacon.

Korolenko, M. D. (1997). *Writing for multimedia: A guide and sourcebook for the digital writer*. Belmont, CA: Wadsworth.

Ladas, H. (1980). Summarizing research: A case study. *Review of Educational Research, 50,* 597–624.

Lane, M. K., Lindenfelser, L. F., & Powell, G. B., Jr. (1993). *Style manual for political science* (Rev. ed.). Washington, DC: American Political Science Association.

Locke, D. (1992). *Science as writing*. New Haven, CT: Yale University Press.

Madigan, R., Johnson, S., & Linton, P. (1995). The language of style: APA style as epistemology. *American Psychologist, 50,* 428–436.

Madsen, D. (1983). *Successful dissertations and theses*. San Francisco, CA: Jossey-Bass.

Matthews, J. R., Bowen, J. M., & Matthews, R. W. (1996). *Successful scientific writing: A step-by-step guide for the biological and medical sciences*. New York: Cambridge University Press.

Mauch, J. E., & Birch, J. W. (1983). *Guide to the successful thesis and dissertation*. New York: Marcel Dekker.

McQuain, J. (1996). *Power of language: Getting the most out of your words.* Boston: Houghton Mifflin.

Morris, D. (1994). *Guidelines for writing a qualitative research report.* Chicago: American Marketing Association.

National Information Standards Organization Staff. (1995). *Scientific and technical reports: Elements, organization, and design.* Bethesda, MD: National Information Standards Organization Press.

Scientific style and format: The CBE manual for authors, editors, and publishers (6th ed.). (1994). New York: Cambridge University Press.

Smith, M. L. (1987). Publishing qualitative research. *American Educational Research Journal, 24,* 173–183.

Sommers, N. (1980). Revision strategies of student writers and experienced adult writers. *College Composition and Communication, 31,* 378–388.

Sternberg, D. (1981). *How to complete and survive a doctoral dissertation.* New York: St. Martin's Press.

Strunk, W., & White, E. B. (1995). *The elements of style.* Needham Heights, MA: Allyn & Bacon.

Tuckman, B. W. (1990). A proposal for improving the quality of published educational research. *Educational Researcher, 19*(9), 22–25.

Van Maanen, J. (1988). *Tales of the field: On writing ethnography.* Chicago: University of Chicago Press.

Westmeyer, P. M. (1994). *A guide for use in planning, conducting, and reporting research projects* (2nd ed.). Springfield, IL: Thomas.

Wilkinson, A. (1991). *A scientist's handbook for writing papers and dissertations.* Englewood Cliffs, NJ: Prentice-Hall.

Wolcott, H. F. (1990). *Writing up qualitative research.* Newbury Park, CA: Sage.

Wolcott, H. F. (1994). *Transforming qualitative data: Description, analysis, and interpretation.* Newbury Park, CA: Sage.

REFERENCES

American Psychological Association. (1994). *Publication manual of the American Psychological Association* (4th ed.). Washington, DC: Author.

Campbell, W. G., Ballou, S. V., & Slade, C. (1990). *Form and style: Theses, reports, term papers* (7th ed.). Boston: Houghton Mifflin.

Chicago manual of style: Fourteenth edition, revised and expanded. (1993). Chicago: University of Chicago Press.

Council for Exceptional Children (1997, Spring). *Exceptional children.* Reston, VA: Author.

Dugdale, K. (1967). *A manual on writing research* (Rev ed.). Bloomington, IN: Author.

Gibaldi, J., & Achtert, W. S. (1988). *MLA handbook for writers of research papers.* New York: Modern Language Association of America.

Hacker, D. (1992). *A writer's reference* (2nd ed.). Boston, MA: St. Martin's Press.

Hebert, E. P., Landin, D., & Solmon, M. A. (1996, March). Practice schedule effects on the performance and learning of low- and high-skilled students: An applied study. *Research Quarterly for Exercise and Sport, 67*(1), 52–58. Reprinted by permission.

Henson, K. T. (1997, June). Writing for publication: Some perennial mistakes. *Phi Delta Kappan, 78*(10), 781–784.

Jones, B. E., Clark, G. M., & Soltz, D. F. (1997, Winter). Characteristics and practices of sign language interpreters in inclusive education programs. *Exceptional Children, 63*(2), 257–268. Reprinted by permission of the publisher.

Lilley, R. (1997, May 18). Academics score big in bad writing contest. *New Hampshire Sunday News,* p. 7A.

Magill, R. A. (Ed.). (1996, March). Guidelines for contributors. *Research Quarterly for Exercise and Sport, 67*(1), n.p.

Pyrczak, F., & Bruce, R. R. (1992). *Writing empirical research reports: A basic guide for students of the social and behavioral sciences.* Los Angeles, CA: Pyrczak.

Riebel, J. P. (1972). *How to write reports, papers, theses, articles: A practical guide to every aspect of effective writing.* New York: Arco.

Turabian, K. L. (1987). *A manual for writers of term papers, theses, and dissertations* (5th ed.). Chicago: University of Chicago Press.

CHAPTER 14

Evaluation of a Research Report

OBJECTIVES

After reading this chapter, you should be able to:

- Discuss the purpose of evaluating research reports.
- Distinguish between general and method-specific evaluatory criteria.
- Identify questions that should be addressed in order to judge the quality of (1) preliminary information, (2) introduction, (3) methods, (4) findings, and (5) discussion.
- Distinguish between the method-specific criteria used to evaluate (1) surveys and experimental studies; (2) interviews and observations; (3) mail, computerized, and telephone questionnaires; (4) correlation and causal-comparative studies; (5) historical and philosophical studies; and (6) qualitative and test-and-measurement studies.
- Demonstrate the competence to evaluate research reports.
- Define key terms, and answer the checkpoint questions.

KEY TERMS

Analytical Procedures

Article Acceptance Date

Article Submission Date

Causal-Comparative Studies

Computerized Questionnaires

Criteria

Evaluation

General Evaluatory Criteria

Historical Studies

Indicators

Interviews

Mail Questionnaires

Measures

Operational Definitions

Preliminary Information

Qualitative Studies

Research Design

Research Evaluation Digest (RED) Form

Specific Evaluatory Criteria

Statement of the Problem

Subjects

Summary Sheet

Survey Studies

Telephone Questionnaires

Test and Measurement Studies

INTRODUCTION

One of the major goals of research is to produce results that are both internally and externally valid. Throughout the book, repeated reference has been made to the importance of thoughtful selection, planning, and implementation of one's design. Each of these points culminated in Chapter 13, Preparing the Research Report.

From the information presented in reports, other researchers make determinations of the relevance of the studies to their own particular investigations. Practitioners take what is reported and apply it to the circumstances within their places of employment. To a great extent, these individuals should feel comfort in knowing that this research has been thoughtfully designed and administered. However, there are reasons to be cautious about accepting what is read simply because it is in print. Every day of the week, newspapers report upon current events, advertise products, and make weather predictions. Sometimes the accounts are accurate; sometimes they are not. The decisions that are made by the public, however, are often prompted by what is "learned" from these sources.

Although we can all identify with the importance of "responsible journalism," there are all too many reports to which one can point that are based upon inadequate information or distortion. It is through experience that we learn of the importance of knowing such things as what, who, where, when, and how, before accepting what is said as truth. Knowledge affects behavior, and every effort must be made to ensure that what is known is accurate and complete. This is in keeping with the underlying purpose of this chapter.

The most notable characteristic of a quality research report is that the investigator has clearly delineated the mechanisms that account for the findings. The problem statement, hypothesis, nature of the sample, instrumentation, and **analytical procedures** are among the elements that need to be clearly annunciated. Through the utilization of appropriate evaluatory criteria, judgments can be made about the relative strengths and weaknesses of the various components of the study. There are generic standards that are applicable to all studies, and there are standards that are unique to the design of the study (for example, whether the study is a survey or an experiment). Each will be discussed in turn within the sections that follow. The first section elaborates upon the purpose of evaluating papers and published research. This is followed by a discussion of general and specific evaluatory criteria and an evaluation practicum. Note that the Recommended Readings list at the end of the chapter contains references that have been selected for their relevance to report assessment practices.

PURPOSE

The fact that a research report is in print does not necessarily mean that the investigation is without flaws. Hittleman and Simon (1997), Huck and Cormier (1996), Tuckman (1994), Vierra and Pollock (1988), and Williamson, Karp, Dalphin, and Gray (1982) are among those who have spoke to the importance of research **evaluation** procedures. Consumers and those seeking to use findings as a basis for further research must be diligent in their assessment practices. All too frequently, published articles have lacked clarity, provided insufficient information, or described research or statistical designs inappropriate to the problem. Hall, Ward, and Comer (1988) conducted a study in which it was requested that a group of experts judge published articles in order to rate their quality. Of those articles that were evaluated, it was observed that only fifty-eight percent met acceptable criteria. Of the forty-two percent judged to be unacceptable or in need of major revisions, the most frequent deficiency was lack of information on validity and reliability for the instruments of assessment used in the studies. This is a concern worth noting because of the importance of this evidence to judging the worth of any data-collection endeavor. After all, how much credibility would a reader want to assign to findings generated by an instrument that she knows very little about? Although investigators may have used instruments of quality in the studies that were judged to be unacceptable, one would not be able to make that determination by reading the articles alone.

Since the writing of a report is an integral part of the entire research process (see Chapter 13, Preparing the Research Report), it is incumbent upon the investigator to be as thorough with that phase of the study as she was with any other. The fewer the number of questions that linger when completing the article, the better able is the reader to render judgment on the value of the study to her own professional interests. Whereas some information may be quite difficult to judge, for example, the adequacy of a literature review on adult learning if your background is in early childhood education, other information would be more easily interpreted, for example, the adequacy of a literature review on inclusionary education if your specialty is in the area of developmental disabilities. Because each of these topics deals with *methods,* however, it is very likely that early childhood, English, *and* special education teachers would have interest in the studies and be curious about what the results would show.

> **NOTE:** When investigators find a dearth of literature in a specific topic, for example, teaching methods in English, it may be helpful for them to branch out to studies of methods in other disciplines. Many of the general teaching methods found to be effective in one field of study have been found to be effective in others (see the section on review of related literature in Chapter 3, Preparation of a Research Plan).

There may be any number of components of a study that may be more difficult than others to judge. Should gender have been controlled in the study? What about a pretest? Would it have been more desirable to have someone other than the investigator work with the experimental group? Something to which all of us might agree, however, is that a questionnaire is an appropriate tool to use when assessing the preferences of high school teachers toward elective courses in the curriculum. On the other hand, if one were to ask whether that questionnaire should be administered through an interview as opposed to through the mail, one might say that questionnaires are more effective if administered face-to-face (so that there can be opportunities to clarify question ambiguity). Would that same view be held, however, if there was cause to be concerned about subject anonymity?

As you can see, there are any number of factors that go into the determination of whether the investigator employed appropriate procedures. The evaluator who is attempting to make an informed judgment in this regard must contrast what is reported against established standards. There is no question, for example, that any research report should make reference to such things as:

1. A problem statement
2. A literature review
3. Hypotheses
4. Analytical procedures
5. Findings, conclusions, and recommendations

And while there may be a question about the *best* way to administer a questionnaire, the evaluator should be satisfied if there is evidence that the investigator gave thoughtful regard to all pertinent issues and selected the method best suited to generating the most valid results.

Although the findings of every study are not going to make the same level of contribution to the profession, it is important that any findings that are presented are based upon optimum investigative practices. It is in this regard that the evaluation of studies holds its rightful place. The next section examines the **criteria** that are considered common to the evaluation of any study.

GENERAL EVALUATORY CRITERIA

In spite of the lack of complete precision when it comes to evaluating written reports, valid studies ordinarily provide evidence of having satisfied generally accepted criteria. Although the following discussion of **general evaluatory criteria** should not be considered an inclusive list, the items presented are considered indicative of what needs to be taken into account when evaluating any research report.

Preliminary Information

Preliminary information includes the title, the abstract, the key terms, and the **article submission and acceptance dates.**

Title.

1. Is it a clear and concise statement of the main topic?
2. Does it include variables (or categories of variables), if applicable?
3. Is it free of unnecessary terms and phrases?
4. Does it lend itself to proper indexing?

Abstract.

1. Has the problem been stated?
2. Have the procedures (including the design) been indicated?
3. Has the number and kind of subjects been identified?
4. Has the instrumentation been reviewed?
5. Have the results (and statistical levels of significance, if applicable) been presented?

Key Terms.

1. Were key terms presented?
2. Have they been defined (clarified) in the introductory portion of the report or, if related to instruments of measurement, in the instrumentation portion of the report?
3. Was each variable in the study clearly defined?

 NOTE: The quality of the title, abstract, and key terms cannot be judged until the entire research report has been read.

Submission/Acceptance of Article.

1. Has the *submission date* for the article been indicated?
2. Has the *revision-acceptance date* for the article been indicated?

Introduction

The introduction includes the **statement of the problem,** the need for the study, a review of related literature, and a statement of the hypothesis or research question.

Statement of the Problem.

1. Is there a problem statement? If so:

   a. What is it?

   b. Is it self-contained—that is, a complete and accurate statement of what was actually studied—or was something left out?

 NOTE: Whether the problem statement is complete and accurate cannot be determined until the report has been read.

   c. Is it clear?

   d. Is it measurable?

2. Has sufficient background information on the problem been presented?

3. Have the variables of interest been indicated and, if applicable, have they been defined? (See **Key Terms,** above.)

4. Did the investigators demonstrate undue bias (positive or negative) in discussing the problem statement?

5. Was the statement of the problem introduced *prior* to the literature review?

Need for the Study.

1. Does the problem have *theoretical* and *practical* educational value, and has that been established?

2. Is the problem to be studied timely?

Review of Related Literature.

1. Is it comprehensive?

2. Does it include studies known to be relevant to the problem?

3. Has it been clearly written and organized? Is it easy to follow, with the studies *least* related to the problem introduced *first,* and those *most* related to the problem introduced *last* (that is, in an inverted pyramid style)?

4. Are most of the sources primary, or are they "as cited in" referrals?

5. Has the related literature been analyzed critically, with similar findings grouped together, or is the "review" simply a compilation of isolated abstracts?

6. Is there a summary of the literature, followed by its implications for the hypothesis?

7. Does the reference list (provided at the conclusion of the article) include all sources introduced within the body of the report?

Statement of the Hypotheses or Research Questions.

1. What are they?

2. Are they clearly stated and leave nothing implied?

3. Are they consistent with the statement of the problem?

4. Are they testable?

5. Did the investigators offer a compelling argument for using research questions instead of hypotheses (or vice versa)?

✓CHECKPOINT

Identify four major elements within the *introductory* portion of the report that should be judged against general evaluatory standards.

Answer

The four components of the introductory section of the report that should be evaluated against the general standards are:

1. Statement of the problem

2. Need for the study

3. Review of related literature

4. Statement of the hypotheses or research questions

Methods

The methods section contains information about the **subjects,** the instrumentation used, and the procedures followed.

Subjects.

1. Is there a description of the size and character of the study group?

2. If random-selection techniques were used:

  a. Was the method of random selection clearly described?

  b. Is it likely that the procedures led to an unbiased sample?

  c. Were subgroups formed and, if so, upon what basis?

  d. Did the study groups meet the recommended guidelines for minimum sample size?

3. How was confidentiality assured?

Instrumentation.

1. Was a rationale provided for selecting the instruments of assessment?

2. Was there a description of the purpose and content of each instrument?

3. If pertinent, were procedures described for calibrating instruments?

4. Is there evidence that each instrument was valid and reliable for the purpose of the study?

5. If a practitioner-made instrument was used, what evidence was provided for its validity, reliability, and objectivity, specifically in regard to:

    a. Jury composition (content and construct validity)?

    b. Criterion **measures** (concurrent and predictive validity)?

    c. Pilot study (test reliability and objectivity; item difficulty; discrimination; and whether alternatives were functioning)?

6. Were descriptions provided for administering and scoring the instruments?

Procedures.

1. Is there evidence that the design was appropriate to the purpose of the study?

2. What measures were taken to control for threats to internal and external validity?

3. Were the procedures described in sufficient detail to permit replication of the study by other investigators?

Findings

The findings section should consider the following questions:

1. If numerical data were generated (that is, nominal, interval, ratio, or interval), did the investigator use appropriate statistical measures for their analysis?

2. Were the statistics employed correctly?

3. Were the statistical findings interpreted correctly?

4. Was every hypothesis tested—that is, accepted or rejected—and, if rejected, at what levels of confidence?

5. What were the findings, and did they address the statement of the problem?

6. Were the findings adequately supported by narrative and graphs?

Discussion

The discussion section covers the conclusions, implications, and recommendations.

Conclusions.

1. Are they consistent with the findings of the study?

2. Was reference made to the relationship of the findings to those of the related literature?

3. Was discussion presented on the possible influence of uncontrolled variables?

4. Was it apparent that the investigator's professional affiliations and personal philosophy impacted inappropriately upon her objective analysis of the data?

Implications.

1. Were adequate explanations provided for the findings?

2. Was there discussion of the practical and theoretical implications of the findings?

3. If inferential analyses were employed, did the investigator distinguish between the *statistical* and *practical* significance of the findings?

Recommendations.

1. Were recommendations made in regard to how practitioners may use the results?

2. Were suggestions offered about possible foci of future research?

✓CHECKPOINT

The following five questions are asked to see if you can identify the areas of the report where the evaluator should expect to find related information. From the list at the top, select the *best* answer and place its letter into the space provided to the left of the numbered item. Answers may be used only once.

> A. Preliminary information
> B. Introduction
> C. Methods
> D. Findings
> E. Discussion

___ **1.** Did the investigator distinguish between *statistical* and *practical* significance?

___ **2.** Has sufficient background information on the problem been presented?

___ **3.** Is it free of unnecessary terminology, and does it lend itself to proper indexing?

___ **4.** Were the statistics interpreted correctly?

___ **5.** Was a rationale provided for selecting the instruments of assessment?

Answers

The answers that follow indicate the section of the report in which information pertinent to the inquiry would ordinarily be found.

1. The *discussion* section (E) is where the investigator would likely distinguish between the statistical and practical significance of any findings.

2. The *introduction* (B) should include the background information on the problem of the study.

3. It is from the title in the *preliminary information* section (A) of the report that the evaluator would judge indexing suitability.

4. It is from what is presented in the *findings* section (D) of the report that the evaluator should be able to determine whether the statistics were interpreted correctly. Although this information may be found in the discussion section of the report, it would be more appropriate to include interpretations of the statistics with the findings [for example, whether $F(2,6) = 6.661$ is significant].

5. The *methods* section (C) of the report is where the writer should provide a rationale for selecting the instruments of assessment.

NOTE: With regard to the illustration presented in response 4, above, $F(2,6)$ = 6.661, $p < .05$. For 2,6 (numerator and denominator degrees of freedom, respectively), an F ratio of 5.143 would have to be equaled or exceeded in order to find significance at the .05 level of confidence. Since the earned value was 6.661, the finding is significant at $< .05$. The ratio does *not* reach the .01 *loc*, however, as an F ratio of 10.925 would have been required.

Were you able to recall the process for determining the significance of F ratios? If so, well done! Should you feel it necessary to review the procedures, refer to Chapter 10, Two-Group Designs, and Chapter 11, Other Experimental Procedures.

Having examined evaluatory criteria common to *all* studies, the next section presents those areas of inquiry that are specific to particular research designs.

SPECIFIC EVALUATORY CRITERIA

The previous section discussed areas of inquiry to which all studies should be subjected. Add to those the questions that are specific to the type of investigation that has been reported, and you will have a battery of items that should serve as a reasonable measure of a study's quality. **Specific evaluatory criteria** for different types of studies are discussed in the following text.

Survey Studies

1. What techniques were used to obtain the data: interview, observation, or mail, computerized, or telephone questionnaires?

2. How were prime sources of information identified?

3. Was discussion presented on the rationale underlying the choice of data-gathering procedures?

4. What form of question was used in the measuring instrument (for example, closed-ended, fixed-response)?

5. Was each area and item weighted according to its relative importance?

6. What procedures were taken to establish dates and times for data collection?

7. Is each question related to a study objective?

8. What precautions were taken to ensure that the data were being obtained from prime sources?

Interviews.

1. Were prime sources of information used?

2. Was the method for recording responses described?

3. Were interviews recorded on tape? If so, was permission granted?

4. Was more than one visit necessary?

Observations.

1. Were observers trained?

2. Was there evidence of inter-rater reliability?

3. Was only one behavior observed at a time?

4. Were observations video-recorded? If so, was permission granted?

5. Were observer bias and obtrusiveness discussed?

Mail Questionnaires.

1. How was it determined that the responses were those of the prime sources of information?

2. Were answer sheets coded?

3. What percentage of returns was obtained? If lower than seventy percent, were explanations provided?

4. What procedures were established for follow-up should responses *not* be received by established dates?

5. How were responses secured?

Computerized Questionnaires.

1. Were procedures described for accessing computers and entering information?

2. Were codes established to ensure confidentiality?

Telephone Questionnaires.

1. Did the investigators discuss provisions for call forwarding, call waiting, conference calls, TTY (telecommunications device for the deaf), voice mail, and so on?

2. Were any special procedures discussed to help ensure that the person responding to questions over the phone was the prime source of information?

3. Was there any discussion of precautions that were taken to reduce interruptions of telephone conversation/interviews?

Correlation Studies

1. What correlation procedure was used?

2. On what basis was a decision made on the method of correlation to employ?

3. Were the criteria for variable selection described?

4. Were interpretations based upon the coefficient, common variance, or levels of significance?

5. Did the conclusions imply causal relationships between the variables under study?

6. In instances where predictions were made:

   a. Was a rationale provided for selecting predictor variables?

   b. Was the criterion variable well-defined?

Qualitative Studies

1. Was there evidence that the subjects selected for study were capable of producing information germane to the topic of interest?
2. Did the investigators appear to be biased when describing the subjects of the study?
3. Did the investigators assume the role of full participant-observers or observers?
4. Is there evidence that each analytical measure was appropriate to the individual, group, or setting?
5. Was more than one strategy employed to enhance the validity and reliability of the data (for example, triangulation)?
6. Was there evidence that the investigators pursued leads to additional information that may have arisen during the course of the study?
7. Were data-coding procedures used and described?
8. Were distinctions made between the reactions of the investigators and descriptive field notes?
9. Were reasonable explanations given to explain the findings?
10. Were numerical data used to support the findings? If so, what did the analyses show?
11. Were there direct quotations provided to support conclusions?
12. Were qualifications attached to any generalizations that were made?

Historical Studies

1. Was the *majority* of the information obtained from primary sources?
2. Were there descriptions of artifacts?
3. Was each piece of data subjected to external and internal criticism?
4. How were data organized for subsequent treatment (for example, documentary analysis)?

Philosophical Studies

1. Were sources of scientific evidence used to generate philosophical positions?
2. Was reference made to the practice of aesthetics, epistemology, ethics, logic, or metaphysics?
3. To what extent did the investigators attribute solutions to personal experiences?

Test and Measurement Studies

1. What are the objectives of the instrument?
2. What category of measuring instrument did the investigators create (for example, achievement, aptitude, attitude, interest, intelligence, and so on)?

3. What types of items were prepared for the instrument (for example, checklist, rating scale, multiple-choice, discussion, and so on)?

4. What criteria were established for jury and pilot group selections?

5. How were validity, reliability, and objectivity determined?

6. What evidence for validity was provided:

   a. Content,

   b. Concurrent,

   c. Construct, or

   d. Predictive?

7. What evidence for reliability was provided:

   a. Equivalence,

   b. Internal consistency, or

   c. Stability?

8. Did the investigator describe how the measurement error (ME) was calculated? If the coefficient was provided:

   a. What is it?

   b. What inferences were made on the basis of the findings?

9. What evidence for objectivity (inter-rater reliability) was provided?

10. Were norms constructed? If so, in what form?

Causal-Comparative Studies

1. Did the investigators provide a description of factors that differentiated the study group?

2. Were extraneous variables identified and discussed?

3. Were *rival* hypotheses tested?

4. Did the investigators attach caution to any causal relationship that was discovered?

Experimental Studies

1. Did the investigators select a **research design** that was appropriate to the study?

2. Was a rationale provided for the design selection, with specific reference to controlling threats to internal validity?

3. Was the assignment of the individuals to groups, and groups to treatments, made on the basis of random selection?

4. Were **operational definitions** provided for the:

   a. Independent (treatment) variables,

   b. Dependent (outcome) variables, and

   c. Sample, person(s), place(s), and time(s)?

5. Did the investigators test the null or directional hypotheses?

6. Was discussion presented on the degree of influence of moderator and intervening variables upon the findings of the study?

At this point, you are aware of the items that should be considered when evaluating research reports. In the next section, you will find a sample form upon which you can summarize your observations (findings).

EVALUATION PRACTICUM

Once a research report has been judged against the general evaluatory criteria, the next step is to determine whether method-specific standards have been satisfied. One way to record your perceptions of the article's compliance with both general and specific standards is to simply place your indicators directly in the margins located to the left (or right) of the items in a list of standards. Although various symbols can be employed, it probably makes the most sense to simply use:

Y = Yes, the standard has been met.

N = No, the standard has *not* been met.

X = Unable to judge.

NA = Standard is *not* applicable.

In order to summarize the findings, the evaluator can then record her perceptions by placing check marks within the appropriate **indicator** columns on a **Research Evaluation Digest (RED) Form** (see Table 14–1). From this **summary sheet**, judgments can be made about the overall quality of the research report. Trends may be revealed by examining the total columns.

NOTE: If there were several occasions when the evaluator was unable to make a judgment about whether the standard was met, it may not necessarily be lack of clarity on the part of the writer. The experience of the evaluator has a great deal to do with the levels of understanding she brings to the task. The more research that is read, however, the easier it will be to make appropriate determinations.

Depending upon one's reason for choosing a particular article to read, there may be some factors that are considered to be more important than others. For example, if an individual is seeking to learn more about what the related literature has to offer on a particular topic, she will pay a great deal of attention to the results pertaining to that section of the report. Conversely, if the individual were interested in examining the degree to which abstracts accurately represent article content, she might not consider the related literature section of the report to be as important.

We all have our reasons for reading various research reports. It is important to remember, however, that the only way that informed judgment can be made as to (1) whether the title of the article appropriately identifies the study, (2) whether the abstract accurately describes the major content elements, (3) whether the related literature is pertinent, and (4) whether the findings are a product of utilizing appropriate

Table 14–1: **Sample Research Evaluation Digest Form**

Name of Journal: _____ Date Published: _____
Article Title:_____ Date Submitted:_____
Author(s): _____

Directions: Upon examining the article against all pertinent standards, place a check mark under the indicator that *best* represents your overall perception of quality as it relates to the category in question. Comments regarding the rating may be entered beneath each category.

Indicators: Y = Yes, the standard has been met.
N = No, the standard has *not* been met.
X = Unable to judge.
NA = Standard is *not* applicable.

Indicator summaries may be calculated by finding the total of each column.

	Y	N	X	NA
1. Preliminary Information				
a. Title	___	___	___	___
b. Abstract	___	___	___	___
c. Key Terms	___	___	___	___
Comment: _____				
2. Introduction				
a. Statement of the Problem	___	___	___	___
b. Need for the Study	___	___	___	___
c. Review of Related Literature	___	___	___	___
d. Statement of Hypothesis (Question)	___	___	___	___
Comment: _____				
3. Method				
a. Subjects	___	___	___	___
b. Instrumentation	___	___	___	___
c. Procedures	___	___	___	___
Comment: _____				
4. Findings	___	___	___	___
Comment: _____				
5. Discussion				
a. Conclusions	___	___	___	___
b. Implications	___	___	___	___
c. Recommendations	___	___	___	___
Comment: _____				
Indicator Totals:	___	___	___	___
Evaluator:_____ Date: _____				

research methods, is to evaluate the entire article against general *and* specific standards of quality.

The task before you now is to use this information as a basis for examining professional documents of interest. The usefulness of the written report you evaluate will determine its appropriateness as a foundation for further research and school reform.

SUMMARY

Hundreds upon hundreds of reports bearing the accounts of research activity are published each year. This is due in part to the recognition of an increasing number of educational professionals that research is the trigger to providing solutions to many of the problems in our schools. Feeling comfort in putting the recommendations of these studies into practice, however, rests with the knowledge that the results have been based upon sound methodology. It is to this purpose that this chapter has been written.

In the preceding sections, both general and method-specific criteria were described. From the *preliminary* overview of the study to the *implications* of the findings, there are standards by which the quality of the research report can be judged. Evaluating the research and writings of others requires the utilization of *quantitative* and *qualitative* measures. The quantitative measures come from the application of the evaluatory criteria to the various elements of the report (see Table 14–1). The qualitative judgment that emerges from the various pieces of quantitative evidence then provides an indication of the overall value of the study.

The process of evaluation is a very important one. Whether standards of quality are applied to the research conducted by you or by others, it is important to know whether the results are appropriate for use as a basis for decision making. Research is a never-ending activity. Always looking to make things better is at the foundation of being an enlightened professional.

 ## RECOMMENDED LABORATORY ASSIGNMENTS

1. Review the recommended readings.

2. Respond to any suggestions offered by the publisher as they relate to your manuscript submitted in response to Recommended Laboratory Assignment 9 in Chapter 13, Preparing the Research Report.

3. Select a published research report, along with two to three colleagues. Working independently, evaluate the article against all pertinent general and method-specific evaluatory criteria.

4. From the notations made in response to item 3, above, complete a summary form (similar to that shown in Table 14–1). Share your findings with those who have read and evaluated the same article. Discuss the relative strengths and weaknesses of the article, the group's overall perceptions of it, and the process of evaluation itself.

5. Apply the general and method-specific evaluatory criteria to a descriptive or experimental research project that was designed and administered in response to recommended assignments of earlier chapters. Identify possible areas of improvement.

6. Select a research report within your professional field of interest. With the exception of the abstract, read its contents up to the point where conclusions are presented. Write your own conclusions and implications. Compare them with those of the written report.

7. For the report read in response to item 6, above, write an abstract (in accordance with the guidelines presented in Chapter 13, Preparing the Research Report). Compare your results with the abstract written by the author of the report.

8. Obtain an article on the basis of an abstract that you have reviewed in a source such as the Educational Resources Information Center (ERIC). Evaluate the abstract against the contents of the article with a view toward how the abstract could be improved.

9. Obtain a copy of a research paper presented at a professional meeting, and compare it against the style and format of a published report written on the same topic.

10. Prepare a list of items that could be added to the general and method-specific evaluation standards that were presented in this chapter.

11. Create a summary evaluation form that would provide a basis for reporting the overall quality of a research report.

12. Continue to conduct critical evaluations of published and nonpublished research.

 RECOMMENDED READINGS

Anisfeld, M. (1987). A course to develop competence in critical reading of empirical research in psychology. *Teaching of Psychology, 14,* 224–227.

Cooper, H. M. (1982). Scientific guidelines for conducting integrative research reviews. *Review of Educational Research, 52,* 291–302.

Cooper, H. M., & Hedges, L. V. (Eds.). (1994). *The handbook of research synthesis.* New York: Sage.

Ericsson, K. A., & Simon, H. A. (1984). *Protocol analysis: Verbal reports as data.* Cambridge, MA: MIT Press.

Johnson, R. W. (1993). Where can teacher research lead? One teacher's daydream. *Educational Leadership, 51*(2), 66–68.

Joint Committee on Standards for Educational Evaluation. (1981). *Standards for evaluation of educational programs, projects, and materials.* New York: McGraw-Hill.

Kamil, M. L., Langer, J. A., & Shanahan, T. (1985). *Understanding research in reading and writing.* Boston: Allyn & Bacon.

Kincheloe, J. L. (1991). *Teachers as researchers: Qualitative inquiry as a path to empowerment.* New York: Falmer Press.

Oakes, J. (1992). Can tracking research inform practice? Technical, normative, and political considerations. *Educational Researcher, 21*(4), 12–21.

Rush, R. T. (1985). Assessing readability: Formulas and alternatives. *The Reading Teacher, 39,* 274–283.

REFERENCES

Hall, B. W., Ward, A. W., & Comer, C. B. (1988). Published educational research: An empirical study of its quality. *Journal of Educational Research, 81,* 182–189.

Hittleman, D. R., & Simon, A. J. (1997). *Interpreting educational research: An introduction for consumers of research* (2nd ed.). Columbus, OH: Merrill.

Huck, S. W., & Cormier, W. H. (1996). *Reading statistics and research* (2nd ed.). New York: HarperCollins.

Tuckman, B. W. (1994). *Conducting educational research* (4th ed.). New York: Harcourt Brace.

Vierra, A., & Pollock, J. (1988). *Reading educational research*. Scottsdale, AZ: Gorsuch Scarisbrick.

Williamson, J. B., Karp, D. A., Dalphin, J. R., & Gray, P. S. (1982). *The research craft: An introduction to social research methods* (2nd ed.). Boston: Little, Brown.

APPENDICES

Appendix A **Table of (10,000) Random Numbers**

Rows	Columns				
1	10480	15011	01536	02011	81647
2	22368	46573	25595	85393	30995
3	24130	48360	22527	97265	76393
4	42167	93093	06243	61680	07856
5	37570	39975	81837	16656	06121
6	77021	06907	11008	42751	27756
7	99562	56420	69994	98872	31016
8	96301	91977	05463	07972	18876
9	89579	14342	63661	10281	17453
10	85475	36857	43342	53988	53060
11	28918	69578	88231	33276	70997
12	63553	40961	48235	03427	49626
13	09429	93969	52636	92737	88974
14	10365	61129	87529	85689	48237
15	07119	97336	74048	08178	77233
16	31862	72040	14302	83351	97769
17	69017	22031	46489	89953	36219
18	50703	39531	88879	20450	66353
19	79042	92001	12591	93511	67872
20	44725	75087	42597	09057	20800
21	91638	50296	68766	92455	25310
22	20985	93804	30522	69907	58928
23	61878	23219	29986	01957	07410
24	26148	10943	30531	30719	52031
25	03876	54579	55069	61745	03107
26	62572	92449	77353	77745	87583
27	73374	25289	67817	01886	37856
28	23693	66496	99425	40359	74487
29	08984	63733	33532	86680	21695
30	15866	89360	72999	95325	60843
31	61362	94280	92434	74739	10087
32	31942	29031	53794	83783	35977
33	61507	05746	86899	10423	64832
34	88356	58846	37532	14319	65491
35	47985	55039	73060	40805	91436

Appendix A **Table of (10,000) Random Numbers (continued)**

Rows	Columns				
36	06756	04494	86590	29153	41919
37	00561	88398	54170	30824	82643
38	21658	32016	51603	93006	28974
39	23548	39715	81538	22663	46611
40	87390	74879	29375	84768	58320
41	19507	82251	26748	69599	79900
42	67156	73174	11078	70878	10689
43	31581	29100	41180	72943	11773
44	34387	93924	33495	88240	45807
45	05674	87123	26279	61056	83663
46	62888	49314	11083	83144	56083
47	45332	02844	47077	59498	57784
48	90978	61205	04876	87411	79988
49	32227	31137	77138	76256	09884
50	53487	96780	97685	70966	10334
51	91114	82089	19705	10546	15519
52	60192	58425	95130	63927	72950
53	14408	38664	02300	84653	74393
54	46768	78192	50956	17331	79478
55	76220	37532	41371	06749	38413
56	71067	49384	13441	82456	00693
57	82195	20470	34174	24962	27806
58	98229	29444	22175	49710	17779
59	46344	38645	78796	04971	32217
60	61714	14498	82780	09547	75596
61	82866	16980	76435	90054	19446
62	73562	26676	88926	05300	03228
63	46509	59719	64413	90811	97331
64	72481	65670	75953	33061	91872
65	03853	35572	59270	16790	04765
66	51329	10574	26787	14686	53813
67	74669	80756	78895	76668	07635
68	88447	41328	05040	65692	86298
69	97665	06569	28629	89766	50480
70	93590	24452	03457	41483	48069

Appendix A **Table of (10,000) Random Numbers (continued)**

Rows	Columns				
71	19635	22753	43007	22592	22488
72	38513	60720	35207	77213	92090
73	23944	21956	47537	83650	12163
74	33312	49483	86637	03810	36309
75	21883	63185	51304	00490	21322
76	20775	79442	26084	74899	67037
77	44639	20293	83414	87989	44873
78	38900	31897	77408	13840	08046
79	02801	45351	13961	30652	72789
80	20103	97339	61608	16898	89134
81	77522	31320	39358	28065	24574
82	02474	74423	95999	04095	50644
83	80805	54726	83218	21079	30989
84	78217	05092	82189	88560	97794
85	01553	28309	05178	96440	27340
86	88260	76845	49341	08505	10461
87	55875	99176	74125	14689	44080
88	12459	02571	70398	00279	60782
89	73356	17648	02925	15263	97553
90	30448	75275	69566	54847	96377
91	48146	71366	81873	23522	30716
92	43594	03121	75795	24542	07290
93	66002	63890	27945	34622	15036
94	54579	44833	77067	94641	81866
95	86934	13232	14702	63452	62051
96	74972	74493	09223	46874	65121
97	15166	97131	41151	04830	98352
98	22026	34800	97914	99139	57766
99	60670	22195	19513	93715	45014
100	78956	05299	78609	35254	28746
101	38518	42843	96714	52028	43341
102	24682	30784	55631	61624	54379
103	84365	47726	49499	71598	88588
104	13493	11608	67135	43156	72483
105	17750	17862	19940	18536	64493

Appendix A **Table of (10,000) Random Numbers (continued)**

Rows	Columns				
106	28205	96718	38249	39559	71957
107	94366	11288	79135	73355	01083
108	76705	38416	75010	35732	80157
109	73084	10594	03837	37953	61212
110	94865	11113	91356	03336	44830
111	40900	42166	04830	40535	89773
112	05489	57089	91446	31904	82620
113	67400	65036	73356	94554	27748
114	56942	46255	71495	62568	97589
115	33596	98510	69735	75338	86800
116	65066	23171	26758	65570	28010
117	86057	78603	58742	09470	93830
118	49641	52097	97957	17468	87102
119	67223	03057	76471	47818	16053
120	86445	46713	38517	94241	21598
121	56910	42623	59761	28664	38464
122	08472	26158	08238	42413	31043
123	54264	71889	07394	44737	28142
124	30074	07516	75125	02534	72142
125	61200	85109	38027	38764	52276
126	38841	38216	66098	13142	57993
127	31938	97545	68219	98093	33553
128	21370	35175	03428	41395	24601
129	04918	18718	71183	76505	31991
130	02575	90495	68899	21075	42852
131	54702	38616	94218	10896	75990
132	81429	90910	73299	28560	58132
133	39720	00913	14706	87083	80220
134	17927	51983	46073	18714	49590
135	36869	90501	19160	20632	59111
136	63472	63191	81254	23886	28999
137	89803	48549	50831	58453	97770
138	29500	54022	73247	57057	34157
139	81818	10351	16155	90521	47531
140	52193	93084	56401	62099	52225

Appendix A **Table of (10,000) Random Numbers (continued)**

Rows	Columns				
141	83952	10364	72578	34629	80314
142	75180	88962	35354	61285	81851
143	58584	33198	85285	29313	78773
144	14474	96046	00882	87668	29228
145	93876	82592	36317	98921	45309
146	06618	42664	94514	09307	49027
147	85545	66900	78506	13209	70979
148	08143	88460	21230	12766	87648
149	76237	20274	90179	25212	06591
150	97604	40499	57523	15401	66332
151	89057	64723	53230	91133	21495
152	43080	42847	35767	66411	76897
153	80940	71290	92492	20708	84975
154	21134	62165	54125	11824	83024
155	61015	52579	46670	64183	38425
156	04719	86586	27883	51867	09370
157	58850	01082	34004	50465	80654
158	11599	06307	26722	85787	81255
159	88749	06783	52361	91449	13184
160	51616	55114	15195	90887	41766
161	32334	03533	17343	37488	14736
162	41752	31539	05165	05979	53136
163	36363	99423	42345	01424	74212
164	24600	73601	23130	24940	38360
165	56052	41689	91544	25342	86511
166	97609	80523	78002	94240	59893
167	40894	43247	79224	29818	47304
168	36397	69077	51372	78160	63524
169	99148	60391	09799	32974	81168
170	57950	85378	69657	68011	98211
171	52895	64185	68136	80545	54337
172	08624	41555	13473	27299	96598
173	20642	20658	93455	09837	49204
174	90065	92962	69976	57287	83970
175	30978	95544	80409	60661	55111

Appendix A **Table of (10,000) Random Numbers (continued)**

Rows	Columns				
176	09346	77223	28996	80876	58033
177	75890	19845	69323	40226	31295
178	82429	89960	82255	79871	06674
179	74537	42399	78304	78196	34109
180	40305	38972	36701	69035	77979
181	91734	91982	59433	79218	69380
182	14761	04055	55184	87533	54256
183	39929	69530	31476	94861	84321
184	01342	19327	69940	45874	88135
185	92000	75223	05886	41163	02800
186	25866	35115	70732	89434	05624
187	03495	29425	06754	80500	20413
188	77853	68823	88129	43660	34882
189	73548	88354	91531	98834	67973
190	46797	31422	66024	10788	74665
191	13580	22689	87717	61540	61600
192	63589	57998	78302	38549	23853
193	20133	03556	89864	40202	26104
194	23867	40519	84250	49220	02799
195	66118	92501	06457	20721	83635
196	00725	34408	28961	33768	45011
197	11197	37792	41763	54125	84873
198	18631	16024	92875	87590	57643
199	92511	83854	69204	39032	20882
200	28537	80317	04516	17569	24676
201	51334	86199	34004	94342	28427
202	52175	65261	87141	30147	16530
203	31420	49916	48530	84040	10242
204	80368	73112	23411	55990	72360
205	18233	73334	72764	08793	27659
206	88179	17124	58977	08187	52024
207	00246	52011	20920	35396	73605
208	12041	85687	90454	51208	63412
209	96912	97110	59137	25576	38754
210	21108	31141	77207	49735	49733

Appendix A **Table of (10,000) Random Numbers (continued)**

Rows	Columns				
211	89969	42738	68363	01646	38942
212	60460	58868	16316	89280	10308
213	14898	16534	56574	00782	17144
214	09313	55316	04831	03119	90285
215	26336	47776	29826	85225	97383
216	49201	48500	69638	24173	11658
217	56784	03496	72357	35735	32730
218	30431	23268	50293	89401	87558
219	23362	19590	65008	97548	95183
220	45569	46496	05901	58729	01441
221	29268	72629	99192	20615	59314
222	59931	45992	93534	93626	05809
223	27446	03692	05269	65741	92892
224	64081	11870	28298	61419	05823
225	11078	54756	28526	21764	76479
226	76762	18702	00697	47243	92940
227	90989	62429	75034	58339	52750
228	66928	25298	71660	04865	04677
229	87673	38330	28564	39478	73111
230	59912	75549	40156	95729	51241
231	49342	99023	15795	02667	36402
232	04207	19743	02037	51753	90066
233	90014	51548	99668	81906	52459
234	03703	94726	81234	27004	19876
235	46322	89890	78278	89205	42872
236	95083	84346	36660	81527	53295
237	34369	71002	19653	66871	99508
238	00871	00283	13078	63941	47072
239	20715	72661	82652	72403	04182
240	57741	81651	39741	44325	97672
241	58120	62716	81613	78244	22638
242	62446	58710	29222	73308	28335
243	95792	76064	35625	89464	00946
244	66477	92680	08941	47780	24018
245	14594	11029	56588	23525	80418

Appendix A **Table of (10,000) Random Numbers (continued)**

Rows			Columns		
246	11820	07625	34882	33556	65707
247	52189	73890	57327	63538	43901
248	30689	57270	18319	90759	31348
249	21991	36978	25649	99916	06533
250	94152	47039	60281	30945	01151
251	42381	87315	94722	22649	53115
252	29265	07670	31652	34109	98099
253	66237	16101	66088	08901	08140
254	10310	05589	29346	70984	50403
255	58366	41464	58063	79292	11663
256	40357	97643	84748	24413	92980
257	71926	59628	50310	28850	28488
258	17015	25427	61462	25902	27265
259	94599	65321	80065	42943	18755
260	67426	60649	34246	16313	47794
261	53839	82125	95509	30221	03354
262	47308	93118	33914	20508	07328
263	87971	11624	38345	42776	31771
264	20146	68363	39402	68942	53109
265	79407	32171	19704	35482	50542
266	74325	00945	41065	97552	92714
267	84585	86775	77722	41782	64726
268	47265	76083	96472	10973	47657
269	80267	02094	26059	53364	83041
270	26044	21029	39719	10396	06038
271	67599	61747	54958	44176	43982
272	42508	19145	18365	68895	98834
273	50365	08066	11776	66570	81431
274	12618	44154	24173	04842	15400
275	77957	63081	89700	31924	15213
276	63618	14475	06866	21954	88314
277	07334	94449	39635	68812	73878
278	86208	53733	06758	75208	22176
279	32492	74176	71251	03645	39879
280	69594	91777	19601	35369	37103

Appendix A **Table of (10,000) Random Numbers (continued)**

Rows	Columns				
281	19277	90165	69018	78580	25282
282	65370	94207	41816	44305	85010
283	31724	91580	64879	41876	11127
284	25569	47943	60827	30560	41977
285	00695	77508	52186	51487	72867
286	88027	26814	65772	19899	98721
287	17037	73620	60238	89057	65992
288	88818	53815	85333	72392	60494
289	51697	91816	03831	72188	31116
290	19876	08923	33937	80327	93374
291	22586	95007	19210	29218	57660
292	54031	99521	66812	90024	19882
293	64422	46213	31382	78587	49239
294	19366	64292	22533	89528	72990
295	48421	51622	22339	94596	62035
296	13003	85501	46962	91685	48692
297	92359	10095	99047	44921	18865
298	04847	01453	08306	75273	38298
299	50329	49228	26059	66219	71377
300	15860	77216	49388	96706	12705
301	30900	79856	00508	29725	28064
302	64298	51765	60973	66596	59464
303	92698	27515	82475	68744	19263
304	33502	43730	18053	99793	28790
305	16580	44651	30013	62959	36394
306	15329	22338	19050	45823	07511
307	22453	90769	45433	88430	40652
308	84302	61139	44306	18416	06291
309	92174	10899	88257	32346	82354
310	23852	20237	35897	68878	77465
311	48560	20891	59863	82774	07009
312	69672	30493	86112	75101	90272
313	23555	76127	37946	79000	60024
314	64794	62274	16897	96950	28736
315	88913	28065	95051	08160	58200

Appendix A **Table of (10,000) Random Numbers (continued)**

Rows			Columns		
316	13039	14615	42501	92380	17427
317	12234	52000	28463	49504	34922
318	91939	25780	87982	95159	66076
319	01350	67208	32280	62445	32529
320	67680	17265	13345	68449	40341
321	90828	46005	76111	22081	15089
322	55866	00218	22422	32865	34709
323	07803	40302	92659	84478	20706
324	12705	09007	98560	05082	07252
325	53090	07985	60050	82072	52806
326	46429	85176	56097	36659	65946
327	49269	82751	58247	57874	41926
328	33350	24373	01805	39979	32879
329	01658	04465	13001	36295	93639
330	41532	92233	81905	04582	30751
331	12245	39076	94543	38843	04065
332	28430	26113	94430	61841	60629
333	19217	41089	98825	73234	68235
334	42385	22023	73589	76887	88746
335	54856	02089	15986	38277	40700
336	96967	23049	38611	27510	19027
337	23555	76127	37946	79000	24647
338	94622	74168	97969	50287	36889
339	13280	65950	51081	60582	00130
340	39146	15425	01923	80174	27122
341	34520	00284	63495	04349	22919
342	39257	80879	82951	59660	76013
343	50672	08322	80624	45325	29676
344	80172	65133	45684	49403	41908
345	28467	05761	11220	81150	89558
346	66002	18224	22328	65347	09078
347	03403	02926	59844	78207	06933
348	73487	70113	18161	81712	55744
349	11797	78231	02170	89485	62078
350	23621	73990	44017	34191	79542

Appendix A **Table of (10,000) Random Numbers (continued)**

Rows	Columns				
351	22670	68517	96289	04421	06014
352	49286	64678	17531	93729	10231
353	26330	66189	25192	32599	76300
354	17822	81487	72026	88417	51963
355	60433	36285	62501	23234	14984
356	51324	03820	27648	02620	76192
357	32147	64992	00997	01331	14160
358	16137	22933	20204	08449	02551
359	58052	50131	71293	33984	15387
360	27214	24457	93875	53237	87532
361	12695	37359	48726	88695	17383
362	87728	65689	89852	22207	95966
363	30086	66638	78601	12799	25455
364	13345	63304	68686	79607	51953
365	77914	81609	58605	53810	91152
366	10953	10440	76087	83401	23135
367	29799	32128	28182	47182	19856
368	51102	62519	58415	60698	68820
369	45078	64910	86451	41885	90366
370	99796	21541	75404	95755	89847
371	80856	73669	71456	55813	43832
372	78961	66766	54272	55048	50167
373	93759	11999	98647	21941	64734
374	34856	73043	27253	93271	50094
375	12425	54702	15004	98876	12939
376	21722	15025	34480	97126	27132
377	24327	77982	17154	95784	33795
378	60986	01097	16913	31610	46145
379	83433	25369	63697	98432	63662
380	28431	33288	53057	55684	42910
381	90077	92428	46647	99781	63764
382	05656	16481	31764	49480	41247
383	44835	21961	67270	28458	53386
384	80249	24766	81410	50565	12993
385	16530	57583	76754	98346	89446

Appendix A **Table of (10,000) Random Numbers (continued)**

Rows	Columns				
386	14526	52440	43189	67137	91706
387	78413	27589	23682	21478	52454
388	11181	39955	70496	70761	89999
389	80002	75996	84115	63491	67703
390	78880	91081	16710	43535	18918
391	20634	60311	37423	99762	43389
392	33158	24440	23702	85511	88233
393	86376	38042	63008	96260	45645
394	45645	58728	74186	46166	41055
395	27030	33767	78289	59122	19371
396	11603	01938	23325	23043	01481
397	20495	70016	22116	80806	44439
398	21878	40547	77597	40675	80601
399	79461	28908	83330	17503	91916
400	79590	66996	70129	42019	24403

Reprinted by permission of Theodore Wisniewski.

Appendix B **Table of Appropriate Sample Sizes**

N	s	N	s	N	s
10	10	220	140	1200	291
15	14	230	144	1300	297
20	19	240	148	1400	302
25	24	250	152	1500	306
30	28	260	155	1600	310
35	32	270	159	1700	313
40	36	280	162	1800	317
45	40	290	165	1900	320
50	44	300	169	2000	322
55	48	320	175	2200	327
60	52	340	181	2400	331
65	56	360	186	2600	335
70	59	380	191	2800	338
75	63	400	196	3000	341
80	66	420	201	3500	346
85	70	440	205	4000	351
90	73	460	210	4500	354
95	76	480	214	5000	357
100	80	500	217	6000	361
110	86	550	226	7000	364
120	92	600	234	8000	367
130	97	650	242	9000	368
140	103	700	248	10000	370
150	108	750	254	15000	375
160	113	800	260	20000	377
170	118	850	265	30000	379
180	123	900	269	40000	380
190	127	950	274	50000	381
200	132	1000	278	75000	382
210	136	1100	285	100000	384

From Krejcie, R.V., and Morgan, D.W., "Determining Sample Size for Research Activities," *Educational and Psychological Measurement,* 30, 608, 1970.
Reprinted by permission of Sage Publications, Inc.

Appendix C **Chi Square Table**

df	Levels of Confidence (*loc*)		
	.05	.02	.01
1	3.841	5.412	6.635
2	5.991	7.824	9.210
3	7.815	9.837	11.345
4	9.488	11.668	13.277
5	11.070	13.388	15.086
6	12.592	15.033	16.812
7	14.067	16.622	18.475
8	15.507	18.168	20.090
9	16.919	19.679	21.666
10	18.307	21.161	23.209
11	19.675	22.618	24.725
12	21.026	24.054	26.217
13	22.362	25.472	27.688
14	23.685	26.873	29.141
15	24.996	28.259	30.578
16	26.296	29.633	32.000
17	27.587	30.995	33.409
18	28.869	32.346	34.805
19	30.144	33.687	36.191
20	31.410	35.020	37.566
21	32.671	36.343	38.932
22	33.924	37.659	40.289
23	35.172	38.968	41.638
24	36.415	40.270	42.980
25	37.652	41.566	44.314
26	38.885	42.856	45.642
27	40.113	44.140	46.963
28	41.337	45.419	48.278
29	42.557	46.693	49.588
30	43.773	47.962	50.892

Reprinted by permission of Addison Wesley Longman Ltd.

Appendix D **Critical Values for _r_**

df (N − 2)	Levels of Confidence		
	.05	.01	.001
1	.99692	.99988	.99999
2	.95000	.99000	.99900
3	.8783	.95873	.99116
4	.8114	.91720	.97406
5	.7545	.8745	.95074
6	.7067	.8343	.92493
7	.6664	.7977	.8982
8	.6319	.7646	.8721
9	.6021	.7348	.8471
10	.5760	.7079	.8233
11	.5529	.6835	.8010
12	.5324	.6614	.7800
13	.5139	.6411	.7603
14	.4973	.6226	.7420
15	.4821	.6055	.7246
16	.4683	.5897	.7084
17	.4555	.5751	.6932
18	.4438	.5614	.6787
19	.4329	.5487	.6652
20	.4227	.5368	.6524
25	.3809	.4869	.5974
30	.3494	.4487	.5541
35	.3246	.4182	.5189
40	.3044	.3932	.4896
45	.2875	.3721	.4648
50	.2732	.3541	.4433
60	.2500	.3248	.4078
70	.2319	.3017	.3799
80	.2172	.2830	.3568
90	.2050	.2673	.3375
100	.1946	.2540	.3211

Reprinted by permission of Addison Wesley Longman Ltd.

Appendix E **Critical Values for *t***

Degrees of Freedom	One-Tailed *p* Value			
	.05	.02	.01	.005
	Two-Tailed *p* Value			
df	.10	.05	.02	.01
1	6.314	12.706	31.821	63.657
2	2.920	4.303	6.965	9.925
3	2.353	3.182	4.541	5.841
4	2.132	2.776	3.747	4.604
5	2.015	2.571	3.365	4.032
6	1.943	2.447	3.143	3.707
7	1.895	2.365	2.998	3.499
8	1.860	2.306	2.896	3.355
9	1.833	2.262	2.821	3.250
10	1.812	2.228	2.764	3.169
11	1.796	2.201	2.718	3.106
12	1.782	2.179	2.681	3.055
13	1.771	2.160	2.650	3.012
14	1.761	2.145	2.626	2.977
15	1.753	2.131	2.602	2.947
16	1.746	2.120	2.583	2.921
17	1.740	2.110	2.567	2.898
18	1.734	2.101	2.552	2.878
19	1.729	2.093	2.539	2.861
20	1.725	2.086	2.528	2.845
21	1.721	2.080	2.518	2.831
22	1.717	2.074	2.508	2.819
23	1.714	2.069	2.500	2.807
24	1.711	2.064	2.492	2.797
25	1.708	2.060	2.485	2.787
26	1.706	2.056	2.479	2.779
27	1.703	2.052	2.473	2.771
28	1.701	2.048	2.467	2.763
29	1.699	2.045	2.462	2.756
30	1.697	2.042	2.457	2.750

Appendix E **Critical Values for _t_ (continued)**

Degrees of Freedom	One-Tailed _p_ Value			
	.05	.02	.01	.005
	Two-Tailed _p_ Value			
_df_	.10	.05	.02	.01
35	1.690	2.030	2.438	2.724
40	1.684	2.021	2.423	2.704
45	1.680	2.014	2.412	2.690
50	1.676	2.008	2.403	2.678
55	1.673	2.004	2.396	2.669
60	1.671	2.000	2.390	2.660
70	1.667	1.994	2.381	2.648
80	1.665	1.989	2.374	2.638
90	1.662	1.986	2.368	2.631
100	1.661	1.982	2.364	2.625
120	1.658	1.980	2.358	2.617
∞	1.645	1.960	2.326	2.576

Appendix F **Critical Values for *F*** (Light print = .05; Bold print = .01)

Degrees of Freedom in Denominator (*N* − *K*)	Degrees of Freedom in Numerator (*K* − 1)				
	1	2	3	4	5
1	161.447	199.500	215.707	224.583	230.162
	4052.176	**4999.492**	**5403.344**	**5624.574**	**5763.641**
2	18.513	19.000	19.164	19.247	19.296
	98.502	**99.000**	**99.166**	**99.249**	**99.299**
3	10.128	9.552	9.277	9.117	9.013
	34.116	**30.816**	**29.457**	**28.710**	**28.237**
4	7.709	6.944	6.591	6.388	6.256
	21.198	**18.000**	**16.694**	**15.977**	**15.522**
5	6.608	5.786	5.409	5.192	5.056
	16.258	**13.274**	**12.060**	**11.392**	**10.967**
6	5.987	5.143	4.757	4.534	4.387
	13.745	**10.925**	**9.780**	**9.148**	**8.746**
7	5.591	4.737	4.347	4.120	3.972
	12.246	**9.547**	**8.451**	**7.847**	**7.460**
8	5.318	4.459	4.066	3.838	3.687
	11.259	**8.649**	**7.591**	**7.006**	**6.632**
9	5.117	4.256	3.863	3.633	3.482
	10.561	**8.022**	**6.992**	**6.422**	**6.057**
10	4.965	4.103	3.708	3.478	3.326
	10.044	**7.559**	**6.552**	**5.994**	**5.636**

From Pearson, E., and Hartley, H., (eds.), "Critical Values for F," *Biometrika Tables for Statisticians,* 1966, Vol. I, 3rd Ed. Used by permission of the Biometrika Trustees.

Appendix F **Critical Values for *F*** (Light print = .05;
Bold print = .01) (continued)

Degrees of Freedom in Denominator (*N – K*)	Degrees of Freedom in Numerator (*K* – 1)				
	6	7	8	10	15
1	233.986	236.768	238.882	241.882	245.950
	5858.977	**5928.348**	**5981.062**	**6055.836**	**6157.273**
2	19.330	19.353	19.371	19.396	19.429
	99.333	**99.356**	**99.374**	**99.399**	**99.432**
3	8.941	8.887	8.845	8.786	8.703
	27.911	**27.672**	**27.489**	**27.229**	**26.872**
4	6.163	6.094	6.041	5.964	5.858
	15.207	**14.976**	**14.799**	**14.546**	**14.198**
5	4.950	4.876	4.818	4.735	4.619
	10.672	**10.456**	**10.289**	**10.051**	**9.722**
6	4.284	4.207	4.147	4.060	3.938
	8.466	**8.260**	**8.102**	**7.874**	**7.559**
7	3.866	3.787	3.726	3.637	3.511
	7.191	**6.993**	**6.840**	**6.620**	**6.314**
8	3.581	3.500	3.438	3.347	3.218
	6.371	**6.178**	**6.029**	**5.814**	**5.515**
9	3.374	3.293	3.230	3.137	3.006
	5.802	**5.613**	**5.467**	**5.257**	**4.962**
10	3.217	3.135	3.072	2.978	2.845
	5.386	**5.200**	**5.057**	**4.849**	**4.558**

Appendix F **Critical Values for *F*** (Light print = .05; **Bold print = .01**) **(continued)**

Degrees of Freedom in Denominator (N – K)	Degrees of Freedom in Numerator (K – 1)				
	1	2	3	4	5
11	4.844 **9.646**	3.982 **7.206**	3.587 **6.217**	3.357 **5.668**	3.204 **5.316**
12	4.747 **9.330**	3.885 **6.927**	3.490 **5.953**	3.259 **5.412**	3.106 **5.064**
13	4.667 **9.074**	3.806 **6.701**	3.411 **5.739**	3.179 **5.205**	3.025 **4.862**
14	4.600 **8.862**	3.739 **6.515**	3.344 **5.564**	3.112 **5.035**	2.958 **4.695**
15	4.543 **8.683**	3.682 **6.359**	3.287 **5.417**	3.056 **4.893**	2.901 **4.556**
16	4.494 **8.531**	3.634 **6.226**	3.239 **5.292**	3.007 **4.773**	2.852 **4.437**
17	4.451 **8.400**	3.592 **6.112**	3.197 **5.185**	2.965 **4.669**	2.810 **4.336**
18	4.414 **8.285**	3.555 **6.013**	3.160 **5.092**	2.928 **4.579**	2.773 **4.248**
19	4.381 **8.185**	3.522 **5.926**	3.127 **5.010**	2.895 **4.500**	2.740 **4.171**
20	4.351 **8.096**	3.493 **5.849**	3.098 **4.938**	2.866 **4.431**	2.711 **4.103**

Appendix F **Critical Values for *F*** (Light print = .05;
Bold print = .01) (continued)

Degrees of Freedom in Denominator (*N − K*)	Degrees of Freedom in Numerator (*K* − 1)				
	6	7	8	10	15
11	3.095	3.012	2.948	2.854	2.719
	5.069	**4.886**	**4.744**	**4.539**	**4.251**
12	2.996	2.913	2.849	2.753	2.617
	4.821	**4.640**	**4.499**	**4.296**	**4.010**
13	2.915	2.832	2.767	2.671	2.533
	4.620	**4.441**	**4.302**	**4.100**	**3.815**
14	2.848	2.764	2.699	2.602	2.463
	4.456	**4.278**	**4.140**	**3.939**	**3.656**
15	2.790	2.707	2.641	2.544	2.403
	4.318	**4.142**	**4.004**	**3.805**	**3.522**
16	2.741	2.657	2.591	2.494	2.352
	4.202	**4.026**	**3.890**	**3.691**	**3.409**
17	2.699	2.614	2.548	2.450	2.308
	4.102	**3.927**	**3.791**	**3.593**	**3.312**
18	2.661	2.577	2.510	2.412	2.269
	4.015	**3.841**	**3.705**	**3.508**	**3.227**
19	2.628	2.544	2.477	2.378	2.234
	3.939	**3.765**	**3.631**	**3.434**	**3.153**
20	2.599	2.514	2.447	2.348	2.203
	3.871	**3.699**	**3.564**	**3.368**	**3.088**

Appendix F **Critical Values for *F*** (Light print = .05;
Bold print = .01) (continued)

Degrees of Freedom in Denominator (*N* – *K*)	Degrees of Freedom in Numerator (*K* – 1)				
	1	2	3	4	5
21	4.325	3.467	3.072	2.840	2.685
	8.017	**5.780**	**4.874**	**4.369**	**4.042**
22	4.301	3.443	3.049	2.817	2.661
	7.945	**5.719**	**4.817**	**4.313**	**3.988**
23	4.279	3.422	3.028	2.796	2.640
	7.881	**5.664**	**4.765**	**4.264**	**3.939**
24	4.260	3.403	3.009	2.776	2.621
	7.823	**5.614**	**4.718**	**4.218**	**3.895**
25	4.242	3.385	2.991	2.759	2.603
	7.770	**5.568**	**4.675**	**4.177**	**3.855**
26	4.225	3.369	2.975	2.743	2.587
	7.721	**5.526**	**4.637**	**4.140**	**3.818**
27	4.210	3.354	2.960	2.728	2.572
	7.677	**5.488**	**4.601**	**4.106**	**3.785**
28	4.196	3.340	2.947	2.714	2.558
	7.636	**5.453**	**4.568**	**4.074**	**3.754**
29	4.183	3.328	2.934	2.701	2.545
	7.598	**5.420**	**4.538**	**4.045**	**3.725**
30	4.171	3.316	2.922	2.690	2.534
	7.562	**5.390**	**4.510**	**4.018**	**3.699**

Appendix F **Critical Values for F** (Light print = .05;
Bold print = .01) (continued)

Degrees of Freedom in Denominator (N – K)	Degrees of Freedom in Numerator (K – 1)				
	6	7	8	10	15
21	2.573	2.488	2.420	2.321	2.176
	3.812	**3.640**	**3.506**	**3.310**	**3.030**
22	2.549	2.464	2.397	2.297	2.151
	3.758	**3.587**	**3.453**	**3.258**	**2.978**
23	2.528	2.442	2.375	2.275	2.128
	3.710	**3.539**	**3.406**	**3.211**	**2.931**
24	2.508	2.423	2.355	2.255	2.108
	3.667	**3.496**	**3.363**	**3.168**	**2.889**
25	2.490	2.405	2.337	2.236	2.089
	3.627	**3.457**	**3.324**	**3.129**	**2.850**
26	2.474	2.388	2.321	2.220	2.072
	3.591	**3.421**	**3.288**	**3.094**	**2.815**
27	2.459	2.373	2.305	2.204	2.056
	3.558	**3.388**	**3.256**	**3.062**	**2.783**
28	2.445	2.359	2.291	2.190	2.041
	3.528	**3.358**	**3.226**	**3.032**	**2.753**
29	2.432	2.346	2.278	2.177	2.027
	3.499	**3.330**	**3.198**	**3.005**	**2.726**
30	2.421	2.334	2.266	2.165	2.015
	3.473	**3.304**	**3.173**	**2.979**	**2.700**

Appendix F **Critical Values for *F*** (Light print = .05;
      Bold print = .01) (continued)

Degrees of Freedom in Denominator (*N* – *K*)	Degrees of Freedom in Numerator (*K* – 1)				
	1	2	3	4	5
40	4.085	3.232	2.839	2.606	2.449
	7.314	**5.179**	**4.313**	**3.828**	**3.514**
50	4.034	3.183	2.790	2.557	2.400
	7.171	**5.057**	**4.199**	**3.720**	**3.408**
60	4.001	3.150	2.758	2.525	2.368
	7.077	**4.977**	**4.126**	**3.649**	**3.339**
70	3.978	3.128	2.736	2.503	2.346
	7.011	**4.922**	**4.074**	**3.600**	**3.291**
80	3.960	3.111	2.719	2.486	2.329
	6.963	**4.881**	**4.036**	**3.563**	**3.255**
90	3.947	3.098	2.706	2.473	2.316
	6.925	**4.849**	**4.007**	**3.535**	**3.228**
100	3.936	3.087	2.696	2.463	2.305
	6.895	**4.824**	**3.984**	**3.513**	**3.206**
150	3.904	3.056	2.665	2.432	2.274
	6.807	**4.749**	**3.915**	**3.447**	**3.142**
200	3.888	3.041	2.650	2.417	2.259
	6.763	**4.713**	**3.881**	**3.414**	**3.110**
300	3.873	3.026	2.635	2.402	2.244
	6.720	**4.677**	**3.848**	**3.382**	**3.079**
400	3.865	3.018	2.627	2.394	2.237
	6.699	**4.659**	**3.831**	**3.366**	**3.063**
500	3.860	3.014	2.623	2.390	2.232
	6.686	**4.648**	**3.821**	**3.357**	**3.054**

Appendix F **Critical Values for F** (Light print = .05;
Bold print = .01) (continued)

Degrees of Freedom in Denominator (N – K)	Degrees of Freedom in Numerator (K – 1)				
	6	7	8	10	15
40	2.336	2.249	2.180	2.077	1.924
	3.291	**3.124**	**2.993**	**2.801**	**2.522**
50	2.286	2.199	2.130	2.026	1.871
	3.186	**3.020**	**2.890**	**2.698**	**2.419**
60	2.254	2.167	2.097	1.993	1.836
	3.119	**2.953**	**2.823**	**2.632**	**2.352**
70	2.231	2.143	2.074	1.969	1.812
	3.071	**2.906**	**2.777**	**2.585**	**2.306**
80	2.214	2.126	2.056	1.951	1.793
	3.036	**2.871**	**2.742**	**2.551**	**2.271**
90	2.201	2.113	2.043	1.938	1.779
	3.009	**2.845**	**2.715**	**2.524**	**2.244**
100	2.191	2.103	2.032	1.927	1.768
	2.988	**2.823**	**2.694**	**2.503**	**2.223**
150	2.160	2.071	2.001	1.894	1.734
	2.924	**2.761**	**2.632**	**2.441**	**2.160**
200	2.144	2.056	1.985	1.878	1.717
	2.893	**2.730**	**2.601**	**2.411**	**2.129**
300	2.129	2.040	1.969	1.862	1.700
	2.862	**2.699**	**2.571**	**2.380**	**2.099**
400	2.121	2.032	1.962	1.854	1.691
	2.847	**2.684**	**2.556**	**2.365**	**2.084**
500	2.117	2.028	1.957	1.850	1.686
	2.838	**2.675**	**2.547**	**2.356**	**2.075**

Appendix G **Standard Score Conversion Table**

z Scores	T Scores	ETS Scores	Deviation IQs	Percentiles
+3.0	80	800	145	99.87
+2.9	79	790	144	99.81
+2.8	78	780	142	99.74
+2.7	77	770	141	99.65
+2.6	76	760	139	99.53
+2.5	75	750	138	99.38
+2.4	74	740	136	99.18
+2.3	73	730	135	98.93
+2.2	72	720	133	98.61
+2.1	71	710	132	98.21
+2.0	70	700	130	97.72
+1.9	69	690	129	97.13
+1.8	68	680	127	96.41
+1.7	67	670	126	95.54
+1.6	66	660	124	94.52
+1.5	65	650	123	93.32
+1.4	64	640	121	91.92
+1.3	63	630	120	90.32
+1.2	62	620	118	88.49
+1.1	61	610	117	86.43
+1.0	60	600	115	84.13
+0.9	59	590	114	81.59
+0.8	58	580	112	78.81
+0.7	57	570	111	75.80
+0.6	56	560	109	72.57
+0.5	55	550	108	69.15
+0.4	54	540	106	65.54
+0.3	53	530	105	61.79
+0.2	52	520	103	57.93
+0.1	51	510	102	53.98
0.0	50	500	100	50.00

Appendix G **Standard Score Conversion Table (continued)**

z Scores	T Scores	ETS Scores	Deviation IQs	Percentiles
−0.1	49	490	99	46.02
−0.2	48	480	97	42.07
−0.3	47	470	96	38.21
−0.4	46	460	94	34.46
−0.5	45	450	93	30.85
−0.6	44	440	91	27.43
−0.7	43	430	90	24.20
−0.8	42	420	88	21.19
−0.9	41	410	87	18.41
−1.0	40	400	85	15.87
−1.1	39	390	84	13.57
−1.2	38	380	82	11.51
−1.3	37	370	81	9.68
−1.4	36	360	79	8.08
−1.5	35	350	78	6.68
−1.6	34	340	76	5.48
−1.7	33	330	75	4.46
−1.8	32	320	73	3.59
−1.9	31	310	72	2.87
−2.0	30	300	70	2.28
−2.1	29	290	69	1.79
−2.2	28	280	67	1.39
−2.3	27	270	66	1.07
−2.4	26	260	64	.82
−2.5	25	250	63	.62
−2.6	24	240	61	.47
−2.7	23	230	60	.35
−2.8	22	220	58	.26
−2.9	21	210	57	.19
−3.0	20	200	55	.13

z Score: $M = 0$, $SD = 1$
T Score: $M = 50$, $SD = 10$ [T Score = $10z + 50$; for example, $10(2) + 50 = 20 + 50 = 70$]
ETS Score: $M = 500$, $SD = 100$ [ETS Score: $100z + 500$; for example, $100(2) + 500 = 200 + 500 = 700$]
Deviation IQ: $M = 100$, $SD = 15$ [Deviation IQ: $15z + 100$; for example, $15(2) + 100 = 30 + 100 = 130$]
Percentiles correspond to points along a normal curve.

From Sax, G., *Principles of Educational and Psychological Measurement and Evaluation, 3rd Ed.*, ©1989 by Wadsworth, Inc. Reprinted by permission of the publisher.

GLOSSARY

A-B-A-B Design A single-subject design in which baseline measurements are taken until the assumption of stability is satisfied; then the treatment phase is introduced accompanied by an appropriate number of measurements, followed by a second baseline phase, which is then followed by a second treatment phase.

A-B-A Design A single-subject design in which baseline measurements are taken until the assumption of stability is satisfied; then the treatment phase is introduced accompanied by an appropriate number of measurements, followed by a second baseline phase.

A-B Design A single-subject design in which baseline measurements are taken until the assumption of stability is satisfied; then the treatment phase is introduced accompanied by an appropriate number of measurements.

Abscissa The horizontal line at the bottom of a graph that represents the independent (or predictor) variable.

Abstract A summary of the most important components of a research report, including major results and conclusions.

Acceptance Page That part of the prefatory section of a document (for example, thesis, dissertation) that includes the names of those individuals who served as degree committee members. It is their signatures that reflect the acceptance of the report (see Chapter 13, Figure 13–7).

Accuracy The correctness or exactness of what is said or done.

Accurate Disclosure Revealing information that is truthful.

Acknowledgment Page That part of the prefatory section of a document (for example, thesis, dissertation) where the writer has the opportunity to express appreciation to those individuals who were particularly helpful in guiding, and providing support for, the work that was done (see Chapter 13, Figure 13–8).

Active Deception The intentional creation of a false impression.

Adjective A class of words that modify nouns or pronouns.

Adverb A class of words that modify verbs, adjectives, or other adverbs.

AERA See American Educational Research Association (AERA).

Aesthetics In philosophical research, the sensitivity one has for art and beauty.

Alternating-Treatment Designs A variation of multiple-baseline research whereby alternating treatments are administered to a single subject.

Alternative Treatment A condition in experimental research whereby one of the groups receives the traditional (alternative) treatment for purposes of contrasting it against the treatment that is new. The traditional treatment is considered to be the control.

American Educational Research Association (AERA) An organization committed to the promotion and dissemination of quality research, the American Educational Research Association sponsors the *American Educational Research Journal, Encyclopedia of Educational Research, Handbook of Research on Curriculum, Handbook of Research on Educational Administration, Handbook of Research on Teaching,* and *Review of Educational Research.* AERA also sponsors an electronic bulletin board called Educational Research List (ERL-L), which can be accessed through the Internet, and has coauthored "Standards for Educational and Psychological Testing" with the American Psychological Association and the National Council for Measurement in Education. This booklet includes the guidelines for instrument reliability and validity recommended by the three corporate organizations.

American Psychological Association (APA) Founded in 1892 and incorporated in 1925, the American Psychological Association is the major organization of psychologists in the United States. The APA presently includes more than 24,000 members. Its mission is to advance psychology as a science, as a profession, and as a means of promoting human welfare. One way APA accommodates this mission is through its publication program, including the production of a document of style, the *Publication Manual of the American Psychological Association.*

Ampersand The abbreviation (&) of the word *and.* It is used between the names of authors in reference citations (*APA* style).

Analysis of Covariance A method of statistical control through which scores on the dependent variable are adjusted according to scores on a related variable.

Analysis of Variance A procedure for estimating the probability that the apparent differences among the means of two or more sets of scores are the result of mere chance fluctuations in those scores.

Analytical Procedures Techniques used to treat data generated by the study.

APA See American Psychological Association (APA).

Applied Research Studies that are done to solve existing problems (usually in the workplace). The major distinction between applied and action research is that, in the latter, there is no intent to generalize results.

Archie A server that enables one to search worldwide sites for program files.

Article Acceptance Date The date when a manuscript is accepted for publication.

Article Citation The process and product of referencing a published document (that is, an article). See also Book Citation.

Article Submission Date The date when a manuscript is submitted to a publisher for consideration.

Attribute-Treatment Interaction Research An experimental form of research that attempts to examine the influence of interacting variables (for example, interests and instructional methods) upon the dependent variable (for example, achievement).

Audit Trail Maintaining records of the observation techniques employed and materials acquired during the course of an investigation.

Bar Graph A visual portrayal of data displayed in lines (bars) parallel with the abscissa (which has been divided into intervals). The number of observations generated by subjects displayed along the ordinate are indicated by the length of the bar (see Chapter 13, Figure 13–4).

Baseline Phase The initial portion of a study in which repeated measurements are taken of subjects in order to establish stability.

Basic Assumptions Conditions considered to be true in order to proceed with the investigation.

Basic Research Investigations that are conducted for the purpose of theory development or refinement.

Baud Rate See Chapter 12, Figure 12–1.

Behavioral Objectives Measurable outcomes that consist of a statement of condition, performance, and criterion for success.

Beneficence The act of refraining from expressing doubts about the credibility of the work of others.

Benefit-to-Risk Ratio The relative difference between the advantages of a study and the potential harm it may create for participating subjects.

Between Group Sum of Squared Deviations In analysis of variance, it is the sum of the squared deviations of each within group score from the grand mean, each weighted by its group sample size.

Between Mean Squares In analysis of variance, it is the quotient of the between group sum of squared deviations divided by the number of groups minus one $(K - 1)$.

Bibliography A list of sources of information on a given subject.

Biserial Correlation A relationship between two variables when one of the variables can be dichotomized.

Bit See Chapter 12, Figure 12–1.

Block Random Sample One that is comprised of randomly selected groups rather than individuals.

Block Sampling Randomly selecting groups rather than individuals.

Body of the Report The section of a document that includes the introduction, review of related literature, method, findings, and discussion.

Book Citation A formal identification of the author, title, publisher, and place and date of publication of a book (per guidelines of a manual of form and style).

Book Guides Publications that identify sources of information (that is, textbooks, reference books).

Boot See Chapter 12, Figure 12–1.

Buckley Amendment The Family Educational Rights and Privacy Act (1974) that put into law the principle of record confidentiality.

Byte See Chapter 12, Figure 12–1.

Capitalization The act of using uppercase letters in writing (for example, at the beginning of sentences and for proper nouns).

Case Sample Individuals or institutions who are selected to participate in a study because they meet a set of recognized criteria.

Case Study An in-depth descriptive investigation of a unique individual, group, or institution.

Causal-Comparative Research Studies that are designed to determine reasons for observed differences between subjects or groups; also referred to as *ex post facto research*.

Causal-Comparative Studies See Causal-Comparative Research.

Causes Variables that produce an effect or result.

Ceiling Effect A condition of having earned near maximum on a pretest.

Central Processing Unit (CPU) See Chapter 12, Figure 12–1.

Chain of Evidence A succession of findings related to the topic of inquiry.

Chapter Headings Titles of the major divisions of a document (for example, theses, dissertations, books).

Checklists Items in which the respondent is asked to select from the alternatives provided, usually two in number (for example, yes/no; agree/disagree; married/single).

Chi Square Test An inferential statistic used to determine if significance exists between expected and obtained results.

Citations Formal references to sources cited in a document (as in a bibliography).

Cluster Random Sample See Block Random Sample.

Cluster Sampling See Block Sampling.

Code of Conduct Standards of behavior (that is, during the administration of research).

Coding Organizing information in a way that facilitates its subsequent entry into a computer.

Coefficient Alpha See Cronbach's Coefficient Alpha.

Coefficient of Contingency A correlation procedure to employ when each of two variables under study can be classified into two or more categories.

Cohort Designs Experimental research that provides for comparable groups of subjects to be examined successively over time. One of the cohorts is considered the treatment group; the other is considered to be the control.

Comparative Group See Comparative-Group Designs.

Comparative-Group Designs Experimental research in which two or more intact groups are studied.

Completion-Type Questions Sentences that have spaces the respondents are requested to fill.

Computer-Assisted Instruction (CAI) See Chapter 12, Introduction.

Computerized Questionnaires Instruments of assessment that research subjects can access through a computer. See also Survey.

Computer-Managed Concept Instruction (CMCI) See Chapter 12, Introduction.

Computer-Managed Drill and Practice (CMDP) See Chapter 12, Introduction.

Computer-Managed Instruction (CMI) See Chapter 12, Introduction.

Computer-Managed Problem Solving (CMPS) See Chapter 12, Introduction.

Computer-Managed Simulation (CMS) See Chapter 12, Introduction.

Computer-Managed Tutorial (CMT) See Chapter 12, Introduction.

Concept/Theory-Based Sample Individuals or institutions selected to participate in a study because they are presently engaged with the topic of interest.

Conclusions A summary of the findings generated by the research.

Concurrent-Related Evidence See Concurrent Validity.

Concurrent Validity The degree to which performance on one test correlates with performance on a test for which validity has already been established (when both instruments are administered at approximately the same time).

Confidence Interval The range within which a criterion measure is likely to fall.

Confidentiality The maintenance of secrecy about the identity of individuals participating in a study. See also Buckley Amendment.

Conflict of Interest The simultaneous influence of mutually exclusive concerns.

Construct-Related Evidence The degree to which an instrument of assessment measures a trait that is not directly observable. See also Internal Behavior.

Contact Summary Sheet A form that has been standardized in order to facilitate the collation of data.

Content-Related Evidence See Content Validity.

Content Validity The extent to which experts believe that the instrument of assessment addresses the research objectives; also known as *face validity*.

Continuous Recording Observing behavior throughout an entire block of time (for example, class period).

Control Group In experimental studies, it is the group from which the treatment is withheld; it is used as a basis of comparison.

Control-Group Designs Experimental research in which one of the groups does not receive the treatment.

Controlled Threats Threats that will have little or no influence on the dependent variable.

Control Program for Microcomputers (CP/M) See Chapter 12, Figure 12–1.

Convenience Sample One that consists of individuals or groups that happen to be available for the study.

Conventional Practice That which is generally accepted, as in the procedures to be used when preparing a research report.

Coordination The assigning of equal emphasis to ideas when combining them in a single sentence (as in a research report).

Corrective True-False A form of question in which selected words have been underlined by its author. If the question is false, it is the underlined word or words that must be corrected (in order to receive credit for the item).

Correlation Coefficient A numerical value representing the degree of relationship between two or more variables. Coefficients range from 0.0 to +/− 1.0.

Correlation Command Used to initiate and complete a computerized transaction, this command tells the computer that the researcher wants to calculate a Pearson product-moment correlation coefficient (SPSS Software).

Correlation Research Studies that examine the relationship of two or more variables for a single group of subjects.

Correlation Studies See Correlation Research.

Counterbalanced Control-Group Designs A research method in which each of the groups in the study receive alternative treatments in rotation.

Covariate The measure used in an analysis of Covariance for adjusting the scores of the dependent variable.

Credibility Believable, plausible; worthy of confidence.

Criteria Standards of performance; plural for criterion.

Criterion A single standard of performance.

Criterion Variable See Dependent Variable.

Critical Values Values found at the intersect point of levels of confidence and degrees of freedom that reveal the ratio that must be equaled or exceeded in order for an obtained value to be considered statistically significant.

Critical Values for *F* Ratios representing the *F* test values (per degrees of freedom) at given levels of confidence in order to establish a finding of significance.

Critical Values for *r* Correlation coefficients representing the values (per degrees of freedom) at given levels of confidence in order to establish a finding of significance.

Critical Values for *t* Ratios representing the *t* test values (per degrees of freedom) at given levels of confidence in order to establish a finding of significance.

Cronbach's Alpha See Cronbach's Coefficient Alpha.

Cronbach's Coefficient Alpha A process that enables one to estimate internal consistency when the scoring of items on a test is not limited to 1 point (for correct) or 0 points (for incorrect) responses.

Cross-Sectional Studies Research in which issues of concern are examined at a particular point in time.

DAI See *Dissertation Abstracts International* (DAI).

Data The plural of datum, they are facts or figures to be processed; evidence, records, statistics, and so on from which conclusions can be inferred.

Data Analysis The processing of statistical information.

Database See Chapter 12, Figure 12–1.

Database Management System (DMS) A computer program that provides a format for organizing information—that is, alphabetizing, arranging scores, and selecting and printing records.

Data List Command Used to initiate and complete a computerized transaction, this command attaches a label designation to each variable, and tells the computer in which column to find it.

Debriefing A procedure whereby a participant who was deceived for a research project is subsequently apprised of the actual circumstances.

Definitive Statements Comments that are decisive, authoritative, to the point.

Degrees of Freedom An expression (*df*) that identifies the point at which a table is entered in order to interpret the significance of a finding. With parametric statistics (for example, *t* tests), degrees of freedom are related to the number of subjects. With nonparametric statistics (for example, chi square), the degrees of freedom are ordinarily based upon the number of categories.

Denominator The term below or to the right of the line in a fraction.

Dependent-Samples *t* Test An inferential statistic used to compare the arithmetic averages of two groups when the scores earned by individuals on one test can be paired with the scores of those same individuals on another test.

Dependent Variable In experimental studies, the criterion (outcome) whose value is dependent upon the effects of an independent (treatment or control) variable.

Descriptive Statistics Statistics that describe some property of the group of numbers on which they are calculated (for example, mean, median, mode, standard deviation).

Descriptive Studies Research that examines the past or present status of individuals, institutions, or processes.

Descriptive Validity The accuracy that can be attributed to the descriptions of events.

Design Alternatives Optional procedures for investigating a research topic.

Deviation Formulas Statistical procedures that are based on the deviation of each score from the mean of the distribution.

Deviation Method for Computing ANOVA A process that depends upon the deviation of each score from the mean of its group and the grand mean. See also Analysis of Variance.

Diachronic Reliability The comparison of observations made on different occasions.

Diagram A graphic display of experimental designs comprised of Os (observations) and Xs (treatments), with or without subscripts (which, if used, identify alternative groups or treatments).

Dichotomized Variables Traits that can be divided into two categories, for example, gender.

Dictionaries Reference books containing alphabetical lists of defined terms.

Differentiating Factors Elements that comprise the composition of a study group (for example, gender, intelligence, socioeconomic background); also referred to as *delimitations*.

Direct Costs Expenses to be borne by the investigator.

Directional Hypothesis A hypothesis that specifies the direction of a difference in means or of a relationship between variables.

Direct Object Pertaining to pronouns, a direct object (objective case) would include: Mark found the *book* and brought *it* home (see Chapter 13, Preparing the Research Report).

Directories Documents that provide sources of names, addresses, and telephone numbers.

Discussion That section of a research report that discusses the findings. It is here that the investigator draws conclusions, presents implications, and makes recommendations for further study.

Disk Drive See Chapter 12, Figure 12–1.

Disk Operating System (DOS) See Chapter 12, Figure 12–1.

Display An exhibit, for example, a visual representation of data, as on a computer video screen.

Dissertation Abstracts International **(DAI)** A source of abstracts of theses.

Documentary Analysis Examining source materials for the purpose of uncovering trends.

Dot Matrix Printer See Chapter 12, Figure 12–1.

Double-Blind An experiment in which neither the participants nor those administering the treatment know which of the groups is the control.

Educational Resources Information Center (ERIC) A resource that includes *Current Index to Journals in Education* (CIJE) and *Resources in Education* (RIE).

Educational Testing Service (ETS) Located in Princeton, New Jersey, it provides information on standardized tests that it publishes.

Education Index **(EI)** A source of citations to journal articles.

Effects In experimental studies, they are the results of the administration or with-holding of a treatment.

Effect Size Used with meta-analysis, it is a standard score that represents the strength of a treatment in an experiment. It is calculated by dividing the difference between the means of the experimental and the control group by the pooled standard deviation.

E-mail See Chapter 12, Introduction.

Emersion The practice of placing oneself into a participatory position at a setting in which qualitative research is being conducted.

Empirical Research Research that is based on practical experience without reference to scientific principles.

Encyclopedias Comprehensive, often multivolume reference works containing articles on a variety of subjects.

Enumeration Questions Items in which the respondent is asked to list the answers in the spaces provided beneath each of the questions.

Epistemology In philosophical research, the study or theory of the nature, sources, and limits of knowledge.

Equivalence The extent to which two forms of a measuring device are able to demonstrate evidence that they generate similar results.

Equivalence-Related Reliability See Equivalence.

ERIC See Educational Resources Information Center (ERIC).

Error Band Based upon the measurement error for a test, it is the range within which one is expected to find a true score 68.26% of the time.

Essay Questions Items in which the respondent is asked to discuss a topic.

Essential Definitions Meanings for terms that are deemed vital to the study. See also Key Terms.

Ethical Safeguards Standards of professional conduct governing the design, administration, writing, and reporting of research.

Ethics The rules or standards governing the conduct of the members of a profession; a body of principles; a system of moral standards and values.

Ethnographic Research See Qualitative Research.

Ethnographic Studies See Qualitative Research.

ETS See Educational Testing Service (ETS).

Evaluation The process of making decisions based on the results of measurements or observations. Evaluation strategies describe the elements that go into this decision-making process.

Evaluative Validity The extent to which legitimacy can be attributed to the judgments that are made about the findings of a study.

Exculpatory Language that is intended to free the investigator from liability should negligence be determined.

Expectancy A threat to the internal validity of a study when the researcher has a bias about the outcome of the study.

Experimental Mortality A threat to the internal validity of a study when changes in the composition of the groups occur during the course of the investigation.

Experimental Research A planned, controlled, and recorded observation or measurement to test a hypothesis concerning the effects of one or more variables (that is, experimental, treatment) upon another variable (that is, dependent, outcome) when all related variables (that is, intervening, moderator) are eliminated or held constant.

Experimental Studies See Experimental Research.

Experiments Studies that involve the administration of treatments. See also Experimental Research.

Exploratory Questions Questions that are asked in order to establish a direction for further inquiry.

Ex Post Facto Research See Causal-Comparative Research.

External Behavior A construct that can be observed directly (for example, math achievement).

External Criticism Accounting for the authenticity of the evidence.

External Validity The extent to which the findings of a study can be generalized to other populations.

Face-to-Face Interviews Oral questionnaires.

Factorial Designs Experimental research in which a large number of variables are sorted into smaller clusters of related variables with a view toward determining the interrelatedness of the variables within these clusters.

Factorial MANCOVA An extension of MANCOVA wherein a moderator variable (for example, gender) is factored into the analysis. See also Multivariate Analysis of Covariance.

Factorial MANCOVA with Repeated Measures An extension of factorial MANCOVA by administering follow-up measures. See also Multivariate Analysis of Covariance.

Field Notes Written descriptions of observations.

Field of Interest A broad area of study (for example, administration, mathematics, special education).

File Transfer Protocol (Ftp) A system for transferring files from a remote computer to a local host.

Findings That section of a report that relates the results of the research. It is in this section where narrative would be augmented by graphs.

Finite Population A population in which all of its members can be identified and counted.

Fixed-Choice Questions Inquiries in which the respondent selects responses from among the choices that are provided.

Form See Format.

Format The pattern or arrangement and organization of a report.

Formatting Organizing (or coding) information for subsequence analysis.

F **Ratio** A quotient that is referred to a Table of Critical Values for *F* in order to determine whether an observed finding is statistically significant. This ratio is found by dividing the between mean squares by the within mean squares (that is, analysis of variance).

Frequency of Mention The process of identifying the occasions in which a finding repeats itself.

F **Test** See Analysis of Variance.

Ftp See File Transfer Protocol (Ftp).

Full Disclosure Complete revelation of information pertinent to research and its design.

Functioning of Alternatives The degree to which the choices in a multiple-choice item appear plausible to those taking the test.

Gantt Chart A matrix consisting of the major phases of a proposed study with corresponding estimated completion dates.

General Evaluatory Criteria Standards that apply to the assessment of all research designs or reports.

Gerund A verb form ending in *-ing* that has all the uses of a noun but retains certain syntactic characteristics of the verb, such as the ability to take an object or an adverbial modifier (for example, *reading* in "reading is her only form of relaxation").

Gopher See Chapter 12, Introduction.

Grand Mean Average of the means.

Grand Sum of Squared Deviations In analysis of variance, the total of the values found in response to the within group sums of squared deviations.

Graph A diagram (for example, bar graph, histogram, polygon) used to display information; ordinarily found in the findings section of a written report.

Group Designs Research procedures that utilize groups rather than individuals as subjects.

Handbook A one-volume overview of generally accepted facts and procedures. A manual providing specific information or instruction about an activity, place, or subject.

Haphazard Sampling See Convenience Sample.

Hardware See Chapter 12, Figure 12–1.

Hawthorne Effect A reaction that may arise when subjects know that they are involved in an experiment or receiving "special attention."

Histogram A visual portrayal of data displayed in lines (bars) parallel with the ordinate. The abscissa represents the various individuals or groups, and the ordinate represents the frequencies or percentages, with the number of observations indicated by the height of the bar over that individual or group (see Chapter 13, Figure 13–5).

Historical Method See Historical Research.

Historical Research The systematic collection and analysis of facts related to persons, places, and events of the past.

Historical Studies See Historical Research.

Historiography The study of the techniques of historical research.

History A threat to the internal validity of a study when events unrelated to the treatment arise in one's environment during the course of the investigation.

Holistic Inquiry Examining the totality of the circumstances surrounding the topic of investigation.

Homogeneity of Variance Considered equivalent to the null hypothesis, it is used to test the hypothesis that there are equal variances for the populations from which the samples were selected.

Honesty The capacity or condition of being trustworthy, having integrity, being truthful. See also Credibility.

HSRC See Human Subjects Research Committee (HSRC).

Human Subjects Research Committee (HSRC) Synonymous with Institutional Review Board, this group, by federal regulation, protects the rights of participants in a study.

Hypothesis A tentative, testable position regarding the expected outcome of a study.

Implications Inferences of the findings.

Independent-Group Designs Experimental designs in which there is no particular relationship between the scores of one group and the scores of another.

Independent-Samples *t* Test A form of *t* test that is used when the members of the groups have not been paired in any way.

Independent Variable In experimental studies, the treatment being tested in order to study its influence upon the dependent variable.

Index An alphabetical listing of names, subjects, and so on, together with the page numbers where they appear in the text; usually placed at the end of a book or other publication.

Indicators Gauges that provide criteria for judging performance.

Indirect Costs Expenses to be borne by those other than the investigator (for example, private grant sources, institution where the researcher is employed, and so on).

Indirect Object Pertaining to pronouns (objective case), an indirect object would include: Mark gave *me* a copy of the book.

Inferential Statistics The use of statistics that test hypotheses or draw conclusions about a population based upon data collected from a sample.

Infinite Population A category of population in which its members cannot be counted.

Informed Consent Having knowledge sufficient to make an intelligent decision about participating in a study.

Instability A threat to the internal validity of a study that is attributed to chance factors.

Instrumentation A threat to the internal validity of a study when the test being used lacks appropriate levels of validity, reliability, and objectivity; also refers to tools used to acquire data.

Intact Group A previously arranged cluster of individuals, as in a class of students.

Integrity See Credibility; Honesty.

Interaction A threat to the internal validity of a study when two or more existing threats combine to influence the dependent variable—for example, history and maturation.

Interactions The effects of two or more independent variables upon the dependent variable.

Interactive Effect The result of interactions.

Interface See Chapter 12, Figure 12–1.

Internal Behavior A construct that cannot be seen directly (for example, attitude, belief).

Internal Consistency The extent to which the questions comprising a single version of a test appear to be measuring similar traits.

Internal Criticism Accounting for the accuracy of information in a source.

Internal Validity The ability of research to produce findings that are valid to the group under study.

Internet Interworking networks (computer).

Interpretive True-False A form of question in which the respondent defends a true or false response in the space provided beneath the item.

Interpretive Validity The degree to which interpretations of the observer agree with those of the subject.

Inter-Rater Reliability See Objectivity.

Interrupted Time Series A design in which a series of measurements is taken before and after the administration of the treatment. There is no control group.

Interrupted Time Series Control-Group Design Two-group experimental research in which there are multiple pre- and posttests. Prior to the posttest, one of the groups is administered a treatment; the second group is the control. This design has the advantage of establishing pre-experiment stability, and studying the effect of the treatment (and control) upon retention.

Interval Data Data that are based on a scale of measurement in which equal differences in scores represent equal differences in amount of the property measured. See also Interval Scale.

Interval Recording Collecting data by observing behavior throughout an abbreviated period of time (for example, the first or last five minutes of a class period).

Interval Scale A level of measurement that provides for equal intervals between numerical values.

Intervening Variable A variable that arises during the course of the study; not directly observed nor controlled; may alter the relationship between the independent and the dependent variable.

Interviews The utilization of oral questionnaires (preferably with prime sources) for the purpose of gaining information about attitudes, interests, and so on. See also Survey.

Introduction That section of a research report that introduces the problem area, provides a literature review, and offers the hypotheses and research questions for testing. It provides a place for the investigator to establish the significance of the problem, and offer his own perspectives regarding its relevance (see Chapter 13, Preparing the Research Report).

Inverted Pyramid A format for displaying the title of one's research, as on a title page (see Chapter 13, Figure 13–3).

Item Analysis A procedure that is used to determine item characteristics, such as difficulty level and discrimination.

Item Difficulty A term that refers to the proportion of individuals responding correctly to an item.

Item Discrimination The extent to which an item distinguishes the most from the least knowledgeable subjects in the group.

John Henry Effect The result of being in competition with another individual or group; performing beyond what would normally be expected.

Judgmental Sampling See Purposive Sample.

Jury An group of experts called upon to validate a process or an instrument of assessment.

K – 1 In analysis of variance, it represents the number of groups minus one.

Key Terms Words that are vital to the report; usually placed immediately before the introduction to the study.

Kuder-Richardson 20 A process that provides an estimate of the reliability of a test based upon the number of questions, item difficulty, and variance of the scores.

Kuder-Richardson 21 Similar to the Kuder-Richardson 20, except for the fact that with this process, one does not need to compute the difficulty coefficient of each test item.

Kurzweil Reading Machine An omni-font reader that employs an optical scanner to "read" printed documents; particularly valuable for the visually impaired.

Laser Printer See Chapter 12, Figure 12–1.

Legal Considerations Circumstances related to the law that must be accounted for when designing and administering studies.

Legal Safeguards The authority of law that is provided to individuals (subjects) who have agreed to participate in a study.

Level of Confidence A term that refers to the number of times out of one hundred that one would be wrong in making a statement.

Limitations Uncontrolled threats; weaknesses of a study.

Linear Relationships Circumstances in which an increase (or decrease) in one variable is associated with a corresponding increase (or decrease) in another variable.

List of Figures That part of the preliminary section of a document that identifies the figures of the report (for example, bar graphs, histograms), and corresponding page numbers where they can be found.

List of Tables That part of the preliminary section of a document that identifies the tables of the report (for example, lists of numbers), and corresponding page numbers where they can be found.

Literature Review The study of documents for information related to the topic of interest.

Logic In philosophical research, the science of inductive and deductive reasoning.

Longitudinal Studies Research in which issues of concern are examined at different points in time.

Lottery Method A process of selecting a random sample (that is, raffle box method). An event regarded as having an outcome on the basis of probability.

Low Inference Descriptions Findings that reflect actual rather than inferred statements of fact.

Mailing List See Chapter 12, Introduction.

Mail Questionnaires Instruments of assessment that are delivered through on- or off-campus postal services. See also Survey.

Main Effect The effect of each independent variable upon the dependent variable. In factorial research, a direct effect of one independent variable on the dependent variable, with all independent variables equal.

Mainframe See Chapter 12, Figure 12–1.

Manipulation In experimental studies, managing the independent (treatment) variable in order to study its influence upon a dependent (outcome) variable.

Master List Questions Items in which the respondent selects the best answer or answers from a list provided at the top of page. In this form of question, it is common to allow answers to be used more than once.

Matched Groups Groups that have been equated on one or more variables. Members of one group have direct counterparts in the second group.

Matching Questions Items in which the respondent selects the best answer from among an extended list of alternatives (usually found to the right of the test page). Directions make clear whether or not answers can be used more than once.

Maturation A threat to internal validity when a study extends over a sustained period of time.

Mean A measure of central tendency that takes into account the weighting of each number. It is found by dividing the sum of scores by N.

Measurement Error Based upon the estimated reliability and standard deviation of a test, *ME* represents the estimated difference between an obtained and a true score.

Measures See Data.

Median The middle score in an ordered list of numbers; also known as the *fiftieth percentile, fifth decile, second quartile.*

Mental Measurements Yearbook (MMY) A source of test reviews.

Meta-Analysis A statistical procedure that provides for the combining of results from related studies to produce a numerical average.

Metaphysics That branch of philosophy that deals with principles; seeks to explain the nature of being or reality; studies nature and knowledge.

Methods That section of a research report that describes in detail the procedures that were used to conduct the study; includes reference to such things as subject selection, instrumentation, design, treatment (if pertinent), and collection of data. The description of research methods usually follows the introduction section of the report.

Microcomputer See Chapter 12, Figure 12–1.

Minimum Sample Size The smallest a sample can be and still be considered statistically representative of the population from which it was selected (see Appendix B).

Mixed Construction Parts of a sentence that do not fit together (see Chapter 13, Preparing the Research Report).

MMY See *Mental Measurements Yearbook* (MMY).

Mode The most frequent response in a distribution.

Modem See Chapter 12, Figure 12–1.

Moderator Variable An identifiable factor that is present at the onset of an experimental study (for example, age, gender, grade level) which, if not accounted for by the design, may influence the findings.

Modifiers A word, phrase, or clause that limits the meaning of another word or phrase (see Chapter 13, Preparing the Research Report).

Mortality Within the context of experimental research, it is a threat to internal validity caused by subjects withdrawing from the study.

Mouse See Chapter 12, Figure 12–1.

Multiple-Baseline Designs Single-subject research in which baseline data are collected on several behaviors for one subject, one behavior for several subjects, or one subject in several settings. Treatments are then applied to each behavior, subject, or setting.

Multiple-Choice Questions Items in which the respondent must select her answer from the alternatives provided (usually four to five in number), usually found beneath the questions.

Multiple Correlation The relationship between one variable and a combination of other variables.

Multiple-Group Designs Experimental research in which two or more treatments are administered while maintaining a control group.

Multiple Posttest Control-Group Design (with Pretest) Experimental research in which a pretest is administered to each of two groups. A treatment is assigned to one of the groups, followed by a series of equivalent posttests. This design is used in order to assess the influence of the treatment upon retention.

Multiple Pretest Control-Group Design (with Posttest) Two-group experimental research in which the investigator repeatedly administers pretests until stability is established. A treatment is then administered to one of the groups, followed by the administration of posttests to both groups.

Multivariate Analysis of Covariance A statistical procedure that extends analysis of covariance to the simultaneous analysis of two or more additional variables (for example, two programs designed to get people to decrease their cholesterol by making lifestyle changes might be compared to each other and to a control group by an analysis of covariance, using posttest cholesterol as the dependent measure and pretest cholesterol as the covariate. If cholesterol, exercise, and rest were all used as variables, a multivariate analysis of covariance could be used with pretest scores on all three measures as covariates, posttest scores as the dependent variable, and type of program as the independent variable).

$N - K$ In analysis of variance, it represents the number of individuals minus the number of groups.

National Research Act A law passed by Congress in 1974 to protect human subjects against emotional, mental, or physical harm by requiring that proposed research be approved by an authorized group within the institution in which the research is designed to occur. See also Human Subjects Research Committee (HSRC).

Naturalistic Setting The place where research data originate (for example, school, hospital). See also Qualitative Research.

Need for the Study A statement providing justification for conducting the investigation.

Negative Correlation A situation in which individuals who scored above the average of their group in one variable, scored below the average of their group in the second variable (or vice versa).

Negative Relationship See Negative Correlation.

Network Sample One that is selected on the basis of having been nominated by prior interviewees as those who would have information pertaining to the subject.

Newsgroup See Chapter 12, Introduction.

Newspaper Index An index that is used to identify sources in which pertinent articles can be found.

Nominal Data Data that are based on a scale of measurement in which scores represent names only but not differences in amount. See also Nominal Scale.

Nominal Scale A level of measurement that provides for the classification of data according to labels or categories—for example, boy, girl; married, single; republican, democrat.

Nonapplicable Threats Within the context of experimental studies, limitations that are without relevance to the specific design in question.

Noncomparative Group Research in which there is no control group; often referred to as a *nondesign investigation*.

Nonequivalent Groups Two-group research designs in which the subjects have not been selected through the process of randomization. This is frequently a product of utilizing intact groups (for example, previously arranged classes of students).

Nonindependent-Samples *t* Test See Dependent-Samples *t* test.

Nonparametric Statistics Inferential statistics (for example, chi square) that are not based on the assumption that the scores upon which they are used fall into a normal distribution.

Nonprobability Sampling A process that does not depend upon the existence of a finite population (that is, nonrandomized).

Noun *(Gram.)* Any class of words naming or denoting a person, place, quality, thing, or action (for example, *man, laboratory, beauty, water, walking*).

Null Hypothesis A hypothesis that states that there is no difference between the variables under study; that if a difference is observed in the dependent variables, the difference can be attributed to chance alone.

Numerator The term above or to the left of the line in a fraction.

Objective Case An element of sentence structure that should be used when pronouns are functioning as objects (for example, *us, you, him/her/it*).

Objectivity The degree to which two or more observers agree on the value of a behavior; also called *inter-rater reliability*.

Observations The acts or practices of noting and recording facts and events. See also Survey.

One-Tailed Test Used with directional hypotheses, it assumes that a difference can occur only in one direction ($A > B$).

Ontology In philosophical research, the study of the nature of being or reality.

Open-Ended Questions Inquiries in which the respondent supplies answers rather than selecting ones from among fixed choices. See also Exploratory Questions.

Operational Definitions Statements that govern the meaning of variables in a study.

Optical Mark Reader (OMR) A device that scans responses placed on computer answer sheets (that is, multiple-choice questions).

Ordinal Data Data that are based on a scale of measurement in which scores indicate only relative amounts or rank order. See also Ordinal Scale.

Ordinal Scale A level of measurement that provides for the ranking of values from high to low. In this scale, the intervals between the ranks are not consistent.

Ordinate The vertical line on a graph that represents the value of the dependent (or predicted) variable.

Outcome See Dependent Variable.

Outcome Variable See Dependent Variable.

Parallelism Maintaining balance between parallel ideas (see Chapter 13, Preparing the Research Report).

Parametric Statistics Inferential statistics (for example, *t* test) that are based on the assumption that the scores on which they are used are normally distributed (that is, bell-shaped curve).

Partial Correlation The relationship between two variables while other variables are held constant. (for example, when two variables are held constant, the designation would be second-order partial correlation).

Participant-Observer One who collects data while engaged in the activity of the research setting.

Passive Deception Circumstances in which the investigator is not lying, but simply avoids mentioning something that he feels the subjects should not know about at the onset of the study.

Passive Voice Denoting the form of a verb whose subject is the object of the action of the verb. When writing research reports, the use of passive voice is preferred over the use of active voice (for example, *the findings seem to indicate that* as opposed to *the investigator found that*).

Past Tense The character of a verb that indicates something *has happened* (for example, the data *revealed*).

Pattern Analysis Examination of the trends in the data.

Percentages A number that indicates the number of times a category was observed out of 100 cases, multiplied by 100.

Percentiles Values that are found by dividing the number of individuals who earned at or below a given value in an ordered list of scores, by the total number of scores, and multiplying by 100.

Percent of Agreement A percentage that is calculated by dividing the numbers of answers that are found to be in agreement on two evaluation forms, by the total number of answers possible on one of the forms, and multiplying by 100. It is used to determine the reliability of nominal test data.

Percent of Attainment The number of those who responded to a given question, divided by the total number of respondents, times 100; or a given score, divided by the maximum score possible, times 100.

Periodical Index An index that is used to identify sources of articles.

Person(s) Within the context of experimental research, it is a threat to the external validity of a study if the sample and the population that it is to represent do not share pertinent characteristics at the onset of the investigation.

Phenomenology See Philosophical Research.

Phi Coefficient The relationship between variables when they fall into distinct (rather than artificial) categories.

Philosophical Method See Philosophical Research.

Philosophical Research A study that examines the principles of laws that underlie knowledge, reality, and the processes that govern thought and behavior.

Pilot Study A preliminary investigation that is conducted with a small group in order to gather information about that group and the research process itself.

Pilot Test See Pilot Study.

Placebo Effect Performing as if the treatment was genuine.

Place(s) Within the context of experimental research, it is a threat to the external validity of the study if the findings are generalized to settings unrelated to those of the research.

Plagiarism Taking another's work and passing it off as one's own.

Polygon A line graph that displays intersect points of data reported on the abscissa and ordinate (see Chapter 11, Figure 11–2).

Population All scores or members of a group that are of interest to a researcher; the group to which the researcher wishes to generalize.

Positive Relationship One in which those who scored above the average of their group in one trait also tended to score above the average of their group in a second trait.

Possessive Case An element of sentence structure that should be used when pronouns are functioning as possessives (for example, *our, your, his/her/its*).

Posttest An instrument of assessment administered at the cessation of a treatment.

Posttest Only Design Considered to be the weakest of all single-group experimental designs, it does not provide for a pretest.

Posttest Only Nonequivalent Control-Group Designs Research in which at least two intact groups are selected, one of which is considered to be the control. No pretest data are collected.

Practical Significance When findings from a study can be applied to real-life settings without undue hardship; may or may not have relevance to statistical significance.

Prediction Studies Investigations that are conducted in order to identify the variable most related to the criterion.

Predictive-Related Evidence The degree to which estimated performance becomes a reality.

Prefatory Section That section of a research document (for example, thesis, dissertation) that includes the title, acceptance, and acknowledgment pages; table of contents; and lists of tables and figures.

Preliminary Information That part of a study that is found in the prefatory section of a report (for example, author, title, abstract, key terms).

Pretest An instrument of assessment administered at the onset of the study in order to establish a baseline. With two-group research, pretests help to control for mortality.

Pretesting Generating data at the onset of the study in order to establish baselines.

Pretest-Posttest Design A design that does not include a control group; it involves administering a test at the beginning of the study in order to establish a baseline, followed by a treatment and a posttest.

Pretest-Posttest Nonequivalent Control-Group Designs Research methods that provide for an assessment in advance of the administration of a treatment in nonequivalent group designs. See also Posttest Only Nonequivalent Control-Group Designs.

Primary Sources Firsthand information—for example, original documents, testimony of a participant.

Prime Sources See Primary Sources.

Principles Rules or standards that govern behavior; guiding rules of conduct.

Privacy The condition of secrecy or confidentiality. See also Buckley Amendment.

Probability Sampling See Random Sampling.

Problem Area A topic for investigation within a field of interest.

Problem Statement A declaration that identifies the variables of interest to the investigator; a topic of investigation.

Procedures See Methods.

Product-Moment Correlation The numerical relationship between two variables; also known as *Pearson product-moment correlation*.

Product-Moment *r* See Product-Moment Correlation.

Pronoun A word that assumes the function of a noun. See also Pronoun Agreement.

Pronoun Agreement Relationship or signal words that assume the function of nouns within clauses or phrases while referring to other locations within the sentence or in other sentences (for example, the *writer* completed *her* report).

Pronoun Case Pronouns that function as subjects or subject complements should be presented in the subjective case (for example, *I*); those that function as objects should appear in the objective case (for example, *me*); those that function as possessives should be in the possessive case (for example, *my*). See Chapter 13, Preparing the Research Report.

Pronoun Clarity The quality or condition of being clear in regard to the noun to which the pronoun is referring (for example, "When Steven set the computer on the table, it broke" is incorrect; "When Steven set the computer on the table, the computer broke" is correct).

Prophecy Formula A procedure that is used to predict the reliability of a complete test based upon the findings of the relationship between the first and second halves, or the odd and even numbered items, of a test; also known as the *Spearman-Brown Prophecy Formula*.

Protection See National Research Act.

Protocol The procedures used for planning and administering a study. See also Treatment Fidelity.

Pseudoreplication Study An investigation in which exact replications are not possible because of the cumulative effects of treatments. For example, in the counterbalanced control-group design, the subjects are first subjected to one of two treatments; the treatments are then rotated. As a consequence, the measured results of the second treatment are compromised by the cumulative effects of the first treatment. Thus, this design does not provide for a pure replication of events.

***Psychological Abstracts* (PsycLit)** A source of citations and abstracts for psychological journal articles.

PsycLit See *Psychological Abstracts* (PsycLit).

Publication The published work of a writer (for example, an article or book).

Punctuation Standardized marks in writing that are used to separate sentences or sentence elements; assists in making sentences clearer to understand.

Purposive Sample One comprised of individuals whom the researcher believes would be representative of what would be found in a given population.

***P* Value** A symbol for significance (for example, $p < .05$).

Qualitative Data Analysis The examination of the words (rather than the numbers) generated by a study.

Qualitative Method See Qualitative Data Analysis.

Qualitative Research A category of inquiry that places emphasis on the meaning of events as expressed by those who experience them.

Qualitative Studies See Qualitative Research.

Quantitative Data Analysis The examination of the numbers (rather than the words) generated by a study.

Quantitative Method See Quantitative Data Analysis.

Quantitative Research A category of inquiry in which the investigator gathers numerical data on observed behavior with a view to subjecting the findings to statistical analysis.

Quasi-Experimental Designs Experimental investigations in which treatments are examined without the benefit of control groups.

Questionnaires Instruments of assessment used to generate information regarding persons, places, things, or events. They may be administered face-to-face, over the telephone/computer, or through the mail.

Quota Sample One that is comprised of individuals or groups that are chosen to be in direct proportion to their frequency in the population.

Raffle Method See Lottery Method.

Random Access Memory (RAM) See Chapter 12, Figure 12–1.

Random Assignment The assignment of individuals to groups, or groups to treatments, on the basis of random selection.

Randomization See Random Sampling.

Randomized Posttest Only Control-Group Designs Experimental studies in which individuals are randomly assigned to one of two groups. One of the groups is subjected to a treatment; both groups are then administered equivalent posttests.

Randomized Pretest-Posttest Control-Group Designs Similar to the randomized posttest only control-group design, except that a pretest on the dependent variable is administered at the onset of the study in order to establish baselines.

Random Sampling Selecting subjects in such a way that each and every member of the population has an equal opportunity to be selected to participate in the study.

Rank-Order Correlation The numerical relationship between two ranked variables; also known as *Spearman rank-order correlation,* or *rho.*

Rating Scales An extension of checklists, they provide for a continuum of choices (for example, always, usually, sometimes, rarely, never).

Ratio Scale A level of measurement that contains all the properties of an interval scale but, in addition, has an absolute zero. This is the only level of measurement in which it is appropriate to calculate ratios—that is, to say that a six-foot jump is twice as high as a three-foot jump.

Raw-Score Formulas Statistical procedures that utilize the earned values that have been generated by the participants in a study.

Raw Scores Numerical values generated by an investigation.

Read Only Memory (ROM) See Chapter 12, Figure 12–1.

Recommendations Suggestions, for example, for future study, or in regard to how the completed research could be improved.

References A list of those information sources that were introduced within the report.

Regression A threat to the internal validity of a study when subjects are significantly above or below average on the dependent variable at the onset of the investigation.

Related-Samples *t* Test See Dependent-Samples *t* test.

Reliability The degree to which a measuring instrument is consistent. See also Equivalence; Internal Consistency; Stability.

Repeated Measures Two or more sets of observations for each of the subjects participating in the study.

Replication Studies Investigations that are repeated in accordance with the protocol of earlier studies.

Reputational Case Sample Sources of information selected for use because of having been recommended by recognized authorities.

Research Assistant An associate (for example, colleague, student) who assists with the administration of the study.

Research Design The process and product of planning an investigation.

Research Diagram See Diagram.

Research Evaluation Digest (RED) Form An instrument used to assess the quality of research reports.

Research Hypothesis Used in descriptive investigations, it is a statement of an expected outcome.

Research Question A query to be resolved through the investigative process.

Results See Findings.

Review of Related Literature That section of a research report that presents a summary of related findings; usually presented in the form of an inverted pyramid with least-related studies discussed first to a discussion of the studies that are most related to the investigation.

RF Modulator See Chapter 12, Figure 12–1.

Risks Hazards (that is, physical, mental, emotional) associated with participating as a subject in research. See also National Research Act.

Rival Hypotheses Alternative suppositions being tested to explain what the findings of a study might reveal.

Running Head An abbreviated title that is placed at the top of each page of a published article in order to identify the topic for the reader.

Sample Individuals or groups selected to participate in a study; the term does not imply that it was selected through the process of randomization.

Sampling The process of selecting subjects to participate in a study; a threat to the external and internal validity of a study when random sampling techniques are not employed.

Sampling Error The mathematical difference between the means of two distributions of scores.

Scatter Diagram A visual representation of the relationship between two variables; also called a *scattergram* or *scatter plot*. Each dot on the diagram represents a pair of scores.

Scheffe Test In analysis of variance, it is a statistical procedure for computing individual comparisons.

Score Stability The degree to which numerical values repeat themselves.

Secondary Sources Secondhand information—for example, those who did not participate directly in nor witness the event being examined.

Selection A threat to the internal validity of a study when subjects are selected in a way that does not provide for representation of the population.

Sentence Structure The arrangement or interrelation of words that state, ask, command, or explain something.

Sentence Variety A combination of simple and compound sentences within paragraphs (see Chapter 13, Preparing the Research Report).

Simple Random Sample See Random Sampling.

Single-Blind An experiment in which the participant does not know to what group (that is, experimental or control) he belongs.

Single-Group Designs Considered quasi-experimental experiments because there are no control groups, they are created to assess the effects of an independent variable upon a dependent variable.

Single-Sample *t* Test A statistical procedure used to test the significance between the means of two distributions. See also Student's *t*-test.

Single-Subject Designs Experimental research that involves the administration of a treatment, and at least one posttest to a single individual.

Software See Chapter 12, Figure 12–1.

Spearman-Brown Formula An equation for estimating what the internal consistency reliability for a measuring instrument would be if the test was increased in length.

Spearman-Brown Prophecy Formula See Spearman-Brown Formula.

Specific Evaluatory Criteria Standards that apply to the assessment of specific research designs or reports (for example, surveys, correlation studies, historical studies, and so on).

Spelling To name, write, or signal the letters that make up a word; to place the correct letters in the correct order.

Split-Half Reliability An internal consistency measure that is computed by comparing the first half to the second half of the test, or the odd- versus the even-numbered questions. See also Spearman-Brown Formula.

Spreadsheet A computer program that organizes information and performs statistical calculations.

SPSS See Statistical Products and Service Solutions (SPSS).

Stability The degree to which scores generated by a test replicate themselves.

Stability-Related Reliability See Stability.

Standard Deviation A measure of the average spread among the individual values in a set of scores; a measure of variability. The square root of the average of the squared deviations from the mean of the distribution. In a normal distribution, six standard deviations cover the range of most scores—three standard deviations above and below the mean.

Standard Error of the Mean The standard deviation of a hypothetical population of sample means. It is found by dividing the standard deviation of the scores by the square root of $N - 1$ (where N represents the number of subjects).

Standards Guidelines governing behavior. See also Criteria; Principles.

Standard Score A value based on the number of standard deviations a person is from the mean. Standard scores include z scores, T scores, and ETS scores.

Standard True-False A question in which the respondent indicates her agreement or disagreement, without qualification.

Statement of Hypothesis See Hypothesis.

Statement of the Problem See Problem Statement.

Statistical Products and Service Solutions (SPSS) A comprehensive computer package that contains software for data analysis, including: central tendency, variability, correlation and regression, *t* test, analysis of variance, and factor analysis.

Statistical Regression A threat to the internal validity of a study when one or more groups in the research score particularly high or low in a pretest.

Statistical Significance Findings that are based on having equaled or exceeded the critical values required of the study; may or may not be related to practical significance.

Statistical Treatments The mathematical procedures applied to the analysis of data generated by the study.

Statistics Command Used to initiate and complete a computerized transaction, it provides for the researcher to identify analyses that he wants the computer to calculate, in addition to, for example, a Pearson product-moment correlation coefficient.

Stratified Cluster A sampling procedure that guarantees representation of heterogeneous blocks (clusters) of subjects.

Stratified Random Sample One in which identifiable subgroups are included in the same proportion as they can be found in the population from which the sample was selected.

Structured Questions Questions that are designed to measure specific issues.

Student's *t*-test A statistical procedure used to compare the means of two distributions of scores in order to determine whether an observed difference can be attributed to something other than chance.

Style The rules of mechanics, including: capitalization, punctuation, sentence structure, spelling, and word usage.

Subject *(Gram.)* The noun or other substantive that is one of the two immediate constituents of a sentence and about which something is said in the predicate.

Subject Complement *(Gram.)* State of agreement, as in subjective, objective, or possessive case.

Subjective Case An element of sentence structure that should be used when pronouns are functioning as subjects or subject complements (for example, *we, you, he/she/it*).

Subjectivity The infusion of judgment into decision making.

Subjects Participants in a study.

Subject-Verb Agreement Correspondence, as in person and number (for example, the investigator *is,* two *are*).

Subordination Assigning unequal emphasis to ideas when combining them in a sentence.

Summary An overview of procedures, findings, and conclusions.

Summary Sheet A single-page document that provides a summation of findings. See also Research Evaluation Digest (RED) Form.

Survey A systematic collection, analysis, interpretation, and report of pertinent facts and findings about the current status of persons, processes, products, or programs. Through the use of interviews and written questionnaires, information is gathered with a view toward identifying relative strengths and weaknesses of topics under study.

Survey Research The utilization of interviews, questionnaires, and/or observation to gather information on the present status of person(s), place(s), or thing(s).

Survey Studies See Survey.

Synchronic Reliability The extent of agreement between two or more individuals who have witnessed the same event.

Systematic Random Sample One comprised of individuals who were selected on the basis of their *n*th position on a randomized list.

Table of Contents That part of the prefatory section of a report that identifies the chapter headings and major subheads, with corresponding page numbers where those sections of the report begin.

Table of Random Numbers A display of randomly displayed digits from which samples are selected (see Appendix A).

Table of Specifications Used in the test planning stages, it is a guide to help ensure that all pertinent objectives are weighted in accordance with their relative importance to the instrument.

Telephone Questionnaires Formal interviews conducted over the telephone. See also Survey.

Telnet See Chapter 12, Introduction.

Template A model of procedures for conducting a study.

Tentative Budget A document consisting of estimated direct and indirect costs for carrying out one's study.

Tentative Interpretations Provisional explanations; subject to change when new findings are available.

Terminal See Chapter 12, Figure 12–1.

Test and Measurement Research Utilizes processes appropriate to the creation and revision of instruments of assessment (for example, achievement tests, attitude scales, personality inventories). Procedures include developing objectives, tables of specifications, and questions; jury validation; pilot testing; and item analysis.

Test and Measurement Studies See Test and Measurement Research.

Test Critiques Edited by Sweetland and Keyser, it provides critical reviews of published tests. See also *Tests*.

Tests Edited by Sweetland and Keyser, it is a reference guide to assessments in psychology, education, and business.

Tests in Print **(TIP)** A source of description and bibliographic information.

Tetrachoric Correlation The relationship between two variables when both of them can be dichotomized.

Textbook Sources References that provide the names of authors, titles, publishers, and copyright dates of books published in assorted fields of interest and problem areas.

Thesaurus A collection of antonyms and synonyms.

Third Person The form of pronoun (such as *he*) or verb (such as *is*) that refers to the person or thing spoken of in an oral or written report.

Threats of Interaction See Interactions.

Threats to External Validity Factors that may influence the degree to which the findings of a study can be generalized to populations outside of the experimental setting.

Threats to Internal Validity Factors that may influence the extent to which one can attribute the observed findings to the manipulation of specific variables (that is, independent).

Threats to the Study Indications of impending design weaknesses that could impact upon the findings in ways unrelated to the treatment. See also External Validity; Internal Validity.

Time(s) Within the context of experimental research, it is a threat to the external validity of the study if one attempts to generalize the findings to times unrelated to those in which the investigation took place.

Time Sampling Observing behavior at a randomly selected point in time.

TIP See *Tests in Print* (TIP).

Title The name of the study, article, book, and so on from which abstracts and indexing are prepared.

Title Command Used to initiate and complete a computerized transaction, it assigns a label that will be placed at the top of each printed output page.

Title Page The first page of a report; includes such things as the name of the study, author, and date.

Topical Heading See Running Head.

Total Regression A situation in which the predicted score is at the mean of the second variable.

Total Sum of Squared Deviations In analysis of variance, it is the total of the squared deviations of each score from the grand mean.

Tracking Monitoring the process and product of data collection.

t **Ratio** A quotient that is referred to a Table of Critical Values for *t* in order to determine whether the finding is statistically significant. This ratio is found by dividing the sampling error by the standard error of the mean.

Treatment The experimental (independent) variable.

Treatment Fidelity The extent to which the administration of a study is in compliance with the protocol of the investigator's design.

Treatment Phase That portion of a study in which the independent variable is administered to the subjects.

Triangulation The employment of multiple data-gathering processes in order to judge the validity of an outcome.

Truncation To cut off (for example, to three places to the right of the decimal point; in this instance, the number would not be carried to four places and rounded).

Two-Tailed Test Used when testing a nondirectional (null) hypothesis, it provides for the possibility that, if the null hypothesis is rejected, the difference between obtained findings may occur in either direction; that is, either group mean may be greater than the other ($A > B$ or $A < B$).

Type I Error An error in which a null hypothesis is rejected when it should have been accepted.

Type II Error An error in which a null hypothesis is accepted when it should have been rejected.

Uncontrolled Threats Within the context of experimental research, they are threats to the internal validity of the investigation because they were not controlled for through the design of the study.

User-Managed Problem Solving (UMPS) See Chapter 12, Introduction.

Validity The degree to which an instrument measures what it claims to measure.

Variable A concept (that is, trait, characteristic, quality) that is capable of assuming any one of a range of values.

Verb Any of a class of words expressing action, existence, or occurrence.

Veronica See Chapter 12, Introduction.

Vita A brief autobiography; includes those professional experiences that have contributed to the investigator's qualifications for conducting the research. A vita sheet is the final page in one's thesis or dissertation.

Voice Synthesizer See Chapter 12, Figure 12–1.

WAIS See Wide Area Information Service (WAIS).

Weighted Averages Averages that consider the relative importance of each value comprising the distribution of factors.

Weighted Rating Scale A measuring device that assigns emphasis to portions of an instrument (that is, rating scale) according to its relative importance.

Wide Area Information Service (WAIS) See Chapter 12, Introduction.

Within Group Sum of Squared Deviations In analysis of variance, it is the sum of the squared deviations of each score from the mean of its group.

Within Mean Squares In analysis of variance, it is the quotient of the within group sum of squared deviations divided by the number of subjects minus the number of groups $(N - K)$.

WordPerfect A software program for Windows that creates, edits, and prints documents; it also provides interface capabilities.

Word Processing See Word Processor.

Word Processor Computer software program that enables one to store, edit, revise, and reformat text.

Word Usage One component of the rules of mechanics to be used when preparing a report (see Chapter 13, Preparing the Research Report).

World Wide Web (WWW) See Chapter 12, Introduction.

X Axis See Abscissa.

Y Axis See Ordinate.

Zero Correlation A circumstance in which there is no statistical relationship between the variables under study.

Zero-Order Correlation The relationship between two variables when other variables are not held constant; also referred to as *Pearson product-moment correlation*.

Zero Relationship See Zero Correlation.

z Score The most basic of standard scores. Contains a mean of 0.0 and a standard deviation of ±1.0.

INDEX

Page numbers in **bold** refer to illustrations.